Systems Programming
and
Operating Systems

Second Revised Edition

D M Dhamdhere

Professor and Head
Department of Computer Science & Engineering
Indian Institute of Technology
Mumbai

Tata McGraw-Hill Publishing Company Limited
NEW DELHI

McGraw-Hill Offices
New Delhi New York St Louis San Francisco Auckland Bogotá
Caracas Lisbon London Madrid Mexico City Milan Montreal
San Juan Singapore Sydney Tokyo Toronto

Tata McGraw-Hill

A Division of The ***McGraw·Hill*** *Companies*

Information contained in this work has been obtained by Tata McGraw-Hill, from sources believed to be reliable. However, neither Tata McGraw-Hill nor its authors guarantee the accuracy or completeness of any information published herein, and neither Tata McGraw-Hill nor its authors shall be responsible for any errors, omissions, or damages arising out of use of this information. This work is published with the understanding that Tata McGraw-Hill and its authors are supplying information but are not attempting to render engineering or other professional services. If such services are required, the assistance of an appropriate professional should be sought.

ISBN 0-07-463579-4

Published by Tata McGraw-Hill Publishing Company Limited, and 7 West Patel Nagar, New Delhi 110 008, printed at Replika Press Pvt. Ltd, A-229 DSIDC Industrial Park, Narela, Delhi 110 040

Cover: Replika

RYLDCRATRCBRB

Dedicated to

Principal Vishwanath Gangadhar Oke
— Professor, philosopher, author
... and a student forever

Preface to the Second Revised Edition

I started work on the second revised edition soon after the second edition was published. The primary motivation was to improve readability and focus, clarity of the fundamental concepts and utility of the examples. This involved a thorough editing of the text, with numerous improvements on each page. Some errors and ambiguities noticed while editing were also corrected.

Apart from these improvements there are plenty of additions to all chapters. The significant ones amongst these are,

- *Evolution of OS Functions (Chapter 9):* A new section on resource allocation and user interface functions.
- *Processes (Chapter 10):* A much enlarged section on threads.
- *Memory Management (Chapter 15):* A new section on the reuse of memory.
- *IO Organization and IO Programming (Chapter 16):* A new section on IO initiation.

I hope the readers will like the new format and compact style. As before, I look forward to comments from the readers.

D M DHAMDHERE

Preface to the Second Edition

This edition presents a more logical arrangement of topics in Systems Programming and Operating Systems than the first edition. This has been achieved by restructuring the following material into smaller chapters with specific focus:

- *Language processors:* Three new chapters on Overview of language processors, Data structures for language processors, and Scanning and parsing techniques have been added. These are followed by chapters on Assemblers, Macro processors, Compilers and interpreters, and Linkers.
- *Process management:* Process management is structured into chapters on Processes, Scheduling, Deadlocks, Process synchronization, and Interprocess communication.
- *Information management:* Information management is now organized in the form of chapters on IO organization and IO programming, File systems, and Protection and security.

Apart from this, some parts of the text have been completely rewritten and new definitions, examples, figures, sections added and exercises and bibliographies updated. New sections on user interfaces, resource instance and resource request models and distributed control algorithms have been added in the chapters on Software tools, Deadlocks and Distributed operating systems, respectively.

I hope instructors and students will like the new look of the book. Feedback from readers, preferably by email (dmd@cse.iitb.ernet.in), are welcome. I thank my wife and family for their forbearance.

D M DHAMDHERE

Preface to the First Edition

This book has grown out of an earlier book *Introduction to System Software* published in 1986, which addressed the recommended curricula in *Systems Programming* (courses 14 of ACM curriculum 68 and CS-11 of ACM curriculum 77), and *Operating Systems and Computer Architecture* (courses CS-6, 7 of ACM curriculum 77 and SE-6, 7 of IEEE curriculum 77). The present book offers a much expanded coverage of the same subject area and also incorporates the recommendations of the ACM-IEEE joint curriculum task force (Computing Curriculum 1991). The contents have also been updated to keep pace with the developments in the field, and the changing emphasis in the teaching of these courses. An example is the way courses titled *Systems Programming* are taught today. As against the 'mostly theory' approach of the previous decade, today the emphasis is on a familiarity with the necessary theory and available software tools. The instructors of these courses have the hard task of finding instructional material on both these aspects. One of the aims of this book is to cater for this requirement through the incorporation of a large number of examples and case studies of the widely used operating systems and software tools available in the field. Treatment of the standard components of system software, viz. assemblers and loaders, is now aimed at the IBM PC. Due to the wide availability of the IBM PC, this makes it possible for students to appreciate the finer aspects in the design of these software components. Case studies of UNIX and UNIX based tools, viz. LEX and YACC, are similarly motivated.

Organization of the book

This book is organized in two parts—*Systems Programming* and *Operating Systems*. The part on Systems Programming introduces the fundamental models of the processing of an HLL program for execution on a computer system, after which separate chapters deal with different kinds of software processors, viz. assemblers, compilers, interpreters and loaders. Each chapter contains examples and case studies so as to offer a comprehensive coverage of the subject matter.

Part II of the book is devoted to an in-depth study of operating systems. The introductory chapter of this part, Chapter 7, identifies the fundamental functions and techniques common to all operating systems. Chapters 8, 9 and 10 offer a detailed treatment of the processor management, storage management and information management functions of the operating systems. These chapters contain motivating discussions, case studies and a set of exercises which would encourage a student to delve deeper into the subject area. Chapter 11 is devoted to an important area of the study of operating systems, that of *concurrent programming*. Evolution of the primitives and contemporary language features for concurrent programming is presented so as to develop an insight into the essentials of concurrent programming. A case study of a disk manager consolidates the material covered in this chapter. Chapter 12, which is on distributed operating systems, motivates the additional functionalities that de-volve on the operating system due to the distributed environment. This chapter is intended as a primer on distributed operating systems. A detailed treatment has not been possible due to space constraints.

Using this book

This book can be used for the courses on *Systems programming* (or *System software*) at the undergraduate and postgraduate levels, and for an undergraduate course on *Operating systems*. For the former, Part I of the book, together with Chapter 7 from Part II, contains the necessary material. Additionally, parts of Chapter 12 could be used as read-for-yourself material. For a course on *operating systems*, Part II of the book contains the necessary material.

In the courses based on this book, use of concurrently running design-and-implementation projects should be mandatory. Typical project topics would be the development of compilers and interpreters using LEX and YACC, concurrent programming projects, development of OS device drivers, etc.

Apart from use as a text, this book can also be used in the professional computer environment as a reference book or as a text for the enhancement of skills, for new entrants to the field as well as for software managers.

The motivation for writing this book comes from the experience in teaching various courses in the area of system software. I thank all my students for their vital contribution to this book.

DM DHAMDHERE

Contents

Systems Programming
and
Operating Systems

Second Revised Edition

Part I

SYSTEMS PROGRAMMING

CHAPTER 1

Language Processors

1.1 INTRODUCTION

Language processing activities arise due to the differences between the manner in which a software designer describes the ideas concerning the behaviour of a software and the manner in which these ideas are implemented in a computer system. The designer expresses the ideas in terms related to the *application domain* of the software. To implement these ideas, their description has to be interpreted in terms related to the *execution domain* of the computer system. We use the term *semantics* to represent the rules of meaning of a domain, and the term *semantic gap* to represent the difference between the semantics of two domains. Fig. 1.1 depicts the semantic gap between the application and execution domains.

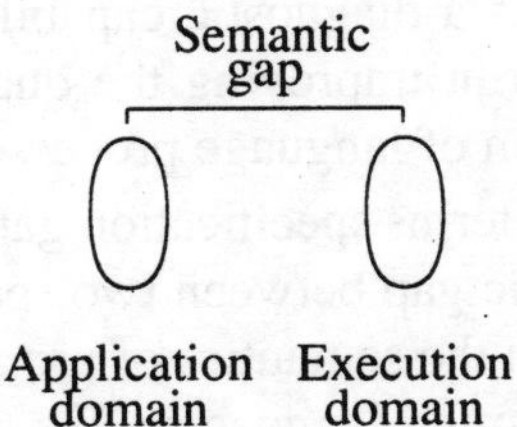

Fig. 1.1 Semantic gap

The semantic gap has many consequences, some of the important ones being large development times, large development efforts, and poor quality of software. These issues are tackled by Software engineering through the use of methodologies and programming languages (PLs). The software engineering steps aimed at the use of a PL can be grouped into

1. Specification, design and coding steps
2. PL implementation steps.

Software implementation using a PL introduces a new domain, the *PL domain.* The semantic gap between the application domain and the execution domain is bridged by the software engineering steps. The first step bridges the gap between the application and PL domains, while the second step bridges the gap between the PL and execution domains. We refer to the gap between the application and PL domains as the *specification-and-design gap* or simply the *specification gap*, and the gap between the PL and execution domains as the *execution gap* (see Fig. 1.2). The specification gap is bridged by the software development team, while the execution gap is bridged by the designer of the programming language processor, viz. a translator or an interpreter.

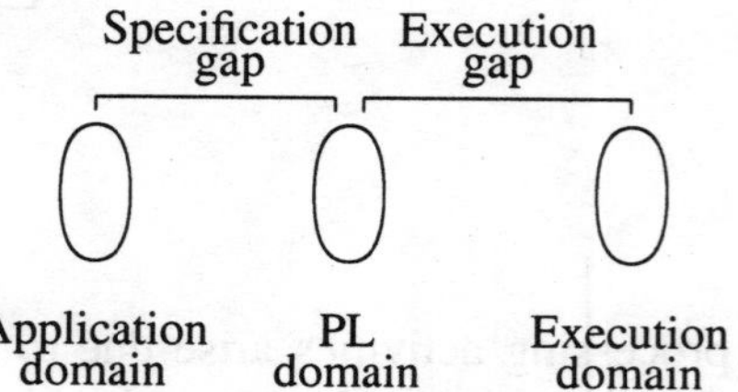

Fig. 1.2 Specification and execution gaps

It is important to note the advantages of introducing the PL domain. The gap to be bridged by the software designer is now between the application domain and the PL domain rather than between the application domain and the execution domain. This reduces the severity of the consequences of semantic gap mentioned earlier. Further, apart from bridging the gap between the PL and execution domains, the language processor provides a diagnostic capability which detects and indicates errors in its input. This helps in improving the quality of the software. (We shall discuss the diagnostic function of language processors in Chapters 3 and 6.)

We define the terms specification gap and execution gap as follows: *Specification gap* is the semantic gap between two specifications of the same task. *Execution gap* is the gap between the semantics of programs (that perform the same task) written in different programming languages. We assume that each domain has a specification language (SL). A specification written in an SL is a *program* in SL. The specification language of the PL domain is the PL itself. The specification language of the execution domain is the machine language of the computer system. We restrict the use of the term execution gap to situations where one of the two specification languages is closer to the machine language of a computer system. In other situations, the term specification gap is more appropriate.

Language processors

Definition 1.1 (Language processor) A *language processor* is a software which bridges a specification or execution gap.

We use the term *language processing* to describe the activity performed by a language processor and assume a diagnostic capability as an implicit part of any form of language processing. We refer to the program form input to a language processor as the *source program* and to its output as the *target program*. The languages in which these programs are written are called *source language* and *target language*, respectively. A language processor typically abandons generation of the target program if it detects errors in the source program.

A spectrum of language processors is defined to meet practical requirements.

1. A *language translator* bridges an execution gap to the machine language (or assembly language) of a computer system. An *assembler* is a language translator whose source language is assembly language. A *compiler* is any language translator which is not an assembler.
2. A *detranslator* bridges the same execution gap as the language translator, but *in the reverse direction.*
3. A *preprocessor* is a language processor which bridges an execution gap but is not a language translator.
4. A *language migrator* bridges the specification gap between two PLs.

Example 1.1 Figure 1.3 shows two language processors. The language processor of part (a) converts a C++ program into a C program, hence it is a preprocessor. The language processor of part (b) is a language translator for C++ since it produces a machine language program. In both cases the source program is in C++. The target programs are the C program and the machine language program, respectively.

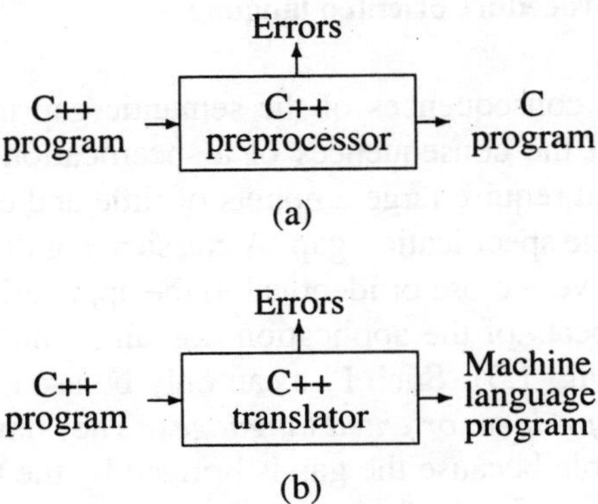

Fig. 1.3 Language processors

Interpreters

An interpreter is a language processor which bridges an execution gap without generating a machine language program. In the classification arising from Definition 1.1, the interpreter is a language translator. This leads to many similarities between translators and interpreters. From a practical viewpoint many differences also exist between translators and interpreters.

The absence of a target program implies the absence of an output interface of the interpreter. Thus the language processing activities of an interpreter cannot be separated from its program execution activities. Hence we say that an interpreter 'executes' a program written in a PL. In essence, the execution gap vanishes totally. Figure 1.4 is a schematic representation of an interpreter, wherein the interpreter domain encompasses the PL domain as well as the execution domain. Thus, the specification language of the PL domain is identical with the specification language of the interpreter domain. Since the interpreter also incorporates the execution domain, it is as if we have a computer system capable of 'understanding' the programming language. We discuss principles of interpretation in Section 1.2.2.

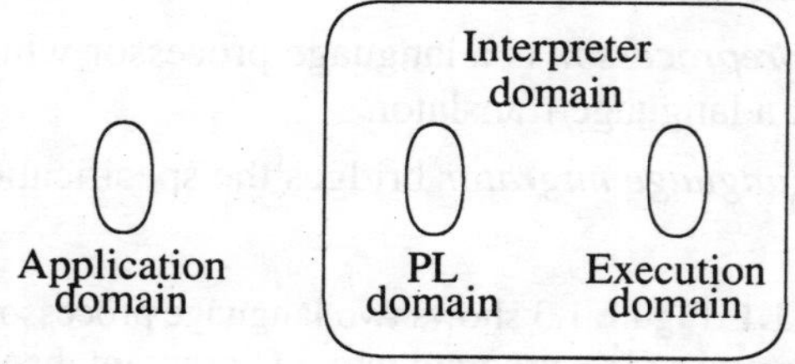

Fig. 1.4 Interpreter

Problem oriented and procedure oriented languages

The three consequences of the semantic gap mentioned at the start of this section are in fact the consequences of a specification gap. Software systems are poor in quality and require large amounts of time and effort to develop due to difficulties in bridging the specification gap. A classical solution is to develop a PL such that the PL domain is very close or identical to the application domain. PL features now directly model aspects of the application domain, which leads to a very small specification gap (see Fig. 1.5). Such PLs can only be used for specific applications, hence they are called *problem oriented languages*. They have large execution gaps, however this is acceptable because the gap is bridged by the translator or interpreter and does not concern the software designer.

A *procedure oriented language* provides general purpose facilities required in most application domains. Such a language is independent of specific application domains and results in a large specification gap which has to be bridged by an application designer.

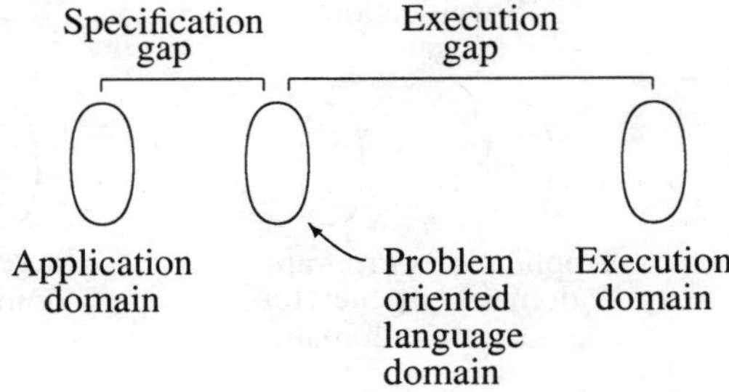

Fig. 1.5 Problem oriented language domain

1.2 LANGUAGE PROCESSING ACTIVITIES

The fundamental language processing activities can be divided into those that bridge the specification gap and those that bridge the execution gap. We name these activities as

1. Program generation activities
2. Program execution activities.

A program generation activity aims at automatic generation of a program. The source language is a specification language of an application domain and the target language is typically a procedure oriented PL. A program execution activity organizes the execution of a program written in a PL on a computer system. Its source language could be a procedure oriented language or a problem oriented language.

1.2.1 Program Generation

Figure 1.6 depicts the program generation activity. The program generator is a software system which accepts the specification of a program to be generated, and generates a program in the target PL. In effect, the program generator introduces a new domain between the application and PL domains (see Fig. 1.7). We call this the *program generator domain*. The specification gap is now the gap between the application domain and the program generator domain. This gap is smaller than the gap between the application domain and the target PL domain.

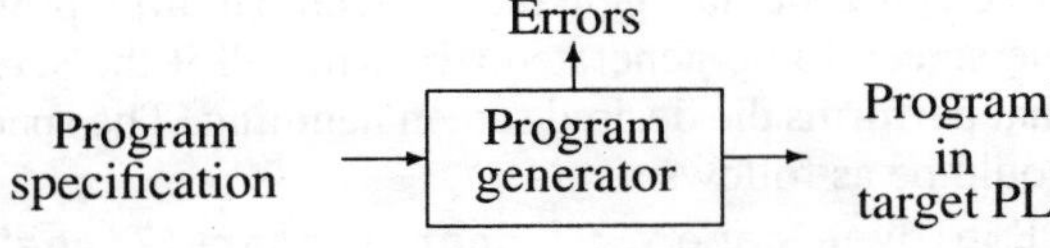

Fig. 1.6 Program generation

Reduction in the specification gap increases the reliability of the generated program. Since the generator domain is close to the application domain, it is easy for the designer or programmer to write the specification of the program to be generated.

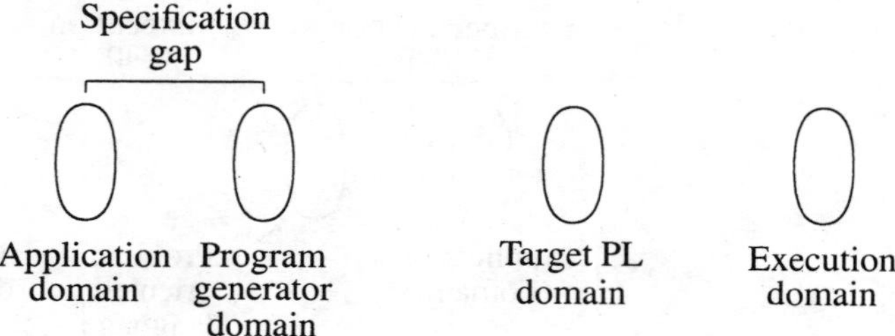

Fig. 1.7 Program generator domain

The harder task of bridging the gap to the PL domain is performed by the generator. This arrangement also reduces the testing effort. Proving the correctness of the program generator amounts to proving the correctness of the transformation of Fig. 1.6. This would be performed while implementing the generator. To test an application generated by using the generator, it is necessary to only verify the correctness of the specification input to the program generator. This is a much simpler task than verifying correctness of the generated program. This task can be further simplified by providing a good diagnostic (i.e. error indication) capability in the program generator which would detect inconsistencies in the specification.

It is more economical to develop a program generator than to develop a problem oriented language. This is because a problem oriented language suffers a very large execution gap between the PL domain and the execution domain (see Fig. 1.5), whereas the program generator has a smaller semantic gap to the target PL domain, which is the domain of a standard procedure oriented language. The execution gap between the target PL domain and the execution domain is bridged by the compiler or interpreter for the PL.

Example 1.2 A screen handling program (also called a form fillin program) handles screen IO in a data entry environment. It displays the field headings and default values for various fields in the screen and accepts data values for the fields. Figure 1.8 shows a screen for data entry of employee information. A data entry operator can move the cursor to a field and key in its value. The screen handling program accepts the value and stores it in a data base.

A screen generator generates screen handling programs. It accepts a specification of the screen to be generated (we will call it the screen spec) and generates a program that performs the desired screen handling. The specification for some fields in Fig. 1.8 could be as follows:

```
Employee name  :  char : start(line=2,position=25)
                  end(line=2,position=80)
Married        :  char : start(line=10,position=25)
                  end(line=10,position=27)
                  default('Yes')
```

Errors in the specification, e.g. invalid start or end positions or conflicting specifications for a field, are detected by the generator. The generated screen handling program validates the data during data entry, e.g. the *age* field must only contain digits, the *sex* field must only contain M or F, etc.

Employee Name
Address
Married Yes
Age Sex

Fig. 1.8 Screen displayed by a screen handling program

1.2.2 Program Execution

Two popular models for program execution are translation and interpretation.

Program translation

The program translation model bridges the execution gap by translating a program written in a PL, called the *source program* (SP), into an equivalent program in the machine or assembly language of the computer system, called the *target program* (TP) (see Fig. 1.9).

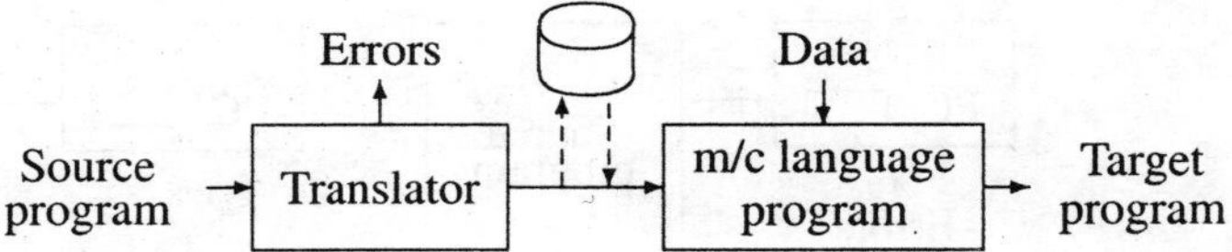

Fig. 1.9 Program translation model

Characteristics of the program translation model are:

- A program must be translated before it can be executed.
- The translated program may be saved in a file. The saved program may be executed repeatedly.
- A program must be retranslated following modifications.

Program interpretation

Figure 1.10(a) shows a schematic of program interpretation. The interpreter reads the source program and stores it in its memory. During interpretation it takes a source statement, determines its meaning and performs actions which implement it. This includes computational and input-output actions.

To understand the functioning of an interpreter, note the striking similarity between the interpretation schematic (Fig. 1.10(a)) and a schematic of the execution of a machine language program by the CPU of a computer system (Fig. 1.10(b)). The CPU uses a *program counter* (PC) to note the address of the next instruction to be executed. This instruction is subjected to the *instruction execution cycle* consisting of the following steps:

1. Fetch the instruction.
2. Decode the instruction to determine the operation to be performed, and also its operands.
3. Execute the instruction.

At the end of the cycle, the instruction address in PC is updated and the cycle is repeated for the next instruction. Program interpretation can proceed in an analogous manner. Thus, the PC can indicate which statement of the source program is to be interpreted next. This statement would be subjected to the *interpretation cycle*, which could consist of the following steps:

1. Fetch the statement.
2. Analyse the statement and determine its meaning, viz. the computation to be performed and its operands.
3. Execute the meaning of the statement.

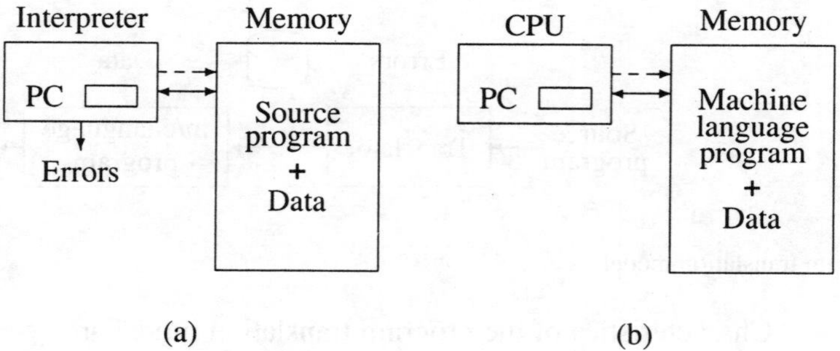

Fig. 1.10 Schematics of (a) interpretation, (b) program execution

From this analogy, we can identify the following characteristics of interpretation:

- The source program is retained in the source form itself, i.e. no target program form exists,
- A statement is analysed during its interpretation.

Section 6.6 contains a detailed description of interpretation.

Comparison

A fixed cost (the translation overhead) is incurred in the use of the program translation model. If the source program is modified, the translation cost must be incurred again irrespective of the size of the modification. However, execution of the target program is efficient since the target program is in the machine language. Use of the interpretation model does not incur the translation overheads. This is advantageous if a program is modified between executions, as in program testing and debugging. Interpretation is however slower than execution of a machine language program because of Step 2 in the interpretation cycle.

1.3 FUNDAMENTALS OF LANGUAGE PROCESSING

Definition 1.2 (Language Processing)
Language Processing ≡ *Analysis of SP* + *Synthesis of TP.*

Definition 1.2 motivates a generic model of language processing activities. We refer to the collection of language processor components engaged in analysing a source program as the *analysis phase* of the language processor. Components engaged in synthesizing a target program constitute the *synthesis phase*.

A specification of the source language forms the basis of source program analysis. The specification consists of three components:

1. *Lexical rules* which govern the formation of valid lexical units in the source language.
2. *Syntax rules* which govern the formation of valid statements in the source language.
3. *Semantic rules* which associate meaning with valid statements of the language.

The analysis phase uses each component of the source language specification to determine relevant information concerning a statement in the source program. Thus, analysis of a source statement consists of lexical, syntax and semantic analysis.

Example 1.3 Consider the statement

```
percent_profit := (profit * 100) / cost_price;
```

in some programming language. Lexical analysis identifies `:=`, `*` and `/` as operators, `100` as a constant and the remaining strings as identifiers. Syntax analysis identifies the statement as an assignment statement with `percent_profit` as the left hand side and `(profit * 100) / cost_price` as the expression on the right hand side. Semantic analysis determines the meaning of the statement to be the assignment of

$$\frac{\texttt{profit} \times 100}{\texttt{cost\_price}}$$

to `percent_profit`.

The synthesis phase is concerned with the construction of target language statement(s) which have the same meaning as a source statement. Typically, this consists of two main activities:

- Creation of data structures in the target program
- Generation of target code.

We refer to these activities as *memory allocation* and *code generation*, respectively.

Example 1.4 A language processor generates the following assembly language statements for the source statement of Ex. 1.3.

```
                MOVER    AREG, PROFIT
                MULT     AREG, 100
                DIV      AREG, COST_PRICE
                MOVEM    AREG, PERCENT_PROFIT
                ...
PERCENT_PROFIT  DW       1
PROFIT          DW       1
COST_PRICE      DW       1
```

where MOVER and MOVEM move a value from a memory location to a CPU register and vice versa, respectively, and DW reserves one or more words in memory. Needless to say, both memory allocation and code generation are influenced by the target machine's architecture.

Phases and passes of a language processor

From the preceding discussion it is clear that a language processor consists of two distinct phases—the analysis phase and the synthesis phase. Figure 1.11 shows a schematic of a language processor. This schematic, as also Examples 1.3 and 1.4 may give the impression that language processing can be performed on a statement-by-statement basis—that is, analysis of a source statement can be immediately followed by synthesis of equivalent target statements. This may not be feasible due to:

- Forward references

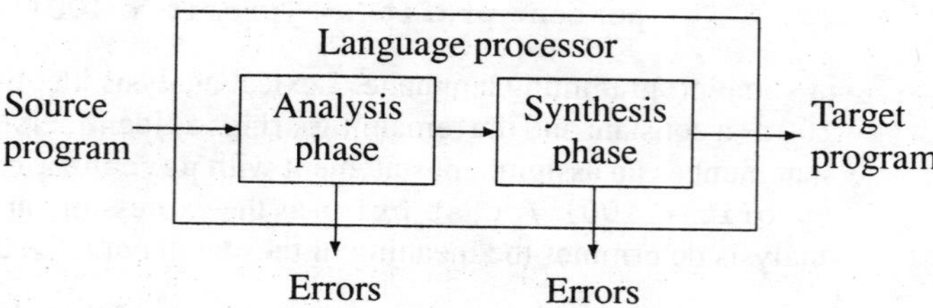

Fig. 1.11 Phases of a language processor

- Issues concerning memory requirements and organization of a language processor.

We discuss these issues in the following.

Definition 1.3 (Forward reference) *A* forward reference *of a program entity is a reference to the entity which precedes its definition in the program.*

While processing a statement containing a forward reference, a language processor does not possess all relevant information concerning the referenced entity. This creates difficulties in synthesizing the equivalent target statements. This problem can be solved by postponing the generation of target code until more information concerning the entity becomes available. Postponing the generation of target code may also reduce memory requirements of the language processor and simplify its organization.

Example 1.5 Consider the statement of Ex. 1.3 to be a part of the following program in some programming language:

```
percent_profit := (profit * 100) / cost_price;
...
long profit;
```

The statement `long profit;` declares `profit` to have a double precision value. The reference to `profit` in the assignment statement constitutes a forward reference because the declaration of `profit` occurs later in the program. Since the type of `profit` is not known while processing the assignment statement, correct code cannot be generated for it in a statement-by-statement manner.

Departure from the statement-by-statement application of Definition 1.2 leads to the *multipass model* of language processing.

Definition 1.4 (Language processor pass) *A* language processor pass *is the processing of every statement in a source program, or its equivalent representation, to perform a* language processing function *(a set of language processing functions).*

Here 'pass' is an abstract noun describing the processing performed by the language processor. For simplicity, the part of the language processor which performs one pass over the source program is also called a pass.

Example 1.6 It is possible to process the program fragment of Ex. 1.5 in two passes as follows:

Pass I	:	Perform analysis of the source program and note relevant information
Pass II	:	Perform synthesis of target program

Information concerning the type of `profit` is noted in pass I. This information is used during pass II to perform code generation.

Intermediate representation of programs

The language processor of Ex. 1.6 performs certain processing more than once. In pass I, it analyses the source program to note the type information. In pass II, it once again analyses the source program to generate target code using the type information noted in pass I. This can be avoided using an *intermediate representation* of the source program.

Definition 1.5 (Intermediate Representation (IR)) *An* intermediate representation (IR) *is a representation of a source program which reflects the effect of some, but not all, analysis and synthesis tasks performed during language processing.*

The IR is the 'equivalent representation' mentioned in Definition 1.4. Note that the words *'but not all'* in Definition 1.5 differentiate between the target program and an IR. Figure 1.12 depicts the schematic of a two pass language processor. The first pass performs analysis of the source program and reflects its results in the intermediate representation. The second pass reads and analyses the IR, instead of the source program, to perform synthesis of the target program. This avoids repeated processing of the source program. The first pass is concerned exclusively with source language issues. Hence it is called the *front end* of the language processor. The second pass is concerned with program synthesis for a specific target language. Hence it is called the *back end* of the language processor. Note that the front and back ends of a language processor need not coexist in memory. This reduces the memory requirements of a language processor.

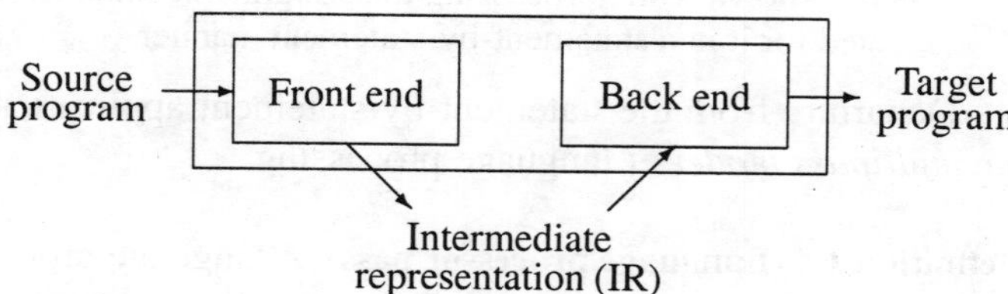

Fig. 1.12 Two pass schematic for language processing

Desirable properties of an IR are:

- *Ease of use:* IR should be easy to construct and analyse.
- *Processing efficiency:* efficient algorithms must exist for constructing and analysing the IR.
- *Memory efficiency:* IR must be compact.

Like the pass structure of language processors, the nature of intermediate representation is influenced by many design and implementation considerations. In the following sections we will focus on the fundamental issues in language processing. Wherever possible and relevant, we will comment on suitable IR forms.

Semantic actions

As seen in the preceding discussions, the front end of a language processor analyses the source program and constructs an IR. All actions performed by the front end, except lexical and syntax analysis, are called *semantic actions*. These include actions for the following:

1. Checking semantic validity of constructs in SP
2. Determining the meaning of SP
3. Constructing an IR.

1.3.1 A Toy Compiler

We briefly describe the front end and back end of a toy compiler for a Pascal-like language.

1.3.1.1 The Front End

The front end performs lexical, syntax and semantic analysis of the source program. Each kind of analysis involves the following functions:

1. Determine validity of a source statement from the viewpoint of the analysis.
2. Determine the 'content' of a source statement.
3. Construct a suitable representation of the source statement for use by subsequent analysis functions, or by the synthesis phase of the language processor.

The word 'content' has different connotations in lexical, syntax and semantic analysis. In lexical analysis, the content is the lexical class to which each lexical unit belongs, while in syntax analysis it is the syntactic structure of a source statement. In semantic analysis the content is the meaning of a statement—for a declaration statement, it is the set of attributes of a declared variable (e.g. type, length and dimensionality), while for an imperative statement, it is the sequence of actions implied by the statement.

Each analysis represents the 'content' of a source statement in the form of (1) tables of information, and (2) description of the source statement. Subsequent analysis uses this information for its own purposes and either adds information to these tables and descriptions, or constructs its own tables and descriptions. For example, syntax analysis uses information concerning the lexical class of lexical units and constructs a representation for the syntactic structure of the source statement. Semantic analysis uses information concerning the syntactic structure and constructs a representation for the meaning of the statement. The tables and descriptions at the end of semantic analysis form the IR of the front end (see Fig. 1.12).

Output of the front end

The IR produced by the front end consists of two components:

1. Tables of information
2. An *intermediate code* (IC) which is a description of the source program.

Tables

Tables contain the information obtained during different analyses of SP. The most important table is the symbol table which contains information concerning all identifiers used in the SP. The symbol table is built during lexical analysis. Semantic analysis adds information concerning symbol attributes while processing declaration statements. It may also add new names designating temporary results.

Intermediate code (IC)

The IC is a sequence of IC units, each IC unit representing the meaning of one action in SP. IC units may contain references to the information in various tables.

Example 1.7 Figure 1.13 shows the IR produced by the analysis phase for the program

```
i : integer;
a,b : real;
a := b+i;
```

Symbol table

	symbol	*type*	*length*	*address*
1	`i`	int		
2	`a`	real		
3	`b`	real		
4	`i*`	real		
5	`temp`	real		

Intermediate code

1. Convert (Id, #1) to real, giving (Id, #4)
2. Add (Id, #4) to (Id, #3), giving (Id, #5)
3. Store (Id, #5) in (Id, #2)

Fig. 1.13 IR for the program of Example 1.8

The symbol table contains information concerning the identifiers and their types. This information is determined during lexical and semantic analysis, respectively. In IC, the specification (Id, #1) refers to the id occupying the first entry in the table. Note that `i*` and `temp` are temporary names added during semantic analysis of the assignment statement.

Lexical analysis (Scanning)

Lexical analysis identifies the lexical units in a source statement. It then classifies the units into different lexical classes, e.g. id's, constants, reserved id's, etc. and enters them into different tables. This classification may be based on the nature of a string or on the specification of the source language. (For example, while an integer constant is a string of digits with an optional sign, a reserved id is an id whose name matches one of the reserved names mentioned in the language specification.) Lexical analysis builds a descriptor, called a *token*, for each lexical unit. A token contains two fields—*class code*, and *number in class*. *class code* identifies the class to which a lexical unit belongs. *number in class* is the entry number of the lexical unit in the relevant table. We depict a token as [*Code #no*], e.g. [*Id #10*]. The IC for a statement is thus a string of tokens.

Example 1.8 The statement `a := b+i;` is represented as the string of tokens

[*Id #2*][*Op #5*][*Id #3*][*Op #3*][*Id #1*][*Op #10*]

where [*Id #2*] stands for 'identifier occupying entry #2 in the Symbol table', i.e. the id `a` (see Fig. 1.13). [*Op #5*] similarly stands for the operator ':=', etc.

Syntax analysis (Parsing)

Syntax analysis processes the string of tokens built by lexical analysis to determine the statement class, e.g. assignment statement, if statement, etc. It then builds an IC which represents the structure of the statement. The IC is passed to semantic analysis to determine the meaning of the statement.

Example 1.9 Figure 1.14 shows IC for the statements `a,b : real;` and `a := b+i;`. A tree form is chosen for IC because a tree can represent the hierarchical structure of a PL statement appropriately. Each node in a tree is labelled by an entity. For simplicity, we use the source form of an entity, rather than its token. IC for the assignment statement shows that the computation `b+i` is a part of the expression occurring on the RHS of the assignment.

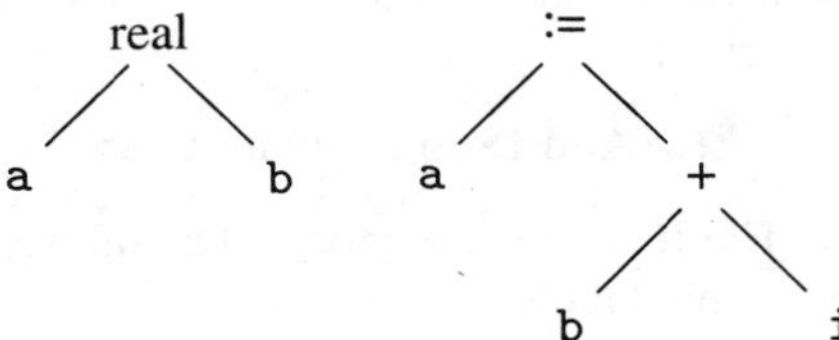

Fig. 1.14 IC for the statements `a,b : real; a := b+i;`

Semantic analysis

Semantic analysis of declaration statements differs from the semantic analysis of imperative statements. The former results in addition of information to the symbol table, e.g. type, length and dimensionality of variables. The latter identifies the sequence of actions necessary to implement the meaning of a source statement. In both cases the structure of a source statement guides the application of the semantic rules. When semantic analysis determines the meaning of a subtree in the IC, it adds information to a table or adds an action to the sequence of actions. It then modifies the IC to enable further semantic analysis. The analysis ends when the tree has been completely processed. The updated tables and the sequence of actions constitute the IR produced by the analysis phase.

Example 1.10 Semantic analysis of the statement `a := b+i;` proceeds as follows:

1. Information concerning the type of the operands is added to the IC tree. The IC tree now looks as in Fig. 1.15(a).
2. Rules of meaning governing an assignment statement indicate that the expression on the right hand side should be evaluated first. Hence focus shifts to the right subtree rooted at '+'.
3. Rules of addition indicate that type conversion of `i` should be performed to ensure type compatibility of the operands of '+'. This leads to the action

   (i) Convert `i` to real, giving `i*`.

   which is added to the sequence of actions. The IC tree under consideration is modified to represent the effect of this action (see Fig. 1.15(b)). The symbol `i*` is now added to the symbol table.

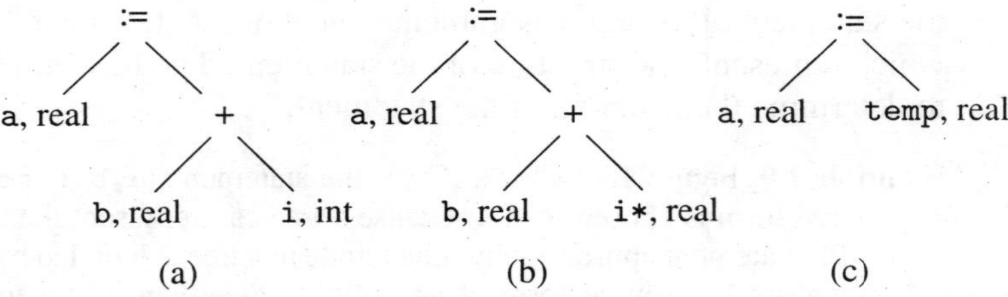

Fig. 1.15 Steps in semantic analysis of an assignment statement

4. Rules of addition indicate that the addition is now feasible. This leads to the action

   (ii) Add `i*` to `b`, giving `temp`.

   The IC tree is transformed as shown in Fig. 1.15(c), and `temp` is added to the symbol table.
5. The assignment can be performed now. This leads to the action

   (iii) Store `temp` in `a`.

This completes semantic analysis of the statement. Note that IC generated here is identical with that shown in Fig. 1.13.

Figure 1.16 shows the schematic of the front end where arrows indicate flow of data.

1.3.1.2 The Back End

The back end performs memory allocation and code generation.

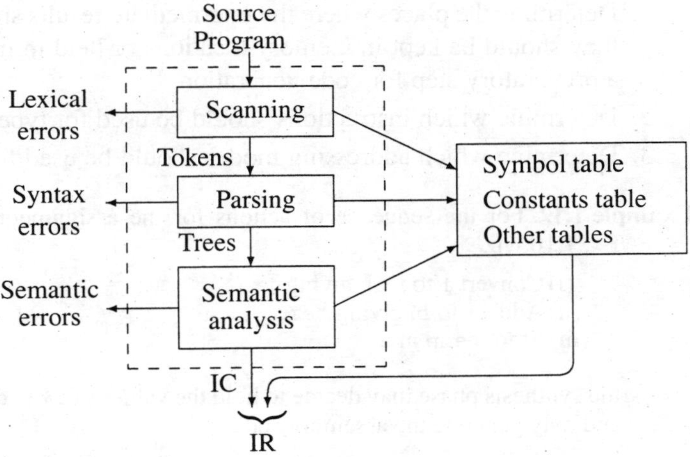

Fig. 1.16 Front end of the toy compiler

Memory allocation

Memory allocation is a simple task given the presence of the symbol table. The memory requirement of an identifier is computed from its type, length and dimensionality, and memory is allocated to it. The address of the memory area is entered in the symbol table.

Example 1.11 After memory allocation, the symbol table looks as shown in Fig. 1.17. The entries for `i*` and `temp` are not shown because memory allocation is not needed for these id's.

	symbol	*type*	*length*	*address*
1	`i`	int		2000
2	`a`	real		2001
3	`b`	real		2002

Fig. 1.17 Symbol table after memory allocation

Note that certain decisions have to precede memory allocation, for example, whether `i*` and `temp` of Ex. 1.10 should be allocated memory. These decisions are taken in the preparatory steps of code generation.

Code generation

Code generation uses knowledge of the target architecture, viz. knowledge of instructions and addressing modes in the target computer, to select the appropriate instructions. The important issues in code generation are:

1. Determine the places where the intermediate results should be kept, i.e. whether they should be kept in memory locations or held in machine registers. This is a preparatory step for code generation.
2. Determine which instructions should be used for type conversion operations.
3. Determine which addressing modes should be used for accessing variables.

Example 1.12 For the sequence of actions for the assignment statement `a := b+i;` in Ex. 1.10, viz.

(i) Convert `i` to real, giving `i*`,
(ii) Add `i*` to `b`, giving `temp`,
(iii) Store `temp` in `a`.

the synthesis phase may decide to hold the values of `i*` and `temp` in machine registers and may generate the assembly code

```
CONV_R    AREG, I
ADD_R     AREG, B
MOVEM     AREG, A
```

where `CONV_R` converts the value of `I` into the real representation and leaves the result in `AREG`. `ADD_R` performs the addition in real mode and `MOVEM` puts the result into the memory area allocated to `A`.

Some issues involved in code generation may require the designer to look beyond machine architecture. For example, whether or not the value of `temp` should be stored in a memory location in Ex. 1.12 would partly depend on whether the value of `b+i` is used more than once in the program. This is an aspect of code optimization.

Figure 1.18 shows a schematic of the back end.

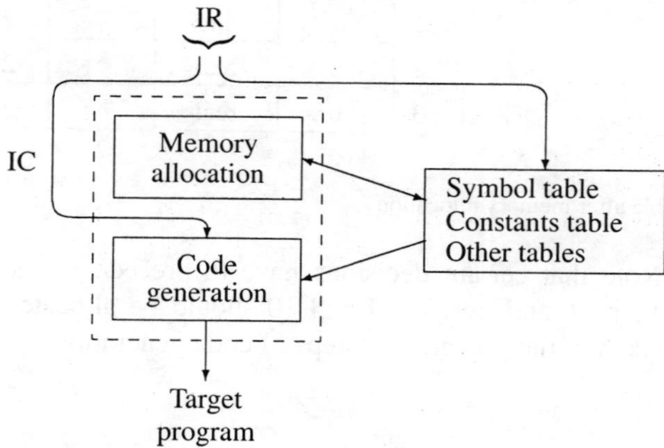

Fig. 1.18 Back end of the toy compiler

1.4 FUNDAMENTALS OF LANGUAGE SPECIFICATION

As mentioned earlier, a specification of the source language forms the basis of source program analysis. In this section, we shall discuss important lexical, syntactic and semantic features of a programming language.

1.4.1 Programming Language Grammars

The lexical and syntactic features of a programming language are specified by its grammar. This section discusses key concepts and notions from formal language grammars. A language L can be considered to be a collection of valid sentences. Each sentence can be looked upon as a sequence of words, and each word as a sequence of letters or graphic symbols acceptable in L. A language specified in this manner is known as a *formal language*. A formal language grammar is a set of rules which precisely specify the sentences of L. It is clear that natural languages are not formal languages due to their rich vocabulary. However, PLs are formal languages.

Terminal symbols, alphabet and strings

The *alphabet* of L, denoted by the Greek symbol Σ, is the collection of symbols in its character set. We will use lower case letters a, b, c, etc. to denote symbols in Σ. A symbol in the alphabet is known as a *terminal symbol* (T) of L. The alphabet can be represented using the mathematical notation of a set, e.g.

$$\Sigma \equiv \{\texttt{a, b, ...z, 0, 1, ...9}\}$$

Here the symbols {, ',' and } are part of the notation. We call them *metasymbols* to differentiate them from terminal symbols. Throughout this discussion we assume that metasymbols are distinct from the terminal symbols. If this is not the case, i.e. if a terminal symbol and a metasymbol are identical, we enclose the terminal symbol in quotes to differentiate it from the metasymbol. For example, the set of punctuation symbols of English can be defined as

$$\{\texttt{:, ;, ',', ...}\}$$

where ',' denotes the terminal symbol 'comma'.

A *string* is a finite sequence of symbols. We will represent strings by Greek symbols α, β, γ, etc. Thus α = axy is a string over Σ. The length of a string is the number of symbols in it. Note that the absence of any symbol is also a string, the *null string* ε. The *concatenation* operation combines two strings into a single string. It is used to build larger strings from existing strings. Thus, given two strings α and β, concatenation of α with β yields a string which is formed by putting the sequence of symbols forming α before the sequence of symbols forming β. For example, if α = ab, β = axy, then concatenation of α and β, represented as α.β or simply αβ, gives the string abaxy. The null string can also participate in a concatenation, thus a.ε = ε.a = a.

Nonterminal symbols

A *nonterminal symbol* (NT) is the name of a syntax category of a language, e.g. noun, verb, etc. An NT is written as a single capital letter, or as a name enclosed between < ... >, e.g. A or < *Noun* >. During grammatical analysis, a nonterminal symbol represents an instance of the category. Thus, < *Noun* > represents a noun.

Productions

A *production*, also called a *rewriting rule*, is a rule of the grammar. A production has the form

A nonterminal symbol :: = String of Ts and NTs

and defines the fact that the NT on the LHS of the production can be rewritten as the string of Ts and NTs appearing on the RHS. When an NT can be written as one of many different strings, the symbol '|' (standing for 'or') is used to separate the strings on the RHS, e.g.

< *Article* > ::= `a` | `an` | `the`

The string on the RHS of a production can be a concatenation of component strings, e.g. the production

< *Noun Phrase* > ::= < *Article* >< *Noun* >

expresses the fact that the noun phrase consists of an article followed by a noun.

Each grammar G defines a language L_G. G contains an NT called the *distinguished symbol* or the *start NT* of G. Unless otherwise specified, we use the symbol S as the distinguished symbol of G. A valid string α of L_G is obtained by using the following procedure

1. Let α = 'S'.
2. While α is not a string of terminal symbols
   (a) Select an NT appearing in α, say X.
   (b) Replace X by a string appearing on the RHS of a production of X.

Example 1.13 Grammar (1.1) defines a language consisting of noun phrases in English

< *Noun Phrase* > ::= < *Article* >< *Noun* >
< *Article* > ::= `a` | `an` | `the` (1.1)
< *Noun* > ::= `boy` | `apple`

< *Noun Phrase* > is the distinguished symbol of the grammar, `the boy` and `an apple` are some valid strings in the language.

Definition 1.6 (Grammar) *A grammar* G *of a language* L_G *is a quadruple* (Σ, *SNT, S, P) where*

Σ	*is the alphabet of* L_G*, i.e. the set of* Ts,
SNT	*is the set of* NTs,
S	*is the distinguished symbol, and*
P	*is the set of productions.*

Derivation, reduction and parse trees

A grammar G is used for two purposes, to generate valid strings of L_G and to 'recognize' valid strings of L_G. The derivation operation helps to generate valid strings while the reduction operation helps to recognize valid strings. A parse tree is used to depict the syntactic structure of a valid string as it emerges during a sequence of derivations or reductions.

Derivation

Let production P_1 of grammar G be of the form

$$P_1 : \quad A ::= \alpha$$

and let β be a string such that $\beta \equiv \gamma A \theta$, then replacement of A by α in string β constitutes a *derivation* according to production P_1. We use the notation $N \Rightarrow \eta$ to denote direct derivation of η from N and $N \overset{*}{\Rightarrow} \eta$ to denote transitive derivation of η (i.e. derivation in zero or more steps) from N, respectively. Thus, $A \Rightarrow \alpha$ only if $A ::= \alpha$ is a production of G and $A \overset{*}{\Rightarrow} \delta$ if $A \Rightarrow \ldots \Rightarrow \delta$. We can use this notation to define a valid string according to a grammar G as follows: δ is a valid string according to G only if $S \overset{*}{\Rightarrow} \delta$, where S is the distinguished symbol of G.

Example 1.14 Derivation of the string `the boy` according to grammar (1.1) can be depicted as

$$\begin{aligned} <\textit{Noun Phrase}> &\Rightarrow <\textit{Article}><\textit{Noun}> \\ &\Rightarrow \texttt{the} <\textit{Noun}> \\ &\Rightarrow \texttt{the boy} \end{aligned}$$

A string α such that $S \overset{*}{\Rightarrow} \alpha$ is a *sentential form* of L_G. The string α is a *sentence* of L_G if it consists of only Ts.

Example 1.15 Consider the grammar G

$$\begin{aligned} <\textit{Sentence}> &::= <\textit{Noun Phrase}><\textit{Verb Phrase}> \\ <\textit{Noun Phrase}> &::= <\textit{Article}><\textit{Noun}> \\ <\textit{Verb Phrase}> &::= <\textit{Verb}><\textit{Noun Phrase}> \\ <\textit{Article}> &::= \texttt{a} \mid \texttt{an} \mid \texttt{the} \\ <\textit{Noun}> &::= \texttt{boy} \mid \texttt{apple} \\ <\textit{Verb}> &::= \texttt{ate} \end{aligned} \qquad (1.2)$$

The following strings are sentential forms of L_G.

< *Noun Phrase* >< *Verb Phrase* >
`the boy` < *Verb Phrase* >
< *Noun Phrase* > `ate` < *Noun Phrase* >
`the boy ate` < *Noun Phrase* >
`the boy ate an apple`

However, only `the boy ate an apple` is a sentence.

Reduction

Let production P_1 of grammar G be of the form

$$P_1 : \quad A ::= \alpha$$

and let σ be a string such that $\sigma \equiv \gamma\alpha\theta$, then replacement of α by A in string σ constitutes a *reduction* according to production P_1. We use the notations $\eta \rightarrow N$ and $\eta \stackrel{*}{\rightarrow} N$ to depict direct and transitive reduction, respectively. Thus, $\alpha \rightarrow A$ only if $A ::= \alpha$ is a production of G and $\alpha \stackrel{*}{\rightarrow} A$ if $\alpha \rightarrow \ldots \rightarrow A$. We define the validity of some string δ according to grammar G as follows: δ is a valid string of L_G if $\delta \stackrel{*}{\rightarrow} S$, where S is the distinguished symbol of G.

Example 1.16 To determine the validity of the string

`the boy ate an apple`

according to grammar (1.2) we perform the following reductions

Step	*String*
0	`the boy ate an apple`
1	< *Article* > `boy ate an apple`
2	< *Article* > < *Noun* > `ate an apple`
3	< *Article* > < *Noun* > < *Verb* > `an apple`
4	< *Article* > < *Noun* > < *Verb* > < *Article* > `apple`
5	< *Article* > < *Noun* > < *Verb* > < *Article* > < *Noun* >
6	< *Noun Phrase* > < *Verb* > < *Article* > < *Noun* >
7	< *Noun Phrase* > < *Verb* > < *Noun Phrase* >
8	< *Noun Phrase* > < *Verb Phrase* >
9	< *Sentence* >

The string is a sentence of L_G since we are able to construct the reduction sequence

`the boy ate an apple` $\stackrel{*}{\rightarrow}$ < *Sentence* >.

Parse trees

A sequence of derivations or reductions reveals the syntactic structure of a string with respect to G. We depict the syntactic structure in the form of a *parse tree*. Derivation according to the production $A ::= \alpha$ gives rise to the following elemental parse tree:

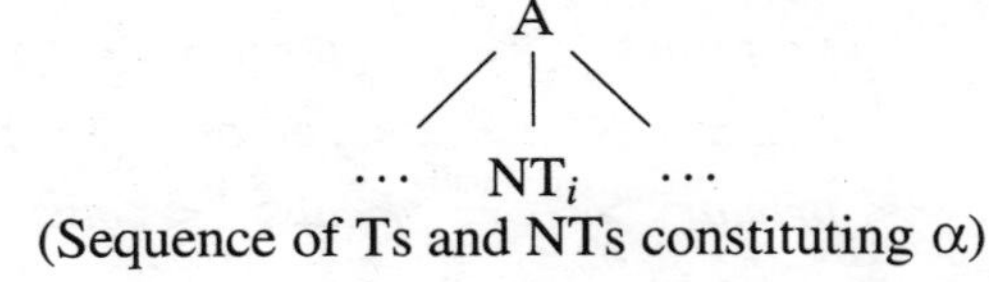

A subsequent step in the derivation replaces an NT in α, say NT_i, by a string. We can build another elemental parse tree to depict this derivation, viz.

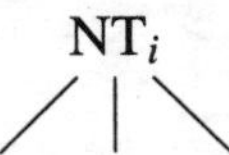

We can combine the two trees by replacing the node of NT_i in the first tree by this tree. In essence, the parse tree has grown in the downward direction due to a derivation. We can obtain a parse tree from a sequence of reductions by performing the converse actions. Such a tree would grow in the upward direction.

Example 1.17 Figure 1.19 shows the parse tree of the string `the boy ate an apple` obtained using the reductions of Ex. 1.16. The superscript associated with a node in the tree indicates the step in the reduction sequence which led to the subtree rooted at that node. Reduction steps 1 and 2 lead to reduction of `the` and `boy` to <Article> and <Noun>, respectively. Step 3 combines the parse trees of < *Article* > and < *noun* > to give the subtree rooted at < *Noun Phrase* >.

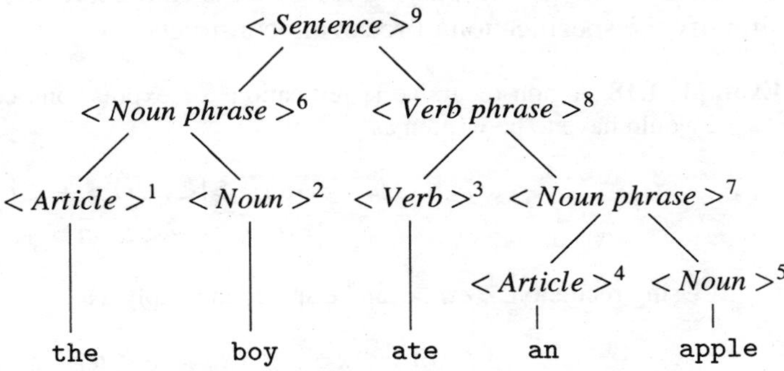

Fig. 1.19 Parse tree

Note that an identical tree would have been obtained if `the boy ate an apple` was derived from S.

Recursive specification

Grammar (1.3) is a complete grammar for an arithmetic expression containing the operators ↑ (exponentiation), * and +.

$$< exp > \ ::= \ < exp > + < term > | < term >$$

$$
\begin{aligned}
< term > &::= < term > * < factor > | < factor > \\
< factor > &::= < factor > \uparrow < primary > | < primary > \\
< primary > &::= < id > | < constant > | \ (< exp >) \\
< id > &::= < letter > | < id > \ [< letter > | < digit >] \\
< const > &::= [+ | -] < digit > | < const > < digit > \\
< letter > &::= \texttt{a} \mid \texttt{b} \mid \texttt{c} \mid \ldots \mid \texttt{z} \\
< digit > &::= \texttt{0} \mid \texttt{1} \mid \texttt{2} \mid \texttt{3} \mid \texttt{4} \mid \texttt{5} \mid \texttt{6} \mid \texttt{7} \mid \texttt{8} \mid \texttt{9}
\end{aligned}
\qquad (1.3)
$$

This grammar uses the notation known as the Backus Naur Form (BNF). Apart from the familiar elements $::=$, $|$ and $< \ldots >$, a new element here is $[\ldots]$, which is used to enclose an optional specification. Thus, the rules for $< id >$ and $< const >$ in grammar (1.3) are equivalent to the rules

$$
\begin{aligned}
< id > &::= < letter > | < id >< letter > | < id >< digit > \\
< const > &::= < digit > + < digit > | - < digit > \\
&\quad | < const >< digit >
\end{aligned}
$$

Grammar (1.3) uses recursive specification, whereby the NT being defined in a production itself occurs in a RHS string of the production, e.g. X ::= ... X .... The RHS alternative employing recursion is called a *recursive rule*. Recursive rules simplify the specification of recurring constructs.

Example 1.18 A non-recursive specification for expressions containing the '+' operator would have to be written as

$$
\begin{aligned}
< exp > &::= < term > | < term > + < term > \\
&\quad | < term > + < term > + < term > | \ldots
\end{aligned}
$$

Using recursion, *<exp>* can be specified simply as

$$
< exp > \ ::= \ < exp > + < term > | < term > \qquad (1.4)
$$

The first alternative on the RHS of grammar (1.4) is recursive. It permits an unbounded number of '+' operators in an expression. The second alternative is non-recursive. It provides an 'escape' from recursion while deriving or recognizing expressions according to the grammar. Recursive rules are classified into *left-recursive rules* and *right-recursive rules* depending on whether the NT being defined appears on the extreme left or extreme right in the recursive rule. For example, all recursive rules of grammar (1.3) are left-recursive rules. Indirect recursion occurs when two or more NTs are defined in terms of one another. Such recursion is useful for specifying nested constructs in a language. In grammar (1.3), the alternative *<primary>* ::= (*<exp>*) gives rise to indirect recursion because $<exp> \stackrel{*}{\Rightarrow} <primary>$. This specification permits a parenthesized expression to occur in any context where an identifier or constant can occur.

Direct recursion is not useful in situations where a limited number of occurrences is required. For example, the recursive specification

$$< id > ::= < letter > | < id > [< letter > | < digit >]$$

permits an identifier string to contain an unbounded number of characters, which is not correct. In such cases, controlled recurrence may be specified as

$$< id > ::= < letter > \{< letter > | < digit >\}_0^{15}$$

where the notation $\{\ldots\}_0^{15}$ indicates 0 to 15 occurrences of the enclosed specification.

1.4.1.1 Classification of Grammars

Grammars are classified on the basis of the nature of productions used in them (Chomsky, 1963). Each grammar class has its own characteristics and limitations.

Type-0 grammars

These grammars, known as *phrase structure grammars*, contain productions of the form

$$\alpha ::= \beta$$

where both α and β can be strings of Ts and NTs. Such productions permit arbitrary substitution of strings during derivation or reduction, hence they are not relevant to specification of programming languages.

Type-1 grammars

These grammars are known as *context sensitive grammars* because their productions specify that derivation or reduction of strings can take place only in specific contexts. A Type-1 production has the form

$$\alpha \, A \, \beta ::= \alpha \, \pi \, \beta$$

Thus, a string π in a sentential form can be replaced by 'A' (or vice versa) only when it is enclosed by the strings α and β. These grammars are also not particularly relevant for PL specification since recognition of PL constructs is not context sensitive in nature.

Type-2 grammars

These grammars impose no context requirements on derivations or reductions. A typical Type-2 production is of the form

$$A ::= \pi$$

which can be applied independent of its context. These grammars are therefore known as *context free grammars* (CFG). CFGs are ideally suited for programming language specification. Two best known uses of Type-2 grammars in PL specification are the ALGOL-60 specification (Naur, 1963) and Pascal specification (Jensen, Wirth, 1975). The reader can verify that grammars (1.2) and (1.3) are Type-2 grammars.

Type-3 grammars

Type-3 grammars are characterized by productions of the form

$$A ::= \texttt{t}\,\texttt{B} \mid \texttt{t} \text{ or}$$
$$A ::= \texttt{B}\,\texttt{t} \mid \texttt{t}$$

Note that these productions also satisfy the requirements of Type-2 grammars. The specific form of the RHS alternatives—namely a single T or a string containing a single T and a single NT—gives some practical advantages in scanning (we shall see this aspect in Chapter 6). However, the nature of the productions restricts the expressive power of these grammars, e.g. nesting of constructs or matching of parentheses cannot be specified using such productions. Hence the use of Type-3 productions is restricted to the specification of lexical units, e.g. identifiers, constants, labels, etc. The productions for <*constant*> and <*identifier*> in grammar (1.3) are in fact Type-3 in nature. This can be seen clearly when we rewrite the production for $< id >$ in the form B t | t, viz.

$$< id > ::= l \mid < id > l \mid < id > d$$

where l and d stand for a letter and digit respectively.

Type-3 grammars are also known as *linear grammars* or *regular grammars*. These are further categorized into left-linear and right-linear grammars depending on whether the NT in the RHS alternative appears at the extreme left or extreme right.

Operator grammars

Definition 1.7 (Operator grammar (OG)) *An* operator grammar *is a grammar none of whose productions contain two or more consecutive NTs in any RHS alternative.*

Thus, nonterminals occurring in an RHS string are separated by one or more terminal symbols. All terminal symbols occurring in the RHS strings are called *operators* of the grammar. As we will discuss later in Chapter 6, OGs have certain practical advantages in compiler writing.

Example 1.19 Grammar (1.3) is an OG. '↑', '*', '+', '(' and ')' are the operators of the grammar.

1.4.1.2 Ambiguity in Grammatic Specification

Ambiguity implies the possibility of different interpretations of a source string. In natural languages, ambiguity may concern the meaning or syntax category of a word, or the syntactic structure of a construct. For example, a word can have multiple meanings or can be both noun and verb (e.g. the word 'base'), and a sentence can have multiple syntactic structures (e.g. 'police ordered to stop speeding on roads'). Formal language grammars avoid ambiguity at the level of a lexical unit or a syntax category. This is achieved by the simple rule that identical strings cannot appear on the RHS of more than one production in the grammar. Existence of ambiguity at the level of the syntactic structure of a string would mean that more than one parse tree can be built for the string. In turn, this would mean that the string can have more than one meaning associated with it.

Example 1.20 Consider the expression grammar

$$\begin{array}{lll} <exp> & ::= & <id> \mid <exp> + <exp> \mid <exp> * <exp> \\ <id> & ::= & \texttt{a} \mid \texttt{b} \mid \texttt{c} \end{array} \quad (1.5)$$

Two parse trees exist for the source string `a+b*c` according to this grammar —one in which `a+b` is first reduced to <*exp*> and another in which `b*c` is first reduced to <*exp*>. Since semantic analysis derives the meaning of a string on the basis of its parse tree, clearly two different meanings can be associated with the string.

Eliminating ambiguity

An ambiguous grammar should be rewritten to eliminate ambiguity. In Ex. 1.20, the first tree does not reflect the conventional meaning associated with `a+b*c`, while the second tree does. Hence the grammar must be rewritten such that reduction of '*' precedes the reduction of '+' in `a+b*c`. The normal method of achieving this is to use a hierarchy of NTs in the grammar, and to associate the reduction or derivation of an operator with an appropriate NT.

Example 1.21 Figure 1.20 illustrates reduction of `a+b*c` according to Grammar 1.3. Part (a) depicts an attempt to reduce `a+b` to <*exp*>. This attempt fails because the resulting string <*exp*> * <*id*> cannot be reduced to <*exp*>. Part (b) depicts the correct reduction of `a+b*c` in which `b*c` is first reduced to <*exp*>. This sequence of reductions can be explained as follows: Grammar (1.3) associates the recognition of '*' with reduction of a string to a <*term*>, which alone can take part in a reduction involving '+'. Consequently, in `a+b*c`, '*' has to be necessarily reduced before '+'. This yields the conventional meaning of the string. Other NTs, viz. <*factor*> and <*primary*>, similarly take care of the operator '↑' and the parentheses '(...)'. Hence there is no ambiguity in grammar (1.3).

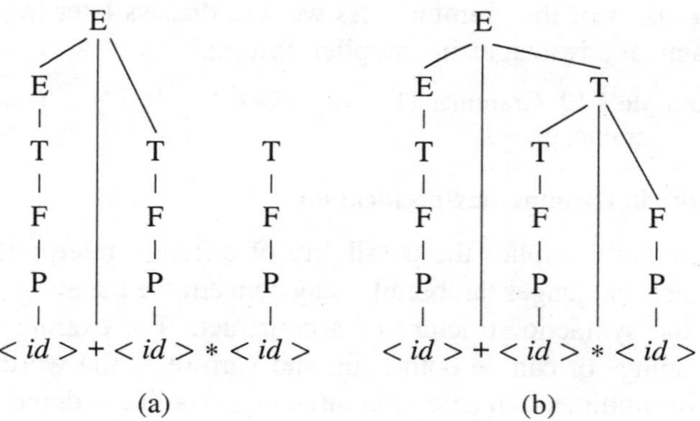

Fig. 1.20 Ensuring a unique parse tree for an expression

EXERCISE 1.4

1. In grammar (1.3), identify productions which could belong to
   (a) an operator grammar.
   (b) a linear grammar.
2. Write productions for the following
   (a) a decimal constant with or without a fractional part,
   (b) a real number with mantissa and exponent specification.
3. In grammar (1.3) what are the priorities of '+', '*' and '↑' with respect to one another?
4. In grammar (1.3) add productions to incorporate relational and boolean operators.
5. *Associativity* of an operator indicates the order in which consecutive occurrences of the operator in a string are reduced. For example '+' is left associative, i.e. in `a+b+c`, `a+b` is performed first, followed by the addition of `c` to its result.
   (a) Find the associativities of operators in grammar (1.3).
   (b) Exponentiation should be right associative so that `a↑b↑c` has the conventional meaning a^{b^c}. What changes should be made in grammar (1.3) to implement right associativity for ↑?
   (c) Is the grammar of problem 3 of Exercise 3.2.2 ambiguous? If so, give a string which has multiple parses.

1.4.2 Binding and Binding Times

Each program entity pe_i in program P has a set of attributes $A_i \equiv \{a_j\}$ associated with it. If pe_i is an identifier, it has an attribute *kind* whose value indicates whether it is a variable, a procedure or a reserved identifier (i.e. a keyword). A variable has attributes like type, dimensionality, scope, memory address, etc. Note that the attribute of one program entity may be another program entity. For example, type is an attribute of a variable. It is also a program entity with its own attributes, e.g. size (i.e. number of memory bytes). The values of the attributes of a type `typ` should be determined some time before a language processor processes a declaration statement using that type, viz. a Pascal-like statement

```
var : type;
```

For simplicity we often use the words 'the a_j attribute of pe_i is ..' instead of the more precise words 'the value of the a_j attribute of pe_i is ..'.

Definition 1.8 (Binding) *A* binding *is the association of an attribute of a program entity with a value.*

Binding time is the time at which a binding is performed. Thus the type attribute of variable `var` is bound to `typ` when its declaration is processed. The size attribute of `typ` is bound to a value sometime prior to this binding. We are interested in the following binding times:

1. Language definition time of L
2. Language implementation time of L
3. Compilation time of P
4. Execution init time of `proc`
5. Execution time of `proc`.

where L is a programming language, P is a program written in L and `proc` is a procedure in P. Note that language implementation time is the time when a language translator is designed. The preceding list of binding times is not exhaustive; other binding times can be defined, viz. binding at the linking time of P. The language definition of L specifies binding times for the attributes of various entities of a program written in L.

Example 1.22 Consider the Pascal program

```
program bindings(input, output);
   var
      i : integer;
      a,b : real;
   procedure proc (x : real; j : integer);
      var
         info : array [1..10, 1..5] of integer;
         p : ↑integer;
      begin
         new(p);
   end;
   begin
   proc(a,i);
end.
```

Binding of the keywords of Pascal to their meanings is performed at language definition time. This is how keywords like **program**, **procedure**, **begin** and **end** get their meanings. These bindings apply to all programs written in Pascal. At language implementation time, the compiler designer performs certain bindings. For example, the size of type 'integer' is bound to n bytes where n is a number determined by the architecture of the target machine. Binding of type attributes of variables is performed at compilation time of program `bindings`. The memory addresses of local variables `info` and `p` of procedure `proc` are bound at every execution init time of procedure `proc`. The value attributes of variables are bound (possibly more than once) during an execution of `proc`. The memory address of `p↑` is bound when the procedure call `new (p)` is executed.

Importance of binding times

The binding time of an attribute of a program entity determines the manner in which a language processor can handle the use of the entity. A compiler can generate code specifically tailored to a binding performed during or before compilation time. However, a compiler cannot generate such code for bindings performed later than compilation time. This affects execution efficiency of the target program.

Example 1.23 Consider the PL/1 program segment

```
procedure pl1_proc (x, j, info_size, columns);
   declare x float;
   declare (j, info_size, columns) fixed;
   declare pl1_info (1:info_size,1:columns) fixed;
   ...
end pl1_proc;
```

Here the size of array `pl1_info` is determined by the values of parameters `info_size` and `columns` in a specific call of `pl1_proc`. This is an instance of execution time binding. The compiler does not know the size of array `pl1_info`. Hence it may not be able to generate efficient code for accessing its elements.

The dimension bounds of array `info` in program `bindings` of Ex. 1.22 are constants. Thus, binding of the dimension bound attributes can be performed at compilation time. This enables the Pascal compiler to generate efficient code to access elements of `info`. Thus the PL/1 program of Ex. 1.23 may execute slower than the Pascal program of Ex. 1.22 (see Section 6.2.3 for more details). However, the PL/1 program provides greater flexibility to the programmer since the dimension bounds can be specified during program execution. From this comparison, we can draw the following inference concerning the influence of binding times on the characteristics of programs: An early binding provides greater execution efficiency whereas a late binding provides greater flexibility in the writing of a program.

Static and dynamic bindings

Definition 1.9 (Static binding) *A* static binding *is a binding performed before the execution of a program begins.*

Definition 1.10 (Dynamic binding) *A* dynamic binding *is a binding performed after the execution of a program has begun.*

Needless to say that static bindings lead to more efficient execution of a program than dynamic bindings. We shall discuss static and dynamic binding of memory in Section 6.2.1 and dynamic binding of variables to types in Section 6.6.

1.5 LANGUAGE PROCESSOR DEVELOPMENT TOOLS

The analysis phase of a language processor has a standard form irrespective of its purpose, the source text is subjected to lexical, syntax and semantic analysis and the results of analysis are represented in an IR. Thus writing of language processors is a well understood and repetitive process which ideally suits the program generation approach to software development. This has led to the development of a set of language processor development tools (LPDTs) focussing on generation of the analysis phase of language processors.

Figure 1.21 shows a schematic of an LPDT which generates the analysis phase of a language processor whose source language is L. The LPDT requires the following two inputs:

1. Specification of a grammar of language L
2. Specification of semantic actions to be performed in the analysis phase.

It generates programs that perform lexical, syntax and semantic analysis of the source program and construct the IR. These programs collectively form the analysis phase of the language processor (see the dashed box in Fig. 1.21).

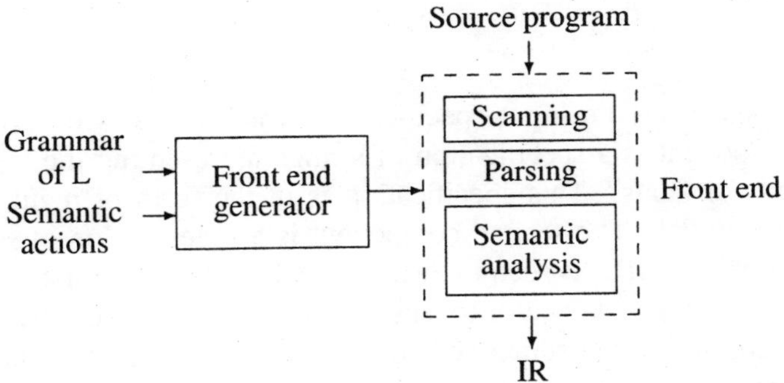

Fig. 1.21 A language processor development tool (LPDT)

We briefly discuss two LPDTs widely used in practice. These are, the lexical analyser generator LEX, and the parser generator YACC. The input to these tools is a specification of the lexical and syntactic constructs of L, and the semantic actions to be performed on recognizing the constructs. The specification consists of a set of *translation rules* of the form

< *string specification* > { < *semantic action* > }

where < *semantic action* > consists of C code. This code is executed when a string matching < *string specification* > is encountered in the input. LEX and YACC generate C programs which contain the code for scanning and parsing, respectively, and the semantic actions contained in the specification. A YACC generated parser can use a LEX generated scanner as a routine if the scanner and parser use same conventions concerning the representation of tokens. Figure 1.22 shows a schematic for developing the analysis phase of a compiler for language L using LEX and YACC. The analysis phase processes the source program to build an intermediate representation (IR). A single pass compiler can be built using LEX and YACC if the semantic actions are aimed at generating target code instead of IR. Note that the scanner also generates an intermediate representation of a source program for use by the parser. We call it IR_l in Fig. 1.22 to differentiate it from the IR of the analysis phase.

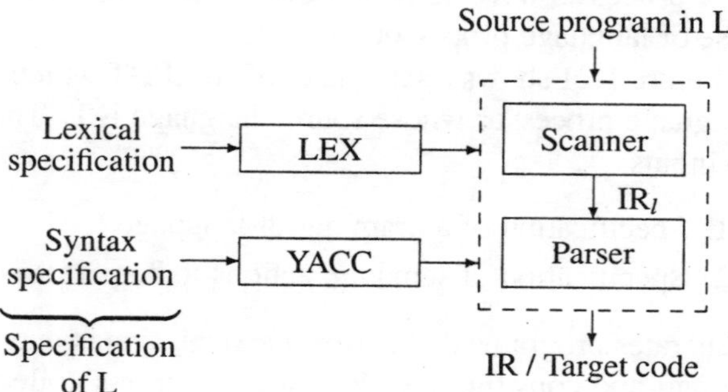

Fig. 1.22 Using LEX and YACC

1.5.1 LEX

LEX accepts an input specification which consists of two components. The first component is a specification of strings representing the lexical units in L, e.g. id's and constants. This specification is in the form of regular expressions defined in Section 3.1. The second component is a specification of semantic actions aimed at building an IR. As seen in Section 1.3.1.1, the IR consists of a set of tables of lexical units and a sequence of tokens for the lexical units occurring in a source statement. Accordingly, the semantic actions make new entries in the tables and build tokens for the lexical units.

Example 1.24 Figure 1.23 shows a sample input to LEX. The input consists of four components, three of which are shown here. The first component (enclosed by %{ and %}) defines the symbols used in specifying the strings of L. It defines the symbol `letter` to stand for any upper or lower case letter, and `digit` to stand for any digit. The second component enclosed between %% and %% contains the translation rules. The third component contains auxiliary routines which can be used in the semantic actions.

```
%{
letter                          [A-Za-z]
digit                           [0-9]
}%

%%
begin                           {return(BEGIN);}
end                             {return(END);}
":= "                           {return(ASGOP);}
{letter} ({letter}|{digit})*    {yylval=enter_id();
                                 return(ID);}
{digit}+                        {yylval=enter_num();
                                 return(NUM);}

%%
enter_id()
{ /* enters the id in the symbol table and returns
     entry number */ }
enter_num()
{ /* enters the number in the constants table and
     returns entry number */}
```

Fig. 1.23 A sample LEX specification

The sample input in Figure 1.23 defines the strings `begin`, `end`, `:=` (the assignment operator), and identifier and constant strings of L. When an identifier is found, it is entered in the symbol table (if not already present) using the routine `enter_id`. The pair (`ID`, *entry #*) forms the token for the identifier string. By convention *entry #* is put in the global variable `yylval`, and the class code `ID` is returned as the value of the call on scanner. Similar actions are taken on finding a constant, the keywords `begin` and `end` and the assignment operator. Note that each operator and keyword has been made into a class by itself to suit the conventions mentioned earlier.

1.5.2 YACC

Each string specification in the input to YACC resembles a grammar production. The parser generated by YACC performs reductions according to this grammar. The actions associated with a string specification are executed when a reduction is made according to the specification. An attribute is associated with every nonterminal symbol. The value of this attribute can be manipulated during parsing. The attribute can be given any user-designed structure. A symbol '$n' in the action part of a translation rule refers to the attribute of the nth symbol in the RHS of the string specification. '$$' represents the attribute of the LHS symbol of the string specification.

Example 1.25 Figure 1.24 shows sample input to YACC. The input consists of four components, of which only two are shown. It is assumed that the attribute of a symbol resembles the attributes used in Fig. 1.15. The routine `gendesc` builds a descriptor containing the name and type of an id or constant. The routine `gencode` takes an operator and the attributes of two operands, generates code and returns with the attribute for the result of the operation. This attribute is assigned as the attribute of the LHS symbol of the string specification. In a subsequent reduction this attribute becomes the attribute of some RHS symbol.

```
%%
E : E+T   {$$ = gencode('+', $1, $3);}
  | T     {$$ = $1;}
  ;
T : T*V   {$$ = gencode('*', $1, $3);}
  | V     {$$ = $1;}
  ;
V : id    {$$ = gendesc($1);}
  ;
%%
gencode (operator, operand_1, operand_2)
{ /* Generates code using operand descriptors.
     Returns descriptor for result */ }
gendesc (symbol)
{ /* Refer to symbol/constant table entry.
     Build and return descriptor for the symbol */ }
```

Fig. 1.24 A sample YACC specification

Parsing of the string `b+c*d` where `b`, `c` and `d` are of type `real`, using the parser generated by YACC from the input of Fig. 1.24 leads to following calls on the C routines:

```
Gendesc ( [Id #1] );
Gendesc ( [Id #2] );
Gendesc ( [Id #3] );
Gencode ( *, [c, real], [d, real] );
Gencode ( +, [b, real], [t, real] );
```

where an attribute has the form [*<name>, <type>*], and `t` is the name of a location (a register or memory word) used to store the result of `c*d` in the code generated by the first call on `gencode`. Details of `gencode` shall be discussed in Chapter 6.

BIBLIOGRAPHY

Elson (1973), Tennent (1981), Pratt (1983) and Maclennan (1983) discuss the influence of programming language design on aspects of compilation and execution, i.e. on the specification and execution gaps. Cleaveland and Uzgalis (1977) and Backhouse (1979) are devoted to programming language grammars. Programming language grammars are also discussed in most compiler books.

Prywes *et al* (1979) discusses automatic program generation. Martin (1982) describes generation of application programs.

(a) Programming languages

1. Elson, M. (1973): *Concepts of Programming Languages*, Science Research Associates, Chicago.

2. Maclennan, B.J. (1983): *Principles of Programming Languages*, Holt, Rinehart & Winston, New York.
3. Pratt, T.W. (1983): *Programming Languages – Design and Implementation*, Prentice-Hall, Englewood Cliffs.
4. Tennent, R.D. (1981): *Principles of Programming Languages*, Prentice-Hall, Englewood Cliffs.

(b) Grammars for programming languages

1. Backhouse, R.C. (1979): *Syntax of Programming Languages*, Prentice-Hall, New Jersey.
2. Cleaveland, J.C. and R.C. Uzgalis (1977): *Grammars for Programming Languages*, Elsevier, New York.
3. Jensen, K. and N. Wirth (1975): *Pascal User Manual and Report*, Springer-Verlag, New York.
4. Lewis, P.M., D.J. Rosenkrantz and R.E. Stearns (1976): *Compiler Design Theory*, Addison-Wesley, Reading.
5. Naur, P. (ed.) (1963): "Revised report on the algorithmic language ALGOL 60," *Commn. of ACM*, **6** (1), 1.
6. Naur, P. (1975): "Programming languages, natural languages and mathematics, *Commn. of ACM*, **18** (12), 676-683.

(c) Program generation

1. Martin, J. (1982): *Application Development Without Programmers*, Prentice-Hall, Englewood Cliffs.
2. Prywes, N.S., A. Pnueli and S. Shastry (1979): "Use of nonprocedural specification language and associated program generator in software development," *ACM TOPLAS*, **1** (2), 196-217.

(d) Language processor development tools

1. Graham, S.L. (1980): "Table driven code generation," *Computer*, **13** (8), 25-34.
2. Johnson, S.C. (1975): "Yacc – Yet Another Compiler Compiler," *Computing Science Technical Report no. 32*, AT & T Bell Laboratories, N.J.
3. Lesk, M.E. (1975): "Lex – A lexical analyzer generator," *Computing Science Technical Report no. 39*, At & T Bell Laboratories, N.J.
4. Schreiner, A.T. and H.G. Fredman, Jr. (1985): *Introduction to Compiler Construction with Unix*, Prentice-Hall, Englewood Cliffs.
5. Levine, J.R., T. Mason and D. Brown (1990): *Lex and Yacc*, 2nd edition, O'Reilly & associates, Sebastopol.

CHAPTER 2

Data Structures for Language Processing

The space–time tradeoff in data structures, i.e. the tradeoff between memory requirements and the search efficiency of a data structure, is a fundamental principle of systems programming. A language processor makes frequent use of the search operation over its data structures. This makes the design of data structures a crucial issue in language processing activities. In this chapter we shall discuss the data structure requirements of language processors and suggest efficient data structures to meet these requirements.

The data structures used in language processing can be classified on the basis of the following criteria:

1. Nature of a data structure—whether a *linear* or *nonlinear* data structure
2. Purpose of a data structure—whether a *search* data structure or an *allocation* data structure.
3. Lifetime of a data structure—whether used during language processing or during target program execution.

A *linear data structure* consists of a linear arrangement of elements in the memory. The physical proximity of its elements is used to facilitate efficient search. However, a linear data structure requires a contiguous area of memory for its elements. This poses problems in situations where the size of a data structure is difficult to predict. In such a situation, a designer is forced to overestimate the memory requirements of a linear data structure to ensure that it does not outgrow the allocated memory. This leads to wastage of memory. The elements of a *nonlinear data structure* are accessed using pointers. Hence the elements need not occupy contiguous areas of memory, which avoids the memory allocation problem seen in the context of linear data structures. However, the nonlinear arrangement of elements leads to lower search efficiency.

Example 2.1 Figure 2.1(a) shows memory allocation for four linear data structures. Parts of the data structures shaded with dotted lines are not in current use. Note that these parts may remain unused throughout the execution of the program, however the memory allocated to them cannot be used for other data structure(s). Figure 2.1(b) shows allocation to four nonlinear data structures. Elements of the data structures are allocated noncontiguous areas of memory as and when needed. This is how two memory areas are allocated to E while three memory areas are allocated to F and two memory areas are allocated to H. No parts of the data structures are currently unused. Free memory existing in the system can be allocated to any new or existing data structures.

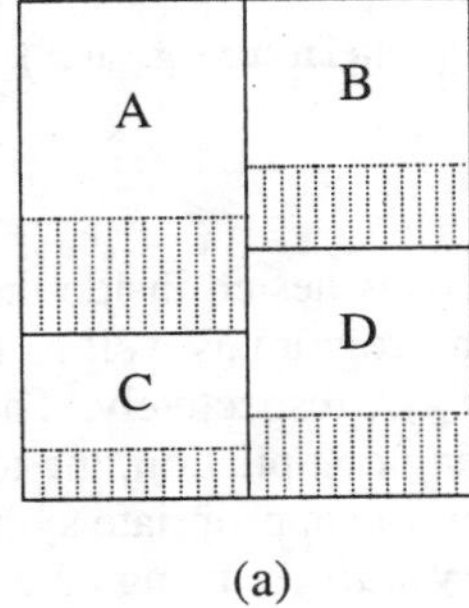

(a)

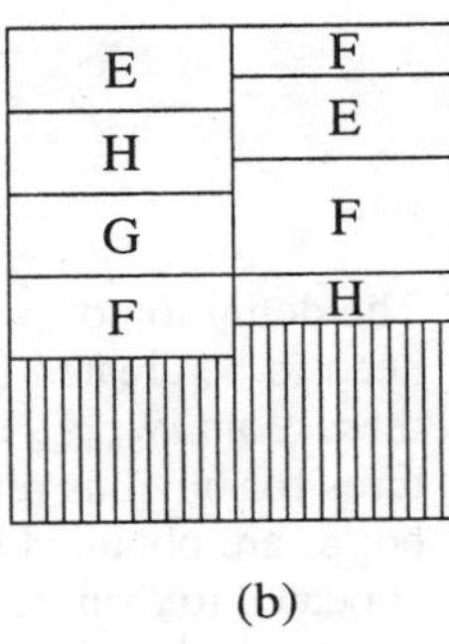

(b)

Fig. 2.1 Linear and nonlinear data structures

Search data structures are used during language processing to maintain attribute information concerning different entities in the source program. These data structures are characterized by the fact that the entry for an entity is created only once but may be searched for a large number of times. Search efficiency is therefore very important. *Allocation data structures* are characterized by the fact that the address of the memory area allocated to an entity is known to the user(s) of that entity. Thus no search operations are conducted on them. Speed of allocation or deallocation and efficiency of memory utilization are the important criteria for the allocation data structures.

A language processor uses both search and allocation data structures during its operation (see Ex. 2.2). Search data structures are used to constitute various tables of information. Allocation data structures are used to handle programs with nested structures of some kind. A target program rarely uses search data structures. However, it may use allocation data structures (see Ex. 2.3).

Example 2.2 Consider the Pascal program

```
Program Sample(input,output);
  var
      x,y : real;
      i   : integer;
  Procedure calc(var a,b : real);
    var
        sum : real;
    begin
        sum := a+b;
        ...
  end calc;
  begin { Main program }
    ...
end.
```

The definition of procedure `calc` is nested inside the main program. Symbol tables need to be created for the main program as well as for procedure `calc`. Let us call these $Symtab_{\texttt{Sample}}$ and $Symtab_{\texttt{calc}}$, respectively. These tables are search data structures for obvious reasons. During compilation, the attributes of a symbol, e.g. symbol `a`, are obtained by searching the appropriate symbol table. Memory needs to be allocated to $Symtab_{\texttt{Sample}}$ and $Symtab_{\texttt{calc}}$ using an allocation data structure. The addresses of these tables are noted in a suitable manner. Hence no searches are involved in locating $Symtab_{\texttt{Sample}}$ or $Symtab_{\texttt{calc}}$.

Example 2.3 Consider the following Pascal and C program segments

```
Pascal  :  var p : ↑integer;
           begin
             new(p);

C       :  float *ptr;
           ptr = (float *) calloc(5, sizeof(float));
```

The Pascal call `new(p)` allocates sufficient memory to hold an integer value and puts the address of this memory area in `p`. The C statement `ptr = ..` allocates a memory area sufficient to hold 5 float values and puts its address in `ptr`. Accesses to these memory areas are implemented through pointers `p` and `ptr`. No search is involved in accessing the allocated memory.

2.1 SEARCH DATA STRUCTURES

A search data structure (or *search structure* for short) is a set of entries, each entry accommodating the information concerning one entity. Each entry is assumed to contain a *key* field which forms the basis for a search. Throughout this section we will use examples of entries in a symbol table used by a language processor. Here, the key field is the *symbol* field containing the name of an entity.

Entry formats

Each entry in a search structure is a set of fields. It is common for an entry in a search structure to consist of two parts, a fixed part and a variant part. Each part consists of a set of fields. Fields of the fixed part exist in each entry of the search structure. The value in a *tag* field of the fixed part determines the information to be stored in the variant part of the entry. For each value v_i in the tag field, the variant part of the entry consists of the set of fields SF_{v_i} (see Ex. 2.4). Note that the fixed and variant parts may be nested, i.e. a variant part may itself consist of fixed and variant parts, etc.

Example 2.4 Entries in the symbol table of a compiler have the following fields:

Fixed part: Fields *symbol* and *class* (*class* is the tag field).

Variant part:

Tag value	*Variant part fields*
variable	*type, length, dimension info.*
procedure name	*address of parameter list, number of parameters.*
function name	*type of returned value, length of returned value, address of parameter list, number of parameters.*
label	*statement number.*

Fixed and variable length entries

An entry may be declared as a *record* or a *structure* of the language in which the language processor is being implemented. (We shall use the word 'record' in our discussion.) In the *fixed length entry* format, each record is defined to consist of the following fields:

1. Fields in the fixed part of the entry
2. $\bigcup_{v_i} SF_{v_i}$, i.e. the set of fields in all variant parts of the entry.

All records in the search structure now have an identical format. This enables the use of homogeneous linear data structures like arrays. In turn, the use of linear organizations enables the use of efficient search procedures (we shall see this later in the section). However, this organization makes inefficient use of memory since many records may contain redundant fields.

In the *variable length entry* format, a record consists of the following fields:

1. Fields in the fixed part of the entry, including the tag field
2. $\{ f_j \mid f_j \in SF_{v_j} \text{ if } tag = v_j \}$.

This entry format leads to a compact organization in which no memory wastage occurs.

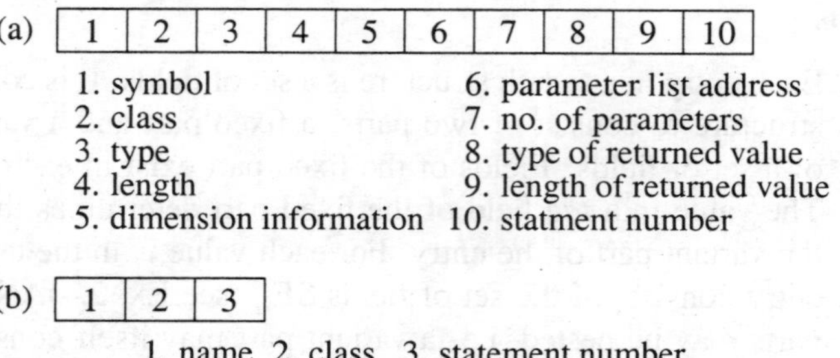

Fig. 2.2 (a) Fixed entry, (b) Variable length entry for label

Example 2.5 Figure 2.2 shows two entry formats for the symbol table of Ex. 2.4. Part (a) shows the fixed length entry format. When *class* = label, all fields excepting *name*, *class* and *statement number* are redundant. Part (b) shows the variable length entry format when *class* = label.

When a variable length entry format is used, the search method may require knowledge of the length of an entry. In such cases a record would consist of the following fields:

1. A *length* field
2. Fields in the fixed part of the entry, including the tag field
3. $\{ f_j \mid f_j \in \mathrm{SF}_{v_j} \text{ if } tag = v_j \}$.

We will depict this format as

length	*entry*

Hybrid entry formats

A Hybrid entry format is used as a compromise between the fixed and variable entry formats to combine the access efficiency of the fixed entry format with the memory efficiency of the variable entry format. In this format each entry is split into two halves, the fixed part and the variable part. A *pointer* field is added to the fixed part. It points to the variable part of the entry. The fixed and variable parts are accommodated in two different data structures. The fixed parts of all entries are organized into an efficient search structure, e.g. a linear data structure. Since the fixed part contains a pointer to the variable part, the variable part does not need to be located through a search. Hence it is put into an allocation data structure which can be linear or nonlinear in nature. The hybrid entry format is depicted as

fixed part	*pointer*

length	*variable part*

Operations on search structures

The following operations are performed on search data structures:

1. Operation *add:* Add the entry of a symbol.
2. Operation *search:* Search and locate the entry of a symbol.
3. Operation *delete:* Delete the entry of a symbol.

The entry for a symbol is created only once, but may be searched for a large number of times during the processing of a program. The deletion operation is not very common.

Generic search procedure

We give the generic procedure to search and locate the entry of symbol s in a search data structure as Algorithm 2.1.

Algorithm 2.1 (Generic search procedure)

1. Make a prediction concerning the entry of the search data structure which symbol s may be occupying. Let this be entry e.
2. Let s_e be the symbol occupying e^{th} entry. Compare s with s_e. Exit with success if the two match.
3. Repeat steps 1 and 2 till it can be concluded that the symbol does not exist in the search data structure.

The nature of the prediction varies with the organization of the search data structure. Each comparison of Step 2 is called a *probe*. Efficiency of a search procedure is determined by the number of probes performed by the search procedure. We use following notation to represent the number of probes in a search:

p_s : Number of probes in a successful search
p_u : Number of probes in an unsuccessful search

2.1.1 Table Organizations

A table is a linear data structure. The entries of a table occupy adjoining areas of the memory. Two points can be made concerning tables as search structures:

1. Given the location of an entry of the table, it is meaningful to talk of the *next* entry of the table or the *previous* entry of the table. A search technique may use this fact to advantage.
2. Tables using the fixed length entry organization possess the property of *positional determinacy*. This property states that the address of an entry in a table can be determined from its entry number. For example, the address of the eth

entry is $a+(e-1).l$, where a is the address of the first entry and l is the length of an entry. This property facilitates the representation of a symbol s by e, its entry number in the search structure, in the intermediate code generated by a language processor (see Section 1.3.1). Positional determinacy may also be used to design efficient search procedures, as we shall see later in this section. Tables using variable length entries do not possess the property of positional determinacy, so one must step through the first $(e-1)$ entries of a table in order to locate the eth entry. Hence variable length entries are generally avoided in linear data structures. In our discussion, we assume the use of fixed length entries in linear data structures.

Sequential search organization

Figure 2.3 shows a typical state of a table using the sequential search organization. We use the following symbols in our discussion:

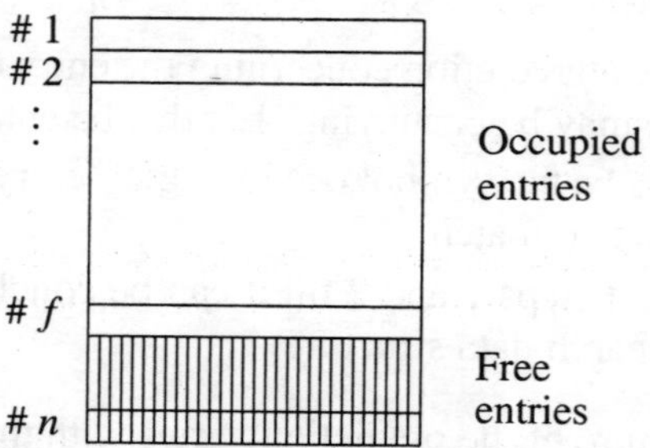

Fig. 2.3 Sequential search table

n : Number of entries in the table
f : Number of occupied entries

Search for a symbol

At any stage the search prediction in Algorithm 2.1 is that symbol s occupies the *next* entry of the table, where *next* = 1 to start with. From Algorithm 2.1, it follows that if all active entries in the table have the same probability of being accessed, we have

$$p_s = f/2 \quad \text{for a successful search}$$
$$p_u = f \quad \text{for an unsuccessful search}$$

Following an unsuccessful search, a symbol may be entered in the table using an *add* operation.

Add a symbol

The symbol is added to the first free entry in the table. The value of f is updated accordingly.

Delete a symbol

Deletion of an entry can be implemented in two ways, physical deletion and logical deletion. In *physical deletion*, an entry is deleted by erasing or by overwriting. Thus, if the dth entry is to be deleted, entries $d+1$ to f can be shifted 'up' by one entry each. This would require $(f-d)$ shift operations in the symbol table. An efficient alternative would be to move the fth entry into the dth position, thus requiring only one shift operation. Physical deletion causes changes in the entry numbers of symbols, which interferes with the representation of a symbol in the IC. Hence physical deletion is seldom used.

Logical deletion of an entry is performed by adding some information to the entry to indicate its deletion. This can be implemented by introducing a field to indicate whether an entry is active or deleted. The complete symbol table entry now looks as follows:

Active/deleted	*Symbol*	*Other info*

Binary search organization

All entries in a table are assumed to satisfy an ordering relation. For example, use of the '$<$' relation implies that the symbol occupying an entry is 'smaller than' the symbol occupying the next entry. At any stage the search prediction in Algorithm 2.1 is that s occupies the middle entry of that part of the table which is expected to contain its entry.

Algorithm 2.2 (Binary search)

1. *start* := 1; *end* := f;
2. While *start* $\leq$ *end*
   (a) $e := \lceil \frac{start+end}{2} \rceil$; where $\lceil \ldots \rceil$ implies a rounded quotient. Exit with success if $s = s_e$.
   (b) If $s < s_e$ then *end* := $e-1$;
   else *start* := $e+1$;
3. Exit with failure.

For a table containing f entries, we have $p_s \leq \lceil log_2 f \rceil$ and $p_u = \lceil log_2 f \rceil$. Thus the search performance is logarithmic in the size of the table. However, the requirement that the entry number of a symbol in the table should not change after an *add* operation (due to its use in the IC), forbids both additions and deletions during language processing. Hence, binary search organization is suitable only for a table containing a fixed set of symbols, e.g. the table of keywords in a PL. For the same reason, it cannot be used for a symbol table unless one can afford a separate pass of the language processor for constructing the table.

Hash table organization

In the hash table organization the search prediction in Algorithm 2.1 depends on the value of s, i.e. e is a function of s. Three possibilities exist concerning the predicted entry—the entry may be occupied by s, the entry may be occupied by some other symbol, or the entry may be empty. The situation in the second case, i.e. $s \neq s_e$, is called a *collision*. Following a collision, the search continues with a new prediction. In the third case, s is entered in the predicted entry.

Algorithm 2.3 (Hash table management)

1. $e := h(s)$;
2. Exit with success if $s = s_e$, and with failure if entry e is unoccupied.
3. Repeat steps 1 and 2 with different functions h', h'', etc.

The function h used in Algorithm 2.3 is called a *hashing function*. We use the following notation to discuss the properties of hashing functions:

n	:	Number of entries in the table
f	:	Number of occupied entries in the table
ρ	:	*Occupation density* in the table, i.e. f/n
k	:	Number of distinct symbols in the source language
k_p	:	Number of symbols used in some source program
S_p	:	Set of symbols used in some source program
N	:	Address space of the table, i.e. the space formed by the entries 1 ... n
K	:	Key space of the system, i.e. the space formed by enumerating all symbols of the source language. We will denote it as 1 ... k
K_p	:	Key space of a program, i.e. 1 ... k_p

A hashing function has the property that $1 \leq h(symb) \leq n$, where *symb* is any valid symbol of the source language. If $k \leq n$, we can select a one-to-one function as the hashing function h. This will eliminate collisions in the symbol table since entry number e given by $e = h(s)$ can only be occupied by symbol s. We refer to this organization as a *direct entry organization.*

However, k is a very large number in practice hence use of a one-to-one function will require a very large symbol table. Fortunately a one-to-one function is not needed. For good search performance it is adequate if the hashing function implements a mapping $K_p \Rightarrow N$ which is nearly one-to-one for any arbitrary set of symbols S_p.

The effectiveness of a hashing organization depends on the average value of p_s. For a given size of a hash table, the value of p_s can be expected to increase with the value of k_p.

Hashing functions

While hashing, the representation of s, the symbol to be searched, is treated as a binary number. The hashing function performs a numerical transformation on this number to obtain e. Let the representation of s have b bits in it and let the host computer use m bit arithmetic. Now, to apply the numerical transformation, we need to obtain an m bit representation of s. Let us call it r_s. If $b \leq m$, the representation of s can be padded with 0's to obtain r_s. If $b > m$, the representation of s is split into pieces of m bits each, and bitwise exclusive OR operations are performed on these pieces to obtain r_s. This process is called *folding*. The hashing function h is now applied to r_s. This method ensures that the effect of all characters in a symbol is incorporated during hashing.

A hashing function h should possess the following properties to ensure good search performance:

1. The hashing function should not be sensitive to the symbols in S_p, that is, it should perform equally well for different source programs. Thus, the value of p_s should only depend on k_p.
2. The hashing function h should execute reasonably fast.

The first property is satisfied by designing a hashing function which is a good randomizer over the table space. This makes its performance insensitive to S_p. Two popular classes of such hashing functions are described in the following.

1. *Multiplication functions:* These functions are analogous to functions used in random number generation, e.g. $h(s) = (a \times r_s + b) \bmod 2^m$, where a, b are constants and fixed point arithmetic is used to compute $h(s)$. The table size should be a power of 2, say 2^g, such that the lower order g bits of $h(s)$ can be used as e.
2. *Division functions:* A typical division hashing function is

$$h(s) = (\textit{remainder of } \frac{r_s}{n}) + 1$$

where n is the size of the table. If n is a prime number, the method is called *prime division hashing*.

Both multiplication and division methods perform well in practice. A multiplication method has the advantage of being slightly faster but suffers from the drawback that the table size has to be a power of 2. Prime division hashing is slower but has the advantage that prime numbers are much more closely spaced than powers of 2. This provides a wider choice of table size.

Collision handling methods

Two approaches to collision handling are to accommodate a colliding entry elsewhere in the hash table using a *rehashing* technique, or to accommodate the colliding entry in a separate table using an *overflow chaining* technique. We discuss these in the following paragraphs.

Rehashing

This technique uses a sequence of hashing functions $h_1, h_2, \ldots$ to resolve collisions. Let a collision occur while probing the table entry whose number is provided by $h_i(s)$. We use $h_{i+1}(s)$ to obtain a new entry number. This provides the new prediction in Algorithm 2.1. A popular technique called *sequential rehashing* uses the recurrence relation

$$h_{i+1}(s) \quad = \quad h_i(s) \; mod \; n+1$$

to provide a series of hashing functions for rehashing.

A drawback of rehashing techniques is that a colliding entry accommodated elsewhere in the table may contribute to more collisions. This may lead to clustering of entries in the table.

Example 2.6 Let $h(\texttt{a}) = h(\texttt{b}) = h(\texttt{c}) = 5$ and $h(\texttt{d}) = 6$ in a language processor using sequential rehashing to handle collisions. If symbols are entered in a table in the sequence a, b, c, d, they would occupy the entries shown below:

Symbol	*Entry number*
a	5
b	6
c	7
d	8

While entering d, collisions occur in entries numbered 6 and 7 before d is accommodated in the 8th entry. Entries 5-8 form a cluster of size 4. A symbol x such that $h(\texttt{x}) = 5$ suffers 4 collisions due to the cluster. Thus, the average number of collisions for a colliding entry = $\frac{1}{2} \times$(average size of cluster+1).

Table 2.1 summarizes the performance of sequential rehashing. For values of ρ in the range 0.6–0.8, performance of the hash table is quite adequate. p_s has values in the range of 1.75 to 3.0, while p_u has values in the range 2.5 to 5.0. This performance is obtained at the cost of over-commitment of memory for the symbol table. Taking $\rho = 0.7$ as a practical figure, the table must have $k_p^m/0.7$ entries, where k_p^m is the largest value of k_p in a practical mix of source programs. If a program contains less symbols, the search performance would be better. However, a larger part of the table would remain unused. Note that unlike the sequential and binary search organizations, the hash table performance is independent of the size of the table; it is determined only by the value of ρ.

Table 2.1 Performance of sequential rehash

ρ	p_u	p_s
0.2	1.25	1.125
0.4	1.67	1.33
0.6	2.5	1.75
0.8	5.0	3.0
0.9	10.0	5.5
0.95	20.0	10.5

Hash table performance can be improved by reducing the clustering effect. Various rehashing schemes like sequential step rehash, quadratic and quadratic quotient rehash have been devised with this in view. Bell (1970) and Ackerman (1974) deal with these schemes. Price (1971) and Dhamdhere (1983) contain comprehensive treatments of hash table organizations.

Overflow chaining

Overflow chaining avoids the problems associated with the clustering effect (see Ex. 2.6) by accommodating colliding entries in a separate table called the *overflow table*. Thus, a search which encounters a collision in the primary hash table has to be continued in the overflow table. To facilitate this, a pointer field is added to each entry in the primary and overflow tables. The entry format is as follows:

Symbol	*Other info*	*Pointer*

A single hashing function h is used. All symbols which encounter a collision are accommodated in the overflow table. Symbols hashing into a specific entry of the primary table are chained together using the pointer field. On encountering a collision in the primary table, that is, in step 3 of Algorithm 2.3, one chain in the overflow table has to be searched.

Example 2.7 Figure 2.4 shows the organization of a hash table with overflow chaining. Symbols a, b, c and d of Ex. 2.6 are entered in the table as follows: a is entered in the 5th entry of the hash table. Symbol b collides with it. Hence b is put in the next available entry of the overflow table and the *pointer* field of the 5th entry of the hash table is set to point at it. c collides with a in the hash table and with b in the overflow table. A new entry is created for c and the *pointer* field of b's entry is set to point to it. d does not suffer a collision.

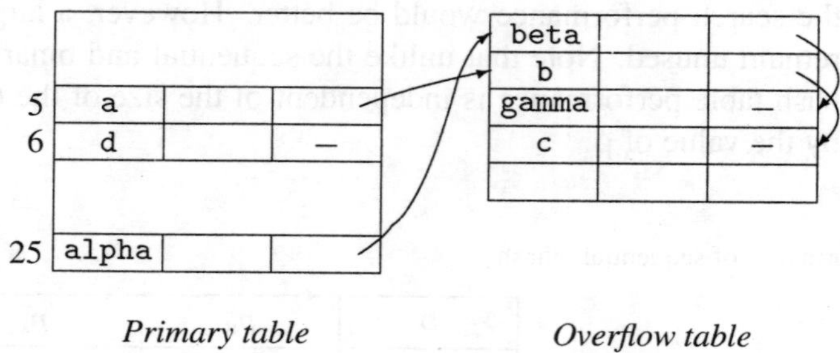

Fig. 2.4 Hash table organization with overflow chaining

Symbols `alpha`, `beta` and `gamma` form another chain since they all hash into entry 25 of the hash table.

The main drawback of the overflow chaining method is the extra memory requirement due to the presence of the overflow table, which must have $(k_p^m - 1)$ entries. An organization called scatter table organization is often used to reduce the memory requirements. In this organization, the hash table merely contains pointers, and all symbol entries are stored in the overflow table. Effectively, the hash table is merely a routing table (hence the name *scatter table*). Now the hash table should be large to ensure low values of ρ in it, and the overflow table needs to contain k_p^m entries.

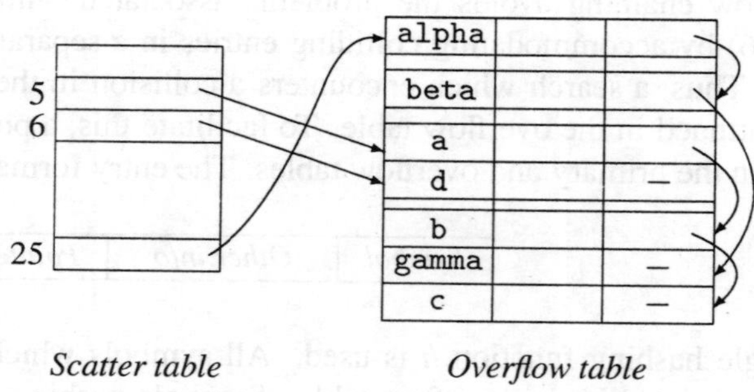

Fig. 2.5 Scatter table organization

Example 2.8 Figure 2.5 shows the scatter table organization for the symbols of Ex. 2.7. If each pointer requires 1 word and each symbol entry requires l words, the memory requirements are

$$
\begin{aligned}
&= \frac{k_p^m}{0.7} + k_p^m \times l \text{ words} \\
&= k_p^m \times (1.43 + l) \text{ words} \\
&\cong k_p^m \times l \text{ words}
\end{aligned}
$$

This compares favourably with the memory requirements if a rehashing technique was used to handle collisions, viz.

$$= (\frac{k_p^m}{0.7}) \times l \text{ words}$$
$$\cong 1.43\ k_p^m \times l \text{ words}$$

Memory requirements in the case of hash with overflow chaining (see Ex. 2.7) would have been

$$= (\frac{k_p^m}{0.7}) \times l + (k_p^m - 1) \times l \text{ words}$$
$$\cong 2.43\ k_p^m \times l \text{ words}$$

Note that both hash with overflow and scatter table organizations would perform better than the sequential rehash organization for the same value of ρ.

2.1.2 Linked List and Tree Structured Organizations

Linked list and tree structured organizations are nonlinear in nature, that is, elements of the search data structure are not located in adjoining memory areas. To facilitate search, each entry contains one or more pointers to other entries.

Symbol	*Other info*	*Pointer*	... *Pointer*

These organizations have the advantage that a fixed memory area need not be committed to the search structure. The system simply allocates a *header* element to start with. This element points to the first entry in the linked list or to the root of the tree. Other entries are allocated as and when needed.

Linked lists

Each entry in the linked list organization contains a single pointer field. The list has to be searched sequentially for obvious reasons. Hence its search performance is identical with that of sequential search tables, i.e. $p_s = l/2$ and $p_u = l$.

Binary trees

Each node in the tree is a symbol entry with two pointer fields—the *left_pointer* and the *right_pointer*. The following relation holds at every node of the tree: If s is the symbol in the entry, the left pointer points to a subtree containing all symbols $< s$ while the right pointer points to a subtree containing all symbols $> s$. This relation is used by the search procedure in a manner analogous to Algorithm 2.2. Algorithm 2.4 contains the search procedure. We use the notation $x.y$ to represent field y of node x and the notation $(p)^*.y$ to represent field y of the node pointed to by pointer p.

Algorithm 2.4 (Binary tree search)

1. *current_node_pointer* := address of root of the binary tree;

2. If $s =$ (*current_node_pointer*)**.symbol*, then exit with success;
3. If $s <$ (*current_node_pointer*)**.symbol* then
   current_node_pointer := (*current_node_pointer*)**.left_pointer*;
   else *current_node_pointer* := (*current_node_pointer*)**.right_pointer*;
4. If *current_node_pointer* = *nil* then
   exit with failure.
   else goto Step 2.

The best search performance is obtained when the tree is balanced. This performance is identical with that of the binary search table. In the worst case, the tree degenerates to a linked list and the search performance is identical with sequential search.

Example 2.9 Parts (a)-(d) of Figure 2.6 show various stages in the building of a binary tree when symbols are entered in the sequence `p`, `c`, `t`, `f`, `h`, `k`, `e`. Part (e) shows a balanced binary tree with the same symbols which gives better search performance.

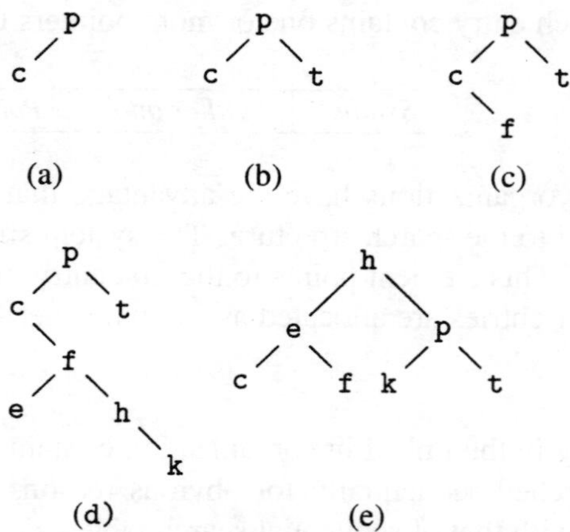

Fig. 2.6 Tree structured table organization

Nested search structures

Nested search structures are used when it is necessary to support a search along a secondary dimension within a search structure. Since the search structure cannot be linear in the secondary dimension, a linked list representation is used for the secondary search. Examples of nested search structures can be found in the handling of records of Pascal, PL/1, Cobol, etc., structures of C or handling of procedure parameters in any source language. Nested search structures are also known as *multi-list structures*.

Example 2.10 Figure 2.7 shows the symbol table entries for the Pascal record

```
personal_info   : record
                    name : array [1..10] of character;
                     sex : character;
                      id : integer;
                  end;
```

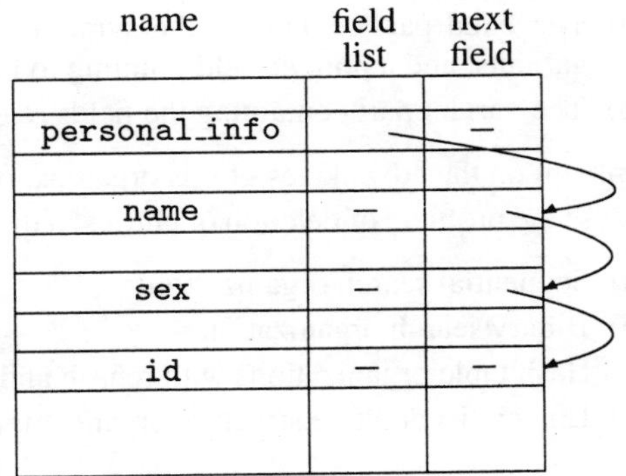

Fig. 2.7 Multi-list structure

Each symbol table entry contains two additional fields, *field list* and *next field*. *field list* of `personal_info` points to the entry for `name`. *next_field* of `name` points to `sex`, etc. This organization permits the field `name` to be searched in the primary as well as secondary dimensions, i.e., as a symbol in the table as well as a field of `personal_info`. This enables efficient handling of occurrences like `name` and `personal_info.name` in the Pascal program.

EXERCISE 2.1

1. Comment on the feasibility of designing a hashing function to implement a direct entry organization for a fixed set of symbols. (Sprugnoli (1977) and Lyon (1978) report some related work).
2. An assembler is to be designed to handle programs containing up to 500 symbols. However, it is found that an average program contains only about 200 symbols. It is decided that a hash organization with sequential rehashing must be used. Evaluate the following three design alternatives in terms of memory requirements and access efficiency.
   (a) Size of the table = 550 entries
   (b) Size of the table = 700 entries
   (c) Size of the table = 500 entries
3. An assembler supports an option by which it produces an alphabetical listing of all symbols used in a program. Comment on the suitability of the following organizations

to organize the symbol table:

(a) Binary search organization
(b) Linked list organization
(c) Binary tree organization
(d) A multi-list organization

4. Many language processors use the concept of split-entry symbol tables. Each entry in such a table consists of two parts:

   (a) The fixed part containing the symbol field, a tag field, fields common to all variants, and a pointer field pointing to the variant part.
   (b) The variant part containing the fields relevant to the variant.

   Comment on the advantages of this organization.
5. Discuss the problem of deletion of entries in the following symbol table organizations:

   (a) Sequential search organization
   (b) Binary search organization
   (c) Hash table organizations with rehash and overflow chaining techniques
   (d) Linked list and tree structure organizations.

2.2 ALLOCATION DATA STRUCTURES

We discuss two allocation data structures, stacks and heaps.

2.2.1 Stacks

A *stack* is a linear data structure which satisfies the following properties:

1. Allocations and deallocations are performed in a *last-in-first-out* (LIFO) manner—that is, amongst all entries existing at any time, the first entry to be deallocated is the last entry to have been allocated.
2. Only the last entry is accessible at any time.

Figure 2.8 illustrates the stack model of allocation. Being a linear data structure, an area of memory is reserved for the stack. A pointer called the *stack base* (SB) points to the first word of the stack area. The stack grows in size as entries are created, i.e. as they are allocated memory. (We shall use the convention that a stack grows towards the higher end of memory. We depict this as downwards growth in the figures.) A pointer called the *top of stack* (TOS) points to the last entry allocated in the stack. This pointer is used to access the last entry. No provisions exist for access to other entries in the stack. When an entry is *pushed* on the stack (i.e. allocated in the stack), TOS is incremented by l, the size of the entry (we assume $l = 1$). When an entry is *popped*, i.e. deallocated, TOS is decremented by l (see Figs. 2.8(a)-(c)). To start with, the stack is *empty*. An empty stack is represented by TOS = SB$-$1 (see Fig. 2.8(d)).

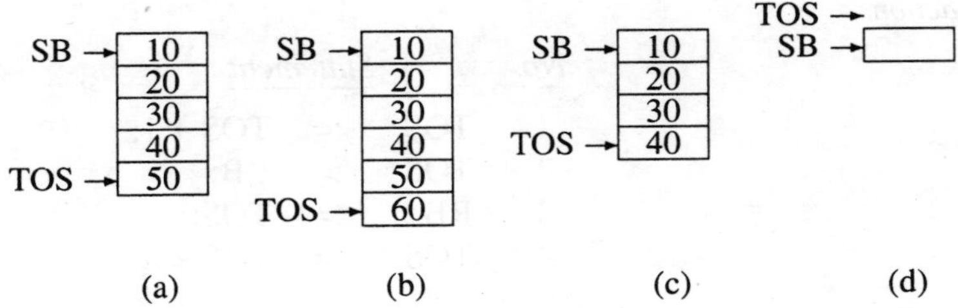

Fig. 2.8 Stack model of allocation

Extended stack model

The LIFO nature of stacks is useful when the lifetimes of the allocated entities follow the LIFO order. However, some extensions are needed in the simple stack model because all entities may not be of the same size. The size of an entity is assumed to be an integral multiple of the size of a stack entry. To allocate an entity, a *record* is created in the stack, where the record consists of a set of consecutive stack entries. For simplicity, the size of a stack entry, i.e. l, is assumed to be one word. Figure 2.9(a) shows the extended stack model. In addition to SB and TOS, two new pointers exist in the model:

1. A *record base pointer* (RB) pointing to the first word of the last record in stack.

2. The first word of each record is a *reserved pointer*. This pointer is used for housekeeping purposes as explained below.

The allocation and deallocation time actions in the extended stack model are described in the following paragraphs (see Fig. 2.9(b)–(c)).

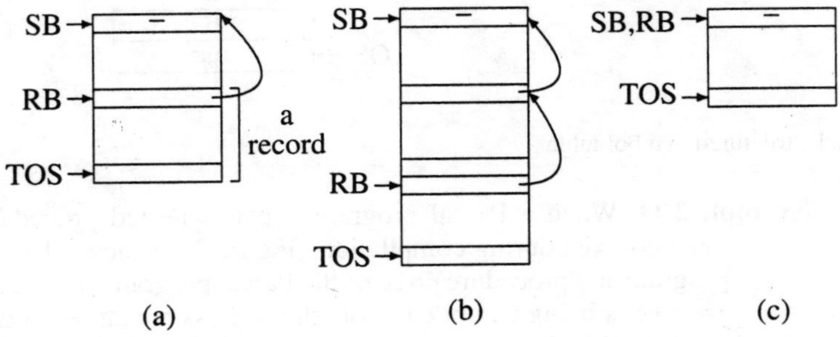

Fig. 2.9 Extended stack model

Allocation time actions

No.	*Statement*		
1.	TOS	:=	TOS + 1;
2.	TOS*	:=	RB;
3.	RB	:=	TOS;
4.	TOS	:=	TOS + n;

The first statement increments TOS by one stack entry. It now points at the *reserved pointer* of the new record. The '*' mark in statement 2 indicates indirection. Hence the assignment TOS* := RB deposits the address of the previous record base into the reserved pointer. Statement 3 sets RB to point at the first stack entry in the new record. Statement 4 performs allocation of n stack entries to the new entity (see Fig. 2.9(b)). The newly created entity now occupies the addresses <RB> $+l$ to <RB> $+l \times n$, where <RB> stands for 'contents of RB'.

Deallocation time actions

No.	*Statement*		
1.	TOS	:=	RB – 1;
2.	RB	:=	RB*;

The first statement pops a record off the stack by resetting TOS to the value it had before the record was allocated. RB is then made to point at the base of the previous record (see Fig. 2.9(c)).

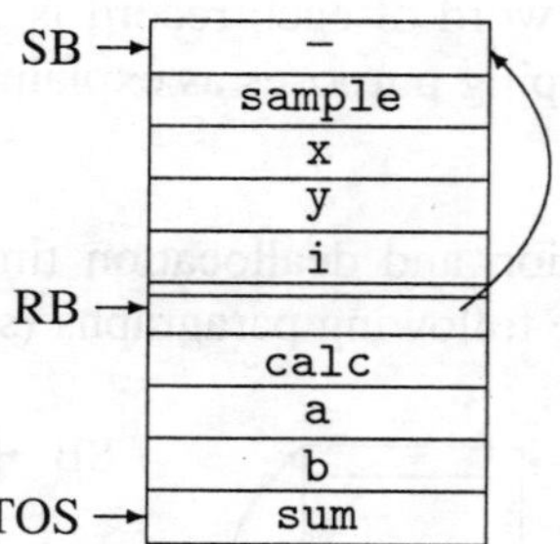

Fig. 2.10 Stack structured symbol table

Example 2.11 When a Pascal program contains nested procedures, many symbol tables must co-exist during compilation. Figure 2.10 shows the symbol tables of the main program and procedure `calc` of the Pascal program of Ex. 2.2 when the statement `sum := a+b` is being compiled. Note the address contained in the *reserved pointer* in the symbol table for procedure `calc`. It is used to pop the symbol table of `calc` off the stack after its `end` statement is compiled.

2.2.2 Heaps

A heap is a nonlinear data structure which permits allocation and deallocation of entities in a random order. An allocation request returns a pointer to the allocated area in the heap. A deallocation request must present a pointer to the area to be deallocated. The heap data structure does not provide any specific means to access an allocated entity. It is assumed that each user of an allocated entity maintains a pointer to the memory area allocated to the entity.

Example 2.12 Figure 2.11 shows the status of a heap after executing the following C program

```
float *floatptr1, *floatptr2;
int *intptr;
floatptr1 = (float *) calloc (5, sizeof (float));
floatptr2 = (float *) calloc (2, sizeof (float));
intptr = (int *) calloc (5, sizeof (int));
free (floatptr2);
```

Three memory areas are allocated by the calls on `calloc` and the pointers `floatptr1`, `floatptr2` and `intptr` are set to point to these areas. `free` frees the area allocated to `floatptr2`. This creates a 'hole' in the allocation. Note that following Section 2.1, each allocated area is assumed to contain a *length* field preceding the actual allocation.

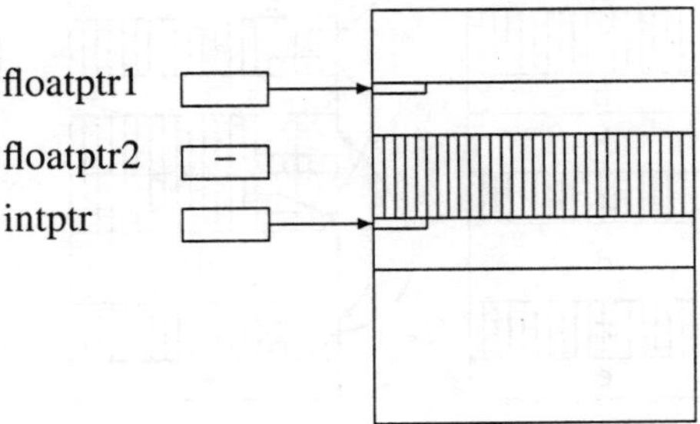

Fig. 2.11 Heap

Memory management

Example 2.12 illustrates how free areas (or 'holes') develop in memory as a result of allocations and deallocations in the heap. Memory management thus consists of identifying the free memory areas and reusing them while making fresh allocations. Speed of allocation/deallocation, and efficiency of memory utilization are the obvious performance criteria of memory management.

Identifying free memory areas

Two popular techniques used to identify free memory areas are:

1. Reference counts
2. Garbage collection.

In the reference count technique, the system associates a *reference count* with each memory area to indicate the number of its active users. The number is incremented when a new user gains access to that area and is decremented when a user finishes using it. The area is known to be free when its reference count drops to zero. The reference count technique is simple to implement and incurs incremental overheads, i.e. overheads at every allocation and deallocation. In the latter technique, the system performs garbage collection when it runs out of memory. Garbage collection makes two passes over the memory to identify unused areas. In the first pass it traverses all pointers pointing to allocated areas and *marks* the memory areas which are in use. The second pass finds all unmarked areas and declares them to be *free*. The garbage collection overheads are not incremental. They are incurred every time the system runs out of free memory to allocate to fresh requests.

To manage the reuse of free memory, the system can enter the free memory areas into a *free list* and service allocation requests out of the free list. Alternatively, it can perform *memory compaction* to combine these areas into a single free area.

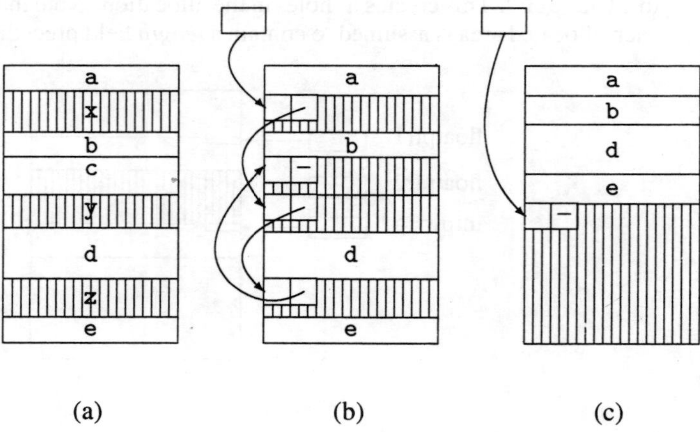

Fig. 2.12 (a) allocation status of heap, (b) free list, (c) after compaction

Example 2.13 Figure 2.12 shows free area management using free lists and memory compaction. Part (a) shows five areas named `a`-`e` in active use, and three free areas named `x`, `y` and `z`. The system has a *free area descriptor* permanently allocated. If a free list is to be used to facilitate memory allocation to fresh requests, the descriptor is used as a list header for the free list. The first word in each area is used to hold the count of words in the area and a pointer to the next free area in the list. Part (b) shows how area `c` is added to the free list consisting of `x`, `y` and `z`. If memory compaction is used, the *free area descriptor* describes the single free area resulting from compaction. The first word in this area contains a count of words in the area and a *null* pointer. Figure 2.12(c) shows the results of memory compaction.

Reuse of memory

When memory compaction is used, fresh allocations are made from the block of free memory. The *free area descriptor* and the count of words in the free area are updated appropriately. When a free list is used, two techniques can be used to perform a fresh allocation:

1. First fit technique
2. Best fit technique.

The first fit technique selects the first free area whose size is $\geq n$ words, where n is the number of words to be allocated. The remaining part of the area is put back into the free list. This technique suffers from the problem that memory areas become successively smaller, hence requests for large memory areas may have to be rejected. The best fit technique finds the smallest free area whose size $\geq n$. This enables more allocation requests to be satisfied. However, in the long run it, too, may suffer from the problem of numerous small free areas.

Example 2.14 Let the free list consist of two areas called $area_1$ and $area_2$ of 500 words and 200 words, respectively. Let allocation requests for 100 words, 50 words and 400 words arise in the system. The first fit technique will allocate 100 words from $area_1$ and 50 words from the remainder of $area_1$. The free list now contains areas of 350 words and 200 words. The request for 400 words cannot be granted. The best fit technique will allocate 100 words and 50 words from $area_2$, and 400 words from $area_1$. This leaves areas of 100 words and 50 words in the free list.

Knuth (1973) discusses methods of overcoming the problems of first fit and best fit techniques. The *buddy* method may be used to merge adjoining free areas into larger free areas.

BIBLIOGRAPHY

(a) Data structures, general

1. Aho, A.V. and J.D. Ullman (1984): *Data Structures*, Addison-Wesley, New York.
2. Horowitz, E. and S. Sahni (1983): *Fundamentals of Data Structures*, Computer Science Press, California and Galgotia, New Delhi.
3. Knuth, D.E. (1985): *The Art of Computer Programming : Vol. I*, Addison-Wesley, Reading and Narosa, New Delhi.
4. Wirth, N. (1976): *Algorithms + Data Structures = Programs*, Prentice-Hall, Englewood Cliffs.

(b) Table management

Table management crucially determines the speed of language processing. Most books on compilers include a good coverage of table management techniques. Gries (1971) and

Dhamdhere (1983) contain comprehensive treatments of this topic. Price (1977) is an important review article on table management. Horowitz and Sahni (1983) and Tremblay and Sorenson (1983) are good sources on algorithms for table management.

1. Ackermann, A.F. (1974): "Quadratic search for hash tables of size p^n," *Commn. of ACM*, **17** (3), 164-165.
2. Bell, J.R. (1970): "The quadratic quotient method," *Commn. of ACM*, **13** (2), 107-109.
3. Dhamdhere, D.M. (1983): *Compiler Construction – Principles and Practice*, Macmillan India, New Delhi.
4. Donovan, J.J. (1972): *Systems Programming*, McGraw-Hill Kogakusha, Tokyo.
5. Gries, D. (1971): *Compiler Construction for Digital Computers*, Wiley, New York.
6. Horowitz, E. and S. Sahni (1983): *Fundamentals of Data Structures*, Computer Science Press, California.
7. Knuth, D. (1973): *The Art of Computer Programming, Vol. III – Sorting and Searching*, Addison-Wesley, Reading.
8. Lyon, G. (1978): "Packed scatter tables," *Commn. of ACM*, **21** (10), 857-865.
9. Price, C.E. (1971): "Table lookup techniques," *Computing Surveys*, **3** (2), 49-65.
10. Sprugnoli, R. (1977): "Perfect hashing functions – a single probe retrieval method for static sets." *Commn. of ACM*, **20** (11), 841-850.
11. Tremblay, J.P. and P.G. Sorenson (1983): *An Introduction to Data Structures with Applications*, McGraw-Hill.

CHAPTER 3

Scanning & Parsing

3.1 SCANNING

Scanning is the process of recognizing the lexical components in a source string. As stated in Section 1.4.1.1, the lexical features of a language can be specified using Type-3 or regular grammars. This facilitates automatic construction of efficient recognizers for the lexical features of the language. In fact the scanner generator LEX generates such recognizers from the string specifications input to it (see Section 1.5.1).

In the early days of compilers, it was not possible to generate scanners automatically because the theory of PL grammars was not sufficiently understood and practiced. Specifications of lexical strings were excessively complex and scanners had to be hand coded to implement them. Fortran is notorious for very complex specifications of this kind.

Example 3.1 Successful scanning of some Fortran constructs requires interaction with the parser, e.g. consider the Fortran statements

```
DO 10 I = 1,2 and
DO 10 I = 1.2
```

The former is a DO statement while the latter is an assignment to a variable named `DO10I` (note that blanks are ignored in Fortran). Thus, scanning can only be performed after presence of the ',' identifies the former as a DO statement and its absence identifies the latter as an assignment statement. Fortunately, modern PL's do not contain such constructs.

Before proceeding with the details of scanning, it is important to understand the reasons for separating scanning from parsing. From Section 1.4.1.1, it is clear that each Type-3 production specifying a lexical component is also a Type-2 production. Hence it is possible to write a single set of Type-2 productions which specifies both lexical and syntactic components of the source language. However, a recognizer for

Type-3 productions is simpler, easier to build and more efficient during execution than a recognizer for Type-2 productions. Hence it is better to handle the lexical and syntactic components of a source language separately.

Finite state automata

Definition 3.1 (Finite state automaton (FSA)) *A* finite state automaton *is a triple (S, Σ, T) where*

S	*is a finite set of states, one of which is the* initial state s_{init}, *and one or more of which are the* final states
Σ	*is the alphabet of source symbols*
T	*is a finite set of state transitions defining transitions out of each* $s_i \in S$ *on encountering the symbols of* Σ.

We label the transitions of FSA using the following convention: A transition out of $s_i \in S$ on encountering a symbol $symb \in \Sigma$ has the label *symb*. We say a symbol *symb* is recognized by an FSA when the FSA makes a transition labelled *symb*. The transitions in an FSA can be represented in the form of a state transition table (STT) which has one row for each state $s_i \in S$ and one column for each symbol $symb \in \Sigma$. An entry STT (s_i, *symb*) in the table indicates the id of the new state entered by the FSA if there exists a transition labelled *symb* in state s_i. If the FSA does not contain a transition out of state s_i for *symb*, we leave STT (s_i, *symb*) blank. A state transition can also be represented by a triple (old state, source symbol, new state). Thus, the entry STT(s_i, *symb*) = s_j and the triple (s_i, *symb*, s_j) are equivalent.

The operation of an FSA is determined by its current state s_c. The FSA actions are limited to the following: Given a source symbol x at its input, it checks to see if STT (s_c, x) is defined—that is, if STT (s_c, x) = s_j, for some s_j. If so, it makes a transition to s_j, else it indicates an error and stops.

Definition 3.2 (DFA) *A* deterministic finite state automaton *(DFA) is an FSA such that* $t_1 \in T,\ t_1 \equiv (s_i,\ symb,\ s_j)$ *implies* $\nexists\ t_2 \in T,\ t_2 \equiv (s_i, symb, s_k)$.

Transitions in a DFA are deterministic—that is, at most one transition exists in state s_i for a symbol *symb*. Figure 3.1 illustrates the operation of a DFA. At any point in time, the DFA would have recognized some *prefix* α of the source string, possibly

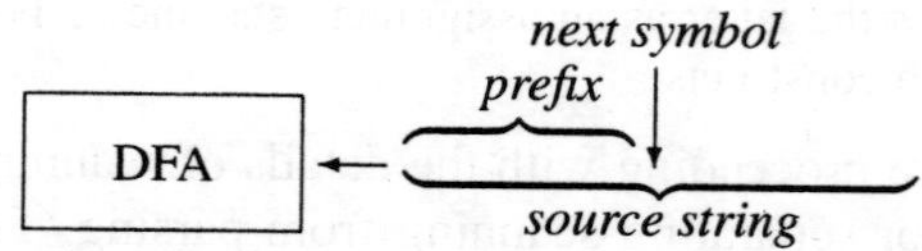

Fig. 3.1 Operation of a DFA

the null string, and would be poised to recognize the symbol pointed to by the pointer *next symbol*. The operation of a DFA is history-sensitive because its current state is a function of the prefix recognized by it. The DFA halts when all symbols in the source string are recognized, or an error condition is encountered. It can be seen that a DFA recognizes the longest valid prefix before stopping.

The validity of a string is determined by giving it at the input of a DFA in its initial state. The string is valid if and only if the DFA recognizes every symbol in the string and finds itself in a final state at the end of the string. This fact follows from the deterministic nature of transitions in the DFA.

Example 3.2 Figure 3.2 shows a DFA to recognize integer strings according to the Type-3 rule

<integer> ::= *d* | *<integer> d*

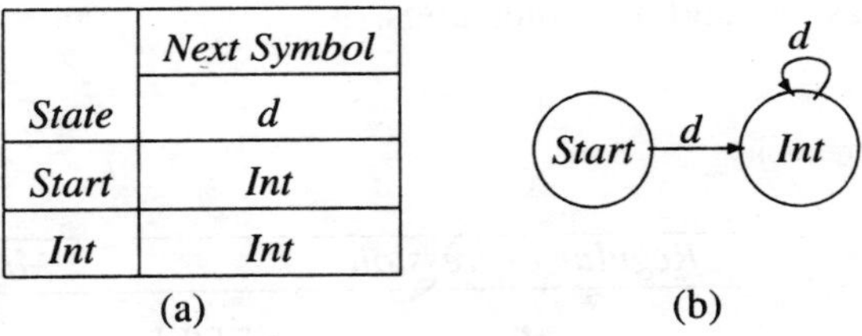

	Next Symbol
State	*d*
Start	*Int*
Int	*Int*

Fig. 3.2 DFA to recognise integer strings

where *d* represents a digit. Part (a) of the figure shows the STT for the DFA. Part (b) shows a diagrammatic representation of the states and state transitions. A transition from state s_i to state s_j on symbol *symb* is depicted by an arrow labelled *symb* from s_i to s_j. The initial and final states of the DFA are *Start* and *Int* respectively. Transitions during the recognition of string `539` are as given in the following table:

Current state	*Input symbol*	*New state*
Start	5	*Int*
Int	3	*Int*
Int	9	*Int*

The string leaves the DFA in state *Int* which is a final state, hence the string is a valid integer string. A string `5ab9` is invalid because no transition marked 'letter' exists in state *Int*.

Regular expressions

In Ex. 3.2 a single Type-3 rule was adequate to specify a lexical component. However, many Type-3 rules would be needed to specify complex lexical components like real constants. Hence we use a generalization of Type-3 productions called a *regular expression*.

Example 3.3 An organization uses an employee code which is obtained by concatenating the section id of an employee, which is alphabetic in nature, with a numeric code. The structure of the employee code can be specified as

<section code> ::= *l* | *<section code> l*
<numeric code> ::= *d* | *<numeric code> d*
<employee code> ::= *<section code> <numeric code>*

Note that a specification like

< s_code > ::= *l* | *d* | *< s_code > l* | *< s_code > d*

would be incorrect !

The regular expression generalizes on Type-3 rules by permitting multiple occurrences of a string form, and concatenation of strings. Table 3.1 shows regular expressions and their meanings.

Table 3.1 Regular expressions

Regular expression	*Meaning*
r	string r
s	string s
$r.s$ or rs	concatenation of r and s
(r)	same meaning as r
$r \mid s$ or $(r \mid s)$	alternation, i.e. string r or string s
$(r) \mid (s)$	alternation
$[r]$	an optional occurrence of string r
$(r)^*$	≥ 0 occurrences of string r
$(r)^+$	≥ 1 occurrences of string r

Example 3.4 The employee codes of Ex. 3.3 can be specified by the regular expression

$$(l)^+(d)^+$$

Some other examples of regular expressions are

integer	$[+ \mid -](d)^+$
real number	$[+ \mid -](d)^+.(d)^+$
real number with optional fraction	$[+ \mid -](d)^+.(d)^*$
identifier	$l(l \mid d)^*$

Building DFAs

A DFA for a Type-3 specification can be built using some simple rules. Building a DFA for a regular expression can be achieved by repeated application of the same simple rules. However it is a tedious process, hence it is best to automate the process of building DFAs. In the following, we shall not discuss the building of DFAs but assume that they can be built by a procedure described in the literature cited at the end of the chapter.

The lexical components of a source language can be specified by a set of regular expressions. Since an input string may contain any one of these lexical components, it is necessary to use a single DFA as a recognizer for valid lexical strings in the language. Such a DFA would have a single initial state and one or more final states for each lexical component.

Example 3.5 Figure 3.3 shows a DFA for recognizing identifiers, unsigned integers and unsigned real numbers with fractions. The DFA has 3 final states – *Id*, *Int* and *Real* corresponding to identifier, unsigned integer and unsigned real respectively. Note that a string like '25.' is invalid because it leaves the DFA in state s_2 which is not a final state.

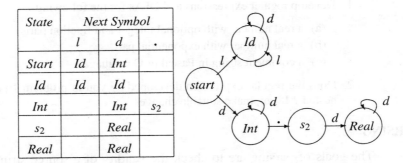

State	*Next Symbol*		
	l	*d*	.
Start	*Id*	*Int*	
Id	*Id*	*Id*	
Int		*Int*	s_2
s_2		*Real*	
Real		*Real*	

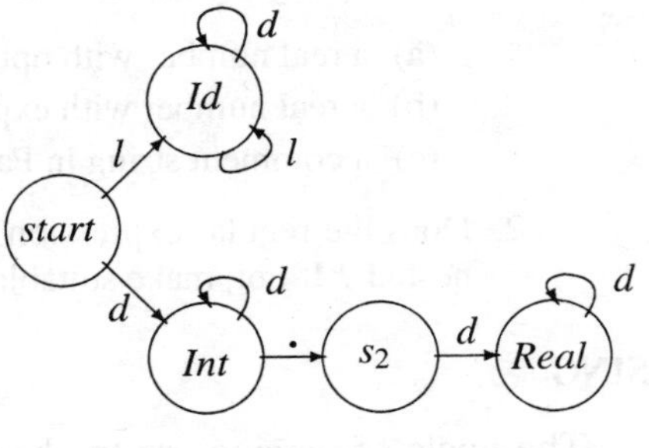

Fig. 3.3 A combined DFA for integers, real numbers and identifiers

Performing semantic actions

Semantic actions during scanning concern table building and construction of tokens for lexical components. These actions are associated with the final states of a DFA. The semantic actions associated with a final state s_f are performed after the DFA recognizes the longest valid prefix of the source string corresponding to s_f.

Writing a scanner

We will use a notation analogous to the LEX notation (see Section 1.5.1) to specify a scanner. A scanner for integer and real numbers, identifiers and reserved words of a language is given in Table 3.1.

Table 3.2 Specification of a scanner

Regular expression	*Semantic actions*
$[+ \mid -](d)^+$	{Enter the string in the table of integer constants, say in entry *n*. Return the token [*Int #n*] }
$[+ \mid -]((d)^+.(d)^* \mid (d)^*.(d)^+)$	{Enter in the table of real constants. Return the token [*Real #m*] }
$l\,(l \mid d)^*$	{Compare with reserved words. If a match is found, return the token [*Kw #k*], else enter in symbol table and return the token [*Id #i*] }

EXERCISE 3.1

1. Develop regular expressions and DFAs for the following
   (a) a real number with optional integer and fraction parts,
   (b) a real number with exponential part,
   (c) a comment string in Pascal or C language.
2. Does the regular expression developed by you in problem 1 permit comments to be nested ? If not, make suitable changes.

3.2 PARSING

The goals of parsing are to check the validity of a source string, and to determine its syntactic structure. For an invalid string the parser issues diagnostic messages reporting the cause and nature of error(s) in the string. For a valid string it builds a parse tree to reflect the sequence of derivations or reductions performed during parsing. The parse tree is passed on to the subsequent phases of the compiler.

As described in Section 1.4.1, the fundamental step in parsing is to derive a string from an NT, or reduce a string to an NT. This gives rise to two fundamental approaches to parsing—*top down parsing* and *bottom up parsing*, respectively.

Parse trees and abstract syntax trees

A parse tree depicts the steps in parsing, hence it is useful for understanding the process of parsing. However, it is a poor intermediate representation for a source string because it contains too much information as far as subsequent processing in the compiler is concerned. An *abstract syntax tree* (AST) represents the structure of a source string in a more economical manner. The word 'abstract' implies that it is a representation designed by a compiler designer for his own purposes. Thus the designer has total control over the information represented in an AST. It thus follows that an AST for a source string is not unique, whereas a parse tree is.

Example 3.6 Figure 3.4(a) shows a parse tree for the source string `a+b*c` according to Grammar (1.3). Figure 3.4(b) shows an AST for the same string. It contains sufficient information to represent the structure of the string. Note its economy compared to the parse tree.

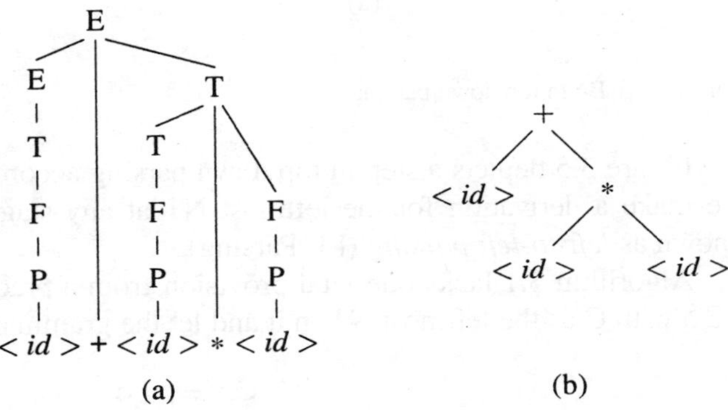

Fig. 3.4 Parse tree and AST

3.2.1 Top Down Parsing

Top down parsing according to a grammar G attempts to derive a string matching a source string through a sequence of derivations starting with the distinguished symbol of G. For a valid source string α, a top down parse thus determines a derivation sequence

$$S \Rightarrow \ldots \Rightarrow \ldots \Rightarrow \alpha.$$

We shall identify the important issues in top down parsing by trying to develop a naive algorithm for it.

Algorithm 3.1 (Naive top down parsing)

1. *Current sentential form* (CSF) := 'S';
2. Let CSF be of the form $\beta A \pi$, such that β is a string of Ts (note that β may be null), and A is the leftmost NT in CSF. Exit with success if CSF = α.
3. Make a derivation $A \Rightarrow \beta_1 B \delta$ according to a production $A ::= \beta_1 B \delta$ of G such that β_1 is a string of Ts (again, β_1 may be null). This makes CSF = $\beta\beta_1 B \delta\pi$.
4. Go to Step 2.

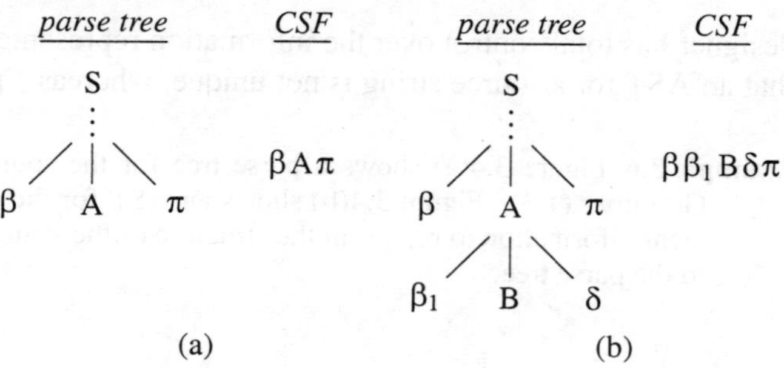

Fig. 3.5 Derivation $A \Rightarrow \beta_1 B \delta$ in top down parsing

Figure 3.5 depicts a step in top down parsing according to Algorithm 3.1. Since we make a derivation for the leftmost NT at any stage, top down parsing is also known as *left-to-left parsing* (LL Parsing).

Algorithm 3.1 lacks one vital provision from a practical viewpoint. Let CSF $\equiv \gamma C \delta$ with C as the leftmost NT in it and let the grammar production for C be

$$C ::= \rho \mid \sigma$$

where each of ρ, σ is a string of terminal and non-terminal symbols. Which RHS alternative should the parser choose for the next derivation ? The alternative we choose may lead us to a string of Ts which does not match with the source string α. In such a case, other alternatives would have to be tried out until we derive a sentence that matches the source string (i.e., a successful parse), or until we have systematically generated all possible sentences without obtaining a sentence that matches the source string (i.e., an unsuccessful parse). A naive approach to top down parsing would be to generate complete sentences of the source language and compare them with α to check if a match exists. However, this approach is inefficient for obvious reasons.

We introduce a check, called a *continuation check*, to determine whether the current sequence of derivations may be able to find a successful parse of α. This check is performed as follows: Let CSF be of the form $\beta A \pi$, where β is a string of n Ts. All sentential forms derived from CSF would have the form $\beta \ldots$. Hence, for a successful parse β must match the first n symbols of α. We can apply this check at every parsing step, and abandon the current sequence of derivations any time this condition is violated. The continuation check may be applied incrementally as follows: Let CSF $\equiv \beta A \pi$, then the source string must be $\beta \ldots$ (else we would have abandoned this sequence of derivations earlier). If the prediction for A is A $\Rightarrow \beta_1 B \delta$, where β_1 is a string of m terminal symbols, then the string β_1 must match m symbols following β in the source string (see Fig. 3.5). Hence we compare β_1 with m symbols to the right of β in the source string. This incremental check is more economical than a continuation check which compares the string $\beta\beta_1$ with $(n+m)$ symbols in the source string.

Predictions and backtracking

A typical stage in top down parsing can be depicted as follows:

$$\begin{array}{rcl} \text{CSF} & \equiv & \beta A \pi \\ & & \quad \text{SSM} \\ & & \quad \downarrow \\ \text{Source string} & : & \beta \ \mathtt{t} \end{array}$$

where CSF $\equiv \beta A\pi$ implies $S \stackrel{*}{\Rightarrow} \beta A\pi$ and the *source string marker* (SSM) points at the first symbol following β in the source string, i.e. at the terminal symbol '`t`'. We have already seen that if CSF = $\beta A\pi$, the source string must have the form $\beta \ldots$.

Parsing proceeds as follows: We identify the leftmost nonterminal in CSF, i.e. A. We now select an alternative on the RHS of the production for A. Since we do not know whether the derived string will satisfy the continuation check, we call this choice a *prediction*. The continuation check is applied incrementally to the terminal symbol(s), if any, occurring in the leftmost position(s) of the prediction. SSM is incremented if the check succeeds and parsing continues. If the check fails, one or more predictions are discarded and SSM is reset to its value before the rejected prediction(s) was made. This is called *backtracking*. Parsing is now resumed.

Implementing top down parsing

The following features are needed to implement top down parsing:

1. *Source string marker* (SSM): SSM points to the first unmatched symbol in the source string.
2. *Prediction making mechanism:* This mechanism systematically selects the RHS alternatives of a production during prediction making. It must ensure that any string in L_G can be derived from S.
3. *Matching and backtracking mechanism:* This mechanism matches every terminal symbol generated during a derivation with the source symbol pointed to by SSM. (This implements the incremental continuation check.) Backtracking is performed if the match fails. This involves resetting CSF and SSM to earlier values.

Continuation check and backtracking is performed in Step 3 of Algorithm 3.1. A complete algorithm incorporating these features can be found in (Dhamdhere, 1983).

Example 3.7 Lexically analysed version of the source string `a+b*c`, viz. $< id > + < id > * < id >$ is to be parsed according to the grammar

$$\begin{array}{lcl} \text{E} & ::= & \text{T} + E \mid \text{T} \\ \text{T} & ::= & \text{V} * T \mid \text{V} \\ \text{V} & ::= & < id > \end{array} \tag{3.1}$$

The prediction making mechanism selects the RHS alternatives of a production in a left-to-right manner. First few steps in the parse are:

1. SSM := 1; CSF := E;
2. Make the prediction $E \Rightarrow T + E$. Now, CSF = T + E.
3. Make the prediction $T \Rightarrow V * T$. CSF = V * T + E.
4. Make the prediction $V \Rightarrow < id >$. CSF = $< id > * T + E$. $< id >$ matches with the first symbol of the source string. Hence, SSM := SSM + 1;
5. Match the second symbol of the prediction in Step 3, viz. '*'. This match fails, hence reject the prediction $T \Rightarrow V * T$. SSM and CSF are reset to 1 and T + E, respectively. (The situation now resembles that at the end of Step 2.)
6. Make a new prediction for T, viz. $T \Rightarrow V$. CSF = V + E.
7. Make the prediction $V \Rightarrow < id >$. CSF = $< id > + E$. $< id >$ matches with the first symbol of the source string. Hence, SSM := SSM + 1;
8. Match the second symbol of the prediction in Step 2, viz. '+'. Match succeeds. SSM := SSM + 1;
9. Make the prediction $E \Rightarrow T + E$. CSF = $< id > + T + E$.
10. Make the prediction $T \Rightarrow V * T$. CSF = $< id > + V * T + E$.
11. ...

The predictions surviving at the end of the parse are listed in Table 3.3.

Table 3.3 Predictions in top sown parsing

Prediction	*Predicted Sentential Form*
$E \Rightarrow T + E$	$T + E$
$T \Rightarrow V$	$V + E$
$V \Rightarrow < id >$	$< id > + E$
$E \Rightarrow T$	$< id > + T$
$T \Rightarrow V * T$	$< id > + V * T$
$V \Rightarrow < id >$	$< id > + < id > * T$
$T \Rightarrow V$	$< id > + < id > * V$
$V \Rightarrow < id >$	$< id > + < id > * < id >$

Comments on top down parsing

Two problems arise due to the possibility of backtracking. First, semantic actions cannot be performed while making a prediction. The actions must be delayed until the prediction is known to be a part of a successful parse. Second, precise error reporting is not possible. A mismatch merely triggers backtracking. A source string is known to be erroneous only after all predictions have failed. This makes it impossible to pinpoint the violations of PL specification.

Grammars containing left recursion are not amenable to top down parsing. For example, consider parsing of the string $<id> + < id > * < id >$ according to the grammar

$$
\begin{aligned}
E &::= E + T \mid T \\
T &::= T * V \mid V \\
V &::= \langle id \rangle
\end{aligned}
$$

The first prediction would be

$$E \Rightarrow E + T$$

which makes E the leftmost NT in CSF once again. Thus, the parser would enter an infinite loop of prediction making. To make top down parsing feasible, it is necessary to eliminate left recursion. This can be achieved by rewriting the grammar using right recursion as follows

$$
\begin{aligned}
E &::= T + E \mid T \\
T &::= V * T \mid V \\
V &::= \langle id \rangle
\end{aligned}
\qquad (3.2)
$$

However, this method is time-consuming and error-prone for large grammars. An alternative is to systematically eliminate left-recursion using the following rule: Rewrite a left recursive production

$$E ::= E + T \mid T$$

as

$$
\begin{aligned}
E &::= T\,E' \\
E' &::= +T\,E' \mid \varepsilon
\end{aligned}
\qquad (3.3)
$$

The rationale for the rewriting is as follows: From the original production, it is clear that E produces a string consisting of one or more Ts separated by '+' symbols. Hence we write the production E ::= T E' with the expectation that E' will produce zero or more occurrences of the string '+ T'. This is what the production of E' achieves. After all left-recursive rules are converted in this manner, the resulting grammar can be used for top down parsing.

Top down parsing without backtracking

Elimination of backtracking in top down parsing would have several advantages—parsing would become more efficient, and it would be possible to perform semantic actions and precise error reporting during parsing. Prediction making becomes very crucial when backtracking is eliminated. The parser must use some contextual information from the source string to decide which prediction to make for the leftmost NT.

This is achieved as follows: If the leftmost NT is A and the source symbol pointed to by SSM is '`t`', parser selects that RHS alternative of A which can produce '`t`' as its first terminal symbol. An error is signalled if no RHS alternative can produce '`t`' as the first terminal symbol.

For the above approach to work, it is essential that at most one RHS alternative should be able to produce the terminal symbol '`t`' in the first position. The grammar may have to be modified to ensure this. As an example, consider parsing of the string $< id > + < id > * < id >$ according to Grammar (3.2). The first prediction is to be made using the production

$$\mathrm{E} ::= \mathrm{T} + \mathrm{E} \mid \mathrm{T}$$

such that the first terminal symbol produced by it would be $< id >$, the first symbol in the source string. From the grammar, we find that T ⇒ V... and V ⇒ $< id >$. Thus, any RHS alternative starting with a T can produce $< id >$ in the first position. However, both alternatives of E start with a T, so which one should the parser choose? To overcome this dilemma, we use *left-factoring* to ensure that the RHS alternatives will produce unique terminal symbols in the first position. The production for E is now rewritten as

$$\begin{aligned} \mathrm{E} &::= \mathrm{T}\,E'' \\ \mathrm{E}'' &::= +E \mid \varepsilon \end{aligned}$$

The first prediction according to this grammar is E ⇒ T E" since the first source symbol is '<*id*>'. When E" becomes the leftmost NT in CSF, we would make the prediction E"⇒ + E if the next source symbol is '+' and the prediction E"⇒ E in all other cases. If the next source symbol is '+', we would make the prediction E" ⇒ + E, else we would make the prediction E" ⇒ ε. Thus, parsing is no longer by trial-and-error. Such parsers are known as *predictive parsers*.

The complete rewritten form of Grammar (3.2) is

$$\begin{aligned} \mathrm{E} &::= \mathrm{T}\,E'' \\ \mathrm{E}'' &::= +E \mid \varepsilon \\ \mathrm{T} &::= \mathrm{V}\,T'' \\ \mathrm{T}'' &::= *\,T \mid \varepsilon \\ \mathrm{V} &::= < id > \end{aligned} \qquad (3.4)$$

Note that grammar (3.3) does not need left factoring since its RHS alternatives produce unique terminal symbols in the first position.

Example 3.8 Parsing of $< id > + < id > * < id >$ according to Grammar (3.4) proceeds as shown in Table 3.4. Note that *Symbol* is the symbol pointed to by SSM.

To start with, CSF = E and SSM points to '<*id*>'. The first three steps are obvious. In the 4th step, SSM points to '+' and the leftmost NT is T″. This leads to the prediction T″⇒ ε.

Table 3.4 Top down parsing without backtracking

Sr. No.	*CSF*	*Symbol*	*Prediction*
1.	E	$<id>$	$\text{E} \Rightarrow \text{T E}''$
2.	$\text{T E}''$	$<id>$	$\text{T} \Rightarrow \text{V T}''$
3.	$\text{V T}''\text{E}''$	$<id>$	$\text{V} \Rightarrow <id>$
4.	$<id>\ \text{T}''\text{E}''$	+	$\text{T}'' \Rightarrow \varepsilon$
5.	$<id>\ \text{E}''$	+	$\text{E}'' \Rightarrow +\text{E}$
6.	$<id> + \text{E}$	$<id>$	$\text{E} \Rightarrow \text{T E}''$
7.	$<id> + \text{T E}''$	$<id>$	$\text{T} \Rightarrow \text{V T}''$
8.	$<id> + \text{V T}''\text{E}''$	id	$\text{V} \Rightarrow <id>$
9.	$<id> + <id>\ \text{T}''\text{E}''$	$*$	$\text{T}'' \Rightarrow *\,\text{T}$
10.	$<id> + <id> * \text{T E}''$	$<id>$	$\text{T} \Rightarrow \text{V T}''$
11.	$<id> + <id> * \text{V T}''\text{E}''$	$<id>$	$\text{V} \Rightarrow <id>$
12.	$<id> + <id> * <id>\ \text{T}''\text{E}''$	–	$\text{T}'' \Rightarrow \varepsilon$
13.	$<id> + <id> * <id>\ \text{E}''$	–	$\text{E}'' \Rightarrow \varepsilon$
14.	$<id> + <id> * <id>$	–	–

3.2.1.1 Practical Top Down Parsing

A recursive descent parser

A recursive descend (RD) parser is a variant of top down parsing without backtracking. It uses a set of recursive procedures to perform parsing. Salient advantages of recursive descent parsing are its simplicity and generality. It can be implemented in any language supporting recursive procedures.

To implement recursive descent parsing, a left-factored grammar is modified to make repeated occurrences of strings more explicit. Grammar (3.4) is rewritten as

$$\begin{aligned} \text{E} &::= \text{T}\,\{+\,T\}^* \\ \text{T} &::= \text{V}\,\{*\,V\}^* \\ \text{V} &::= <id> \end{aligned} \tag{3.5}$$

where the notation $\{..\}^*$ indicates zero or more occurrences of the enclosed specification. A parser procedure is now written for each NT of G. It handles prediction making, matching and error reporting for that NT. The structure of a parser procedure is dictated by the grammar production for the NT. If A ::= ..B.. is a production of G, the parser procedure for A contains a call on the procedure for B.

Example 3.9 A skeletal recursive descent parser for Grammar (3.5) is shown in Fig. 3.6. The parser returns an AST for a valid source string, and reports an error for an invalid string. The procedures `proc_E`, `proc_T` and `proc_V` handle the parsing for E, T and

```
procedure proc_E : (tree_root);
   /* This procedure constructs an AST for 'E'
      and returns a pointer to its root */
  var
     a,b : pointer to a tree node;
  begin
     proc_T(a);
        /* Returns a pointer to the root of tree for T */
     while (nextsymb = '+') do
        match ('+');
        proc_T(b);
        a := treebuild ('+', a, b);
              /* Builds an AST and returns pointer
                 to its root */
     tree_root := a;
     return;
end proc_E;

procedure proc_T (tree_root);
  var
     a,b : pointer to a tree node;
  begin
     proc_V(a);
     while (nextsymb = '*') do;
        match ('*');
        proc_V(b);
        a := treebuild ('*', a, b);
     tree_root := a;
     return;
end proc_T;

procedure proc_V (tree_root);
  var
     a : pointer to a tree node;
  begin
     if (nextsymb = <id>) then
        tree_root := treebuild (<id>, -, -);
        else print "Error !";
     return;
end proc_V;
```

Fig. 3.6 A recursive descent parser

V, respectively, and build ASTs for these NTs using the procedure `treebuild`. Procedure `match` increments SSM. Procedure `proc_E`, the procedure for E, always calls `proc_T` to perform parsing and AST building for a T. If the next source symbol (which is assumed to be contained in the parser variable `nextsymb`) is a '+', then another T is expected. Hence `proc_T` is called again. This process is repeated until the symbol following a T is not a '+'. At this point, `proc_E` returns to the parser control routine. The control routine should now check whether the entire source string has been successfully parsed, else indicate an error. Error detection and reporting is restricted to those parser procedures which produce terminal symbol(s) in the first position. For grammar (3.5) only the routine for V would declare error if anything but an $< id >$ is encountered. The reader can verify that error indication would be precise.

Note that the parser procedures do not call themselves recursively. However, indirect recursion would result if the grammar specification contains indirect recursion—for example, if a rule like

$$\text{V} ::= < id > \mid (\text{E})$$

existed in grammar (3.5).

An LL(1) parser

An LL(1) parser is a table driven parser for left-to-left parsing. The '1' in LL(1) indicates that the grammar uses a look-ahead of one source symbol—that is, the prediction to be made is determined by the next source symbol. A major advantage of LL(1) parsing is its amenability to automatic construction by a parser generator.

Figure 3.7 shows the parser table for an LL(1) parser for Grammar (3.6).

$$\begin{array}{lcl} \text{E} & ::= & \text{T}\, E' \\ \text{E}' & ::= & +\, T\, E' \mid \varepsilon \\ \text{T} & ::= & \text{V}\, T' \\ \text{T}' & ::= & *\, V\, T' \mid \varepsilon \\ \text{V} & ::= & < id > \end{array} \tag{3.6}$$

The parsing table (PT) has a row for each NT $\in$ SNT and a column for each T $\in \Sigma$. A parsing table entry PT (nt_i, t_j) indicates what prediction should be made if nt_i is the leftmost NT in a sentential form and t_j is the next source symbol. A blank entry in PT indicates an error situation. A source string is assumed to be enclosed between the symbols '$\vdash$' and '$\dashv$'. Hence the parser starts with the sentential form $\vdash$ E $\dashv$.

Example 3.10 The sequence of predictions made by the parser of Fig. 3.7 for the source string

$$\vdash < id > + < id > * < id > \dashv$$

can be seen in Table 3.5 where *symbol* is the next source symbol. At every stage the parser refers to the table entry PT (nt_i, t_j) where nt_i is the leftmost nonterminal in the string and t_j is the next source symbol. Note that these steps are equivalent to the steps in Ex. 3.8.

Non-terminal	*Source symbol*			
	<id>	+	∗	⊣
E	E ⇒ TE′			
E′		E′ ⇒ +TE′		E′ ⇒ ε
T	T ⇒ VT′			
T′		T′ ⇒ ε	T′ ⇒ ∗VT′	T′ ⇒ ε
V	V ⇒ *<id>*			

Fig. 3.7 LL(1) parser table

Table 3.5 LL parsing

Current sentential form	*Symbol*	*Prediction*
⊢E⊣	< *id* >	E ⇒ TE′
⊢ TE′ ⊣	< *id* >	T ⇒ VT′
⊢ VT′E′⊣	< *id* >	V ⇒ < *id* >
⊢< *id* > T′E′ ⊣	+	T′ ⇒ ε
⊢< *id* > E′ ⊣	+	E′ ⇒ + TE′
⊢< *id* > + TE′ ⊣	< *id* >	T ⇒ VT′
⊢< *id* > + VT′E′ ⊣	< *id* >	V ⇒ < *id* >
⊢< *id* > +< *id* > T′E′ ⊣	∗	T′ ⇒ ∗VT′
⊢< *id* > +< *id* > ∗ VT′E′ ⊣	< *id* >	V ⇒ < *id* >
⊢< *id* > +< *id* > ∗ < *id* >T′E′ ⊣	⊣	T′ ⇒ ε
⊢< *id* > +< *id* > ∗ < *id* >E′ ⊣	⊣	E′ ⇒ ε
⊢< *id* > +< *id* > ∗ < *id* > ⊣	–	–

The procedure for the construction of the parser table is described in the literature cited at the end of the chapter.

EXERCISE 3.2.1

1. Study the operation of the recursive descent parser described in this section for the following input strings:

   (a) < *id* > + < *id* > ∗ < *id* >
   (b) < *id* > ∗ < *id* >< *id* >

   Verify that precise error indication is provided by the parser.
2. A recursive descent parser is to be developed for Grammar (1.3).

(a) What changes will you make in the grammar to make it suitable for recursive descent parsing?
(b) Code the parser procedures.
(c) Identify the procedures that perform error indication.

3. Compare and contrast recursive descent parsing with LL(1) parsing. What grammar forms are acceptable to each of these?

3.2.2 Bottom Up Parsing

A bottom up parser constructs a parse tree for a source string through a sequence of reductions. The source string is valid if it can be reduced to S, the distinguished symbol of G. If not, an error is to be detected and reported during the process of reduction. Bottom up parsing proceeds in a left-to-right manner, i.e. attempts at reduction start with the first symbol(s) in the string and proceed to the right. A typical stage during bottom up parsing is depicted as follows:

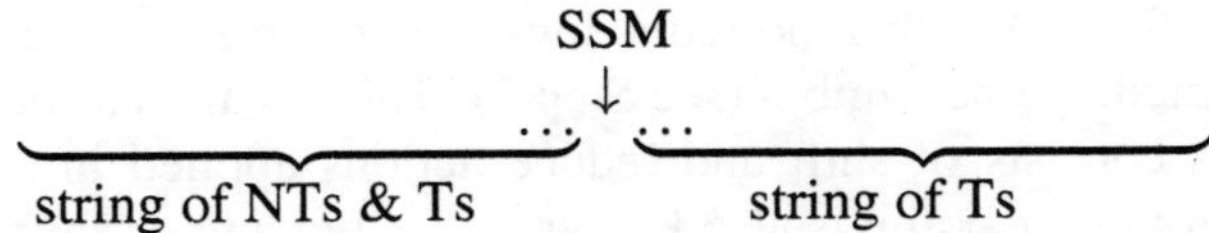

Reductions have been applied to the string on the left of SSM. Hence this string is composed of NTs and Ts. Remainder of the string, yet to be processed by the parser, consists of Ts alone.

We try the following naive approach to bottom up parsing: Let there be n symbols to the left of SSM in the current string form. We try to reduce some part of the string to the immediate left of SSM. Let this part have r symbols in it, and let it be reduced to the NT A. This reduction can be depicted as follows:

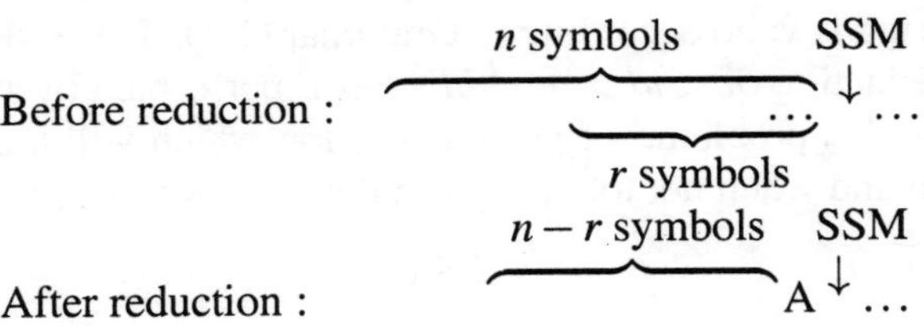

Since we do not know the value of r, we try the values $r = n$, $r = n - 1$, ... $r = 1$. This approach is summarized in Algorithm 3.2.

Algorithm 3.2 (Naive bottom up parsing)

1. SSM := 1; n := 0;
2. r := n;
3. Compare the string of r symbols to the left of SSM with *all* RHS alternatives in G which have a length of r symbols.

4. If a match is found with a production A :: = α, then
   reduce the string of *r* symbols to the NT A.
   $n := n - r + 1;$
   Go to Step 2;
5. $r := r - 1;$
   If $r > 0$, go to Step 3;
6. If no more symbols exist to the right of SSM then
   if current string form = 'S' then
   exit with success
   else report error and exit with failure
7. SSM := SSM + 1;
   $n := n + 1;$
   Go to Step 2;

Thus the parser makes as many reductions as possible at the current position of SSM (see Step 5). When no reductions are possible at the current position, SSM is incremented by one symbol (see Step 7). This is called a *shift* action. The parsing process thus consists of shift and reduce actions applied in a left-to-right manner. Hence bottom up parsing is also known as *LR parsing* or *shift-reduce parsing*.

Algorithm 3.2 is unsatisfactory for two reasons. First, it is inefficient due to the large number of comparisons made in Step 3. Second, it performs reductions in a manner which may conflict with operator priorities. For example, consider Grammar (1.3) and the input string $< id > + < id > * < id >$. The correct parse tree is as shown in Fig. 3.8(b), where the symbols E, T, F and P stand for <*exp*>, <*term*>, <*factor*> and <*primary*>, respectively. The parser of Algorithm 3.2 builds the parse tree of Fig. 3.8(a) by erroneously reducing $< id > + < id >$ to an E. Further, since E $*$ T does not appear on the RHS of any production, the parser indicates an error. However, the string is valid according to Grammar (1.3). This difficulty arises due to the premature reduction of $< id > + < id > \rightarrow$ E performed by Algorithm 3.2.

To overcome this problem, we need a criterion which will indicate when to perform a reduction and when not to, viz. given the current stage of parsing

$$\begin{array}{c} \text{SSM} \\ \downarrow \\ \ldots \alpha \mathtt{t} \gamma \ldots \end{array}$$

the criterion should indicate which of the following should be performed:

1. Apply a reduction involving α, and possibly some symbols to its left, to obtain an NT A.
2. Perform a shift action and now apply a reduction to some string δα`t` or σ`t` to obtain an NT B. (Here σ is a substring of α.)
3. Perform one or more shift actions and apply a reduction to the string `t`. . . to obtain an NT C. Now apply a reduction to some string δαC or σC.

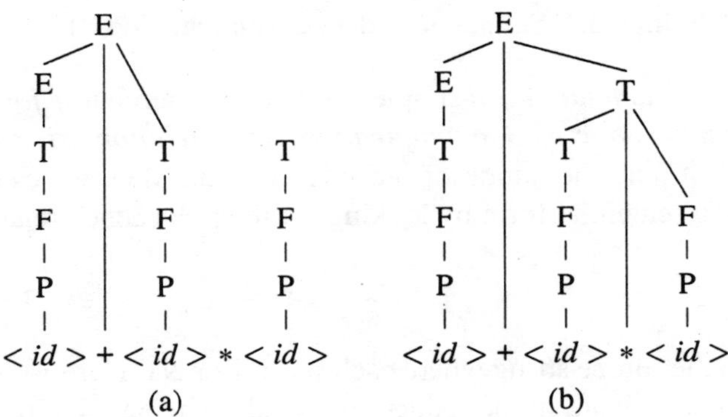

Fig. 3.8 Parse trees in bottom up parsing

In other words, given the sentential form ... αtγ..., the criterion should indicate whether to reduce (a substring of) α before, along with, or after some string t... appearing to its right. Such a criterion is provided by the notion of *precedence* of grammar symbols.

Simple precedence

Definition 3.3 (Simple precedence) *A grammar symbol* a precedes *symbol* b*, where each of* a*,* b *is a T or NT of G, if in a sentential form* ... a b ...*,* a *should be reduced prior to* b *in a bottom up parse.*

We use the notation a $\cdot\!>$ b for the words 'a precedes b'. Two possibilities arise if a does not precede b,

1. b precedes a, (i.e. b should be reduced prior to a), represented as b $\cdot\!>$ a, or
2. a and b have equal precedence (i.e. a and b should be reduced in the same step), represented as a $\doteq$ b.

Note that a precedence relation is defined between grammar symbols a and b only if a and b can occur side by side in a sentential form. We use this fact to obtain the precedence relation between a and b as follows:

1. Consider some sentential form ... a b ... .
2. Determine the sequence of derivations S $\stackrel{*}{\Rightarrow}$ ... a b ... such that the last derivation derives a string containing a or b or both. Number the derivations in this sequence from 1 to *q*.
3. Consider the derivation numbered *q*. This is the last derivation for obtaining ... a b ... . Let this be of the form A $\Rightarrow$ β. Then $\beta \rightarrow$ A must be the first reduction in the bottom up parse of the string ... a b ... . Now (3.7)
   (a) a $\cdot\!>$ b if $\beta \equiv$ ...a
   (b) a $<\!\cdot$ b if $\beta \equiv$ b...
   (c) a $\doteq$ b if $\beta \equiv$ ...a b... .

Definition 3.4 (Simple precedence grammar (SPG))

Grammar G is a simple precedence grammar *if for all terminal and nonterminal symbols* a, b *of G, a unique precedence relation exists for* a, b.

Using the notion of precedence in an SPG, we can identify a unit for reduction in a sentential form by looking for the precedence relations

$$<\cdot\ s_1 \doteq s_2 \doteq \ldots \doteq s_r \cdot>$$

in the source string where each s_i is a T or NT. Here s_1, s_r are the first and last symbols to participate in the reduction. Needless to say that the string $s_1 s_2 \ldots s_r$ would form some RHS alternative in the grammar.

We will now formally state the problem of bottom up parsing as follows:

Definition 3.5 (Simple phrase) α *is a* simple phrase *of the sentential form* $\ldots\alpha\beta\ldots$ *if there exists a production of the grammar* A ::= α *and* $\alpha \rightarrow$ A *is a reduction in the sequence of reductions* $\ldots\alpha\beta\ldots \rightarrow \ldots \rightarrow$ S.

Definition 3.6 (Handle) *A* handle *of a sentential form is the left-most simple phrase in it.*

Example 3.11 E + T is not a simple phrase of the sentential form E + T ∗ F according to grammar (1.3) since its reduction to E does not lead to the distinguished symbol. However, T ∗ F is a simple phrase of the sentential form (see Fig. 3.8).

The deficiency of Algorithm 3.2 lies in its failure to identify simple phrases and handles. Algorithm 3.3 rectifies this deficiency.

Algorithm 3.3 (Bottom up parsing)

1. Identify the handle of the current string form.
2. If a handle exists, reduce it. Go to Step 1.
3. If the current string form = 'S' then exit with success
   else report error and exit with failure.

In practice, most grammars are not SPGs. Hence we will illustrate bottom up parsing for the class of operator grammars.

Example 3.12 Grammar (1.3) is not an SPG because of the following: In the string E + T ∗ F, + $<\cdot$ T due to the production T ::= T ∗ F. However, in E + T, + $\doteq$ T due to the production E ::= E + T.

Operator precedence grammars

In Section 1.4.1.1, we defined an operator grammar as a grammar none of whose productions contain two NTs appearing side-by-side. By induction, NTs cannot appear side-by-side in any sentential form of an operator grammar. Hence it is possible to ignore the presence of NTs and define precedence relations between operators for making parsing decisions. An operator precedence grammar (OPG) is an operator grammar in which the precedences between operators are unique. Such grammars typically arise in expressions.

Operator precedence

Precedence between *operators* a and b appearing in a sentential form ...aPb... where P is an NT or a null string, is termed *operator precedence*. The rules of procedure (3.7) can be used to determine operator precedences by considering the sentential form ...aPb... instead of the form ...ab.... Alternatively, it is possible to determine precedence relations from the productions of G as follows

1. a $\doteq$ b iff there exists a grammar production
   C ::= βabγ or C ::= βaAbγ.
2. a ·> b iff there exist grammar productions
   C ::= βAbγ and
   A ::= πa | πaD
3. a <· b iff there exist grammar productions
   C ::= βaBγ and
   B ::= bδ | Dbδ

(3.8)

An *operator precedence matrix* (OPM) represents operator precedence relations between pairs of operators. The entry OPM (a, b) represents the precedence of operator a with respect to operator b in a sentential form ...aPb... , where P may be a null string.

Example 3.13 The precedence relations for the grammar

$$\begin{aligned} E &::= E + T \mid T \\ T &::= T * V \mid V \\ V &::= \ <id> \end{aligned}$$

are shown in Fig. 3.9. The entry OPM (+, ∗) = <·, represents the precedence of '+' as a left operator and '∗' as the right operator of a pair of adjoining operators in a string, e.g. '+' and '∗' of the string $<id> + <id> * <id>$. This precedence relation is obtained by applying procedure (3.7) to the sequence of derivations E ⇒ E + T, T ⇒ T ∗ V, or by applying rule 3 of the rules (3.8) to the same productions.

There is a simpler way to obtain the precedence relations which works well for most grammars. This is based on the notions of associativity and relative priority of

LHS operator	RHS operator	
	+	*
+	·>	<·
*	·>	·>

Fig. 3.9

operators. A high priority operator always precedes a low priority operator appearing to its left or right. When two occurrences of an operator occupy adjoining positions of a string, the left occurrence precedes the right occurrence if the operator is left associative, else the right occurrence precedes the left occurrence.

Example 3.14 Consider the following grammar

$$\begin{array}{lll} S & ::= & \vdash E \dashv \\ E & ::= & E + T \mid T \\ T & ::= & T * V \mid V \\ V & ::= & \langle id \rangle \mid (E) \end{array} \qquad (3.9)$$

Figure 3.10 shows the operator precedence matrix for the grammar. The entry OPM ('+', '+') = ·> follows from the fact that '+' is left associative. The entries for '(' and ')' can be explained as follows: Consider an expression string

... b * (c + d) * e ...

Since a parenthesized expression is to be evaluated before its left and right neighbours, any operator would have <· relation with '(' appearing to its right, viz. '* <· '(' in the above string, and '(' would have a <· relation with any operator appearing to its right, viz. '(' <· '+'. Similarly, any operator would have ·> relation with ')' appearing to its right, while ')' would have a ·> relation with any operator appearing to its right. This is seen from the fact that '+' ·> ')', while ')' ·> '* in the above string. When '(' and ')' occur side by side, they would have $\doteq$ precedence with one another. In fact, this is the only instance of equal precedence in expressions. Same precedence relations would be obtained by applying procedure (3.7) or rules (3.8).

Note that '⊣' cannot be the LHS operator of a pair. Similarly '⊢' cannot be the RHS operator of a pair. Hence no rows and columns exist for these operators in OPM, respectively. The entries OPM ('(', '⊣') and OPM ('⊢', ')') are blank. Both these entries represent erroneous combinations of operators.

Operator precedence parsing

Example 3.15 Consider parsing of the string

$$\vdash \langle id \rangle + \langle id \rangle * \langle id \rangle \dashv$$

LHS operator	RHS operator				
	+	*	(	)	⊣
+	·>	<·	<·	·>	·>
*	·>	·>	<·	·>	·>
(	<·	<·	<·	≐	
)	·>	·>		·>	·>
⊢	<·	<·	<·		≐

Fig. 3.10 Operator precedence matrix

according to Grammar (3.9). The precedence relations from Figure 3.10 are marked below the string

Initial string : ⊢ <*id*> + <*id*> * <*id*> ⊣
<· <· ·>

The first <· is the precedence relation ⊢ <· +, the second <· represents + <· * etc. The handle is the string consisting of '* and its operands. After its reduction, the reduced string is

Reduced string : ⊢ <*id*> + ... ⊣
<· ·>

which leads to reduction of '+'.

Since operator precedence parsing ignores the NTs in a string, it is not easy to build a parse tree for a source string. However, an AST can be built easily. To develop an algorithm for AST building, we begin with some terminology and observations. We call the operator pointed to by SSM as the *current operator* and the operator to its left as the *previous operator*. From Ex. 3.15 it is clear that the previous operator must be reduced if previous operator ·> current operator, else a shift action must be performed. Thus end of the handle is known when previous operator ·> current operator. To find the beginning of the handle, we use the fact that the only instance of ≐ is '(' ≐ ')'. Hence the handle merely consists of the previous operator and its operands unless the previous operator is '('. If the previous operator is '(', the handle consists of '(..)'.

From these observations it is clear that apart from the current operator, only the previous operator needs to be considered at any point. A stack is therefore an appropriate data structure to use. An operator is pushed on the stack during a shift action and popped off during a reduce action. We can accommodate the right operand of an operator in the stack entry of the operator. The left operand, if present, would exist in the previous stack entry. We refer to the stack entry below the TOS entry as (TOS-1) entry, or TOSM entry for short.

Algorithm 3.4 (Operator Precedence Parsing)
Data structures

Stack : Each stack entry is a record with two fields, *operator* and *operand_pointer*.
Node : A *node* is a record with three fields, *symbol*, *left_pointer*, and *right_pointer*.

Functions

newnode (*operator, l_operand_pointer, r_operand_pointer*) creates a *node* with appropriate pointer fields and returns a pointer to the node.

1. TOS := SB − 1; SSM := 0;
2. Push '$\vdash$' on the stack.
3. SSM := SSM + 1;
   If current source symbol is an operator, then go to Step 5.
4. *x* := *newnode* (*source symbol, null, null*);
   TOS.*operand_pointer* := *x*;
   Go to Step 3;
5. While TOS operator $\cdot\!>$ current operator
   x := *newnode* (TOS *operator*, TOSM.*operand_pointer*, TOS.*operand_pointer*);
   Pop an entry off the stack.
   TOS.*operand_pointer* := *x*;
6. If TOS operator $<\!\cdot$ current operator, then
   Push the current operator on the stack.
   Go to Step 3;
7. If TOS operator $\doteq$ current operator, then
   If TOS operator = '$\vdash$', then exit successfully.
   If TOS operator = '(', then
   temp := TOS.*operand_pointer*;
   Pop an entry off the stack.
   TOS.*operand_pointer* := *temp*;
   Go to Step 3;
8. If no precedence defined between TOS operator and current operator then
   Report error and exit unsuccessfully.

Example 3.16 Consider parsing of the string

$$\vdash <id>_{\mathsf{a}} + <id>_{\mathsf{b}} * <id>_{\mathsf{c}} \dashv$$

according to grammar (3.9), where $<id>_{\mathsf{a}}$ represents a. Figure 3.11 shows steps in its parsing. Figures 3.11(a)-3.11(c) show the stack and the AST when current operator is '+', '∗' and '$\dashv$', respectively. In Fig. 3.11(c), TOS operator $\cdot\!>$ current operator.

This leads to reduction of '∗' (see Step 5 of Algorithm 3.4). Figure 3.11(d) shows the situation after the reduction. The new TOS operator, i.e. '+', ·> current operator. This leads to reduction of '+' as shown in Fig. 3.11(e).

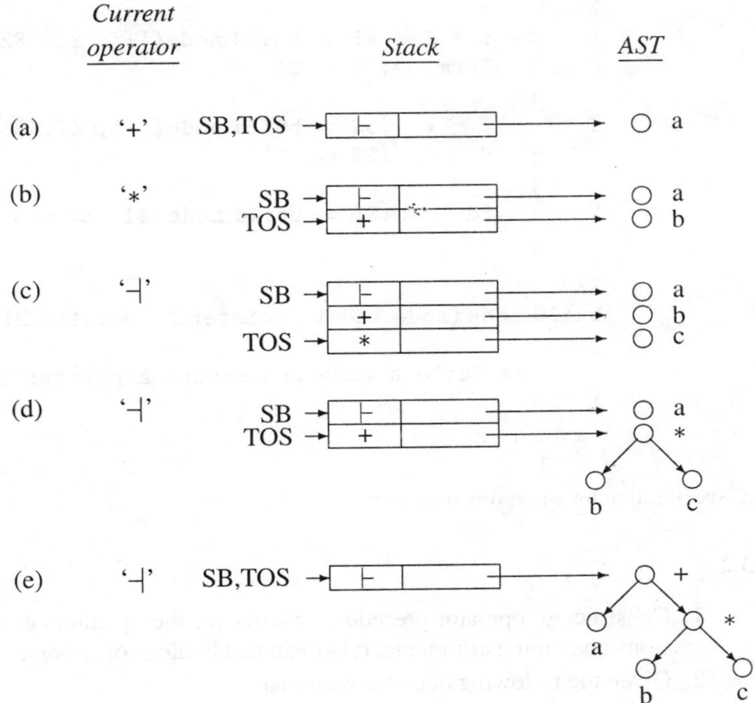

Fig. 3.11 Operator precedence parsing using a stack

LALR parsing

Practical LR parsers are table driven in nature, i.e. the parsing actions are governed by the table entry corresponding to the current state of the parser and the next few source symbols. The parser tables are typically generated using a parser generator. The information in the LR parsing tables and the operation of the LR parsers are described in Dhamdhere(1983) and Aho, Sethi, Ullman (1986). Here, we shall see a simple example containing specification of grammar productions and semantic actions in a YACC like manner. Note that YACC generates a parser which uses the LALR(1) variant of LR parsing.

Example 3.17 Figure 3.12 shows the YACC like specification for an expression parser. The parser builds an AST analogous to the parser of Ex. 3.16. As described in Section 1.5.2, the semantic action specified for a production is executed when a reduction is performed according to that production. The `build_node` routine builds a node and returns a pointer to it. The node description consists of three parts—node label and pointers to its left and right child nodes. The pointer returned by `build_node` is remembered as the attribute of the left hand side symbol of a production.

```
%%
E    :  E + T   {$$ = build_node('+', $1, $3)}
     |  Term    {$$ = $1}
     ;
T    :  T * V   {$$ = build_node('*', $1, $3)}
     |  V       {$$ = $1}
     ;
V    :  id      {$$ = build_node ($1, nil , nil)}
     ;

%%
build_node (node_label, pointer_1, pointer_2);
{
      /* Build a node and return a pointer to it */
}
```

Fig. 3.12 YACC specification for an expression parser

EXERCISE 3.2

1. Construct an operator precedence matrix for the operators of a grammar for expressions containing arithmetic, relational and boolean operators.
2. Given the following operator grammar

S	::=	⊢A⊣
A	::=	VaB | ε
B	::=	VaC
C	::=	VbA
V	::=	*<id>*

   (a) Construct an operator precedence matrix for the operators of the grammar.
   (b) Give a bottom up parse for a string containing nine *<id>* symbols.
3. An **if** statement may be written with or without an **else** part. Given the following operator grammar for **if**

$$
\begin{aligned}
< if\_stmt > \; &::= \; \textbf{if} < exp > \textbf{then} < stmt > \textbf{else} < stmt > \\
&\quad\;\; | \; \textbf{if} < exp > \textbf{then} < stmt > \\
< assignment > \; &::= \; < var > := < exp > \\
< stmt > \; &::= \; < assignment > | < if\_stmt >
\end{aligned}
$$

   where **if, then** and **else** are operators, find whether the operator precedence relations in this grammar are unique.

BIBLIOGRAPHY

Aho, Sethi and Ullman (1986) discuss automatic construction of scanners. Lewis, Rosenkrantz and Stearns (1976), Dhamdhere (1983) and Aho, Sethi and Ullman (1986) discuss parsing techniques in detail.

1. Aho, A.V., R. Sethi and J.D. Ullman (1986) : *Compilers – Principles, Techniques and Tools*, Addison-Wesley, Reading.
2. Barrett, W.A. and J.D. Couch (1977): *Compiler Construction*, Science Research Associates, Pennsylvania.
3. Dhamdhere, D.M. (1983): *Compiler Construction – Principles & Practice*, Macmillan India, New Delhi.
4. Fischer, C.N. and R.J. LeBlanc (1988): *Crafting a Compiler*, Benjamin/Cummings, Menlo Park, California.
5. Gries, D. (1971): *Compiler Construction for Digital Computers*, Wiley, New York.
6. Lewis, P.M., D.J. Rosenkrantz, and R.E. Stearns (1976): *Compiler Design Theory*, Addison-Wesley, Reading.
7. Tremblay, J.P. and P.G. Sorenson (1984): *The Theory and Practice of Compiler Writing*, McGraw-Hill.

CHAPTER 4

Assemblers

4.1 ELEMENTS OF ASSEMBLY LANGUAGE PROGRAMMING

An assembly language is a machine dependent, low level programming language which is specific to a certain computer system (or a family of computer systems). Compared to the machine language of a computer system, it provides three basic features which simplify programming:

1. *Mnemonic operation codes:* Use of mnemonic operation codes (also called *mnemonic opcodes*) for machine instructions eliminates the need to memorize numeric operation codes. It also enables the assembler to provide helpful diagnostics, for example indication of misspelt operation codes.
2. *Symbolic operands:* Symbolic names can be associated with data or instructions. These symbolic names can be used as operands in assembly statements. The assembler performs memory bindings to these names; the programmer need not know any details of the memory bindings performed by the assembler. This leads to a very important practical advantage during program modification as discussed in Section 4.1.2.
3. *Data declarations:* Data can be declared in a variety of notations, including the decimal notation. This avoids manual conversion of constants into their internal machine representation, for example, conversion of -5 into $(11111010)_2$ or 10.5 into $(41A80000)_{16}$.

Statement format

An assembly language statement has the following format:

[Label] <*Opcode*> <*operand spec*>[,<*operand spec*> ..]

where the notation [..] indicates that the enclosed specification is optional. If a label is specified in a statement, it is associated as a symbolic name with the memory word(s) generated for the statement. <*operand spec*> has the following syntax:

<symbolic name> [+*<displacement>*][(*<index register>*)]

Thus, some possible operand forms are: `AREA`, `AREA+5`, `AREA(4)`, and `AREA+5(4)`. The first specification refers to the memory word with which the name `AREA` is associated. The second specification refers to the memory word 5 words away from the word with the name `AREA`. Here '5' is the *displacement* or *offset* from `AREA`. The third specification implies indexing with index register 4—that is, the operand address is obtained by adding the contents of index register 4 to the address of `AREA`. The last specification is a combination of the previous two specifications.

A simple assembly language

In the first half of the chapter we use a simple assembly language to illustrate features of assembly languages and techniques used in assemblers. In this language, each statement has two operands, the first operand is always a register which can be any one of `AREG`, `BREG`, `CREG` and `DREG`. The second operand refers to a memory word using a symbolic name and an optional displacement. (Note that indexing is not permitted.)

Instruction opcode	*Assembly mnemonic*	*Remarks*
00	`STOP`	Stop execution
01	`ADD`	*First operand is modified* *Condition code is set*
02	`SUB`	
03	`MULT`	
04	`MOVER`	Register ← memory move
05	`MOVEM`	Memory ← register move
06	`COMP`	Sets condition code
07	`BC`	Branch on condition
08	`DIV`	Analogous to SUB
09	`READ`	*First operand is not used*
10	`PRINT`	

Fig. 4.1 Mnemonic operation codes

Figure 4.1 lists the mnemonic opcodes for machine instructions. The `MOVE` instructions move a value between a memory word and a register. In the MOVER instruction the second operand is the source operand and the first operand is the target operand. Converse is true for the MOVEM instruction. All arithmetic is performed in a register (i.e. the result replaces the contents of a register) and sets a *condition code*. A comparison instruction sets a condition code analogous to a subtract instruction without affecting the values of its operands. The condition code can be tested by a Branch on Condition (`BC`) instruction. The assembly statement corresponding to it has the format

`BC` *<condition code spec>*, *<memory address>*

It transfers control to the memory word with the address <*memory address*> if the current value of condition code matches <*condition code spec*>. For simplicity, we assume <*condition code spec*> to be a character string with obvious meaning, e.g. `GT`, `EQ`, etc. A `BC` statement with the condition code spec `ANY` implies unconditional transfer of control. In a machine language program, we show all addresses and constants in decimal rather than in octal or hexadecimal.

Figure 4.2 shows the machine instructions format. The opcode, register operand and memory operand occupy 2, 1 and 3 digits, respectively. The sign is not a part of the instruction. The condition code specified in a `BC` statement is encoded into the first operand position using the codes 1-6 for the specifications `LT`, `LE`, `EQ`, `GT`, `GE` and `ANY`, respectively. Figure 4.3 shows an assembly language program and an equivalent machine language program.

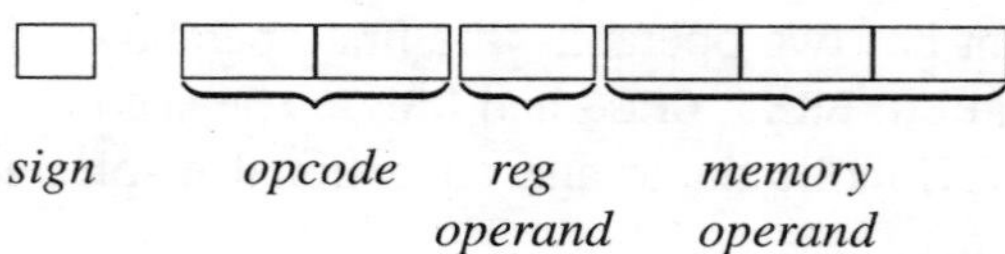

Fig. 4.2 Instruction format

```
         START  101
         READ   N                  101)  + 09 0 113
         MOVER  BREG, ONE          102)  + 04 2 115
         MOVEM  BREG, TERM         103)  + 05 2 116
AGAIN    MULT   BREG, TERM         104)  + 03 2 116
         MOVER  CREG, TERM         105)  + 04 3 116
         ADD    CREG, ONE          106)  + 01 3 115
         MOVEM  CREG, TERM         107)  + 05 3 116
         COMP   CREG, N            108)  + 06 3 113
         BC     LE, AGAIN          109)  + 07 2 104
         MOVEM  BREG, RESULT       110)  + 05 2 114
         PRINT  RESULT             111)  + 10 0 114
         STOP                      112)  + 00 0 000
N        DS     1                  113)
RESULT   DS     1                  114)
ONE      DC     '1'                115)  + 00 0 001
TERM     DS     1                  116)
         END
```

Fig. 4.3 An assembly and equivalent machine language program

4.1.1 Assembly Language Statements

An assembly program contains three kinds of statements:

1. Imperative statements

2. Declaration statements
3. Assembler directives.

Imperative statements

An imperative statement indicates an action to be performed during the execution of the assembled program. Each imperative statement typically translates into one machine instruction.

Declaration statements

The syntax of declaration statements is as follows:

```
[Label]   DS      <constant>
[Label]   DC      '<value>'
```

The DS (short for *declare storage*) statement reserves areas of memory and associates names with them. Consider the following DS statements:

```
A         DS      1
G         DS      200
```

The first statement reserves a memory area of 1 word and associates the name A with it. The second statement reserves a block of 200 memory words. The name G is associated with the first word of the block. Other words in the block can be accessed through offsets from G, e.g. G+5 is the sixth word of the memory block, etc.

The DC (short for *declare constant*) statement constructs memory words containing constants. The statement

```
ONE       DC      '1'
```

associates the name ONE with a memory word containing the value '1'. The programmer can declare constants in different forms—decimal, binary, hexadecimal, etc. The assembler converts them to the appropriate internal form.

Use of constants

Contrary to the name 'declare constant', the DC statement does not really implement constants, it merely initializes memory words to given values. These values are not protected by the assembler; they may be changed by moving a new value into the memory word. For example, in Fig. 4.3 the value of ONE can be changed by executing an instruction MOVEM BREG, ONE.

An assembly program can use constants in the sense implemented in an HLL in two ways—as immediate operands, and as literals. Immediate operands can be used in an assembly statement only if the architecture of the target machine includes the necessary features. In such a machine, the assembly statement

```
ADD     AREG,5
```

is translated into an instruction with two operands—AREG and the value '5' as an immediate operand. Note that our simple assembly language does not support this feature, whereas the assembly language of Intel 8086 supports it (see Section 4.5).

```
                                   ADD    AREG, FIVE
ADD   AREG, ='5'     ⇒             -- --
                            FIVE   DC      '5'
        (a)                             (b)
```

Fig. 4.4 Use of literals in an assembly program

A *literal* is an operand with the syntax ='<*value*>'. It differs from a constant because its location cannot be specified in the assembly program. This helps to ensure that its value is not changed during execution of a program. It differs from an immediate operand because no architectural provision is needed to support its use. An assembler handles a literal by mapping its use into other features of the assembly language. Figure 4.4(a) shows use of a literal ='5'. Figure 4.4(b) shows an equivalent arrangement using a DC statement `FIVE   DC   '5'`. When the assembler encounters the use of a literal in the operand field of a statement, it handles the literal using an arrangement similar to that shown in Fig. 4.4(b)—it allocates a memory word to contain the value of the literal, and replaces the use of the literal in a statement by an operand expression referring to this word. The value of the literal is protected by the fact that the name and address of this word is not know to the assembly language programmer.

Assembler directives

Assembler directives instruct the assembler to perform certain actions during the assembly of a program. Some assembler directives are described in the following.

START <*constant*>

This directive indicates that the first word of the target program generated by the assembler should be placed in the memory word with address <*constant*>.

END [<*operand spec*>]

This directive indicates the end of the source program. The optional <*operand spec*> indicates the address of the instruction where the execution of the program should begin. (By default, execution begins with the first instruction of the assembled program.)

4.1.2 Advantages of Assembly Language

The primary advantages of assembly language programming vis-a-vis machine language programming arise from the use of symbolic operand specifications. Consider the machine and assembly language statements of Fig. 4.3 once again. The programs presently compute N!. Figure 4.5 shows a changed program to compute $\frac{1}{2} \times$N!, where rectangular boxes are used to highlight changes in the program. One statement has been inserted before the PRINT statement to implement division by 2. In the machine language program, this leads to changes in addresses of constants and reserved memory areas. Because of this, addresses used in most instructions of the program had to change. Such changes are not needed in the assembly program since operand specifications are symbolic in nature.

```
         START   101
         READ    N                    101)   + 09 0 [114]
         MOVER   BREG, ONE            102)   + 04 2 [116]
         MOVEM   BREG, TERM           103)   + 05 2 [117]
AGAIN    MULT    BREG, TERM           104)   + 03 2 [117]
         MOVER   CREG, TERM           105)   + 04 3 [117]
         ADD     CREG, ONE            106)   + 01 3 [116]
         MOVEM   CREG, TERM           107)   + 05 3 [117]
         COMP    CREG, N              108)   + 06 3 [114]
         BC      LE, AGAIN            109)   + 07 2 104
        [DIV     BREG, TWO]           110)  [+ 08 2 118]
         MOVEM   BREG, RESULT         111)   + 05 2 [115]
         PRINT   RESULT               112)   + 10 0 [115]
         STOP                         113)   + 00 0 000
N        DS      1                    114)
RESULT   DS      1                    115)
ONE      DC      '1'                  116)   + 00 0 001
TERM     DS      1                    117)
TWO      DC      '2'                  118)   + 00 0 001
         END
```

Fig. 4.5 Modified assembly and machine language programs

Assembly language programming holds an edge over HLL programming in situations where it is necessary or desirable to use specific architectural features of a computer—for example, special instructions supported by the CPU.

4.2 A SIMPLE ASSEMBLY SCHEME

The fundamental translation model is motivated by Definition 1.2. In this section we use this model to develop preliminary ideas on the design of an assembler. We will use these ideas in Sections 4.4 and 4.5.

Design specification of an assembler

We use a four step approach to develop a design specification for an assembler:

1. Identify the information necessary to perform a task.

2. Design a suitable data structure to record the information.
3. Determine the processing necessary to obtain and maintain the information.
4. Determine the processing necessary to perform the task.

The fundamental information requirements arise in the synthesis phase of an assembler. Hence it is best to begin by considering the information requirements of the synthesis tasks. We then consider how to make this information available, i.e. whether it should be collected during analysis or derived during synthesis.

Synthesis phase

Consider the assembly statement

```
MOVER    BREG, ONE
```

in Fig. 4.3. We must have the following information to synthesize the machine instruction corresponding to this statement:

1. Address of the memory word with which name `ONE` is associated,
2. Machine operation code corresponding to the mnemonic `MOVER`.

The first item of information depends on the source program. Hence it must be made available by the analysis phase. The second item of information does not depend on the source program, it merely depends on the assembly language. Hence the synthesis phase can determine this information for itself.

Based on the above discussion, we consider the use of two data structures during the synthesis phase:

1. Symbol table
2. Mnemonics table.

Each entry of the symbol table has two primary fields—*name* and *address*. The table is built by the analysis phase. An entry in the mnemonics table has two primary fields—*mnemonic* and *opcode*. The synthesis phase uses these tables to obtain the machine address with which a name is associated, and the machine opcode corresponding to a mnemonic, respectively. Hence the tables have to be searched with the symbol name and the mnemonic as keys.

Analysis phase

The primary function performed by the analysis phase is the building of the symbol table. For this purpose it must determine the addresses with which the symbolic names used in a program are associated. It is possible to determine some addresses directly, e.g. the address of the first instruction in the program, however others must be inferred. Consider the assembly program of Fig. 4.3. To determine the address of

N, we must fix the addresses of all program elements preceding it. This function is called *memory allocation*.

To implement memory allocation a data structure called *location counter* (LC) is introduced. The location counter is always made to contain the address of the next memory word in the target program. It is initialized to the constant specified in the `START` statement. Whenever the analysis phase sees a label in an assembly statement, it enters the label and the contents of LC in a new entry of the symbol table. It then finds the number of memory words required by the assembly statement and updates the LC contents. (Hence the word 'counter' in 'location counter'.) This ensures that LC points to the next memory word in the target program even when machine instructions have different lengths and `DS`/`DC` statements reserve different amounts of memory. To update the contents of LC, analysis phase needs to know lengths of different instructions. This information simply depends on the assembly language, hence the mnemonics table can be extended to include this information in a new field called *length*. We refer to the processing involved in maintaining the location counter as *LC processing*.

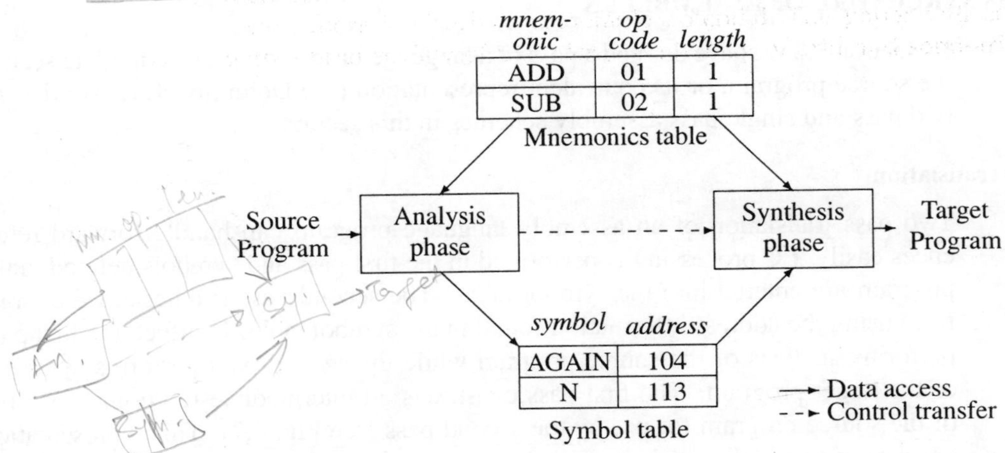

Fig. 4.6 Data structures of the assembler

Figure 4.6 illustrates the use of the data structures by the analysis and synthesis phases. Note that the Mnemonics table is a fixed table which is merely accessed by the analysis and synthesis phases, while the Symbol table is constructed during analysis and used during synthesis. The tasks performed by the analysis and synthesis phases are as follows:

Analysis phase 1. Isolate the label, mnemonic opcode and operand fields of a statement.

2. If a label is present, enter the pair (*symbol*, <*LC contents*>) in a new entry of symbol table.
3. Check validity of the mnemonic opcode through a look-up in the Mnemonics table.
4. Perform LC processing, i.e. update the value contained in LC by considering the opcode and operands of the statement.

Synthesis phase

1. Obtain the machine opcode corresponding to the mnemonic from the Mnemonics table.
2. Obtain address of a memory operand from the Symbol table.
3. Synthesize a machine instruction or the machine form of a constant, as the case may be.

4.3 PASS STRUCTURE OF ASSEMBLERS

In Section 1.3 we have defined a pass of a language processor as one complete scan of the source program, or its equivalent representation (see Definition 1.4). We discuss two pass and single pass assembly schemes in this section.

Two pass translation

Two pass translation of an assembly language program can handle forward references easily. LC processing is performed in the first pass and symbols defined in the program are entered into the symbol table. The second pass synthesizes the target form using the address information found in the symbol table. In effect, the first pass performs analysis of the source program while the second pass performs synthesis of the target program. The first pass constructs an intermediate representation (IR) of the source program for use by the second pass (see Fig. 4.7). This representation consists of two main components—data structures, e.g. the symbol table, and a processed form of the source program. The latter component is called *intermediate code* (IC).

Single pass translation

LC processing and construction of the symbol table proceed as in two pass translation. The problem of forward references is tackled using a process called *backpatching*. The operand field of an instruction containing a forward reference is left blank initially. The address of the forward referenced symbol is put into this field when its definition is encountered. In the program of Fig. 4.3, the instruction corresponding to the statement

```
MOVER    BREG, ONE
```

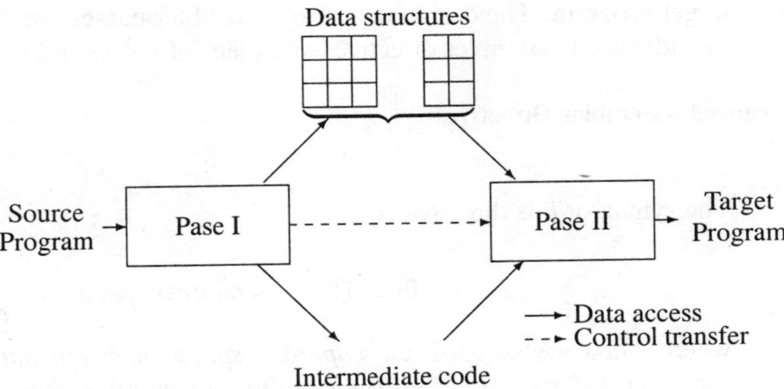

Fig. 4.7 Overview of two pass assembly

can be only partially synthesized since `ONE` is a forward reference. Hence the instruction opcode and address of `BREG` will be assembled to reside in location 101. The need for inserting the second operand's address at a later stage can be indicated by adding an entry to the Table of Incomplete Instructions (TII). This entry is a pair (<*instruction address*>, <*symbol*>), e.g. (101, `ONE`) in this case.

By the time the `END` statement is processed, the symbol table would contain the addresses of all symbols defined in the source program and TII would contain information describing all forward references. The assembler can now process each entry in TII to complete the concerned instruction. For example, the entry (101, `ONE`) would be processed by obtaining the address of `ONE` from symbol table and inserting it in the operand address field of the instruction with assembled address 101. Alternatively, entries in TII can be processed in an incremental manner. Thus, when definition of some symbol *symb* is encountered, all forward references to *symb* can be processed.

4.4 DESIGN OF A TWO PASS ASSEMBLER

Tasks performed by the passes of a two pass assembler are as follows:

Pass I
1. Separate the symbol, mnemonic opcode and operand fields.
2. Build the symbol table.
3. Perform LC processing.
4. Construct intermediate representation.

Pass II — Synthesize the target program.

Pass I performs analysis of the source program and synthesis of the intermediate representation while Pass II processes the intermediate representation to synthesize the target program. The design details of assembler passes are discussed after introducing advanced assembler directives and their influence on LC processing.

4.4.1 Advanced Assembler Directives

ORIGIN

The syntax of this directive is

ORIGIN *<address spec>*

where *<address spec>* is an *<operand spec>* or *<constant>*. This directive indicates that LC should be set to the address given by *<address spec>*. The ORIGIN statement is useful when the target program does not consist of consecutive memory words. The ability to use an *<operand spec>* in the ORIGIN statement provides the ability to perform LC processing in a *relative* rather than *absolute* manner. Example 4.1 illustrates the differences between the two.

Example 4.1 Statement number 18 of Fig. 4.8(a), viz. ORIGIN LOOP+2, sets LC to the value 204, since the symbol LOOP is associated with the address 202. The next statement, viz.

```
MULT      CREG, B
```

is therefore given the address 204. The statement ORIGIN LAST+1 sets LC to address 217. Note that an equivalent effect could have been achieved by using the statements ORIGIN 202 and ORIGIN 217 at these two places in the program, however the absolute addresses used in these statements would need to be changed if the address specification in the START statement is changed.

EQU

The EQU statement has the syntax

<symbol> EQU *<address spec>*

where *<address spec>* is an *<operand spec>* or *<constant>*.

The EQU statement defines the symbol to represent *<address spec>*. This differs from the DC/DS statement as no LC processing is implied. Thus EQU simply associates the name *<symbol>* with *<address spec>*.

Example 4.2 Statement 22 of Fig. 4.8(a), viz. BACK EQU LOOP introduces the symbol BACK to represent the operand LOOP. This is how the 16th statement, viz.

```
BC        LT, BACK
```

is assembled as '+ 07 1 202'.

```
1            START    200
2            MOVER    AREG, ='5'        200)   +04 1 211
3            MOVEM    AREG, A           201)   +05 1 217
4    LOOP    MOVER    AREG, A           202)   +04 1 217
5            MOVER    CREG, B           203)   +05 3 218
6            ADD      CREG, ='1'        204)   +01 3 212
7            ...

12           BC       ANY, NEXT         210)   +07 6 214
13           LTORG
                      ='5'              211)   +00 0 005
                      ='1'              212)   +00 0 001
14           ...
15   NEXT    SUB      AREG, ='1'        214)   +02 1 219
16           BC       LT, BACK          215)   +07 1 202
17   LAST    STOP                       216)   +00 0 000
18           ORIGIN   LOOP+2
19           MULT     CREG, B           204)   +03 3 218
20           ORIGIN   LAST+1
21   A       DS       1                 217)
22   BACK    EQU      LOOP
23   B       DS       1                 218)
24           END
25                    ='1'              219)   +00 0 001
```

Fig. 4.8 An assembly program illustrating ORIGIN

`LTORG`

Fig. 4.4 has shown how literals can be handled in two steps. First, the literal is treated as if it is a <*value*> in a `DC` statement, i.e. a memory word containing the value of the literal is formed. Second, this memory word is used as the operand in place of the literal. Where should the assembler place the word corresponding to the literal? Obviously, it should be placed such that control never reaches it during the execution of a program. The `LTORG` statement permits a programmer to specify where literals should be placed. By default, assembler places the literals after the `END` statement.

At every `LTORG` statement, as also at the `END` statement, the assembler allocates memory to the literals of a *literal pool.* The pool contains all literals used in the program since the start of the program or since the last `LTORG` statement.

Example 4.3 In Fig. 4.8, the literals ='5' and ='1' are added to the literal pool in statements 2 and 6, respectively. the first `LTORG` statement (statement number 13) allocates the addresses 211 and 212 to the values '5' and '1'. A new literal pool is now started. The value '1' is put into this pool in statement 15. This value is allocated the address 219 while processing the `END` statement. The literal ='1' used in statement 15 therefore refers to location 219 of the second pool of literals rather than location 212 of the first pool. Thus, all references to literals are forward references by definition.

The LTORG directive has very little relevance for the simple assembly language we have assumed so far. The need to allocate literals at intermediate points in the program rather than at the end is critically felt in a computer using a base displacement mode of addressing, e.g. computers of the IBM 360/370 family.

EXERCISE 4.4.1

1. An assembly program contains the statement

```
X        EQU        Y+25
```

   Indicate how the EQU statement can be processed if
   (a) Y is a back reference,
   (b) Y is a forward reference.
2. Can the operand expression in an ORIGIN statement contain forward references? If so, outline how the statement can be processed in a two pass assembly scheme.

4.4.2 Pass I of the Assembler

Pass I uses the following data structures:

OPTAB	A table of mnemonic opcodes and related information
SYMTAB	Symbol table
LITTAB	A table of literals used in the program

Figure 4.9 illustrates sample contents of these tables while processing the program of Fig. 4.8. OPTAB contains the fields *mnemonic opcode*, *class* and *mnemonic info*. The *class* field indicates whether the opcode corresponds to an imperative statement (IS), a declaration statement (DL) or an assembler directive (AD). If an imperative, the *mnemonic info* field contains the pair (*machine opcode, instruction length*), else it contains the id of a routine to handle the declaration or directive statement. A SYMTAB entry contains the fields *address* and *length*. A LITTAB entry contains the fields *literal* and *address*.

Processing of an assembly statement begins with the processing of its label field. If it contains a symbol, the symbol and the value in LC is copied into a new entry of SYMTAB. Thereafter, the functioning of Pass I centers around the interpretation of the OPTAB entry for the mnemonic. The *class* field of the entry is examined to determine whether the mnemonic belongs to the class of imperative, declaration or assembler directive statements. In the case of an imperative statement, the length of the machine instruction is simply added to the LC. The length is also entered in the SYMTAB entry of the symbol (if any) defined in the statement. This completes the processing of the statement.

For a declaration or assembler directive statement, the routine mentioned in the *mnemonic info* field is called to perform appropriate processing of the statement. For example, in the case of a DS statement, routine R#7 would be called. This routine

mnemonic opcode	*class*	*mnemonic info*
MOVER	IS	(04,1)
DS	DL	R#7
START	AD	R#11
	:	

OPTAB

symbol	*address*	*length*
LOOP	202	1
NEXT	214	1
LAST	216	1
A	217	1
BACK	202	1
B	218	1

SYMTAB

	literal	*address*
1	='5'	
2	='1'	
3	='1'	

LITTAB

literal no
#1
#3
–

POOLTAB

Fig. 4.9 Data structures of assembler Pass I

processes the operand field of the statement to determine the amount of memory required by this statement and appropriately updates the LC and the SYMTAB entry of the symbol (if any) defined in the statement. Similarly, for an assembler directive the called routine would perform appropriate processing, possibly affecting the value in LC.

The use of LITTAB needs some explanation. The first pass uses LITTAB to collect all literals used in a program. Awareness of different literal pools is maintained using the auxiliary table POOLTAB. This table contains the literal number of the starting literal of each literal pool. At any stage, the current literal pool is the last pool in LITTAB. On encountering an LTORG statement (or the `END` statement), literals in the current pool are allocated addresses starting with the current value in LC and LC is appropriately incremented. Thus, the literals of the program in Fig. 4.8(a) will be allocated memory in two steps. At the `LTORG` statement, the first two literals will be allocated the addresses 211 and 212. At the `END` statement, the third literal will be allocated address 219.

We now present the algorithm for the first pass of the assembler. Intermediate code forms for use in a two pass assembler are discussed in the next section.

Algorithm 4.1 (Assembler First Pass)

1. *loc_cntr* := 0; (default value)
   pooltab_ptr := 1; POOLTAB [1] := 1;
   littab_ptr := 1;
2. While next statement is not an END statement
   (a) If label is present then
       this_label := symbol in label field;
       Enter (*this_label, loc_cntr*) in SYMTAB.
   (b) If an LTORG statement then
       (i) Process literals LITTAB [POOLTAB [*pooltab_ptr*]] ... LITTAB [*littab_ptr*−1] to allocate memory and put the address in the *address* field. Update *loc_cntr* accordingly.
       (ii) *pooltab_ptr* := *pooltab_ptr* + 1;
       (iii) POOLTAB [*pooltab_ptr*] := *littab_ptr*;
   (c) If a START or ORIGIN statement then
       loc_cntr := value specified in operand field;
   (d) If an EQU statement then
       (i) *this_addr* := value of <*address spec*>;
       (ii) Correct the symtab entry for *this_label* to (*this_label, this_addr*).
   (e) If a declaration statement then
       (i) *code* := code of the declaration statement;
       (ii) *size* := size of memory area required by DC/DS.
       (iii) *loc_cntr* := *loc_cntr* + *size*;
       (iv) Generate IC '(DL, *code*) ···'.
   (f) If an imperative statement then
       (i) *code* := machine opcode from OPTAB;
       (ii) *loc_cntr* := *loc_cntr* + instruction length from OPTAB;
       (iii) If operand is a literal then
           this_literal := literal in operand field;
           LITTAB [*littab_ptr*] := *this_literal*;
           littab_ptr := *littab_ptr* + 1;
         else (i.e. operand is a symbol)
           this_entry := SYMTAB entry number of operand;
           Generate IC '(IS, *code*)(S, *this_entry*)';
3. (Processing of END statement)
   (a) Perform step 2(b).
   (b) Generate IC '(AD,02)'.
   (c) Go to Pass II.

4.4.3 Intermediate Code Forms

In Section 1.3 two criteria for the choice of intermediate code, viz. processing efficiency and memory economy, have been mentioned. In this section we consider some variants of intermediate codes and compare them on the basis of these criteria.

The intermediate code consists of a set of IC units, each IC unit consisting of the following three fields (see Fig. 4.10):

1. Address
2. Representation of the mnemonic opcode
3. Representation of operands.

Address	Opcode	Operands

Fig. 4.10 An IC unit

Variant forms of intermediate codes, specifically the operand and address fields, arise in practice due to the tradeoff between processing efficiency and memory economy. These variants are discussed in separate sections dealing with the representation of imperative statements, and declaration statements and directives, respectively. The information in the mnemonic field is assumed to have the same representation in all the variants.

Mnemonic field

The mnemonic field contains a pair of the form

(*statement class, code*)

where *statement class* can be one of IS, DL and AD standing for imperative statement, declaration statement and assembler directive, respectively. For an imperative statement, *code* is the instruction opcode in the machine language. For declarations and assembler directives, *code* is an ordinal number within the class. Thus, (AD, 01) stands for assembler directive number 1 which is the directive START. Figure 4.11 shows the codes for various declaration statements and assembler directives.

Declaration statements		*Assembler directives*	
DC	01	START	01
DS	02	END	02
		ORIGIN	03
		EQU	04
		LTORG	05

Fig. 4.11 Codes for declaration statements and directives

4.4.4 Intermediate Code for Imperative Statements

We consider two variants of intermediate code which differ in the information contained in their operand fields. For simplicity, the address field is assumed to contain identical information in both variants.

Variant I

The first operand is represented by a single digit number which is a code for a register (1-4 for AREG-DREG) or the condition code itself (1-6 for LT-ANY). The second operand, which is a memory operand, is represented by a pair of the form

(operand class, code)

where *operand class* is one of C, S and L standing for constant, symbol and literal, respectively (see Fig. 4.12). For a constant, the *code* field contains the internal representation of the constant itself. For example, the operand descriptor for the statement START 200 is (C, 200). For a symbol or literal, the *code* field contains the ordinal number of the operand's entry in SYMTAB or LITTAB. Thus entries for a symbol XYZ and a literal ='25' would be of the form (S, 17) and (L, 35) respectively.

```
        START   200          (AD,01)  (C,200)
        READ    A            (IS,09)  (S,01)
LOOP    MOVER   AREG, A      (IS,04)  (1)(S,01)
          .                     .
          .                     .
        SUB     AREG, ='1'   (IS,02)  (1)(L,01)
        BC      GT, LOOP     (IS,07)  (4)(S,02)
        STOP                 (IS,00)
A       DS      1            (DL, 02) (C,1)
        LTORG                (DL,05)
        ...                  ...
```

Fig. 4.12 Intermediate code - variant I

Note that this method of representing symbolic operands gives rise to one peculiarity. We have so far assumed that an entry is made in SYMTAB only when a symbol occurs in the label field of an assembly statement, e.g. an entry (A, 345, 1) if symbol A is allocated one word at address 345. However, while processing a forward reference

MOVER AREG, A

it is necessary to enter A in SYMTAB, say in entry number *n*, so that it can be represented by (S, *n*) in IC. At this point, the *address* and *length* fields of A's entry cannot be filled in. This implies that two kinds of entries may exist in SYMTAB at any time—for defined symbols and for forward references. This fact should be noted for use during error detection (see Section 4.4.7).

Variant II

This variant differs from variant I of the intermediate code in that the operand fields of the source statements are selectively replaced by their processed forms (see Fig. 4.13). For declarative statements and assembler directives, processing of the operand fields is essential to support LC processing. Hence these fields contain the processed forms. For imperative statements, the operand field is processed only to identify literal references. Literals are entered in LITTAB, and are represented as (L, *m*) in IC. Symbolic references in the source statement are not processed at all during Pass I.

```
          START   200            (AD,01)  (C,200)
          READ    A              (IS,09)  A
LOOP      MOVER   AREG, A        (IS,04)  AREG, A
            :                       :
          SUB     AREG, ='1'     (IS,02)  AREG, (L,01)
          BC      GT, LOOP       (IS,07)  GT, LOOP
          STOP                   (IS,00)
A         DS      1              (DL,02)  (C,1)
          LTORG                  (DL,05)
          ...                    ...
```

Fig. 4.13 Intermediate code - variant II

Comparison of the variants

Variant I of the intermediate code appears to require extra work in Pass I since operand fields are completely processed. However, this processing considerably simplifies the tasks of Pass II—a look at the IC of Fig. 4.12 confirms this. The functions of Pass II are quite trivial. To process the operand field of a declaration statement, we only need to refer to the appropriate table and obtain the operand address. Most declarations do not require any processing, e.g. `DC`, `DS` (see Section 4.4.5), and `START` statements, while some, e.g. `LTORG`, require marginal processing. The IC is quite compact—it can be as compact as the target code itself if each operand reference like (S, *n*) can be represented in the same number of bits as an operand address in a machine instruction.

Variant II reduces the work of Pass I by transferring the burden of operand processing from Pass I to Pass II of the assembler. The IC is less compact since the memory operand of a typical imperative statement is in the source form itself. On the other hand, by making Pass II to perform more work, the functions and memory requirements of the two passes get better balanced. Figure 4.14 illustrates the advantages of this aspect. Part (a) of Fig. 4.14 shows memory utilization by an assembler using variant I of IC. Some data structures, viz. symbol table, are passed in the memory while IC is presumably written in a file. Since Pass I performs much more processing than Pass II, its code occupies more memory than the code of Pass II. Part

(b) of Fig. 4.14 shows memory utilization when variant II of IC is used. The code sizes of the two passes are now comparable, hence the overall memory requirement of the assembler is lower.

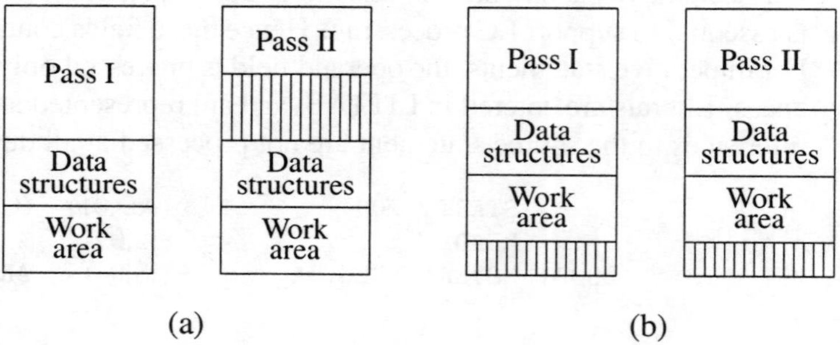

Fig. 4.14 Memory requirements using (a) variant I, (b) variant II

Variant II is particularly well-suited if expressions are permitted in the operand fields of an assembly statement. For example, the statement

```
MOVER      AREG, A+5
```

would appear as

```
(IS,05)    (1) (S,01)+5
```

in variant I of IC. This does not particularly simplify the task of Pass II or save much memory space. In such situations, it would have been preferable not to have processed the operand field at all.

4.4.5 Processing of Declarations and Assembler Directives

The focus of this discussion is on identifying alternative ways of processing declaration statements and assembler directives. In this context, it is useful to consider how far these statements can be processed in Pass I of the assembler. This depends on answers to two related questions:

1. Is it necessary to represent the address of each source statement in IC?
2. Is it necessary to have an explicit representation of `DS` statements and assembler directives in IC?

Let the answer to the first question be 'yes'. Now consider the following source program fragment and its intermediate code:

	START	200		—)	(AD,01)	(C,200)
AREA1	DS	20	⇒	200)	(DL,02)	(C,20)
SIZE	DC	5		220)	(DL,01)	(C,5)

Here, it is redundant to have the representations of the START and DS statements in IC, since the effect of these statements is implied in the fact that the DC statement has the address 220 ! Thus, it is not necessary to have a representation for DS statements and assembler directives in IC if the IC contains an *address* field. If the *address* field of the IC is omitted, a representation for the DS statements and assembler directives becomes essential. Now, Pass II can determine the address for SIZE only after analyzing the intermediate code units for the START and DS statements. The first alternative avoids this processing but requires the existence of the address field. Yet another instance of space–time tradeoff !

DC statement

A DC statement must be represented in IC. The mnemonic field contains the pair (DL,01). The operand field may contain the value of the constant in the source form or in the internal machine representation. No processing advantage exists in either case since conversion of the constant into the machine representation is required anyway. If a DC statement defines many constants, e.g.

```
DC        '5, 3, -7'
```

a series of (DL,01) units can be put in the IC.

START and ORIGIN

These directives set new values into the LC. It is not necessary to retain START and ORIGIN statements in the IC if the IC contains an address field.

LTORG

Pass I checks for the presence of a literal reference in the operand field of every statement. If one exists, it enters the literal in the current literal pool in LITTAB. When an LTORG statement appears in the source program, it assigns memory addresses to the literals in the current pool. These addresses are entered in the *address* field of their LITTAB entries.

After performing this fundamental action, two alternatives exist concerning Pass I processing. Pass I could simply construct an IC unit for the LTORG statement and leave all subsequent processing to Pass II. Values of literals can be inserted in the target program when this IC unit is processed in Pass II. This requires the use of POOLTAB and LITTAB in a manner analogous to Pass I.

Example 4.4 Figure 4.9 shows the LITTAB and POOLTAB for the program of Fig. 4.8 at the end of Pass I. Literals of the first pool are copied into the target program when the IC unit for LTORG is encountered in Pass II. Literals of the second pool are copied into the target program when the IC unit for END is processed.

Alternatively, Pass I could itself copy out the literals of the pool into the IC. This avoids duplication of Pass I actions in Pass II. The IC for a literal can be made identical to the IC for a DC statement so that no special processing is required in Pass II.

Example 4.5 Figure 4.15 shows the IC for the first half of the program of Fig. 4.8. The literals of the first pool (see Fig. 4.9) are copied out at LTORG statement. Note that the opcode field of the IC units, i.e (DL,01), is same as that for DC statements.

```
        START   200              (AD,01)  (C,200)
        MOVER   AREG, ='5'       (IS,04)  (1)(L,01)
        MOVEM   AREG, A          (IS,05)  (1)(S,01)
LOOP    MOVER   AREG, A          (IS,04)  (1)(S,01)
          :
        BC      ANY, NEXT        (IS,07)  (6)(S,04)
        LTORG                    (DL,01)  (C,5)
                                 (DL,01)  (C,1)
          :
```

Fig. 4.15 Copying of literal values into intermediate code

However, this alternative increases the tasks to be performed by Pass I, consequently increasing its size. This might lead to an unbalanced pass structure for the assembler with the consequences illustrated in Fig. 4.14. Secondly, the literals have to exist in two forms simultaneously, in the LITTAB along with the address information, and also in the intermediate code.

EXERCISE 4.4

1. Given the following source program:

```
        START    100
A       DS       3
L1      MOVER    AREG, B
        ADD      AREG, C
        MOVEM    AREG, D
D       EQU      A+1
L2      PRINT    D
        ORIGIN   A-1
C       DC       '5'
        ORIGIN   L2+1
        STOP
B       DC       '19'
        END      L1
```

(a) Show the contents of the symbol table at the end of Pass I.
(b) Explain the significance of EQU and ORIGIN statements in the program and explain how they are processed by the assembler.
(c) Show the Intermediate code generated for the program.

4.4.6 Pass II of the Assembler

Algorithm 4.2 is the algorithm for assembler Pass II. Minor changes may be needed to suit the IC being used. It has been assumed that the target code is to be assembled in the area named *code_area.*

Algorithm 4.2 (Assembler Second Pass)

1. *code_area_address* := address of *code_area*;
   pooltab_ptr := 1;
   loc_cntr := 0;
2. While next statement is not an END statement
   - (a) Clear *machine_code_buffer*;
   - (b) If an LTORG statement
     - (i) Process literals in LITTAB [POOLTAB [*pooltab_ptr*]] ... LITTAB [POOLTAB [*pooltab_ptr*+1]]−1 similar to processing of constants in a DC statement, i.e. assemble the literals in *machine_code_buffer*.
     - (ii) *size* := size of memory area required for literals;
     - (iii) *pooltab_ptr* := *pooltab_ptr* + 1;
   - (c) If a START or ORIGIN statement then
     - (i) *loc_cntr* := value specified in operand field;
     - (ii) *size* := 0;
   - (d) If a declaration statement
     - (i) If a DC statement then
       Assemble the constant in *machine_code_buffer*.
     - (ii) *size* := size of memory area required by DC/DS;
   - (e) If an imperative statement
     - (i) Get operand address from SYMTAB or LITTAB.
     - (ii) Assemble instruction in *machine_code_buffer*.
     - (iii) *size* := size of instruction;
   - (f) If *size* ≠ 0 then
     - (i) Move contents of *machine_code_buffer* to the address *code_area-_address* + *loc_cntr*;
     - (ii) *loc_cntr* := *loc_cntr* + *size*;
3. (Processing of END statement)
   - (a) Perform steps 2(b) and 2(f).
   - (b) Write *code_area* into output file.

Output interface of the assembler

It has been assumed that the assembler produces a target program which is the machine language of the target computer. This is rarely (if ever !) the case. The assembler produces an *object module* in the format required by a linkage editor or loader. The information contained in object modules is discussed in Chapter 7.

4.4.7 Listing and Error Reporting

Design of an error indication scheme involves some decisions which influence the effectiveness of error reporting and the speed and memory requirements of the assembler. The basic decision is whether to produce program listing and error reports in Pass I or delay these actions until Pass II. Producing the listing in the first pass has the advantage that the source program need not be preserved till Pass II. This conserves memory and avoids some amount of duplicate processing.

This design decision also has very important implications from a programmer's viewpoint. A listing produced in Pass I can report only certain errors in the most relevant place, that is, against the source statement itself. Examples of such errors are syntax errors like missing commas or parentheses and semantic errors like duplicate definitions of symbols. Other errors like references to undefined variables can only be reported at the end of the source program (see Fig. 4.16). The target code can be printed later in Pass II, however it is difficult to locate the target code corresponding to a source statement and vice versa. All these factors make debugging difficult.

```
Sr. No.         Statement              Address
001          START   200
002          MOVER   AREG, A             200
                 :
003
009          MVER    BREG, A             207
          ** error ** Invalid opcode
010          ADD     BREG, B             208
014       A  DS      1                   209
                 :
015
021       A  DC      '5'                 227
          ** error ** Duplicate definition of symbol A
                 :
022
035          END
          ** error ** Undefined symbol B in statement 10
```

Fig. 4.16 Error reporting in pass I

For effective error reporting, it is necessary to report all errors against the erroneous statement itself. This can be achieved by delaying program listing and error reporting till Pass II. Now the error reports as well as the target code can be printed against each source statement (see Ex. 4.6).

Example 4.6 Figure 4.16 illustrates error reporting in Pass I. Detection of errors in statements 9 and 21 is straightforward. In statement 9, the opcode is known to be invalid because it does not match with any mnemonic in OPTAB. In statement 21, `A` is known to be a duplicate definition because an entry for `A` already exists in the symbol table. Use of the undefined symbol `B` is harder to detect because at the end of Pass I we have no record that a forward reference to `B` exists in statement 10. This problem can be resolved by making an entry for `B` in the symbol table with an indication that a forward reference to `B` exists in statement 10. All such entries would be processed at the end of Pass I to check if a definition of the symbol has been encountered. If not, the symbol table entry contains sufficient information for error reporting. Note that the target instructions cannot be printed because they have not yet been generated. The memory address is printed against each statement in a weak attempt to provide a cross-reference between source statements and target instructions.

Example 4.7 Figure 4.17 illustrates error reporting performed in Pass II. Indication of errors in statements 9 and 21 is as easy as in Ex. 4.6. Indication of the error in statement 10 is equally easy—the symbol table is searched for an entry of `B` and an error is reported when no matching entry is found. Note that target program instructions appear against the source statements to which they belong.

```
Sr. No.         Statement                Address   Instruction

001             START  200
002             MOVER  AREG, A            200      + 04 1 209
                  :
003
009             MVER   BREG, A            207      + -- 2 209
           ** error ** Invalid opcode

010             ADD    BREG, B            208      + 01 2 ---
           ** error ** Undefined symbol B in operand field

014        A    DS     1                  209
                  :
015
021        A    DC     '5'                227      + 00 0 005
           ** error ** Duplicate definition of symbol A
                  :
022
035             END
```

Fig. 4.17 Error reporting in pass II

EXERCISE 4.4.7

1. A two pass assembler performs program listing and error reporting in Pass II using the following strategy: Errors detected in Pass I are stored in an error table. These are reported along with Pass II errors while producing the program listing.
   (a) Design the error table for use by Pass I. What is its entry format? What is the table organization?
   (b) Let the error messages (e.g. DUPLICATE LABEL...) be stored in an error message table. Comment on the organization of this table.

   (*Note:* Readers may refer to Dhamdhere (1983) for some interesting error reporting strategies.)

4.4.8 Some Organizational Issues

We discuss some organizational issues in assembler design, like the placement and access of tables and IC, with respect to the schematic shown in Fig. 4.18.

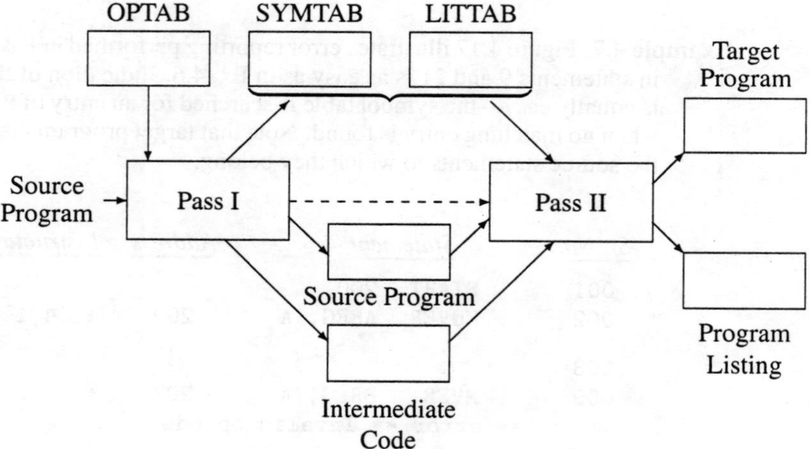

Fig. 4.18 Data structures and files in a two pass assembler

Tables

For efficiency reasons SYMTAB must remain in main memory throughout Passes I and II of the assembler. LITTAB is not accessed as frequently as SYMTAB, however it may be accessed sufficiently frequently to justify its presence in the memory. If memory is at a premium, it is possible to hold only part of LITTAB in the memory because only the literals of the current pool need to be accessible at any time. For obvious reasons, no such partitioning is feasible for SYMTAB. OPTAB should be in memory during Pass I.

Source program and intermediate code

The source program would be read by Pass I on a statement by statement basis. After processing, a source statement can be written into a file for subsequent use in Pass II. The IC generated for it would also be written into another file. The target code and the program listings can be written out as separate files by Pass II. Since all these files are sequential in nature, it is beneficial to use appropriate blocking and buffering of records.

EXERCISE 4.4.8

1. Develop complete program specifications for the passes of a two pass assembler indicating
   (a) Tables for internal use of the passes
   (b) Tables to be shared between passes
   (c) Inputs (files and tables) for every pass
   (d) Outputs (files and tables) of every pass.

   You must clearly specify why certain information is in the form of tables in main memory while other information is in the form of files.
2. Recommend appropriate organizations for the tables and files used in the two pass assembler of problem 1.

4.5 A SINGLE PASS ASSEMBLER FOR IBM PC

We shall discuss a single pass assembler for the intel 8088 processor used in the IBM PC. The discussion focuses on the design features for handling the forward reference problem in an environment using segment-based addressing.

4.5.1 The architecture of Intel 8088

The intel 8088 microprocessor supports 8 and 16 bit arithmetic, and also provides special instructions for string manipulation. The CPU contains the following features (see Fig. 4.19):

- Data registers AX, BX, CX and DX
- Index registers SI and DI
- Stack pointer registers BP and SP
- Segment registers Code, Stack, Data and Extra.

Each data register is 16 bits in size, split into the upper and lower halves. Either half can be used for 8 bit arithmetic, while the two halves together constitute the data register for 16 bit arithmetic. The architecture supports stacks for storing subroutine and interrupt return addresses, parameters and other data. The index registers SI and DI are used to index the source and destination addresses in string manipulation instructions. They are provided with the auto-increment and auto-decrement facility.

(a)

AH	AL	AX
BH	BL	BX
CH	CL	CX
DH	DL	DX

(b)

BP
SP

(c)

SI
DI

(d)

Code
Stack
Data
Extra

Fig. 4.19 (a) Data, (b) Base, (c) Index and (d) Segment registers

Two stack pointer registers called SP and BP are provided to address the stack. SP points into the stack implicitly used by the architecture to store subroutine and interrupt return addresses. BP can be used by the programmer in any desired manner. Push and Pop instructions are provided for this purpose.

The Intel 8088 provides addressing capability for 1 MB of primary memory. The memory is used to store three components of a program, program code, data and stack. The Code, Stack and Data segment registers are used to contain the start addresses of these three components. The Extra segment register points to another memory area which can be used to store data. To address a memory location, an instruction designates a segment register and provides a 16 bit logical address. The address contained in the segment register is extended by adding four lower order zeroes to yield the segment base address. The logical address is now added to it to obtain a 20 bit memory address. The size of each segment is thus limited to 2^{16}, i.e. 64K, bytes. A large program may contain many segments, only four of which can be addressed at any given time. Segment-based addressing facilitates easy relocation of programs. If the memory area allocated to a program is changed, it is sufficient to change the addresses loaded in the segment registers. The memory addresses generated would now automatically lie in the new memory area occupied by the program.

The 8088 architecture provides 24 addressing modes. These are summarized in Fig. 4.20. In the immediate addressing mode, the instruction itself contains the data that is to participate in the instruction. This data can be 8 or 16 bits in length. In the direct addressing mode, the instruction contains a 16 bit number which is taken to be a displacement from the segment base contained in a segment register. The segment

Addressing mode	*Example*	*Remarks*
Immediate	`MOV SUM, 1234H`	Data = 1234H
Register	`MOV SUM, AX`	AX contains the data
Direct	`MOV SUM, [1234H]`	Data disp. = 1234H
Register indirect	`MOV SUM, [BX]`	Data disp. = (BX)
Register indirect	`MOV SUM, CS: [BX]`	Segment override : Segment base = (CS) Data disp. = (BX)
Based	`MOV SUM, 12H [BX]`	Data disp. = 12H+(BX)
Indexed	`MOV SUM, 34H [SI]`	Data disp. = 34H+(SI)
Based & indexed	`MOV SUM, 56H [SI] [BX]`	Data disp. `= 56H + (SI) + (BX)`

Fig. 4.20 Addressing modes of 8088 ('(..)' implies 'contents of')

register may be explicitly indicated in a prefix of the instruction, else a default segment register is used. In the indexed mode, contents of the index register indicated in the instruction (SI or DI) are added to the 8 or 16 bit displacement contained in the instruction. The result is taken to be the displacement from the segment base of the data segment. In the based mode, contents of the base register (BP or BX) are added to the displacement. The result is taken to be the displacement from the data segment base unless BP is specified, in which case it is taken as a displacement from the stack segment base. The based-and-indexed-with-displacement mode combines the effect of the based and indexed modes.

4.5.2 Intel 8088 Instructions

Arithmetic instructions

The operands can be in one of the four 16 bit registers, or in a memory location designated by one of the 24 addressing modes. Three instruction formats shown in Fig. 4.21 are supported. The *mod* and *r/m* fields specify the first operand, which can be in a register or in memory, while the *reg* field describes the second operand, which is always a register. The instruction opcode indicates which instruction format is applicable. The direction field (*d*) in the instruction indicates which operand is the destination operand in the instruction. If $d = 0$, the register/memory operand is the destination, else the register operand indicated by *reg* is the destination. The *width* field (*w*) indicates whether 8 or 16 bit arithmetic is to be used. The conventions for determining the operands are described in Fig. 4.21.

Figure 4.22 contains some sample instructions. Note that in the first statement, AL could be encoded into the first or the second operand of the instruction. In the second statement, however, it has to be encoded into second operand since the first operand has to be `12H [SI]`. Here, *mod* = 01 since only one byte of displacement is

(a) *Register/Memory to Register*

opcode d w	*mod reg r/m*

(b) *Immediate to Register/Memory*

opcode d w	*mod op r/m*	*data*	*data*

(c) *Immediate to Accumulator*

opcode w	*data*	*data*

r/m	*mod* = 00	*mod* = 01	*mod* = 10	*mod* = 11	
				w=0	*w*=1
000	(BX) + (SI)	(BX) + (SI) + d8	Note 2	AL	AX
001	(BX) + (DI)	(BX) + (DI) + d8	Note 2	CL	CX
010	(BP) + (SI)	(BP) + (SI) + d8	Note 2	DL	DX
011	(BP) + (DI)	(BP) + (DI) + d8	Note 2	BL	BX
100	(SI)	(SI) + d8	Note 2	AH	SP
101	(DI)	(DI) + d8	Note 2	CH	BP
110	Note 1	(BP) + d8	Note 2	DH	SI
111	(BX)	(BX) + d8	Note 2	BH	DI

Note 1 : (BP) + DISP for indirect addressing, d16 for direct
Note 2 : Same as previous column, except d16 instead of d8

reg	*Register* 8-bit (*w*=0)	16-bit (*w*=1)
000	AL	AX
001	CL	CX
010	DL	DX
011	BL	BX
100	AH	SP
101	CH	BP
110	DH	SI
111	BH	DI

Fig. 4.21 Instruction formats of Intel 8088

Assembly statement	*Opcode d w*	*mod reg r/m*	*data/ displacement*
`ADD AL, BL`	000000 0 0	11 011 000	
`ADD AL, 12H[SI]`	000000 1 0	01 000 100	00010010
`ADD AX, 3456H`	100000 0 1	11 000 000	01010110 00110100
`ADD AX, 3456H`	000001 0 1	01 010 110	00110100

Fig. 4.22 Sample instructions of 8088

adequate. The third instruction contains 16 bits of immediate data. Note that the low byte of immediate data comes first, followed by its high byte. The fourth assembly statement is identical to the third, however it has been encoded using the immediate to accumulator instruction format. Here, w = 1 implies that the accumulator is the AX register. This instruction is only 3 bytes in length as against the previous instruction which is 4 bytes. This illustrates the fact that the assembler has to perform an analysis of the available options before determining the best instruction to use in a specific case.

Segment overrides

For arithmetic and `MOV` instructions, the architecture uses the data segment by default. To override this, an instruction can be preceded by a 1-byte segment override prefix with the following format:

001 *seg* 110

where *seg*, represented in 2 bits, has the meanings shown in Fig. 4.23.

seg	*segment register*
00	ES
01	CS
10	SS
11	DS

Fig. 4.23 Segment codes

Example 4.8 If the code segment is to be used instead of the data segment in the second statement of Fig. 4.22, it can be rewritten as

```
ADD        AL, CS:12H[SI]
```

The assembler would encode this as

segment override	*instruction*
001 01 110	000000 1 0 01 000 100 00010010

Control transfer instructions

Two groups of control transfer instructions are supported. These are:

1. Calls, jumps and returns
2. Iteration control instructions.

The calls, jumps and returns can occur within the same segment, or can cross segment boundaries. Intra-segment transfers are preferably assembled using a self-relative displacement in the range of −128 to +127. The longer form of intra-segment transfer uses a 16 bit logical address within the segment. Inter-segment transfers indicate a new segment base and an offset. Their execution is expensive since the code segment register has to be modified. Control transfers can be both direct and indirect. Their instruction formats are as shown in Fig. 4.24.

(a) *Intrasegment*

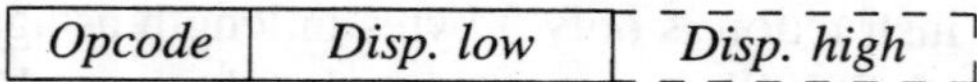

(b) *Intersegment*

Opcode	*Offset*	*Offset*	*Segment*	*base*

(c) *Indirect*

Opcode	*mod 100 r/m*	*Disp. low*	*Disp. high*

Fig. 4.24 Formats of control transfer instructions

A call pushes the offset of the next instruction's address from the segment base on the stack. This address is used to return to the calling program. In the case of an inter-segment call, the CS segment register is pushed first, followed by the offset.

Iteration control operations perform looping decisions in string operations. A self-relative jump of −128 to +127 permits the decision to be made at the beginning or end of the loop.

Example 4.9 Consider the program

```
MOV          SI, 100H    ; Source address
MOV          DI, 200H    ; Destination address
MOV          CX, 50H     ; No.  of bytes
CLD                      ; Clear direction flag
REP          MOVSB       ; Move 80 bytes
```

The MOVSB instruction moves one byte from the address contained in SI to the address contained in DI. After the move, the SI and DI registers are incremented/decremented by one byte depending on the direction flag. Since the CLD instruction resets the direction flag, the registers will be incremented in this case. The REP prefix of MOVSB will cause CX to be decremented after MOVSB is performed. The new value of CX is tested and the loop is repeated until CX becomes zero.

4.5.3 The Assembly Language of Intel 8088

Statement format

The format of an assembly statement is as follows:

```
[Label:]  opcode     operand(s)  ; comment string
```

where the label is optional. In the operand field, operands are separated by commas. Figure 4.22 contains some examples of assembly statements. The parentheses [..] in the operand field represent the words 'contents of'. Base and index register specifications, as also direct addresses specified as numeric offsets from the segment base are enclosed in these parentheses. A segment override is specified in the operand to which it applies, viz. CS:12H [SI]. More details of operand specification can be found in Sections 4.5.1 and 4.5.2.

Assembler directives

The ORG, EQU and END directives are analogous to the ORIGIN, EQU and END directives described in Sections 4.4 and 4.1. The start directive is not supported since ORG subsumes its functionality. The concept of literals, and the LTORG directive, are redundant since the 8088 architecture supports immediate operands.

Declarations

Declaration of constants and reservation of storage are both achieved in the same directive, viz.

```
A    DB    25        ;Reserve byte & initialize
B    DW    ?         ;Reserve word, no initialization
C    DD    6DUP(0)   ;6 Double words, all 0's
```

DQ and DT reserve a quad-word (8 bytes) and ten bytes respectively. Since logical addresses (16 bits) are required to occupy a word, the DW declaration is used for some special purposes, viz.

```
ADDR_A    DW    A
```

initializes the word to the logical address of A (i.e. offset from the segment base).

EQU *and* PURGE

EQU defines symbolic names to represent values or other symbolic names as described in Section 4.4. The names so defined can be 'undefined' through a PURGE statement. Such a name can be reused for other purposes later in the program.

Example 4.10 Following program illustrates EQU and PURGE.

```
XYZ        DB        ?
ABC        EQU       XYZ  ; ABC represents name XYZ
           PURGE     ABC  ; ABC no longer XYZ
ABC        EQU       25   ; ABC now stands for '25'
```

SEGMENT, ENDS *and* ASSUME

All memory addressing is segment directed. Hence as assembly program consists of a set of segments. SEGMENT and ENDS directives demarcate the segments in an assembly program. To assemble a symbolic reference, the assembler must determine the offset of the symbol from the start of the segment containing it. To facilitate this, the programmer must perform the following actions in the assembly program: (a) load a segment register with the segment base, and (b) let the assembler know which segment register contains the segment base. The second task is performed using the ASSUME directive, which has the syntax

ASSUME <*register*> : <*segment name*>

and tells the assembler that it can 'assume' the address of the indicated segment to be present in <*register*>. The directive ASSUME <*register*> : NOTHING cancels any prior assumptions indicated for <*register*>.

Example 4.11 Consider the following program:

```
SAMPLE_DATA  SEGMENT
ARRAY        DW            100 DUP ?
SUM          DW            0
SAMPLE_DATA  ENDS
SAMPLE_CODE  SEGMENT

             ASSUME        DS:SAMPLE_DATA
HERE:        MOV           AX, SAMPLE_DATA
             MOV           DS, AX
             MOV           AX, SUM
             - -
SAMPLE_CODE  ENDS
             END           HERE
```

The program consists of two segments, a code segment and a data segment. The ASSUME directive tells the assembler that the start address of SAMPLE_DATA can be assumed to be in the DS register. While assembling the statement MOV AX, SUM the assembler first computes the offset of SUM from the start of its segment. This is 200 bytes. It now finds whether the segment in which SUM exists is addressable at the current moment. Since it is, it would encode SUM to be an offset of 200 bytes from the DS register. Note that it is the programmer's responsibility to ensure that the correct address is loaded in the DS register before executing the reference to SUM. If the address of SAMPLE_DATA were to be loaded into some other segment register, e.g. register ES, this fact would be indicated through the statement ASSUME ES:SAMPLE_DATA. The assembler would then generate a segment override prefix while assembling the statement MOV AX, SUM.

PROC, ENDP, NEAR *and* FAR

PROC and ENDP delimit the body of a procedure. The keywords NEAR and FAR appearing in the operand field of PROC indicate whether the call to the procedure is to be assembled as a *near* or *far* call. A RET statement must appear in the body of the procedure to return execution control to the calling program. Parameters for the called procedure can be passed through registers or on the stack.

Example 4.12 Consider the following assembly program:

```
SAMPLE_CODE  SEGMENT
CALCULATE    PROC       FAR         ; a FAR procedure
             - -
             RET
CALCULATE    ENDP
SAMPLE_CODE  ENDS
PGM          SEGMENT
             - -
             CALL       CALCULATE   ; a FAR call
             - -
PGM          ENDS
             END
```

Since CALCULATE is a far procedure, it need not be addressable at the point of call. The assembler will encode a far call instruction which specifies the segment base and the offset of CALCULATE within the segment.

PUBLIC *and* EXTRN

When a symbolic name declared in one assembly module is to be accessible in other modules, it is specified in a PUBLIC statement. Another module wishing to use this name must specify it in an EXTRN statement which has the syntax

EXTRN <*symbolic name*>:<*type*>

For labels of DC, DS statements, the type can be word, byte, etc. For labels of instructions, the type can be FAR or NEAR.

Analytic operators

The analytic operators split a memory address into its components, or provide information regarding the type and memory requirements of operands. Five analytic operators exist. These are SEG, OFFSET, TYPE, SIZE and LENGTH. SEG and OFFSET provide the segment and offset components of the memory address of an operand.

Example 4.13 The instruction

```
MOV         AX, OFFSET ABC
```

loads the offset of symbol ABC within its segment into the AX register.

TYPE indicates the manner in which an operand is defined and returns the following numeric codes: 1 (byte), 2 (word), 4 (double word), 8 (quad-word), 10 (ten bytes), −1 (near instruction) and −2 (far instruction). SIZE indicates the number of units declared for an operand, while LENGTH indicates the number of bytes allocated to the operand.

Example 4.14 The symbol BUFFER defined in

```
BUFFER      DW          100 DUP (0)
```

has the SIZE of 100 and LENGTH of 200 bytes. SIZE and LENGTH can be used as in

```
MOV         CX, LENGTH XYZ
```

which loads length of XYZ into the CX register.

Synthetic operators

It is sometimes necessary to have different types associated with the same memory operand, e.g. when a byte in an operand of type 'word' is to be accessed as an operand of type 'byte'. This is achieved through the PTR and THIS operators. The PTR operator creates a new memory operand with the same segment and offset addresses as an existing operand, but having a different type. No memory allocation is implied by its use. The THIS operator performs the special function of creating a new memory operand with the same address as the next memory byte available for allocation.

Example 4.15 Consider the program

```
XYZ         DW          312
NEW_NAME    EQU         BYTE PTR XYZ
LOOP:       CMP         AX, 234
            JMP         LOOP
FAR_LOOP    EQU         FAR PTR LOOP
            JMP         FAR_LOOP
```

Here, NEW_NAME is a byte operand with the same address as XYZ, while FAR_LOOP is a FAR symbolic name with the same address as LOOP. Thus, while JMP LOOP is a near jump, JMP FAR_LOOP is a far jump. Exactly the same effect could be achieved by rewriting the program using THIS as follows:

```
                DW
NEW_NAME        EQU         THIS BYTE
XYZ             DW          312
FAR_LOOP        EQU         THIS FAR
LOOP            CMP         AX, 234
                JMP         LOOP
                -- --
                JMP         FAR_LOOP
```

4.5.4 Problems of Single Pass Assembly

A single pass assembler for Intel 8088 shares some problems with other single pass assemblers, viz. problems in assembling forward references and in error reporting. The forward reference problem is aggravated by the nature of the 8088 architecture. We discuss two aspects of this problem. The sample program of Fig. 4.25 is used to illustrate these problems.

```
Statement                                          Offset

CODE    SEGMENT
        ASSUME  CS:CODE, DS:DATA
        MOV     AX, DATA                           0000
        MOV     DS, AX                             0003
        MOV     CX, LENGTH STRNG                   0005
        MOV     COUNT,0000                         0008
        MOV     SI, OFFSET STRNG                   0011
        ASSUME  ES:DATA, DS:NOTHING
        MOV     AX, DATA                           0014
        MOV     ES, AX                             0017
COMP:   CMP     [SI],'A'                           0019
        JNE     NEXT                               0022
        MOV     COUNT, 1                           0024
NEXT:   INC     SI                                 0027
        DEC     CX                                 0029
        JNE     COMP                               0030
CODE    ENDS

DATA    SEGMENT
        ORG     1
COUNT   DB      ?                                  0001
STRNG   DW      50 DUP (?)                         0002
DATA    ENDS
        END
```

Fig. 4.25 Sample assembly program of Intel 8088

Forward references

A symbolic name may be forward referenced in a variety of ways. When used as a data operand in a statement, its assembly is straightforward. An entry can be made in the table of incomplete instructions (TII) discussed in Section 4.3. This entry would identify the bytes in code where the address of the referenced symbol should be put. When the symbol's definition is encountered, this entry would be analysed to complete the instruction. However, use of a symbolic name as the destination in a branch instruction gives rise to a peculiar problem. Some generic branch opcodes like `JMP` in the 8088 assembly language can give rise to instructions of different formats and different lengths depending on whether the jump is *near* or *far*—that is, whether the destination symbol is less than 128 bytes away from the `JMP` instruction. However, this would not be known until sometime later in the assembly process! This problem is solved by assembling such instructions with a 16 bit logical address unless the programmer indicates a short displacement, e.g. `JMP SHORT LOOP`. The program of Fig. 4.25 contains the forward branch instruction `JNE NEXT`. However, the above problem does not arise here since the opcode `JNE` dictates that the instruction should be in the self-relative format.

A more serious problem arises when the type of a forward referenced symbol is used in an instruction. The type may be used in a manner which influences the size/length of a declaration. Such usage will have to be disallowed to facilitate single pass assembly.

Example 4.16 Consider the statements

```
XYZ     DB      LENGTH ABC DUP(0)
- -
ABC     DD      ?
```

Here the forward reference to `ABC` makes it impossible to assemble the `DB` statement in a single pass.

Segment registers

An `ASSUME` statement indicates that a segment register contains the base address of a segment. The assembler represents this information by a pair of the form (*segment register, segment name*). This information can be stored in a *segment registers table* (SRTAB). SRTAB is updated on processing an `ASSUME` statement. For processing the reference to a symbol *symb* in an assembly statement, the assembler accesses the symbol table entry of *symb* and finds (seg_{symb}, $offset_{symb}$) where seg_{symb} is the name of the symbol containing the definition of *symb*. It uses the information in SRTAB to find the register which contains seg_{symb}. Let it be register *r*. It now synthesizes the pair (*r*, $offset_{symb}$). This pair is put in the address field of the target instruction.

However, this strategy would not work while assembling forward references. Consider statements 6 and 13 in Fig. 4.25 which make forward references to `COUNT`.

When the definition of `COUNT` is encountered in statement 20, information concerning these forward references can be found in the table of incomplete instructions (TII). What segment register should be used to assemble these references? The first reference was made in statement 6 when DS was the segment register containing the segment base of `DATA`. However, SRTAB presently contains the pair (ES, `DATA`) as a result of statement 8, viz. `ASSUME ES:DATA` . . . A similar problem may arise while assembling forward references contained in branch instructions. The following provisions are made to handle this problem:

1. A new SRTAB is created while processing an `ASSUME` statement. This SRTAB differs from the old SRTAB only in the entries for the segment registers named in the `ASSUME` statement. Since many SRTAB's exist at any time, an array named SRTAB_ARRAY is used to store the SRTAB's. This array is indexed using a counter *srtab_no*.
2. Instead of TII, a *forward reference table* (FRT) is used. Each entry of FRT contains the following entries:
   (a) Address of the instruction whose operand field contains the forward reference
   (b) Symbol to which forward reference is made
   (c) Kind of reference (e.g. T : analytic operator `TYPE`, D : data address, S : self relative address, L : length, F : offset, etc.)
   (d) Number of the SRTAB to be used for assembling the reference.

Example 4.17 illustrates how these provisions are adequate to handle the problem concerning forward references mentioned earlier.

Example 4.17 Two SRTAB's would be built for the program of Fig. 4.25. SRTAB#1 contains the pairs (CS, `CODE`) and (DS, `DATA`) while SRTAB#2 contains the pairs (CS, `CODE`) and (ES, `DATA`). While processing statement 6, SRTAB#1 is the current SRTAB. Hence the FRT entry for this statement is (008, `COUNT`, D, SRTAB#1). Similarly the FRT entry for statement 13 is (024, `COUNT`, D, SRTAB#2). These entries are processed on encountering the definition of `COUNT`, giving the address pairs (DS, 001) and (ES, 001). (Note that FRT entries would also exist for statements 5, 7 and 12. However, none of them require the use of a base register.)

4.5.5 Design of the Assembler

Algorithm for the Intel 8088 assembler, Algorithm 4.3, is given at the end of this section. LC processing in this algorithm differs from LC processing in the first pass of a two pass assembler (see Algorithm 4.1) in one significant respect. In Intel 8088, the unit for memory allocation is a byte, however certain entities require their starting byte to be aligned on specific boundaries in the address space. For example, a word requires alignment on an even boundary, i.e. it must have an even start address. Such alignment requirements may force some bytes to be left unused during memory allocation. Hence while processing `DB` statements and imperatives, assembler first aligns

LC on the requisite boundary. We call this *LC alignment*. Allocation of memory for a statement and entering its label in the symbol table is performed after LC alignment.

The data structures of the assembler are illustrated in Fig. 4.26, where numbers in parentheses indicate the number of bytes required for a field. The mnemonics table (MOT) is hash organized and contains the following fields: *mnemonic opcode, machine opcode, alignment/format info* and *routine id*. The *routine id* field of an entry specifies the routine which processes that opcode. *Alignment/format info* is specific to a given routine. For example, the code of '00H' for routine R2 implies that only one instruction format, that with self-relative displacement, is supported. 'FFH' for the same routine implies that all formats are supported, hence the routine must decide which machine opcode to use. The symbol table (SYMTAB) is also hash-organized and contains all relevant information about symbols defined and used in the source program. The contents of some important fields are as follows: The *owner segment* field indicates id of the segment in which a symbol is defined. It contains the SYMTAB entry # of the segment name. For a non-EQU symbol the *type* field indicates the alignment information. For an EQU symbol, *type* field indicates whether the symbol is to be given a numeric value or a textual value. The owner segment and offset fields are used to accommodate the value.

An SRTAB can contain upto four entries, one for each register. The current SRTAB exists in the last entry of SRTAB_ARRAY. SRTAB's are accessed by their entry numbers in SRTAB_ARRAY.

Forward references

Information concerning forward references to a symbol is organized in the form of a linked list. Thus, the *forward reference table* (FRT) contains a set of linked lists. The *FRT pointer* field of a SYMTAB entry points to the head of this list. Since ordering of FRT entries is not important, for efficiency reasons new entries are added at the beginning of the list. Each FRT entry contains SRTAB # to be used to assemble the forward reference. It also contains the instruction address and a *usage code* indicating where and how the reference is to be assembled. When the definition of a symbol is encountered, its forward references (if any) are processed, and the forward references list is discarded. This minimizes the size of FRT at any time.

Cross references

A cross reference directory is a report produced by the assembler which lists all references to a symbol sorted in the ascending order of statement numbers. The assembler uses the *cross reference table* (CRT) to collect the information concerning references to all symbols in the program. Each SYMTAB entry points to the head and tail of a linked list in the CRT. New entries are added at the end of the list.

Being linked lists, FRT and CRT can be organized in a single memory area. The tables grow from the high end of storage to its low end. The freed entries of FRT are reused by maintaining a free list. The target code generated by the assembler grows

(a) Mnemonics table (MOT)

Mnemonic opcode (6)	*Machine opcode* (2)	*Alignment/ format info* (1)	*Routine id* (4)
JNE	75H	OOH	R2

(b) Symbol table (Symtab)

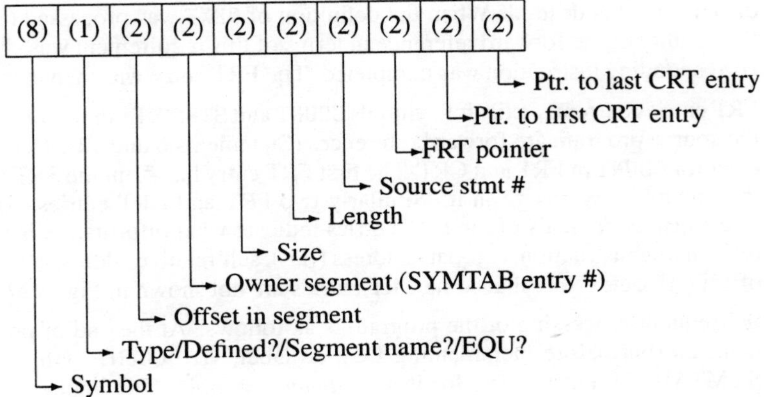

(c) Segment Register Table Array (SRTAB_ARRAY)

Segment Register (1)	*Segment name* (2)	
00(ES)	23	SRTAB #1
:		SRTAB #2

(d)Forward Reference table (FRT)

Pointer (2)	*SRTAB #* (1)	*Instruction address* (2)	*Usage code* (1)	*Source stmt #* (2)

(e) Cross Reference table (CRT)

Pointer (2)	*Source Stmt #* (2)

Fig. 4.26 Data structures of the assembler

from the low end to the high end of storage. As a result, no size restrictions need to be placed on individual tables. The assembler fails to handle a source program only if its target code overlaps with its tables.

Example 4.18 Figure 4.27 illustrates contents of important data structures after processing Statement 19 of the source program of Fig. 4.25. The symbol table contains entries for symbols `COMP` and `NEXT` whose definitions have already been processed. The *defined* flag of these entries is = 'Yes' and the address and type fields contain appropriate values. `NEXT` was forward referenced in Statement 12 of the program. An FRT entry was created for this reference with the *usage code* ='S' to indicate that a self-relative displacement is desired. When the definition of `NEXT` was processed (Statement 14), the validity of the forward reference in terms of this requirement was checked and the corresponding instruction was completed. The FRT entry was then discarded.

FRT entries currently exist for symbols `COUNT` and `STRNG`. Both references to `COUNT` in the source program are forward references (Statements 6 and 13). Hence, two entries exist for `COUNT` in FRT and CRT. The first FRT entry has #1 in the SRTAB field, while the second entry has #2 in it. Similarly two FRT and CRT entries exist for `STRNG`. The *usage code* fields of the FRT entries indicate what information is required in the referencing instruction, e.g. data address ('D'), self relative address ('S'), length ('L'), offset ('F'), etc. Note that some CRT entries are not shown in Fig. 4.27.

Subsequent processing of the program is as follows: At the end of processing statement 20 (but before incrementing LC), its label, viz. `COUNT`, will be looked up in SYMTAB. An entry exists for it with *defined* = '*no*'. This implies that `COUNT` has been forward referenced. Its *segment* and *offset* fields are now set. The forward reference chain is then traversed and each forward reference is processed to perform error detection, and to complete the machine instruction containing the forward reference. The second forward reference to `COUNT` passes the error detection step and leads to completion of the machine instruction with offset 0024. The first forward reference, however, expects a word alignment for `COUNT` (since immediate data is 2 bytes in length) which is not the case. An error is indicated at this point. The *FRT pointer* field of `COUNT`'s SYMTAB entry is now reset and the FRT entries for `COUNT` are destroyed.

Listing and error indication

The program listing and error reporting function faces the problems discussed in Section 4.4.7. The program listing can contain the statement in source form, its serial number in the program and the memory address assigned to it. The target code can only be printed at the end of assembly. Error reporting also suffers due to the single pass assembly scheme. An error cannot be reported against the statement containing a forward reference since the statement would have been already listed out. If the error is simply reported at the end of the source program, it is rather cumbersome for the programmer to identify the erroneous statement.

The following strategy is used to overcome this problem (see Ex. 4.19):

1. The serial number of the source statement containing a forward reference is stored in the FRT entry along with other relevant information (see Fig. 4.27).

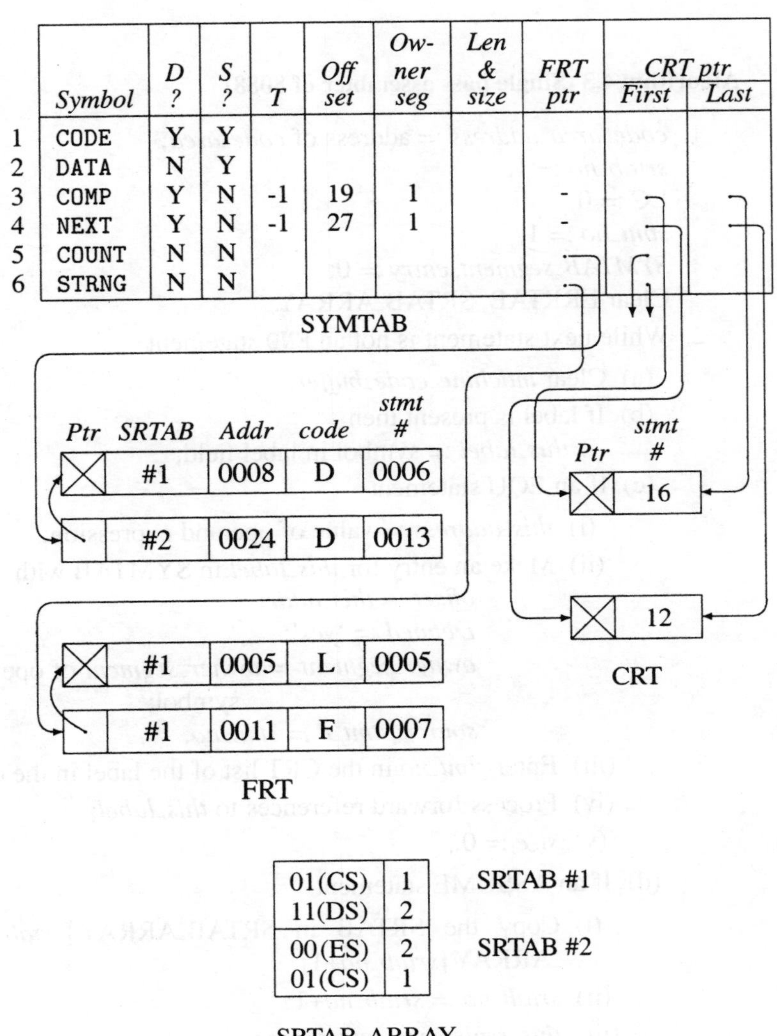

Fig. 4.27 Data structures after processing Statement 19

2. Whenever a symbol's definition is encountered, all forward references to the symbol are processed and errors, if any, are reported against this statement. Though this is not as effective as reporting the error against the erroneous statement, it is the next best thing.

Algorithm 4.3 (Single pass assembler of 8088)

1. *code_area_address* := address of *code_area*;
   srtab_no := 1;
   LC := 0;
   stmt_no := 1;
   SYMTAB_segment_entry := 0;
   Clear ERRTAB, SRTAB_ARRAY.
2. While next statement is not an `END` statement
   (a) Clear *machine_code_buffer*.
   (b) If label is present then
       this_label := symbol in label field;
   (c) If an EQU statement
      (i) *this_address* := value of operand expression;
      (ii) Make an entry for *this_label* in SYMTAB with
           offset := *this_addr*;
           Defined := '*yes*';
           owner_segment := *owner_segment* of operand symbol;
           source_stmt_# := *stmt_no*;
      (iii) Enter *stmt_no* in the CRT list of the label in the operand field.
      (iv) Process forward references to *this_label*;
      (v) *size* := 0;
   (d) If an ASSUME statement
      (i) Copy the SRTAB in SRTAB_ARRAY [*srtab_no*] into SRTAB_ARRAY [*srtab_no*+1];
      (ii) *srtab_no* := *srtab_no*+1;
      (iii) *this_register* := register mentioned in the statement.
      (iv) *this_segment* := entry number of SYMTAB entry of the segment appearing in operand field.
      (v) Make the entry (*this_register, this_segment*) in SRTAB_ARRAY [*srtab_no*]. (This overwrites an existing entry for *this_register*.)
      (vi) *size* := 0;
   (e) If a SEGMENT statement

(i) Make an entry for *this_label* in SYMTAB.
(ii) Set *segment name ? := true*;
(iii) *SYMTAB_segment_entry* := entry no. in SYMTAB;
(iv) LC := 0;
(v) *size* := 0;

(f) If an ENDS statement then
SYMTAB_segment_entry := 0;

(g) If a declaration statement
(i) Align LC according to the specification in the operand field.
(ii) Assemble the constant(s), if any, in the *machine_code_buffer*.
(iii) *size* := size of memory area required;

(h) If an imperative statement
(i) If operand is a symbol *symb* then
enter *stmt_no* in CRT list of *symb*.
(ii) If operand symbol is already defined then
Check its alignment and addressibility.
Generate the address specification (segment register, *offset*) for the symbol using its SYMTAB entry and SRTAB_ARRAY [*srtab_no*].
else
Make an entry for *symbol* in SYMTAB.
Defined := '*no*';
Enter (*srtab_no*, LC, *usage code, stmt_no*) in FRT.
(iii) Assemble instruction in *machine_code_buffer*.
(iv) *size* := size of the instruction;

(i) If *size* $\neq$ 0 then
(i) If label is present then
Make an entry for *this_label* in SYMTAB.
owner_segment := *SYMTAB_segment_entry*;
Defined := '*yes*';
offset := LC;
source_stmt_# := *stmt_no*;
(ii) Move contents of *machine_code_buffer* to the address *code_area-address*;
(iii) *code_area_address* := *code_area_address* + *size*;
(iv) Process forward references to the symbol. Check for alignment and addressability errors. Enter errors in ERRTAB.
(v) List the statement with errors contained in ERRTAB.
(vi) Clear ERRTAB.

3. (Processing of END statement)
   (a) Report undefined symbols from SYMTAB.
   (b) Produce cross reference listing.
   (c) Write *code_area* into output file.

Example 4.19 Error in the forward reference to COUNT in Statement 6 of Fig. 4.25 would be reported as:

Stmt no.	*Source statement*	*Offset*	*Instrn*
006	MOV COUNT, 0000	0005	...
...	...	...	...
020	COUNT DB ?	0001	...

** error ** Illegal forward reference (alignment) from Stmt 6.

BIBLIOGRAPHY

Most books on computer architecture discuss assembly languages of particular computer systems, e.g. Stone and Siewiorek (1975), Gear (1980), and Macewen (1980). Leeds and Weinberg (1966) is one of the first books devoted to assembly language programming. Flores (1971) covers assembly language of IBM/360. Books by Leventhal deal with assembly language programming for microcomputers.

(a) Assembly language programming

1. Leeds, H.D. and M.W. Weinberg (1966): *Computer Programming Fundamentals*, McGraw-Hill, New York.
2. Leventhal, L.A., A. Osborne, and C. Collins (1980): *Z8000 Assembly Language Programming*, Osborne/McGraw-Hill, Berkeley.
3. Rudd, W.G. (1976): *Assembly Language Programming and the IBM 360/370 Computers*, Prentice-Hall, Englewood Cliffs.
4. Stone, H.S. and D.P. Siewiorek (1975): *Introduction to Computer Organization and Data Structures*, McGraw-Hill, New York.
5. Weller, W.J. (1975): *Assembly Level Programming for Small Computers*, Heath & Co., Lexington.
6. Yarmish, R. and J. Yarmish (1979): *Assembly Language Fundamentals 360/370, OS/VS, DOS/VS*, Addison-Wesley, Reading.

(b) Assemblers

1. Barron, D.W. (1969): *Assemblers and Loaders*, Macdonald Elsevier, London.
2. Calingaert, P. (1979): *Assemblers, Compilers and Program Translation*, Computer Science Press, Maryland.
3. Donovan, J.J. (1972): *Systems Programming*, McGraw-Hill Kogakusha, Tokyo.
4. Flores, I. (1971): *Assemblers and BAL*, Prentice-Hall, Englewood Cliffs.

CHAPTER 5

Macros and Macro Processors

Macros are used to provide a *program generation* facility (see Section 1.2.1) through *macro expansion*. Many languages provide built-in facilities for writing macros. Well known examples of these are the higher level languages PL/I, C, Ada and C++. Assembly languages of most computer systems also provide such facilities. When a language does not support built-in macro facilities, a programmer may achieve an equivalent effect by using generalized preprocessors or software tools like Awk of Unix. The discussion in this chapter is confined to macro facilities provided in assembly languages.

Definition 5.1 (Macro) *A* macro *is a unit of specification for program generation through expansion.*

A macro consists of a name, a set of formal parameters and a body of code. The use of a macro name with a set of actual parameters is replaced by some code generated from its body. This is called *macro expansion*. Two kinds of expansion can be readily identified:

1. *Lexical expansion:* Lexical expansion implies replacement of a character string by another character string during program generation. Lexical expansion is typically employed to replace occurrences of formal parameters by corresponding actual parameters.
2. *Semantic expansion:* Semantic expansion implies generation of instructions tailored to the requirements of a specific usage—for example, generation of type specific instructions for manipulation of byte and word operands. Semantic expansion is characterized by the fact that different uses of a macro can lead to codes which differ in the number, sequence and opcodes of instructions.

Example 5.1 The following sequence of instructions is used to increment the value in a memory word by a constant:

1. Move the value from the memory word into a machine register.
2. Increment the value in the machine register.
3. Move the new value into the memory word.

Since the instruction sequence MOVE-ADD-MOVE may be used a number of times in a program, it is convenient to define a macro named INCR. Using lexical expansion the macro call INCR A, B, AREG can lead to the generation of a MOVE-ADD-MOVE instruction sequence to increment A by the value of B using AREG to perform the arithmetic.

Use of semantic expansion can enable the instruction sequence to be adapted to the types of A and B. For example, for Intel 8088, an INC instruction could be generated if A is a byte operand and B has the value '1', while a MOV-ADD-MOV sequence can be generated in all other situations.

Note that macros differ from subroutines in one fundamental respect. Use of a macro name in the mnemonic field of an assembly statement leads to its *expansion*, whereas use of a subroutine name in a call instruction leads to its *execution*. Thus, programs using macros and subroutines differ significantly in terms of program size and execution efficiency. In fact, macros can be said to trade program size for execution efficiency of a program. Other differences between macros and subroutines will be discussed along with the discussion of advanced macro facilities in Section 5.4.

5.1 MACRO DEFINITION AND CALL

Macro definition

A *macro definition* is enclosed between a *macro header* statement and a *macro end* statement. Macro definitions are typically located at the start of a program. A macro definition consists of

1. A *macro prototype* statement
2. One or more *model statements*
3. Macro *preprocessor statements*.

The macro prototype statement declares the name of a macro and the names and kinds of its parameters. A model statement is a statement from which an assembly language statement may be generated during macro expansion. A preprocessor statement is used to perform auxiliary functions during macro expansion.

The macro prototype statement has the following syntax:

$$<macro\ name>\quad [<formal\ parameter\ spec>[,..]]$$

where *<macro name>* appears in the mnemonic field of an assembly statement and *<formal parameter spec>* is of the form

$$\&<parameter\ name>[<parameter\ kind>] \tag{5.1}$$

Macro call

A macro is called by writing the macro name in the mnemonic field of an assembly statement. The macro call has the syntax

<*macro name*> [<*actual parameter spec*> [,..]] (5.2)

where an actual parameter typically resembles an operand specification in an assembly language statement.

Example 5.2 Figure 5.1 shows the definition of macro INCR. MACRO and MEND are the macro header and macro end statements, respectively. The prototype statement indicates that three parameters called MEM_VAL, INCR_VAL and REG exist for the macro. Since parameter kind is not specified for any of the parameters, they are all of the default kind 'positional parameter'. Statements with the operation codes MOVER, ADD and MOVEM are model statements. No preprocessor statements are used in this macro.

```
MACRO
INCR        &MEM_VAL, &INCR_VAL, &REG
MOVER       &REG, &MEM_VAL
ADD         &REG, &INCR_VAL
MOVEM       &REG, &MEM_VAL
MEND
```

Fig. 5.1 A macro definition

5.2 MACRO EXPANSION

A macro call leads to *macro expansion*. During macro expansion, the macro call statement is replaced by a sequence of assembly statements. To differentiate between the original statements of a program and the statements resulting from macro expansion, each expanded statement is marked with a '+' preceding its label field.

Two key notions concerning macro expansion are:

1. *Expansion time control flow:* This determines the order in which model statements are visited during macro expansion.
2. *Lexical substitution:* Lexical substitution is used to generate an assembly statement from a model statement.

Flow of control during expansion

The default flow of control during macro expansion is *sequential*. Thus, in the absence of preprocessor statements, the model statements of a macro are visited sequentially starting with the statement following the macro prototype statement and ending with the statement preceding the MEND statement. A preprocessor statement can alter the flow of control during expansion such that some model statements are either never visited during expansion, or are repeatedly visited during expansion. The former results in *conditional expansion* and the latter in *expansion time loops*.

The flow of control during macro expansion is implemented using a *macro expansion counter* (MEC).

Algorithm 5.1 (Outline of macro expansion)

1. MEC := statement number of first statement following the prototype statement;
2. While statement pointed by MEC is not a MEND statement
   (a) If a model statement then
      (i) Expand the statement.
      (ii) MEC := MEC + 1;
   (b) Else (i.e. a preprocessor statement)
      (i) MEC := new value specified in the statement;
3. Exit from macro expansion.

MEC is set to point at the statement following the prototype statement. It is incremented by 1 after expanding a model statement. Execution of a preprocessor statement can set MEC to a new value to implement conditional expansion or expansion time loops. These features are discussed in Section 5.4.

Lexical substitution

A model statement consists of 3 types of strings

1. An ordinary string, which stands for itself.
2. The name of a formal parameter which is preceded by the character '&'.
3. The name of a preprocessor variable, which is also preceded by the character '&'.

During lexical expansion, strings of type 1 are retained without substitution. Strings of types 2 and 3 are replaced by the 'values' of the formal parameters or preprocessor variables. The value of a formal parameter is the corresponding actual parameter string. The rules for determining the value of a formal parameter depend on the kind of parameter.

Positional parameters

A positional formal parameter is written as &<*parameter name*>, e.g. &SAMPLE where SAMPLE is the name of a parameter. In other words, <*parameter kind*> of syntax rule (5.1) is omitted. The <*actual parameter spec*> in a call on a macro using positional parameters [see syntax rule (5.2)] is simply an <*ordinary string*>.

The value of a positional formal parameter XYZ is determined by the rule of *positional association* as follows:

1. Find the ordinal position of XYZ in the list of formal parameters in the macro prototype statement.
2. Find the actual parameter specification occupying the same ordinal position in the list of actual parameters in the macro call statement (see syntax rule (5.2)). Let this be the ordinary string ABC. Then, the value of formal parameter XYZ is ABC.

Example 5.3 Consider the call

```
INCR      A, B, AREG
```

on macro INCR of Fig. 5.1. Following the rule of positional association, values of the formal parameters are:

formal parameter	*value*
MEM_VAL	A
INCR_VAL	B
REG	AREG

Lexical expansion of the model statements now leads to the code

```
+        MOVER      AREG, A
+        ADD        AREG, B
+        MOVEM      AREG, A
```

Keyword parameters

For keyword parameters, *<parameter name>* is an ordinary string and *<parameter kind>* is the string '=' in syntax rule (5.1). The *<actual parameter spec>* is written as *<formal parameter name>* = *<ordinary string>*. The value of a formal parameter XYZ is determined by the rule of *keyword association* as follows:

1. Find the actual parameter specification which has the form XYZ= *<ordinary string>*.
2. Let *<ordinary string>* in the specification be the string ABC. Then the value of formal parameter XYZ is ABC.

Note that the ordinal position of the specification XYZ=ABC in the list of actual parameters is immaterial. This is very useful in situations where long lists of parameters have to be used.

Example 5.4 Figure 5.2 shows macro INCR of Fig. 5.1 rewritten as macro INCR_M using keyword parameters. The following macro calls

```
INCR_M      MEM_VAL=A, INCR_VAL=B, REG=AREG
...
INCR_M      INCR_VAL=B, REG=AREG, MEM_VAL=A
```

are now equivalent.

```
MACRO
INCR_M      &MEM_VAL=, &INCR_VAL=, &REG=
MOVER       &REG, &MEM_VAL
ADD         &REG, &INCR_VAL
MOVEM       &REG, &MEM_VAL
MEND
```

Fig. 5.2 A macro definition using keyword parameters

Default specifications of parameters

A *default* is a standard assumption in the absence of an explicit specification by the programmer. Default specification of parameters is useful in situations where a parameter has the same value in most calls. When the desired value is different from the default value, the desired value can be specified explicitly in a macro call. This specification overrides the default value of the parameter for the duration of the call.

Default specification of keyword parameters can be incorporated by extending syntax (5.1), the syntax for formal parameter specification, as follows:

$$\&<parameter\ name>[<parameter\ kind>[<default\ value>]] \tag{5.3}$$

Example 5.5 Register AREG is used for all arithmetic in a program. Hence most calls on macro INCR_M contain the specification ®=AREG. The macro can be redefined to use a default specification for the parameter REG shown in Fig. 5.3 (see macro INCR_D). Consider the following calls

```
INCR_D      MEM_VAL=A, INCR_VAL=B
INCR_D      INCR_VAL=B, MEM_VAL=A
INCR_D      INCR_VAL=B, MEM_VAL=A, REG=BREG
```

The first two calls are equivalent to the calls in Ex. 5.4. The third call overrides the default value for REG with the value BREG. BREG will be used to perform the arithmetic in its expanded code.

```
MACRO
INCR_D      &MEM_VAL=, &INCR_VAL=, &REG=AREG
MOVER       &REG, &MEM_VAL
ADD         &REG, &INCR_VAL
MOVEM       &REG, &MEM_VAL
MEND
```

Fig. 5.3 A macro definition with default parameter

Macros with mixed parameter lists

A macro may be defined to use both positional and keyword parameters. In such a case, all positional parameters must precede all keyword parameters. For example, in the macro call

```
SUMUP    A,B,G=20,H=X
```

A, B are positional parameters while G, H are keyword parameters. Correspondence between actual and formal parameters is established by applying the rules governing positional and keyword parameters separately.

Other uses of parameters

The model statements of Examples 5.2-5.5 have used formal parameters only in operand fields. However, use of parameters is not restricted to these fields. Formal parameters can also appear in the label and opcode fields of model statements.

Example 5.6

```
                MACRO
                CALC        &X, &Y, &OP= MULT, &LAB=

&LAB            MOVER       AREG, &X
                &OP         AREG, &Y
                MOVEM       AREG, &X
                MEND
```

Expansion of the call `CALC A, B, LAB=LOOP` leads to the following code:

```
+ LOOP     MOVER     AREG, A
+          MULT      AREG, B
+          MOVEM     AREG, A
```

5.3 NESTED MACRO CALLS

A model statement in a macro may constitute a call on another macro. Such calls are known as *nested macro calls*. We refer to the macro containing the nested call as the *outer* macro and the called macro as the *inner* macro. Expansion of nested macro calls follows the *last-in-first-out* (LIFO) rule. Thus, in a structure of nested macro calls, expansion of the latest macro call (i.e. the innermost macro call in the structure) is completed first.

Example 5.7 Macro COMPUTE of Fig. 5.4 contains a nested call on macro INCR_D of Fig. 5.3. Figure 5.5 shows the expanded code for the call

```
COMPUTE    X, Y
```

After lexical expansion, the second model statement of COMPUTE is recognized to be a call on macro INCR_D. Expansion of this macro is now performed. This leads to generation of statements marked [2], [3] and [4] in Fig. 5.5. The third model statement of COMPUTE is now expanded. Thus the expanded code for the call on COMPUTE is:

```
            +         MOVEM         BREG, TMP
            +         MOVER         BREG, X
            +         ADD           BREG, Y
            +         MOVEM         BREG, X
            +         MOVER         BREG, TMP

MACRO
COMPUTE     &FIRST, &SECOND
MOVEM       BREG, TMP
INCR_D      &FIRST, &SECOND, REG=BREG
MOVER       BREG, TMP
MEND
```

Fig. 5.4 A nested macro call

```
                  + MOVEM    BREG,TMP [1]
                                           + MOVER   BREG,X [2]
COMPUTE  X,Y  {   + INCR_D   X,Y        {  + ADD     BREG,Y [3]
                                           + MOVEM   BREG,X [4]
                  + MOVER    BREG,TMP [5]
```

Fig. 5.5 Expanded code for a nested macro call

5.4 ADVANCED MACRO FACILITIES

Advanced macro facilities are aimed at supporting semantic expansion. These facilities can be grouped into

1. Facilities for alteration of flow of control during expansion
2. Expansion time variables
3. Attributes of parameters.

This section describes some advanced facilities and illustrates their use in performing conditional expansion of model statements and in writing expansion time loops.

Alteration of flow of control during expansion

Two features are provided to facilitate alteration of flow of control during expansion:

1. Expansion time sequencing symbols
2. Expansion time statements AIF, AGO and ANOP.

A sequencing symbol (SS) has the syntax

$$. < ordinary\ string > \tag{5.4}$$

As SS is defined by putting it in the label field of a statement in the macro body. It is used as an operand in an AIF or AGO statement to designate the destination of an expansion time control transfer. It never appears in the expanded form of a model statement.

An AIF statement has the syntax

`AIF` (<*expression*>) <*sequencing symbol*>

where <*expression*> is a relational expression involving ordinary strings, formal parameters and their attributes, and expansion time variables. If the relational expression evaluates to *true*, expansion time control is transferred to the statement containing <*sequencing symbol*> in its label field. An AGO statement has the syntax

`AGO` <*sequencing symbol*>

and unconditionally transfers expansion time control to the statement containing <*sequencing symbol*> in its label field. An ANOP statement is written as

<*sequencing symbol*> `ANOP`

and simply has the effect of defining the sequencing symbol.

Expansion time variables

Expansion time variables (EV's) are variables which can only be used during the expansion of macro calls. A local EV is created for use only during a particular macro call. A global EV exists across all macro calls situated in a program and can be used in any macro which has a declaration for it. Local and global EV's are created through declaration statements with the following syntax:

`LCL` <*EV specification*>[,<*EV specification*> ..]
`GBL` <*EV specification*>[,<*EV specification*> ..]

and <*EV specification*> has the syntax &<*EV name*>, where <*EV name*> is an ordinary string.

Values of EV's can be manipulated through the preprocessor statement SET. A SET statement is written as

<*EV specification*> `SET` <*SET-expression*>

where <*EV specification*> appears in the label field and SET in the mnemonic field. A SET statement assigns the value of <*SET-expression*> to the EV specified in <*EV specification*>. The value of an EV can be used in any field of a model statement, and in the expression of an AIF statement.

Example 5.8

```
                    MACRO
                    CONSTANTS
                    LCL          &A
        &A          SET          1
                    DB           &A
        &A          SET          &A+1
                    DB           &A
                    MEND
```

A call on macro CONSTANTS is expanded as follows: The local EV A is created. The first SET statement assigns the value '1' to it. The first DB statement thus declares a byte constant '1'. The second SET statement assigns the value '2' to A and the second DB statement declares a constant '2'.

Attributes of formal parameters

An attribute is written using the syntax

<attribute name>'<formal parameter spec>

and represents information about the value of the formal parameter, i.e. about the corresponding actual parameter. The type, length and size attributes have the names T, L and S.

Example 5.9

```
                    MACRO
                    DCL_CONST    &A
                    AIF          (L'&A EQ 1) .NEXT
                    - -
        .NEXT       - -
                    - -
                    MEND
```

Here expansion time control is transferred to the statement having .NEXT in its label field only if the actual parameter corresponding to the formal parameter A has the length of '1'.

5.4.1 Conditional Expansion

While writing a general purpose macro it is important to ensure execution efficiency of its generated code. Conditional expansion helps in generating assembly code specifically suited to the parameters in a macro call. This is achieved by ensuring that a model statement is visited only under specific conditions during the expansion of a macro. The AIF and AGO statements are used for this purpose.

Example 5.10 It is required to develop a macro EVAL such that a call

```
        EVAL      A, B, C
```

generates efficient code to evaluate A−B+C in AREG. When the first two parameters of a call are identical, EVAL should generate a single MOVER instruction to load the 3rd parameter into AREG. This is achieved as follows:

```
             MACRO
             EVAL          &X, &Y, &Z
             AIF           (&Y EQ &X) .ONLY
             MOVER         AREG, &X
             SUB           AREG, &Y
             ADD           AREG, &Z
             AGO           .OVER
.ONLY        MOVER         AREG, &Z
.OVER        MEND
```

Since the value of a formal parameter is simply the corresponding actual parameter, the AIF statement effectively compares names of the first two actual parameters. If the names are same, expansion time control is transferred to the model statement MOVER AREG, &Z. If not, the MOVE-SUB-ADD sequence is generated and expansion time control is transferred to the statement .OVER MEND which terminates the expansion. Thus efficient code is generated under all conditions.

Expansion time loops

It is often necessary to generate many similar statements during the expansion of a macro. This can be achieved by writing similar model statements in the macro.

Example 5.11

```
MACRO
CLEAR          &A
MOVER          AREG, ='0'
MOVEM          AREG, &A
MOVEM          AREG, &A+1
MOVEM          AREG, &A+2
MEND
```

When called as CLEAR B, the MOVER statement puts the value '0' in AREG, while the three MOVEM statements store this value in 3 consecutive bytes with the addresses B, B+1 and B+2.

Alternatively, the same effect can be achieved by writing an expansion time loop which visits a model statement, or a set of model statements, repeatedly during macro expansion. Expansion time loops can be written using expansion time variables (EV's) and expansion time control transfer statements AIF and AGO.

Example 5.12

```
            MACRO
            CLEAR       &X, &N
            LCL         &M
&M          SET         0
            MOVER       AREG, ='0'
.MORE       MOVEM       AREG, &X+&M
&M          SET         &M+1
            AIF         (&M NE N) .MORE
            MEND
```

Consider expansion of the macro call

```
CLEAR      B, 3
```

The LCL statement declares M to be a local EV. At the start of expansion of the call, M is initialized to zero. The expansion of model statement MOVEM AREG, &X+&M thus leads to generation of the statement MOVEM AREG, B. The value of M is incremented by 1 and the model statement MOVEM .. is expanded repeatedly until its value equals the value of N, which is 3 in this case. Thus the macro call leads to generation of the statements

```
+        MOVER       AREG, ='0'
+        MOVEM       AREG, B
+        MOVEM       AREG, B+1
+        MOVEM       AREG, B+2
```

Comparison with execution time loops

Most expansion time loops can be replaced by execution time loops. For example, instead of generating many MOVEM statements as in Ex. 5.12 to clear the memory area starting on B, it is possible to write an execution time loop which moves 0 into B, B+1 and B+2. An execution time loop leads to more compact assembly programs. However, such programs would execute slower than programs containing expansion time loops. Thus a macro can be used to trade program size for execution efficiency.

5.4.2 Other Facilities for Expansion Time Loops

Many assemblers provide other facilities for conditional expansion, an ELSE clause in AIF being an obvious example. The assemblers for M 68000 and Intel 8088 processors provide explicit expansion time looping constructs. We discuss two such facilities here.

The REPT statement

REPT *<expression>*

<*expression*> should evaluate to a numerical value during macro expansion. The statements between REPT and an ENDM statement would be processed for expansion <*expression*> number of times. Example 5.13 illustrates the use of this facility to declare 10 constants with the values 1, 2, .. 10.

Example 5.13

```
        MACRO
        CONST10
        LCL     &M
&M      SET     1
        REPT    10
        DC      '&M'
&M      SETA    &M+1
        ENDM
        MEND
```

The IRP statement

```
IRP          <formal parameter> , <argument-list>
```

The formal parameter mentioned in the statement takes successive values from the argument list. For each value, the statements between the IRP and ENDM statements are expanded once.

Example 5.14

```
MACRO
CONSTS     &M, &N, &Z
IRP        &Z, &M, 7, &N
DC         '&Z'
ENDM
MEND
```

A macro call `CONSTS 4, 10` leads to declaration of 3 constants with the values 4, 7 and 10.

5.4.3 Semantic Expansion

Semantic expansion is the generation of instructions tailored to the requirements of a specific usage. It can be achieved by a combination of advanced macro facilities like AIF, AGO statements and expansion time variables. The CLEAR macro of Ex. 5.12 is an instance of semantic expansion. Here, the number of `MOVEM AREG, ..` statements generated by a call on CLEAR is determined by the value of the second parameter of CLEAR. Macro EVAL of example 5.10 is another instance of conditional expansion wherein one of two alternative code sequences is generated depending on the peculiarities of actual parameters of a macro call. Example 5.15 illustrates semantic expansion using the type attribute.

Example 5.15

```
                MACRO
                CREATE_CONST  &X, &Y
                AIF           (T'&X EQ B) .BYTE
&Y              DW            25
                AGO           .OVER
.BYTE           ANOP
&Y              DB            25
.OVER           MEND
```

This macro creates a constant '25' with the name given by the 2nd parameter. The type of the constant matches the type of the first parameter.

EXERCISE 5.4

1. Write a macro that moves 8 numbers from the first 8 positions of an array specified as the first operand into first 8 positions of an array specified as the second operand.
2. Generalize the macro of problem 1 above to move *n* numbers from the first operand to the second operand, where *n* is specified as the third operand of the macro.
3. Write a macro which takes A, B, C and D as parameters and calculates A*B + C*D in AREG.
   (a) Where would you store the temporary result?
   (b) Would you reserve space for the temporary result within the macro body or outside it (i.e. in the main program)? Why? What are the advantages and disadvantages of these alternatives?
   (c) Space reserved within the macro would be replicated in every expansion. If this space is named then the name would also be repeated in every expansion. This can lead to duplicate declarations. Can you think of a method to avoid this conflict?
4. Many macro processors permit the operation of concatenation within a macro body to form larger strings. For example, if &C is a parameter with the value M2 then the string XY.&C has the meaning XYM2. (*note:* '.' stands for the concatenation operation.) Could you use this concept to advantage in problem 3(c)?
5. A global EV carries over its value from one macro expansion to another. Can global EV's be used to advantage in problem 3(c)?
6. Study the conditional expansion and SET variable facilities of a macro language accessible to you and code problems 1 to 5 in this macro language.
7. A general purpose macro is to be written to move the contents of one area of memory into another area of memory. Two key issues here are: If the source area is larger in size than the destination area, some of its contents should be ignored (i.e. contents should be *truncated*). If the destination area is larger in size, some part of it should be *padded* with zeroes or blanks. Both truncation and padding can occur at the start or end of the area.

   Code the macro such that user can specify whether truncation and padding should occur at the start or end of the areas.

5.5 DESIGN OF A MACRO PREPROCESSOR

The macro preprocessor accepts an assembly program containing definitions and calls and translates it into an assembly program which does not contain any macro definitions or calls. Figure 5.6 shows a schematic of a macro preprocessor. The program form output by the macro preprocessor can now be handed over to an assembler to obtain the target language form of the program.

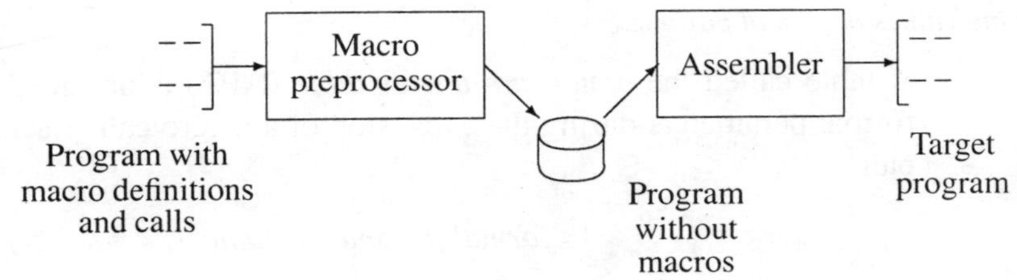

Fig. 5.6 A schematic of a macro preprocessor

Thus the macro preprocessor segregates macro expansion from the process of program assembly. It is economical because it can use an existing assembler. However, it is not as efficient as a macro-assembler, i.e. an assembler that performs macro expansion as well as assembly.

5.5.1 Design Overview

We begin the design by listing all tasks involved in macro expansion.

1. Identify macro calls in the program.
2. Determine the values of formal parameters.
3. Maintain the values of expansion time variables declared in a macro.
4. Organize expansion time control flow.
5. Determine the values of sequencing symbols.
6. Perform expansion of a model statement.

The following 4 step procedure is followed to arrive at a design specification for each task:

1. Identify the information necessary to perform a task.
2. Design a suitable data structure to record the information.
3. Determine the processing necessary to obtain the information.
4. Determine the processing necessary to perform the task.

Application of this procedure to each of the preprocessor tasks is described in the following.

Identify macro calls

A table called the *macro name table* (MNT) is designed to hold the names of all macros defined in a program. A macro name is entered in this table when a macro definition is processed. While processing a statement in the source program, the preprocessor compares the string found in its mnemonic field with the macro names in MNT. A match indicates that the current statement is a macro call.

Determine values of formal parameters

A table called the *actual parameter table* (APT) is designed to hold the values of formal parameters during the expansion of a macro call. Each entry in the table is a pair

(*<formal parameter name>*, *<value>*)

Two items of information are needed to construct this table, names of formal parameters, and default values of keyword parameters. For this purpose, a table called the *parameter default table* (PDT) is used for each macro. This table would be accessible from the MNT entry of a macro and would contain pairs of the form (*<formal parameter name>*, *<default value>*). If a macro call statement does not specify a value for some parameter *par*, its default value would be copied from PDT to APT.

Maintain expansion time variables

An *expansion time variables' table* (EVT) is maintained for this purpose. The table contains pairs of the form

(*<EV name>*, *<value>*)

The value field of a pair is accessed when a preprocessor statement or a model statement under expansion refers to an EV.

Organize expansion time control flow

The body of a macro, i.e. the set of preprocessor statements and model statements in it, is stored in a table called the *macro definition table* (MDT) for use during macro expansion. The flow of control during macro expansion determines when a model statement is to be visited for expansion. Algorithm 5.1 can be used for this purpose. MEC is initialized to the first statement of the macro body in the MDT. It is updated after expanding a model statement or on processing a macro preprocessor statement.

Determine values of sequencing symbols

A *sequencing symbols table* (SST) is maintained to hold this information. The table contains pairs of the form

(*<sequencing symbol name>*, *<MDT entry #>*)

where *<MDT entry #>* is the number of the MDT entry which contains the model statement defining the sequencing symbol. This entry is made on encountering a statement which contains the sequencing symbol in its label field (in the case of a back reference to the symbol), or on encountering a reference prior to its definition (in the case of a forward reference).

Perform expansion of a model statement

This is a trivial task given the following:

1. MEC points to the MDT entry containing the model statement.
2. Values of formal parameters and EV's are available in APT and EVT, respectively.
3. The model statement defining a sequencing symbol can be identified from SST.

Expansion of a model statement is achieved by performing a lexical substitution for the parameters and EV's used in the model statement.

5.5.2 Data Structures

Section 5.5.1 has identified the key data structures of the macro preprocessor. To obtain a detailed design of the data structures it is necessary to apply the practical criteria of processing efficiency and memory requirements

The tables APT, PDT and EVT contain pairs which are searched using the first component of the pair as a key—for example, the formal parameter name is used as the key to obtain its value from APT. This search can be eliminated if the position of an entity within a table is known when its value is to be accessed. We will see this in the context of APT.

The value of a formal parameter `ABC` is needed while expanding a model statement using it, viz.

```
MOVER     AREG, &ABC
```

Let the pair (`ABC`, `ALPHA`) occupy entry #5 in APT. The search in APT can be avoided if the model statement appears as

```
MOVER     AREG, (P,5)
```

in the MDT, where (`P, 5`) stands for the words 'parameter #5'.

Thus, macro expansion can be made more efficient by storing an intermediate code for a statement, rather than its source form, in the MDT. All parameter names could be replaced by pairs of the form (`P`, *n*) in model statements and preprocessor statements stored in MDT. An interesting offshoot of this decision is that the first component of the pairs stored in APT is no longer used during macro expansion, e.g. the information (`P, 5`) appearing in a model statement is sufficient to access the value of formal parameter `ABC`. Hence APT containing (*<formal parameter name>*, *<value>*) pairs is replaced by another table called APTAB which only contains *<value>*'s.

To implement this simplification, ordinal numbers are assigned to all parameters of a macro. A table named *parameter name table* (PNTAB) is used for this purpose. PNTAB is used while processing the definition of a macro. Parameter names are entered in PNTAB in the same order in which they appear in the prototype statement. The entry # of a parameter's entry in PNTAB is now its ordinal number. This entry is used to replace the parameter name in the model and preprocessor statements of the macro while storing it in the MDT. This implements the requirement that the statement `MOVER AREG, &ABC` should appear as `MOVER AREG, (P, 5)` in MDT.

In effect, the information (*<formal parameter name>*, *<value>*) in APT has been split into two tables -

PNTAB	which contains formal parameter names
APTAB	which contains formal parameter values (i.e. contains actual parameter)

Note again that PNTAB is used while processing a macro definition while APTAB is used during macro expansion.

Similar analysis leads to splitting of EVT into EVNTAB and EVTAB and SST into SSNTAB and SSTAB. EV names are entered in EVNTAB while processing EV declarations. SS names are entered in SSNTAB while processing an SS reference or definition, whichever occurs earlier.

This arrangement leads to some simplifications concerning PDT. The positional parameters (if any) of a macro appear before keyword parameters in the prototype statement. Hence in the prototype statement for a macro BETA which has p positional parameters and k keyword parameters, the keyword parameters have the ordinal numbers p+1 ... p+k. Due to this numbering, two kinds of redundancies appear in PDT, the first component of each entry is redundant as in APTAB and EVTAB. Further, entries 1 ... p are redundant since positional parameters cannot have default specifications. Hence entries only need to exist for parameters numbered p+1 ... p+k. To accommodate these changes, we replace the parameter default table (PDT) by a *keyword parameter default table* (KPDTAB). KPDTAB of macro BETA would only have k entries in it. To note the mapping that the first entry of KPDTAB corresponds to parameter numbered p+1, we store p, the number of positional parameters of macro BETA, in a new field of the MNT entry.

MNT has entries for all macros defined in a program. Each MNT entry contains three pointers MDTP, KPDTP and SSTP, which are pointers to MDT, KPDTAB and SSNTAB for the macro, respectively. Instead of using different MDT's for different macros, for simplicity we can create a single MDT and use different sections of this

Table	*Fields in each entry*
Macro name table (MNT)	*Macro name*, *Number of positional parameters* (#PP), *Number of keyword parameters* (#KP), *Number of expansion time variables* (#EV), *MDT pointer* (MDTP), *KPDTAB pointer* (KPDTP), *SSTAB pointer* (SSTP)
Parameter Name Table (PNTAB)	*Parameter name*
EV Name Table (EVNTAB)	*EV name*
SS Name Table (SSNTAB)	*SS name*
Keyword Parameter Default Table (KPDTAB)	*parameter name*, *default value*
Macro Definition Table (MDT)	*Label*, *Opcode*, *Operands*
Actual Parameter Table (APTAB)	*Value*
EV Table (EVTAB)	*Value*
SS Table (SSTAB)	*MDT entry #*

Fig. 5.7 Tables of the macro preprocessor

table for different macros. A similar arrangement can be used with KPDTAB and SSNTAB. The data structures are now summarized in Fig. 5.7.

Construction and use of the macro preprocessor data structures can be summarized as follows: PNTAB and KPDTAB are constructed by processing the prototype statement. Entries are added to EVNTAB and SSNTAB as EV declarations and SS definitions/references are encountered. MDT entries are constructed while processing the model statements and preprocessor statements in the macro body. An entry is added to SSTAB when the definition of a sequencing symbol is encountered. APTAB is constructed while processing a macro call. EVTAB is constructed at the start of expansion of a macro.

Example 5.16

```
             MACRO
             CLEARMEM    &X, &N, &REG=AREG
             LCL         &M
     &M      SET         0
             MOVER       &REG, ='0'
     .MORE   MOVEM       &REG, &X+&M
     &M      SET         &M+1
             AIF         (&M NE N) .MORE
             MEND
```

Figure 5.8 shows the contents of the data structures for the call

```
CLEARMEM    AREA, 10
```

Data structures above the broken line are used during the processing of a macro definition, while the data structures between the broken and firm lines are constructed during macro definition processing and used during macro expansion. Data structures below the firm line are used for the expansion of a macro call.

Note how APTAB has been constructed using the actual parameters in the macro call and the default value AREG of the parameter REG. Note also the SSTAB entry for .MORE.

5.5.3 Processing of Macro Definitions

The following initializations are performed before initiating the processing of macro definitions in a program

KPDTAB_pointer := 1;
SSTAB_ptr := 1;
MDT_ptr := 1;

Algorithm 5.2 is invoked for every macro definition in the program.

Algorithm 5.2 (Processing of a macro definition)

1. *SSNTAB_ptr* := 1;
   PNTAB_ptr := 1;
2. Process the macro prototype statement and form the MNT entry
   (a) *name* := macro name;
   (b) For each positional parameter
      (i) Enter *parameter name* in PNTAB [*PNTAB_ptr*].
      (ii) *PNTAB_ptr* := *PNTAB_ptr* + 1;

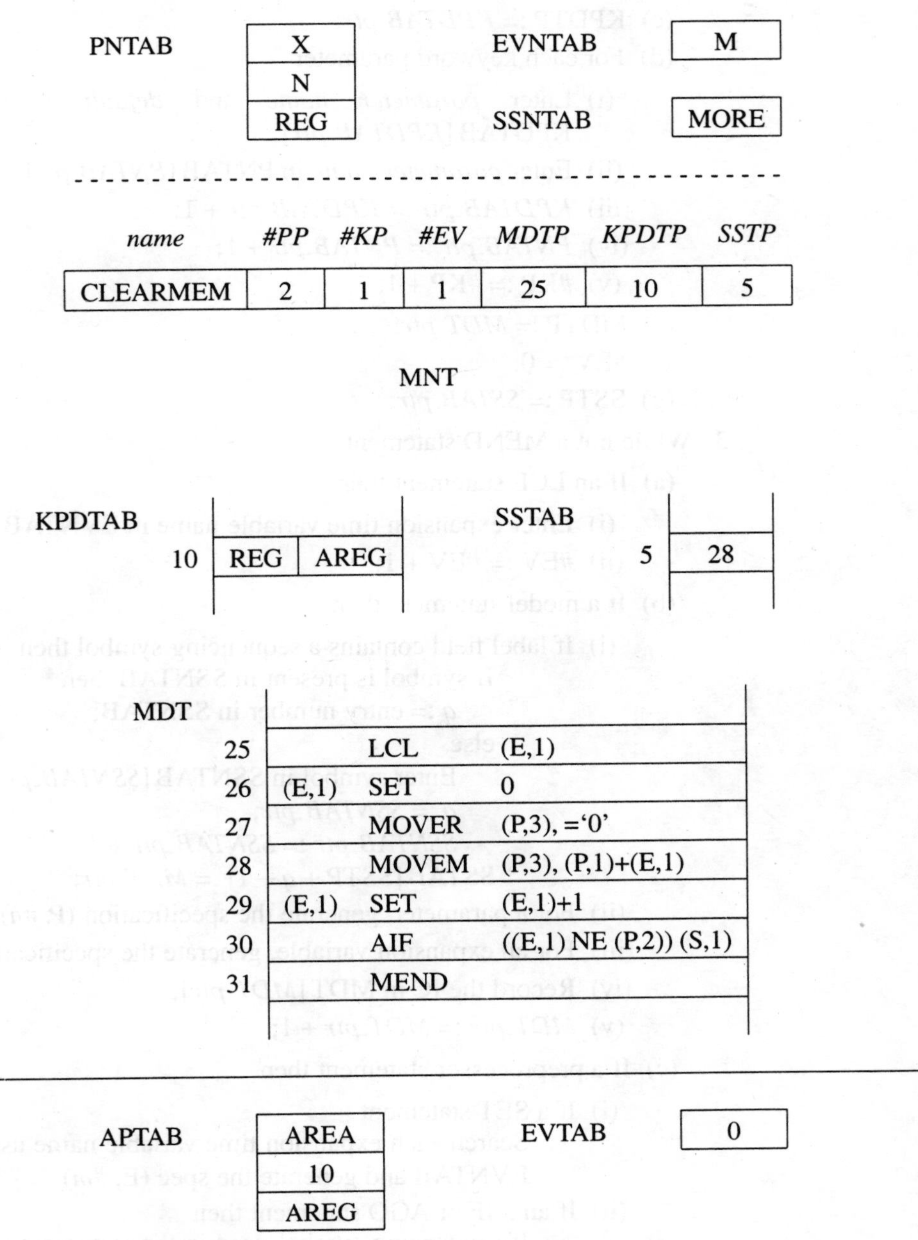

Fig. 5.8 Data structures of the macro preprocessor

(iii) #PP := #PP + 1;

(c) KPDTP := *KPDTAB_ptr*;

(d) For each keyword parameter

(i) Enter *parameter name* and *default value* (if any), in KPDTAB [*KPDTAB_ptr*].

(ii) Enter *parameter name* in PNTAB [*PNTAB_ptr*].

(iii) *KPDTAB_ptr* := *KPDTAB_ptr* + 1;

(iv) *PNTAB_ptr* := *PNTAB_ptr* + 1;

(v) #KP := #KP + 1;

(e) MDTP := *MDT_ptr*;

(f) #EV := 0;

(g) SSTP := *SSTAB_ptr*;

3. While not a MEND statement

(a) If an LCL statement then

(i) Enter expansion time variable name in EVNTAB.

(ii) #EV := #EV + 1;

(b) If a model statement then

(i) If label field contains a sequencing symbol then
If symbol is present in SSNTAB then
q := entry number in SSNTAB;
else
Enter symbol in SSNTAB [*SSNTAB_ptr*].
q := *SSNTAB_ptr*;
SSNTAB_ptr := *SSNTAB_ptr* + 1;
SSTAB [SSTP + $q - 1$] := *MDT_ptr*;

(ii) For a parameter, generate the specification (P, #*n*).

(iii) For an expansion variable, generate the specification (E, #*m*).

(iv) Record the IC in MDT [*MDT_ptr*];

(v) *MDT_ptr* := *MDT_ptr* + 1;

(c) If a preprocessor statement then

(i) If a SET statement
Search each expansion time variable name used in the statement in EVNTAB and generate the spec (E, #*m*).

(ii) If an AIF or AGO statement then
If sequencing symbol used in the statement is present in SSNTAB then
q := entry number in SSNTAB;

else
Enter symbol in SSNTAB [*SSNTAB_ptr*].
q := *SSNTAB_ptr*;
SSNTAB_ptr := *SSNTAB_ptr* + 1;
Replace the symbol by (S, SSTP + $q - 1$).
(iii) Record the IC in MDT [*MDT_ptr*].
(iv) *MDT_ptr* := *MDT_ptr* + 1;

4. (MEND statement)
If *SSNTAB_ptr* = 1 (i.e. SSNTAB is empty) then
SSTP := 0;
Else *SSTAB_ptr* := *SSTAB_ptr* + *SSNTAB_ptr* − 1;
If #KP = 0 then KPDTP = 0;

5.5.4 Macro Expansion

We use the following data structures to perform macro expansion:

APTAB	Actual parameter table
EVTAB	EV table
MEC	Macro expansion counter
APTAB_ptr	APTAB pointer
EVTAB_ptr	EVTAB pointer

The number of entries in APTAB (i.e., $\#e_{APTAB}$) equals the sum of values in the #PP and #KP fields of the MNT entry of a macro. Number of entries in EVTAB (i.e., $\#e_{EVTAB}$) is given by the value in #EV field of the MNT. APTAB and EVTAB are constructed when a macro call is recognized. *APTAB_ptr* and *EVTAB_ptr* are set to point at these tables. As in Algorithm 5.1, MEC always points to the next statement to be expanded.

Algorithm 5.3 (Macro expansion)

1. Perform initializations for the expansion of a macro
   (a) MEC := MDTP field of the MNT entry;
   (b) Create EVTAB with #EV entries and set *EVTAB_ptr*.
   (c) Create APTAB with #PP+#KP entries and set *APTAB_ptr*.
   (d) Copy keyword parameter defaults from the entries KPDTAB [KPDTP] ... KPDTAB [KPDTP+#KP−1] into APTAB [#PP+1] ... APTAB [#PP+#KP].
   (e) Process positional paremeters in the actual parameter list and copy them into APTAB [1] ... APTAB [#PP].

(f) For keyword parameters in the actual parameter list
Search the keyword name in *parameter name* field of KPDTAB [KPDTP] ... KPDTAB [KPDTP+#KP−1]. Let KPTDAB [*q*] contain a matching entry. Enter value of the keyword parameter in the call (if any) in APTAB [#PP+*q*−KPDTP+1].

2. While statement pointed by MEC is not MEND statement
   (a) If a model statement then
      (i) Replace operands of the form (P, #*n*) and (E, #*m*) by values in APTAB [*n*] and EVTAB [*m*] respectively.
      (ii) Output the generated statement.
      (iii) MEC := MEC + 1;
   (b) If a SET statement with the specification (E, #*m*) in the label field then
      (i) Evaluate the expression in the operand field and set an appropriate value in EVTAB [*m*].
      (ii) MEC := MEC + 1;
   (c) If an AGO statement with (S, #*s*) in operand field then
      MEC := SSTAB [SSTP+*s* − 1];
   (d) If an AIF statement with (S, #*s*) in operand field then
      If condition in the AIF statement is *true* then
         MEC := SSTAB [SSTP+*s* − 1];
3. Exit from macro expansion.

Figure 5.9 shows the data structures at some point during the expansion of macro CLEARMEM of Ex. 5.16.

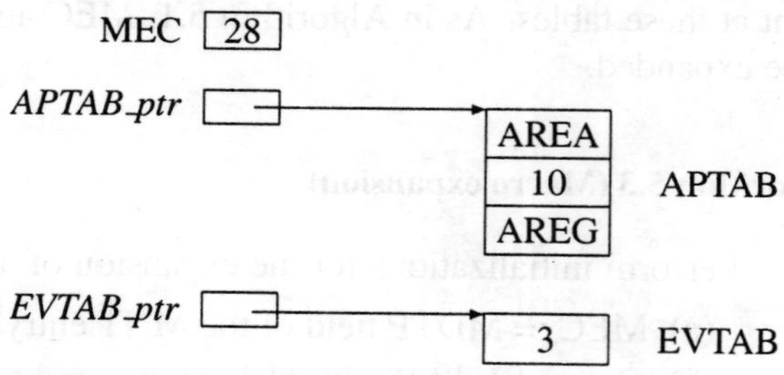

Fig. 5.9 Data structures during macro expansion

5.5.5 Nested Macro Calls

Figure 5.5 in Section 5.3 illustrates nested macro calls. Two basic alternatives exist for processing nested macro calls. We can apply the macro expansion schematic of

Section 5.5.4 to obtain the first level expanded code, viz.

```
                 - - -
        +        MOVEM     BREG, TMP
        +        INCR_D    X, Y, REG=BREG
        +        MOVER     BREG, TMP
                 - - -
```

In this code macro calls appearing in the source program have been expanded but statements resulting from the expansion may themselves contain macro calls. The macro expansion schematic can be applied to the first level expanded code to expand these macro calls and so on, until we obtain a code form which does not contain any macro calls. This scheme would require a number of passes of macro expansion, which makes it quite expensive.

A more efficient alternative would be to examine each statement generated during macro expansion to see if it is itself a macro call. If so, a provision can be made to expand this call before continuing with the expansion of the parent macro call. This avoids multiple passes of macro expansion, thus ensuring processing efficiency. This alternative requires some extensions in the macro expansion scheme of Section 5.5.4.

Consider the situation when the ADD statement marked [3] in Fig. 5.5 is being generated. Expansion of two macro calls is in progress at this moment. This happened because the outer macro COMPUTE gave rise to a macro call on macro INCR_D during the expansion of its current model statement. The model statements of INCR_D are currently being expanded using the expansion time data structures MEC, APTAB, EVTAB, *APTAB_ptr* and *EVTAB_ptr*. A MEND statement encountered during the expansion must lead to resumption of expansion of the outer macro. This requires that MEC, APTAB, EVTAB, *APTAB_ptr* and *EVTAB_ptr* should be restored to the values contained in them while the macro COMPUTE was being expanded. Control returns to the processing of the source program when the MEND statement is encountered during the processing of COMPUTE.

Thus, two provisions are required to implement the expansion of nested macro calls:

1. Each macro under expansion must have its own set of data structures, viz. MEC, APTAB, EVTAB, *APTAB_ptr* and *EVTAB_ptr*.
2. An *expansion nesting counter* (*Nest_cntr*) is maintained to count the number of nested macro calls. *Nest_cntr* is incremented when a macro call is recognized and decremented when a MEND statement is encountered. Thus *Nest_cntr* > 1 indicates that a nested macro call is under expansion, while *Nest_cntr* = 0 implies that macro expansion is not in progress currently.

The first provision can be implemented by creating many copies of the expansion time data structures. These can be stored in the form of an array. For example, we can have an array called APTAB_ARRAY, each element of which is an APTAB. APTAB for the innermost macro call would be given by APTAB_ARRAY[*Nest_cntr*]. This arrangement provides access efficiency. However, it is expensive in terms of memory requirements. It also involves a difficult design decision—how many copies of the data structures should be created? If too many copies are created, some may never be used. If too few are created, some assembly programs may have to be rejected because their macro call nesting depth exceeds the number of copies of the data structures.

Since macro calls are expanded in a LIFO manner, a practical solution is to use a stack to accommodate the expansion time data structures. The stack consists of *expansion records*, each expansion record accommodating one set of expansion time data structures. The expansion record at the top of the stack corresponds to the macro call currently being expanded. When a nested macro call is recognized, a new expansion record is pushed on the stack to hold the data structures for the call. At MEND, an expansion record is popped off the stack. This would uncover the previous expansion record in the stack which houses the expansion time data structures of the outer macro. The extended stack model of Section 2.2.1 is used for this purpose.

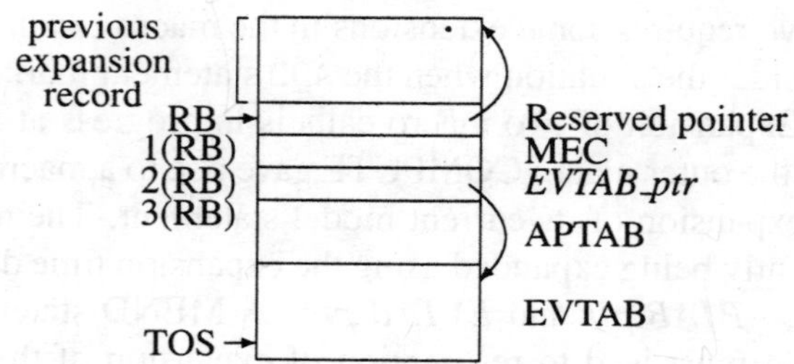

Fig. 5.10 Use of stack for macro preprocessor data structures

Figure 5.10 illustrates the stack oriented management of expansion time data structures. The expansion record on top of the stack contains the data structures in current use. *Record base* (RB) is a pointer pointing to the start of this expansion record. TOS points to the last occupied entry in stack. When a nested macro call is detected, another set of data structures is allocated on the stack. RB is now set to point to the start of the new expansion record. MEC, *EVTAB_ptr*, APTAB and EVTAB are allocated on the stack in that order. During macro expansion, the various data structures are accessed with reference to the value contained in RB. This is performed using the following addresses:

Data structure	*Address*
Reserved pointer	0(RB)
MEC	1(RB)

EVTAB_ptr	2(RB)
APTAB	3(RB) to e_{APTAB}+2(RB)
EVTAB	contents of *EVTAB_ptr*

where 1(RB) stands for 'contents of RB+1'. Note that the first entry of APTAB always has the address 3(RB). This eliminates the need for *APTAB_ptr*.

At a MEND statement, a record is popped off the stack by setting TOS to the end of the previous record. It is now necessary to set RB to point to the start of previous record in stack. This is achieved by using the entry marked 'reserved pointer' in the expansion record. This entry always points to the start of the previous expansion record in stack. While popping off a record, the value contained in this entry can be loaded into RB. This has the effect of restoring access to the expansion time data structures used by the outer macro.

Actions at start and end of a macro expansion are based on the extended stack model of Section 2.2.1.

At start of expansion

Actions at the start of expansion are summarized in Table 5.1.

Table 5.1 Actions at start of macro expansion

No.			*Statement*
1.	TOS	:=	TOS+1;
2.	TOS*	:=	RB;
3.	RB	:=	TOS;
4.	1(RB)	:=	MDTP entry of MNT;
5.	2(RB)	:=	RB+3+#e_{APTAB};
6.	TOS	:=	TOS + #e_{APTAB} + #e_{EVTAB}+2;

The first statement increments TOS to point at the first word of the new expansion record. This is the *reserved pointer*. The '*' mark in the second statement TOS* := RB indicates indirection. This statement deposits the address of the previous record base into this word. New RB is now established in statement 3. Statements 4 and 5 set MEC and *EVTAB_ptr* respectively. Statement 6 sets TOS to point to the last entry of the expansion record.

At end of expansion

Actions at the end of expansion are summarized in Table 5.2.

The first statement pops an expansion record off the stack by resetting TOS to the value it had while the outer macro was being expanded. RB is then made to point at the base of the previous record. Data structures in the old expansion record are now accessible as displacements from the new value in RB, e.g. MEC is 1(RB).

Table 5.2 Actions at end of macro expansion

No.	*Statement*
1.	TOS := RB−1;
2.	RB := RB*;

Example 5.17 Figure 5.11 illustrates the stack during the expansion of nested macro calls of Fig. 5.4. The statement `INCR_D &FIRST, &SECOND` of macro COMPUTE is assumed to occupy entry 18 in MDT. The body of macro INCR_D is assumed to occupy entries 73-75. Parts (a), (b) and (c) of the figure show the stack before, during and after the expansion of the nested macro call `INCR_D X,Y`. In part (a) of the figure, RB points at the bottom-most entry of the stack and TOS points at the last entry of the expansion record, i.e. at the entry of `Y` in APTAB. When the nested call is encountered, the *reserved pointer* of the new record would be made to point at the start of the previous expansion record. MEC and APTAB for the call would now be established.

After completing the expansion of the call on INCR_D, RB would be reset to the bottom-most entry of the stack, and TOS would once again point at the entry of `Y` in APTAB of the first record. MEC now contains the value 18, which would be incremented to 19. Macro expansion thus continues with the next statement in macro COMPUTE.

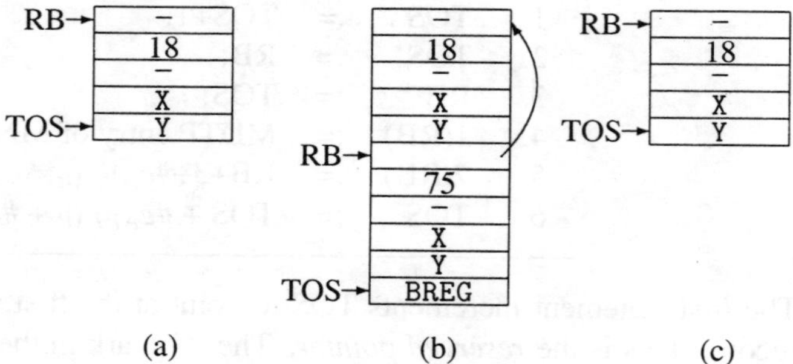

Fig. 5.11 An illustration of the expansion of nested macro calls

EXERCISE 5.5

1. Modify Algorithm 5.3 to enable expansion of nested macro calls.

5.5.6 Design of a Macro-assembler

As mentioned in Section 5.5, use of a macro preprocessor followed by a conventional assembler (see Fig. 5.6) is an expensive way of handling macros since the number of passes over the source program is large and many functions get duplicated. For example, analysis of a source statement to detect macro calls requires us to process the mnemonic field. A similar function is required in the first pass of the assembler. Similar functions of the preprocessor and the assembler can be merged if macros are handled by a macro assembler which performs macro expansion and program assembly simultaneously. This may also reduce the number of passes.

The discussion in the previous section may give rise to the impression that it is always possible to perform macro expansion in a single pass. This is not true, as certain kinds of forward references in macros cannot be handled in a single pass.

Example 5.18 Consider the assembly program of Fig. 5.12. Here the type attribute `T'&X` in macro CREATE_CONST is a forward reference to symbol `A`. Processing of the type attribute cannot be postponed because it determines the nature of the constant defined by the macro. In turn, this affects memory allocation and hence the address of `A` !

```
            MACRO
            CREATE_CONST  &X, &Y
            AIF           (T'&X EQ B) .BYTE
&Y          DW            25
            AGO           .OVER
.BYTE       ANOP
&Y          DB            25
.OVER       MEND

            CREATE_CONST  A, NEW_CON
                 :
A           DB            ?
            END
```

Fig. 5.12 Forward reference in type attribute of a parameter

This problem leads to the classical two pass organization for macro expansion. The first pass collects information about the symbols defined in a program and the second pass performs macro expansion.

Pass structure of a macro-assembler

To design the pass structure of a macro-assembler we identify the functions of a macro preprocessor and the conventional assembler which can be merged to advantage. After merging, the functions can be structured into passes of the macro-assembler. This process leads to the following pass structure:

Pass I

1. Macro definition processing
2. SYMTAB construction.

Pass II

1. Macro expansion

2. Memory allocation and LC processing
3. Processing of literals
4. Intermediate code generation.

Pass III

1. Target code generation.

Pass II is large in size since it performs many functions. Further, since it performs macro expansion as well as Pass I of a conventional assembler, all the data structures of the macro preprocessor and the conventional assembler need to exist during this pass.

The pass structure can be simplified if attributes of actual parameters are not to be supported. The macro preprocessor would then be a single pass program. Integrating Pass I of the assembler with the preprocessor would give us the following two pass structure:

Pass I

1. Macro definition processing
2. Macro expansion
3. Memory allocation, LC processing and SYMTAB construction
4. Processing of literals
5. Intermediate code generation.

Pass II

1. Target code generation.

There is obvious imbalance between the sizes of the two passes. A 3-pass structure might be preferred for this reason alone.

EXERCISE 5.5

1. Compare and contrast the properties of macros and subroutines with respect to the following:
   (a) code space requirements
   (b) execution speed
   (c) processing required by the assembler
   (d) flexibility and generality.
2. In an assembly language program, a certain action is required at 10 places in the program. Under what conditions would you code this action as
   (a) a macro?
   (b) a subroutine?

   Justify your answer with the help of appropriate examples.
3. Solve the problems of exercise 5.4.3 using REPT and IRP statements.

4. Extend the macro preprocessor described in this chapter to support the following features:
   (a) REPT and IRP statements discussed in section 5.4.2
   (b) Global EV's
   (c) Nested macro calls.

BIBLIOGRAPHY

Flores (1971), Donovan (1972) and Cole (1981) are few of the texts covering macro processors and macro assemblers in detail. Macros have been used as a tool for writing portable programs. Brown (1974) and Wallis (1982) discuss these aspects in detail.

1. Brown, P.J. (1974): *Macro Processors and Techniques for Portable Software*, Wiley, London.
2. Cole, A.J. (1981): *Macro Processors*, Cambridge University Press, Cambridge.
3. Donovan, J.J. (1972): *Systems Programming*, McGraw-Hill Kogakusha, Tokyo.
4. Flores, I. (1971): *Assemblers and BAL*, Prentice-Hall, Englewood Cliffs.
5. Wallis, P.J.L. (1982): *Portable Programming*, Macmillan, London, 1982.

CHAPTER 6

Compilers and Interpreters

6.1 ASPECTS OF COMPILATION

A compiler bridges the semantic gap between a PL domain and an execution domain. Two aspects of compilation are:

1. Generate code to implement meaning of a source program in the execution domain.
2. Provide diagnostics for violations of PL semantics in a source program.

To understand the issues involved in implementing these aspects, we briefly discuss PL features which contribute to the semantic gap between a PL domain and an execution domain. These are:

1. Data types
2. Data structures
3. Scope rules
4. Control structure.

Data types

Definition 6.1 (Data type) A data type *is the specification of* (i) *legal values for variables of the type, and* (ii) *legal operations on the legal values of the type.*

Legal operations of a type typically include an assignment operation and a set of data manipulation operations. Semantics of a data type require a compiler to ensure that variables of a type are assigned or manipulated only through legal operations. The following tasks are involved in ensuring this:

1. Checking legality of an operation for the types of its operands. This ensures that a variable is subjected only to legal operations of its type.
2. Use type conversion operations to convert values of one type into values of another type wherever necessary and permissible according to the rules of a PL.
3. Use appropriate instruction sequences of the target machine to implement the operations of a type.

Example 6.1 Consider the Pascal program segment

```
var
   x, y : real;
   i, j : integer;
begin
   y := 10;
   x := y + i;
```

While compiling the first assignment statement, the compiler must note that y is a real variable, hence every value stored in y must be a real number. Therefore it must generate code to convert the value '10' to the floating point representation. In the second assignment statement, the addition cannot be performed on the values of y and i straightaway as they belong to different types. Hence the compiler must first generate code to convert the value of i to the floating point representation and then generate code to perform the addition as a floating point operation.

Having checked the legality of each operation and determined the need for type conversion operations, the compiler must generate *type specific code* to implement an operation. In a type specific code the value of a variable of type $type_i$ is always manipulated through instructions which know how values of $type_i$ are represented.

Example 6.2 In example 1.12, we have seen how the instructions

```
CONV_R    AREG, I
ADD_R     AREG, B
MOVEM     AREG, A
```

are generated for the program segment

```
i : integer;
a,b : real;
a := b+i;
```

Each instruction is type specific, i.e. it expects the operand to be of a specific type.

Generation of type specific code achieves two important things. It implements the second half of a type's definition, viz. a value of $type_i$ is only manipulated through a legal operation of $type_i$. It also ensures execution efficiency since type related issues do not need explicit handling in the execution domain.

Data structures

A PL permits the declaration and use of data structures like arrays, stacks, records, lists, etc. To compile a reference to an element of a data structure, the compiler must develop a memory mapping to access the memory word(s) allocated to the element. A record, which is a heterogeneous data structure, leads to complex memory mappings. A user defined type requires mappings of a different kind—those that map the values of the type into their representations in a computer, and vice versa.

Example 6.3 Consider the Pascal program segment

```
program example (input, output);
  type
    employee = record
      name : array [1..10] of character;
      sex : character;
      id : integer
    end;
    weekday = (mon, tue, wed, thu, fri);
  var
    info : array [1..500] of employee;
    today : weekday;
    i,j : integer;
  begin { Main program }
      today := mon;
      info[i].id := j;
      if today = tue then ..
end.
```

Here, `info` is an array of records. The reference `info[i].id` involves use of two different kinds of mappings. The first one is the homogeneous mapping of an array reference. This is used to access `info[i]`. The second mapping is used to access the field `id` within an element of `info`, which is a data item of type `employee`. `weekday` is a user defined data type. The compiler must first decide how to represent different values of the type, and then develop an appropriate mapping between the values `mon .. fri` and their representations. A popular technique is to map these values into a subrange of integers. For example, `mon .. fri` can be mapped into the subrange 1 .. 5. This does not lead to confusion between these values and integers because the legality check is applied to each operation. Thus `tue+10` is an illegal expression even if `tue` is represented by the value '2', because '+' is not a legal operation of type `weekday`.

Scope rules

Scope rules determine the accessibility of variables declared in different blocks of a program. The *scope* of a program entity (e.g. a data item) is that part of a program where the entity is accessible. In most languages the scope of a data item is restricted to the program block in which the data item is declared. It extends to an enclosed block unless the enclosed block declares a variable with an identical name.

Example 6.4

```
  ┌ x,y : real;
  │   ┌ y,z : integer;
  │   │
A │ B │ x := y;
  │   │
  │   └
  └
```

Variable x of block A is accessible in block A and in the enclosed block B. However, variable y of block A is not accessible in block B since y is redeclared in block B. Thus, the statement x := y uses y of block B.

The compiler performs operations called *scope analysis* and *name resolution* to determine the data item designated by the use of a name in the source program. The generated code simply implements the results of the analysis. Section 6.2.2 contains a detailed discussion of the implementation of scope rules.

Control structure

The *control structure* of a language is the collection of language features for altering the flow of control during the execution of a program. This includes conditional transfer of control, conditional execution, iteration control and procedure calls. The compiler must ensure that a source program does not violate the semantics of control structures.

Example 6.5 In the Pascal program segment

```
for i := 1 to 100 do
begin
   lab1: if i = 10 then ..
end;
```

a control transfer to the statement bearing label `lab1` from outside the loop is forbidden. Some languages (though not Pascal !) also forbid assignments to the control variable of a **for** loop within the body of the loop.

6.2 MEMORY ALLOCATION

Memory allocation involves three important tasks

1. Determine the amount of memory required to represent the value of a data item.
2. Use an appropriate memory allocation model to implement the lifetimes and scopes of data items.
3. Determine appropriate memory mappings to access the values in a non scalar data item, e.g. values in an array.

The first task is implemented during semantic analysis of data declaration statements. In this section, we discuss the static and dynamic memory allocation models, and memory mappings used in the case of arrays. Discussion of advanced memory mappings to handle data alignment requirements in vector data, e.g. records, can be found in the literature cited at the end of the chapter.

6.2.1 Static and Dynamic Memory Allocation

Following Definition 1.8, we can define memory binding as follows:

Definition 6.2 (Memory binding) A memory binding *is an association between the 'memory address' attribute of a data item and the address of a memory area.*

Memory allocation is the procedure used to perform memory binding. The binding ceases to exist when memory is deallocated. Memory bindings can be static or dynamic in nature (see Definitions 1.9 and 1.10), giving rise to the static and dynamic memory allocation models. In *static memory allocation*, memory is allocated to a variable *before* the execution of a program begins. Static memory allocation is typically performed during compilation. No memory allocation or deallocation actions are performed during the execution of a program. Thus, variables remain permanently allocated; allocation to a variable exists even if the program unit in which it is defined is not active. In *dynamic memory allocation*, memory bindings are established and destroyed *during* the execution of a program. Typical examples of the use of these memory allocation models are Fortran for static allocation and block structured languages like PL/I, Pascal, Ada, etc., for dynamic allocation.

Example 6.6 Figure 6.1 illustrates static and dynamic memory allocation to a program consisting of 3 program units—A, B and C. Part (a) shows static memory allocation. Part (b) shows dynamic allocation when only program unit A is active. Part (c) shows the situation after A calls B, while Part (d) shows the situation after B returns to A and A calls C. C has been allocated part of the memory deallocated from B. It is clear that static memory allocation allocates more memory than dynamic memory allocation except when all program units are active.

Dynamic memory allocation has two flavours—automatic allocation and program controlled allocation. According to the terminology of Section 1.4.2, the former implies memory binding performed at execution init time of a program unit, while the latter implies memory binding performed during the execution of a program unit. We describe the details of these bindings in the following.

In *automatic dynamic allocation*, memory is allocated to the variables declared in a program unit when the program unit is entered during execution and is deallocated when the program unit is exited. Thus the same memory area may be used for the variables of different program units (see Fig. 6.1). It is also possible that different memory areas may be allocated to the same variable in different activations of a program unit, e.g. when some procedure is invoked in different blocks of a program. In

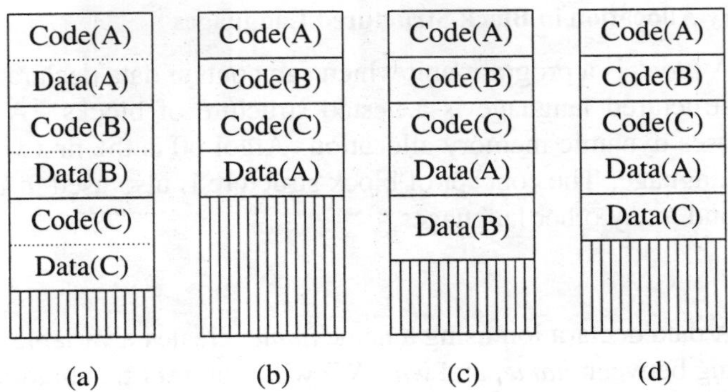

Fig. 6.1 Static and dynamic memory allocation

program controlled dynamic allocation, a program can allocate or deallocate memory at arbitrary points during its execution. It is obvious that in both automatic and program controlled allocation, address of the memory area allocated to a program unit cannot be determined at compilation time.

Dynamic memory allocation is implemented using stacks and heaps, thus necessitating pointer based access to variables. This tends to make it slower in execution than static memory allocation. Automatic dynamic allocation is implemented using a stack since entry and exit from program units is LIFO in nature (see Section 6.2.2 for more details). When a program unit is entered during the execution of a program, a record is created in the stack to contain its variables. A pointer is set to point to this record. Individual variables of the program unit are accessed using displacements from this pointer. Program controlled dynamic allocation is implemented using a heap. A pointer is now needed to point to each allocated memory area.

Example 6.7 Let program unit A contain a declaration for a simple variable `alpha`. When static memory allocation is used the compiler can use the absolute address of `alpha` to implement accesses to it. When dynamic allocation is used, let the compiler maintain the address of the memory record created for A in some register *r*. Address of variable `alpha` is now

$$< r > + d_{\texttt{alpha}}$$

where $d_{\texttt{alpha}}$ is the displacement of the memory area allocated to `alpha` from the start of the record for A. The constant $d_{\texttt{alpha}}$ is determined during compilation.

Dynamic allocation provides some significant advantages. Recursion can be implemented easily because memory is allocated when a program unit is entered during execution. This leads to allocation of a separate memory area for each recursive activation of a program unit. (We discuss this aspect later in the section.) Dynamic allocation can also support data structures whose sizes are determined dynamically, e.g. an array declaration `a [m,n]`, where `m` and `n` are variables.

6.2.2 Memory Allocation in Block Structured Languages

A *block* is a program unit which can contain data declarations. A program in a block structured language is a nested structure of blocks. A block structured language uses dynamic memory allocation. Algol-60 is the first widely used block structured language. The concept of block structure is also used in PL/I, Algol-68, Pascal, Ada and many other languages.

Scope rules

A data declaration using a name $name_i$ creates a variable var_i and establishes a binding between $name_i$ and var_i. We will represent this binding as ($name_i$, var_i), and call it the name–var binding. Variable var_i is *visible* at a place in the program if some binding ($name_l$, var_i) is effective at that place. A visible variable can be accessed using its name, $name_l$ in the above case. It is possible for data declarations in many blocks of a program to use a same name, say, $name_i$. This would establish many bindings of the form ($name_i$, var_k) for different values of k. Scope rules determine which of these bindings is effective at a specific place in the program.

Consider a block b which contains a data declaration using the name $name_i$. This establishes a binding ($name_i$, var_i) for a variable var_i. This binding only exists within block b. If a block b' nested inside block b also contains a declaration using $name_i$, a binding ($name_i$, var_j) exists in b' for some variable var_j. This suppresses the binding ($name_i$, var_i) over block b'. Thus variable var_i is not visible in b'. However, if b' did not contain a declaration using $name_i$, the binding ($name_i$, var_i) would have been effective over b' as well. Thus, var_i would have been visible in b'. We summarize the rules governing visibility of a variable in the following.

Scope of a variable

If a variable var_i is created with the name $name_i$ in a block b,

1. var_i can be accessed in any statement situated in block b.
2. var_i can be accessed in any statement situated a block b' which is enclosed in b, unless b' contains a declaration using the same name (i.e. using the name $name_i$).

A variable declared in block b is called a *local variable* of block b. A variable of an enclosing block, that is accessible within block b, is called a *nonlocal variable* of block b. The following notation is used to differentiate between variables created using the same name in different blocks:

$name_{block\_name}$: variable created by a data declaration using the name *name* in block *block_name*

Thus $\texttt{alpha}_\texttt{A}$, $\texttt{alpha}_\texttt{B}$ are variables created using the name `alpha` in blocks A and B.

Example 6.8 Consider the block-structured program in Fig. 6.2. The variables accessible within the various blocks are as follows:

```
  ┌x,y,z : integer;
  │  ┌g : real;
  │ B│ C┌h,z : real;
  │  │  └
  │  └
 A│
  │  ┌i,j : integer;
  │ D│
  │  └
  └
```

Fig. 6.2 Block structured program

Block	*Accessible variables*	
	local	*nonlocal*
A	x_A, y_A, z_A	–
B	g_B	x_A, y_A z_A
C	h_C, z_C	x_A, y_A, g_B
D	i_D, j_D	x_A, y_A, z_A

Variable z_A is not accessible inside block C since C contains a declaration using the name z. Thus z_A and z_C are two distinct variables. This would be true even if they had identical attributes, i.e. even if z of C was declared to be an integer.

Memory allocation and access

Automatic dynamic allocation is implemented using the extended stack model (see Section 2.2.1) with a minor variation—each record in the stack has *two* reserved pointers instead of one (see Fig. 6.3). Each stack record accommodates the variables for one activation of a block, hence we call it an *activation record* (AR). The following notation is used to refer to the activation record of a block:

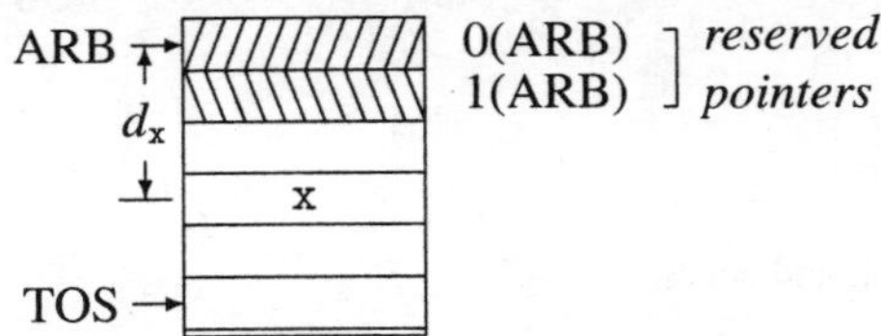

Fig. 6.3 Stack record format

AR^i_A : Activation record for the ith activation of A wherein we omit the superscript *i* unless multiple activations of a block exist. During the execution of a block structured program, a register called the *activation record base* (ARB) always points to the start address of the TOS record. This record belongs to the block which contains the statement being executed. A local variable `x` of this block is accessed using the address d_x(ARB), where d_x is the displacement of variable `x` from the start of AR. The address may also be written as <ARB> + d_x, where <ARB> stands for the words 'contents of ARB'.

Dynamic pointer

The first reserved pointer in a block's AR points to the activation record of its dynamic parent. This is called the *dynamic pointer* and has the address 0(ARB). The dynamic pointer is used for deallocating an AR. Actions at block entry and exit are analogous to those described in Section 2.2.1.

Example 6.9 Figure 6.4 depicts memory allocation for the following program:

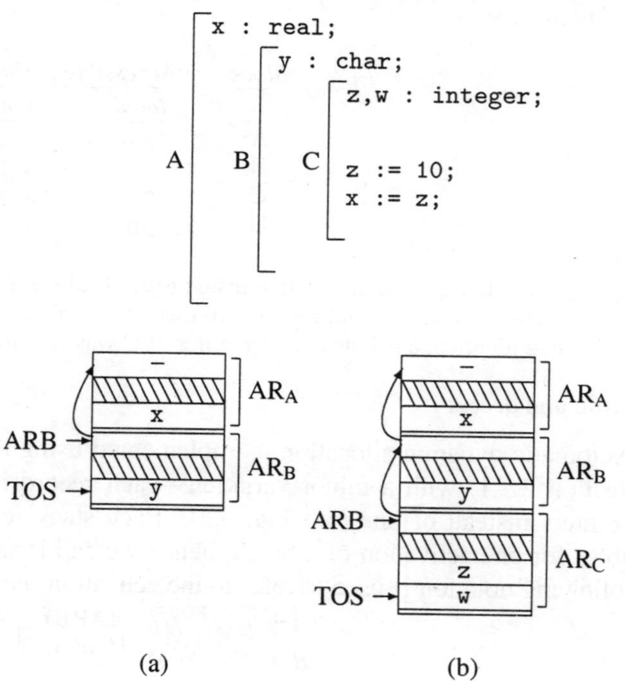

Fig. 6.4 Dynamic allocation and access

where each block could be a **begin** block in Algol, PL/I or a procedure without parameters in some block structured language. It is assumed that the blocks are entered in the sequence A, B, C during the execution of the program.

Figure 6.4(a) shows the situation when blocks A and B are active. Figure 6.4(b) shows the situation after entry to C. Situation after exit from C would again be as shown in

Fig. 6.4(a).

Actions at entry

The actions at entry of block C are described in Table 6.1.

Table 6.1 Actions at block entry

No.	*Statement*		
1.	TOS	:=	TOS + 1;
2.	TOS*	:=	ARB; {Set the dynamic pointer}
3.	ARB	:=	TOS;
4.	TOS	:=	TOS + 1;
5.	TOS*	:=	...; {Set reserved pointer 2}
6.	TOS	:=	TOS + n;

where n is the number of memory words allocated to variables of block C, i.e. n = 2. After step 1, TOS points to the dynamic pointer of the AR being created. Step 2 sets the dynamic pointer to point to the previous activation record. Step 3 sets ARB to the start of the new AR. Step 6 is the memory allocation step. Note that positions of local variables z and w in AR_C are determined during compilation using their type and length information. d_z and d_w are 2 and 3 assuming an integer to occupy 1 word. Thus the address of variable z is <ARB> + 2.

Actions at exit

The actions at entry of block C are described in Table 6.2.

Table 6.2 Actions at block exit

No.	*Statement*		
1.	TOS	:=	ARB – 1;
2.	ARB	:=	ARB*;

The first statement sets TOS to point to the last word of the previous activation record. The second statement sets ARB to point to the start of the previous activation record. These actions effectively deallocate the TOS AR in the stack.

Accessing nonlocal variables

A nonlocal variable *nl_var* of a block *b_use* is a local variable of some block *b_defn* enclosing *b_use* (trivially *b_defn* and *b_use* could be the same block). The following terminology is used for a block and its enclosing blocks. A *textual ancestor* or *static ancestor* of block *b_use* is a block which encloses block *b_use*. The block immediately enclosing *b_use* is called its Level 1 ancestor. A Level m ancestor is a block which immediately encloses the Level (m–1) ancestor. The *level difference* between *b_use* and its Level m ancestor is m. If $s\_nest_{b\_use}$ represents the static nesting level of block *b_use* in the program, *b_use* has a Level i ancestor, $\forall i < s\_nest_{b\_use}$.

According to the rules of a block structured language, when *b_use* is in execution, *b_defn* must be active. Hence AR_{b_defn} exists in the stack, and *nl_var* is to be accessed as

$$\text{start address of } AR_{b\_defn} + d_{nl\_var}$$

where d_{nl_var} is the displacement of *nl_var* in AR_{b_defn}.

Static pointer

Access to nonlocal variables is implemented using the second reserved pointer in AR. This pointer, which has the address 1(ARB), is called the *static pointer.* When an AR is created for a block b, its static pointer is set to point to the AR of the static ancestor of b. The code to access a nonlocal variable *nl_var* declared in a Level m ancestor of *b_use*, $m \geq 1$, is as follows:

1. r := ARB; where r is some register.
2. Repeat step 3 m times.
3. r := 1(r); i.e. load the static pointer into register r.
4. Access *nl_var* using the address $< r > + d_{nl\_var}$. (6.1)

Thus a nonlocal variable defined in a Level m ancestor is accessed using m indirections through the static pointer. Note that the value of m is known during compilation from the static structure of the program.

Example 6.10 Figure 6.5 shows the status of memory allocation after executing statement `z := 10;` of block `C` in the program of Ex. 6.9. Steps 4 and 5 of the actions at block entry are:

No.	*Statement*		
4.	TOS	:=	TOS + 1;
5.	TOS*	:=	address of AR of Level 1 ancestor.

When block `C` is entered, these actions set the static pointer in AR_C to point at the start of AR_B. When `B` was entered, the static pointer in AR_B would have been set to point at the start of AR_A. The code generated to access variable `x` in the statement `x := z;` is

1. r := ARB;
2. r := 1(r);
3. r := 1(r);
4. Access `x` using the address $< r > + d_x$.

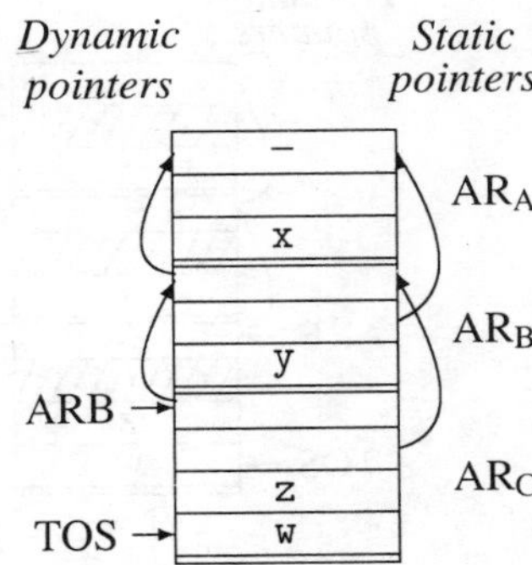

Fig. 6.5 Accessing nonlocal variables with static pointers

Displays

For large values of level difference, it is expensive to access nonlocal variables using static pointers. *Display* is an array used to improve the efficiency of nonlocal accesses. When a block B is in execution, the entries of *Display* contain the following information:

$$
\begin{aligned}
\text{Display}[1] &= \text{address of Level } (s\_nest_b{-}1) \text{ ancestor of B.}\\
\text{Display}[2] &= \text{address of Level } (s\_nest_b{-}2) \text{ ancestor of B.}\\
&\vdots\\
\text{Display}[s\_nest_b{-}1] &= \text{address of Level 1 ancestor of B.}\\
\text{Display}[s\_nest_b] &= \text{address of AR}_\text{B}.
\end{aligned}
$$

Let block B refer to some variable v_j defined in an ancestor block b_i. The address of v_j is calculated as

$$\text{Display}[s\_nest_{b_i}] + d_{v_j}$$

Hence the code generated for the access would be

$$
\begin{array}{l}
1.\ r := \text{Display}[s\_nest_{b_i}];\\
2.\ \text{Access } v_j \text{ using the address } <r> + d_{v_j};
\end{array}
\tag{6.2}
$$

which is more efficient compared with the steps in (6.1).

Example 6.11 Figure 6.6 illustrates the contents of *Display* while executing the program of Ex. 6.9. The reference to variable x in block C is implemented using the code

1. $r :=$ Display[1];
2. Access x using the address $<r> + d_\text{x}$.

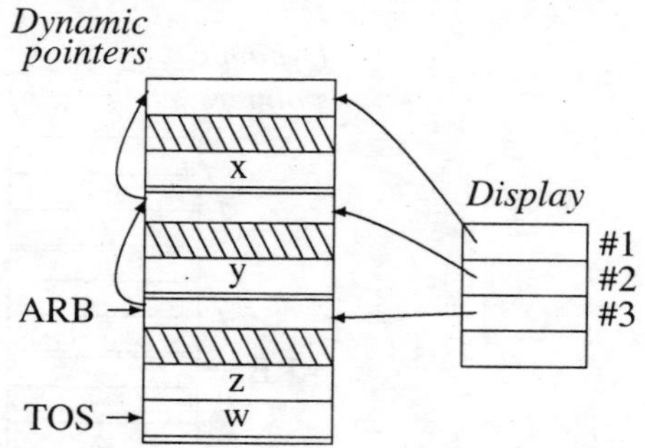

Fig. 6.6 Accessing nonlocal variables using display

Symbol table requirements

In order to implement dynamic allocation and access, a compiler should perform the following tasks while compiling the use of a name v in *b_current*, the block being compiled:

1. Determine the static nesting level of *b_current*.
2. Determine the variable designated by the name v. This should be done in accordance with the scope rules.
3. Determine the static nesting level of the block in which v is defined. Determine the value of d_v.
4. Generate the code indicated in (6.1) or (6.2).

We present a simple scheme to implement functions 1, 2 and 3. This scheme uses the extended stack model of Section 2.2.1 to organize the symbol table. When the start of block *b_current* is encountered during compilation, a new record is pushed on the stack. It contains

1. Nesting level of *b_current*
2. Symbol table for *b_current*.

The reserved pointer of the new record points to the previous record in the stack. This record contains the symbol table of the static ancestor of *b_current*. Each entry in the symbol table contains a variable's name, type, length and displacement in the AR.

Scope rules are implemented by searching the name v referenced in *b_current* in the symbol table as follows: Symbol table in the topmost record of the stack is searched first. Existence of name v there implies that v designates a local variable of *b_current*. If an entry for v does not exist there, the previous record in the stack is searched. It contains the symbol table for the Level 1 ancestor of *b_current*. Existence of v in it implies that v is a variable declared in the Level 1 ancestor block, and not redeclared in *b_current*. If v is not found there, it is searched in the previous record of the stack, i.e. in the symbol table of the Level 2 ancestor, and so on. When `v` is found in a symbol table, its displacement d_v in the AR is obtained from its symbol table entry. The nesting level of the block defining `v` is obtained from the first field of the stack record containing the symbol table. Code can now be generated to implement the access to variable `v` as in (6.1) or (6.2).

Example 6.12 Figure 6.7 shows the symbol table for the program of Ex. 6.9. For simplicity, each symbol table entry only shows a symbol and its displacement in AR. The search for variable `x` accessed in the statement `x := z;` terminates on finding the entry of `x` in the symbol table for block A. The nesting level of A is 1. $d_x = 2$ and nesting level of C, the current block, is 3. This information is sufficient to generate code as in Ex. 6.10 or Ex. 6.11.

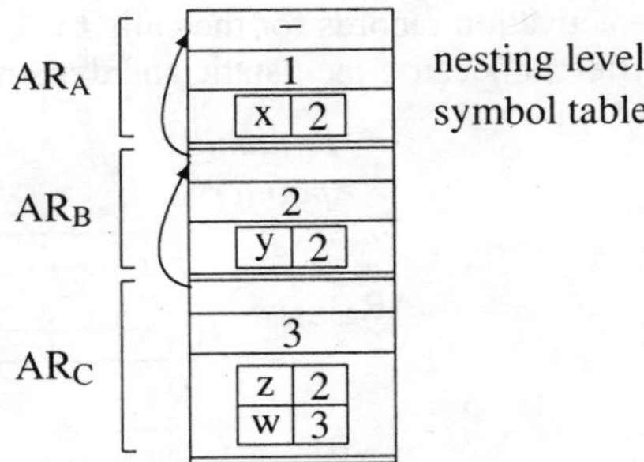

Fig. 6.7 Stack structured symbol table

Recursion

Recursive procedures (or functions) are characterized by the fact that many invocations of a procedure coexist during the execution of a program. A copy of the local variables of the procedure must be allocated for each invocation. This does not pose any problems when a stack model of memory allocation is used because an activation record is created for every invocation of a procedure or function.

Example 6.13 A Pascal program `sample2` contains a function `fib` which computes the nth term of the Fibonacci series.

```
Program sample2 (input, output);
  var
     a,b : integer;
  function fib(n) : integer;
    var
      x : integer;
    begin
      if n > 2 then
         x := fib(n-1) + fib(n-2);
      else x := 1;
      return(x);
```

```
end fib;
begin
    fib(4);
end.
```

For the call `fib(4)`, the function makes recursive calls `fib(3)` and `fib(2)`, each of which makes further recursive calls, and so on. Assuming that a formal parameter is allocated memory analogous to a local variable, Fig. 6.8 shows the allocation status after the recursive call `fib(2)`. Creation of multiple AR's for function `fib` is handled naturally by the actions at block entry. Note that the static and dynamic pointers in the activation record for `fib(4)`, i.e. in AR^1_{fib} are identical because `sample2` is both a static and dynamic ancestor of this invocation. However static and dynamic pointers in the activation records for the calls `fib(3)` and `fib(2)`, i.e. in AR^2_{fib} and AR^3_{fib}, are different because their static and dynamic ancestors are different.

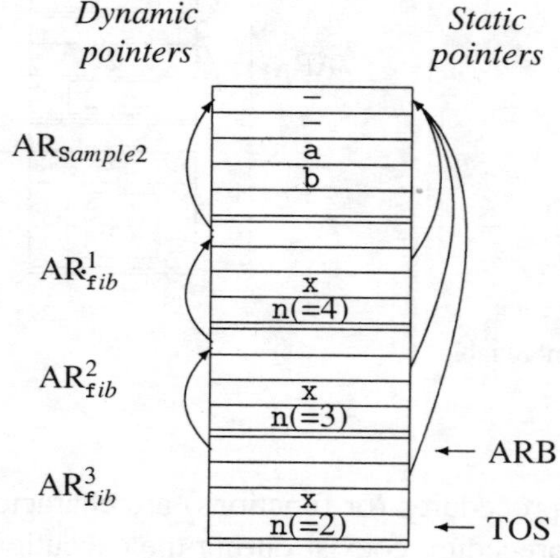

Fig. 6.8 Memory allocation in recursion

Limitations of stack based memory allocation

The stack based memory allocation model is not adequate for program controlled memory allocation, e.g. when the **new** or **dispose** statements of Pascal or `calloc` and `free` functions of C are used to allocate and free memory areas. The compiler must resort to the use of heaps for such allocation. Accesses to variables are now implemented through pointers associated with individual variables rather than with AR's. Free lists or garbage collection are used to implement the reuse of deallocated memory. The stack model is also inadequate for multi-activity programs, i.e. concurrent programs, because in such a program, program blocks may be entered in exited in a non-LIFO manner.

6.2.3 Array Allocation and Access

When an n dimensional array is organized in a computer's memory, the order in which the array elements are arranged in the memory is governed by the rules of the PL. In our discussion, we shall assume array elements to be ordered such that elements occupying adjoining memory locations always differ in the first subscript. For two dimensional arrays, this implies a column-wise arrangement of elements. Figure 6.9 shows the allocation for an array a [5, 10]. It is obvious that static memory allocation is feasible only if dimension bounds of an array are known at compilation time.

```
a [1, 1]
   :
a [5, 1]
a [1, 2]
   :
a [5, 2]
   :
   :
a [1, 10]
   :
a [5, 10]
```

Fig. 6.9 Memory allocation for a 2 dimensional array

The arrangement of array elements in the memory determines the memory mapping to be used in computing the address of an array element. In Fig. 6.9, it has been assumed that the lower bound of each dimension to be 1. Under this assumption, address of an array element a $[s_1, s_2]$ can be determined as follows:

$$Ad.\ \mathtt{a}[s_1, s_2] \quad = \quad Ad.\ \mathtt{a}[1,1] + \{(s_2 - 1) \times n + (s_1 - 1)\} \times k$$

where n is the number of rows in the array and k is the number of memory locations (words or bytes) occupied by each element of the array. For a general two dimensional array

$$\mathtt{a}\,[\,l_1 : u_1,\ l_2 : u_2\,]$$

where l_i and u_i are the lower and upper bounds of the ith subscript, respectively; address of a $[s_1, s_2]$ is given by the formula

$$Ad.\ \mathtt{a}[s_1, s_2] \quad = \quad Ad.\ \mathtt{a}[l_1, l_2] + \{(s_2 - l_2) \times (u_1 - l_1 + 1) + (s_1 - l_1)\} \times k$$

Defining $range_i$ to be the range of the ith subscript, we have

$$range_1 \quad = \quad u_1 - l_1 + 1,$$
$$range_2 \quad = \quad u_2 - l_2 + 1, \text{ and}$$

$$
\begin{aligned}
Ad.\ \mathtt{a}[s_1,s_2] &= Ad.\ \mathtt{a}[l_1,l_2]+\{(s_2-l_2)\times range_1+(s_1-l_1)\}\times k \\
&= Ad.\ \mathtt{a}[l_1,l_2]-(l_2\times range_1+l_1)\times k \\
&\quad +(s_2\times range_1+s_1)\times k \\
&= Ad.\ \mathtt{a}[0,0]+(s_2\times range_1+s_1)\times k \qquad (6.3)
\end{aligned}
$$

Note that a [0,0]—which we will call the *base element* of array a—does not exist unless $l_i \le 0\ \forall i$. However, this fact is irrelevant to the address calculation formula. Generalizing for an m dimensional array

$$
\begin{aligned}
Ad.\mathtt{a}[s_1,..,s_m] &= Ad.\mathtt{a}[0,..,0] \\
&\quad +\{((\dots(s_m\times range_{m-1}+s_{m-1})\times range_{m-2} \\
&\quad +s_{m-2})\times range_{m-3}+..)\times range_1+s_1\}\times k \qquad (6.4) \\
&= Ad.\mathtt{a}[0,..,0]+\Sigma_{i=1}^{m}\ s_i\ \times\ (\Pi_{j=1}^{i-1} range_j)\ \times k \qquad (6.5)
\end{aligned}
$$

where $\Pi_{j=1}^{i-1} range_j\ = 1$ for $i = 1$. Values of l_i, u_i and $range_i$ for all dimentions of the array can be computed at compilation time (if subscript bounds are constants), or at array allocation time. These values can be stored in an array descriptor called a *dope vector* (DV). Figure 6.10 shows the dope vector format for an m dimensional array. If dimension bounds are known at compilation time, the dope vector needs to exist only during program compilation; it is accommodated in the symbol table entry for the array and its contents are used while generating code for an array reference (see Ex. 6.14). In some machine architectures, (6.5) can be computed more efficiently than (6.4) if $\forall j\ \Pi_{j=1}^{i-1} range_j\ \times\ k$ is a precomputed constant. In such cases $\Pi_{j=1}^{i-1} range_j\ \times\ k$ can be computed and stored in the dope vector instead of $range_j$.

Ad. a [0,...,0]		
No. of dimensions (m)		
l_1	u_1	$range_1$
l_2	u_2	$range_2$
⋮	⋮	⋮
l_m	u_m	$range_m$

Fig. 6.10 Dope vector

Example 6.14 The code generated for an array reference `a[i, j]` of a two dimensional array a [1:5, 1:10] is shown in Fig. 6.11. Note that the various subscript bounds and subscript ranges used here become constants of the generated program. Provision is made to call an error routine if any subscript value falls outside the corresponding range.

If array dimension bounds are not known during compilation, the dope vector has to exist during program execution. The number of dimensions of an array determines the format and size of its DV. The dope vector is allocated in the AR of a block and

```
MOVER    AREG, I
COMP     AREG, ='5'
BC       GT, ERROR_RTN     Error if i>5
COMP     AREG, ='1'
BC       LT, ERROR_RTN     Error if i<1
MOVER    AREG, J
COMP     AREG, ='10'
BC       GT, ERROR_RTN     Error if j>10
COMP     AREG, ='1'
BC       LT, ERROR_RTN     Error if j<1
MULT     AREG, ='5'        Multiply by range_1
ADD      AREG, I
MULT     AREG, ='2'        Multiply by element size
ADD      AREG, ADDR_ABASE  Add Address of a[0,0]
```

Fig. 6.11 Code for an array reference

d_{DV}, its displacement in AR, is noted in the symbol table entry of the array. The array is allocated dynamically by repeating step 6 of Table 6.1 for the array. Its start address, values of l_j, u_j and $range_j$ are entered in the DV. The generated code uses d_{DV} to access the contents of DV to check the validity of subscripts and compute the address of an array element.

Example 6.15 Figure 6.12 shows the memory allocation for the following program segment:

```
var
   x,y : real;
   alpha : array [l_1:u_1, l_2:u_2] of integer;
   i,j : integer;
begin
   alpha[i,j] := ...;
```

where l_1, l_2, u_1 and u_2 are nonlocal variables. Since the dimension bounds are not known during compilation, the dope vector must exist during execution. Hence DV is allocated in the AR. d_{alpha_DV}, its displacement in AR, is thus known at compilation time. Array alpha is allocated when the program segment is activated. The address of its base element is recorded in its DV. The generated code uses knowledge of d_{alpha_DV} to access the contents of DV. For example, 4 (ARB) is the *address* field in DV, 6 (ARB) gives information about its first dimension, etc. Note that the field *no. of dimensions* may be omitted from DV since this information is implicit in the generated code.

EXERCISE 6.2

1. Develop an algorithm to build the stack structured symbol table shown in Fig. 6.7.
2. In this section we have not described how memory mapping is performed for records of Pascal, Cobol or structures of C. Refer to Dhamdhere (1997) for a discussion of the same.

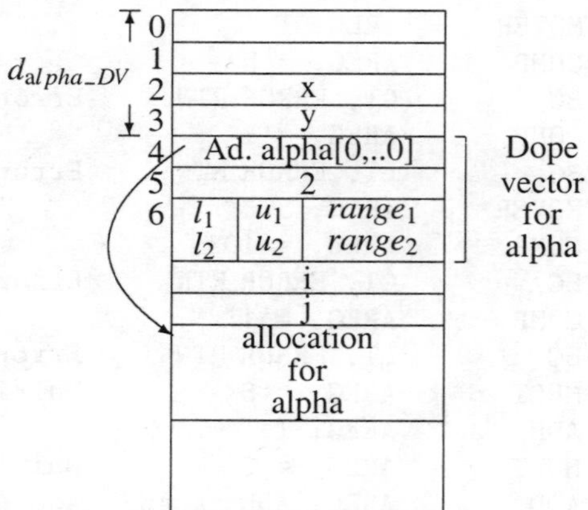

Fig. 6.12 Dope vector for array with dynamic dimension bounds

3. Many languages support bit and character strings with dynamically varying lengths. Would these language features interfere with the use of a stack model for memory allocation?
4. For the recursive procedure `fib`, show contents of the *Display* before and after each recursive call.

6.3 COMPILATION OF EXPRESSIONS

6.3.1 A Toy Code Generator for Expressions

The major issues in code generation for expressions are as follows:

1. Determination of an evaluation order for the operators in an expression.
2. Selection of instructions to be used in the target code.
3. Use of registers and handling of partial results.

The evaluation order of operators depends on operator precedences in an obvious way—an operator which precedes its left and right neighbours must be evaluated before either of them. Hence, a feasible evaluation order is the order in which operators are reduced during a bottom-up parse, or the reverse of the order in which operators are produced during a top down parse. (Other feasible evaluation orders are discussed in the next section.) In the following discussion the use of a bottom up parser to determine the evaluation order has been assumed.

The choice of an instruction to be used in the target code depends on the following:

1. The *type* and *length* of each operand
2. The *addressability* of each operand, i.e. *where* the operand is located and *how* it can be accessed.

The addressability of an operand indicates *where* an operand is located and *how* it can be accessed.

We introduce the notion of an *operand descriptor* to maintain the type, length and addressability information for each operand. Thus the choice of an instruction can be made by analysing an operator and the descriptors of its operands.

A *partial result* is the value of some subexpression computed while evaluating an expression. In the interests of efficiency, partial results are maintained in CPU registers as far as possible. However, some of them have to be moved to memory if the number of results exceeds the number of available CPU registers. An important issue in code generation is when and how to move partial results between memory and CPU registers, and how to know which partial result is contained in a register. We use a *register descriptor* to maintain information for the latter purpose.

We develop a toy code generator for expressions using a YACC like bottom-up parser generator. For simplicity we present a code generator which uses a single CPU register. However, it can be easily extended to handle multiple registers.

Operand descriptors

An operand descriptor has the following fields:

1. *Attributes:* Contains the subfields *type*, *length* and *miscellaneous information.*
2. *Addressability:* Specifies *where* the operand is located, and *how* it can be accessed. It has two subfields
   (a) *Addressability code:* Takes the values 'M' (operand is in memory), and 'R' (operand is in register). Other addressability codes, e.g. address in register ('AR') and address in memory ('AM'), are also possible, however we do not consider them in this section.
   (b) *Address:* Address of a CPU register or memory word.

An operand descriptor is built for every operand participating in an expression, i.e. for *id*'s, constants and partial results. A descriptor is built for an *id* when the *id* is reduced during parsing. A partial result pr_i is the result of evaluating some operator op_j. A descriptor is built for pr_i immediately after code is generated for operator op_j. For simplicity we assume that all operand descriptors are stored in an array called *Operand_descriptor*. This enables us to designate a descriptor by its index in *Operand_descriptor*, e.g. descriptor #*n* is the descriptor in *Operand_descriptor*[*n*].

Example 6.16 The code generated for the expression a*b is as follows:

```
MOVER    AREG, A
MULT     AREG, B
```

Three operand descriptors are used during code generation. Assuming a, b to be integers occupying 1 memory word, these are:

1	(int,1)	M, addr(a)	Descriptor for a
2	(int,1)	M, addr(b)	Descriptor for b
3	(int,1)	R, addr(AREG)	Descriptor for a*b

A skeleton of the code generator is shown in Fig. 6.13. Operand descriptor numbers are used as attributes of NT's. The routine `build_descriptor` called from the semantic action for the production <*F*> ::= <*id*> builds a descriptor for <*id*> and returns its entry number in *Operand_descriptor*. The code generation routine generates code for an operator and builds an operand descriptor for the partial result. Semantic actions of other rules merely copy the operand descriptors as attributes of NT's.

```
%%
E   :   E + T   {$$ = codegen('+', $1, $3)}
    |   T       {$$ = $1}
    ;
T   :   T * F   {$$ = codegen('*', $1, $3)}
    |   F       {$$ = $1}
    ;
F   :   id      {$$ = build_descriptor ($1)}
    ;
%%
build_descriptor (operand)
{
      i = i + 1;
      operand_descr[i] = ((type), (addressability_code, address))
                            of operand;
      return i;
}
```

Fig. 6.13 Skeleton of the code generator

Register descriptors

A register descriptor has two fields

1. *Status:* Contains the code *free* or *occupied* to indicate register status.
2. *Operand descriptor #:* If *status* = *occupied*, this field contains the descriptor # for the operand contained in the register.

Register descriptors are stored in an array called *Register_descriptor*. One register descriptor exists for each CPU register.

Example 6.17 The register descriptor for AREG after generating code for a*b as in Ex. 6.16 would be

Occupied	#3

This indicates that register AREG contains the operand described by descriptor #3.

Generating an instruction

When an operator op_i is reduced by the parser, the function `codegen` is called with op_i and descriptors of its operands as parameters. A single instruction can be generated to evaluate op_i if the descriptors indicate that one operand is in a register and the other is in memory, If both operands are in memory, an instruction is generated to move one of them into a register. This is followed by an instruction to evaluate op_i.

Saving partial results

If all registers are occupied (i.e. they contain partial results) when operator op_i is to be evaluated, a register r is freed by copying its contents into a *temporary location* in the memory. r is now used to evaluate operator op_i. For simplicity we assume that an array `temp` is declared in the target program (i.e. in the generated code) to hold partial results. A partial result is always stored in the next free entry of `temp`. Note that when a partial result is moved to a temporary location, the descriptor of the partial result must change. The *operand descriptor #* field of the register descriptor is used to achieve this.

Example 6.18 Consider the expression `a*b+c*d`. After generating code for `a*b`, the operand and register descriptors would be as shown in Ex. 6.16 and 6.17. After the partial result `a*b` is moved to a temporary location, say `temp[1]`, the operand descriptors must become

1	(int,1)	M, addr(a)
2	(int,1)	M, addr(b)
3	(int,1)	M, addr(temp[1])

to indicate that the value of the operand described by operand descriptor # 3 (viz. `a*b`) has been moved to memory location `temp[1]`.

Figure 6.14 shows the complete code generation routine. It first checks the addressabilities of its operands to decide whether one of them exists in a register. If so, it generates a single instruction to perform the operation. If none of the operands is in a register, it needs to move one operand into the register before performing the operation. For this purpose, it first frees the register if it is occupied and changes the operand descriptor of the result it contained previously. (Note how it uses the register descriptor for this purpose.) It now moves one operand into the register and generates an instruction to perform the operation. At the end of code generation, it builds a descriptor for the partial result.

Example 6.19 Code generation steps for the expression `a*b+c*d` are shown in Tab. 6.3, where the superscript of an NT shows the operand descriptor # used as its attribute, and the notation $<id>_{\mathtt{v}}$ represents the token <*id*> constructed for symbol `v`.

Figure 6.15(a) shows the parse tree and operand and register descriptors after step 8. Figure 6.15(b) shows the parse tree and descriptors after step 9. Note that operand descriptor #3 has been changed to indicate that the partial result `a*b` has been moved

```
codegen (operator, opd1, opd2)
{
    if opd1.addressability_code = 'R'
        /* Code generation -- case 1 */
      if operator = '+' generate 'ADD AREG, opd2';
        /* Analogous code for other operators */
    else if opd2.addressability_code = 'R'
        /* Code generation -- case 2 */
      if operator = '+' generate 'ADD AREG, opd1';
        /* Analogous code for other operators */
    else
        /* Code generation -- case 3 */
      if Register_descr.status = 'Occupied'
        /* Save partial result */
        generate  ('MOVEM AREG, Temp[j]');
        j = j + 1;
        Operand_descr[Register_descr.Operand_descriptor#]
                = (<type>, (M, Addr(Temp[j])));
      /* Generate code */
      generate 'MOVER AREG, opd1';
      if operator = '+' generate 'ADD AREG, opd2';
        /* Analogous code for other operators */
    /* Common part -- Create a new descriptor
    Saying operand value is in register AREG */
    i = i + 1;
    operand_descr[i] = (<type>,('R', Addr(AREG)));
    Register_descr = ('Occupied', i);
    return i;
}
```

Fig. 6.14 Code generation routine

to the temporary location `temp[1]`. The register descriptor now points to operand descriptor #6 which describes the partial result `c*d`.

To see how temporary locations are used to hold partial results, consider the source string `a*b+c*d*(e+f)+c*d`. Figure 6.16 shows the expression tree for the string wherein operator numbers indicate the bottom up evaluation order. Figure 6.17(a) shows the code generated for this string using the code generation routine of Fig. 6.14. The contents of the temporary locations and their usage are summarized in Table 6.4.

The general rule concerning the use of partial results is that the partial result saved last is always used before the results saved earlier. For example, the value of `c*d` is used before the value of `a*b`. (It is easy to prove the rule by contradiction—if this fact does not hold, we must have evaluated the operators in some order other than the bottom up evaluation order!) It is therefore possible to use a LIFO data structure,

Table 6.3 Code generation actions for `a*b+c*d`

Step no.	*Parsing action*	*Code generation action*
1.	$<id>_{a} \rightarrow F^1$	Build descriptor # 1
2.	$F^1 \rightarrow T^1$	–
3.	$<id>_{b} \rightarrow F^2$	Build descriptor # 2
4.	$T^1 * F^2 \rightarrow T^3$	Generate `MOVER AREG, A` `MULT AREG, B` Build descriptor # 3
5.	$T^3 \rightarrow E^3$	–
6.	$<id>_{c} \rightarrow F^4$	Build descriptor # 4
7.	$F^4 \rightarrow T^4$	–
8.	$<id>_{d} \rightarrow F^5$	Build descriptor # 5

9.	$T^4 * F^5 \rightarrow T^6$	Generate `MOVEM AREG, TEMP_1`
		`MOVER AREG, C`
		`MULT AREG, D`
		Build descriptor # 6

10.	$E^3 + T^6 \rightarrow E^7$	Generate `ADD AREG, TEMP_1`

Table 6.4

Temporary	*Contents*	*Used in*
temp [1]	Value of node 1 (i.e. value of `a*b`)	evaluating node 5
temp [2]	Value of node 2	evaluating node 4
temp [3]	Value of node 5	evaluating node 7

i.e. a stack, to organize the temporary locations. Use of a stack permits the reuse of temporary locations during the evaluation of an expression, thus reducing the number of temporary locations required. Figure 6.17(b) shows the code for the expression resulting from the reuse of *temp* [1]. The contents of the temporary locations and their usage are summarized in Table 6.5.

Note that *temp* [1] is reused to store the value of node 5. This is realized as follows: When the value contained in *temp* [2] is used in evaluating node 4, *temp* [2] is marked free (see the 9th instruction in Fig. 6.17(b)). Similarly *temp* [1] is marked free

Table 6.5

Temporary	*Contents*	*Used in*
temp [1]	Value of node 1	evaluating node 5
temp [2]	Value of node 2	evaluating node 4
temp [1]	Value of node 5	evaluating node 7

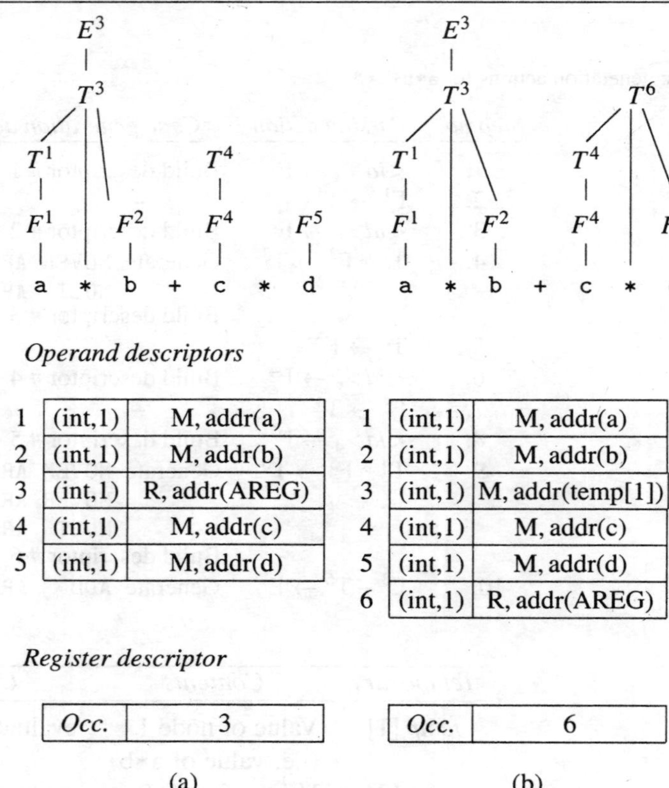

(a)

1	(int,1)	M, addr(a)
2	(int,1)	M, addr(b)
3	(int,1)	R, addr(AREG)
4	(int,1)	M, addr(c)
5	(int,1)	M, addr(d)

Occ.	3

(b)

1	(int,1)	M, addr(a)
2	(int,1)	M, addr(b)
3	(int,1)	M, addr(temp[1])
4	(int,1)	M, addr(c)
5	(int,1)	M, addr(d)
6	(int,1)	R, addr(AREG)

Occ.	6

Fig. 6.15 Code generation actions

when the value contained in it is used in evaluating node 5 (see the 10th instruction). While generating the code for node 6, the partial result contained in the register is saved in the first available location. This happens to be *temp* [1].

To implement a stack of temporaries, variable `i` of routine `codegen` is used as a stack pointer. Now, `i` needs to be decremented whenever an operand of an instruction is a temporary location. If dynamic memory allocation is used, it is best to locate the stack *after* the activation record for a block. Now we can increment/decrement TOS instead of variable `i`. Figure 6.18 illustrates this arrangement.

EXERCISE 6.3.1

1. Extend the toy code generator to incorporate the following:
   (a) Parentheses in an expression,
   (b) Non-commutative operators like '−' and '/'.
2. Extend the toy code generator to handle multiple registers in the CPU. Show various steps in the code generation for the expression `(a+b)/(c+d)` using 2 CPU registers.

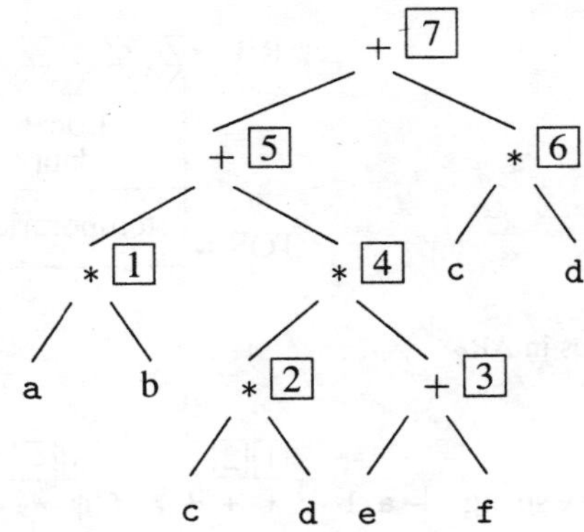

Fig. 6.16 Expression tree

(a)		(b)	
MOVER	AREG, A	MOVER	AREG, A
MULT	AREG, B	MULT	AREG, B
MOVEM	AREG, TEMP_1	MOVEM	AREG, TEMP_1
MOVER	AREG, C	MOVER	AREG, C
MULT	AREG, D	MULT	AREG, D
MOVEM	AREG, TEMP_2	MOVEM	AREG, TEMP_2
MOVER	AREG, E	MOVER	AREG, E
ADD	AREG, F	ADD	AREG, F
MULT	AREG, TEMP_2	MULT	AREG, TEMP_2
ADD	AREG, TEMP_1	ADD	AREG, TEMP_1
MOVEM	AREG, TEMP_3	MOVEM	AREG, TEMP_1
MOVER	AREG, C	MOVER	AREG, C
MULT	AREG, D	MULT	AREG, D
ADD	AREG, TEMP_3	ADD	AREG, TEMP_1

Fig. 6.17 Illustration for temporary location usage

6.3.2 Intermediate Codes for Expressions

Postfix strings

In the postfix notation, each operator appears immediately after its last operand. Thus, a binary operator op_i appears after its second operand. If any of its operands is itself an expression involving an operator op_j, op_j must appear before op_i. Thus operators can be evaluated in the order in which they appear in the string.

Example 6.20 Consider the following strings:

$$\text{Source string : } \vdash \mathtt{a} \overset{\boxed{2}}{+} \mathtt{b} \overset{\boxed{1}}{*} \mathtt{c} \overset{\boxed{5}}{+} \mathtt{d} \overset{\boxed{4}}{*} \mathtt{e} \overset{\boxed{3}}{\uparrow} \mathtt{f} \dashv \qquad (6.6)$$

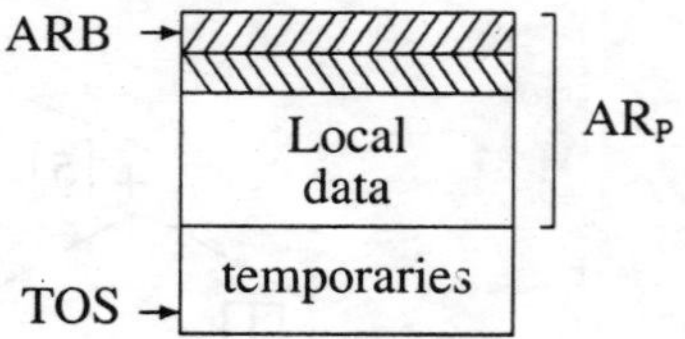

Fig. 6.18 Stack of temporaries in ARp

Postfix string : ⊢a b c * [1] + [2] d e f ↑ [3] * [4] + [5] ⊣

The numbers appearing over the operators indicate their evaluation order. The second operand of the operator '+' marked [2] in the source string is the expression `b*c`. Hence its operands `b`, `c` and its operator '*' appear before '+' in the postfix string.

The postfix string is a popular intermediate code in non-optimizing compilers due to ease of generation and use. We perform code generation from the postfix string using a stack of operand descriptors. Operand descriptors are pushed on the stack as operands appear in the string. When an operator with arity k appears in the string, k descriptors are popped off the stack. A descriptor for the partial result generated by the operator is now pushed on the stack. Thus in Ex. 6.20, the operand stack would contain descriptors for `a` , `b` and `c` when '*' is encountered. The stack contains the descriptors for `a` and the partial result `b*c` when '+' is encountered.

Conversion from infix to postfix is performed using a slight modification of Algorithm 3.4. Each stack entry simply contains an operator. Operands appearing in the source string are copied into the postfix string straightaway. The TOS operator is popped into the postfix string if TOS operator ·> current operator.

Triples and quadruples

A *triple* is a representation of an elementary operation in the form of a pseudo-machine instruction

Operator	*Operand 1*	*Operand 2*

Triples are numbered in some convenient manner. Each operand of a triple is either a variable/constant or the result of some evaluation represented by another triple. In the latter case, the operand field contains that triple's number. Conversion of an infix string into triples can be achieved by a slight modification of Algorithm 3.4.

Example 6.21 Figure 6.19 contains the triples for the expression string (6.6). [1] in the operand field of triple 2 indicates that the operand is the value of `b*c` represented by triple number 1.

	operator	*operand 1*	*operand 2*
1	*	b	c
2	+	[1]	a
3	↑	e	f
4	*	d	[3]
5	+	[2]	[4]

Fig. 6.19 Triples for string 6.6

A program representation called *indirect triples* is useful in optimizing compilers. In this representation, a table is built to contain all distinct triples in the program. A program statement is represented as a list of triple numbers. This arrangement is useful to detect the occurrences of identical expressions in a program. For efficiency reasons, a hash organization can be used for the table of triples. The indirect triples representation provides memory economy. It also aids in certain forms of optimization, viz. common subexpression elimination.

Example 6.22 Figure 6.20 shows the indirect triples' representation for the program segment

```
z := a+b*c+d*e↑f;
y := x+b*c;
```

Use of `b*c` in both statements is reflected by the fact that triple number 1 appears in the list of triples for both statements. As we shall see in Section 6.5.2, this fact is used to advantage in local common subexpression elimination.

	operator	*operand 1*	*operand 2*
1	*	b	c
2	+	[1]	a
3	↑	e	f
4	*	d	[3]
5	+	[2]	[4]
6	+	x	[1]

triples' table

stmt no.	*triple nos.*
1	1,2,3,4,5
2	1,6

statement table

Fig. 6.20 Indirect triples

A *quadruple* represents an elementary evaluation in the following format:

Operator	*Operand 1*	*Operand 2*	*Result name*

Here, *result name* designates the result of the evaluation. It can be used as the operand of another quadruple. This is more convenient than using a number (as in the case of triples) to designate a subexpression.

	operator	*operand 1*	*operand 2*	*result name*
1	*	b	c	t_1
2	+	t_1	a	t_2
3	↑	e	f	t_3
4	*	d	t_3	t_4
5	+	t_2	t_4	t_5

Fig. 6.21 Quadruples

Example 6.23 Quadruples for the expression string (6.6) are shown in Fig. 6.21.

Note that $t_1, t_2, ... t_5$ in Fig. 6.21 are not temporary locations for holding partial results. They are result names. Some of these become temporary locations when common subexpression elimination is implemented. For example, if an expression `x+b*c` were also present in the program, then `b*c` may be a common subexpression. t_1 would then become a compiler generated temporary location. We discuss details of optimization by elimination of common subexpressions in Section 6.5.2.

Expression trees

We have so far assumed that operators are evaluated in the order determined by a bottom up parser. This evaluation order may not lead to the most efficient code for an expression. Hence a compiler back end must analyse an expression to find the best evaluation order for its operators. An *expression tree* is an abstract syntax tree (see Section 3.2) which depicts the structure of an expression. This representation simplifies the analysis of an expression to determine the best evaluation order.

Example 6.24 Figure 6.22 shows two alternative codes to evaluate the expression `(a+b)/(c+d)`. The code in part (b) uses fewer MOVER/MOVEM instructions. It is obtained by deviating from the evaluation order determined by a bottom up parser.

```
MOVER   AREG, A
ADD     AREG, B
MOVEM   AREG, TEMP_1
MOVER   AREG, C
ADD     AREG, D
MOVEM   AREG, TEMP_2
MOVER   AREG, TEMP_1
DIV     AREG, TEMP_2
```

(a)

```
MOVER   AREG, C
ADD     AREG, D
MOVEM   AREG, TEMP_1
MOVER   AREG, A
ADD     AREG, B
DIV     AREG, TEMP_1
```

(b)

Fig. 6.22 Alternative codes for `(a+b)/(c+d)`

A two step procedure is used to determine the best evaluation order for the operations in an expression. The first step associates a *register requirement label* (RR label) with each node in the expression. It indicates the number of CPU registers required to evaluate the subtree rooted at the node without moving a partial result to memory. Labelling is performed in a bottom up pass of the expression tree. The second step, which consists of a top down pass, analyses the RR labels of the child nodes of a node to determine the order in which they should be evaluated.

Algorithm 6.1 (Evaluation order for operators)

1. Visit all nodes in an expression tree in post order (i.e., such that a node is visited *after* all its children).

   For each node n_i

   (a) If n_i is a leaf node then
          if n_i is the left operand of its parent then RR(n_i) := 1;
             else RR(n_i) := 0;

   (b) If n_i is not a leaf node then
          If RR($l\_child_{n_i}$) $\neq$ RR($r\_child_{n_i}$) then
             RR(n_i) := max (RR($r\_child_{n_i}$), RR($l\_child_{n_i}$));
          else RR(n_i) := RR($l\_child_{n_i}$) + 1;

2. Perform the procedure call *evaluation_order* (*root*) (See Fig. 6.23), which prints a postfix form of the source string in which operators appear in the desired evaluation order.

```
procedure evaluation_order (node);
   if node is not a leaf node then
      if RR(l_child_node) ≤ RR(r_child_node) then
         evaluation_order (r_child_node);
         evaluation_order (l_child_node);
      else
         evaluation_order (l_child_node);
         evaluation_order (r_child_node);
   print node;
end evaluation_order;
```

Fig. 6.23 Procedure *evaluation_order*

Let RR=q for the root node. This implies that the evaluation order can evaluate the expression without moving any partial result(s) to memory if q CPU registers are available. It thus provides the most efficient way to evaluate the expression. When the number of available registers $< q$, some partial results have to be saved in memory. However, the evaluation order still leads to the most efficient code. The code generation algorithm is described in Dhamdhere (1997) and Aho, Sethi, Ullman (1986).

Example 6.25 Figure 6.24 shows the expression tree for the string `f+(x+y)*((a+b)/(c-d))`. The boxed numbers indicate operator positions in the source string. The RR label of each node is shown as the superscript of the operand or operator at that node. The evaluation order according to algorithm 6.1 is [6], [4], [5], [2], [3], [1]. This evaluation order is determined as follows: When *evaluation_order* is called with the root node, i.e. operator [1], as the parameter, it decides that the right child of the node should be evaluated before its left child since RR([3]) > RR(node for `f`). This leads to a recursive call with node [3] as the parameter. Here RR([5]) > RR([2]) leads to a recursive call with node [5] as the parameter. At node [5] also decision is made to visit its right child before its left child. This leads to the postfix string `cd-ab+/xy+*f+` in which operators appear in the evaluation order mentioned above.

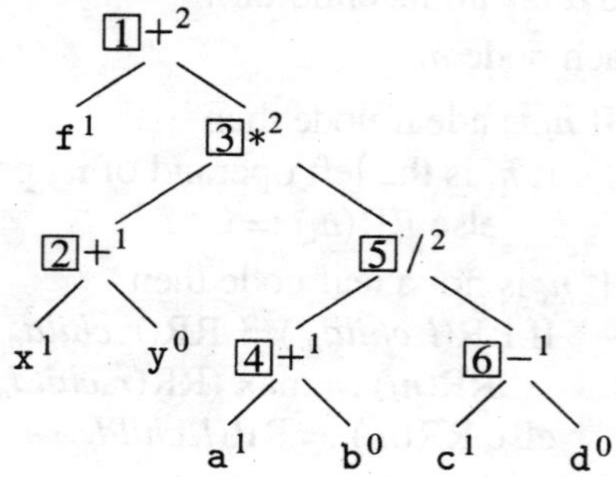

Fig. 6.24 Register requirement labels

EXERCISE 6.3.2

1. Modify the code generator of Fig. 6.13 to
   (a) Generate a postfix string as an IR,
   (b) Generate an expression tree as an IR.

6.4 COMPILATION OF CONTROL STRUCTURES

Definition 6.3 (Control structure) *The* control structure *of a programming language is the collection of language features which govern the sequencing of control through a program.*

The control structure of a PL consists of constructs for control transfer, conditional execution, iteration control and procedure calls. In this section we outline the fundamentals of control structure compilation and describe the compilation of procedure calls in some detail.

Control transfer, conditional execution and iterative constructs

Control transfers implemented through conditional and unconditional **goto**'s are the most primitive control structure. When the target language of a compiler is a machine language, compilation of control transfers is analogous to the assembly of forward or backward **goto**'s in an assembly language program. Hence similar techniques based around the use of a label table can be used. When the target language is an assembly language (as is mostly the case in practice), a statement **goto lab** can be simply compiled as the assembly statement `BC  ANY, LAB`. In the following, the target language of a compiler is assumed to be an assembly language.

Control structures like **if**, **for** or **while** cause significant semantic gap between the PL domain and the execution domain because the control transfers are implicit rather than explicit. This semantic gap is bridged in two steps. In the first step a control structure is mapped into an equivalent program containing explicit **goto**'s. Since the destination of a **goto** may not have a label in the source program, the compiler generates its own labels and puts them against the appropriate statements. Figure 6.25 illustrates programs equivalent to the **if** and **while** statements wherein the labels int_1, int_2 are introduced by the compiler for its own purposes. In the second step, these programs are translated into assembly programs. Note that the first step need not be carried out explicitly. It can be implied in the compilation action, as seen in Ex. 6.26.

if (e_1) **then**		**if** $(\overline{e_1})$ **then goto** int_1;
S_1;		S_1;
else	⇒	**goto** int_2;
S_2;		int_1: S_2;
S_3;		int_2: S_3;

(a)

while (e_2) **do**		int_3: **if** $(\overline{e_2})$ **then goto** int_4;
S_1;		S_1;
S_2;	⇒	S_2;
⋮		⋮
S_n;		S_n;
endwhile;		**goto** int_3;
<next statement>		int_4: *<next statement>*

(b)

Fig. 6.25 Control structure compilation

Example 6.26 Compilation of an **if** statement proceeds as follows (see Fig. 6.25): The compiler selects a pair of labels, viz. int_1 and int_2 in Fig. 6.25, to be associated with the **else** statement and the end of the **if** statement, respectively. Code is generated to evaluate the expression $\overline{e}_1$. This is followed by an instruction `BC  ..`, int_1 which transfers control to int_1 if $\overline{e}_1$ is *true*. Code is now generated for the statements in the **then** part, followed by an instruction `BC ANY`, int_2. int_1 is now associated with the first statement of the **else** clause. int_2 is similarly associated with the statement following the **if** statement. The resulting code is:

if (e_1) **then**		{ instructions for $\overline{e}_1$ }
		BC ..., int_1 {Branch if true}
S_1;		{ instructions for S_1 }
	⇒	BC ANY, int_2
else		
S_2;		int_1: { instructions for S_2 }
S_3;		int_2: { instructions for S_3 }

6.4.1 Function and Procedure Calls

A function call, viz. the call on fn_1 in the statement

```
x := fn_1(y,z)+b*c;
```

executes the body of `fn_1`, and returns its value to the calling program. In addition, the function call may also result in some side effects.

Definition 6.4 (Side effect) *A* side effect *of a function (procedure) call is a change in the value of a variable which is not local to the called function (procedure).*

A procedure call only achieves side effects, it does not return a value. Since all considerations excepting the return of a value are analogous for function and procedure calls, in the following only compilation of function calls are discussed.

Example 6.27 A side effect of the call `fn_1(y,z)` could be a change in the value of an actual parameter, viz. y or z, or of a nonlocal variable of `fn_1`.

While implementing a function call, the compiler must ensure the following:

1. Actual parameters are accessible in the called function.
2. The called function is able to produce side effects according to the rules of the PL.
3. Control is transferred to, and is returned from, the called function.
4. The function value is returned to the calling program.
5. All other aspects of execution of the calling programs are unaffected by the function call.

The compiler uses a set of features to implement function calls. These are described below.

1. *Parameter list:* The parameter list contains a *descriptor* for each actual parameter of the function call. The notation D_p is used to represent the descriptor corresponding to formal parameter p.
2. *Save area:* The called function saves the contents of CPU registers in this area before beginning its execution. The register contents are restored from this area before returning from the function.

3. *Calling conventions:* These are execution time assumptions shared by the called function and its caller(s). The conventions include the following:
   (a) How the parameter list is accessed
   (b) How the save area is accessed
   (c) How the transfers of control at call and return are implemented
   (d) How the function value is returned to the calling program.

   Most machine architectures provide special instructions to implement items (c) and (d).

Calling conventions

In a static memory allocation environment, the parameter list and the save area are allocated in the calling program. The calling conventions require the addresses of the function, the parameter list and the save area to be contained in specific CPU registers at the time of call. Let r_{par_list} denote the register containing the address of the parameter list and let $(d_{D_p})_{par\_list}$ denote the displacement of D_p in the parameter list. $(d_{D_p})_{par\_list}$ is computed while processing the formal parameter list of the function and is stored in the symbol table entry of p. During execution, D_p has the address $< r_{par\_list} > + (d_{D_p})_{par\_list}$. Hence every reference to p in the function body is compiled using this address. At return, the function value may be returned in a CPU register or in a memory location.

In a dynamic memory allocation environment, the calling program constructs the parameter list and the save area on the stack. These become a part of the called function's AR when its execution is initiated. Start of the parameter list has a known displacement d_{par_list} in the AR. For every formal parameter p, the displacement of D_p in the AR, denoted as $(d_{D_p})_{AR}$, is computed and stored in the symbol table entry of p. During execution, D_p has the address $<ARB> + (d_{D_p})_{AR}$. Ex. 6.28 illustrates calling conventions in the static and dynamic allocation environments.

Example 6.28 Figure 6.26 illustrates the calling conventions used in IBM mainframe systems to implement a call on function `fn_1` with the formal parameters `a` and `b`. The use of registers can be summarized as follows:

Register no.	Purpose
0	Function value
1	Address of parameter list
13	Address of save area
14	Return address
15	Address of function

Figure 6.27 illustrates a simplified version of the calling conventions used in a dynamic memory allocation environment. The calling program constructs the parameter list on the stack before invoking the function. At call, ARB is set to point at a location prior to the parameter list. Thus the parameter list is accessible as part of the function's AR. Register contents are now saved in the save area. Before returning, the function

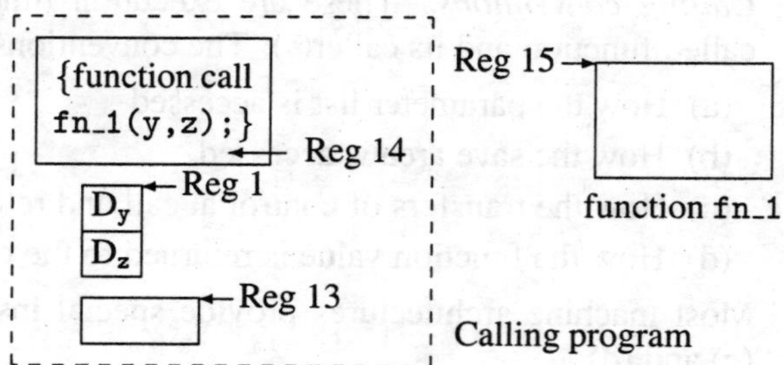

Fig. 6.26 Calling conventions in static memory allocation

value is stored in the AR. At return, TOS is set to <ARB>+2. Thus, the function value is available at the top of the run-time stack. (The stack locations allocated to the static and dynamic pointers would be wasted on return from the function. To avoid this, a practical compiler would put these pointers *after* the function value in the AR format.)

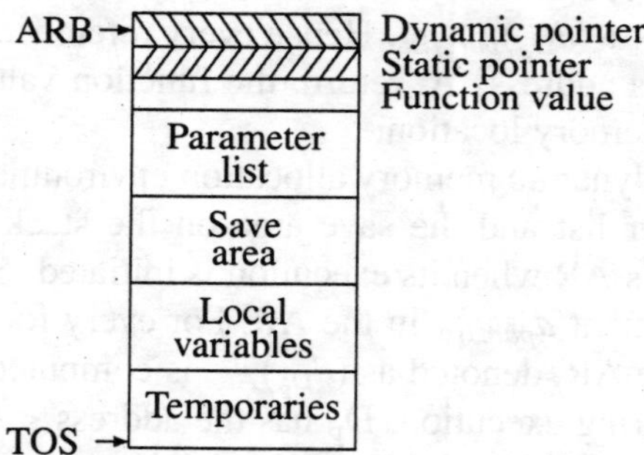

Fig. 6.27 Calling conventions in dynamic memory allocation

Parameter passing mechanisms

Language rules for parameter passing define the semantics of parameter usage inside a function, thereby defining the kind of side effects a function can produce on its actual parameters. The side effect characteristics and the execution efficiency of common parameter passing mechanisms are briefly described.

Call by value

In this mechanism, values of actual parameters are passed to the called function. These values are assigned to the corresponding formal parameters. Note that the passing of values only takes place in one direction—from the calling program to the called function. If a function changes the value of a formal parameter, the change is not reflected on the corresponding actual parameter. Thus a function cannot produce any side effects on its parameters.

Call by value is commonly used for built-in functions of the language. Its main advantage is its simplicity. A called function may allocate memory to a formal parameter and copy the value of the actual parameter into this location at every call. Thus a formal parameter appears like an initialized local variable, hence the compiler can treat it as if it were a local variable. This simplifies compilation considerably. This mechanism is very efficient if parameters are scalar variables.

Call by value-result

This mechanism extends the capabilities of the call by value mechanism by copying the values of formal parameters back into corresponding actual parameters at return. Thus, side effects are realized *at return*. This mechanism inherits the simplicity of the call by value mechanism but incurs higher overheads.

Call by reference

In this mechanism, the address of an actual parameter is passed to the called function. If the parameter is an expression, its value is computed and stored in a temporary location and the address of the temporary location is passed to the called function. If the parameter is an array element, its address is similarly computed at the time of call.

The parameter list is thus a list of addresses of actual parameters. At every access of a formal parameter in the function, the address of the corresponding actual parameter is obtained from the parameter list. This is used as the address of the formal parameter. The code generated to access the value of formal parameter p is

1. $r \leftarrow$ <ARB> + $(d_{\mathrm{D_p}})_{AR}$ or $r \leftarrow < r_{par\_list} > + (d_{\mathrm{D_p}})_{par\_list}$.
2. Access the value using the address contained in register r.

Thus each access to a parameter in the function body incurs the overheads of step 1. Step 2 produces instantaneous side effects if the address in r is used on the left hand side of an assignment. This mechanism is very popular because it has 'cleaner' semantics than call by value-result.

Example 6.29 Consider a function

```
function alpha (a,b : integer) : integer;
   z := a;
   i := i+1;
   b := a+5;
return;
end alpha;
```

where z, i are nonlocal variables of alpha. Let the parameters be passed by reference and let alpha be called as alpha(d[i],x). The address of d[i] is evaluated at the time of call and put into the parameter list. This address is used as the address of a in alpha. Note that a change in the value of i in the body of alpha does not change this address. The assignment `b := ..` changes the value of `x` instantaneously. This is important in case a nested function call accesses `x` as a nonlocal variable. (If parameters are passed by value-result, the side effect on `x` would be realized at return. Thus a nested function call would access the old value of `x` rather than its new value assigned in function `alpha`.)

Call by name

This parameter transmission mechanism has the same effect as if every occurrence of a formal parameter in the body of the called function is replaced by the name of the corresponding actual parameter.

Example 6.30 In the program of Ex. 6.29, name substitution implies replacement of `a` by `d[i]` in the body of `alpha` during the execution of `alpha`. Thus the call `alpha (d[i],x)` has the same effect as execution of the statements

```
z := d[i];
i := i+1;
x := d[i]+5;
```

Apart from achieving instantaneous side effects, call by name has the implication of changing its actual parameter corresponding to a formal parameter *during* the execution of a function, e.g. formal parameter `a` in the above code corresponds to two different elements of `d` at different times in the execution of `alpha`.

Call by name is implemented as follows: Each parameter descriptor in the parameter list is the address of a routine which computes the address of the corresponding actual parameter. The code generated for every access of formal parameter `p` in the function body is

1. $r \leftarrow <\text{ARB}> + (d_{D_p})_{AR}$ or $r \leftarrow <r_{par\_list}> + (d_{D_p})_{par\_list}$.
2. Call the function whose address is contained in r.
3. Use the address returned by the function to access `p`.

As seen in Ex. 6.30, the actual parameter corresponding to a formal parameter can change dynamically during the execution of a function. This makes the call by name mechanism immensely powerful. However, the high overheads of step 2 in the code make it less attractive in practice.

Most languages use call by value for built-in functions. C also uses it for programmer defined functions. Pascal permits a programmer to choose between call by value and call by reference. Fortran and PL/I use call by reference only. Ada leaves the choice between call by value-result and call by reference to the compiler writer. Algol-60 used call by value and call by name.

EXERCISE 6.4

1. Many block structured languages permit nonlocal `goto`'s. Comment on the compilation of such **goto**'s. (Hint: Think of memory deallocation.)

2. Most PLs forbid control transfers into the iteration control constructs, e.g. goto's to statements situated in **for** loops. Devise a scheme to detect such control structure violations.
3. Compare and contrast the following parameter passing mechanisms in terms of execution efficiency and power to produce side effects.
   (a) call by value-result
   (b) call by reference
   (c) call by name.
4. What are the results produced by the following program for the different parameter passing mechanisms discussed in this section?

```
a : array[1..20] of real;      procedure sub_1(x,y,z,w);
k := 7;                        x, y : integer;
i := 11;                       y := x;
a[11] := 0.0;                  x := x + 1;
a[12] := -0.5;                 z := w;
sub_1(i,k,a[i],i+k);           return;
print k,i,a[i],a[k];           end;
```

5. A compiler uses a stack to compile nested control structures in a program. Each entry in the stack indicates information about one control structure. This information is used for error detection and code generation. An entry for a control structure is pushed/popped when the start/end of the control structure is encountered during compilation.
   Design a scheme to compile **if** and **for** statements using this approach. (Hint: see Ex. 6.26.)
6. Study the **case** control structure of Pascal and its generated code. Comment on how the code differs from nested **if** statements. Design a code generation model for the **case** statement.

6.5 CODE OPTIMIZATION

Code optimization aims at improving the execution efficiency of a program. This is achieved in two ways:

1. Redundancies in a program are eliminated.
2. Computations in a program are rearranged or rewritten to make it execute efficiently.

It is axiomatic that code optimization must not change the meaning of a program. Two points concerning the scope of optimization should also be noted. First, optimization seeks to improve a program rather than the algorithm used in a program. Thus replacement of an algorithm by a more efficient algorithm is beyond the scope of optimization. Second, efficient code generation for a specific target machine (e.g. by fully exploiting its instruction set) is also beyond its scope; it belongs in the back end of a compiler. The optimization techniques are thus independent of both the PL and the target machine.

Figure 6.28 contains a schematic of an optimizing compiler. It differs from the schematic in Fig. 1.12 in the presence of the optimization phase. The front end generates an IR which could consist of triples, quadruples or ASTs. The optimization phase transforms this to achieve optimization. The transformed IR is input to the back end.

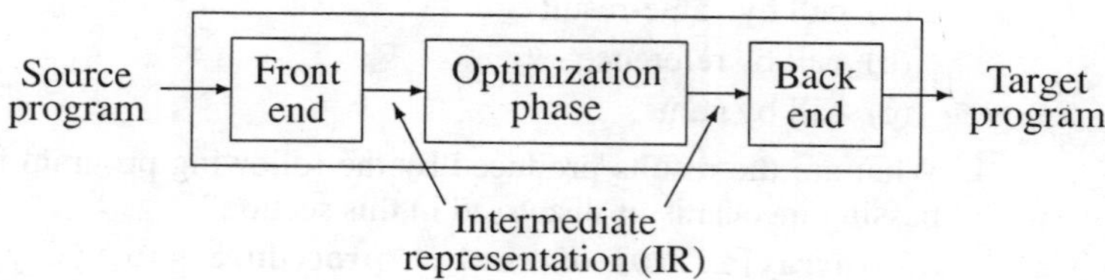

Fig. 6.28 Schematic of an optimising compiler

The structure of a program and the manner in which it manipulates its data provide vital clues for optimization. The compiler analyses a program to collect information concerning these aspects. The cost and benefits of optimization depend on how exhaustively a program is analysed. Experience with the Fortran 'H' optimizing compiler for the IBM/360 system (Lowry, Medlock, 1969) gives a quantitative feel for the cost and benefits of code optimization. The compiler was found to consume 40 percent extra compilation time due to optimization. The optimized program occupied 25 percent less storage and executed three times as fast as the unoptimized program.

6.5.1 Optimizing Transformations

An *optimizing transformation* is a rule for rewriting a segment of a program to improve its execution efficiency without affecting its meaning. Optimizing transformations are classified into *local* and *global* transformations depending on whether they are applied over small segments of a program consisting of a few source statements, or over larger segments consisting of loops or function bodies. The reason for this distinction is the difference in the costs and benefits of the optimizing transformations. A few optimizing transformations commonly used in compilers are discussed below.

Compile time evaluation

Execution efficiency can be improved by performing certain actions specified in a program during compilation itself. This eliminates the need to perform them during execution of the program, thereby reducing the execution time of the program. *Constant folding* is the main optimization of this kind. When all operands in an operation are constants, the operation can be performed at compilation time. The result of the operation, also a constant, can replace the original evaluation in the program. Thus, an assignment a := 3.14157/2 can be replaced by a := 1.570785, thereby eliminating a division operation. An instance of compile time evaluation can be found in array address arithmetic. The products $(\Pi_{j=1}^{i-1} range_j) \times k$ can be evaluated at compilation time (see Section 6.2.3) if $range_j$ $\forall j$ and k are constants. This avoids evaluation of these products while executing every array reference.

Elimination of common subexpressions

Common subexpressions are occurrences of expressions yielding the same value. (Such expressions are called *equivalent expressions.*) Let CS_i designate a set of common subexpressions. It is possible to eliminate an occurrence $e_j \in \mathrm{CS}_i$ if, no matter how the evaluation of e_j is reached during the execution of the program, the value of some $e_k \in \mathrm{CS}_i$ would have been already computed. Provision is made to save this value and use it at the place of occurrence of e_j.

Example 6.31

```
                         t := b*c;
a := b*c                 a := t;
- - -           ⇒        - - -
x := b*c+5.2;            x := t+5.2;
```

Here CS_i contains the two occurrences of `b*c`. The second occurrence of `b*c` can be eliminated because the first occurrence of `b*c` is always evaluated before the second occurrence is reached during execution of the program. The value computed at the first occurrence is saved in `t`. This value is used in the assignment to `x`.

This optimization is implemented as follows: First, expressions which yield the same value are identified. Many compilers simplify this task by restricting its scope to congruent, i.e. identical, subexpressions. These can be easily identified using triples or quadruples (see indirect triples, Section 6.3.2). Their equivalence is determined by considering whether their operands have the same values in all occurrences. Occurrences of the subexpression which satisfy the criterion mentioned earlier for expressions e_j can be eliminated. Some compilers also use rules of algebraic equivalence in common subexpression elimination. In the following program:

```
..:= b*c ..
d := b;
..:= d*c..
```

`d*c` is a common subexpression since `d` has the same value as `b`. Use of algebraic equivalence improves the effectiveness of optimization. However, it also increases the cost of optimization.

Dead code elimination

Code which can be omitted from a program without affecting its results is called *dead code*. Dead code is detected by checking whether the value assigned in an assignment statement is used anywhere in the program.

Example 6.32 An assignment x := <*exp*> constitutes dead code if the value assigned to x is not used in the program, no matter how control flows after executing this assignment. Note that <*exp*> constitutes dead code only if its execution does not produce side effects, i.e. only if it does not contain function or procedure calls.

Frequency reduction

Execution time of a program can be reduced by moving code from a part of a program which is executed very frequently to another part of the program which is executed fewer times. For example, the transformation of *loop optimization* moves loop invariant code out of a loop and places it prior to loop entry.

Example 6.33

```
                              x := 25*a;
for i := 1 to 100 do          for i := 1 to 100 do
begin                         begin
   z := i;              ⇒        z := i;
   x := 25*a;                    y := x+z;
   y := x+z;                  end;
end;
```

Here x := 25*a; is loop invariant. Hence in the optimized program it is computed only once before entering the **for** loop. y := x+z; is not loop invariant. Hence it cannot be subjected to frequency reduction.

Strength reduction

The strength reduction optimization replaces the occurrence of a time consuming operation (a 'high strength' operation) by an occurrence of a faster operation (a 'low strength' operation), e.g. replacement of a multiplication by an addition.

Example 6.34 In Fig. 6.29, the 'high strength' operator '*' in i*5 occurring inside the loop is replaced by a low strength operator '+' in itemp+5.

```
                              itemp := 5;
for i := 1 to 10 do           for i := 1 to 10 do
begin                         begin
   - - -                         - - -
   k := i*5;                     k := itemp;
   - - -                ⇒        - - -
                                 itemp := itemp+5;
end;                          end;
```

Fig. 6.29 Strength reduction

Strength reduction is very important for array accesses occurring within program loops. For example, an array reference a[i,j] within a Pascal loop gives rise to the high strength computation `i*`n in the address arithmetic, where n is the number of rows in the array (see Section 6.2.3). Strength of `i*`n can be reduced as in Fig. 6.29. Note that strength reduction optimization is not performed on operations involving floating point operands because finite precision of floating point arithmetic cannot guarantee equivalence of results after strength reduction.

Local and global optimization

Optimization of a program is structured into the following two phases:

1. *Local optimization:* The optimizing transformations are applied over small segments of a program consisting of a few statements,
2. *Global optimization:* The optimizing transformations are applied over a program unit, i.e. over a function or a procedure.

Local optimization is a preparatory phase for global optimization. It can be performed by the front end while converting a source program into the IR (see Fig. 6.36). Local optimization also simplifies certain aspects of global optimization. For example, let a program segment seg_i contain n occurrences of an expression `a+b`. After local common subexpression elimination has been performed over seg_i, global optimization only needs to consider elimination of the first occurrence of `a+b`—other occurrences of `a+b` are either not redundant, or would have been already eliminated!

6.5.2 Local Optimization

Local optimization provides limited benefits at a low cost. The scope of local optimization is a *basic block* which is an 'essentially sequential' segment in the source program. The cost of local optimization is low because the sequential nature of the basic block simplifies the analysis needed for optimization. The benefits are limited because certain optimizations, e.g. loop optimization, are beyond the scope of local optimization.

Definition 6.5 (Basic block) A basic block *is a sequence of program statements* $(s_1, s_2, \ldots, s_n)$ *such that only* s_n *can be a transfer of control statement and only* s_1 *can be the destination of a transfer of control statement.*

A basic block b is a program segment with a single entry point. If control reaches statement s_1 during program execution, all statements $s_1, s_2, \ldots, s_n$ will be executed. The 'essentially sequential' nature of a basic block simplifies optimization. Example 6.35 discusses this aspect. We shall also see this aspect while discussing the value numbering technique to perform local optimization.

Example 6.35 Consider the following program segment:

```
                a := x*y;              t := x*y;
                - - -                  a := t;
                            ⇒          - - -
                b := x*y;              b := t;
      labi :    c := x*y;    labi :    c := x*y;
```

where lab_i is a label. Local optimization identifies two basic blocks in the program. The first block extends up to the statement `b := x*y;`. Its optimization leads to elimination of the second occurrence of `x*y`. The third occurrence is not eliminated because it belongs to a different basic block. If the label lab_i did not exist, the entire program segment would constitute a single basic block and the third occurrence `x*y` can also be eliminated during local optimization.

Value numbers

Value numbers provide a simple means to determine if two occurrences of an expression in a basic block are equivalent. The value numbering technique is applied on the fly while identifying basic blocks in a source program. A value number $vn_{\texttt{alpha}}$ is associated with variable `alpha`. It identifies the last assignment to `alpha` processed so far. Thus, the value number of variable `alpha` changes on processing an assignment `alpha := ....` Now two expressions e_i and e_j are equivalent if they are congruent and their operands have the same value numbers.

For simplicity all statements of a basic block are numbered in some convenient manner. If statement n, the current statement being processed, is an assignment to `alpha`, we set $vn_{\texttt{alpha}}$ to n. A new field is added to each symbol table entry to hold the value number of a variable. The IC for a basic block is a list of quadruples stored in a tabular form. Each operand field in a quadruple holds the pair (*operand, value number*). A boolean flag *save* is associated with each quadruple to indicate whether its value should be saved for use elsewhere in the program. The flag is initialized to *false* in every new quadruple entered in the table.

Let expression e be a subexpression of e', the expression being compiled. While forming a quadruple for e, the value numbers of its operands are copied from the symbol table. The new quadruple is now compared with all existing quadruples in the IC. Existence of a matching quadruple q_i in the IC implies that the current occurrence of expression e has the same value as a previous occurrence represented by quadruple q_i. If a match is found, the newly generated quadruple is not entered in the IC. Instead, the result name of q_i is used as an operand of e'. In effect, this occurrence of e is eliminated from the program. The result name of q_i should now become a compiler generated temporary variable. This requirement is noted by setting the *save* flag of q_i to *true*. During code generation, this flag is checked to see if the value of q_i needs to be saved in a temporary location.

Example 6.36 Figure 6.30 shows the symbol table and the quadruples table during local optimization of the following program:

Symbol table

Symbol	...	*Value number*
y		0
x		15
g		14
z		0
d		5
w		0

Quadruples table

	Operator	*Operand 1*		*Operand 2*		*Result name*	*Use flag*
		Operand	*Value no.*	*Operand*	*Value no.*		
20	:=	g	–	25.2	–	t_{20}	*f*
21	+	z	0	2	–	t_{21}	*f*
22	:=	x	0	t_{21}	–	t_{22}	*f*
23	*	x	15	y	0	t_{23}	*ft*
24	+	t_{23}	–	d	5	t_{24}	*f*
⋮							
57	:=	w	0	t_{23}	–	t_{57}	*f*

Fig. 6.30 Local optimization using value numbering

stmt no.	statement
14	`g := 25.2;`
15	`x := z+2;`
16	`h := x*y+d;`
..	...
34	`w := x*y;`

Local optimization proceeds as follows: All variables are assumed to have the value numbers '0' to start with. Processing of Statements 14 and 15 leads to generation of quadruples numbered 20–22 shown in the table. Value numbers of g, x and y at this stage are 14, 15 and 0, respectively (see the symbol table). Quadruple for x*y is generated next, and the value numbers of x and y are copied from the symbol table. This quadruple is assigned the result name t_{23}, and its *save* flag is set to *false*. This quadruple is entered in entry number 23 of the quadruple table. When the statement w := x*y (i.e., Statement 34) is processed, the quadruple for x*y is formed using the value numbers found in the symbol table entries of x and y. Since these are still 15 and 0, the new quadruple is identical with quadruple 23 in the table. Hence it is not entered in the table. Instead, the *save* flag of quadruple 23 is set to *true*. The only quadruple generated for this statement is therefore the assignment to w (quadruple number 57). While generating code for quadruple 23, its save flag indicates that the value of expression x*y needs to be saved in a temporary location for later use. t_{23} can itself become the name of this temporary location.

This schematic can be easily extended to implement *constant propagation*, which is the substitution of a variable *var* occurring in a statement by a constant *const*, and constant folding. When an assignment of the form *var* := *const* is encountered, we enter *const* into a table of constants, say in entry *n*, and associate the value number '–*n*' with *var*. Constant propagation and folding is implemented while generating a quadruple if each operand is either a constant or has a negative value number.

Example 6.37 In the following program, variable a is given a negative value number, say '−10', on processing the first statement.

```
a := 27.3;            a := 27.3;
- - -         ⇒       - - -
b := a*3.0;           b := 81.9;
```

This leads to the possibility of constant propagation and folding in the third statement. The value of a, viz. '27.3', is obtained from the 10th entry of constants table. Its multiplication with 3.0 yields 81.9. This value is treated as a new constant and a quadruple for b := 81.9 is now generated.

6.5.3 Global Optimization

Compared to local optimization, global optimization requires more analysis effort to establish the feasibility of an optimization. Consider global common subexpression elimination. If some expression x*y occurs in a set of basic blocks SB of program P, its occurrence in a block $b_j \in$ SB can be eliminated if the following two conditions are satisfied for every execution of P:

1. Basic block b_j is executed only after some block $b_k \in$ SB has been executed one or more times. (6.7)
2. No assignments to x or y have been executed after the last (or only) evaluation of x*y in block b_k.

Condition 1 ensures that x*y is evaluated before execution reaches block b_j, while condition 2 ensures that the evaluated value is equivalent to the value of x*y in block b_j. The optimization is realized by saving the value of x*y in a temporary location in all blocks b_k which satisfy condition 1.

To ensure that *every possible execution* of program P satisfies conditions 1 and 2 of (6.7), the program is analysed using the techniques of *control flow analysis* and *data flow analysis*. Note the emphasis on the words 'every possible execution'. This requirement is introduced to ensure that the meaning of the program is unaffected by the optimization. In this section we use the word 'always' to imply 'in every possible evaluation'.

6.5.3.1 Program Representation

A program is represented in the form of a *program flow graph.*

Definition 6.6 (Program flow graph (PFG))

A program flow graph *for a program P is a directed graph* $G_P = (N, E, n_0)$ *where*

N	:	*set of basic blocks in P*
E	:	*set of directed edges* (b_i, b_j) *indicating the possibility of control flow from the last statement of* b_i *(the* source node*) to the first statement of* b_j *(the* destination node*)*
n_0	:	*start node of P.*

A basic block, which is a sequence of statements $s_1, s_2, \ldots s_n$, is visualized as a sequence of *program points* $p_1, p_2, \ldots p_n$ such that a statement s_i is said to exist at program point p_i. This notion is used to differentiate between different occurrences of identical statements. For example, an occurrence of *e* at program point p_i is distinct from the occurrence of *e* at program point p_j.

6.5.3.2 Control and Data Flow Analysis

The techniques of control and data flow analysis are together used to determine whether the Conditions governing an optimizing transformation are satisfied in a program, e.g. conditions 1 and 2 of (6.7).

Control flow analysis

Control flow analysis analyses a program to collect information concerning its structure, e.g. presence and nesting of loops in the program. Information concerning program structure is used to answer specific questions of interest, e.g. condition 1 of (6.7). The control flow concepts of interest are:

1. *Predecessors and successors:* If $(b_i, b_j) \in E$, b_i is a *predecessor* of b_j and b_j is a *successor* of b_i.

2. *Paths:* A path is a sequence of edges such that the destination node of one edge is the source node of the following edge.

3. *Ancestors and descendants:* If a path exists from b_i to b_j, b_i is an ancestor of b_j and b_j is a descendant of b_i.

4. *Dominators and post-dominators:* Block b_i is a dominator of block b_j if every path from n_0 to b_j passes through b_i. b_i is a post-dominator of b_j if every path from b_j to an exit node passes through b_i.

Table 6.6 Data flow concepts

Data flow concept	*Optimization in which used*
Available expression	Common subexpression elimination
Live variable	Dead code elimination
Reaching definition	Constant and variable propagation

Control flow concetps can be used to answer certain questions in a straightforward manner, e.g. the question posed by condition 1 of (6.7). However, this incurs the overheads of control flow analysis for every expression in the program. It may sometimes be possible to reduce the overheads by restricting the scope of optimization. For example, only those expressions may be considered which occur in a block b_j and a dominator block b_k of b_j. Now condition 1 of (6.7) is automatically satisfied.

Data flow analysis

Data flow analysis techniques analyse the use of data in a program to collect information for the purpose of optimization. This information, called *data flow information*, is computed at the entry and exit of each basic block in G_P. It is used to decide whether an optimizing transformation (see Section 6.5.1) can be applied to a segment of code in the program.

Design of the global optimization phase begins with the identification of an appropriate *data flow concept* to support the application of each optimizing transformation. The data flow information concerning a program entity—for example a variable or an expression—is now a boolean value indicating whether the data flow concept is applicable to that entity. Table 6.6 contains a summary of important data flow concepts used in optimization. The first two data flow concepts are discussed in detail.

Available expressions

The transformation of global common subexpression elimination can be defined as follows: Consider a subexpression `x*y` occurring at program point p_i in basic block b_i. This occurrence can be eliminated if

1. Conditions 1 and 2 of (6.7) are satisfied at entry to b_i.
2. No assignments to `x` or `y` precede the occurrence of `x*y` in b_i.

The data flow concept of *available expressions* is used to implement common subexpression elimination. An expression e is *available* at program point p_i if a value equivalent to its value is always computed before program execution reaches p_i. Thus, the concept of available expressions captures the essence of Conditions 1 and 2 of (6.7). The availability of an expression at entry or exit of basic block b_i is computed using the following rules:

1. Expression e is available at the exit of b_i if

   (i) b_i contains an evaluation of e which is not followed by assignments to any operands of e, or
   (ii) the value of e is available at the entry to b_i and b_i does not contain assignments to any operands of e. (6.8)

2. Expression e is available at entry to b_i if it is available at the exit of each predecessor of b_i in G_P.

Available expressions is termed a *forward* data flow concept because availability at the exit of a node determines availability at the entry of its successor(s). It is an *all paths* concept because availability at entry of a basic block requires availability at the exit of all predecessors.

We use the boolean variables $Avail\_in_i$ and $Avail\_out_i$ to represent the availability of expression e at entry and exit of basic block b_i, respectively. Further, we associate the following boolean properties with block b_i to summarize the effect of computations situated in it:

$Eval_i$	:	'true' only if expression e is evaluated in b_i and none of its operands are modified following the evaluation
$Modify_i$	:	'true' only if some operand of e is modified in b_i.

$Eval_i$ and $Modify_i$ are determined solely by the computations situated in b_i. Hence they are called local properties of block b_i. $Avail\_in_i$ and $Avail\_out_i$ are 'global' properties which are computed using the following equations (see Eq. (6.8)):

$$Avail\_in_i = \Pi_{b_j \in pred(b_i)} Avail\_out_j \tag{6.9}$$

$$Avail\_out_i = Eval_i + Avail\_in_i \,.\, \neg Modify_i \tag{6.10}$$

where $\Pi_{b_j \in pred(b_i)}$ is the boolean 'and' operation over all predecessors of b_i. This operation ensures that $Avail\_in_i$ is true only if $Avail\_out$ is true for all predecessors of b_i. Equations (6.9) and (6.10) are called *data flow equations*.

It is to be noted that every basic block in G_P has a pair of equations analogous to (6.9)–(6.10). Thus, we need to solve a system of simultaneous equations to obtain the values of *Avail_in* and *Avail_out* for all basic blocks in G_P. Data flow analysis is the process of solving these equations. Iterative data flow analysis is a simple method which assigns some initial values to *Avail_in* and *Avail_out*, and iteratively recomputes them for all blocks according to Eqs. (6.9)–(6.10) until they converge onto consistent values.

The initial values are:

$$\begin{aligned} Avail\_in_i &= \mathit{true} \;\text{ if } b_i \in N - \{n_o\} \\ & \mathit{false} \;\text{ if } b_i = n_o \\ Avail\_out_i &= \mathit{true} \;\; \forall b_i \end{aligned}$$

After solving the system of equations (6.9)–(6.10) for all blocks, an evaluation of expression e can be eliminated from a block b_i if

1. $Avail\_in_i = true$, and
2. The evaluation of e in b_i is not preceded by an assignment to any of its operands.

Example 6.38 Available expression analysis for the PFG of Fig. 6.31 gives the following results:

`a*b` : *Avail_in* = *true* for blocks 2, 5, 6, 7, 8, 9
Avail_out = *true* for blocks 1, 2, 5, 6, 7, 8, 9, 10

`x+y` : *Avail_in* = *true* for blocks 6, 7, 8, 9
Avail_out = *true* for blocks 5, 6, 7, 8, 9

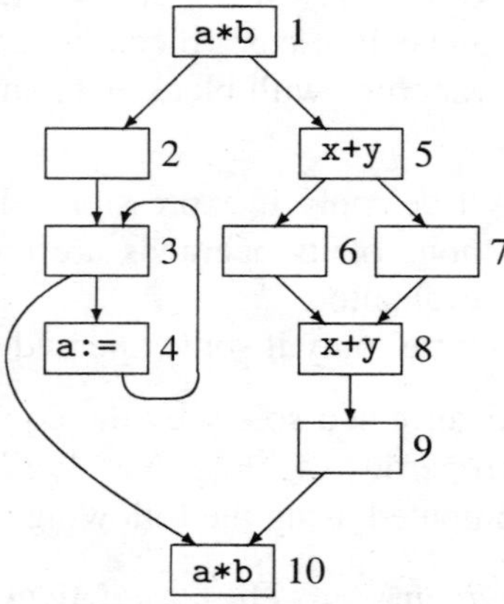

Fig. 6.31 A PFG

The values of *Avail_in* and *Avail_out* for `a*b` can be explained as follows: The assignment `a := ..` in block 4 makes $Avail\_out_4 = false$ (eq. (6.10)). This makes $Avail\_in_3 = false$ (eq. (6.9)), which makes $Avail\_out_3 = Avail\_in_{10} = false$. For `x*y`, $Avail\_in_1 = false$ makes $Avail\_out_1 = false$, which makes $Avail\_in = Avail\_out = false$ for blocks 2, 3, 4 and 10.

Live variables

A variable *var* is said to be *live* at a program point p_i in basic block b_i if the value contained in it at p_i is likely to be used during subsequent execution of the program. If *var* is not live at the program point which contains a definition *var* := ..., the value assigned to *var* by this definition is redundant in the program. Such a definition constitutes dead code which can be eliminated from the program without changing its meaning.

The liveness property of a variable can be determined as follows:

1. Variable v is live at the entry of b_i if

   (i) b_i contains a use of e which is not preceded by assignment(s) to v, or
   (ii) v is live at the exit of b_i and b_i does not contain assignment(s) to v.

2. v is live at exit of b_i if it is live at the entry of some successor of b_i in G_P.

Data flow information concerning live variables can be collected as follows:

$Live\_in_i$	:	*var* is live at entry of b_i
$Live\_out_i$	:	*var* is live at exit of b_i
Ref_i	:	*var* is referenced in b_i and no assignment of *var* precedes the reference
Def_i	:	An assignment to *var* exists in b_i

$$Live\_in_i = Ref_i + Live\_out_i \,.\, \neg Def_i \tag{6.11}$$

$$Live\_out_i = \Sigma_{b_j \in succ(b_i)} Live\_in_j \tag{6.12}$$

where $\Sigma_{b_j \in succ(b_i)}$ is the boolean 'or' operation over all successors of b_i.

Live variables is termed a *backward* data flow concept because availability at the entry of a block determines availability at the exit of its predecessor(s). It is an *any path* concept because liveness at the entry of one successor is sufficient to ensure liveness at the exit of a block. The data flow problem can be solved by iterative data flow analysis using the initializations $Live\_in_i = Live\_out_i = false \; \forall b_i$.

Example 6.39 In the PFG of Fig. 6.31, variable b is live at the entry of all blocks, a is live at the entry of all blocks excepting block 4 and variables x, y are live at the entry of blocks 1,5,6,7 and 8.

EXERCISE 6.5

1. Write a program to generate code from a table of quadruples (see Fig. 6.30).
2. Build a program flow graph for the following program:

```
z := 5;
w := z;
for i := 1 to 100 do
   x := a*b;
   y := c+d;
   if y < 0 then
      a := 25;
      f := c+d;
   else
      g := w;
      h := a*b+f;
      d := z+10;
```

```
end;
g := c+d;
print g,h,d,x,y;
```

Apply the following transformations to optimize the program:

(a) common subexpression elimination

(b) dead code elimination

(c) constant propagation

(d) frequency reduction.

3. Apply the data flow concepts of available expressions and live variables to the flow graph of the program in problem 2 and verify whether you obtain the same answers as in parts (a) and (b) of problem 2.
4. A definition def_i is an assignment of the form *var* := *<exp>*. def_i located at program point p_i is said to reach a program point p_j if the value assigned to *var* by def_i may be the value of *var* when program execution reaches p_j.

   Write the data flow equations to collect the information concerning reaching definitions. (*Hint:* Consider whether the data flow concept is a forward or backward concept and any path or all paths concept.)
5. Constant propagation is the substitution of a variable *var* by a constant $const_i$ in a statement. State the conditions under which constant propagation can be performed. (*Hint:* See problem 4.)
6. Loop invariant movement of an assignment *var* := *<exp>* (see Ex. 6.33) is performed if the following conditions are met:

   (a) *<exp>* is loop invariant.

   (b) The assignment is the only assignment to *var* inside the loop.

   (c) The assignment dominates all loop exist.

   (d) *var* is not live on entry to the loop.

   Discuss the need for each condition.

6.6 INTERPRETERS

In Section 1.2.2 we have seen that use of interpretation avoids the overheads of compilation. This is an advantage during program development, because a program may be modified very often—in fact, it may be modified between every two executions. However, interpretation is expensive in terms of CPU time, because each statement is subjected to the interpretation cycle. Hence, conventional wisdom warns against interpreting a program with large execution requirements. However, to make an informed decision in practice, we need a quantitative basis for a comparison of compilers and interpreters. We introduce the following notation for this purpose:

t_c	:	average compilation time per statement
t_e	:	average execution time per statement
t_i	:	average interpretation time per statement

Note that both compilers and interpreters analyse a source statement to determine its meaning. During compilation, analysis of a statement is followed by code generation, while during interpretation it is followed by actions which implement its meaning. Hence we could assume $t_c \cong t_i$. t_e, which is the execution time of the compiler generated code for a statement, can be several times smaller than t_c. Let us assume $t_c = 20.t_e$.

Consider a program P. Let $size_P$ and $stmts\_executed_P$ represent the number of statements in P and the number of statements executed in some execution of P, respectively. We use these parameters to compute the CPU time required to execute a program using compilation or interpretation. Example 6.40 illustrates how this can be done.

Example 6.40 Let $size_P = 200$. For a specific set of data, let program P execute as follows: 20 statements are executed for initialization purposes. This is followed by 10 iterations of a loop containing 8 statements, followed by the execution of 20 statements for printing the results. Thus, $stmts\_executed_P = 20 + 10 \times 8 + 20 = 120$. Thus,

Total execution time using the compilation model

$$= 200.t_c + 120.t_e$$
$$\cong 206.t_c.$$

Total execution time using the interpretation model

$$= 120.t_i$$
$$\cong 120.t_c.$$

Clearly, interpretation is beneficial in this case.

Use of interpreters

Use of interpreters is motivated by two reasons—efficiency in certain environments and simplicity. The findings of Ex. 6.40 concerning efficiency can be generalized as follows: It is better to use interpretation for a program P if P is modified between executions, and $stmts\_executed_P < size_P$. These conditions are satisfied during program development, hence interpretation should be preferred during program development. In all other situations, it is best to use compilation.

It is simpler to develop an interpreter than to develop a compiler because interpretation does not involve code generation (see Section 6.6.1). This simplicity makes interpretation more attractive in situations where programs or commands are not executed repeatedly. Hence interpretation is a popular choice for commands to an operating system or an editor. User interfaces of many software packages prefer interpretation for similar reasons.

6.6.1 Overview of Interpretation

In this section we discuss an interpretation schematic which implements the meaning of a statement without generating code for it. The interpreter consists of three main components:

1. *Symbol table:* The symbol table holds information concerning entities in the source program.
2. *Data store:* The data store contains values of the data items declared in the program being interpreted. The data store consists of a set of components $\{comp_i\}$. A component $comp_i$ is an array named $name_i$ containing elements of a distinct type $type_i$.
3. *Data manipulation routines:* A set of data manipulation routines exist. This set contains a routine for every legal data manipulation action in the source language.

On analysing a declaration statement, say a statement declaring an array `alpha` of type `typ`, the interpreter locates a component $comp_j$ of its data store, such that $type_j$ = `typ`. `alpha` is now mapped into a part of $name_j$ (this is 'memory allocation'). The memory mapping for `alpha` is remembered in its symbol table entry. An executable statement is analysed to identify the actions which constitute its meaning. For each action, the interpreter finds the appropriate data manipulation routine and invokes it with appropriate parameters. For example, the meaning of statement `a := b+c;` where `a`, `b`, `c` are of the same type can be implemented by executing the calls

```
add (b, c, result);
assign (a, result);
```

in the interpreter.

This schematic has two important advantages. First, the meaning of a source statement is implemented through execution of the interpreter routines rather than through code generation. This simplifies the interpreter. Second, avoiding generation of machine language instructions helps to make the interpreter portable. For example, if the interpreter is itself coded in a higher level programming language it can be ported to a new computer system with ease.

6.6.2 A Toy Interpreter

This section discusses the design and operation of an interpreter for Basic written in Pascal. The interpreter is itself a Pascal program (we will call this the *interpreter program*), which is compiled by a Pascal compiler. The data store of the interpreter consists of two large arrays named `rvar` and `ivar` which are used to store real and integer values respectively. Last few locations in the `rvar` and `ivar` arrays are used as stacks for expression evaluation with the help of the pointers `r_tos` and `i_tos` respectively. (Note that these stacks grow 'upwards' in the arrays.)

The interpreter program contains a set of data manipulation routines for use in expression evaluation (see Fig. 6.32)—one routine for each kind of legal subexpression in the language. A routine performs all subtasks involved in the evaluation of a subexpression, namely type compatibility checks, type conversion and evaluation of the subexpressions. Since the interpreter is a Pascal program, it can be ported to any computer system possessing a Pascal compiler.

```
program interpreter (source,output);
   type
      symentry = record
         symbol : array [1..10] of character;
         type : character;
         address : integer
         end;
   var
      symtab : array [1..100] of symentry;
      rvar : array [1..100] of real;
      ivar : array [1..100] of integer;
      r_tos : 1..100;
      i_tos : 1..100;
   procedure assignint (addr1 : integer; value : integer);
      begin
         ivar[addr1] := value;
      end;
   procedure add (sym1, sym2 : symentry);
      begin
      ...
      if (sym1.type = 'real' and sym2.type = 'int') then
         addrealint(sym1.address, sym2.address);
      ...
      end;
   procedure addrealint (addr1, addr2 : integer);
      begin
         rvar[r_tos] := rvar[addr1] + ivar[addr2]
      end;
   begin { Main Program }
      r_tos := 100;
      i_tos := 100;
      {Analyse a statement and call
       appropriate procedure}
   end.
```

Fig. 6.32 Basic interpreter written in Pascal

Example 6.41 Consider the basic program

```
real a, b
integer c
let c = 7
let b = 1.2
a = b+c
```

Figure 6.33 illustrates the symbol table for the program and the memory allocation for variables a, b and c. Each symbol table entry contains information about the type and memory allocation for a variable. The values 'real' and '8' in the symbol table entry of a indicate that a is allocated the word rvar [8].

symbol	*type*	*address*
a	real	8
b	real	13
c	int	5

Symbol table

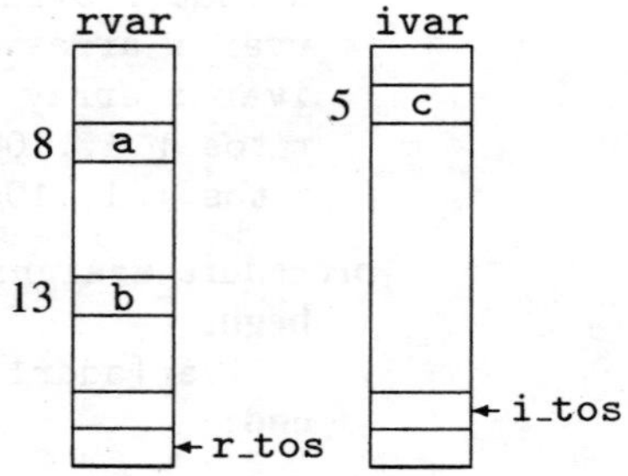

Fig. 6.33 Interpreter data structures

The operation of the interpreter can be explained as follows: The interpreter analyses a source statement to determine its meaning. It implements the meaning by invoking appropriate routines. Consider the assignment statement c = 7 in the Basic program, where both c and '7' are of type integer. The Pascal procedure assignint of Fig. 6.32 is invoked with two parameters. The first parameter is the address of c in ivar and the second parameter is the RHS value. Execution of procedure assignint effectively executes the Pascal statement

```
ivar [5] := 7;
```

Similarly, the assignment to b is executed as rvar [13] := 1.2; by a routine assignreal.

Interpretation of a = b+c proceeds as follows: The interpreter procedure add is called with the symbol table entries of b and c. add analyses the types of b and c and decides that procedure addrealint will have to be called to realize the addition. addrealint now executes a single Pascal statement which is equivalent to

```
rvar [r_tos] := rvar [13] + ivar [5];
```

Note that b+c involves a type conversion operation, which is performed implicitly by the above Pascal statement. In other words, while compiling the expression

```
rvar [addr1] + ivar [addr2]
```

in the interpreter program, the Pascal compiler would have made provision for type conversion of the second operand from integer to real. The interpreter simply arranges to execute this statement under the right conditions.

6.6.3 Pure and Impure Interpreters

The schematic of Fig. 6.34(a) is called a *pure* interpreter. The source program is retained in the source form all through its interpretation. This arrangement incurs substantial analysis overheads while interpreting a statement.

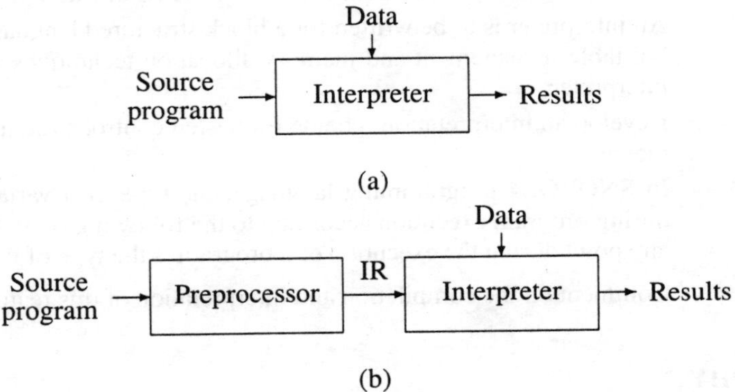

Fig. 6.34 Pure and impure interpreter

An *impure interpreter* performs some preliminary processing of the source program to reduce the analysis overheads during interpretation. Figure 6.34(b) contains a schematic of impure interpretation. The preprocessor converts the program to an intermediate representation (IR) which is used during interpretation. This speeds up interpretation as the code component of the IR, i.e. the IC, can be analysed more efficiently than the source form of the program. However, use of IR also implies that the entire program has to be preprocessed after any modification. This involves fixed overheads at the start of interpretation.

Example 6.42 Postfix notation is a popular intermediate code for interpreters. The intermediate code for a source string `a+b*c` could look like the following:

S #17	S #4	S #29	*	+

where each IC unit resembles a token (see Section 1.3.1.1).

IC of Ex. 6.42 eliminates most of the analysis during interpretation excepting type analysis to determine the need for type conversion. Even this can be eliminated if the preprocessor performs type analysis before generating IC.

Example 6.43 The preprocessor of an interpreter performs type analysis to generate following IC for the expression `a+b*c`, where `a`, `b` are of type real and `c` is of type integer:

S #17	S #4	S #29	$t_{i \to r}$	$*_r$	$+_r$

where the unary operator $t_{i \to r}$ indicates type conversion of an operand (in this case, c) from 'integer' to 'real'. The arithmetic operators are also type specific now.Thus '$*_r$' indicates multiplication in the 'real' representation. This eliminates most analysis during interpretation.

EXERCISE 6.6

1. Modify the interpreter of Ex. 6.41 to use the IC of Ex. 6.43.
2. An interpreter is to be written for a block structured language. Comment on the symbol table management and memory allocation techniques which can be used by the interpreter.
3. Develop an interpretation scheme for nested control structures, e.g. nested `for` statements.
4. In SNOBOL4 programming language, the type of a variable changes dynamically during program execution according to the following rule: The type of a variable x at any point during the execution of a program is the type of the last value assigned to it.

   Comment on the compilation and interpretation of this feature of SNOBOL4.

BIBLIOGRAPHY

Elson (1973), Tennent (1981), Pratt (1983) and Maclennan (1983) have discussed different aspects of the design of programming languages and their influence on programming ease, compilation strategies and execution efficiencies. It is recommended that the reader should acquaint himself with the material covered in one of these texts before reading specialized material.

Gries (1971), Weingarten (1973) and Bauer and Eickel (1974) are important early books on compilers. Later books include those by Lewis, Rosenkrantz and Stearns (1976), Barrett and Couch (1977), Dhamdhere (1997), Tremblay and Sorenson (1984), Aho, Sethi and Ullman (1986), Fischer and LeBlanc (1988), and Watson (1989).

Good discussions on storage allocation can be found in books by Gries (1971) and Dhamdhere (1997). Expression compilation is discussed by Hopgood (1967), Rohl (1975), Dhamdhere (1997) and Aho, Sethi and Ullman (1986). Compilation of control structures and code optimization is discussed by Dhamdhere (1997) and Aho, Sethi and Ullman (1986).

(a) Programming languages

1. Elson, M. (1973): *Concepts of Programming Languages*, Science Research Associates, Chicago.
2. Maclennan, B.J. (1983): *Principles of Programming Languages*, Holt, Rinehart & Winston, New York.
3. Pratt, T.W. (1983): *Programming Languages – Design and Implementation*, Prentice-Hall, Englewood Cliffs.
4. Tennent, R.D. (1981): *Principles of Programming Languages*, Prentice-Hall, Englewood Cliffs.

(b) Computer architecture and compilers

1. Doran, R.W. (1979): *Computer Architecture – A Structured Approach*, Academic Press, London.
2. Organick, E.I. (1973): *Computer System Architecture*, Academic Press, London.
3. Wulf, W.A. (1981): "Compilers and computer architecture," *Computer*, **14** (7), 41-48.

(c) Compilers, general

1. Aho, A.V., R. Sethi and J.D. Ullman (1986) : *Compilers – Principles, Techniques and Tools*, Addison-Wesley, Reading.
2. Barrett, W.A. and J.D. Couch (1977): *Compiler Construction*, Science Research Associates, Pennsylvania.
3. Bauer, F.L. and J. Eickel (1974): *Compiler Construction : An Advanced Course*, Springer-Verlag, Berlin.
4. Calingaert, P. (1979): *Assemblers, Compilers and Program Translation*, Computer Science Press, Maryland.
5. Dhamdhere, D.M. (1997): *Compiler Construction – Principles and Practice*, 2nd *edition*, Macmillan India, New Delhi.
6. Fischer, C.N. and R.J. LeBlanc (1988) : *Crafting a compiler*, Benjamin/ Cummings, Menlo Park, California.
7. Gries, D. (1971): *Compiler Construction for Digital Computers*, Wiley, New York.
8. Hansen, P.B. (1985): *Brinch Hansen on Pascal compilers*, Prentice-Hall, Englewood Cliffs, N.J.
9. Hill, U. (1974): "Special run time organization techniques for Algol-68," in *Compiler Construction : An advanced course*, Bauer, F.L., Eickel, J. (eds), Springer-Verlag, Berlin.
10. Lewis, P.M., D.J. Rosenkrantz, and R.E. Stearns (1976): *Compiler Design Theory*, Addison-Wesley, Reading.
11. Peck, J.E.L. (ed.) (1971): *Algol-68 Implementation*, North Holland, Amsterdam.
12. Tremblay, J.P. and P.G. Sorenson (1984): *The Theory and Practice of Compiler Writing*, McGraw-Hill, New York.
13. Watson, D. (1989): *High Level Languages and their Compilers*, Addison-Wesley, Reading.
14. Weingarten, F.W. (1973): *Translation of Computer Languages*, Holden-Day, San Francisco.

(d) Interpreters and related topics

1. Ayres, R.B. and R.L. Derrenbacher (1971): "Partial recompilation," *Proceedings of AFIPS SJCC*, **38**, 497-502.
2. Berthaud, M. and M. Griffiths (1973): "Incremental compilation and conversational interpretation," *Annual Review in Automatic Programming*, **7** (2), 95-114.
3. Brown, P.J. (1979): *Writing Interactive Compilers and Interpreters*, Wiley, New York.
4. Early, J. and P. Caizergues (1972): "A method of incrementally compiling languages with nested statement structure," *Commn. of ACM*, **15** (12), 1040-1044.

5. Klint, P. (1981): "Interpretation techniques," *Software – Practice and Experience*, **11**, 963-973.
6. Kornerup, P., B.B. Kristensen and O.L. Madsen (1980): "Interpretation and code generation based on intermediate languages," *Software – Practice and Experience*, **10** (8), 636-658.
7. McIntyre, T.C. (1978): *Software Interpreters for Micro computers*, Wiley, New York.
8. Ryan, J.L., R.L. Crandall and M.C. Medwedeff (1966): "A conversational system for incremental compilation and execution in a time sharing environment," *Proceedings of AFIPS FJCC*, **29**, 1-22.

CHAPTER 7

Linkers

Execution of a program written in a language L involves the following steps:

1. *Translation* of the program
2. *Linking* of the program with other programs needed for its execution
3. *Relocation* of the program to execute from the specific memory area allocated to it
4. *Loading* of the program in the memory for the purpose of execution.

These steps are performed by different language processors. Step 1 is performed by the translator for language L. Steps 2 and 3 are performed by a *linker* while Step 4 is performed by a *loader*. The terms linking, relocation and loading are defined in a later section.

Figure 7.1 contains a schematic showing steps 1–4 in the execution of a program. The translator outputs a program form called *object module* for the program. The linker processes a set of object modules to produce a ready-to-execute program form, which we will call a *binary program*. The loader loads this program into the memory for the purpose of execution. As shown in the schematic, the object module(s) and ready-to-execute program forms can be stored in the form of files for repeated use.

Translated, linked and load time addresses

While compiling a program P, a translator is given an origin specification for P. This is called the *translated origin* of P. (In an assembly program, the programmer can specify the origin in a `START` or `ORIGIN` statement.) The translator uses the value of the translated origin to perform memory allocation for the symbols declared in P. This results in the assignment of a *translation time address* t_{symb} to each symbol *symb* in the program. The *execution start address* or simply the *start address* of a program is the address of the instruction from which its execution must begin. The start address specified by the translator is the *translated start address* of the program.

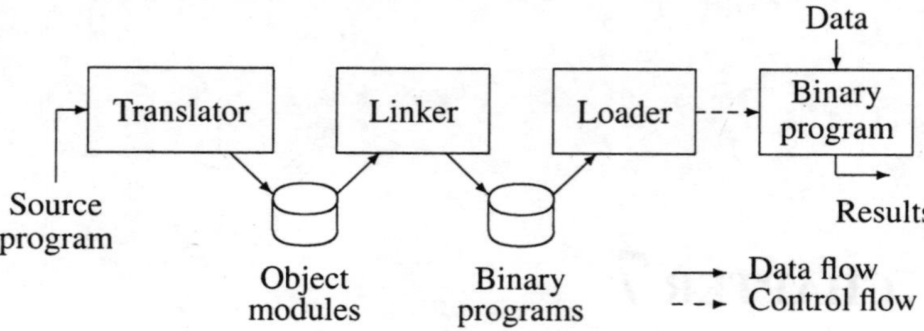

Fig. 7.1 A schematic of program execution

The origin of a program may have to be changed by the linker or loader for one of two reasons. First, the same set of translated addresses may have been used in different object modules constituting a program, e.g. object modules of library rotines often have the same translated origin. Memory allocation to such programs would conflict unless their origins are changed. Second, an operating system may require that a program should execute from a specific area of memory. This may require a change in its origin. The change of origin leads to changes in the execution start address and in the addresses assigned to symbols. The following terminology is used to refer to the address of a program entity at different times:

1. *Translation time* (or *translated*) *address:* Address assigned by the translator.
2. *Linked address:* Address assigned by the linker.
3. *Load time* (or *load*) *address:* Address assigned by the loader.

The same prefixes *translation time* (or *translated*), *linked* and *load time* (or *load*) are used with the origin and execution start address of a program. Thus,

1. *Translated origin:* Address of the origin assumed by the translator. This is the address specified by the programmer in an ORIGIN statement.
2. *Linked origin:* Address of the origin assigned by the linker while producing a binary program.
3. *Load origin:* Address of the origin assigned by the loader while loading the program for execution.

The linked and load origins may differ from the translated origin of a program due to one of the reasons mentioned earlier.

Example 7.1 Consider the assembly program and its generated code shown in Fig. 7.2. The translated origin of the program is 500. The translation time address of `LOOP` is therefore 501. If the program is loaded for execution in the memory area starting with the address 900. the load time origin is 900. The load time address of `LOOP` would be 901.

Statement			Address	Code
	START	500		
	ENTRY	TOTAL		
	EXTRN	MAX, ALPHA		
	READ	A	500)	+ 09 0 540
LOOP			501)	
	⋮			
	MOVER	AREG, ALPHA	518)	+ 04 1 000
	BC	ANY, MAX	519)	+ 06 6 000
	⋮			
	BC	LT, LOOP	538)	+ 06 1 501
	STOP		539)	+ 00 0 000
A	DS	1	540)	
TOTAL	DS	1	541)	
	END			

Fig. 7.2 A sample assembly program and its generated code

7.1 RELOCATION AND LINKING CONCEPTS

7.1.1 Program Relocation

Let AA be the set of absolute addresses—instruction or data addresses—used in the instructions of a program P. AA $\neq \phi$ implies that program P assumes its instructions and data to occupy memory words with specific addresses. Such a program—called an *address sensitive program*—contains one or more of the following:

1. An *address sensitive instruction:* an instruction which uses an address $a_i \in$ AA.
2. An *address constant:* a data word which contains an address $a_i \in$ AA.

In the following, we discuss relocation of programs containing address sensitive instructions. Address constants are handled analogously.

An address sensitive program P can execute correctly only if the start address of the memory area allocated to it is the same as its translated origin. To execute correctly from any other memory area, the address used in each address sensitive instruction of P must be 'corrected'.

Definition 7.1 (Program relocation) Program relocation *is the process of modifying the addresses used in the address sensitive instructions of a program such that the program can execute correctly from the designated area of memory.*

If linked origin $\neq$ translated origin, relocation must be performed by the linker. If load origin $\neq$ linked origin, relocation must be performed by the loader. In general, a linker always performs relocation, whereas some loaders do not. For simplicity, in the first part of the chapter it has been assumed that loaders do not perform relocation—that is, load origin = linked origin. Such loaders are called *absolute loaders*. Hence the terms 'load origin' and 'linked origin' are used interchangeably. However, it would have been more precise to use the term 'linked origin'. (Loaders that perform relocation, i.e. *relocating loaders*, are discussed in Section 7.6.)

Example 7.2 The translated origin of the program in Fig. 7.2 is 500. The translation time address of symbol `A` is 540. The instruction corresponding to the statement `READ A` (existing in translated memory word 500) uses the address 540, hence it is an address sensitive instruction. If the linked origin is 900, `A` would have the link time address 940. Hence the address in the `READ` instruction should be corrected to 940. Similarly the instruction in translated memory word 538 contains 501, the address of `LOOP`. This should be corrected to 901. (Note that the operand addresses in the instructions with the addresses 518 and 519 also need to be corrected. This is explained in Section 7.1.2.)

Performing relocation

Let the translated and linked origins of program P be t_origin_P and l_origin_P, respectively. Consider a symbol *symb* in P. Let its translation time address be t_{symb} and link time address be l_{symb}. The relocation factor of P is defined as

$$relocation\_factor_P \quad = \quad l\_origin_P - t\_origin_P \tag{7.1}$$

Note that $relocation\_factor_P$ can be positive, negative or zero.

Consider a statement which uses *symb* as an operand. The translator puts the address t_{symb} in the instruction generated for it. Now,

$$t_{symb} \quad = \quad t\_origin_P + d_{symb}$$

where d_{symb} is the offset of *symb* in P. Hence

$$l_{symb} \quad = \quad l\_origin_P + d_{symb}$$

Using (7.1),

$$\begin{aligned} l_{symb} &= t\_origin_P + relocation\_factor_P + d_{symb} \\ &= \underbrace{t\_origin_P + d_{symb}} + relocation\_factor_P \\ &= t_{symb} + relocation\_factor_P \end{aligned} \tag{7.2}$$

Let IRR_P designate the set of instructions requiring relocation in program P. Following (7.2), relocation of program P can be performed by computing the relocation factor for P and adding it to the translation time address(es) in every instruction $i \in IRR_P$.

Example 7.3 For the program of Fig. 7.2

relocation factor = 900 − 500
= 400.

Relocation is performed as follows: IRR_P contains the instructions with translated addresses 500 and 538. The instruction with translated address 500 contains the address 540 in the operand field. This address is changed to (540+400) = 940. Similarly, 400 is added to the operand address in the instruction with translated address 538. This achieves the relocation explained in Ex. 7.2.

7.1.2 Linking

Consider an application program AP consisting of a set of program units SP = $\{P_i\}$. A program unit P_i interacts with another program unit P_j by using addresses of P_j's instructions and data in its own instructions. To realize such interactions, P_j and P_i must contain public definitions and external references as defined in the following:

Public definition — a symbol *pub_symb* defined in a program unit which may be referenced in other program units

External reference — a reference to a symbol *ext_symb* which is not defined in the program unit containing the reference.

The handling of public definitions and external references is described in the following.

EXTRN and ENTRY statements

The `ENTRY` statement lists the public definitions of a program unit, i.e. it lists those symbols defined in the program unit which may be referenced in other program units. The `EXTRN` statement lists the symbols to which external references are made in the program unit.

Example 7.4 In the assembly program of Fig. 7.2, the `ENTRY` statement indicates that a public definition of `TOTAL` exists in the program. Note that `LOOP` and `A` are not public definitions even though they are defined in the program. The `EXTRN` statement indicates that the program contains external references to `MAX` and `ALPHA`. The assembler does not know the address of an external symbol. Hence it puts zeroes in the address fields of the instructions corresponding to the statements `MOVER AREG, ALPHA` and `BC ANY, MAX`. If the `EXTRN` statement did not exist, the assembler would have flagged references to `MAX` and `ALPHA` as errors.

Resolving external references

Before the application program AP can be executed, it is necessary that for each P_i in SP, every external reference in P_i should be bound to the correct link time address.

Definition 7.2 (Linking) Linking *is the process of binding an external reference to the correct link time address.*

An external reference is said to be *unresolved* until linking is performed for it. It is said to be *resolved* when its linking is completed.

```
                Statement           Address    Code
                START   200
                ENTRY   ALPHA
                - -
                - -
        ALPHA   DS      25          231)       + 00 0 025
                END
```

Fig. 7.3 Program unit Q

Example 7.5 Let the program unit of Fig. 7.2 (referred to as program unit P) be linked with the program unit Q described in Fig. 7.3.

Program unit P contains an external reference to symbol `ALPHA` which is a public definition in Q with the translation time address 231. Let the link origin of P be 900 and its size be 42 words. The link origin of Q is therefore 942, and the link time address of `ALPHA` is 973. Linking is performed by putting the link time address of `ALPHA` in the instruction of P using `ALPHA`, i.e. by putting the address 973 in the instruction with the translation time address 518 in P.

Binary programs

Definition 7.3 (Binary program) A binary program *is a machine language program comprising a set of program units SP such that* $\forall\ P_i \in SP$

1. P_i *has been relocated to the memory area starting at its link origin, and*
2. *Linking has been performed for each external reference in* P_i.

To form a binary program from a set of object modules, the programmer invokes the linker using the command

`linker` <*link origin*>, <*object module names*>
[, <*execution start address*>]

where <*link origin*> specifies the memory address to be given to the first word of the binary program. <*execution start address*> is usually a pair (program unit name, offset in program unit). The linker converts this into the linked start address. This is stored along with the binary program for use when the program is to be executed. If specification of <*execution start address*> is omitted the execution start address is assumed to be the same as the linked origin.

Note that a linker converts the object modules in the set of program units SP into a binary program. Since we have assumed link address = load address, the loader simply loads the binary program into the appropriate area of memory for the purpose of execution.

7.1.3 Object Module

The object module of a program contains all information necessary to relocate and link the program with other programs. The object module of a program P consists of 4 components:

1. *Header:* The header contains *translated origin, size* and *execution start address* of P.
2. *Program:* This component contains the machine language program corresponding to P.
3. *Relocation table:* (RELOCTAB) This table describes IRR_P. Each RELOCTAB entry contains a single field:

   Translated address : Translated address of an address sensitive instruction.

4. *Linking table* (LINKTAB): This table contains information concerning the public definitions and external references in P.
   Each LINKTAB entry contains three fields:

   Symbol : Symbolic name
   Type : PD/EXT indicating whether public definition or external reference
   Translated address : For a public definition, this is the address of the first memory word allocated to the symbol. For an external reference, it is the address of the memory word which is required to contain the address of the symbol.

Example 7.6 Consider the assembly program of Fig. 7.2. The object module of the program contains the following information:

1. *translated origin* = 500, *size* = 42, *execution start address* = 500.
2. Machine language instructions shown in Fig. 7.2.
3. Relocation table

500
538

4. Linking table

ALPHA	EXT	518
MAX	EXT	519
A	PD	540

Note that the symbol LOOP does not appear in the linking table. This is because it is not declared as a public definition, i.e. it does not appear in an ENTRY statement.

7.2 DESIGN OF A LINKER

7.2.1 Relocation and Linking Requirements in Segmented Addressing

The relocation requirements of a program are influenced by the addressing structure of the computer system on which it is to execute. Use of the segmented addressing structure reduces the relocation requirements of a program.

Example 7.7 Consider the program of Fig. 7.4 written in the assembly language of Intel 8088. The `ASSUME` statement declares the segment registers CS and DS to be available for memory addressing. Hence all memory addressing is performed by using suitable displacements from their contents. Translation time address of `A` is 0196. In statement 16, a reference to `A` is assembled as a displacement of 196 from the contents of the CS register. This avoids the use of an absolute address, hence the instruction is not address sensitive. Now no relocation is needed if segment `SAMPLE` is to be loaded in the memory starting at the address 2000 because the CS register would be loaded with the address 2000 by a calling program (or by the OS). The effective operand address would be calculated as <CS> + 0196, which is the correct address 2196. A similar situation exists with the reference to `B` in statement 17. The reference to `B` is assembled as a displacement of 0002 from the contents of the DS register. Since the DS register would be loaded with the execution time address of `DATA_HERE`, the reference to `B` would be automatically relocated to the correct address.

Sr. no.		*Statement*		*Offset*
0001	DATA_HERE	SEGMENT		
0002	ABC	DW	25	0000
0003	B	DW ?		0002
⋮		⋮		
0012	SAMPLE	SEGMENT		
0013		ASSUME	CS:SAMPLE, DS:DATA_HERE	
0014		MOV	AX, DATA_HERE	0000
0015		MOV	DS, AX	0003
0016		JMP	A	0005
0017		MOV	AL,B	0008
⋮		⋮		
0027	A	MOV	AX,BX	0196
⋮		⋮		
0043	SAMPLE	ENDS		
0044		END		

Fig. 7.4 An 8088 assembly program for linking

Though use of segment registers reduces the relocation requirements, it does not completely eliminate the need for relocation. Consider statement 14 of Fig. 7.4, viz.

```
MOV        AX, DATA_HERE
```

which loads the segment base of `DATA_HERE` into the AX register preparatory to its transfer into the DS register. Since the assembler knows `DATA_HERE` to be a segment, it makes provision to load the higher order 16 bits of the address of `DATA_HERE` into the AX register. However, it does not know the link time address of `DATA_HERE`, hence it assembles the `MOV` instruction in the immediate operand format and puts zeroes in the operand field. It also makes an entry for this instruction in RELOCTAB so that the linker would put the appropriate address in the operand field. Inter-segment calls and jumps are handled in a similar way.

Relocation is somewhat more involved in the case of intra-segment jumps assembled in the FAR format. For example, consider the following program:

```
FAR_LAB  EQU    THIS FAR   ; FAR_LAB is a FAR label
         - - -
         JMP    FAR_LAB    ; A FAR jump
```

Here the displacement and the segment base of `FAR_LAB` are to be put in the `JMP` instruction itself. The assembler puts the displacement of `FAR_LAB` in the first two operand bytes of the instruction, and makes a RELOCTAB entry for the third and fourth operand bytes which are to hold the segment base address. A statement like

```
ADDR_A      DW         OFFSET A
```

(which is an 'address constant') does not need any relocation since the assembler can itself put the required offset in the bytes. In summary, the only RELOCTAB entries that must exist for a program using segmented memory addressing are for the bytes that contain a segment base address.

For linking, however, both segment base address and offset of the external symbol must be computed by the linker. Hence there is no reduction in the linking requirements.

7.2.2 Relocation Algorithm

Algorithm 7.1 (Program relocation)

1. *program_linked_origin* := <*link origin*> from `linker` command;
2. For each object module
   (a) *t_origin* := *translated origin* of the object module;
       OM_size := *size* of the object module;
   (b) *relocation_factor* := *program_linked_origin* − *t_origin*;
   (c) Read the machine language program in *work_area*.
   (d) Read RELOCTAB of the object module.
   (e) For each entry in RELOCTAB
       (i) *translated_addr* := address in the RELOCTAB entry;
       (ii) *address_in_work_area* := address of *work_area*
                + *translated_address* − *t_origin*;

(iii) Add *relocation_factor* to the operand address in the word with the address *address_in_work_area*.

(f) *program_linked_origin* := *program_linked_origin* + *OM_size*;

The computations performed in the algorithm are along the lines described in Section 7.1.1. The only new action is the computation of the work area address of the word requiring relocation (step 2(e)(ii)). Step 2(f) increments *program_linked_origin* so that the next object module would be granted the next available load address.

Example 7.8 Let the address of *work_area* be 300. While relocating the object module of Ex. 7.6, *relocation factor* = 400. For the first RELOCTAB entry, *address_in_work_area* = 300 + 500 − 500 = 300. This word contains the instruction for `READ A`. It is relocated by adding 400 to the operand address in it. For the second RELOCTAB entry, *address_in_work_area* = 300 + 538 − 500 = 338. The instruction in this word is similarly relocated by adding 400 to the operand address in it.

7.2.3 Linking Requirements

Features of a programming language influence the linking requirements of programs. In Fortran all program units are translated separately. Hence all subprogram calls and `common` variable references require linking. Pascal procedures are typically nested inside the main program. Hence procedure references do not require linking—they can be handled through relocation. References to built in functions, however, require linking. In C, program files are translated separately. Thus, only function calls that cross file boundaries and references to global data require linking.

A reference to an external symbol `alpha` can be resolved only if `alpha` is declared as a public definition in some object module. This observation forms the basis of program linking. The linker processes all object modules being linked and builds a table of all public definitions and their load time addresses. Linking for `alpha` is simply a matter of searching for `alpha` in this table and copying its linked address into the word containing the external reference.

A *name table* (NTAB) is defined for use in program linking. Each entry of the table contains the following fields:

Symbol	:	symbolic name of an external reference or an object module.
Linked_address	:	For a public definition, this field contains linked address of the symbol. For an object module, it contains the linked origin of the object module.

Most information in NTAB is derived from LINKTAB entries with *type* = PD.

Algorithm 7.2 (Program Linking)

1. *program_linked_origin* := <*link origin*> from `linker` command.
2. For each object module

(a) *t_origin* := *translated origin* of the object module;
OM_size := *size* of the object module;

(b) *relocation_factor* := *program_linked_origin* − *t_origin*;

(c) Read the machine language program in *work_area*.

(d) Read LINKTAB of the object module.

(e) For each LINKTAB entry with *type* = PD
name := *symbol*;
linked_address := *translated_address* + *relocation_factor*;
Enter (*name*, *linked_address*) in NTAB.

(f) Enter (object module name, *program_linked_origin*) in NTAB.

(g) *program_linked_origin* := *program_linked_origin* + *OM_size*;

3. For each object module

(a) *t_origin* := translated origin of the object module;
program_linked_origin := *load_address* from NTAB;

(b) For each LINKTAB entry with *type* = EXT

(i) *address_in_work_area* := address of *work_area* +
program_linked_origin − *<link origin>*
+ *translated address* − *t_origin*;

(ii) Search *symbol* in NTAB and copy its linked address. Add the linked address to the operand address in the word with the address *address_in_work_area*.

Example 7.9 While linking program P of Ex. 7.2 and program Q of Ex. 7.5 with *linked_origin* = 900, NTAB contains the following information

symbol	*linked address*
P	900
A	940
Q	942
ALPHA	973

Let the address of *work_area* be 300. When the LINKTAB entry of ALPHA is processed during linking, *address_in_work area* := 300 + 900 − 900 + 518 − 500, i.e. 318. Hence, the linked address of ALPHA, i.e. 973, is copied from the NTAB entry of ALPHA and added to the word in address 318 (step 3(b)(ii)).

EXERCISE 7.2

1. It is required to merge a set of object modules $\{om_i\}$ to construct a single object module *om*'. This reduces the linking and relocation time in situations where the object modules in $\{om_i\}$ are interdependent—that is, they call or use each other.

(a) What are the public definitions of *om*'?

(b) What are the external references in *om*'?

(c) Explain how the RELOCTAB's and LINKTAB's can be merged.

2. Comment on the feasibility of reconstructing the original object modules from *om*'. Is any additional information required to facilitate it?

7.3 SELF-RELOCATING PROGRAMS

The manner in which a program can be modified, or can modify itself, to execute from a given load origin can be used to classify programs into the following:

1. Non relocatable programs,
2. Relocatable programs,
3. Self-relocating programs.

A non relocatable program is a program which cannot be executed in any memory area other than the area starting on its translated origin. Non relocatability is the result of address sensitivity of a program and lack of information concerning the address sensitive instructions in the program. The difference between a relocatable program and a non relocatable program is the availability of information concerning the address sensitive instructions in it. A relocatable program can be processed to relocate it to a desired area of memory. Representative examples of non relocatable and relocatable programs are a hand coded machine language program and an object module, respectively.

A self-relocating program is a program which can perform the relocation of its own address sensitive instructions. It contains the following two provisions for this purpose:

1. A table of information concerning the address sensitive instructions exists as a part of the program.
2. Code to perform the relocation of address sensitive instructions also exists as a part of the program. This is called the *relocating logic*.

The start address of the relocating logic is specified as the execution start address of the program. Thus the relocating logic gains control when the program is loaded in memory for execution. It uses the load address and the information concerning address sensitive instructions to perform its own relocation. Execution control is now transferred to the relocated program.

A self-relocating program can execute in any area of the memory. This is very important in time sharing operating systems where the load address of a program is likely to be different for different executions.

EXERCISE 7.3

1. Comment on the following statements:

   (a) Self-relocating programs are less efficient than relocatable programs.

(b) There would be no need for linkers if all programs are coded as self relocating programs.

2. A self-relocating program needs to find its load address before it can execute its relocating logic. Comment on how this information can be determined by the program.

7.4 A LINKER FOR MS DOS

We discuss the design of a linker for the Intel 8088/80x86 processors which resembles LINK of MS DOS in many respects. The design uses the schematics of the previous section. It may be noted that the object modules of MS DOS differ from the Intel specifications in some respects. Further simplifications are made for the purpose of this discussion.

Object Module Format

An Intel 8088 object module is a sequence of *object records*, each object record describing specific aspects of the programs in the object module. There are 14 types of object records containing the following five basic categories of information:

1. Binary image (i.e. code generated by a translator)
2. External references
3. Public definitions
4. Debugging information (e.g. line number in source program)
5. Miscellaneous information (e.g. comments in the source program).

We only consider the object records corresponding to first three categories—a total of eight object record types.

The names and purpose of the object record types is summarized in Table 7.1. The formats of the records are shown in Fig. 7.5. The object records of an object module must appear in the specific order shown in Table 7.1. Each object record contains variable length information and may refer to the contents of previous object records. Each name in an object record is represented in the following format:

length (1 byte)	name

THEADR, LNAMES and SEGDEF records

The module name in the THEADR record is typically derived by the translator from the source file name. This name is used by the linker to report errors. An assembly programmer can specify the module name in the NAME directive. The LNAMES record lists the names for use by SEGDEF records. A SEGDEF record designates a segment name using an index into this list. The *attributes* field of a SEGDEF record indicates whether the segment is relocatable or absolute, whether (and in what manner) it can be combined with other segments, as also the alignment requirement of its base address (e.g. byte, word or paragraph, i.e. 16 byte, alignment). Stack segments

THEADR record

80H	length	T-module name	check-sum

LNAMES record

96H	length	name list	check-sum

SEGDEF record

98H	length	attributes (1-4)	segment length (2)	name index (1)	check-sum

EXTDEF record

8CH	length	external reference list	check-sum

PUBDEF record

90H	length	base (2-4)	name	offset (2)	···	check-sum

LEDATA record

A0H	length	segment index (1-2)	data offset (2)	data	check-sum

FIXUPP record

9CH	length	locat (1)	fix dat (1)	frame datum (1)	target datum (1)	target offset (2)	···	check sum

MODEND record

8AH	length	type (1)	start addr (5)	check-sum

Fig. 7.5 Object record formats

Table 7.1 Object Records of Intel 8088

Record type	*Id (Hex)*	*Description*
THEADR	80	Translator header record
LNAMES	96	List of names record
SEGDEF	98	Segment definition record
EXTDEF	8C	External names definition record
PUBDEF	90	Public names definition record
LEDATA	AO	Enumerated data (binary image)
FIXUPP	9C	Fixup record
MODEND	8A	Module end record

with the same name are concatenated with each other, while common segments with the same name are overlapped with one another. The *attribute* field also contains the origin specification for an absolute segment.

EXTDEF and PUBDEF records

The EXTDEF record contains a list of external references used by the programs of this module. A FIXUPP record designates an external symbol name by using an index into this list. A PUBDEF record contains a list of public names declared in a segment of the object module. The *base specification* identifies the segment. Each (*name*, *offset*) pair in the record defines one public name, specifying the name of the symbol and its offset within the segment designated by the base specification.

LEDATA records

An LEDATA record contains the binary image of the code generated by the language translator. *segment index* identifies the segment to which the code belongs, and *offset* specifies the location of the code within the segment.

FIXUPP records

A FIXUPP record contains information for one or more relocation and linking fixups to be performed. The *locat* field contains a numeric code called *loc code* to indicate the type of a fixup. The meanings of these codes are given in Table 7.2.

Table 7.2 FIXUPP codes

Loc code	*Meaning*
0	low order byte is to be fixed
1	offset is to be fixed
2	segment is to be fixed
3	pointer (i.e., segment : offset) is to be fixed

locat also contains the offset of the fixup location in the previous LEDATA record. The *frame datum* field, which refers to a SEGDEF record, identifies the segment to which the fixup location belongs. The *target datum* and *target offset* fields specify the relocation or linking information. *target datum* contains a segment index or an external index, while *target offset* contains an offset from the name indicated in *target datum*. The *fix dat* field indicates the manner in which the *target datum* and *target offset* fields are to be interpreted. The numeric codes used for this purpose are given in Table 7.3.

Table 7.3 Codes in *fixdat* field

code	*contents of target datum and offset fields*
0	segment index and displacement
2	external index and target displacement
4	segment index (offset field is not used)
6	external index (offset field is not used)

Example 7.10 Consider the assembly program

```
EXTRN     ABC, XYZ
LEA       BX, ABC+25H
MOV       AX, OFFSET XYZ
- - -
```

In the LEA statement, the assembler can put zeroes in the second operand field of the instruction and use code '2' in *fix dat* to indicate the linking requirement. ABC would be identified through the external index put in *target datum*, while 25H would be put in the *target offset* field. *loc code* would be '3'. An alternative would have been to put 25H in the operand field of the instruction and simply use code '6' in *fix dat* and '2' in *loc code* to indicate the linking requirement. For the MOV statement code '6' would be used in *fix dat*. *locat* would contain '1' indicating that offset of the effective address is to be put in the designated location.

MODEND record

The MODEND record signifies the end of the module, with the *type* field indicating whether it is the main program. This record also optionally indicates the execution start address. This has two components: (a) the segment, designated as an index into the list of segment names defined in SEGDEF record(s), and (b) an offset within the segment. The exact format in which this information is represented is not important for our discussion.

Example 7.11 Figure 7.6 illustrates two assembly language programs, each consisting of a single segment, which are assembled separately. From the viewpoint of linking, only the two MOV statements of segment COMPUTE and the CALL, LEA and MOV statements of segment PART2 are of interest. Hence only the object module records concerning these statements are shown in Fig. 7.7. Note that the object modules have been given

Sr. no.		*Statement*		*Offset*
0001		NAME	FIRST	
0002	COMPUTE	SEGMENT		
0003		EXTRN	PHI:BYTE, PSI:WORD	
0004		PUBLIC	ALPHA, BETA	
0007	ALPHA	...		0015
⋮		⋮		
0012		MOV	AX, SEG PHI	0028
⋮		⋮		
0022		MOV	AX, OFFSET PSI	0056
⋮		⋮		
0029	BETA	...		0084
⋮		⋮		
0035		DB	25	0123
0036	COMPUTE	ENDS		
0037		END		

0001		NAME	SECOND	
0002	PART2	SEGMENT	PARA	
0003		EXTRN	ALPHA,BETA:FAR,GAMMA	
0004		PUBLIC	PHI, PSI	
0010		JMP	BETA	0018
⋮		⋮		
0017	PHI	...		0033
⋮		⋮		
0027	PSI	...		0059
⋮		⋮		
0051		LEA	BX, ALPHA+20H	0245
⋮		⋮		
0057		MOV	AX, SEG GAMMA	0279
⋮		⋮		
0069	PART2	ENDS		
0070		END		

Fig. 7.6 Sample MS DOS assembly language programs

Object Module FIRST

Type	*Length*	*Other fields*	*Check sum*	
80H	···	05 FIRST	···	THEADR
96H	···	07 COMPUTE	···	LNAMES
98H	···	20H 124 01	···	SEGDEF
90H	···	01 05 ALPHA 0015	···	PUBDEF
90H	···	01 04 BETA 0084	···	PUBDEF
8CH	···	03 PHI 03 PSI	···	EXTDEF
A0H	···	01 0028 A1 00 00	···	LEDATA
9CH	···	8801 06 01 01	···	FIXUPP
A0H	···	01 0056 A1 00 00	···	LEDATA
9CH	···	8401 06 01 02	···	FIXUPP
8AH	···	C0H 01 00	···	MODEND

Object Module SECOND

Type	*Length*	*Other fields*	*Check sum*	
80H	···	06 SECOND	···	THEADR
96H	···	05 PART2	···	LNAMES
98H	···	60H 398 01	···	SEGDEF
90H	···	01 03 PHI 0033	···	PUBDEF
90H	···	01 03 PSI 0059	···	PUBDEF
8CH	···	05 ALPHA 04 BETA 05 GAMMA	···	EXTDEF
A0H	···	01 0018 EA 00 00 00 00	···	LEDATA
9CH	···	8C01 06 01 02	···	FIXUPP
A0H	···	01 0245 8D 1E 00 00	···	LEDATA
9CH	···	C402 02 01 01 00 20H	···	FIXUPP
A0H	···	01 0279 A1 00 00	···	LEDATA
9CH	···	8801 06 01 03	···	FIXUPP
8AH	···	80H	···	MODEND

Fig. 7.7 MS DOS object modules

the names `FIRST` and `SECOND` through the `NAME` directive. For simplicity, we show addresses in decimal.

In the object module `FIRST`, the `SEGDEF` code of `20H` indicates that the segment is byte aligned and relocatable. For both `MOV` statements involving the use of external symbols, the assembler generates identical code with zeroes in the second operand field. In the first FIXUPP record, 88 in the first byte of *locat* implies *loc code* = '2' indicating that fixing is to be performed by putting the segment base of the external symbol in the generated code. *fix dat* contains the code '6', indicating that an external symbol is involved in the fixup. The next two fields indicate that fixing is to be performed in the first segment of the module, according to the external symbol #1 (i.e., `PHI`). The second FIXUPP record is similar except that 84 in *locat* implies *loc code* = '1' (offset to be put in the target location) and *target datum* = '2' implying that fixing is to be performed according to external symbol and target displacement. (Note that code '6' could have been used as discussed in Ex. 7.10). The next two fields indicate that fixing is to be performed in the first segment of the module according to the external symbol #2 (i.e. `PSI`). In `SECOND`, the `JMP` statement is fixed using the code `8C` in *locat*, implying *loc code* = '3' which indicates that both segment base and offset are to be put into the generated code. The statement

```
LEA          BX, ALPHA+20H
```

is assumed to have been assembled with zeroes in the operand field. It is fixed by using the code `C4` in *locat* (i.e. *loc* = 2) and *code* = 2 in *fix dat*. The displacement 20H appears in *target offset* field of the FIXUPP record.

7.4.1 Design of the Linker

We shall present the design of a program named LINKER which performs both linking and relocation. The output of LINKER is a binary program which resembles a program with .COM extension in MS DOS. It is assumed that the binary program cannot be relocated by the loader. (Note that LINK program of MS DOS produces a program with .EXE extension, which is relocated by the loader prior to execution. The reader would do well to note this difference.)

Specification

The LINKER invocation command has the following format:

`LINKER` *<object module names>*, *<executable file>*,
<load origin>, *<list of library files>*

LINKER performs relocation and linking of all named object modules to produce a binary program with the specified load origin. The program is stored in *<executable file>*. When LINKER comes across an external name ext_symb_i not defined in any of the object modules named in the LINKER command, it locates an object module om_i in *<list of library files>* which contains ext_symb_i as a public definition. om_i is now included in the set of object modules to be linked and relocated. This process of resolving an external reference by including the object module containing its definition from a library file is called *autolinking*. LINKER execution terminates when all external references have been resolved, or when the unresolved external references cannot be found in any of the library files.

Example 7.12 In the LINKER command

```
LINKER alpha+beta+min, calculate, 10000, pas.lib
```

`alpha`, `beta` and `min` are names of the object modules to be linked and `calculate` is the name to be given to the executable file generated by LINKER. The load origin of the executable program is 10,000. Any external names not defined in object modules `alpha`, `beta` and `min` are to be searched in the library `pas.lib`.

Data structures and algorithm

LINKER uses a two pass strategy. In the first pass, the object modules are processed to collect information concerning segments and public definitions. The second pass performs relocation and linking.

First pass

In the first pass, LINKER only processes the object records relevant for building NTAB.

Algorithm 7.3 (First pass of LINKER)

1. *program_linked_origin* := <*load origin*>; (Use a default value if <*load origin*> is not specified.)
2. Repeat step 3 for each object module to be linked.
3. Select an object module and process its object records.
   (a) If an LNAMES record, enter the names in NAMELIST.
   (b) If a SEGDEF record
      (i) *i* := *name index*; *segment_name* := NAMELIST [i]; *segment_addr* := start address in *attributes* (if any);
      (ii) If an absolute segment, enter (*segment_name*, *segment_addr*) in NTAB.
      (iii) If the segment is relocatable and cannot be combined with other segments
         – Align the address contained in *program_linked_origin* on the next word or paragraph as indicated in the *attributes* field.
         – Enter (*segment_name*, *program_linked_origin*) in NTAB.
         – *program_linked_origin* := *program load origin* + *segment length*;
   (c) For each PUBDEF record
      (i) *i* := *base*; *segment_name* := NAMELIST [i]; *symbol* := *name*;
      (ii) *segment_addr* := load address of *segment_name* in NTAB;
      (iii) *sym_addr* := *segment_addr* + *offset*;
      (iv) Enter (*symbol*, *sym_addr*) in NTAB.

Example 7.13 For the LINKER command

```
LINKER FIRST+SECOND, demo, 10000, math.lib
```

where object modules FIRST and SECOND are as shown in Ex. 7.11, NTAB at the end of first pass is as follows:

Symbol	Load address
COMPUTE	10000
ALPHA	10015
BETA	10084
PART2	10128
PHI	10161
PSI	10187

Note that PART2 has the load address of 10128 even though the first byte following the segment COMPUTE has the address 10124. This is because PART2 has a paragraph alignment.

Second pass

Second pass of LINKER constructs the executable program in *work_area*. Data from the LEDATA records is moved to appropriate parts of *work_area*. FIXUPP records are then processed to effect relocation and linking. At the end of the pass, the executable program is written into the current directory under the name <*executable file*> specified in the LINKER command.

It is simple to move the data from an LEDATA record into the appropriate part of *work_area* using *segment index* and *data offset*. The segment index is used to obtain the load origin of the segment from NTAB. Adding the data offset to it gives load address of the first byte of the data in the LEDATA record. Address of this byte in *work_area* is now obtained by a computation analogous to step 2(e)(ii) of Algorithm 7.1.

Some complications arise from the fact that *segment index* contains a numeric value rather than the name of a segment. The segment name can be obtained by using this value as an index into LNAMES record(s). This name can be searched in NTAB to obtain its load origin. Similarly, while processing a FIXUPP record, the target datum can be used as an index into EXTDEF or SEGDEF records to obtain the target name. This name can be searched in NTAB to obtain its load origin.

The second pass constructs a number of tables to eliminate indirect references to NTAB. To eliminate search in the LNAMES records, the NAMELIST table can be constructed once again in the second pass, and *segment index* can be used to index NAMELIST. However, the search in NTAB is still needed. To overcome this problem, LINKER builds another table called the *segment table* (SEGTAB) to contain all segment names defined in the object module. A SEGTAB entry has the following format:

segment name	*load address*

where the load address information is copied from NTAB. Now, while processing an LEDATA record, the segment index can be used to index SEGTAB to obtain the segment's load address. A similar use can be made while processing FIXUPP records.

Since a linking specification in a FIXUPP record may contain a reference to an external symbol, LINKER builds an *external symbols table* (EXTTAB) with a similar entry-format, viz.

external symbol	*load address*

EXTTAB is built by processing the EXTDEF records and copying the load addresses from NTAB. (Actually the *name* fields of the SEGTAB and EXTTAB entries are redundant since access to an entry in these tables is through an index rather than through a name.)

When some external name `alpha` is not found in the set of object modules named in the LINKER command, LINKER performs autolinking. The object module containing `alpha` is included in the set of object modules being linked. To implement this, the first pass of LINKER is performed on the new object module. Processing of the FIXUPP record which triggered off autolinking for `alpha` is then resumed.

Algorithm 7.4 (Second pass of LINKER)

1. *list_of_object_modules* := Object modules named in LINKER command;
2. Repeat step 3 until *list_of_object_modules* is empty.
3. Select an object module and process its object records.
   (a) If an LNAMES record
       Enter the names in NAMELIST.
   (b) If a SEGDEF record
       i := *name index*; *segment_name* := NAMELIST [i];
       Enter (*segment_name*, *load address* from NTAB) in SEGTAB.
   (c) If an EXTDEF record
       (i) *external_name* := name from EXTDEF record;
       (ii) If *external_name* is not found in NTAB, then
           – Locate an object module in the library which contains *external_name* as a segment or public definition.
           – Add name of object module to *list_of_object_modules*.
           – Perform first pass of LINKER, i.e. Algorithm 7.3, for the new object module.
       (iii) Enter (*external_name*, *load address* from NTAB) in EXTTAB.
   (d) If an LEDATA record
       (i) *i* := *segment index*; *d* := *data offset*;
       (ii) *program_load_origin* := SEGTAB [i].*load address*;
       (iii) *address_in_work_area* := address of *work_area* +
             program_load_origin − <*load origin*> + *d*;

(iv) Move data from LEDATA into the memory area starting at the address *address_in_work_area*.

(e) If a FIXUPP record, for each FIXUPP specification

(i) f := *offset* from *locat* field;

(ii) *fix_up_address* := *address_in_work_area* + f;

(iii) Perform required fix up using a load address from SEGTAB or EXTTAB and the value of code in *locat* and *fix dat*.

(f) If a MODEND record

If start address is specified, compute the corresponding load address (analogous to the computation while processing an LEDATA record) and record it in the executable file being generated.

Example 7.14 Figure 7.8(a) illustrates the contents of the various data structures before object module `SECOND` is processed by the second pass of LINKER. While linking the object modules of Ex. 7.11 autolinking would be performed for the external name `GAMMA` of object module `SECOND`. Let `GAMMA` be a public definition in object module `THIRD`. First pass of LINKER is performed for `THIRD`. Thus, the segments and public symbols defined in `THIRD` are added to NTAB. This includes `PRECISE`, a segment name and `EMP_DATA`, another public definition (see Fig. 7.8(b)). The name `THIRD` is also added to the list of object modules. This ensures that the second pass would be performed for `THIRD`.

EXERCISE 7.4

1. Explain the purpose of the *segment index* field in an LEDATA record.
2. Answer problems 1 and 2 of Exercise 7.2 with respect to the Intel 8086 object module.
3. Modify Algorithm 7.4 to incorporate the processing of `common` and `stack` segments as follows:
   (a) All `common` segments with the same name overlap one another,
   (b) All `stack` segments with the same name are concatenated.
4. After a program has been translated to obtain the object module, it is found that certain n instructions from the translated address *aaaa* are redundant. These instructions can be replaced by *no-op* instructions, by introducing an LEDATA record with *aaaa* in its *data offset* field. However, this would leave the program length unchanged and also waste execution time due to the *no-op* instructions. It is therefore required to physically delete these n instructions from the object module.
   Indicate what modifications need to be made to implement physical deletion.
5. Suggest an entry format for the symbol table of an assembler which incorporates all information required to generate the SEGDEF, PUBDEF, EXTDEF and FIXUPP records of the object module.
6. Autolinking is a slow and laborious process because it involves library searches for every unresolved address constant. Comment on the effectiveness of the following schemes aimed at speeding up autolinking:

a) After processing FIRST

NTAB

Symbol	*Load address*
COMPUTE	10000
ALPHA	10015
BETA	10084
PART2	10128
PHI	10161
PSI	10187

NAMELIST

Symbol
COMPUTE

SEGTAB

Segment name	*Load address*
COMPUTE	10000

EXTTAB

External symbol	*Load address*
PHI	10161
PSI	10187

b) After processing SECOND

NTAB

Symbol	*Load address*
COMPUTE	10000
ALPHA	10015
BETA	10084
PART2	10128
PHI	10161
PSI	10187
PRECISE	10528
GAMMA	10586
EMP_DATA	10619

NAMELIST

Symbol
PART2

SEGTAB

Segment name	*Load address*
PART2	10128

EXTTAB

External symbol	*Load address*
ALPHA	10015
BETA	10084
GAMMA	10586

Fig. 7.8 LINKER data structures for autolinking

(a) A few unresolved address constants are grouped together for library searching.

(b) The directory entries for the object modules library are extended to include information about all public definitions in an object module.

7. In Section 7.4.1 we have assumed that *work_area* is large enough to accommodate the entire binary program. Comment on the changes required if *work_area* is smaller than the binary program.

7.5 LINKING FOR OVERLAYS

Definition 7.4 (Overlay) *An* overlay *is a part of a program (or software package) which has the same load origin as some other part(s) of the program.*

Overlays are used to reduce the main memory requirement of a program.

Overlay structured programs

We refer to a program containing overlays as an *overlay structured program*. Such a program consists of

1. A permanently resident portion, called the *root*
2. A set of overlays.

Execution of an overlay structured program proceeds as follows: To start with, the *root* is loaded in memory and given control for the purpose of execution. Other overlays are loaded as and when needed. Note that the loading of an overlay overwrites a previously loaded overlay with the same load origin. This reduces the memory requirement of a program. It also makes it possible to execute programs whose size exceeds the amount of memory which can be allocated to them.

The overlay structure of a program is designed by identifying mutually exclusive modules—that is, modules which do not call each other. Such modules do not need to reside simultaneously in memory. Hence they are located in different overlays with the same load origin.

Example 7.15 Consider a program with 6 sections named `init`, `read`, `trans_a`, `trans_b`, `trans_c`, and `print`. `init` performs some initializations and passes control to `read`. `read` reads one set of data and invokes one of `trans_a`, `trans_b` or `trans_c` depending on the values of the data. `print` is called to print the results.

`trans_a`, `trans_b` and `trans_c` are mutually exclusive. Hence they can be made into separate overlays. `read` and `print` are put in the root of the program since they are needed for each set of data. For simplicity, we put `init` also in the root, though it could be made into an overlay by itself. Figure 7.9 shows the proposed structure of the program. The overlay structured program can execute in 40 K bytes though it has a total size of 65 K bytes. It is possible to overlay parts of `trans_a` against each other by analyzing its logic. This will further reduce the memory requirements of the program.

The overlay structure of an object program is specified in the linker command.

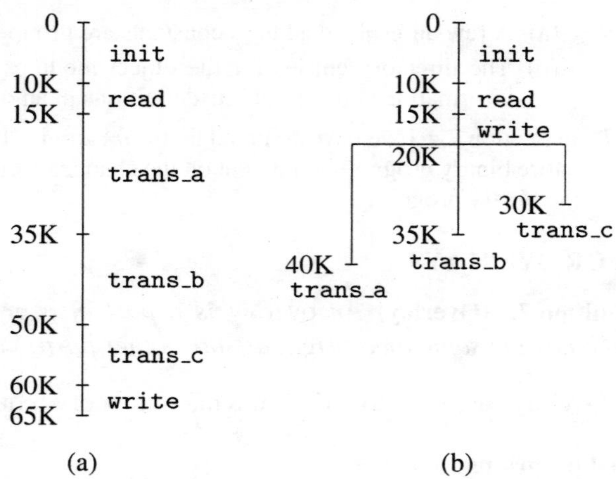

Fig. 7.9 An overlay tree

Example 7.16 The MS-DOS LINK command to implement the overlay structure of Fig. 7.9 is

```
LINK   init + read + write + (trans_a) + (trans_b)
       + (trans_c), <executable file>, <library files>
```

The object module(s) within parenthesis become one overlay of the program. The object modules not included in any overlay become part of the root. LINK produces a single binary program containing all overlays and stores it in <*executable file*>.

Example 7.17 The IBM mainframe linker commands for the overlay structure of Fig. 7.9 are as follows:

```
Phase main:      PHASE     MAIN,+10000
                 INCLUDE   INIT
                 INCLUDE   READ
                 INCLUDE   WRITE
Phase a_trans:   PHASE     A_TRANS,*
                 INCLUDE   TRANS_A
Phase b_trans:   PHASE     B_TRANS,A_TRANS
                 INCLUDE   TRANS_B
Phase c_trans:   PHASE     C_TRANS,A_TRANS
                 INCLUDE   TRANS_C
```

Each overlay forms a binary program (i.e. a *phase*) by itself. A PHASE statement specifies the object program name and linked origin for one overlay. The linked origin can be specified in many different ways. It can be an absolute address specification as in the first PHASE statement. In the second PHASE statement, the '*' indicates contents of the counter *program_linked_origin*. Thus, the linked origin is the next available memory byte. The specifications in the last two PHASE statements indicate the same linked origin as that of A_TRANS.

Execution of an overlay structured program

For linking and execution of an overlay structured program in MS DOS the linker produces a single executable file at the output, which contains two provisions to support overlays. First, an overlay manager module is included in the executable file. This module is responsible for loading the overlays when needed. Second, all calls that cross overlay boundaries are replaced by an interrupt producing instruction. To start with, the overlay manager receives control and loads the root. A procedure call which crosses overlay boundaries leads to an interrupt. This interrupt is processed by the overlay manager and the appropriate overlay is loaded into memory.

When each overlay is structured into a separate binary program, as in IBM mainframe systems, a call which crosses overlay boundaries leads to an interrupt which is attended by the OS kernel. Control is now transferred to the OS loader to load the appropriate binary program.

Changes in LINKER algorithms

The basic change required in LINKER algorithms of Section 7.4.1 is in the assignment of load addresses to segments. *program_load_origin* can be used as before while processing the root portion of a program. The size of the root would decide the load address of the overlays. *program_load_origin* would be initialized to this value while processing every overlay. Another change in the LINKER algorithm would be in the handling of procedure calls that cross overlay boundaries. LINKER has to identify an inter-overlay call and determine the destination overlay. This information must be encoded in the software interrupt instruction.

An open issue in the linking of overlay structured programs is the handling of object modules added during autolinking. Should these object modules be added to the current overlay or to the root of the program? The former has the advantage of cleaner semantics (think of procedures with *static* or *own* data), however it may increase the memory requirement of the program.

EXERCISE 7.5

1. A call matrix (CM) is a square matrix with boolean values in which CM [i, j] = *true* only if procedure i calls procedure j (directly or indirectly). Describe how a programmer can use this information to design the overlay structure of a program.
2. Modify the passes of LINKER to perform the linking of an overlay structured program. (*Hint:* Should each overlay have a separate NTAB?)
3. This chapter has discussed *static relocation*. *Dynamic relocation* implies relocation during the execution of a program, e.g. a program executing in one area of memory may be suspended, relocated to execute in another area of memory and resumed there. Discuss how dynamic relocation can be performed.
4. An inter-overlay call in an overlay structured program is expensive from the execution viewpoint. It is therefore proposed that if sufficient memory is available during program execution, all overlays can be loaded into memory so that each inter-overlay call can simply be executed as an inter-segment call. Comment on the feasibility of

this proposal and develop a design for it.

7.6 LOADERS

As described in Section 7.1.1, an absolute loader can only load programs with load origin = linked origin. This can be inconvenient if the load address of a program is likely to be different for different executions of a program. A *relocating loader* performs relocation while loading a program for execution. This permits a program to be executed in different parts of the memory.

Linking and loading in MS DOS

MS DOS operating system supports two object program forms. A file with a .COM extension contains a non relocatable object program whereas a file with a .EXE extension contains a relocatable program. MS DOS contains a program EXE2BIN which converts a .EXE program into a .COM program. The system contains two loaders—an absolute loader and a relocating loader. When the user types a filename with the .COM extension, the absolute loader is invoked to simply load the object program into the memory. When a filename with the .EXE extension is given, the relocating loader relocates the program to the designated load area before passing control to it for execution.

EXERCISE 7.6

1. Compare the .COM files in MS DOS with an object module. (MS DOS object modules are contained in files with .OBJ extension.)
2. It is proposed to perform dynamic linking and loading of the program units constituting an application. Comment on the nature of the information which would have to be maintained during the execution of a program.

BIBLIOGRAPHY

Most literature on loaders and linkage editors is proprietary. Some public domain literature is listed below.

1. Barron, D. W. (1969): *Assemblers and Loaders,* Macdonald Elsevier, London.
2. Presser, L. and J. R. White (1972): "Linkers and Loaders," *Computing Surveys,* **4** (3).
3. Wilder, W. L. (1980): "Comparing load and go and link/load compiler organizations," *Proc. AFIPS NCC,* **49**, 823-825.
4. Schwartz, R. L. (1978): "Parallel compilation: A design and its application to SIMULA-67," *Computer Languages*, **3** (2), 75-94.

CHAPTER 8

Software Tools

Computing involves two main activities—program development and use of application software. Language processors and operating systems play an obvious role in these activities. A less obvious but vital role is played by programs that help in developing and using other programs. These programs, called *software tools*, perform various housekeeping tasks involved in program development and application usage.

Definition 8.1 A software tool *is a system program which*

1. *interfaces a program with the entity generating its input data, or*
2. *interfaces the results of a program with the entity consuming them.*

The entity generating the data or consuming the results may be a program or a user. Figure 8.1 shows a schematic of a software tool.

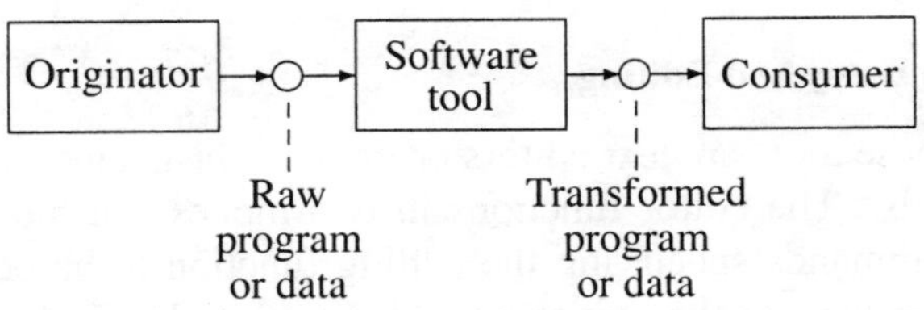

Fig. 8.1 A software tool

Example 8.1 A file rewriting utility organizes the data in a file in a format suitable for processing by a program. The utility may perform blocking/deblocking of data (see Section 16.5.2), padding and truncation of fields and records, sorting of records, etc. The file rewriting utility is a software tool according to Part 1 of Definition 8.1.

In this chapter we discuss two kinds of software tools—software tools for program development, and user interfaces.

8.1 SOFTWARE TOOLS FOR PROGRAM DEVELOPMENT

The fundamental steps in program development are:

1. Program design, coding and documentation
2. Preparation of programs in machine readable form
3. Program translation, linking and loading
4. Program testing and debugging
5. Performance tuning
6. Reformatting the data and/or results of a program to suit other programs.

Step 3 requires use of language processors. All other steps involve transformations of programs or data which fall within the purview of Definition 8.1. The software tools performing these transformations are described in the following Sections.

8.1.1 Program Design and Coding

Two categories of tools used in program design and coding are

1. Program generators
2. Programming environments.

As described in Section 1.2.1, a *program generator* generates a program which performs a set of functions described in its specification. Use of a program generator saves substantial design effort since a programmer merely specifies *what* functions a program should perform rather than *how* the functions should be implemented. Coding effort is saved since the program is generated rather than coded by hand. A *programming environment* (see Section 8.4) supports program coding by incorporating awareness of the programming language syntax and semantics in the language editor.

8.1.2 Program Entry and Editing

These tools are text editors or more sophisticated programs with text editors as front ends. The editor functions in two modes. In the *command mode*, it accepts user commands specifying the editing function to be performed. In the *data mode*, the user keys in the text to be added to the file. Failure to recognize the current mode of the editor can lead to mix up of commands and data. This can be avoided in two ways. In one approach, a quick exit is provided from the data mode, e.g. by pressing the `escape` key, such that the editor enters the command mode. The `vi` editor of Unix uses this approach. Another popular approach is to use the screen mode (also called the what-you-see-is-what-you-get mode), wherein the editor is in the data mode most of the time. The user is provided special keys to move the cursor on the screen. A stroke of any other key is taken to imply input of the corresponding character at the current cursor position. Certain keys pressed along with the `control` key signify commands like erase character, delete line, etc. Thus end of data need not be explicitly indicated by the user. Most Turbo editors on PC's use this approach.

Editors are discussed in greater detail in Section 8.2.

8.1.3 Program Testing and Debugging

Important steps in program testing and debugging are selection of test data for the program, analysis of test results to detect errors (if any), and debugging, i.e. localization and removal of errors. Software tools to assist the programmer in these steps come in the following forms:

1. *Test data generators* help the user in selecting test data for his program. Their use helps in ensuring that a program is thoroughly tested.
2. *Automated test drivers* help in *regression testing*, wherein a program's correctness is verified by subjecting it to a standard set of tests after every modification. Regression testing is performed as follows: Many sets of test data are prepared for a program. These are given as inputs to the test driver (see Fig. 8.2). The driver selects one set of test data at a time and organizes execution of the program on the data.

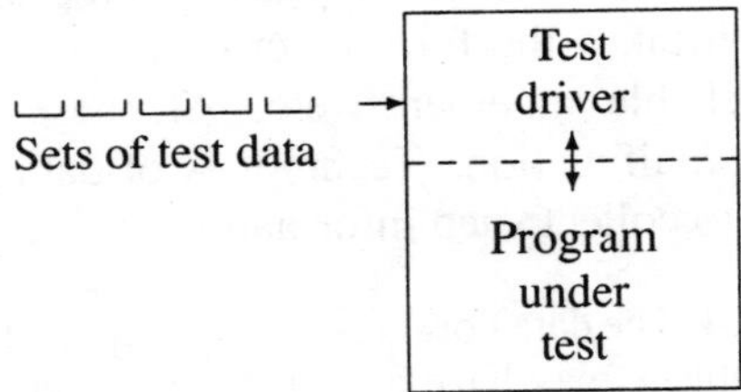

Fig. 8.2 Automated test driver

3. *Debug monitors* help in obtaining information for localization of errors.
4. *Source code control systems* help to keep track of modifications in the source code.

Test data selection uses the notion of an *execution path* which is a sequence of program statements visited during an execution. For testing, a program can be viewed as a set of execution paths. A test data generator determines the conditions which must be satisfied by the program's inputs for control to flow along a specific execution path. A test data is a set of input values which satisfy these conditions.

Example 8.2 The execution path involving the statement `a := a + 1.0;` in Fig. 8.3 is traversed during execution only if `x > z`. To test this path, the test data generator must select a value for y such that $x > z$, e.g. $y = z^2$.

Two problems exist in automated testing of programs. One concerns wastage of testing effort on infeasible paths, i.e. paths which are never followed during the

```
x := sqrt(y) + 2.5;
if x > z then
    a := a + 1.0;
else
    ...
```

Fig. 8.3 Program for Example 8.2

execution of a program. The second concerns testing of complex loop structures. It is best to leave both these aspects to manual testing. Thus automated testing can be used to show up a first batch of errors at low cost. This would free the programmer and system analyst to tackle more complex aspects of testing.

Example 8.3 In Fig. 8.3, if a statement `z := y + 10;` precedes `x := sqrt(y) + 2.5;` then the statement `a := a + 1.0;` lies along an infeasible path.

Producing debug information

Classically, localization and removal of errors has been aided by special purpose debug information. Such information can be produced statically by analysing the source program or dynamically during program execution. Statically produced debug information takes the form of cross reference listings, lists of undefined variables and unreachable statements, etc. All these are useful in determining the cause of a program malfunction. Techniques of data flow analysis (see Section 6.5.3.2) are employed to collect such information.

Example 8.4 The data flow concept of reaching definitions can be used to determine whether variable `x` may have a value when execution reaches statement 10 in the following program

```
No.      Statement
            ...
10.      sum := x + 10;
            ...
```

If no definitions of `x` reach statement 10, then `x` is surely undefined in statement 10. If some definition(s) reach statement 10, then `x` *may* have a value when control reaches the statement. Whether `x` is defined in a specific execution of the program would depend on how control flows during the execution.

Dynamically produced debug information takes the form of value dumps and execution traces produced during the execution of a program. This information helps to determine the execution path followed during an execution and the sequence of values assumed by a variable. Most programming languages provide facilities to produce dynamic debug information.

Example 8.5 Figure 8.4 illustrates the trace and dump facility supported by most Fortran compilers. `debug unit` specifies the kind of dynamic debug information desired, and the file in which it is to be written. The `at` specification is used to enable or disable the production of `trace` and `display` data when control reaches a specified statement during program execution.

1. `debug unit` (<*file_number*>, <*list_of_options*>)

   Debug output is written in the file <*file_number*>.
   <*list_of_options*> can contain:

`trace`	:	Trace of labelled statements executed
`subtrace`	:	Trace of subprograms called
`init` (<*list*>)	:	Trace of assignments made to each variable in <*list*>
`subchk` (<*list*>)	:	Subscript range check: Report error if subscript in any reference to an array in <*list*> is out of bounds

2. `at` <*label*>

   Indicated actions are executed when statement bearing <*label*> is encountered during execution

`trace on`	:	Trace is enabled
`trace off`	:	Trace is disabled
`display` <*list*>	:	Values of variables in the list are written in the debug file

Fig. 8.4 Trace and dump facilities in Fortran

Use of trace and dump facilities is cumbersome due to the volume of information produced. To improve the effectiveness of debugging, it should be possible for the user to dynamically control the production of debug information, i.e. to dynamically specify the trace or dump actions. These facilities can be provided by the language compiler or interpreter, or by a language independent tool.

Example 8.6 Figure 8.5 illustrates the use of dynamic debugging facilities supported by many Basic interpreters. The programmer can set breakpoints at many statements using the `stop on` command. The system initiates a debug conversation with the programmer when control reaches any breakpoint during program execution. During a debug conversation, the programmer can display or change values of variables and set or remove breakpoints.

A debug monitor is a software which provides debugging support for a program. The debug monitor executes the program being debugged under its own control. This provides execution efficiency during debugging. It also enables the monitor to perform dynamically specified debugging actions. A debug monitor can be made language independent, in which case it can handle programs written in many languages. The dynamic debugging technique (DDT) of DEC-10 is a well known example of this approach. The working principles of debug monitors are discussed in Section 8.3.

1. Breakpoint and Dump facilities:
   (a) `stop on` <*list of labels*>
   Sets breakpoint(s) at labelled statement(s).
   (b) `dump at` <*label*> <*list of variables*>
   Dumps values of variables at given label
2. Interactive debugging facilities :

   These commands can be issued when program reaches a breakpoint

`display` <*list of variables*>	:	Displays values of variables
`set` <*var*> = <*exp*>	:	Assigns value of <*exp*> to <*var*>
`resume`	:	Resumes execution
`run`	:	Restarts execution

Fig. 8.5 Debugging facilities in Basic

8.1.4 Enhancement of Program Performance

Program efficiency depends on two factors—the efficiency of the algorithm and the efficiency of its coding. An optimizing compiler can improve efficiency of the code but it cannot improve efficiency of the algorithm. Only a program designer can improve efficiency of an algorithm by rewriting it. However, this is a time consuming process hence some help should be provided to improve its cost-effectiveness. For example, it is better to focus on only those sections of a program which consume a considerable amount of execution time. A performance tuning tool helps in identifying such parts. It is empirically observed that less than three percent of program code generally accounts for more than 50 percent of program execution time. This observation promises major economies of effort in improving a program.

Example 8.7 A program consists of three modules A, B and C. Sizes of the modules and execution times consumed by them in a typical execution as given in Table 8.1.

Table 8.1

Name	*# of statements*	*% of total execution time*
A	150	4.00
B	80	6.00
C	35	90.00

It is seen that module C, which is roughly 13 percent of the total program size, consumes 90 percent of the program execution time. Hence optimization of module C would result in optimization for 90 percent of program execution time at only 13 percent of the cost.

A *profile monitor* is a software tool that collects information regarding the execution behaviour of a program, e.g. the amount of execution time consumed by its modules, and presents it in the form of an *execution profile*. Using this information, the programmer can focus attention on the program sections consuming a significant amount of execution time. These sections can be improved either through code optimization (see Chapter 6), or through improvement of the algorithm.

Example 8.8 Figure 8.6 shows a sample execution profile. The column '# of executions' in the profile indicates the number of times a statement was executed. '# of true' indicates how many times the condition in an `if` statement was found to be true. '% time' gives the percentage of execution time spent in executing a statement, the body of a loop, or a module.

```
Program alpha execution profile

program name   % execution time

main program        11.15
      sub1          41.59
      sub2          15.54
      meor          31.72

Program 'meor' consumed 31.72% of total time

        statement                          # of          %      # of
                                        executions     time     true

    subroutine meor(eoper)                   5         31.72
    integer eoper(10)                        0
    k = 9                                    5          0.08
    do 10 i1 = 1,10                         39         30.74
    j = i1 + k                              39          4.35
    if(sw.eq.1) goto 50                     39          9.53      3
    if(eoper(j).eq.bl) goto 15              36          4.44     26
    if(eoper(j).eq.zero) goto 20            10          2.06      4
    pr = eoper(j)                            6          0.21
    goto 10                                  6          0.21
15  ...
    ...
10  continue                                39          2.01
    ...
    end                                      5          0.59
```

Fig. 8.6 An execution profile

The profile indicates that subroutine `meor` consumed 31.72 percent of the total execution time. The DO loop in `meor` consumed 30.74 percent of the time consumed by subroutine `meor`. This shows that it is important to optimize the loop. It is further seen that the three `if` statements consume more than half of the loop execution time. It is possible to interchange the second and third `if` statements, however this is counterproductive since the second `if` is mostly true while the third `if` is mostly false (see '# of true' column). Hence there appears to be little scope for optimization of `meor` short of replacing the algorithm by a better one. An analysis of the profile would reveal this information in a couple of minutes, thereby saving considerable time and effort.

Information regarding execution counts, etc. is obtained by introducing counters in the program or in its generated code. This can be done by the language compiler as in IITFORT [Dhamdhere *et al*, 1979] or by a preprocessor [Ingalls, 1972].

8.1.5 Program Documentation

Most programming projects suffer from lack of up-to-date documentation. Automatic documentation tools are motivated by the desire to overcome this deficiency. These tools work on the source program to produce different forms of documentation, e.g. flow charts, IO specifications showing files and their records, etc.

8.1.6 Design of Software Tools

Program preprocessing and instrumentation

Program preprocessing techniques are used to support static analysis of programs. Tools generating cross reference listings and lists of unreferenced symbols; test data generators, and documentation aids use this technique. *Program instrumentation* implies insertion of statements in a program. The instrumented program is translated using a standard translator. During execution, the inserted statements perform a set of desired functions. Profile and debug monitors typically use this technique. In a profile monitor, an inserted statement updates a counter indicating the number of times a statement is executed, whereas in debug monitors an inserted statement indicates that execution has reached a specific point in the source program.

Example 8.9 A debug monitor instruments a program to insert statements of the form

```
call debug_mon (const_i);
```

before every statement in the program, where `const_i` is an integer constant indicating the serial number of the statement in the program. During execution of the instrumented program, the debug monitor receives control after every statement. Assume that the user has specified the following debug actions:

```
at 10, display total
at 20, display term
```

Every time debug monitor receives control, it checks to see if statement 10 or 20 is about to be executed. It then performs the debug action indicated by the user.

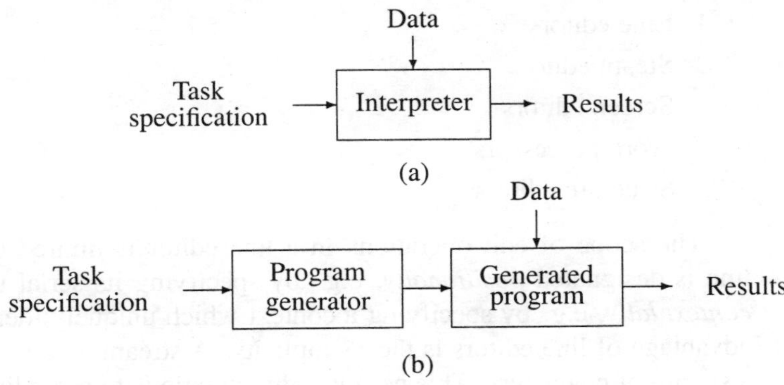

Fig. 8.7 Software tools using interpretation and program generation

Program interpretation and program generation

Figure 8.7 shows the schematic of software tools using the techniques of interpretation and program generation. Use of interpreters in software tools is motivated by the same reasons that motivate the use of interpreters in program development, viz. absence of a translation phase in processing a program. Since most requirements met by software tools are ad hoc, it is useful to eliminate the translation phase. However, interpreter based tools suffer from poor efficiency and poor portability, since an interpreter based tool is only as portable as the interpreter it uses. A generated program is more efficient and can be made portable.

Example 8.10 An organization specializing in the development of interactive applications needs to design user friendly screens for form fillin functions (see Ex. 1.2). It has been decided to use a software tool to obviate repeated coding efforts.

Use of the interpretive approach involves development of a general purpose interpreter for screen handling (we will call it the *screen handler*). Every application that needs to use the tool will have to interface with the screen handler. Whenever the application needs to use a screen, it will have to call the screen handler with the specification of the screen. If the program generator schematic is used, specification of the screen will have to be input to the program generator. The generated program will be in the form of a function which will become a part of the application.

From Fig. 8.7 it can be seen that the interpreter, besides being slow in execution, will require more memory. It will, however, permit dynamic changes in the specifications. The program generator provides execution efficiency. It also provides code space efficiency because only a routine tailored to a desired screen format needs to exist in the application. Any change in the specification of a screen will now imply generation of a new function and its integration with the application.

8.2 EDITORS

Text editors come in the following forms:

1. Line editors
2. Steam editors
3. Screen editors
4. Word processors
5. Structure editors

The scope of edit operations in a line editor is limited to a line of text. The line is designated *positionally*, e.g. by specifying its serial number in the text, or *contextually*, e.g. by specifying a context which uniquely identifies it. The primary advantage of line editors is their simplicity. A stream editor views the entire text as a stream of characters. This permits edit operations to cross line boundaries. Stream editors typically support character, line and context oriented commands based on the current editing context indicated by the position of a *text pointer*. The pointer can be manipulated using positioning or search commands.

Line and steam editors typically maintain multiple representations of text. One representation (the *display form*) shows the text as a sequence of lines. The editor maintains an *internal form* which is used to perform the edit operations. This form contains end-of-line characters and other edit characters. The editor ensures that these representations are compatible at every moment.

8.2.1 Screen editors

A line or stream editor does not display the text in the manner it would appear if printed. A screen editor uses the what-you-see-is-what-you-get principle in editor design. The editor displays a screenful of text at a time. The user can move the cursor over the screen, position it at the point where he desires to perform some editing and proceed with the editing directly. Thus it is possible to see the effect of an edit operation on the screen. This is very useful while formatting the text to produce printed documents.

8.2.2 Word Processors

Word processors are basically document editors with additional features to produce well formatted hard copy output. Essential features of word processors are commands for moving sections of text from one place to another, merging of text, and searching and replacement of words. Many word processors support a spell-check option. With the advent of personal computers, word processors have seen widespread use amongst authors, office personnel and computer professionals. Wordstar is a popular editor of this class.

8.2.3 Structure Editors

A structure editor incorporates an awareness of the structure of a document. This is useful in browsing through a document, e.g. if a programmer wishes to edit a specific function in a program file. The structure is specified by the user while creating or modifying the document. Editing requirements are specified using the structure. A special class of structure editors, called syntax directed editors, are used in programming environments.

Example 8.11 NLS (short form for 'on line system') is an early structure editor [Engelbart, English 1968] oriented towards document editing. A document has a hierarchic structure, with different levels like group, plex, branch and statement. Items within a higher level item are siblings (i.e. brothers) with predecessor-successor relationships. Thus, one can talk of a group, the preceding or succeeding group, first statement in a group, etc.

Contemporary editors support a combination of line, string and screen editing functions. This makes it hard to classify them into the categories defined in this section. The `vi` editor of Unix and the editors in desk top publishing systems are typical examples of these.

8.2.4 Design of an Editor

The fundamental functions in editing are travelling, editing, viewing and display. Travelling implies movement of the editing context to a new position within the text. This may be done explicitly by the user (e.g. the line number command of a line editor) or may be implied in a user command (e.g. the search command of a stream editor). Viewing implies formatting the text in a manner desired by the user. This is an abstract view, independent of the physical characteristics of an IO device. The display component maps this view into the physical characteristics of the display device being used. This determines where a particular view may appear on the user's screen. The separation of viewing and display functions gives rise to interesting possibilities like multiple windows on the same screen, concurrent edit operations using the same display terminal, etc. A simple text editor may choose to combine the viewing and display functions.

Figure 8.8 illustrates the schematic of a simple editor. For a given position of the editing context, the editing and viewing filters operate on the internal form of text to prepare the forms suitable for editing and viewing. These forms are put in the editing and viewing buffers respectively. The viewing-and-display manager makes provision for appropriate display of this text. When the cursor position changes, the filters operate on a new portion of text to update the contents of the buffers. As editing is performed, the editing filter reflects the changes into the internal form and updates the contents of the viewing buffer.

Apart from the fundamental editing functions, most editors support an `undo` function to nullify one or more of the previous edit operations performed by the user. The `undo` function can be implemented by storing a stack of previous views or by devising an inverse for each edit operation. Multilevel `undo` commands pose obvious difficulties in implementing overlapping edits.

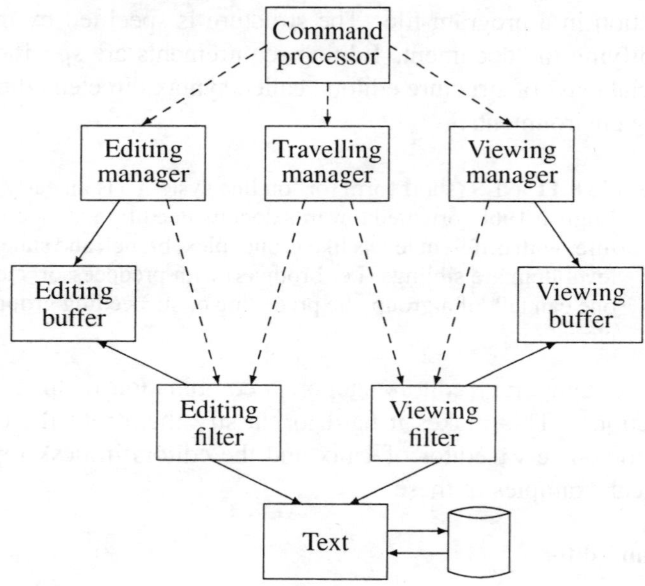

Fig. 8.8 Editor structure

8.3 DEBUG MONITORS

Debug monitors provide the following facilities for dynamic debugging:

1. Setting breakpoints in the program
2. Initiating a debug conversation when control reaches a breakpoint
3. Displaying values of variables
4. Assigning new values to variables
5. Testing user defined assertions and predicates involving program variables.

The debug monitor functions can be easily implemented in an interpreter. However interpretation incurs considerable execution time penalties. Debug monitors therefore rely on instrumentation of a compiled program to implement its functions. To enable the use of a debug monitor, the user must compile the program under the `debug` option. The compiler now inserts the following instructions:

A few `no-op` instructions of the form
`no-op` <*statement no*>

before each statement, where <*statement no*> is a constant indicating the serial number of the statement in the program. The compiler also generates a table containing the pairs (variable name, address). When a user gives a command to set a breakpoint at, say, statement 100, the debug monitor instruments the program to introduce the instruction

$$< SI\_instrn >< Code >$$

in place of the `no-op` instructions preceding `no-op 100`.

The compiled code for the program executes directly on the CPU until it reaches an <*SI_instrn*>. Execution of the <*SI_instrn*> produces a software interrupt with the interrupt code <*Code*>. This signifies a debug interrupt. (Alternatively the debug monitor can use a `BC ANY, DEBUG_MON` instruction instead of < *SI_instrn* >). The debug monitor now gains control and opens a debug conversation. The user may ask for display or modification of program variables. This is implemented using the (variable name, address) information produced by the compiler.

The sequence of steps involved in dynamic debugging of a program is as follows:

1. The user compiles the program under the `debug` option. The compiler produces two files—the compiled code file and the debug information file.
2. The user activates the debug monitor and indicates the name of the program to be debugged. The debug monitor opens the compiled code and debug information files for the program.
3. The user specifies his debug requirements—a list of breakpoints and actions to be performed at breakpoints. The debug monitor instruments the program, and builds a *debug table* containing the pairs (statement number, debug action).
4. The instrumented program gets control and executes up to a breakpoint.
5. A software interrupt is generated when the <*SI_instrn*> is executed. Control is given to the debug monitor which consults the debug table and performs the debug actions specified for the breakpoint. A debug conversation is now opened during which the user may issue some debug commands (which are implemented through interpretation) or modify breakpoints and debug actions associated with breakpoints. Control now returns to the instrumented program.
6. Steps 4 and 5 are repeated until the end of the debug session.

Unix supports two debuggers—`sdb` which is a PL level debugger and `adb` which is an assembly language debugger. `debug` of IBM PC is an object code level debugger.

8.3.1 Testing Assertions

A debug assertion is a relation between the values of program variables. An assertion can be associated with a program statement. The debug monitor verifies the assertion when execution reaches that statement. Program execution continues if the assertion is fulfilled, else a debug conversation is opened. The user can now perform actions to locate the cause of the program malfunction. Use of debug assertions eliminates the need to produce voluminous information for debugging purposes.

8.4 PROGRAMMING ENVIRONMENTS

A programming environment is a software system that provides integrated facilities for program creation, editing, execution, testing and debugging. It consists of the following components:

1. A *syntax directed editor* (which is a structure editor)
2. A language processor—a compiler, interpreter, or both
3. A debug monitor
4. A dialog monitor.

All components are accessed through the dialog monitor. The syntax directed editor incorporates a front end for the programming language. As a user keys in his program, the editor performs syntax analysis and converts it into an intermediate representation (IR), typically an abstract syntax tree. The compiler (or interpreter) and the debug monitor share the IR. If a compiler is used, it is activated after the editor has converted a statement to IR. The compiler works incrementally to generate code for the statement. Thus, program execution or interpretation can be supported immediately after the last statement has been input. At any time during execution the programmer can interrupt program execution and enter the debug mode or return to the editor. In the latter case he can modify the program and resume or restart its execution.

The main simplification for the user is the easy accessibility of all functions through the dialog monitor. The system may also provide other program development and testing functions. For example, it may permit a programmer to execute a partially completed program. The programmer can be alerted if an undeclared variable or an incomplete statement is encountered during execution. The programmer can insert necessary declarations or statements and resume execution. This permits major interfaces in the program to be tested prior to the development of a module. Some programming environments also support reversible execution, whereby a program's execution can be 'stepped back' by one or more statements.

The Cornell Program Synthesizer

The Cornell Program Synthesizer (CPS) [Teitelman, Reps, 1981] is a syntax directed programming environment for a subset of PL/I known as PL/CS. It contains a syntax directed editor, a compilation-and-interpretation schematic for program execution, and a collection of debugging tools.

The editor guides the user to develop a well structured program through the use of templates. A *template* is a unit of information concerning PL/CS. It consists of some fixed syntax information and a few placeholders. A *placeholder* signifies a position in the program where a specific language construct, e.g. a statement or an expression, may be inserted by the programmer. (It is equivalent to a nonterminal symbol in a sentential form.) A program development session starts when the user keys in the command `main`. The editor now displays the template for a program, viz.

```
/* comment */
name :  procedure options(main);
  □{declaration}
  {statement}
  END name;
```

where □ marks the position of the cursor, and { `declaration` } and { `statement` } are placeholders. The user can bring the cursor to a placeholder and begin to expand it by indicating the kind of entity he wishes to put there. CPS now replaces the placeholder by the template for that entity. Use of templates avoids syntax errors. Thus, errors like more **else**'s than **if**'s or missing **end**'s for **do** statements cannot arise in a CPS generated program.

Example 8.12 A user wishes to place an **if** statement in the placeholder { `statement` } in the initial template. When he indicates this, the program becomes

```
/* comment */
name :  procedure options(main);
  {declaration}
  if □{condition} then {statement}
                  else {statement}
  END name;
```

The user can move the cursor to the new placeholder {`statement`}, indicate that an assignment statement is to be inserted in its place and type `a = b;` followed by the `return` key. The placeholder { `statement` } is now replaced by the statement `a = b;`. Moving the cursor to { `statement` } in the **else** part and pressing `return` indicates that the **else** clause is empty.

As the user keys in program statements, they are converted into an IR. Cursor position on the screen is mapped into the correct node of IR to support expansion of a placeholder. CPS supports execution of a partially complete program. When an unexpanded placeholder is encountered during execution, the user is prompted to expand it before resuming execution. The screen is split into two during execution. The lower half is used to display execution results and debug output, if any. The upper half displays a part of the user program in which the statement under execution is marked with the cursor symbol □. Thus, as execution proceeds, the flow of execution through the program is displayed on the screen. The user can interrupt execution at any moment and open a debug conversation or modify the program before resuming or restarting execution.

Experience with the use of CPS has uncovered some significant strengths and weaknesses. The template governed approach guarantees that every CPS generated program is syntactically valid. However, it makes certain operations, like insertion of a loop in an existing program, quite difficult. Another significant drawback is the absence of an undo facility. Later programming environments have removed some of these deficiencies. For example, the programming environment Poe offers unlimited undo facilities. It also offers on line help. The user can query the various expansion options available at a placeholder and the scope and accessibility of variables at a given point in the program. All these facilities further enhance the utility of programming environments.

EXERCISE 8.4

1. Comment on the statement "Dynamic debugging is easier to implement in interpreters than in compilers".
2. Comment on whether you would prefer a generative schematic or an interpretive schematic for following purposes:
   (a) Implementing `display` commands issued during dynamic debugging
   (b) Producing a report from a file
   (c) Writing a general purpose screen handling system
   (d) Handling data base queries.

   Give reasons for your answers.
3. A program profiling package is to be implemented for a Pascal compiler. The following options are being considered for its design:
   (a) Write a preprocessor which would introduce Pascal statements in a program to collect information during execution of the program,
   (b) Support a `profile` option in the compiler to perform program instrumentation.

   Which option would you use? Why?

8.5 USER INTERFACES

A *user interface* (UI) plays a vital role in simplifying the interaction of a user with an application. Classically, UI functionalities have two important aspects—issuing of commands and exchange of data. In early days of computing, a user was often the application designer or developer. Hence an understanding of commands and data was implicit in the use of an application. In those days UI's did not have an independent identity. This situation changed because of two reasons. First, as applications became larger a user was no longer expected to know all details concerning an application. Hence presentation of commands and prompts for data became important. Second, as applications grew to newer fields, it became necessary to assume a lower level of computer skills in an application user. This increased the importance of UI's by adding a new aspect, viz. on line help, to their functionality. The on line help component of the UI serves the function of educating the user in the capabilities of an application and the modalities of its usage. A well designed UI can make the difference between a grudging set of users and an excited user population (and even a fan following!) for an application.

A UI can be visualized to consist of two components—a *dialog manager* and a *presentation manager*. The dialog manager manages the conversation between the user and the application. This involves prompting the user for a command and transmitting the command to the application. The presentation manager displays the data produced by the application in an appropriate manner on the user's display or printer device.

8.5.1 Command Dialogs

Commands are issued to an application through a command dialog. Three ways to implement command dialogs are:

1. Command languages
2. Command menus
3. Direct manipulation.

Command languages for computer applications are similar to command languages for operating systems. Primitive command languages support imperative commands with the syntax *<action>* *<parameters>*. More sophisticated command languages have both declarative and imperative commands and a syntax and semantics of their own. A practical difficulty in the use of a command language is the need to learn it before using the application. This implies a large commitment of time and effort on the part of the user, which makes casual use of the application forbidding. On line help can provide some relief by avoiding the need to memorize the syntax of commands, however it cannot eliminate the need to invest time and effort in initial learning of the command language.

Command menus provide obvious advantages to the casual user of an application, as the basic functionalities of the application are reflected in the menu choices. A hierarchy of menus can be used to guide the user into the details concerning a functionality. Interesting variations like pull-down menus are designed to simplify the use of menu systems. Most Turbo compilers use pull down command menus.

A *direct manipulation system* provides the user with a visual display of the universe of the application. The display shows the important objects in the universe. Actions or operations over objects are indicated using some kind of pointing device, e.g. a cursor or a mouse.

Example 8.13 `Lotus 1-2-3` is an example of a direct manipulation system. The universe of the application is the spreadsheet. The user can select a specific cell in the spreadsheet, change its contents and study the effect of this change on other cells.

Examples of direct manipulation can also be found in screen editors and video games.

Principles of command dialog design

Psychologists and human factors engineers have formulated a set of principles to ensure the effectiveness of command dialogs. Some of these are:

1. Ease of use

2. Consistency in command structure
3. Immediate feedback on user commands
4. Error handling
5. On line help to avoid memorizing command details
6. Undo facility
7. Shortcuts for experienced users.

Command menus score over command languages on the basis of principles 1, 2 and 5, while command languages are superior on the basis of principle 7. Some menu systems provide a *type ahead* facility while entering menu choices. This permits the user of a hierarchical menu system to type the menu choices for menus which are yet to be displayed on the user screen. This improves the appeal of the menu system for experienced users. Recent trends in command dialog design have been towards the use of direct manipulation systems with a graphics capability.

8.5.2 Presentation of Data

Data for an application can be input through free form typing. Alternatively, a form fillin approach may be used (see Ex. 1.2) when large volume of data is involved. Application results can be presented in the form of tables. Summary data can be presented in the form of graphs, pie charts, etc.

8.5.3 On Line Help

On line help is very important to promote and sustain interest in the use of an application. It minimizes the effort of initial learning of commands and avoids the distraction of having to consult a printed document to resolve every doubt. On line help to the users can be organized in the form of on line explanations, demonstrations, tutorials or on line manuals concerning commands. The on line help facility should be organized such that desired information can be efficiently located using the structure of the information, e.g. by searching for section headings, subtitles, figure or table names, footnotes, etc. Another effective method of organizing on line help is to provide context sensitive help, whereby a query can fetch different responses depending on the current position of the user in the application.

Hypertext

Hypertext visualizes a document to consist of a hierarchical arrangement of information units, and provides a variety of means to locate the required information. This takes the form of

1. Tables and indexes
2. String searching functions
3. Means to navigate within the document
4. Backtracking facilities.

Effectiveness of a hypertext document depends on the care with which it is organized. Hypertext authoring systems have been developed to help the application designer in the design of hypertext documents.

8.5.4 Structure of a User Interface

Figure 8.9 shows a UI schematic using a standard graphics package. The UI consists of two main components, presentation manager and dialog manager. The *presentation manager* is responsible for managing the user's screen and for accepting data and presenting results. The *dialog manager* is responsible for interpreting user commands and implementing them by invoking different modules of the application code. The dialog manager is also responsible for error messages and on line help functions, and for organizing changes in the visual context of the user.

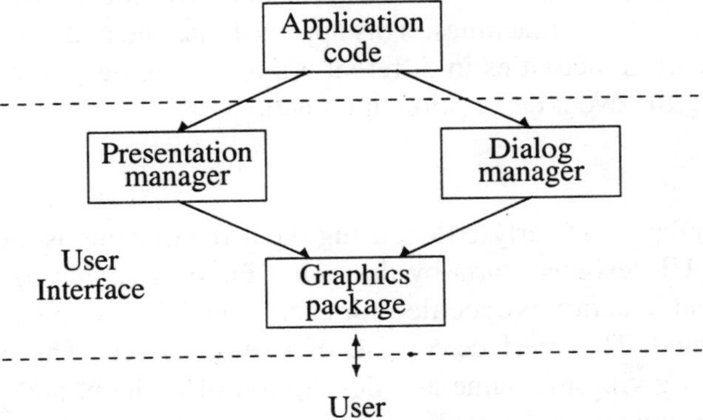

Fig. 8.9 User Interface

Example 8.14 The fields Employee name and Married in the form fillin screen of Fig. 1.8 (see Ex. 1.2) can be displayed by issuing the following commands to the graphics package:

```
Display ((2,5) Employee name :)
Drawbox ((2,25)(55,1))
Display ((10,5) Married :)
Drawdoublebox ((10,25)(2,1)(yes))
```

The dialog monitor is trivial in this application.

8.5.5 User Interface Management Systems

A *user interface management system* (UIMS) automates the generation of user interfaces. The UIMS accepts specification of the presentation and dialog semantics to produce the presentation and dialog managers of the UI respectively. The presentation and data managers could be generated programs specific to the presentation and dialog semantics. Alternatively, the presentation and dialog managers could use interpretive schematics to implement the presentation and dialog semantics.

A variety of formalisms have been used to describe dialog semantics. These include grammars, event descriptions and finite state machines. In a grammar based description, the syntax and semantics of commands are specified in a YACC like manner. Thus, the interface is activated when a user types in a command. The event based approach uses a visual model of the interface. A screen with icons is displayed to the user. Selection of an icon by clicking the mouse on it causes an event. The action specified against the event is now performed.

The grammar and event description approaches lack the notion of a sequence of actions. The finite state machine approach can efficiently incorporate this notion. The basic principle in this approach is to associate a finite state machine with each window or each icon. Actions are specified on the basis of conditions involving the states of these machines. This approach has the additional power of coordinating the concurrent activities in different windows. In the following we describe two UIMSs using the event description approach.

Menulay

Menulay is an early UIMS using the screen layout as the basis for the dialog model. The UI designer starts by designing the user screen to consist of a set of icons. A semantic action is specified for each icon. This action is performed when the icon is selected. The interface consists of a set of screens. The system generates a set of icon tables giving the name and description of an icon, and a list of (event, function_id) pairs indicating the application function to be called when an event is selected.

Hypercard

This UIMS from Apple incorporates object orientation in the event oriented approach. A *card* has an associated screen layout containing buttons and fields. A button can be selected by clicking the mouse on it. A field contains editable text. Each card has a specific background, which itself behaves like a card. Many cards can share the same background. A hypercard program is thus a hierarchy of cards called a *stack*. UI behaviour is specified by associating an action, in the form of a HyperTalk script, with each button, field and card. The action for an event is determined by using the hierarchy of cards as an inheritance hierarchy. Hypercard uses an interpretive schematic to implement a UI.

EXERCISE 8.5

1. A library information system is to provide three functions—
   (a) Query the issue status of a book
   (b) Search the catalog by author and title
   (c) Issue or return a book.

Design a set of screens for these functions. Visualize the design of a UI using a Menulay or Hypercard like system.

BIBLIOGRAPHY

Kernighan and Plauger (1981) discuss various software tools based on the program preprocessing approach. Miller (1979) is a tutorial on software tools. Text editors are widely discussed in the literature. Meyrowitz and Dam (1981) is a comprehensive survey article on text editors. Myers (1979), Miller and Howden (1981) and Beizer (1983) are important sources on various aspects of program testing. Myers (1979) also describes software tools for program testing. Huang (1978) discusses fundamentals of program instrumentation for software testing. Ingalls (1972), Arthur and Ramanathan (1981) and Power (1983) describe use of instrumentation in different kinds of program analysis. Howden (1975), Koster (1980), Voges (1980) and Woodward and Hedley (1980) discuss aspects of test data generation. Prywes *et al* (1979) is an important article on automatic program generation. Martin (1982) describes generation of application programs. Allison (1983) discusses syntax directed editing. Barstow (1983) and Hunke (1981) are important sources on integrated programming environments.

(a) Software tools in general

1. Kernighan, B.W. and P.J.Plauger (1981): *Software Tools in Pascal*, Addison-Wesley, Reading.
2. Miller, E.(ed.) (1979): *Tutorial: Automated Tools for Software Engineering*, IEEE Computer Society Press.
3. Reifer, D.J. and S. Trattner (1977): "A glossary of software tools and techniques," *Computer*, **10** (7), 52-61.
4. Rochkind, M.J. (1975): "The source code control system," *IEEE Transactions on Software Engineering*, **1** (4), 364-370.

(b) Text editors

1. Embley, D.W. and G. Nagy (1981): "Behavioral aspects of text editors," *Computing Surveys*, **13** (1), 33-70.
2. Engelbart, D.C. and W.K. English (1968): "A research centre for augmenting human intellect," *AFIPS SJCC*, 33, 395-410.
3. Fraser, C.W.(1980): "A generalised text editor," *Commn. of ACM*, **23** (1), 27-60.
4. Macleod, I.A. (1977): "Design and implementation of a display oriented text editor," *Software – Practice and Experience*, **7** (6), 771-778.
5. Meyrowitz, N. and A. Van Dam (1982): "Interactive editing systems," Parts I and II, *Computing Surveys*, **14** (3), 321-352 and 353-416.

(c) Program testing and debugging

1. Beizer, B. (1983): *Software Testing Techniques*, Van Nostrand, New York, 1983.
2. Fairly, R.E.(1979):"ALADDIN: Assembly language assertion driven debug interpreter," *IEEE Transactions on Software Engineering*, **5** (4), 426-428.

3. Foster, K.A.(1980): "Error sensitive test cases analysis," *IEEE Transactions on Software Engineering*, **6**, 258-265.
4. Howden, W.F. (1975): "Methodology for generation of software test data," *IEEE Transactions on Computers*, **24** (5), 554-559.
5. Miller, E. and W.E. Howden (eds.) (1981): *Tutorial: Software Testing and Validation Techniques*, IEEE Computer Society Press.
6. Myers, G.J. (1979): The Art of Software Testing, Wiley, New York.
7. Tratner, M. (1979): "A fundamental approach to debugging," *Software – Practice and Experience*, **9** (2), 97-100.
8. Voges, U. *et al* (1980): "SADAT: an automated testing tool," *IEEE Transactions on Software Engineering*, **6** (3), 286-290.
9. Wilcox, T.R. *et al* (1976): "The design and implementation of a table driven, interactive diagnostic programming system," *Commn. of ACM*, **19** (11), 609-616.
10. Woodward, M.R. and D. Hedley (1980): "Experience with path analysis and testing of programs," *IEEE Transactions on Software Engineering*, **6** (3), 278-286.

(d) Program instrumentation and Performance enhancement

1. Allen, F.E. and J. Cocke (1972): "A catalogue of optimizing transformations," in *Design and Optimization of Compilers*, R. Rustin (ed.), Prentice-Hall, Englewood Cliffs.
2. Arthur, J. and J. Ramanathan (1981): "Design of analyzers for selective program analysis," *IEEE Transactions on Software Engineering*, **7** (1), 39-51.
3. Dhamdhere, D.M., K.S. Shastry, C.V. Ravishankar and N.P.S. Bajwa, (1979): *IITFORT User Manual*, Publications Division, IIT Bombay.
4. Huang, J.C.(1978): "Program instrumentation and software testing," *Computer*, **11** (4), 25-33.
5. Ingalls, D. (1972): "The execution time profile as a programming tool," in *Design and Optimization of Compilers*, R. Rustin (ed.), Prentice-Hall, Englewood Cliffs.
6. Power, L.R.(1983): "Design and use of a program execution analyser," *IBM Systems Journal*, **22** (3), 271-294.

(e) Program generators

1. Martin, J.(1982): *Application Development Without Programmers*, Prentice-Hall, Englewood Cliffs.
2. Prywes, N.S., A. Pnueli and S. Shastry (1979): "Use of nonprocedural specification language and associated program generator in software development," *ACM TOPLAS*, **1** (2), 196-217.

(f) Structure editors and Programming environments

1. Allison, L. (1983): "Syntax directed program editing," *Software – Practice and Experience*, **13**, 453-465.
2. Barstow, D.R., H.E. Shrobe, and E. Sandewall (1983): *Interactive Programming Environments*, McGraw-Hill, New York.
3. Fischer, C.N. *et al* (1981): "An introduction to release I of editor Allan Poe," *Computer Science Technical Report 451*, University of Wisconsin.

4. Hunke, H. (1981): *Software Engineering Environments*, North Holland Publ. Co., Amsterdam.
5. Shapiro, E. *et al* (1981): "PASES – A programming environment for Pascal," *SIGPLAN Notices*, **16** (8), 50-57.
6. Teitelman, T. and T. Reps (1981): "The Cornell Program Synthesizer – a syntax directed programming environment," *Commn. of ACM*, **24** (9), 563-573.

(g) User Interfaces

1. Barth, P.S. (1986): "An OO approach to graphical interfaces," *ACM transactions on Graphics*, **5** (2), 142-172.
2. Hayes, F., N. Baran (1989): "A guide to GUI", *Byte*, July 1989, 250-257.
3. Larson (1991): *Interactive software: Tools for Building Interactive User Interfaces*, Prentice-Hall, Reading.
4. Mayhew (1992): *Principles and Guidelines in Software User Interface Design*, Prentice-Hall, Reading.
5. Olsen, D.R. (1992): *User Interface Management Systems*, Morgan Kaufmann, San Mateo, California.
6. Pfaff, G.E. (1985): *User Interface Management Systems*, Springer Verlag.
7. Schneiderman, B. (1983): "Direct manipulation : A step beyond programming languages," *Computer*, **16** (8), 57-69.
8. Schneiderman, B. (1993): *Designing the User Interface*, (2nd edition), Addison-Wesley, New York.

Part II

OPERATING SYSTEMS

CHAPTER 9

Evolution of OS Functions

9.1 OS FUNCTIONS

OS functions can be classified into

- Resource allocation and related functions
- User interface functions.

The resource allocation function implements resource sharing by the users of a computer system. Basically, it performs *binding* of a set of resources with a requesting program—that is, it associates resources with a program. The related functions implement protection of users sharing a set of resources against mutual interference. The user interface function facilitates creation and use of appropriate computational structures by a user. This function typically involves the use of a command language or a menu.

9.1.1 Resource allocation and related functions

The resource allocation function allocates resources for use by a user's computation. Resources can be divided into system-provided resources like CPUs, memory areas and IO devices, or user-created resources like files which are entrusted to the OS. Resource allocation criteria depend on whether a resource is a system resource or a user-created resource. Allocation of system resources is driven by considerations of efficiency of resource utilization. Allocation of user-created resources is based on a set of constraints specified by its creator and typically embodies the notion of access privileges.

Two popular strategies for resource allocation are:

- Partitioning of resources

- Allocation from a pool.

In the resource partitioning approach, the OS decides *a priori* what resources should be allocated to a user computation. This approach is called *static allocation* because the allocation is made before the execution of a program starts. Static resource allocation is simple to implement, however, it could lead to suboptimal utilization because the allocation is made on the basis of perceived needs of a program, rather than its actual needs. In the latter approach, the OS maintains a common pool of resources and allocates from this pool on a need basis. Thus, OS considers allocation of a resource when a program raises a request for a resource. This approach is called *dynamic allocation* because the allocation takes place during the execution of a program. Dynamic resource allocation can lead to better utilization of resources because the allocation is made when a program requests a resource.

An OS can use a resource table as the central data structure for resource allocation. The table contains an entry for each resource unit in the system. The entry contains the name or address of the resource unit and its present status, i.e. whether it is free or allocated to some program. When a program raises a request for a resource, the resource would be allocated to it if it is presently free. If many resource units of a resource class exist in the system, a resource request only indicates the resource class and the OS checks if any resource unit of that class is available for allocation.

In the partitioned resource allocation approach, the OS decides on the resources to be allocated to a program based on the number of resources and the number of programs in the system. For example, an OS may decide that a program can be allocated 1 MB of memory, 2000 disk blocks and a monitor. Such a collection of resources is referred to as a partition. In effect, a set of partitions can be predefined in the system. The resource table can have an entry for each resource partition. When a new program is to be started, an available partition is allocated to it.

Resource preemption

There are different ways in which resources can be shared by a set of programs. Some of these are:

- Sequential sharing
- Concurrent sharing.

In sequential sharing, a resource is allocated for exclusive use by a program. When the resource is de-allocated, it is marked *free* in the resource table. Now it can be allocated to another program. In concurrent sharing, two or more programs can concurrently use the same resource. Examples of concurrent sharing are data files. Most other resources cannot be shared concurrently. Unless otherwise mentioned, all through this text resources are assumed to be only sequentially shareable.

When a resource is sequentially shareable, the system can deallocate a resource when the program makes an explicit request for deallocation. Alternatively, it can deallocate a resource by force. This is called resource preemption.

Definition 9.1 (Resource Preemption) Resource preemption *is forceful deallocation of a resource.*

Preemption of system resources is used by the OS to enforce fairness in their use by programs, or to realize certain system-level goals. A preempted program cannot execute unless the preempted resource unit, or some other resource unit of the same resource class, is allocated to it once again. The shorter term *preemption* is used for preemption of the CPU, and the full term *resource preemption* is used for premption of other resources.

CPU sharing

The CPU can be shared in a sequential manner only. Hence only one program can execute at any time. Other programs in the system have to wait their turn. It is often important to provide fair service to all programs in the system. Hence preemption is used to free the CPU so that it can be given to another program. Deciding which program should be given the CPU and for how long is a critical function. This function is called *CPU scheduling*, or simply *scheduling*. Partitioning is a bad approach for CPU sharing, allocation from a pool is the obvious approach to use.

Memory sharing

Like the CPU, the memory also cannot be shared concurrently. However, unlike the CPU, its availability can be increased by treating different parts of memory as different resources. Both the partitioning and the pool-based allocation approaches can be used to manage the memory resource. Memory preemption can also be used to increase the availability of memory to programs. Special terms are used for different memory preemption techniques, hence the term 'memory preemption' is rarely used in our discussions.

9.1.2 User interface related functions

The purpose of a user interface is to provide for the use of OS resources, primarily the CPU, for processing a user's computational requirements. OS user interfaces typically use command languages. The user uses a command to set up an appropriate computational structure to fulfill a computational requirement.

A variety of computational structures can be defined by an OS. A sample list of computational structures is as follows:

1. A single program
2. A sequence of single programs
3. A collection of programs.

These computational structures will be defined and described in later chapters; here we only point out a few salient features. It is assumed that each program is individually initiated by the user through the user interface. The single program consists of the execution of a program on a given set of data. The user initiates execution of the program through a command. Two kinds of programs can exist—sequential and concurrent. A sequential program, which matches with the conventional notion of a program, is the simplest computational structure. In a concurrent program, different parts of the program can execute concurrently. For this, the OS has to be aware of the identities of the different parts which can execute concurrently. This function is typically *not* served by the user interface of the OS; Chapter 10 indicates how it is achieved. In this chapter it is assumed that each program is sequential in nature.

In a sequence of programs, each program is initiated by the user individually. However, the programs are not independent of each other—execution of a program is meaningful only if the previous programs in the sequence execute successfully. However, since the programs are initiated individually, their interface with one another is set up explicitly by the user. In a collection of programs, the user names the programs involved in the collection in his command. Thus, their identities are indicated to the OS through the user interface itself. The interface between the programs is handled by the OS.

Example 9.1 An MS DOS .bat file contains a sequence of commands, each command indicating the execution of a program. This forms a sequence of programs. If the user tries to terminate the execution of a program after initiation of the .bat file, the OS responds with a query as to whether execution of the entire .bat file should be terminated.

Example 9.2 The Unix command

```
cat names | sort | uniq | wc -l
```

initiates execution of a collection of programs which count the number of unique names in file `names`. The collection contains four programs—`cat`, `sort`, `uniq` and `wc`. The output of `cat` is fed to `sort` as its input. Likewise the outputs of `sort` and `uniq` are given to `uniq` and `wc` as their inputs. `cat` puts the contents of file `names` on its standard output file, `sort` accepts and sorts these names in alphabetical order. `uniq` removes duplicate names and outputs the unique names appearing in its input. `wc` counts and reports the number of names in its input. Note that the programs run concurrently rather than sequentially. The OS ensures that a program consumes some data only after it is produced by the preceding program in the command.

9.2 EVOLUTION OF OS FUNCTIONS

Operating system (OS) functions have evolved in response to the following considerations and issues:

1. Efficient utilization of computing resources
2. New features in computer architecture
3. New user requirements.

Different operating systems address these issues in different manner, however most operating systems contain components which have similar functionalities. For example, all operating systems contain components for functions of memory management, process management and protection of users from one another. The techniques used to implement these functions may vary from one OS to another, but the fundamental concepts are the same. These inherent similarities between OSs make their study manageable. Thus, it is not necessary to study a large number of OSs to understand operating system principles. A study of the fundamental concepts in OS design followed by a few case studies of OS implementations are sufficient to understand operating systems.

In this chapter we study the concepts in OS design by studying the evolution of OS functions and identifying the fundamental concepts and techniques used in their implementation. We also introduce formal definitions of concepts and relevant terminology.

Jobs, programs and processes

The primary function of an OS is to organize the execution of user computations in a computer system. A suitable characterization of user computations is therefore fundamental to its design. Three characterizations of user computations have been used to date—jobs, programs and processes. A *program* is the classical view of a computation. It consists of a set of program units, including program units obtained from libraries, which constitute an object code to be executed. A *process* is an execution of a program or of a part of a program. It differs from a program when concurrent programming techniques are used for coding the program. In such a case many processes can execute a program or a part of a program. Processes are discussed in chapters 10 and 13.

A *job* is a computational structure which is a sequence of programs. It consists of a sequence of *job steps*, each job step constituting the execution of a program. Thus, a job for the compilation and execution of a Pascal program involves the following three job steps—execution of the Pascal compiler to compile the Pascal program, execution of the linker to prepare the compiled program for execution, and execution of the object program which has just been linked. Note that it is not meaningful to execute a job step unless each of the previous job steps has executed successfully, e.g. linking is not meaningful unless compilation was successful. The notion of a job was important in early computer systems which did not support interactive computing. It is of marginal relevance in most contemporary systems, for example the BAT files of MS DOS and shellscripts of Unix resemble the notion of jobs.

In this chapter, the terms job and program are used interchangeably. In later chapters, particularly in the chapter on scheduling, we shall be more specific about the use of these terms.

9.3 BATCH PROCESSING SYSTEMS

When punched cards were used to record user jobs, processing of a job involved physical actions by the system operator, e.g. loading a deck of cards into the card reader, pressing switches on the computer's console to initiate a job, etc. These actions wasted a lot of CPU time. Batch processing (BP) was introduced to avoid this wastage.

A *batch* is a sequence of user jobs. A computer operator forms a batch by arranging user jobs in a sequence and inserting special marker cards to indicate the start and end of the batch. After forming a batch, the operator submits it to the batch processing operating system. The primary function of the BP system is to implement the processing of the jobs in a batch without requiring any intervention of the operator. This is achieved by automating the transition from the execution of one job to that of the next job in the batch. Results of a job are released to the user at the end of the batch. Note that a batch is not a computational structure of a user; each job in the batch is independent of other jobs in the batch.

Batch processing is implemented by locating a component of the BP system, called the *batch monitor* or *supervisor*, permanently in one part of the computer's memory. The remaining memory is used to process a user job—the current job in the batch. The batch monitor is responsible for implementing the various functions of the batch processing system. It accepts a command from the system operator for initiating the processing of a batch and sets up the processing of the first job of the batch. At the end of the job, it performs job termination processing and initiates execution of the next job. At the end of the batch, it performs batch termination processing and awaits initiation of the next batch by the operator.

Figure 9.1 shows a schematic of a BP system. The batch consists of n jobs, job_1, job_2, ... job_n, one of which is currently in execution. The left half of the figure depicts a *memory map* showing the arrangement of the batch monitor and the current job of the batch in the computer's memory. The part of memory occupied by the batch monitor is called the *system area*, and the part occupied by the user job is called the *user area*.

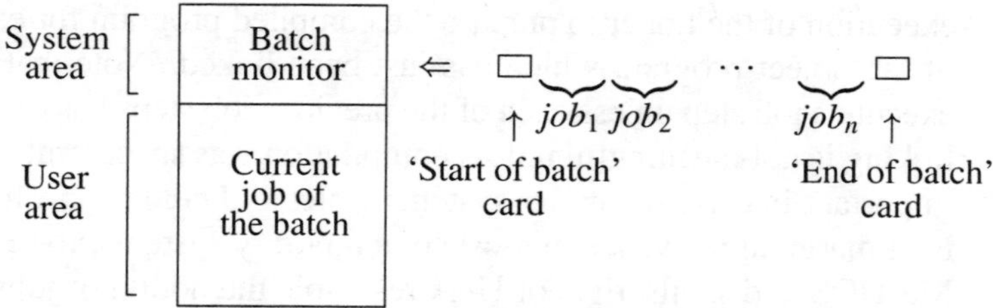

Fig. 9.1 Schematic of a batch processing system

9.3.1 User Service

A user evaluates the performance of an OS on the basis of the service accorded to his or her job. The notion of *turn-around time* is used to quantify user service in a batch processing system.

Definition 9.2 (Turn-around time) *The* turn-around time *of a user job is the time since its submission to the time its results become available to the user.*

The turn around time of a job, say job_i, includes the following:

1. Time till a batch is formed (i.e. time till the jobs $job_{i+1}, \ldots job_n$ are submitted)
2. Time spent in executing all jobs of the batch
3. Time spent in printing and sorting the results belonging to different jobs.

Thus, the turn-around time for job_i is a function of many factors, its own execution time being only one of them. It is clear that use of batch processing does not guarantee improvements in the turn-around times of jobs. In fact, the service to individual users would probably deteriorate due to the three factors mentioned above. This is not surprising because batch processing does not aim at improving user service—it aims at improving CPU utilization.

9.3.2 Batch Monitor Functions

The basic task of the batch monitor is to exercise effective control over the BP environment. This task can be classified into the following three functions:

1. Scheduling
2. Memory management
3. Sharing and protection.

The batch monitor performs the first two functions before initiating the execution of a job. The third function is performed during the execution of a job.

9.3.2.1 Scheduling

Definition 9.3 (Scheduling) Scheduling *is the activity of determining which service request should be handled next by a server.*

In a batch processing system, the CPU of the computer system is the server and the user jobs are the service requests. The nature of batch processing dictates use of the first-come-first-served (FCFS) scheduling criterion. The batch monitor performs scheduling by always selecting the next job in the batch for execution. Scheduling does not influence user service in a BP system because the turn-around time of each job in a batch is subject to the factors mentioned before. Scheduling is non-preemptive since only one job exists in the system at any time.

Due to the use of the FCFS criterion, some amount of job scheduling is implicit in batch formation. This fact can be used by the operations personnel of a computer installation to influence turn around times of jobs to some extent. For example, jobs with different priorities could be put in different batches, and higher priority batches could be processed earlier than others. This would ensure that jobs with higher priorities would have smaller turn around times.

9.3.2.2 Memory Management

At any time during a BP system's operation, the memory is divided into the system area and the user area (see Fig. 9.1). The user area of memory is sequentially shared by the jobs in a batch. This arrangement leads to an obvious allocation issue—how much memory should be allocated to the system area and how much to the user area? An OS designer would like to make the user area as large as possible. At the same time, it is necessary to implement many functions in the batch monitor. A practical solution to this problem is to devise an overlay structure (see Section 7.5) for the monitor, such that unrelated parts of monitor code do not coexist in the memory.

Figure 9.2 illustrates an arrangement using the overlay technique. Some part of the monitor code (called *resident part* of the monitor) is permanently situated in the memory, while other parts (called the *transient parts*) are loaded into a *transient area* whenever required. Frequently needed monitor functions, e.g. IO control, interrupt processing, etc., exist in the resident part of monitor, while infrequently required services like device error recovery, file open and close, etc., belong to the transient part of the monitor. Note that this is a static decision; it is taken while designing the batch monitor and *not* during the operation of the BP system.

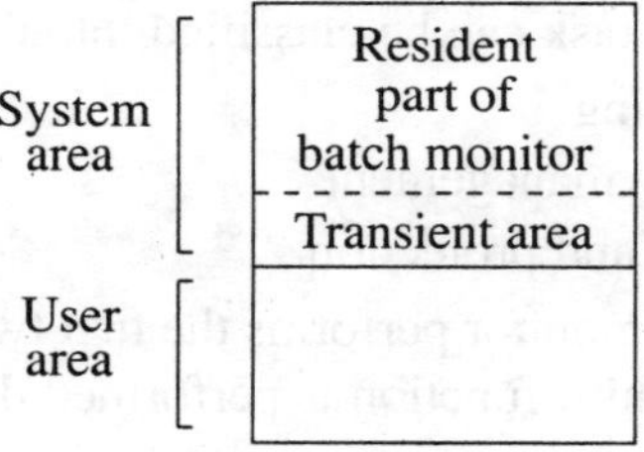

Fig. 9.2 Resident and transient parts of a batch monitor

9.3.2.3 Sharing and Protection

An OS needs to provide two guarantees when its hardware and software resources are shared among its users: Fair treatment to each user's requirements, and absence of interference from other users in the system. These are termed the fairness and protection issues, respectively.

An OS deals with these issues through two distinct functions—the resource allocation function, and the protection function. The resources of a BP system are used sequentially by user jobs. The resource allocation and deallocation function is implicitly performed during job initiation and termination. Once a job is initiated, the entire collection of system resources is available to it till its completion.

The protection function is more complex. User jobs cannot interfere with each other's execution directly because they never co-exist in a computer's memory. However, contrary to one's intuition, sequential sharing of resources can sometimes lead to loss of protection.

Protection problems in card based systems

As mentioned at the start of this section, early BP systems were card-based systems of the 1960's. These systems possessed very limited secondary memories like tapes and disks. Hence system commands, user programs and data were all derived from a single input source—the card reader. This could lead to a situation where the execution of one job interferes with the execution of the next job in the batch (see Ex. 9.3).

Example 9.3 Two jobs A and B exist in a batch, each job consisting of a program and its data. The user who submitted job A has included five data cards in it whereas the program of job A requires ten data cards. When job A executes, it reads its five data cards and the first five cards of job B as its own data. When job B is processed, the compiler finds many errors since the first five cards of B are missing.

Control statements and the command interpreter

A BP system requires a user to insert a set of control statements in a job. The control statements are used for two purposes—to implement a job as a 'sequence of programs' (see Section 9.1.2), and to avoid mutual interference between jobs. Figure 9.3 shows the control statements used to compile and execute a Pascal program. For simplicity we have omitted statements concerning data-set definitions or device assignments which would be necessary in most systems. The `// JOB` statement indicates the start of a job. It contains accounting information for the user, e.g. accounting code, user status, resource limits, etc. An `// EXEC` statement names the program to be executed. Thus, `// EXEC PASCAL` indicates that the Pascal compiler is to be executed. The Pascal program to be compiled follows this statement. The end-of-data statement '`/*`' marks the end of the source program. An `// EXEC` statement without a program name indicates that the just-compiled program should be loaded for the purpose of execution. The second '`/*`' statement indicates the end of data for the program, and the '`/&`' statement indicates the end of the job.

A control statement is processed by the *command interpreter* component of the BP supervisor. The command interpreter reads a control statement, analyses it and carries out the required action. It also checks for errors which might lead to interference between jobs. On encountering a `// JOB` statement, it verifies the validity of the user's account and initializes its own data bases to note that the processing of a new job has started. On seeing an `// EXEC` statement, it organizes loading of the appropriate program for the purpose of execution. On encountering a '`/*`' or '`/&`' statement, it realizes that the program has reached the end of its data and should not be permitted to read any more cards. If the program tries to read more cards, it is terminated by the command interpreter. Since a job is a sequence of programs, abnormal termination of a program implies that remaining job steps of the job should not be processed. The command interpreter implements this by skipping to the '`/&`'

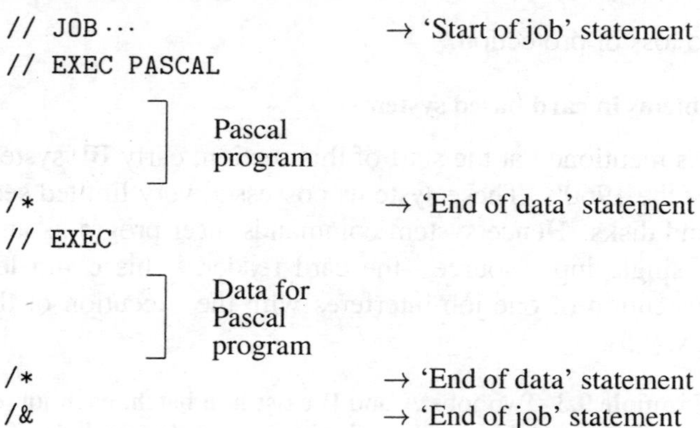

Fig. 9.3 Control statements in IBM 360/370 systems

statement. At the '/&' statement, it updates the resource utilization information for the user.

The command interpreter exists in the resident part of the batch monitor. To implement the processing of control statements as described above, the command interpreter should obtain control between every two job steps of a job, i.e. whenever a program completes its execution. If the execution was successful it initiates the processing of the next job step after skipping the left-over data cards of the previous program. If the previous program did not execute successfully, the command interpreter organizes termination of the current job and initiation of the next job.

The command interpreter algorithm is given in the following. Figure 9.4 contains the procedures used by the algorithm. The algorithm uses the following flags:

mode	:	indicates whether the program in execution is a system program or a user program
abnormal_eoj	:	indicates whether the previous job has been abnormally terminated
end_of_job_seen	:	indicates whether the end-of-job statement has been processed

Algorithm 9.1 (Batch processing command interpreter)

1. *mode* := '*system*';
   abnormal_eoj := '*no*';
   end_of_job_seen := '*no*';
   user_id := '*nil*';
2. *read_a_card*;
3. (a) **if** *abnormal_eoj* = '*yes*' **then**
   job_end_processing;

(b) **else if** *abnormal_eoj* = '*no*' & *mode* = '*user*' **then**
    validate_a_data_card;
    Return to user program.

(c) **else if** *abnormal_eoj* = '*no*' & *mode* = '*system*' **then**
  (i) **if** `//` `JOB` statement **then**
      if *end_of_job_seen* := '*no*' **then**
        job_termination_processing;
      Set user_id from `//` `JOB` statement
  (ii) **if** '`/&`' statement **then**
      job_termination_processing;
  (iii) **else if** an `//` `EXEC` statement **then**
      mode := '*user*';
      if *user_id* ≠ *nil* **then**
        Load the program named in `//` `EXEC` statement and transfer control to it for execution.
        mode := '*system*';
        if *abnormal_eoj* = '*yes*' on completion of the program's execution **then**
          end_of_job_seen := '*no*';
          goto Step 3;
        else goto Step 2;
  (iv) **else if** some other control statement & *user_id* ≠ *nil* **then**
      process the control statement.
  (v) **else** ignore the card.

4. **goto** step 2;

A simple arrangement is used to ensure that the command interpreter gets control when a control statement is read—the command interpreter reads *all* cards. The *mode* flag indicates whether a problem program is in execution. If *mode* = *user*, the command interpreter checks to see if a card contains a control statement. If it does, the command interpreter initiates abnormal termination of the job, else it returns to the user program (see Step 3(b)).

System operation starts with *abnormal_eoj* = '*no*', *mode* = '*system*', and *user_id* = *nil*; With these flag settings, all control statements encountered before a `//` `JOB` statement are ignored (see steps 3(c)(iii)–3(c)(iv)). When a `//` `JOB` statement is encountered, the command interpreter copies the user name from the statement into *user_id* so that resource accounting can be performed at the end of the job. When a `//` `EXEC` statement is encountered, a program is loaded for execution after setting *mode* = '*user*'. Control is transferred to step 2 of the algorithm when a program wishes to read a data card. Step 3(b) is now executed because *abnormal_eoj* = '*no*' and *mode* = '*user*'. It invokes procedure *validate_a_card* which reads the next card. If the card is a control card procedure *validate_a_card* terminates the program. Control now

```
procedure job_end_processing;
if an end_of_batch card then
    job_termination_processing;
    terminate batch processing.
else if an '/&' statement then
    job_termination_processing;
else if a job statement then
    if end_of_job_seen = 'no' then
        job_termination_processing;
        set user_id from // JOB statement.
    else ignore the statement.
end job_end_processing;

procedure job_termination_processing;
    if user_id ≠ nil then
        terminate the job.
        close all open files.
        perform resource accounting using user_id.
        user_id := nil;
        abnormal_eoj := 'no';
        end_of_job_seen := 'yes';
end job_termination_processing;

procedure read_a_card;
    Read a card and put it in card_buffer.
end read_a_card;

procedure validate_a_data_card;
    if card in card_buffer is a control card then
        abnormal_eoj := 'yes';
        terminate the program.
end validate_a_data_card;
```

Fig. 9.4 Routines of the command interpreter

returns to the statement **if** *abnormal_eoj* = .. of step 3(c)(iii). Else control is returned to the user program which resumes execution. Subsequent actions of the command interpreter are explained in the following.

Abnormal_eoj = '*yes*' puts the command interpreter into a loop which reads and ignores all cards until a `// JOB` or `/&` statement is encountered (step 3(a)). On exiting the loop, it performs job termination processing and initiates the processing of the next job. The *end_of_job_seen* flag is used to indicate whether job termination processing has been performed for the current job. *end_of_job_seen* = '*no*' while processing the `// JOB` statement of a job implies that the `/&` statement of the previous job was missing. Hence job termination processing is performed before initiating the next job. On encountering an `// EXEC` statement, the command interpreter loads the required program and passes control to it. This is only done if *user_id* $\neq$ *nil*, i.e. only if a valid `// JOB` statement precedes the `// EXEC` statement.

Note that correct processing of the control statements requires the command interpreter to examine every card read by a user job. Section 9.3.3 describes an arrangement which ensures this.

Example 9.4 Figure 9.5 describes the actions of the command interpreter while processing the first two jobs of a batch. In the first job the program terminates after reading only a few of its data cards. When control returns to the command interpreter it encounters the remaining data cards of the job, and ignores them in step 3(c)(v). The end-of-job card is also missing in the first job. The command interpreter performs job termination processing when it encounters the `// JOB` statement of the next job and finds *end_of_job_seen = no* in step 3(c)(i). The Pascal program of the second job contains compilation errors. Hence the compiler sets *abnormal_eoj = yes* before returning to the command interpreter. On sensing this condition, the command interpreter goes into a loop which reads and ignores all cards until a `// JOB` or `/&` statement is encountered (step 3(a)). It now performs job termination processing for the job.

Statement	*Comment*	*System action*
`// JOB ...`	Start of job	Set user id
`// EXEC PASCAL`	Compile program	Load Pascal compiler
`...`	Data card	Pass to Pascal compiler
`...`	Data card	Pass to Pascal compiler
`/*`	End of data (Normal compilation)	Normal termination
`// EXEC`	Execute program	Load compiled program
`...`	Data card	Pass to program
`...`	Data card	Pass to program
`...`	Process card and Terminate	Normal termination
`...`	Data card	Ignore card
`/*`	End of data	Ignore card
`// JOB ...`	Start of job	Terminate previous job Set user id
`// EXEC PASCAL`	Compile program	Load Pascal compiler
`...`	Data card	Pass to Pascal compiler
`...`	Data card	Pass to Pascal compiler
`/*`	End of data (Compilation errors)	Abnormal termination
`// EXEC`	Execute program	Ignore card
`...`	Data card	Ignore card
`...`	Data card	Ignore card
`/*`	End of data	Ignore card
`/&`	End of job	Terminate job

Fig. 9.5 Illustarion of batch processing

Protection problems in the IBM PC

IBM PC is not a batch processing system. However, a situation analogous to BP, and a problem analogous to the protection problem of the card based BP systems, can be observed if each use of a PC by a user is viewed to constitute a 'job'. IBM PC is a disk based system, hence programs and data reside on the disk in the form of files. The user only inputs commands to the system from the keyboard. This segregates commands from programs and data of the user, thereby avoiding much of the complexity of Algorithm 9.1.

The protection problem arises from the fact that different users of a PC share the same file system. Thus, it is possible for a user to corrupt the program or data files of another user. This could lead to indirect interference in the jobs of other users. To avoid this, protection must be implemented in the file system. File protection techniques are discussed in Section 17.2 (however, note that the IBM PC file system does not implement protection).

9.3.3 Special Features to Support Batch Processing

Hardware features

As shown in Fig. 9.1, a user job shares the memory with the batch monitor. A *memory protection* feature is needed to ensure that the user job does not corrupt the batch monitor code. The memory protection hardware should examine each memory address generated by a program, and prevent invalid references. Memory protection is discussed in Section 9.4.3.2.

Software features

The command interpreter must have an opportunity to examine every card read during the execution of a job. In algorithm 9.1 this is achieved by entrusting the task of reading all cards to the command interpreter. Whenever a program wishes to read a card, it makes a request to the command interpreter. The command interpreter returns the next card in the batch only if it is not a control statement. This arrangement can be implemented through the run-time library of the compiler. The library contains standard routines which are used by programs to perform IO, to terminate themselves, etc. These routines can be coded such that all IO requests are routed to the command interpreter, and control is passed to the command interpreter when a program completes its execution.

EXERCISE 9.3

1. A job contains 10 data cards in a job step. However, execution of the job step program terminates after reading only 5 of these cards. Clearly explain the behavior of the batch processing system in this situation.
2. A user program has included a card `// EXEC ...` in the data for a program. Comment on the handling of this data card by the BP system.

3. The command interpreter of Algorithm 9.1 permits a compiled program to be executed on only one set of data. What changes would you make to enable execution of a program on multiple sets of data? Explain how this differs from use of independent jobs for the different sets of data. (*Hint:* Consider programmer convenience and behavior in the case of execution errors.)
4. Study the .BAT files of MS DOS and the shells of Unix. Comment on their merits and demerits for batch processing.

9.4 MULTIPROGRAMMING SYSTEMS

Early computer systems implemented IO operations as CPU instructions. Thus the reading of a card was conceptually similar to the adding of two numbers: On decoding an IO instruction the CPU realized that an IO operation, viz. a card read operation, was to be performed. It sent a signal to the card reader to read a card and waited for the operation to complete before initiating the next operation. However, the speeds of operation of IO devices were much lower than the speed of the CPU, hence the CPU spent a lot of its time waiting for an IO operation to complete. Consequently programs took long to complete their execution. A new feature was introduced in the machine architecture when this weakness was realized. This feature permitted the CPU to delink itself from an IO operation so that it could execute instructions while an IO operation was in progress. Thus the CPU and the IO devices could now operate concurrently. (This feature is described in Section 9.4.1.)

Following this development in the machine architecture it became necessary to evolve suitable OS techniques to exploit the concurrency of operation between the CPU and the IO subsystem. One approach to this goal is based on the premise that if many user programs exist in the memory, the CPU can execute instructions of one program while the IO subsystem is busy with an IO operation for another program. The term *multiprogramming* (MP) is used to describe this arrangement.

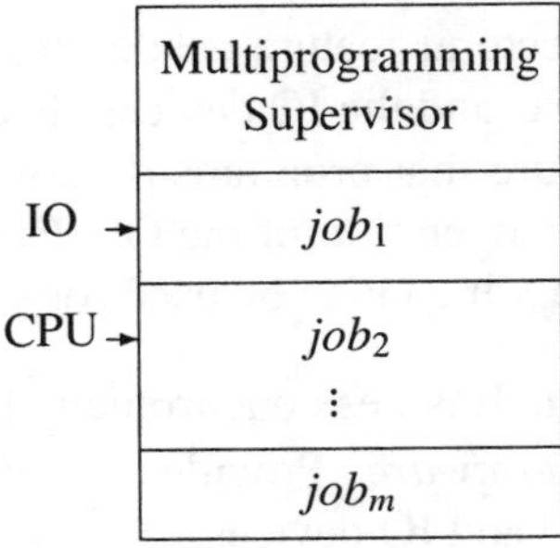

Fig. 9.6 Schematic of a multiprogramming system

Figure 9.6 illustrates a schematic of a multiprogramming OS. Jobs job_1, .. job_m are situated in the memory of the computer system. At any moment the program corresponding to the current job step of each job is in execution. The IO devices and memory are allocated using the partitioned resource allocation approach. At any time, the CPU and the IO subsystem are busy with programs belonging to different jobs. Thus they access different areas of memory. This ensures that their activities would not interfere with one another. In principle the CPU and the IO subsystem could operate on the same program. However, in this case the program must explicitly synchronize the activities of the CPU and the IO subsystem to ensure correctness. Example 9.5 illustrates the need for synchronization. As shown in Fig. 9.1, each job in the memory could be the current job of a batch of jobs. Thus one could have both batch processing and multiprogramming at the same time. One part of the main memory is occupied by the multiprogramming supervisor. Analogous to a BP supervisor, the MP supervisor also consists of a permanently resident part and a transient part (see Section 9.3.2.2).

Example 9.5 Consider the following program segment

Stmt no.	*Statement*
1.	`a := ...;`
	`...`
5.	`b := a+5;`

The value of a should not be used in the fifth statement before its reading is completed by the first statement! Special buffering techniques need to be used in the program to ensure this (see Section 16.5). Use of these techniques would ensure concurrent operation of the CPU and the IO subsystem over statements 2–4 of the program.

The multiprogramming arrangement ensures concurrent operation of the CPU and the IO subsystem without requiring a program to use the special buffering techniques described in Ex. 9.5. It simply ensures that the CPU is allocated to a program only when it is not performing an IO operation.

9.4.1 Architectural Support for Multiprogramming

The basic architectural feature needed for multiprogramming is concurrency of operation of the CPU and the IO devices. However other architectural features become necessary to ensure that programs do not interfere with the execution of other programs or with the operation of the OS. Hence the following features are needed in a computer system which is to be used for multiprogramming:

- *IO channel:* Ensures concurrency of operation of the CPU and an IO device.
- *Interrupt hardware:* Provides facilities for utilizing concurrency of operation of the CPU and IO devices.
- *Memory protection:* Ensures that a program does not destroy contents of memory areas allocated to other programs or to the OS.
- *Privileged mode of CPU operation:* Ensures that memory protection and other measures to avoid interference between programs can be implemented in a foolproof manner.

IO Channels and the interrupt hardware

Figure 9.7 illustrates the IO subsystem which consists of one or more *IO channels* (also called *IO processors*). Each IO channel has an independent data path to the memory. IO devices are connected to IO channels. When an IO instruction is executed, say a *read* instruction on device *d*, CPU transfers details of the IO operation to the channel. The CPU is not involved in the IO operation beyond this point; it is free to execute instructions while the operation is in progress. The channel initiates the *read* operation on device *d* and the data transfer between device *d* and the memory takes place over the channel's data path to memory. Thus the CPU and the IO subsystem can operate concurrently. At the end of the IO operation the channel generates an *IO interrupt*. The interrupt hardware switches the CPU to the execution of the MP supervisor which processes the interrupt and realizes that the IO operation is complete. Details of the interrupt hardware are discussed in Section 9.4.1.1. Note that IO operations can be concurrent with one another. This is possible if a computer system contains many IO channels, or if it contains a *multiplexor channel* which is capable of supporting concurrent IO operations (see Section 16.1).

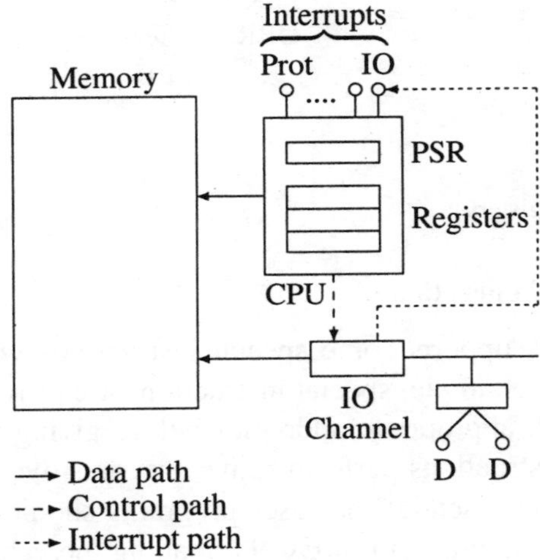

Fig. 9.7 The IO subsystem

Memory protection

Since the supervisor partitions the memory and allocates one partition to each job, memory protection is implemented by checking whether memory addresses used by any program of a job fall outside the memory partition allocated to it. A popular memory protection technique uses the notion of *memory bound registers* (also called *fence registers*). The start and end addresses of the memory area allocated to a program are loaded in the *lower bound register* (LBR) and *upper bound register* (UBR) of the CPU, respectively. Before making any memory reference, say reference to a memory location with address *aaaa*, the memory protection hardware compares *aaaa* with the addresses in LBR and UBR. An interrupt to signal a memory protection violation is generated if *aaaa* lies outside the range defined by contents of LBR and UBR. This interrupt switches the CPU to the execution of the MP supervisor, which terminates the erring program.

Example 9.6 A job is allocated the memory area 200K–250K by the supervisor. Figure 9.8 illustrates memory protection for this job using memory bound registers. LBR is loaded with the start address of the allocated area (i.e. 200K) while UBR is loaded with the end address (i.e. 250K). A memory protection violation interrupt would be generated if an address used during the execution of the programs of job_2 lies outside the range 200K–250K.

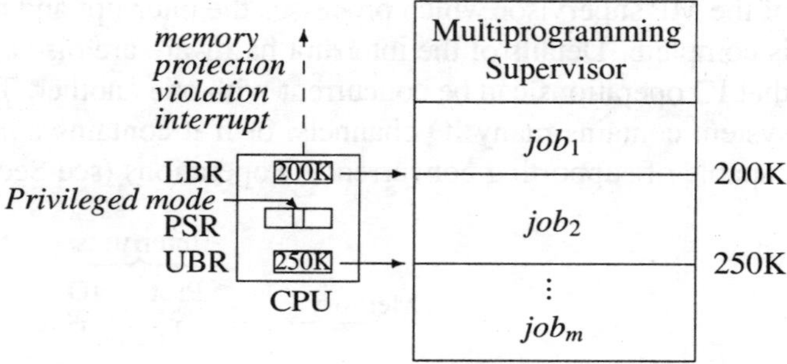

Fig. 9.8 Memory bound registers

Privileged mode of CPU operation

The CPU supports some special instructions which help the MP supervisor in its tasks. For example, special instructions are provided to load the LBR and UBR registers with appropriate addresses before giving the CPU to a user program. These special instructions perform some very sensitive control functions for the supervisor. Hence it is essential that user programs should not be permitted to execute them. (Imagine the program of Ex. 9.6 loading the value 300K in UBR and then making a reference to a memory location which lies outside its allocated area of 200K–250K!) This is ensured as follows: The special instructions can only be executed in a special mode of CPU operation called the *privileged mode*. A bit in the *processor status word* (PSW) indicates whether the CPU is in the privileged mode of operation. All user programs are executed with the CPU in the non-privileged mode. Only the multiprogramming supervisor executes with the CPU in the privileged mode. Hence it alone can use these special instructions. This arrangement ensures that user programs do not possess the means to interfere with other programs.

Other privileged mode instructions are: IO initiation, termination and status sensing instructions; instructions to manipulate important fields of the PSW, e.g. the field indicating whether the CPU is in the privileged mode, fields containing interrupt masks, etc.

9.4.1.1 Interrupt Hardware and Interrupt Processing

The function of the interrupt hardware of a computer system is to draw the supervisor's attention to the occurrence of an interrupt and to provide it with sufficient information for processing the interrupt. This involves diverting the CPU from whatever computation it is engaged in executing, and directing it to an interrupt processing routine in the supervisor. The interrupt hardware achieves this by changing the contents of the PSW. The new contents of the PSW direct the CPU to the execution of the interrupt processing routine. In the same action the interrupt hardware also saves the old contents of the PSW in the memory. These contents are useful for determining the cause of the interrupt and the state of the interrupted program. The supervisor analyses the cause of the interrupt and takes appropriate actions. At the end of its processing it may return to the interrupted program using the state information. The important fields of the are described before discussing the interrupt hardware.

Figure 9.9 shows the important fields in the PSW. The field *memory protection information* contains the LBR and UBR registers. The *privileged mode* field indicates whether the CPU is currently in the privileged mode. This field consists of a single bit. The *interrupt mask* field indicates which interrupts are permitted to occur at any moment of time. The field may contain an integer *m* which indicates that only interrupts with priority $\geq m$ are permitted to occur. Alternatively, it may contain a bit encoded value, each bit indicating whether a specific kind of interrupt is permitted to occur. Interrupts which are permitted to occur are said to be *enabled*, others are said to be *masked* (or *masked off*). Masked interrupts remain pending until they are permitted to occur. Contents of all these fields, along with those of the *program counter* (PC) field, determine the behaviour of the CPU at any instant of time. The *interrupt code* field, which typically contains an integer, records the nature and cause of the last interrupt to have occurred. Its contents do not influence the current behaviour of the CPU. However, as discussed in a later section, the field plays an important role in the processing of interrupts.

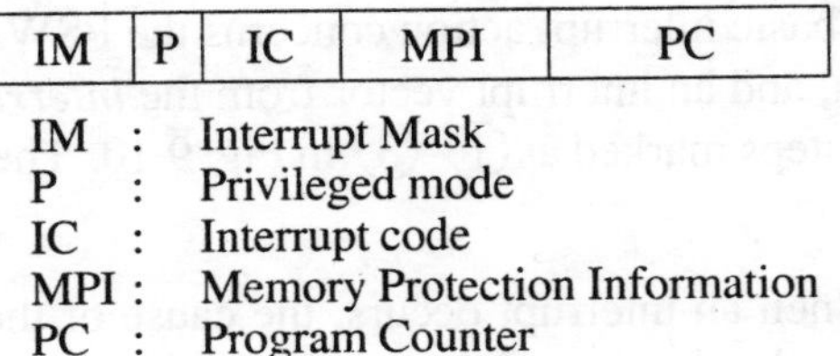

Fig. 9.9 Processor Status Register (PSW)

Figure 9.10 contains a schematic of the interrupt action. As mentioned earlier, the basic purpose of the interrupt action is to transfer control to an appropriate routine in the supervisor. Two areas of memory called the *interrupt vectors* area and the *saved PSW information* area participate in these actions. Each area consists of a set of units; the number of units in each area equals the number of distinct kinds of interrupts defined in the system. Each unit in the *interrupt vectors* area is an interrupt vector which controls the processing of a specific kind of interrupt. It contains the following information:

1. Address of an OS routine to process the interrupt
2. An interrupt mask indicating whether other interrupts can be permitted to occur during the processing of this interrupt
3. Whether the CPU should be in privileged mode while processing the interrupt.

For simplicity it has been assumed that an interrupt vector has the same format as a PSW and contains these items of information in appropriate fields. The interrupt vectors are formed and initialized to appropriate values while booting the system. Each unit in the *saved PSW information* area contains information copied from the PSW.

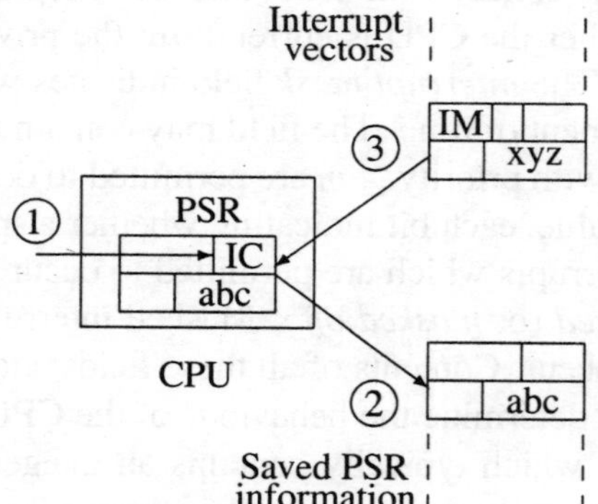

Fig. 9.10 Actions of the interrupt hardware

The basic interrupt action concerns the PSW, a unit from the *saved PSW information* area, and an interrupt vector from the *interrupt vectors* area. The action consists of three steps marked as ①–③ in Fig. 9.10. The details of these steps are as follows:

1. When an interrupt occurs, the cause of the interrupt is identified by the interrupt hardware and a code describing the cause is stored in the *interrupt code* field of the PSW. For example, for an 'IO completion' interrupt, the code could be the address of the IO device causing the interrupt.
2. The PSW is copied into the *saved PSW information* area in the unit corresponding to the kind of the interrupt.

3. The interrupt vector corresponding to the interrupt is accessed. Information from the interrupt vector is loaded into the corresponding fields of the PSW.

Subsequent actions of the CPU depend on the new contents of the PSW, specifically the fields *privileged mode*, *interrupt mask* and *program counter*. Since the interrupt vector contains the address of the OS routine which is supposed to handle the interrupt, the interrupt action effectively transfers control to the appropriate routine in the MP supervisor. Only the interrupts enabled in the new interrupt mask can occur now, others will remain pending until they are enabled by changing the interrupt mask. Note that the interrupt action must put the CPU in the privileged mode if the processing of an interrupt requires the use of privileged instructions. This is achieved by putting the appropriate information in the interrupt vector field corresponding to the *privileged mode* field of the PSW.

Interrupt processing

Apart from interrupt processing actions, which are specific to an interrupt, an interrupt processing routine also has to perform some housekeeping actions at the start and end of interrupt processing. These actions become necessary because the CPU was diverted from whatever computation it was executing when the interrupt was raised, and it should be able to resume that computation sometime in the future. A typical interrupt processing routine contains the following actions:

1. Save contents of CPU registers. (This action is not necessary if the CPU registers are saved by the interrupt action itself, as in the VAX/11 family of computers).
2. Process the interrupt and take appropriate actions. The *interrupt code* field of the *saved PSW information* unit corresponding to this interrupt contains useful information for this purpose.
3. Return from interrupt processing.

Note that the interrupt processing routine does not restore the contents of the CPU registers and return to the interrupted program. Instead, it hands the control to the supervisor. The supervisor performs scheduling to decide which program should be given the CPU. Contents of CPU registers which were saved while entering an interrupt processing routine are used the next time the supervisor schedules the interrupted program.

Example 9.7 Figure 9.11 shows the interrupt processing routines and the interrupt vectors used in the supervisor. The interrupt vector for the IO completion interrupt contains *bbb* in the field corresponding to the PC of the PSW and '1' in the field corresponding to the *privileged mode* field. When an IO interrupt occurs, contents of the PSW are saved in the *saved PSW information* area and the contents of this interrupt vector are loaded in the PSW. Effectively, control is transfered to the OS routine with the start address *bbb*. The CPU is put in the privileged mode since the *privileged mode* field contains '1'. This routine first saves contents of the CPU registers. It then queries the

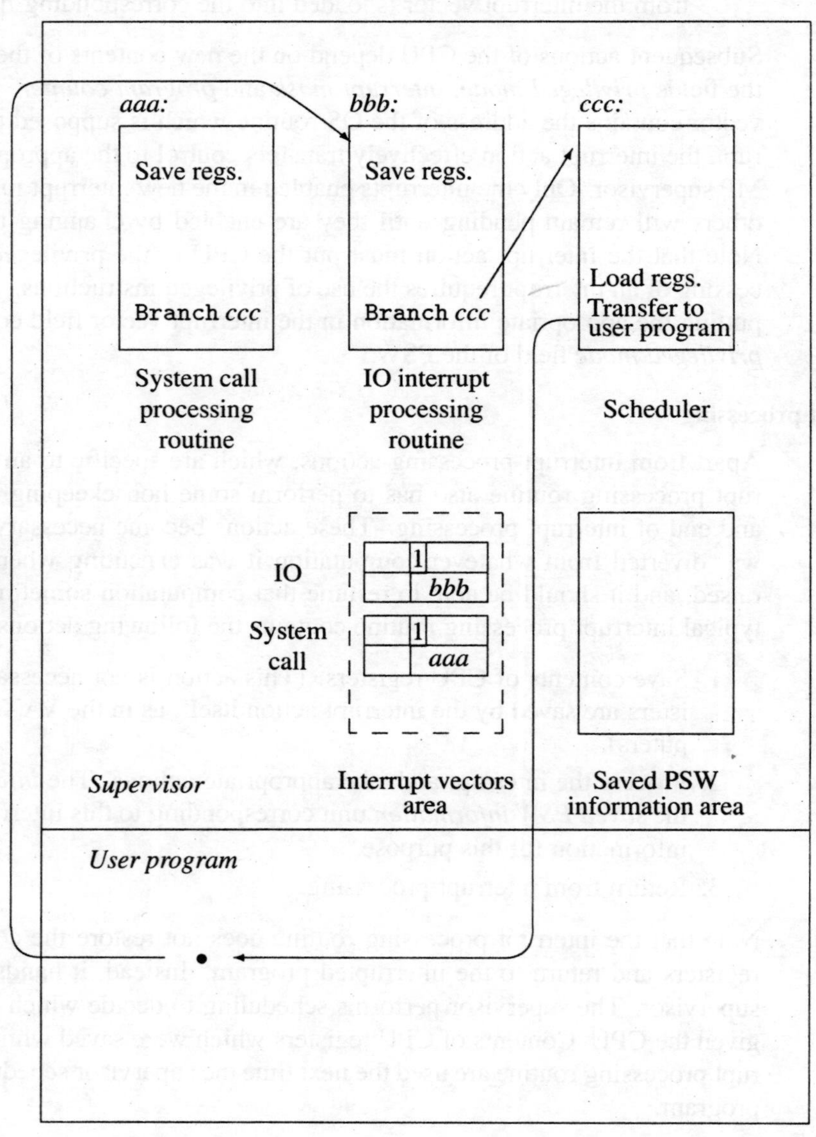

Fig. 9.11 Interrupt processing in an OS

IC field of the *saved PSW information* unit to find the address of the IO device which has completed its operation. At the end of its operation, this routine transfers control to the scheduler. If the scheduler selects the interrupted program itself for execution, the supervisor transfers control to it after loading back the contents of CPU registers. The program resumes execution at the place where it was interrupted.

9.4.1.2 System Calls

Definition 9.4 (System call) *A* system call *is a method by which a program makes a request to the OS.*

System calls are implemented using the interrupt hardware of a computer system. A new kind of interrupt called a *software interrupt* is defined for this purpose. A special instruction is introduced whose sole purpose is to produce a software interrupt. This instruction has the format

<SI_instrn> *<int_code>*

A software interrupt occurs when this instruction is executed. *<int_code>* is put into the IC field of PSW before switching of PSWs takes place. Different values of *<int_code>* are used to designate different requests made to the OS. The interrupt processing routine analyses the IC field to determine the nature of the request made by the program. In most computer systems *<int_code>* is at least 8 bits in size, so upto 256 distinct requests can be defined in the system.

9.4.2 User Service

In an MP system the turn-around time of a job is affected by the amount of CPU attention devoted to the execution of other jobs in the system. This depends on the number of jobs in the system, and on relative priorities assigned to different jobs by the scheduler. Hence there does not exist a direct relation between the execution requirements of a job and its turn around time. The influence of priorities on user service is discussed in Section 9.4.3.1.

9.4.3 Functions of the Multiprogramming Supervisor

Important functions of the multiprogramming supervisor are:

1. Scheduling
2. Memory management
3. IO management.

The MP supervisor uses simple techniques to implement its functions. Function 1, i.e. scheduling, implies sharing of the CPU between the jobs existing in the MP system. This function is performed after servicing every interrupt using a simple priority based scheme described in the next section. Functions 2 and 3 involve allocation of memory and IO devices. The allocation is performed by static partitioning of resources. Thus a part of the memory and some IO devices are allocated to each job. Resource sharing necessitates protection against mutual interference. It is thus necessary to protect the instructions, data, and IO operations of one program from interference by other programs. This is achieved simply by using the memory protection hardware and by putting the CPU in the non-privileged mode while executing a user program. Any effort by a user program to access memory locations situated outside its memory area, or to use a privileged instruction, now leads to an interrupt. The interrupt processing routines for these interrupts simply terminate the program causing the interrupt.

Scheduling and memory management are discussed in the following sections. IO management, which involves almost identical issues in all operating systems, is discussed in chapters 17 and 16.

9.4.3.1 Scheduling

The goal of multiprogramming is to exploit the concurrency of operation between the CPU and the IO subsystem to achieve high levels of system utilization. A useful characterization of system utilization is offered by the notion of *throughput* of a system.

Definition 9.5 (Throughput) *The* throughput *of a system is the number of programs processed by it per unit time.*

Consider a multiprogramming OS which starts its operation at t_0 and stops at time t_f after processing a collection of programs $\{P_i\}$ containing n programs. Its throughput is given by

$$\begin{aligned} \text{Throughput} &= \frac{\text{Number of programs completed}}{\text{Total time taken}} \\ &= \frac{n}{t_f - t_0} \end{aligned} \tag{9.1}$$

The throughput depends on the nature of programs in the collection $\{P_i\}$ and on the manner in which the supervisor switches the CPU between the programs present in the system. To optimize the throughput, an MP system uses the following concepts:

1. *A proper mix of programs:* For good throughput it is important to keep both the CPU and the IO subsystem busy. Hence the system tries to keep an appropriate number of CPU-bound and IO-bound programs in execution, where
   (a) A *CPU-bound program* is a program involving a lot of computation and very little IO. Such a program uses the CPU in long bursts—that is, it uses the CPU for a long time before starting an IO operation.

(b) An *IO-bound program* is a program involving very little computation and a lot of IO. Such a program uses the CPU in small bursts.

2. *Preemptive and priority based scheduling:* Scheduling is priority based, i.e. the CPU is always allocated to the highest priority program which wishes to use it. Further, the scheduling is preemptive. Thus, a low priority program executing on the CPU is preempted if a higher priority program wishes to use the CPU. The priority of a program is determined by the nature of the program, i.e. whether it is CPU-bound or IO-bound.
3. *Degree of multiprogramming:* The degree of multiprogramming (m) is the number of programs existing simultaneously in the system's memory. The MP supervisor uses an appropriate value of m to ensure good throughput.

A proper mix of programs

To see why an OS must keep a proper mix of programs in execution, consider an MP system with $m = 2$. Let $prog_1$ and $prog_2$ be the two programs under processing. Let us assume that both programs are heavily CPU-bound and $prog_1$ is currently executing. Being CPU-bound, $prog_1$ would perform a long burst of CPU activity before performing an IO operation. CPU is given to $prog_2$ when $prog_1$ initiates an IO operation. $prog_2$ also performs a long burst of CPU activity before performing an IO operation. $prog_1$ would have finished its IO operation by this time. Hence it can use the CPU for another burst of computation. In this manner the CPU is kept busy most of the time. It remains idle only when both programs simultaneously perform IO. However, the IO subsystem is underloaded. In fact, it is idle most of the time. Hence periods of concurrent CPU and IO activity are rare. This leads to low values of throughput.

To analyse the throughput of this MP system we will compare it with a BP system processing the same two programs. The BP system would process the programs one after another, i.e. either in the sequence $prog_1$, $prog_2$ or in the sequence $prog_2$, $prog_1$. From Eq. (9.1), the throughput would be the same in either case. For comparing the throughput of the BP and MP systems, a program is said to 'make progress' when either the CPU is executing its instructions or its IO operation is in progress. $prog_1$ and $prog_2$ make concurrent progress only when one of them performs IO and the other executes on the CPU, i.e. only when the CPU and the IO subsystem execute concurrently. Since such periods are rare, periods when both programs make progress are also rare. Hence the throughput of the MP system is likely to be much the same as the BP system.

A practical way to improve the throughput is to select a mix of programs which contains some CPU-bound programs and some IO-bound programs. For example, let an MP system with $m = 2$ contain the following programs:

$prog_{cb}$	:	CPU-bound program
$prog_{iob}$	:	IO-bound program

$prog_{cb}$ can keep the CPU occupied while $prog_{iob}$ keeps the IO channels busy. Thus, both programs would make good progress, and the throughput would be higher than in a BP system.

Program priority

Definition 9.6 (Priority) Priority *is a tie-breaking notion used in a scheduler to decide which request should be scheduled on the server when many requests await service.*

We assume a simple implementation scheme in which each program has a numeric priority where each number is an integer and a larger integer implies higher priority. When many programs are ready to use the CPU the MP supervisor gives the CPU to the program with the highest priority. This rule leads to preemption of a low priority program when a high priority program becomes ready to use the CPU. This is seen when the situation in Fig. 9.11 of Ex. 9.7 is contrasted with that in Fig. 9.12. In Fig. 9.11 it has been assumed that the program which was executing when an interrupt occurred is scheduled again for execution. This implies that the IO operation whose completion was signaled by the interrupt must have belonged to some lower priority program. The interrupted program still remains the highest priority program which can use the CPU so it is selected for execution by the scheduler. In Fig. 9.12, the IO interrupt signals completion of IO for a higher priority program. Hence the scheduler selects the higher priority program for execution and the supervisor starts executing this program on the CPU. Effectively, the lower priority program which was executing on the CPU has been preempted.

The supervisor of the MP system has to assign priorities to programs. Since the program mix consists of some CPU-bound programs and some IO-bound programs, the supervisor has to decide whether CPU-bound programs should have higher priority or whether IO-bound programs should have higher priority. This is a very crucial decision which can influence system throughput. This fact is illustrated by considering the multiprogramming of $prog_{cb}$ and $prog_{iob}$. The CPU and IO activities are plotted in the form of a timing chart. The chart shows when the CPU and the IO subsystem are busy with $prog_{cb}$ and $prog_{iob}$. Figure 9.13 contains such a chart. Note that the chart is not to scale. The CPU activity of $prog_{iob}$ and the IO activities of both programs have been exaggerated for clarity. We draw the timing charts for different priority assignments to $prog_{cb}$ and $prog_{iob}$ and make qualitative remarks on what we find in a chart.

Higher priority to CPU-bound programs

Example 9.8 Figure 9.13 contains a timing chart showing the behaviour of the system when $prog_{cb}$, the CPU bound program, has higher priority. Note that the chart is not to scale and that interval t_0–t_{11} $\gg$ interval t_{11}–t_{12}, i.e. the CPU burst of a CPU bound program is larger than the time taken by an IO operation.

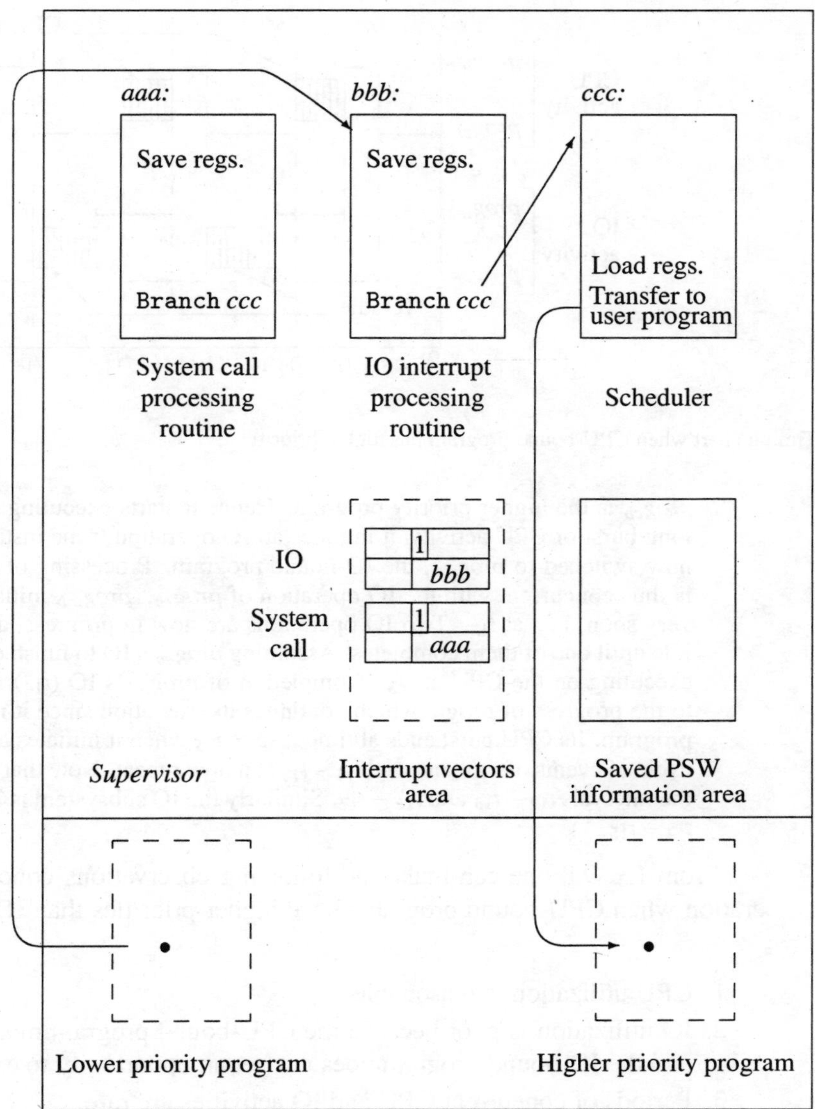

Fig. 9.12 Program switching at an IO interrupt

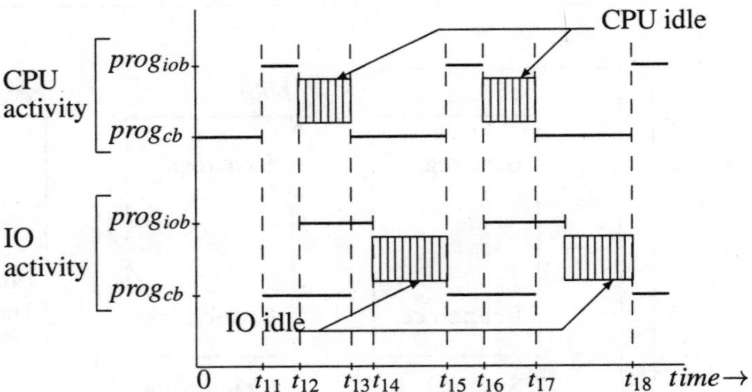

Fig. 9.13 Timing chart when CPU-bound program has higher priority

$prog_{cb}$ is the higher priority program. Hence it starts executing at time t=0. After a long burst of CPU activity, it initiates an IO operation (time instant t_{11}). The CPU is now switched to $prog_{iob}$, the IO-bound program. Processing of $prog_{iob}$ by the CPU is thus concurrent with the IO operation of $prog_{cb}$. $prog_{iob}$ initiates an IO operation very soon, i.e. at t_{12}. Two IO operations are now in progress, and the CPU will be idle until one of them completes. Assuming $prog_{cb}$'s IO to finish earlier, it would start executing on the CPU at t_{13}. Completion of $prog_{iob}$'s IO (t_{14}) makes no difference to the progress of $prog_{cb}$ which continues its execution since it is the higher priority program. Its CPU burst ends at time instant t_{15} when it initiates an IO operation. The cycle of events of time interval $t_{11} - t_{15}$ can now repeat. Note that the CPU is idle over the intervals $t_{12} - t_{13}$ and $t_{16} - t_{17}$. Similarly the IO subsystem is idle over the interval $t_{14} - t_{15}$.

From Ex. 9.8 one can make the following observations concerning system operation when CPU-bound programs have higher priorities than IO-bound programs:

1. CPU utilization is reasonable.
2. IO utilization is poor because the CPU-bound program monopolizes the CPU and the IO-bound program does not get an opportunity to execute.
3. Periods of concurrent CPU and IO activities are rare.

From observation 3 it is clear that only one of the two programs is able to make progress most of the time. Hence the throughput is not much better than in a BP system. Attempts to improve the throughput by increasing the degree of multiprogramming meet with little success. For example, let us increase the degree of multiprogramming (m) to 3 and introduce a CPU-bound program $prog_3$ with a priority between those of $prog_{cb}$ and $prog_{iob}$. This action improves the CPU utilization since the new program can keep the CPU busy over intervals where it would have been idle if m was 2 (see interval t_{12}–t_{13}). However, it leads to further deterioration of the

IO utilization because $prog_{iob}$ receives lesser opportunity to execute. Addition of an IO-bound program (say, $prog_4$) instead of $prog_3$ makes very little difference to the CPU and IO utilizations because $prog_4$ would have the lowest priority. Hence it does not get much opportunity to execute.

Higher priority to IO-bound programs

Example 9.9 Figure 9.14 depicts the operation of the system when the IO-bound program has higher priority. $prog_{iob}$ is the higher priority program, hence it is given the CPU whenever it wishes to use it, i.e. whenever it is not performing IO. When $prog_{iob}$ initiates an IO operation, $prog_{cb}$ gets the CPU. Being a CPU-bound program, $prog_{cb}$ keeps the CPU busy until $prog_{iob}$'s IO completes. $prog_{iob}$ is given the CPU when it completes its IO since its priority is greater than that of $prog_{cb}$. This explains the system behaviour in the period 0–t_{26}. Deviations from this behaviour occur when $prog_{cb}$ initiates an IO operation. Now both programs are engaged in IO and the CPU remains idle until one of them completes its IO. This explains the CPU-idle periods t_{26}–t_{27} and t_{28}–t_{29}. IO-idle periods occur whenever $prog_{iob}$ executes on the CPU and $prog_{cb}$ is not performing IO (see intervals $t_{22} - t_{23}$ and $t_{24} - t_{25}$).

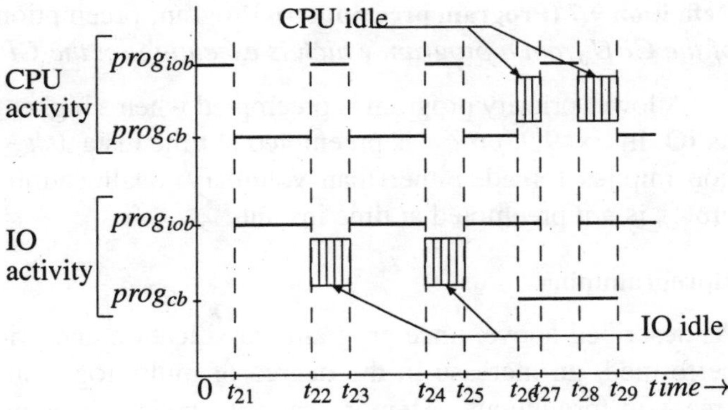

Fig. 9.14 Timing chart when IO-bound program has higher priority

From Ex. 9.9 one can make the following observations concerning system operation when IO-bound programs have higher priorities than CPU-bound programs:

1. CPU utilization is reasonable.
2. IO utilization is reasonable (however, IO idling would exist if many IO channels exist).
3. Frequent periods of concurrent CPU and IO activities exist.

$prog_{iob}$ makes very good progress since it is the highest priority program. It makes very light use of the CPU. Hence $prog_{cb}$ also makes very good progress. The throughput is thus substantially higher than in the BP system. Another important feature of this priority assignment is that an increase in the degree of multiprogramming can improve the system throughput. For example, consider the following possibilities:

1. A CPU-bound program (say, $prog_3$) can be introduced to utilize some CPU time which is wasted in Ex. 9.9 (e.g. the intervals t_{26}–t_{27} and t_{28}–t_{29}). $prog_3$ would have the lowest priority. Hence its presence would not affect the progress made by $prog_{cb}$ and $prog_{iob}$.
2. An IO-bound program (say, $prog_4$) can be introduced. Its priority would be between the priorities of $prog_{cb}$ and $prog_{iob}$. Presence of $prog_4$ would improve the IO utilization. However it would not affect the progress of $prog_{cb}$ since $prog_4$ does not use a significant amount of CPU time.

From the above discussion one can conclude that assignment of higher priorities to IO-bound programs leads to good throughput. It also enables the OS to combat poor throughput in the system by varying the degree of multiprogramming.

Program preemption

Definition 9.7 (Program preemption) Program preemption *is the forced deallocation of the CPU from a program which is executing on the CPU.*

A lower priority program is preempted when a higher priority program completes its IO. In Ex. 9.9, $prog_{cb}$ is preempted at time instants t_{22} and t_{24}. Note that preemption implies forced, rather than voluntary, deallocation of CPU. Thus, in Ex. 9.9 $prog_{cb}$ is *not* preempted at time instant t_{26}.

Degree of multiprogramming

As described above, once program classification and priority assignment have been performed, an increase in the degree of multiprogramming would result in an increase in throughput. Memory capacity and the average memory requirements of user programs determine practical values of m.

9.4.3.2 Memory Management

Early MP systems used a partitioned approach to memory management. Each memory partition was a single contiguous area in the memory. Memory allocation was typically performed for a job as a unit. Thus while initiating a job the supervisor allocated a memory partition larger than the size of the largest program in the job. Use of this memory management model often gave rise to the problem of *memory fragmentation.*

Definition 9.8 (Memory fragmentation) Memory fragmentation *implies the existence of unusable memory areas in a computer system.*

There are two kinds of fragmentation—internal fragmentation and external fragmentation. Example 9.10 illustrates how these arise in a multiprogramming OS.

Example 9.10 Three jobs named A, B and C exist in a multiprogramming system (Fig. 9.15(a)). Job A consists of compilation, linking and execution of a Pascal program. The compiler and linker require 100 Kbytes each. This requirement exactly matches the amount of memory allocated to job A. Let the size of the compiled program be 80 Kbytes. Figure 9.15(b) illustrates the situation when the compiled Pascal program is executing. 20 Kbytes of the memory allocated to job A is currently unused. However, from the OS viewpoint the memory stands allocated to job A. Hence it cannot be allocated to any other job. This is *internal fragmentation.*

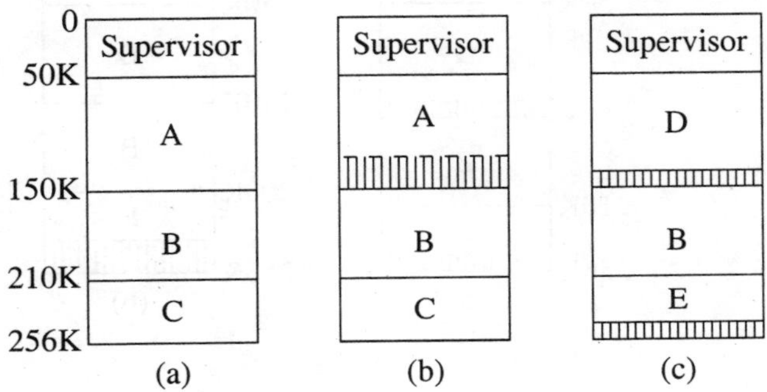

Fig. 9.15 Internal and external fragmentation

Let job A complete and job D whose memory requirement is 90 Kbytes be started in its place. An area of 10 Kbytes of free memory now exists between jobs D and B. However, this cannot be used because it is too small to accommodate a job. Now let job C complete and let job E be started in its place. This leads to another free area, say a 20 Kbytes area, between jobs B and E. A total of 30 Kbytes of unallocated memory now exists in the system but a job, say Job F, requiring 25K bytes cannot be initiated because a single contiguous free area of 25 Kbytes is not available. Hence these areas of 10 Kbytes and 20 Kbytes are unusable. This is *external fragmentation.*

Two approaches can be used to overcome the problem of external fragmentation. One approach forces the contiguity of free memory areas by physically shifting the jobs in memory. This approach is called *memory compaction.* For example, the situation of Fig. 9.15(c) can be transformed by shifting jobs B and E to create a single contiguous free area (see Fig. 9.16). The second approach, called *virtual memory,* favours the use of a special feature in the machine architecture which enables a program to execute from non-contiguous areas of memory. These approaches are discussed in detail in Chapter 15.

Both the approaches to memory fragmentation are expensive in practice. In the memory compaction approach addresses assigned to the instructions and data of a program change when the program is moved around in memory. Hence instructions using these addresses need to be modified before the program can execute correctly from the new memory area allocated to it. This process, called *dynamic relocation,* requires complex software support. Virtual memory implementations require expensive hardware. Due to these software and hardware costs most early MP systems used a simple approach to memory management. The computer's memory was partitioned in such a manner that external fragmentation was eliminated. This was ensured by making each memory partition large enough to accommodate a job. Internal fragmentation during the execution of a job was ignored. This resulted in a memory allocation policy which was very easy to implement.

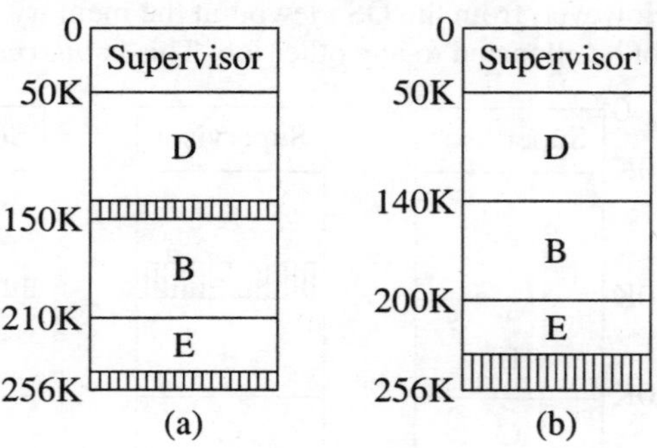

Fig. 9.16 Memory compaction

EXERCISE 9.4

1. The throughput of a MP system depends on the degree of multiprogramming and the classification of programs into CPU-bound and IO-bound programs. Describe the consequences of wrong classification of a program for a user, and for the throughput of the system.
2. System resources consumed by the MP supervisor while performing housekeeping tasks constitute OS overheads. Analyse the functioning of the MP supervisor and list all actions of the supervisor which contribute to overheads.
3. An MP system uses a degree of multiprogramming $m \gg 1$. It is proposed to double the throughput of the system by augmentation/replacement of its hardware components. The following possibilities are being considered in this context:
   (a) Replace the CPU by a CPU with twice the speed.
   (b) Expand the main memory to twice its present size.
   (c) Add new IO channels and IO devices.
   (d) Replace the CPU by a CPU with twice the speed and expand the main memory to twice its present size.

   Which of these is the best solution? Justify your answer.
4. Answer the following questions in the context of the interrupt hardware described in Section 9.4.1.1:
   (a) How does the MP supervisor gain control when an interrupt arises during the execution of a user program?
   (b) The user program must execute in the nonprivileged mode, while the supervisor must execute in the privileged mode. How is this achieved? (*Hint:* Think of the

interrupt action and the new PSR's of Fig. 9.10.)

9.5 TIME SHARING SYSTEMS

Through 1960's and early 1970's card readers and printers remained the primary input and output devices of a computer system, respectively. Hence computing was an *off-line* activity. A user had no contact with his computation during its execution. In such an environment, batch processing was a very natural paradigm for an OS to use. Development of IO channels did not change the basic paradigm. Multiprogramming features were superimposed on batch processing to ensure good utilization of IO channels. Both BP and MP systems provided poor user service. However this was considered inevitable due to the nature of IO devices in use.

Development of interactive terminals changed the scenario. Computation became an *on-line* activity. A user could provide inputs to a computation from a terminal and could also examine the output of the computation on the same terminal. Batch processing and multiprogramming were no longer relevant OS paradigms. Computer users started demanding interactive service rather than the turn around service provided by BP and MP systems. A new OS paradigm was evolved for use in an interactive computing environment. In this paradigm the OS serviced the computations belonging to different users by turn. Hence each user computation was guaranteed some service at short intervals, so a user could interact meaningfully with a computation during its execution. This fact created an illusion that each user had a computer system—somewhat slower than the actual computer system—at his/her sole disposal. This paradigm was called *time sharing* (TS) and an operating system based on this paradigm was called a time sharing OS.

User Service

In an interactive computing environment the execution of a user's computation consists of a sequence of interactions. Each interaction consists of a computational request made by a user and a response from the OS. Hence it is natural to characterize user service in terms of the speed with which a TS operating system implements an interaction.

Definition 9.9 (Response time) *The* response time *(rt) provided to a computational request is the time between the submission of the computational request by a user and the reporting of its results to the user.*

Benefits of good response times in an interactive environment are best illustrated by considering the process of program development. A user engaged in program development typically compiles and tests a program a large number of times. A computational request by the user concerns compilation of a statement or an execution of the program on given data. The OS response consists of a message from the compiler or the results of the program. Good response times would lead to an improvement in the productivity of the user. Any application in which a user has to interact with a computation would derive similar benefits from good response times.

Emphasis on good response times, rather than good utilization efficiency or throughput, requires the use of new design principles and techniques. The notion of a job is no longer relevant, an interactive user interface has to be designed, and new scheduling and memory management techniques are needed to provide good response times to a large number of users.

9.5.1 Scheduling

Since user service in a time sharing system is characterized by response times to user requests, the TS supervisor must strive to provide good response times to *all* users. To realize this goal all users must get *equal* opportunity to present their computational requests and have them serviced. Each user must also get a *reasonable* opportunity. Two provisions are made to ensure this.

1. Programs are not assigned fixed priorities because such assignment of priorities may deny OS attention to low priority programs.
2. A program is prevented from consuming unreasonable amounts of CPU time when scheduled to execute. This ensures that every request will receive OS attention without unreasonable delays.

These provisions are implemented using the techniques of *round robin scheduling* and *time slicing*, respectively.

Round robin scheduling

The round robin scheduling policy schedules user programs in such a manner that a program finishing its turn on the CPU gets another turn only after all other programs which wish to execute get their turn on the CPU. This policy can be implemented by arranging all programs which wish to use the CPU in a list called the *scheduling list*. The scheduler always selects the first program in the scheduling list for execution on the CPU. When it finishes its execution it is put at the end of the list and the first program in the new list is selected for execution. Figure 9.17 illustrates this arrangement. It is obvious that round robin scheduling provides comparable opportunities to all programs in the system. In terms of priorities its operation can be explained as follows: Programs are arranged in the order of decreasing priority. The highest priority program is selected for execution on the CPU. When it finishes its execution, its priority changes from the highest to the lowest in the system. Thus, program priorities are time dependent—that is, they change during the program's existence in the system.

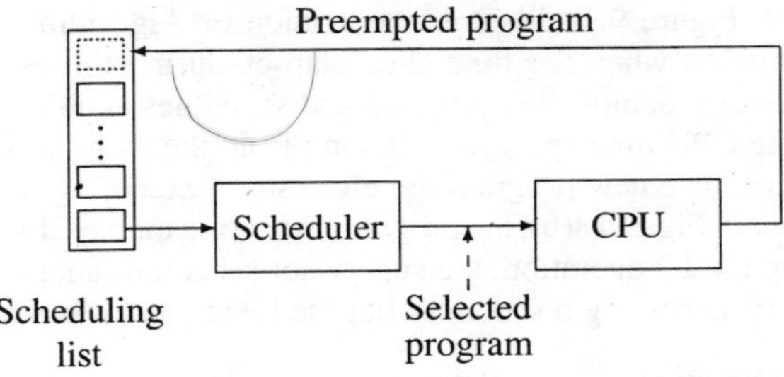

Fig. 9.17 A schematic of round robin scheduling

Time slicing

Definition 9.10 (Time slice) *The* time slice δ *is the largest amount of CPU time any program can consume when scheduled to execute on the CPU.*

Every program is subjected to the time limit imposed by the time slice. A program exceeding this limit is preempted. Thus a program cannot monopolize the CPU. This helps in ensuring good response times. The term *time slicing* is used to imply use of the notion of time slice. The TS supervisor uses the interval timer of the computer to implement time slicing. The interval timer consists of a register called *timer register* which can store an integer number representing a time interval in hours, minutes and seconds. The contents of the register are decremented with an appropriate periodicity, e.g. once every second. A *timer interrupt* is raised when the time interval elapses, that is, when the contents of the timer register become zero. Algorithm 9.2 shows the time slicing actions of the TS supervisor.

Algorithm 9.2 (Time slicing)

1. Perform scheduling to select the program to be executed next. Let the selected program be P.
2. Load the value of the time slice (δ) into the interval timer.
3. Start execution of program P on the CPU. Let this be done at time instant t.
4. If P initiates an IO operation, goto step 1.
5. When a timer interrupt occurs, preempt P and put it at the end of the scheduling list. Go to step 1.

In step 5 the preempted program is put at the end of the scheduling list to implement round robin scheduling. If a program does not consume δ seconds of CPU time, e.g. if it starts an IO operation, the supervisor simply removes it from the scheduling list. When an IO completion interrupt is raised the supervisor identifies the program whose IO operation has completed and enters it into the scheduling list.

Example 9.11 Figure 9.18 illustrates operation of Algorithm 9.2. Figure 9.18(a) depicts the situation when the time slice elapses during the execution of a program. The supervisor preempts this program and schedules another program for execution. Let σ be the CPU time spent in switching from the execution of one program to the next program. The new program therefore starts executing σ seconds after the time slice elapses. In Fig. 9.18(b), the program executing on the CPU makes an IO request. After starting the IO operation, the supervisor schedules another program for execution. It too starts executing σ seconds after the IO request was made.

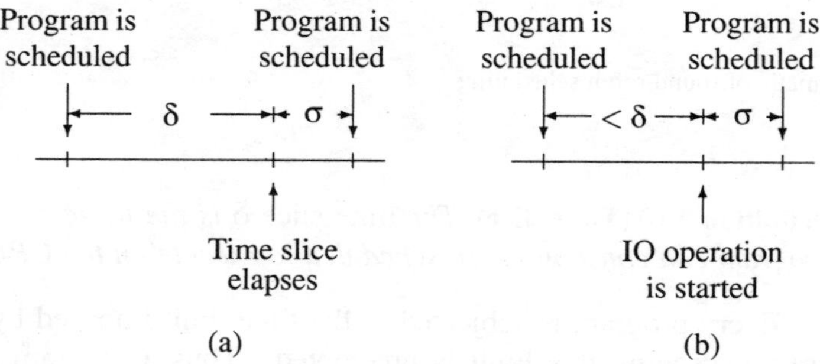

Fig. 9.18 Time sharing

When a combination of round robin scheduling and time slicing is used, the response time for each user request can be estimated in the following manner: Let the number of users using the system at any time be *n*. Let each user request require exactly δ CPU seconds for completion. As in Ex. 9.11, let σ be the CPU time spent in switching from the execution of one program to the next program. Under these conditions, the response time and the CPU utilization efficiency (η) are given by

$$rt = n.(\delta + \sigma) \tag{9.2}$$

$$\eta = \frac{\delta}{\delta + \sigma} \tag{9.3}$$

The actual response time may be different from the value of *rt* predicted by Eq. (9.2). There are several reasons for this. Even in the ideal case where each request requires exactly δ CPU seconds to produce a response, the value of *rt* would be smaller than that predicted by Eq. (9.2). This happens because users need to do some thinking between two interactions. Hence *rt* would not be influenced by the total number of users in the system; it would be influenced by the number of active users (n_a), $n_a < n$.

In practice, user requests do not require exactly δ CPU seconds to produce a response. Two possibilities now arise:

1. *Very small values of* δ: δ may be smaller than the time needed by a program to produce a response. Hence a program may be preempted before it can produce

a response. Such a program would have to be scheduled two or more times before a response is produced. Hence response time would be larger than $n_a \times (\delta + \sigma)$ seconds. The system needs to perform scheduling very often. This leads to lower values of η than predicted by Eq. (9.3).

2. *Large values of* δ*:* Most user requests may be processed in less than δ CPU seconds. Thus most programs release the CPU before δ seconds (see step 4 of Algorithm 9.2). Hence $rt < n_a \times (\delta + \sigma)$ and η is better than the value predicted by Eq. (9.3).

Hence one can conclude that rt is not linearly related to δ and the choice of δ is a very sensitive design decision.

9.5.2 Memory Management

A large number of time sharing users can be supported by a computer system possessing a fast CPU. This would require the computer system to possess a large memory, which is an expensive proposition. The technique of *swapping* provides an alternative whereby a computer system can support a large number of users without having to possess a large memory.

Definition 9.11 (Swapping) Swapping *is the technique of temporarily removing inactive programs from the memory of a computer system.*

An inactive program is one which is neither executing on the CPU, nor performing an IO operation. Figure 9.19 illustrates swapping as used in a practical situation. The programs existing in the memory are classified into three categories:

1. Active programs—one active program executes on the CPU while others perform IO.
2. Programs being swapped out of the memory.
3. Programs being swapped into the memory.

Whenever an active program becomes inactive, the OS begins to swap it out. This involves writing the program's instruction and data areas onto the secondary storage, typically a disk. Once a program is completely swapped out, the memory area allocated to it becomes free. The system allocates it to another program and starts loading the program into this memory area. The program is put at the end of the scheduling list after it is completely swapped in.

Use of swapping is feasible in time sharing systems because the TS supervisor can estimate when a program is likely to be scheduled next. It can use this estimate to ensure that the program is swapped in before its turn on the CPU. Note that swapping increases the OS overheads due to the need to perform swap-in and swap-out operations.

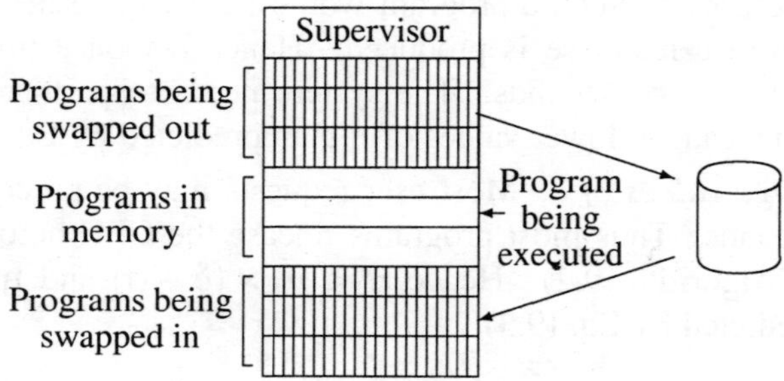

Fig. 9.19 A schematic of swapping

EXERCISE 9.5

1. Justify the following statement:
   "It is possible to support multiprogramming without using time sharing. However, it is impractical to support time sharing without using multiprogramming".
2. A time sharing system is to be designed to support a large number of users. List all considerations which influence the choice of the time slice. Justify each consideration.
3. Two persons using the same time sharing system at the same time notice that the OS requires widely different amounts of time to process their requests and provide a response. What are the possible reasons for this difference in service?
4. The two techniques of *program overlays* and *program swapping* aim to use the same memory area for executing different pieces of code. List all differences between program overlays and program swapping.
5. Clearly explain the advantages of swapping in an operating system.
   (a) Does swapping improve/degrade efficiency of system utilization?
   (b) Does it increase the effective degree of multiprogramming?
   (c) Can swapping be used in a multiprogramming system?

   Clearly justify your answers.
6. A time sharing system uses swapping as the fundamental memory management technique. It uses the following lists to govern its actions: a scheduling list, a swap-out list containing programs to be swapped out, and a swap-in list containing programs to be swapped in.

   When should the TS supervisor put a program in
   (a) the scheduling list,
   (b) the swap-out list,
   (c) the swap-in list?
7. An OS swaps out a program P which was executing in the memory area 200K-250K. What conditions should be satisfied by P if the OS wishes to swap-in P into another area of memory, e.g. the memory area 400K-450K?

9.6 REAL TIME OPERATING SYSTEMS

The advent of time sharing provided 'good' response times to computer users. While the actual response times varied with load conditions in the system, time slicing ensured that response times were maintained within tolerable limits. This satisfied most interactive computer users. However, time sharing could not satisfy the requirements of some applications. Real time operating systems were developed to meet the response requirements of such applications.

Definition 9.12 (Real time application) A real time application *is an application which requires a 'timely' response from the computer system to prevent failures.*

The *worst-case response time* of an application is the largest value of the response time for which it can still function correctly. The nature of a real time application can be analysed to determine its worst-case response time. The timeliness of a response to a request made by the application can now be judged in the context of the worst-case response time. As an example, consider the real time application depicted in Fig. 9.20. The satellite sends digitized samples at the rate of 1000 samples per second. The application program is simply required to store these samples in a file. Since a new sample arrives every millisecond, the computer must respond to every "store the sample" request in less than 1 msec. Failure to do so would result in the loss of a sample, which constitutes a failure of the application. The worst-case response time is thus 1 msec. Other examples of real time applications can be found in process control applications in chemical plants, airline reservations systems, weather warning systems, etc. It can be seen that the worst-case response times of these systems vary greatly. This explodes the myth that all real time applications require very quick response.

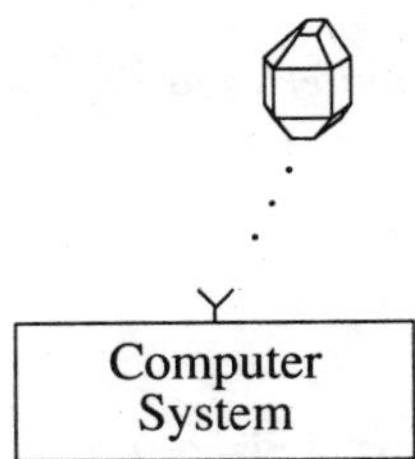

Fig. 9.20 A real time application

A real time (RT) OS is one which helps to fulfill the worst-case response time requirements of an application. An RT OS provides the following facilities for this purpose:

1. Multi-tasking within an application
2. Ability to define the priorities of tasks

3. Priority driven or deadline oriented scheduling
4. Programmer defined interrupts.

A *task* is a subcomputation in an application program which can be executed concurrently with other subcomputations in the program, except at specific places in its execution called synchronization points. Multi-tasking, which permits the existence of many tasks within an application program, provides the possibility of overlapping the CPU and IO activities of the application with one another. This helps in reducing its elapsed time. The ability to specify priorities for the tasks provides additional controls to a designer while structuring an application to meet its response requirements. Example 9.12 illustrates this aspect.

Example 9.12 Consider the real time application of Fig. 9.20. Assume that each sample arriving from the satellite is put into a special register and a special interrupt is raised to signal this fact. The application program has to perform the following three functions:

1. Copy the sample out of the special register.
2. Write the sample into a disk file.
3. Perform some housekeeping operations (e.g. copy some selected fields of the incoming samples into another file).

A task is defined for each function (see Fig. 9.21). The first task copies the sample from the register into *buffer_area* which can hold, say, 50 samples. The second task writes a sample from *buffer_area* into a disk file. The third task performs housekeeping. Execution of the three tasks can overlap as follows: While task 2 is writing a previous sample to the disk, task 1 can copy the next sample into *buffer_area*. This reduces the response time of the application.

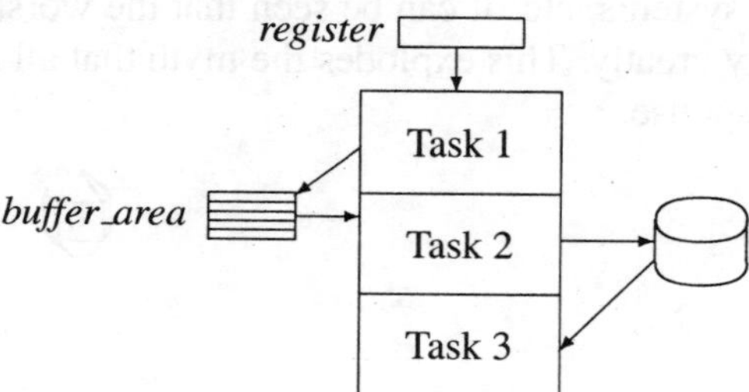

Fig. 9.21 Tasks in the real time application of Figure 9.20

Multi-tasking within the application also helps in another vital way. So long as *buffer_area* has some free space, only the first task has to complete before the next sample arrives. The other tasks can be performed later. This possibility is exploited by associating the highest priority with the first task and lower priorities with other tasks.

An RT system also permits the application program to define new kinds of interrupts relevant in the application domain, assign processing priorities for these interrupts, and provide its own routines to perform interrupt processing. This enables the application to react to events in its environment in an appropriate manner. In Ex. 9.12 a special interrupt may be devised to signal the arrival of a sample into the register. The application would provide an interrupt processing routine which would wake up task 1.

EXERCISE 9.6

1. A real time application requires a response time of 2 seconds. Discuss the suitability of a time sharing system for the real time application if the average response time in the system is
   (a) 20 seconds,
   (b) 2 seconds,
   (c) 0.2 seconds.
2. An application program is being developed for a microprocessor based controller for an automobile. The application is required to perform the following functions:
   (a) Monitor and display the speed of the automobile.
   (b) Monitor the fuel level and raise an alarm, if necessary.
   (c) Display the fuel efficiency, i.e. kilometers/litre at current speed.
   (d) Monitor the engine condition and raise an alarm if an unusual condition arises.
   (e) Periodically record some auxiliary information like speed, fuel level, etc.

   Answer the following questions concerning the application:
   (a) Is this a real time application? Justify your answer.
   (b) It is proposed to use multi-tasking to reduce the response time of the application. What are the tasks in it? What should be their priorities?
   (c) Is it necessary to define any application-specific interrupts? If so, specify the interrupts and their priorities.

9.7 OS STRUCTURE

OS design strongly depends on two factors: architectural features of the computer on which it operates, and features of its application domain. Dependence on architectural features is caused by the need to exercise complete control over all functional units of the system. Hence, the OS needs to know the addressing structure, interrupt structure, IO organization and memory protection features of the computer system. OS policies typically depend on its application domain. For example, the CPU scheduling policy depends on whether the OS will be used for time sharing, or for real time applications. The dependence on these two factors poses obvious difficulties in using an OS on computers with different architectures and different application domains.

Consider the development of an OS for a similar application domain on two computer systems c_1 and c_2. These two OSs differ in terms of architecture specific OS code. Remainder of the code, which forms the bulk of the total OS code, does not have any architectural dependencies. It would be tempting to consider development of the OS for c_1 and c_2 in the following manner:

1. Develop the OS for computer system c_1. Let this be called OS_1.
2. Modify OS_1 to obtain the OS for computer system c_2, i.e. OS_2.

That is, OS_2 is obtained by *porting* OS_1 to c_2.

In early operating systems, this approach faced several difficulties due to the monolithic structure of the OS. Thus, OSs did not provide clean interfaces between the architecture specific and architecture independent parts of their code. Hence the total porting effort was determined by the total size of OS code, rather than by the size of its architecture specific part. Historically, this difficulty has been addressed by developing an OS structure which separates the architecture specific and architecture independent parts of an OS. This enables OSs for different computer systems to share much of their design. When OSs are coded in a high level language, this even permits code sharing across OSs. To see how the separation of architecture specific and architecture independent parts can be implemented, consider the nature of a typical OS component. The component governs a class of resources, e.g. the processor(s) of the computer system, its memory, etc. Resource control actions of the module can be classified into

1. Policies governing the use of resources.
2. Mechanisms to implement the policy.

Policies are usually architecture independent, while mechanisms are often architecture dependent. Hence the policy routines and mechanisms should be segregated to achieve separation of the architecture specific and architecture independent parts of OS. Figure 9.22 shows an OS structure which separates the architecture specific and architecture independent parts into two modules. The module containing the policy routines is architecture independent and the part containing the mechanisms is architecture specific. The policy routines invoke the mechanisms as and when necessary. Such an OS can be ported to a new computer system by rewriting the mechanisms module for the new system, and integrating it with the policy module.

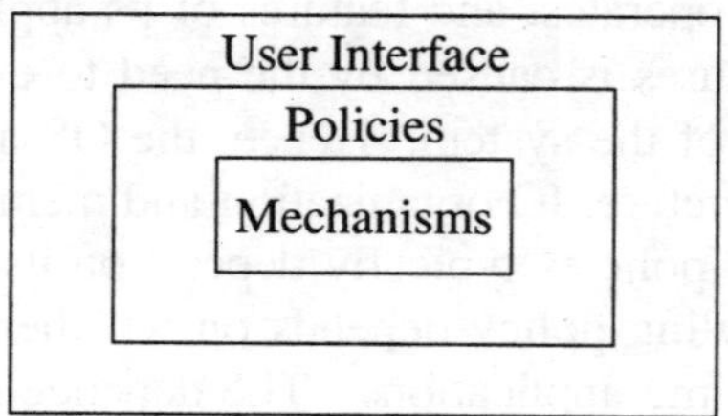

Fig. 9.22 Structure of an OS

Example 9.13 The processor scheduling component of a TS system employs the round robin policy. The policy is implemented through two mechanisms: (i) CPU dispatching, and (ii) program preemption. When the policies and mechanisms are implemented in a monolithic manner, i.e. in a single program module, the entire processor scheduling component of the OS becomes architecture dependent. If the two are separated as shown in Fig. 9.22, the dispatching and preemption mechanisms belong to the mechanisms module. The round robin policy belongs to the policies module.

The structuring principle shown in Fig. 9.22 is implemented using the layered organization shown in Fig. 9.23 which is based on the notion of *extended machines*. Each software layer enhances the capabilities of the architecture by adding new features. In effect, it elevates the architectural interface closer to the user interface. For example, the lowest layer offers a machine which has in-built mechanisms for scheduling, memory management and IO control. This simplifies the functioning of the layer above it. Each layer only communicates with the adjoining layers through well defined interfaces. Thus, a user command may percolate through the layers to reach the lowest layer which directly interacts with the architecture. This layer is called the *OS kernel*. Many modern OSs, particularly Unix, use such OS structure. The porting effort of such an OS is determined by the size of the OS kernel.

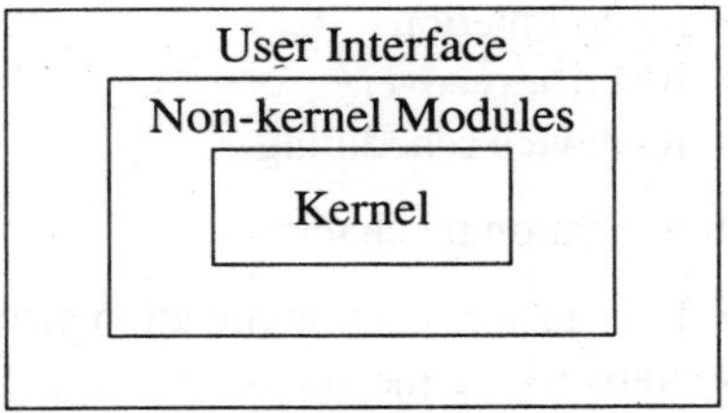

Fig. 9.23 OS layers

OS kernel

The typical mechanisms contained in the OS kernel are listed in Tab. 9.1. The kernel gets control when

1. An exceptional situation arises in the system.
2. An OS policy module explicitly invokes a kernel mechanism.

In the former case, the entry is through the interrupt processing mechanism which senses the occurrence of a hardware interrupt. In the latter case, the OS policy module typically transfers control to the kernel through a software interrupt. Thus, in either case the entry to the kernel is through the interrupt processing mechanism. For this reason, the OS kernel is often said to be *interrupt-driven*.

Many well-known OS kernels include functionalities not shown in Tab. 9.1, for example, process scheduling, device drivers, core file system services and certain memory management functions. This simplifies the writing of non-kernel software. However, it tends to detract from the porting advantages of the kernel based OS structure.

Table 9.1 Typical mechanisms in an OS kernel

1. Interrupt processing mechanism
2. Scheduling mechanisms
   - Program dispatching
   - Program preemption
3. Memory management mechanisms
   - Memory protection
   - Memory swapping mechanisms, e.g. swapping-in/out
   - Virtual memory mechanisms, e.g. page fault handling, page replacement
4. IO mechanisms
   - IO initiation
   - IO completion
   - IO error recovery
   - IO device scheduling
5. Communication mechanisms
   - Inter-process communication mechanisms
   - Networking mechanisms

OS microkernel

The notion of microkernels was developed in the early 1990's to enhance the portability, extensibility and reliability of operating systems. The primary motivation for a microkernel arises from disadvantages of the layered OS model based on kernels. The main problem with the layered model is that every OS functionality is stratified into a hierarchy of layers. Thus, every part of the functionality is subject to the constraints imposed by the interface of the OS layer to which it belongs.

Example 9.14 A certain functionality F of the OS consists of two modules, F_{l1} and F_{l2}, belonging to layers l_1 and l_2 respectively. If layer l_2 can only be entered through an interrupt, F_{l1} must cause an interrupt to communicate with F_{l2}.

Problems with the layered OS model can be summarized as follows: The OS kernel has the potential to offer good portability. However it may also contain architecture independent code, which detracts from the goal of portability. The layered architecture of the kernel-based design offers poor extensibility. This is due to the fact that addition of a new functionality requires changes in the interfaces of many OS layers, e.g. new software interrupts have to be devised to activate the code located in the kernel. The reliability of the kernel may be poor because of its not-so-small size. The kernel supports a large number of calls, many of which are infrequently used. Their implementations across different versions of the kernel are likely to be unreliable.

The OS microkernel is an essential core of the OS code. It provides the minimal functionalities necessary to support architecture independent code. It does not provide a layered interface, instead it supports a few well documented OS calls. This enhances the portability and reliability in an obvious manner. Extensibility is enhanced because many components previously considered to be parts of the OS kernel, e.g. process scheduling, now reside outside it in the OS. These components can be replaced at will to modify or extend the OS behaviour. It is thus possible to use the same microkernel to implement time sharing or dedicated real time systems. This simplifies the development of an OS for a new application domain.

Example 9.15 A microkernel includes a process dispatching mechanism, but does not include a process scheduler. A scheduler can exist outside the microkernel. It would invoke the process dispatcher after selecting the process to be executed. Different schedulers can be written to operate on top of the microkernel (see Fig. 9.24). A scheduler may be configured to become an essential part of the OS, or it may be loaded dynamically depending on the operational requirements.

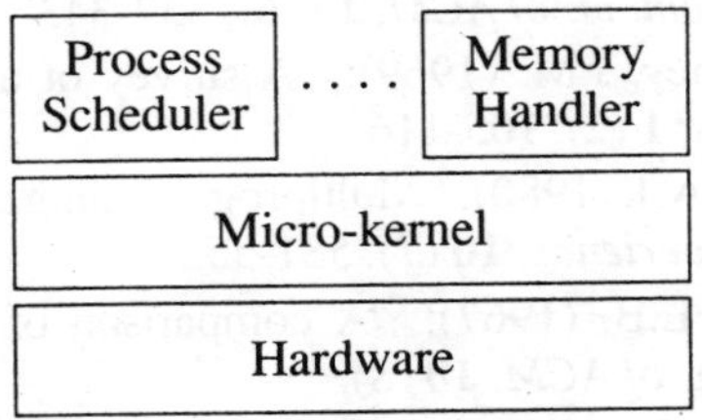

Fig. 9.24 OS microkernel

It is to be noted that microkernel designs vary greatly due to different interpretations of the term 'essential core of OS code'. Variations mainly concern the location of the process scheduler and the device drivers within the OS. For example, the Mach microkernel by IBM leaves the process scheduling policy and the device drivers outside the kernel while certain other microkernels include both these features. Some well-known microkernels include the QNX kernel which is only 8K bytes in size and includes process scheduling, interrupt handling, inter-process communication and core network services.

BIBLIOGRAPHY

Most books on operating systems cover the fundamental aspects of batch processing, multiprogramming and time sharing systems. Considerable literature also exists on efficiencies and response times in multiprogramming and time sharing systems. Metzner (1982) is a comprehensive bibliography covering all aspects of operating system literature.

(a) Job control and command languages

1. Brown, G.D. (1977): *System/370 Job Control Language*, Wiley Interscience, New York.
2. Flores, I. (1971): *Job Control Language and File Definition*, Prentice-Hall, Englewood Cliffs.
3. Unger, C. (ed.) (1975): *Command Languages*, North Holland, Amsterdam.

(b) Batch processing, multiprogramming and time sharing

1. Arden, B. and D. Boettner (1969): "Measurement and Performance of a Multiprogramming System," *Second ACM Symposium on Operating System Principles*.
2. Bard, Y. (1971): "Performance criteria and measurement for a time-sharing system," *IBM Systems Journal*, **10** (3), 193.
3. Bull, G.M. and S.F.G. Packham (1971): *Time-Sharing Systems*, McGraw-Hill, London.
4. Cantrell, H.N. and A.L. Ellison (1968): "Multiprogramming system performance measurement and analysis", *Proc. AFIPS SJCC*, **30**, 213-221.
5. Gold, M.M. (1969): "Time-sharing and batch processing : an experimental comparison of their values in a problem solving situation," *Commn. of ACM*, **12** (5), 249-259.
6. Hamlet, R.G. (1973): "Efficient multiprogramming resource allocation and accessing," *Commn. of ACM*, **16** (6), 337-343.
7. Mckinney, J.M. (1969): "A survey of analytical time-sharing models," *Computing Surveys*, **1** (2), 105-116.
8. Smith, A.J. (1980): "Multiprogramming and memory contention," *Software —Practice and Experience*, **10** (7), 531-552.
9. Smith, L.B. (1967): "A comparison of batch processing and instant turnaround," *Commn. of ACM*, **10** (8).
10. Stimler, S. (1969): "Some criteria for time-sharing system performance," *Commn. of ACM*, **12** (1), 47-53.
11. Watson, R.W. (1970): *Time Sharing System Design Concepts*, McGraw-Hill, New York.
12. Wirth, N. (1969): "On multiprogramming, machine coding, and computer organization," *Commn. of ACM*, **12** (9), 489-491.
13. Wilkes, M.V. (1968): *Time Sharing Computer Systems*, Macdonald, London.
14. Wright, J.D. and J.W. White (1983): "Real time operating systems and multitask programming," in *Real time computing*, Mellichamp, D.A. (ed.), Van Nostrand Reinhold, New York.

(c) General operating system literature

1. Deitel, H.M. (1984): *An Introduction to Operating Systems*, Addison-Wesley, Reading.
2. Denning, P.J. (1971): "Third generation operating systems," *Computing Surveys*, **4** (1), 175-216.
3. Hansen, P.B. (1975): *Operating System Principles*, Prentice-Hall, Englewood Cliffs.
4. Lister, A.M. (1979): *Fundamentals of Operating Systems*, Macmillan, London.

5. Lynch, W.C. (1967): "Description of a high capacity fast turnaround university computing centre," *Proc. ACM National Meeting*, 273-278.
6. Madnick, S.E. and J.J. Donovan (1974): *Operating Systems*, McGraw-Hill, New York.
7. Mckell, L.J., J.V. Hansen and L.E. Heitger (1979): "Charging for computing resources," *Computing Surveys*, **11** (2), 105-120.
8. Metzner, J. R. (1982): "Structuring operating systems literature for the graduate course," *Operating Systems Review*, **16** (4), 10-25.
9. Parmelee, R.P. *et al* (1972): "Virtual storage and virtual machine concepts," *IBM Systems Journal*, **11** (2), 99-130.
10. Silberschatz A. and P. Galvin (1994) : *Operating System Concepts* (4th edition), Addison-Wesley, Reading.
11. Rosin, R.F. (1969): "Supervisory and monitor systems," *Computing Surveys*, **1** (1), 15-32.
12. Shaw, A.C. (1974): *The Logical Design of Operating Systems*, Prentice-Hall, Englewood Cliffs.

CHAPTER 10

Processes

10.1 PROCESS DEFINITION

A *process* is a program in execution.

Definition 10.1 (Process) *A* process *is a tuple*

(process id, code, data, register values, pc value)

where process id *is unique in the system,*
code *is the program code,*
data *is the data used during its execution, i.e. the data space and the values of the data,*
register values *are the values in the machine registers, and*
pc value *is the address in the the program counter.*

At birth, a process is represented by the tuple (*id, code, data*, ϕ, *pc value*) where *id* is the unique process id assigned to the process by the OS, *data* is the initialized or uninitialized data of the program, no values are contained in registers, and *pc value* is the execution start address of the program. The last three components change as the process executes. Note that program data also includes any data entities dynamically created during the execution of the program, including the stack. As process id's are unique in the OS, processes could be identical in other components of the tuple without causing any difficulties for the OS.

Note that a process is *sequential* in nature—that is, instructions in the program code are executed one after another.

Example 10.1 The following processes exist in an OS:

$$\begin{array}{rcl} \text{process } p_1 & : & (p_1, C_1, D_1, rv_1, pc_1) \\ p_2 & : & (p_2, C_2, D_2, rv_2, pc_2) \\ p_3 & : & (p_3, C_1, D_3, rv_3, pc_3) \end{array}$$

Processes p_1 and p_3 represent different executions of the same program, while p_2 represents execution of another program. Note that p_1 and p_3 could be identical in all components other than *process id*. The OS differentiates between them by their identities.

Note that processes p_1 and p_2 represent *concurrent* executions of the same program. Operating systems (e.g. Unix) often use such processes to provide concurrent servicing of user requests.

Execution of user programs in a multiprogramming or time sharing system is represented by a set of processes. At any moment, only one of these processes is actively executing—this is the process which has been given the CPU. Other processes are in a state of suspension. When an interrupt arises, the process executing on the CPU is suspended. After processing the interrupt, OS passes control to the scheduler which selects one process for execution on the CPU. A process is thus the basic unit for CPU scheduling in the OS.

A process may be independent of other processes in the system, or may interact with some of them. An interaction between processes involves sharing of data or exchange of messages and control signals to co-ordinate their activities with respect to one another. The OS provides some means of *synchronization* to implement desired interactions between processes.

Programs and Processes

A program is a static entity whereas a process, since it represents the execution of a program, is dynamic in nature. Example 10.1 has illustrated that concurrent executions of a program lead to multiple processes. It would be interesting to see whether a single execution of a program can lead to multiple processes.

Consider the execution of a Pascal program. The program consists of a main program and a set of procedures, each of which implements a certain computation. The sequencing of control between the main program and the processes is implicitly performed by the code generated for the Pascal program. The OS is not aware of the different computations in the program. Hence the main program and its procedures together constitute a single process.

In some programming languages (e.g. Concurrent Pascal, Ada, etc.) different parts of a program can execute concurrently with one another. The compiler makes the OS aware of the existence of these parts. The OS assigns distinct id's to these parts and considers them as separate entities for the purpose of scheduling. Here, processes have a many-to-one relationship to a program. Such processes must interact with one another to fulfill a common goal. Possible modes of interaction are discussed in Section 10.3 and implementation of interacting processes is discussed in Section 10.4.

EXERCISE 10.1

1. Explain which of the following constitutes a valid reason for creating multiple pro-

cesses in a program:

(a) to enable execution of the program on multiple CPUs in the system
(b) to enable execution of the program so as to consume less CPU time
(c) to minimize the elapsed time for the execution of the program.

2. It is proposed to design an OS kernel to consist of different processes. Can the following components of the kernel be considered as different processes?

(a) process scheduling
(b) program swapping
(c) interrupt processing
(d) IO initiation.

Define their interactions with one another.

10.2 PROCESS CONTROL

10.2.1 Process Creation

OS creates a user process to represent the execution of a user program. This is done when a user types the name of a program to be executed. Alternatively, a user process may be explicitly created by another user process through a system call (this aspect shall be discussed later). A *system process* may be created by an OS for its own purposes, e.g. to service a request made by a user. In this chapter only user processes are discussed.

OS performs the following actions when a new process is created:

1. Create a *process control block* (PCB) for the process
2. Assign process id and priority
3. Allocate memory and other resources to the process
4. Set up the process environment
5. Initialize resource accounting information for the process.

Setting up of a process environment includes loading the process code in the memory, setting up the data space to consist of private and shared data areas of the process, setting up file pointers for standard files, etc. At the end of these actions, the state of the process is set to *ready* and the PCB of the process is entered in the data structures of the process scheduler (see Section 10.2.4). From this point onwards, the process will compete for CPU time in accordance with its priority.

10.2.2 Process State

The notion of *process state* is used by an OS to simplify process scheduling. A process p_i is said to be in a state s_i, if s_i is an appropriate description of p_i's activity. The four fundamental states for a process are:

1. *Running:* A CPU is currently allocated to the process and the process is in execution.
2. *Blocked:* The process is waiting for a request to be satisfied, or an event to occur. Such a process cannot execute even if a CPU is available.
3. *Ready:* The process is not *running*, however it can execute if a CPU is allocated to it (i.e. the process is not *blocked*).
4. *Terminated:* The process has finished its execution.

A *state transition* is a change from one state to another. A state transition is caused by the occurrence of some event in the system. When a process in the *running* state makes an IO request, it has to enter the *blocked* state awaiting completion of the IO. When the IO completes, the process state changes from *blocked* to *ready*. Similar state changes occur when a process makes some request which cannot be satisfied by the OS straightaway. The process state changes to *blocked* until the request is satisfied, when its state changes to *ready* once again. A *ready* process becomes *running* when the CPU is allocated to it. Figure 10.1 shows the fundamental state transitions for a process. Other state transitions and their causes are discussed in chapter 11.

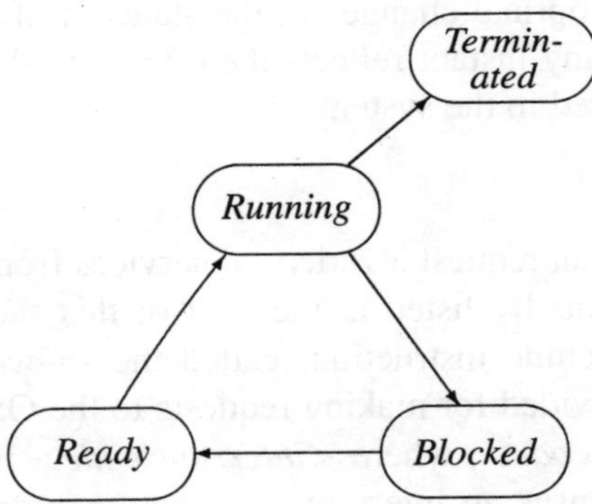

Fig. 10.1 Fundamental state transitions for a process

Note that the state of a process is a function of two components—recent behaviour of the process and occurrence of events pertaining to it. For example, state of a process indicates whether the process made a request recently and whether the request has been satisfied. This makes it possible to design the functioning of the process scheduler around the states of processes existing in the system. This can be done as follows: The OS maintains a list of processes in the *ready* state. This is called the *process scheduling list.* The scheduler picks one process from this list and allocates the CPU to it.

10.2.3 Events Pertaining to a Process

Process state transitions are caused by the occurrence of events in the system. A sample list of events is as follows:

1. *Request event:* Process makes a resource request.
2. *Allocation event:* A requested resource is allocated.
3. *IO initiation event:* Process wishes to start IO.
4. *IO termination event:* An IO operation completes.
5. *Timer interrupt:* The system timer indicates end of a time interval.
6. *Process creation event:* A new process is created.
7. *Process termination event:* A process finishes its execution.
8. *Message arrival event:* An interprocess message is received.

An event may be *internal* to a *running* process, or it may be *external* to it. For example, a request event is internal to the *running* process, whereas the allocation, IO termination and timer interrupt events are external to it. When an internal event occurs, the change of state, if any, concerns the *running* process. When an external event occurs, OS must determine the process affected by the event, and mark an appropriate change of state. Chapter 11 discusses how this function is implemented. For now, we simply state that OS monitors occurrence of events in the system and makes appropriate changes in the states of affected processes. Thus, the state of a process at any instant reflects the effect of all events concerning the process which have occurred in the system.

System call

A process can request a variety of services from an OS. Some of these services have been individually listed at the start of this section. In practice, however, a single generic machine instruction, called the *software interrupt instruction* (SI instruction), is provided for making requests to the OS. It has the format *<SI_instruction>* *<interrupt_code>*, where *<interrupt_code>* is an integer. When executed, the instruction causes an interrupt to occur. *<interrupt_code>* is put in the IC field of PSR when the interrupt action described in Section 9.4.1.1 takes place. This code indicates which service is requested by the process.

We will refer to the execution of SI instructions with appropriate interrupt code as a *system call*. Thus the system call is a major source of events internal to a process. Other internal events are exceptional situations like zero divide, addressing error, etc. which occur during the execution of an instruction.

10.2.4 Process Control Block

A process is more than simply a program in execution. An OS considers a process to be the fundamental unit for resource allocation. Following resources could be allocated to a process

1. Memory
2. Secondary memory, i.e. the swap space
3. IO Devices
4. Files opened by the process
5. CPU time consumed by the process.

A data structure called the *process control block* (PCB) is used by an OS to keep track of all information concerning a process (see Fig. 10.2). The PCB of a process contains the following information:

Process ID
Priority
Process state
PSR
Registers
Event information
Memory allocation
Resources held
PCB pointer

Fig. 10.2 Process Control Block (PCB)

1. *Process scheduling information:* This information consists of three fields containing process id, priority and process state.
2. *PSR and machine registers:* These fields hold contents of the *processor status register* (PSR) and the machine registers when execution of the process was last suspended (i.e. tuple components 4 and 5 of Definition 10.1).
3. *Event information:* When a process is in the blocked state, this field contains information concerning the event for which the process is waiting.
4. *Memory and resources information:* This information is useful for deallocating memory and resources when the process terminates.
5. *PCB pointer:* It is a pointer to the next PCB in the process scheduling list.

The PSR and machine registers fields represent a snapshot of the CPU when it was released by a process. When the process is scheduled once again, this information from its PCB can simply be loaded into the processor to resume its execution. The *event information* field of the PCB plays an important role in effecting appropriate state transitions in the system. Consider a process p_i which is *blocked* on an IO operation. The *event information* field in p_i's PCB indicates the id of the device, say device d, on which the IO operation is to be performed. When the IO operation on device d completes, the operating system must find the process which awaits that event. Since *event information* field of p_i's PCB mentions this event, the operating system concludes that state of p_i should change from *blocked* to *ready*.

10.2.5 Process Scheduling

Process scheduling consists of the following sub-functions:

1. *Scheduling:* Selects the process to be executed next on the CPU.
2. *Dispatching:* Sets up execution of the selected process on the CPU.
3. *Context save:* Saves the status of a running process when its execution is to be suspended.

The scheduling function uses information from the PCB's and selects a process based on the scheduling policy in force. Dispatching involves setting up the execution environment of the selected process, and loading information from the PSR and registers fields of the PCB into the CPU. The context save function performs housekeeping whenever a process releases the CPU or is pre-empted. It involves saving the PSR and registers in appropriate fields of the PCB, and changing the process state. In practice, this function is performed by the interrupt processing module and not by the scheduling module of the OS.

The schematic in Fig. 10.3 illustrates the use of scheduling subfunctions. Occurrence of an event invokes the context save function. The kernel now processes the event which has occurred. This processing may lead to a change of state for some process. The scheduling function is now invoked to select a process for execution on the CPU. The dispatching function arranges execution of the selected function on the CPU.

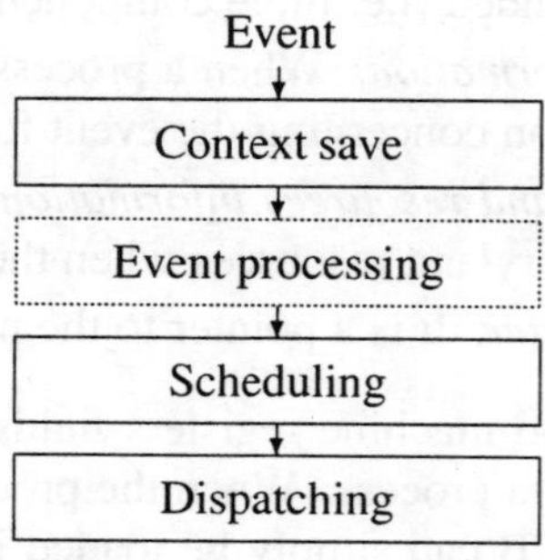

Fig. 10.3 Subfunctions in scheduling

10.2.6 Process Termination

When a process p_i terminates, the kernel has to release all resources allocated to p_i. This function is performed using the information in appropriate fields of p_i. If the terminated process was created by another user process p_c, some additional actions are necessary to implement process synchronization. For example, process p_c may be waiting for p_i to terminate. The kernel can find if this is the case by looking into the *event information* field of p_c. It is also possible that p_c may wait for termination of p_i sometime in the future. For this purpose, the kernel remembers a *termination code* for p_i. This code is used if p_c waits for p_i's termination in future. We discuss these issues in Section 10.4.

10.2.7 Putting It Together

Example 10.2 illustrates use of the data structures and techniques described in this section for controlling the execution of user processes.

Example 10.2 An OS contains 2 processes p_1 and p_2, with p_2 having a higher priority than p_1. Let p_2 be *blocked* on an IO operation and let p_1 be *running*. The sequence of OS actions when an IO termination event occurs is as follows:

1. A context save is performed for p_1.
2. The IO termination event is processed and the state of p_2 is changed from *blocked* to *ready*.
3. Scheduling is performed. Being the highest priority *ready* process, p_2 is selected.
4. p_2 is dispatched.

The term 'switching between processes' is used to collectively describe Functions 1, 3 and 4 of Ex. 10.2.

10.3 INTERACTING PROCESSES

As discussed before, execution of an application program may lead to creation of many processes. This is done to avail of the following advantages:

1. Computation speed up by utilizing multiple CPU's
2. Improved response times or elapsed times of an application
3. Reflecting real world requirements.

Computation speed up can be achieved in computer systems having multiple CPU's. In single CPU systems, existence of multiple processes permits different sections of the application code to be executed concurrently. This is analogous to multiprogramming within the application. It leads to improved response or elapsed times if some of the processes are IO-bound while others are CPU bound. This feature is particularly important for real time applications. Less important activities of the application can be run at a lower priority to further enhance this advantage (see Ex. 9.12).

Certain real world systems are multi-activity by nature. It is natural to structure such systems in the form of multiple processes. Example 10.3 illustrates this aspect.

Example 10.3 An airline reservations application uses a number of terminals connected to a central computer system. The computer stores the data in a centralized fashion and permits agents at all terminals to access this data in real time. The execution of the application may be structured in the form of multiple processes, each process servicing one agent terminal (see Fig. 10.4). Now, while the agent at one terminal keys in the requirements of a customer, other agents could access and update the data on behalf of other customers.

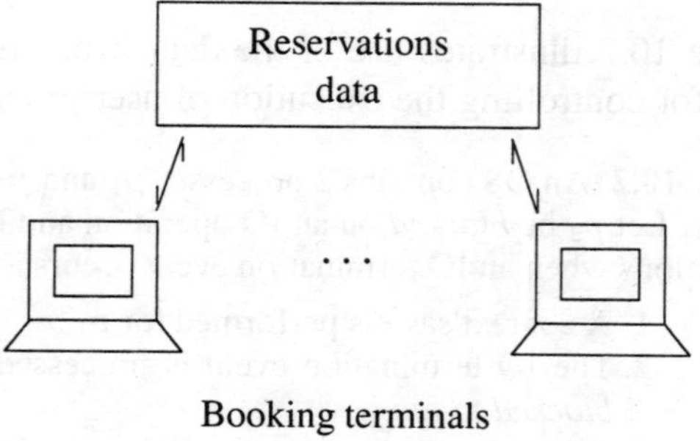

Fig. 10.4 An airline reservation system

The processes of an application interact with one another to co-ordinate their activities or to share some data. The nature of their interaction is described in the following sections. However, before doing that we give a generalized definition of the term *interacting processes* using the following notation:

$read\_set_i$	:	set of data items read by process p_i
$write\_set_i$	:	set of data items modified by process p_i

Definition 10.2 (Interacting processes) *Processes p_i and p_j are* interacting processes *if*

$$(read\_set_i \cup write\_set_i) \cap (read\_set_j \cup write\_set_j) \neq \phi.$$

Definition 10.2 implies that processes p_i and p_j share some data. Note that data sharing may be explicit, as in Ex. 10.3, or implicit as in the following

1. process p_i performs some action a_1,
2. process p_j performs action a_2 two minutes after a_1 was completed.

Here processes implicitly share the clock.

10.3.1 Control Synchronization

In control synchronization, interacting processes co-ordinate their execution with respect to one another. Synchronization can occur at any point in the lifetime of a process, including at the start or end of its lifetime. Example 10.4 illustrates the need for control synchronization when an application is structured into a set of interacting processes to improve the response time.

Example 10.4 A program is to be designed to minimize the elapsed time of the following calculation: Compute Y = HCF (A_{max}, X), where A_{max} is the maximum value in array A, which contains *n* elements. Insert Y in array A and arrange A in ascending order.

The problem can be split into the following steps:

1. Read *n* elements of array A.
2. Find the maximum magnitude A_{max}.
3. Read X.
4. Compute Y = HCF(A_{max}, X).
5. Include Y in array A and arrange the elements of A in ascending order.

Steps 1 and 3 can be performed concurrently. Steps 2, 4 and 5 cannot be performed concurrently in their present form. However, concurrency can be achieved by splitting Steps 2 and 5 into two parts each as

2(a). Copy array A into array B.
2(b). Find A_{max}.
5(a). Arrange array B in ascending order.
5(b). Include Y in array B at the appropriate place.

Now Step 2(b) can be performed concurrently with Step 5(a). Once 2(b) has been performed, Step 4 can also be performed concurrently with Step 5(a). Thus the problem can be coded as the set of processes shown in Fig. 10.5.

Process p_1	*Process p_2*	*Process p_3*
Read *n* elements of A Copy A into array B	Find A_{max}	Read X

Process p_4	*Process p_5*	*Process p_6*
Compute Y = HCF(A_{max},X)	Arrange B in ascending order	Include Y in array B

Fig. 10.5 Concurrent processes for Example 10.4

Processes p_1 and p_3 can be initiated concurrently. Process p_2 can start executing when process p_1 finishes. Process p_4 can be initiated only when both p_2 and p_3 terminate. Process p_5 can be initiated as soon as process p_1 terminates, while p_6 can start only after p_4 and p_5 have terminated.

The motivation for structuring the application into a set of concurrent processes in the manner of Ex. 10.4 is to obtain the benefits of multiprogramming and multiprocessing within a program. Process p_3 is an IO-bound process whose execution partially overlaps with p_2, which is a CPU-bound process, and p_1 which is CPU-bound in later half of its lifetime. This enables the program to make faster progress than if it were to be coded as a single process. Overlapped execution of p_4 and p_5—both of which are CPU-bound processes—yields an advantage if the computer system has multiple CPUs.

10.3.2 Data Access Synchronization

An application may consist of a set of processes sharing some data. Such arrangements are common in systems supporting data base query and update services. The need for data access synchronization arises because use of the shared data by interacting processes may lead to unpredictable results due to race conditions. Let a_i and a_j be operations on shared data d_s performed by two interacting concurrent processes p_i and p_j. Let $f_i(d_s)$, $f_j(d_s)$ represent the value of d_s resulting from the changes, if any, in the values of d_s caused by operations a_i, a_j, respectively.

Definition 10.3 (Race condition) A race condition *arises due to the execution of operations a_i and a_j on shared data d_s if the value of d_s after completing the execution of a_i and a_j is neither $f_i(f_j(d_s))$ nor $f_j(f_i(d_s))$.*

Race conditions arise when values of shared data are not accessed and updated in a mutually exclusive manner.

Example 10.5 Processes of the airline reservations system of Ex. 10.3 execute identical code as shown in Fig. 10.6. To make a reservation, each process examines the value of *nextseatno* and updates it using a load-add-store sequence of instructions. When both processes wish to make a reservation on the same flight, they share the variables *nextseatno*, *capacity*, etc. Assume *nextseatno* < *capacity* and process p_j is incrementing *nextseatno* when process p_i begins to execute the **if** statement. The value of *nextseatno* may increase by 1 or 2 depending on the order in which p_i and p_j execute their load–add–store instruction sequences for incrementing *nextseatno*. Thus, a race condition can arise due to concurrent accesses to *nextseatno*.

Behaviour of programs containing race conditions is not reproduceable because values of shared data depend on the order of execution of instructions in different processes. This makes debugging of such programs very difficult in practice.

In Ex. 10.5, race conditions would be avoided if accesses to *nextseatno* by processes p_i and p_j are implemented in a mutually exclusive manner. Hence to avoid race conditions in an application containing multiple processes, we must

1. Determine whether a pair of processes (p_i, p_j) requires data access synchronization.

process p_i	*process* p_j
$\Rightarrow$**if** *nextseatno* < *capacity*	**if** *nextseatno* < *capacity*
then	**then**
nextseatno:=nextseatno+1;	$\Rightarrow$ *nextseatno:=nextseatno+1;*
allotedno:=nextseatno;	*allotedno:=nextseatno;*
else	**else**
display "sorry, no seats available"	*display "sorry, no seats available"*

Fig. 10.6 Data sharing by processes of a reservations system

2. Use data access synchronization techniques to ensure that the shared data is accessed in a mutually exclusive manner.

Processes p_i, p_j of an application require data access synchronization if one of the following conditions is satisfied:

1. $(read\_set_i \cap write\_set_j) \neq \phi$
2. $(write\_set_i \cap read\_set_j) \neq \phi$
3. $(write\_set_i \cap write\_set_j) \neq \phi$.

Techniques to implement mutual exclusion are discussed in Chapter 13.

10.3.3 Interprocess Communication

Concurrent processes may need to interact in ways other than control and data access synchronization. Such needs are satisfied using *interprocess messages*. Figure 10.7 shows a popular model of communication using interprocess messages. Process p_i sends a message msg_i to process p_j by executing the OS call *send*. The OS copies the message into a buffer area, and awaits execution of a *receive* call by process p_j. When p_j executes a *receive* call, the OS copies msg_i out of the buffer and into the data area with the address <*area_address*>. If no message has been sent by the time p_j executes a *receive* call, the OS blocks p_j pending arrival of a message for it. If many messages have been sent to p_j, the OS queues them and delivers them in FIFO order when p_j executes *receive* calls.

process p_i	*process* p_j
...	...
send (p_j, <*message*>);	*receive* (p_i, <*area_address*>);
...	...

Fig. 10.7 Interprocess messages

In principle, the interprocess communication requirements can be satisfied using shared variables. Processes p_i and p_j can declare some shared variables, and agree to leave messages for each other in these shared variables. Compared to this model, interprocess messages have the following advantages:

1. Processes do not need to guess the size of shared data area required for interprocess communication.
2. Processes need not define a complex protocol for communication. For example, consider the situation when the shared data area is full.
3. The scheme is tamper-proof as messages reside in the system area till delivery.
4. The OS takes the responsibility to block a process executing a *receive* when no messages exist for it.
5. The processes may exist in different computer systems.

Interprocess communication is discussed in chapter 14.

EXERCISE 10.3

1. If the process scheduling, memory management and IO management components of an OS are structured in the form of processes
   (a) What are their control synchronization requirements?
   (b) What are their data access synchronization requirements?

10.4 IMPLEMENTATION OF INTERACTING PROCESSES

In this section we describe the following facilities for implementing interacting processes in programming languages and OSs:

1. **Fork–Join** primitives
2. **Parbegin–Parend** control structure
3. Unix processes
4. OSF pthreads.

This discussion is not a survey of all important language or OS features. It is simply an overview of the features that interest us most at present. In chapter 13 we discuss other methods of implementing interacting processes.

10.4.1 Fork–Join

Fork and **Join** are primitives in a higher level programming language. The syntax of these primitives is as follows:

```
fork <label>;
join <var>;
```

where <*label*> is a label associated with some program statement, and <*var*> is a variable. A statement `fork lab1` causes creation of a new process which starts executing at the statement with the label `lab1`. This process is concurrent with the process which executed the statement `fork lab1`. A **join** statement synchronizes the birth of a process with the termination of one or more processes. Execution of a statement `join v;` has the following effect:

1. Value of variable `v` is decremented by 1.
2. The process executing the `join` statement terminates.
3. A new process is created if the new value of `v` is zero. This process begins execution of the statement following the `join v` statement.

Thus, if `v` is initialized to some value *n*, *n* processes need to execute the statement `join v` before the new process is created.

The program in Fig. 10.8 implements the computation $result := max(a)/min(a)$, where *a* is an array, using the **fork** and **join** primitives. Since `m` is initialized to 3, `join m;` will have to be executed by all three processes before the execution of `result := y/x;` is initiated.

```
                for i := 1 to 100
                    read a[i];
                m := 3;
                fork lab1;
                fork lab2;
                Goto lab3;
lab1      :     x := min(a);
                Goto lab3;
lab2      :     y := max(a);
lab3      :     join m;
                result := y/x;
```

Fig. 10.8 Computing *result* := *max*(*a*)/*min*(*a*) using **Fork–Join**

Fork–Join provide a functionally complete facility for control synchronization. Hence it can be used to implement arbitrary synchronizations. However, being unstructured primitives, their use is cumbersome and error-prone.

10.4.2 Parbegin–Parend

The **Parbegin–Parend** control structure has the following syntax:

```
Parbegin
    <list of statements>
Parend
```

Execution of the control structure results in concurrent execution of each statement in *<list of statements>*. The control structure is implemented as follows: Consider *<list of statements>* to contain *n* statements. Execution of the control structure spawns *n* processes, each process consisting of the execution of one statement in *<list of statements>*. Execution of the statement following `Parend` is initiated only after all the processes spawned by the **Parbegin–Parend** have terminated. The statement grouping facilities of the language, e.g. **begin–end**, can be used if a process is to consist of a block of code instead of a single statement.

The program of Fig. 10.9 illustrates use of the **Parbegin–Parend** control structure to perform the computation $result := max(a)/min(a)$. After reading values of array `a`, the `Parbegin` statement creates two processes to execute the computations of *max* and *min* respectively. `result := y/x;` is executed after both these processes have terminated. This code is simpler than the code using **Fork–Join** for obvious reasons.

```
for i := 1 to 100
     read a[i];
Parbegin
     x := min(a);
     y := max(a);
Parend
result := y/x;
```

Fig. 10.9 Computing *result* := *max*(*a*)/*min*(*a*) using **Parbegin–Parend**

10.4.3 Processes in Unix

Unix permits a user process to create child processes and to synchronize its activities with respect to its child processes. The following features are provided for this purpose:

1. Creation of a child process
2. Termination of a process
3. Waiting for termination of a child process.

Process creation

A process creates a child process through the system call `fork`. `fork` creates a child process and sets up its execution environment. It then allocates an entry in the process table (i.e. a PCB) for the newly created process and marks its state as *ready*. `fork` also returns the id of the child process to its creator (also called the parent process). The child process shares the address space and file pointers of the parent process, hence data and files can be directly shared. A child process can in turn create its own child processes, thus leading to the creation of a process tree. The system keeps track of the parent–child relationships throughout the lives of the parent and child processes.

The child process environment (called its context) is a copy of the parent's environment. Hence the child executes the same code as the parent. At creation, the program counter of the child process is set at the instruction at which the `fork` call returns. The only difference between the parent and the child processes is that in the parent process `fork` returns with the process id of the child process, while in the child process it returns with a '0'.

Process termination

Any process p_i can terminate itself through the exit system call

exit (*status_code*);

where the value of *status_code* is saved in the kernel for access by the parent of p_i. If the parent is waiting for the termination of p_i, a signal is sent to it. The child processes of p_i are made the children of a kernel process.

Waiting for process termination

A process p_i can wait for the completion of a child process through the system call

wait(*adr*(xyz));

Where `xyz` is a variable. When a child of p_i terminates (or if one has already terminated) the `wait` call returns after storing the termination status of the terminated child process into `xyz`. The `wait` call returns with a '-1' if p_i has no children.

```
main()
{
        int saved_status;
        for (i = 0; i < 3; i++)
        {
            if (fork() == 0)
            { /* code for child processes */
                exit();
            }
        }
        while(wait(&saved_status) != -1);
                /* All child processes terminated?   */
}
```

Fig. 10.10 Process creation and termination in Unix

Example 10.6 Figure 10.10 shows a process which creates three child processes and awaits their completion. Due to the peculiarity of the value returned by the `fork` call, the child processes execute the code in the `if` statement, while the parent process skips the `if` statement and executes a `wait`. The wait is satisfied whenever a child process terminates. However, the parent issues another `wait` if the value returned is not '-1'. The fourth `wait` call returns with a '-1', which brings the parent process out of the loop. The parent process code does not contain an explicit `exit()` call. The language compiler would automatically add this at the end of `main()`.

10.5 THREADS

Use of concurrency within an application code has several advantages as described in Section 10.3. Concurrency can be implemented by structuring an application as a set of concurrent processes. However, use of traditional processes in this manner incurs considerable overheads due to process management and scheduling functions. *Threads* are a low cost alternative to processes for certain kinds of concurrent applications.

There are two sets of reasons for high overheads of switching between processes.

- *Intrinsic reasons:* These reasons follow from the definition of a process. A process is defined as an execution of a program. Hence while switching between processes, the execution context of a running process has to be saved and that of a new process has to be loaded. The execution context of a process consists of two parts, the process environment and the CPU state. The process environment consists of the code and data of the process and some control information concerning standard resources allocated to a process. Switching of the process context thus involves saving or loading of pointers to the process environment and the CPU state. These are unavoidable overheads which follow from the process concept directly.
- *OS related reasons:* These reasons follow from the way the process abstraction is implemented in an OS. The process abstraction as implemented in most operating systems is different from that of Def. 10.1 because an OS looks upon a process not only as a unit of computation, but also as a unit for resource allocation, resource accounting, interprocess communication, etc. These aspects add to the switching overheads by requiring the state of resource allocation, etc. of a process to be saved or loaded along with the process environment and the CPU state. Thus the process state becomes fatter than that dictated by Def. 10.1. These aspects are OS-specific, so their effect on process switching overheads differs from one OS to another.

It has been found that these overheads affect the performance of an OS and often result in poor response times in the system. This finding motivated the search for a low-overheads alternative for processes. The basic approach followed in this search was to reduce the overheads of context switching by either reducing the size of process state or by reducing the frequency with which context switching needs to be performed during the operation of an OS. A conceptual advance was made to attack the intrinsic reasons and practical techniques were developed to attack the OS-related reasons mentioned above.

To see how the switching overheads can be reduced in an OS, consider the scheduling subfunctions depicted in Fig. 10.3. Occurrence of an event in the system involves a context save and event handling followed by scheduling and dispatching of a process. This may result in switching between processes. Consider a situation in which the CPU is switched from the execution of a process p_i to a process p_j, where both p_i, p_j belong to the same application. Further, consider the application to involve interacting processes which execute the same code (see Fig. 10.6). Thus, the processes share all code and data barring values in CPU registers and stacks. Much of the process context saved and restored during a switch is thus redundant.

When the redundancies in context-switching actions were realized, a new entity was designed to designate concurrent activities which share code and data. This new entity was called a *thread*. It was defined to be a unit of concurrency *within* a process and had access to the entire code and data parts of the process. Thus threads of the same process would share their code and data with one another. However they would have their own stacks and their own CPU state. The process abstraction would continue to be used as before; processes would typically have distinct code and data parts. Figure 10.11 depicts this arrangement wherein the circle represents a process and the wavy lines represent threads. Thus process p_i contains three threads. These threads execute within the execution environment of process p_i.

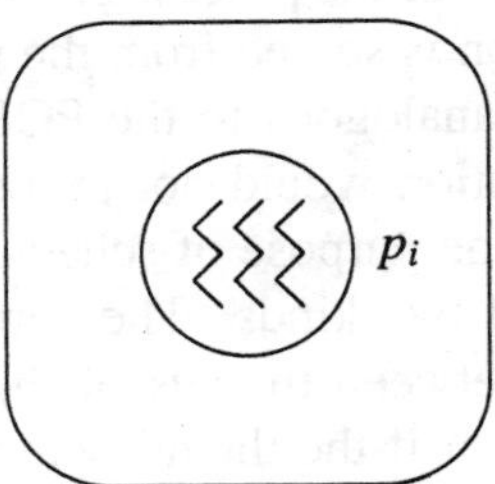

Fig. 10.11 Threads in process p_i

Now consider the reservations system of Fig. 10.6 once again to see the implications of this arrangement. The OS creates a single process for the application. The process does not create other processes. It creates threads. All threads share complete address space of the process. Each thread behaves like a process as described in Sections 10.1–10.2. The OS also treats threads exactly like processes except for one difference—it does not save and restore the execution environment while switching between threads of a process. This avoids redundancies in the context switch function. Use of threads splits the process state of older systems into two parts—resource state remains with the process while execution state is associated with a thread. The cost of concurrency is replication of the execution state for each concurrent entity. The resource state is not replicated. In older systems concurrency was obtained at the cost of replicating both execution and resource states.

Threads come in different flavours. The main difference lies in how much the kernel and the application program knows about threads. These differences lead to differences in the overheads implications and practical limitations on the threads as units of concurrency in an application program. Two representative approaches to the implementation of threads are discussed. These are:

- Kernel level threads
- User level threads

Kernel level threads

The identity of a kernel level thread is known to the OS kernel. A process creates threads in a manner analogous to the `create_process` call discussed earlier. Let us call this the `create_thread` call. One of the parameters of this call is the start address of the thread in the code of the creating process. The kernel creates appropriate data structures for the new thread and assigns it an id. The call returns with the id of the thread. The process creating the thread can use this id for synchronization purposes. The kernel data structures for a thread would be a subset of the data structures for a process described earlier—that is, a subset of the process environment and the PCB. No equivalent of the process environment would be needed since the code, data and file information is shared from the process environment. A *thread control block* would be needed analogous to the PCB, however PCB fields which store resource allocation information would not be needed. The scheduler would use the thread control block for the purpose of scheduling (see Fig. 10.12). The context switching actions are now of two kinds. The kernel would only save and load the CPU state while switching between threads of the same process. It would save and load the process environment if the thread being interrupted and the thread being scheduled to run belong to different processes.

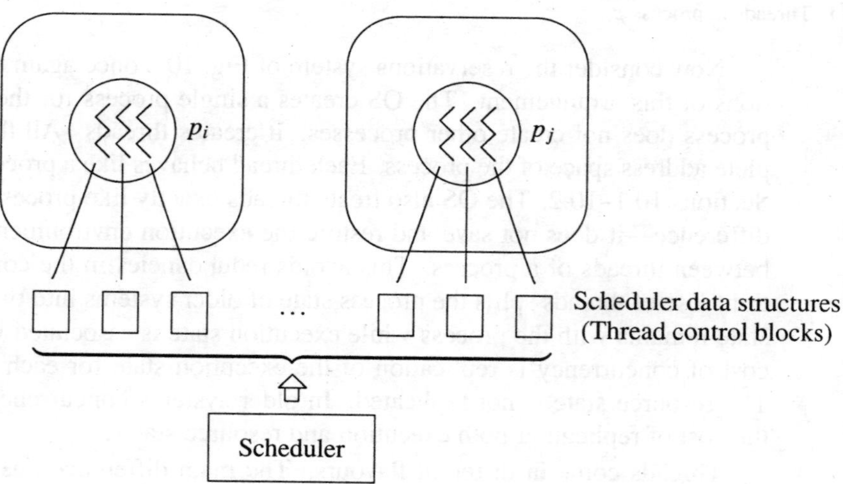

Fig. 10.12 Kernel level threads

Kernel level threads can enjoy all the privileges and facilities enjoyed by processes themselves. Thus, they can make system calls to convey their resource and I/O requirements to the OS. The thread making a system call can block for completion of an I/O operation or grant of a resource. Kernel level threads have some disadvantages too. Threads are like processes except that they have a smaller state. All switching is performed by the kernel. Hence switching between threads incurs the cost of a system call even if threads involved in a switch belong to the same process. Thus, the situation in which each process has exactly one thread is similar to the conventional scenario discussed in earlier sections of this chapter. In other words, overheads are smaller but may not be much smaller than when processes alone are used.

User level threads

In user level threads, a process does not create threads using a `create_thread` system call. Instead, it manages its own threads. The id of a user level thread is thus not known to the kernel. So as not to burden an application programmer with the coding of threads, thread management is performed through a threads library. This library provides functions to create and terminate threads, to synchronize their activities and to permit them to make requests to the OS. These functions are linked with an application program while creating an executable file for the program.

Creation and execution of threads proceeds as follows: A process invokes a library function to create a thread. The library function makes a note of the thread being created, and its associated details, in its own data structures. The library provides functions using which a thread can suspend itself while waiting for a request to be satisfied or a resource to be allocated to it. When a thread calls this function the threads library performs a thread switch and starts executing another thread of the process. All this is done without involving the kernel. This way the kernel is oblivious to the presence of threads in a process, and continues to believe that the process is in execution. If a thread wishes to suspend itself and the threads library does not find another ready thread in the same process, then it makes a 'block me' system call. The kernel now blocks the process. The process will wake up when the condition mentioned in the 'block me' call is satisfied. In effect, user level threads achieve concurrent and interleaved execution of the code of a process. Figure 10.13 illustrates user level threads. The scheduler only sees the PCBs for scheduling purposes; it is unaware of the existence of threads in the processes.

The main advantage of user level threads is that the kernel is not aware of the existence and identities of the threads in a process. Thus kernel resources like data structures for process environments and PCBs are not tied up for the threads. The kernel schedules processes in a conventional manner. Within a process threads schedule themselves through library calls. This arrangement avoids the overheads of a system call. Thus, thread switching overheads in user level threads are much lower than switching overheads in kernel level threads. However, managing threads without in-

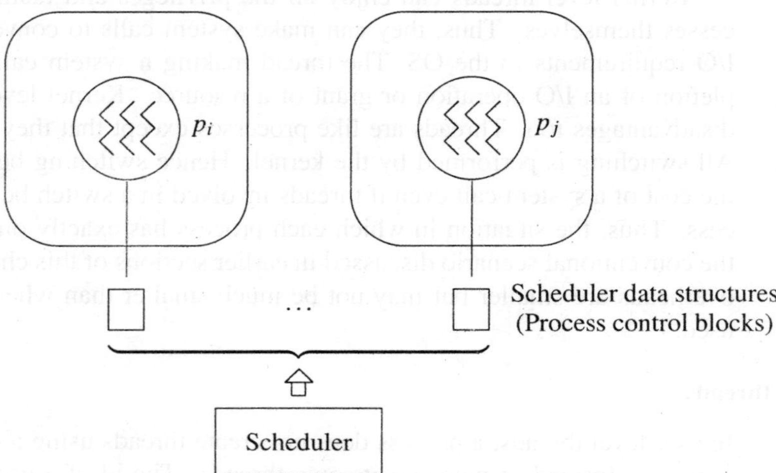

Fig. 10.13 User level threads

volving the kernel has its drawbacks. An application program must ensure that none of its threads makes a system call which can lead to blocking. Since the kernel does not know the distinction between a thread and a process, if a thread were to block in a system call it would block the process containing the thread. In effect, *all* threads of the process would get blocked; none of them can execute until the cause of blocking is removed.

We describe threads of OSF/1 in the following.

Creation of a pthread

A process creates a pthread through a call on the system routine

```
pthread_create(id_ptr, attr, start_routine, arg);
```

where `id_ptr` points to the memory word where the pthread ID will be stored, and `attr` specifies an attributes object defining the attributes to be used while creating the pthread. `start_routine` is the routine to be executed by the pthread, and `arg` is the single argument which can be passed to the pthread. On creation, the pthread begins to execute `start_routine` within the environment of the creating process.

Termination of a pthread

A pthread terminates in one of the following ways:.

1. When it calls the routine `pthread_exit(`*`status_code`*`)`.
2. When it returns from its `start_routine` (`pthread_exit` is implicitly called).

3. When it is cancelled by another pthread by calling the pthread_cancel routine.
4. When the process creating the pthread terminates.

The termination status of a pthread is used by other pthreads in the pthread_join routine.

Detaching a pthread

A pthread is detached through a call pthread_detach(<*pthread_id*>). The detached pthread continues its execution till it terminates. The effect of a detach is that no other pthread can synchronize its activities with respect to the detached pthread.

Waiting for pthread termination

A pthread can await the termination of another pthread through the call

```
pthread_join(<pthread_id>, adr(xyz));
```

where <*pthread_id*> is the id of the target thread, and xyz is a variable in which status of the target thread is to be saved. The pthread(s) performing a pthread_join on a pthread are suspended till that pthread terminates. A join call is refused if the target pthread has been detached. A deadlock is caused if two pthreads perform a join on each other.

Example 10.7 Figure 10.14 illustrates creation of 3 threads to execute the routine thread_routine. The process creating the pthreads waits for all three pthreads to complete before terminating itself.

```
main()
{
    int id1,id2,id3;
    pthread_create(&id1,..,thread_routine,..);
    pthread_create(&id2,..,thread_routine,..);
    pthread_create(&id3,..,thread_routine,..);
                /* 3 pthreads are created */

    pthread_join(&id1,..);
    pthread_join(&id2,..);
    pthread_join(&id3,..);
                /* All pthreads have terminated */
}
thread_routine()
{ ... }
```

Fig. 10.14 Pthreads creation

Apart from the advantage of lower OS overheads, OSF pthreads enjoy two advantages over Unix child processes. First, an execution start address can be explicitly specified for each pthread. Second, the pthreads of a process have a symmetrical relationship with one another. Hence, pthreads can wait on each other while Unix processes cannot.

EXERCISE 10.5

1. Implement the application of Ex. 10.4 using the following synchronization constructs:
   (a) **Fork–Join**
   (b) **Parbegin–Parend**
2. A synchronization construct is said to be functionally complete if it can implement arbitrary control synchronization requirements. Comment on whether the following constructs are functionally complete:
   (a) **Fork–Join**
   (b) **Parbegin–Parend**

   (*Hint* : See Problem 1 above.)
3. Comment on the following in the context of interacting processes in Unix:
   (a) Implementation of the *wait* call using the PCB data structure,
   (b) Comparative lifetimes of a process and its PCB.

BIBLIOGRAPHY

Bach and Vahalia discuss processes and threads in Unix. Tanenbaum discusses processes and threads in Mach.

1. Bach, M.J. (1986): *The Design of the Unix Operating System*, Prentice-Hall, Englewood Cliffs.
2. Hansen, P.B. (1975): *Operating System Principles*, Prentice-Hall, Englewood Cliffs.
3. Silberschatz A. and P. Galvin (1994) : *Operating System Concepts* (4th edition), Addison-Wesley, Reading.
4. Tanenbaum, A.S. (1992): *Modern Operating Systems*, Prentice-Hall, Englewood cliffs.
5. Vahalia, U. (1996): *Unix Internals—The New frontiers*, Prentice-Hall, Enclewood Cliffs.

CHAPTER 11

Scheduling

Scheduling is the activity of determining which service request should be handled next by a server. A scheduling policy specifies criteria for use during scheduling. In an OS, the server in question is the CPU of the system. Scheduling is important because it influences user service and efficiency of CPU utilization. In this chapter we first discuss some fundamental scheduling policies. Implementation of these policies to perform job and process scheduling in an OS shall be discussed later in the chapter.

11.1 SCHEDULING POLICIES

We define four events related to scheduling:

1. *Arrival:* A request arrives in the system when a user submits it to the OS. When a request arrives, the system takes note of its arrival time, and other characteristics like the kind and quantum of the request, etc. This information is entered into a list of pending requests. Some information associated with a request, e.g. elapsed time since arrival, may be updated as it awaits attention of the server. The scheduler uses this information while making a scheduling decision.
2. *Scheduling:* A request is scheduled when the scheduler selects it for servicing. The scheduled request is removed from the list of pending requests.
3. *Preemption:* A request is preempted when the server switches to servicing of another request before completing the request. A preempted request is put back into the list of pending requests. Its processing is resumed when it is scheduled again.
4. *Completion:* The processing of a request gets completed. Scheduling is performed to select another request for processing.

Figure 11.1 shows the movement of requests in the system. All requests waiting to be serviced are kept in a list of pending requests. Whenever scheduling is to be performed, the scheduler examines the pending requests and selects one for servicing (this is shown by the broken arrow in Fig. 11.1). This request is handed over to the server. A request leaves the server when it completes, or when it is preempted by the scheduler, in which case it is put back into the list of pending requests. In either situation, scheduler performs scheduling to select the next request to be serviced. Broken arrows can be drawn from the scheduler to the server, and vice versa, to indicate control flow concerning preemption and completion of requests, respectively. These arrows are omitted in the interest of simplicity.

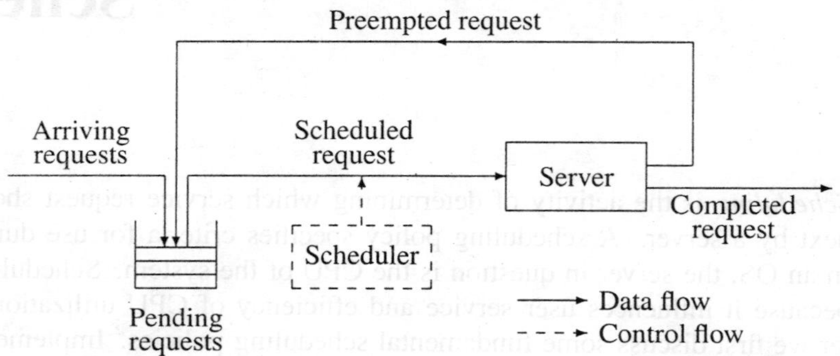

Fig. 11.1 A schematic of scheduling

A scheduling policy typically considers arrival order of requests and information concerning their nature and servicing in the system. In CPU scheduling, this information may include the following:

1. Size of a request in CPU seconds
2. CPU time already consumed by a request
3. Deadline by which its results are required.

Some typical scheduling policies are:

1. First-Come-First-Served (FCFS) service to all requests
2. Service according to request priority
3. Service according to request size.

Table 11.1 summarizes the definitions and notation used in CPU scheduling. Each request is assumed to be a job. The CPU time requirement X_i (also called the execution requirement of job), is a basic characteristic of a job. The arrival time (A_i) is a characteristic of the application environment, whereas the deadline (D_i) is a characteristic of an application (for example, a real time application—see Section 9.6). For simplicity we assume that a deadline is specified as an absolute time rather than as time since arrival of a request. $(C_i - D_i)$ indicates the deadline overrun, i.e. the amount of time by which a job has missed its deadline. A negative value of deadline overrun indicates that a job was completed before its deadline. The job turn around time is a measure of service received by a job. It differs from the CPU time requirement of a job due to two factors—the job may spend some time performing IO operations, and there may be periods of time when the CPU is executing some other job in the system. The mean turn around time ($\overline{ta}$) is a measure of the average service provided to jobs. The weighted turn around relates the turn around time of a job to its execution requirements. Throughput is a measure of system performance. It indicates the number of jobs processed per unit time (see Section 9.4). The schedule length indicates the total elapsed time needed to execute a set of jobs.

Table 11.1 Scheduling definitions and notation

(*note:* subscript indicates the identity of a job)

Notation		*Meaning*
n	:	Number of jobs
A_i	:	Job arrival time
X_i	:	CPU time required for job execution
D_i	:	Deadline for the job
C_i	:	Job completion time
$(C_i - A_i)$	:	Job turn around time (ta_i)
$(C_i - D_i)$	:	Deadline overrun for the job
$\frac{(C_i - A_i)}{X_i}$	:	Weighted turn around (w_i)
$\frac{1}{n}\Sigma_i(C_i - A_i)$	:	Mean turn around time ($\overline{ta}$)
$\frac{1}{n}\Sigma_i\frac{(C_i - A_i)}{X_i}$	:	Mean weighted turn around ($\bar{w}$)
$max(C_i) - min(A_i)$	:	Schedule length
$\frac{n}{max(C_i) - min(A_i)}$	:	Throughput (H)

From the system administrator's viewpoint, schedule length and throughput are important indices of system performance. For a user, the turn around time of a request is an absolute index of service obtained from the system. Weighted turn arounds of different jobs reflect on the comparative service given to them—closely spaced values of weighted turn arounds reflect 'fair' service.

11.1.1 Non-preemptive Scheduling

Definition 11.1 (Non-preemptible server) A non-preemptible server *always processes a scheduled request to completion.*

A scheduler schedules a request for a non-preemptible server only when processing of the previously scheduled request gets completed. In other words, the data flow representing preemption of a request in Fig. 11.1 does not exist. Non-preemptive scheduling is attractive due to its simplicity. Since scheduling is performed only when the previously scheduled request gets completed, the list of pending requests never contains a preempted request. In other words, requests complete in the order in which they are scheduled.

FCFS scheduling

Requests are scheduled in the order in which they arrive in the system. The list of pending requests is organized as a queue. The scheduler always schedules the first request in the list. A batch processing system is a good example of FCFS scheduling if jobs are ordered according to their arrival times (or arbitrarily if their arrival times are identical), and results of a job are released to the user immediately on job completion.

Example 11.1 Table 11.2 depicts the performance of FCFS scheduling for a batch consisting of 5 jobs. The first job in the batch gets the best turn around time, while the last job suffers the worst turn around time. The last two jobs in the batch receive turn around times of 57 and 62 minutes, however their weighted turn arounds are 2.28 and 12.4 respectively.

Table 11.2 Performance of FCFS scheduling

(*note:* job execution requirements are in minutes)

Position in batch	*Execution Requirement* (X_i)	*Turn around time* (ta_i)	*Weighted turn around* (w_i)
1	5	5	1.00
2	15	20	1.33
3	12	32	2.67
4	25	57	2.28
5	5	62	12.40

Mean turn around time ($\overline{ta}$) = 35.2 minutes
Mean weighted turn around ($\bar{w}$) = 3.94
Throughput (H) = 4.84 jobs/hour

Example 11.1 shows that wide disparity exists in the service received by jobs in FCFS scheduling. From this, one can conclude that short jobs may suffer high weighted turn arounds, i.e. poorer service, compared to other jobs. Jobs in the batch may be re-ordered to reduce turn around times and weighted turn arounds of individual jobs. However this would not reduce the spread of turn around times or increase the throughput.

Shortest Job Next (SJN) scheduling

The SJN scheduler always schedules the shortest of arrived requests. Thus, a request remains pending until all shorter requests have been serviced.

Example 11.2 Table 11.3 depicts the performance of SJN scheduling for the jobs of Tab. 11.2. Turn around times of the individual jobs differ from those in FCFS scheduling, however the worst turn around time and throughput remain same. The mean turn around and the mean weighted turn around are better than in FCFS scheduling.

Table 11.3 Performance of SJN scheduling

Position in batch	*Execution Requirement* (X_i)	*Turn around time* (ta_i)	*Weighted turn around* (w_i)
1	5	5	1.00
2	15	37	2.47
3	12	22	1.83
4	25	62	2.48
5	5	10	2.00

Mean turn around time ($\overline{ta}$) = 27.2 minutes
Mean weighted turn around ($\bar{w}$) = 1.96
Throughput (H) = 4.84 jobs/hour

It is not easy to implement the SJN policy in practice since execution times of jobs are not known a priori. Many systems expect users to provide estimates of job execution times. However, results obtained using such data can be erratic owing to the inexperience of users in estimating job execution times. Dependence on user estimates also leaves the system open to abuse or manipulation, as users might try to obtain better service by specifying low values for job execution times. Another factor against SJN scheduling is the poor service offered to long jobs. A steady stream of short jobs arriving in the system can lead to starvation of a long job, i.e. denial of the CPU to it.

Deadline scheduling

The scheduler always selects the request with the earliest deadline. This is done to eliminate (or at least minimize) deadline overruns. No deadline overrun occurs for a request R_i if

$$\Sigma_{k=1,i}\, X_k \leq D_i$$

where $R_1, R_2, .., R_n$ is a sequence of requests ordered according to deadlines. If this condition is not satisfied, an overrun would occur for request R_i. Like in SJN scheduling, erratic performance would result if deadline data is not reliable.

Example 11.3 Table 11.4 illustrates deadline scheduling applied to the jobs of Tab. 11.2. Jobs are processed in the order 1, 3, 5, 2, 4 due to their deadlines. Note that values of mean turn around times, etc., are irrelevant in the case of deadline scheduling.

Table 11.4 Performance of Deadline scheduling

Position in batch	*Execution Requirement* (X_i)	*Deadline* (D_i)	*Turn around time* (ta_i)
1	5	5	27
2	15	25	37
3	12	10	17
4	25	50	62
5	5	12	22

In Ex. 11.3, deadline scheduling only manages to meet the deadline of one job. All other jobs miss their deadlines. It would have been better to process the jobs in the order 1, 5, 2, 4, 3 as that would meet the deadlines of four out of five jobs. However, such considerations can make the scheduling algorithm more complex, hence more expensive to implement.

EXERCISE 11.1.1

Study the performance of the FCFS, SJN and Deadline scheduling algorithms on the jobs of Ex. 11.1 if jobs have the arrival times of 0, 1, 3, 7 and 10 minutes, respectively.

11.1.2 Preemptive Scheduling

A preemptible server can be switched to the processing of a new request before completing the processing of a request scheduled earlier. Thus, scheduling can be performed asynchronously with the processing of requests on the server. If a scheduling decision is made while some request R_i is being processed, processing of R_i is preempted and R_i is put back into the list of pending requests (see Fig. 11.1). R_i would be resumed sometime in future when it is scheduled again. Thus, a request may have to be scheduled many times before completing.

Preemptive scheduling is motivated by a desire to improve system performance. Preemption can be used in one of two ways: A process may be preempted when it enters a *passive* state to free the server for processing another request. For example, in a reservations system, a process may need additional information from a user while processing his request. The process may be preempted at the start of the passive phase, and may be scheduled again when it enters the active phase. Preemption is also useful in another context—it permits the scheduler to respond to developments within the system, e.g. arrival of new requests, changes in process priorities, etc. In chapter 9 we have seen that multiprogramming and time sharing systems use preemptive scheduling for these two reasons, respectively.

In the following, we compare the round robin scheduling policy with other scheduling policies which use preemption to respond to the changing scenario within a system.

Round-Robin scheduling

Round-robin (RR) scheduling with time slicing is aimed at providing fair service to all requests. This is achieved by limiting the amount of CPU time a process may use when scheduled. The request is preempted if it requires more CPU time, or if it encounters an IO operation before the time slice elapses. The effect of this policy is to keep the weighted turn arounds of the requests at approximately equal values at any given time. Variations may arise only due to the nature of the requests, e.g. an IO-bound request may lag behind others in its utilization of the CPU. The RR policy does not fare very well in terms of system performance indices like throughput since it treats all requests alike and does not give a favoured treatment to short requests.

Policies using resource consumption information

These policies aim at eliminating some of the problems of preemptive policies discussed so far, e.g. poor weighted turn arounds of short jobs and starvation of long jobs. We discuss the following three policies:

1. Least Completed Next (LCN) policy
2. Shortest Time to Go (STG) policy
3. Response Ratio Scheduling policy.

The LCN policy schedules the request which has consumed the least amount of processor time. Thus, the nature of a request, whether CPU-bound or IO-bound, does not influence its progress in the system. All requests make approximately equal progress in terms of the processor time consumed by them, and short requests are guaranteed to finish ahead of long requests. However, this policy has the familiar drawback of starving long requests of CPU attention.

The STG policy is a preemptive version of the SJN policy. A request is scheduled when its remaining processing requirements are the smallest in the system. Thus, the STG policy favours any request which is nearing completion, irrespective of the CPU time already consumed by it. Thus, a long request nearing completion may be favoured over short requests entering the system. The long request would finish first, thus improving its weighted turn around, however this may affect turn around times and weighted turn arounds of a number of short requests in the system. On the other hand, long requests have problems receiving service in early stages of their life in the system. Hence, favoured service to long jobs nearing completion may not achieve much in practice.

The notion of response ratio is mooted to overcome the drawbacks of the LCN and STG policies. The response ratio of a request at any moment is computed as follows:

$$\text{Response ratio} = \frac{\text{Elapsed time in the system}}{\text{Execution time received so far}} \quad (11.1)$$

Thus, if x_i^r is the amount of processor time received by request R_i up to some time instant T_r, its response ratio is $(T_r - A_i)/x_i^r$. All requests in the system would receive comparable service if their response ratios are roughly equal. The highest response ratio next (HRN) policy tries to achieve this by scheduling the request with the highest response ratio. This policy can perform well due to the following reasons: No requests are starved of attention at the beginning, as a newly arrived request would have a very high response ratio. Similarly requests nearing completion would also not starve as their response ratio would increase while they wait for service. In this manner, the policy incorporates the desirable aspects of both the LCN and STG policies. Longer requests would not face difficulties either in starting or finishing their execution, while the weighted turn arounds of short requests are not adversely affected by the presence of long requests in the system.

Comparison between preemptive scheduling policies

It is interesting to compare the RR and HRN policies. Consider a set of jobs (say, the jobs of Ex. 11.1 in a time sharing system). Let δ be one CPU second. If IO requirements of jobs are ignored, it can be observed that RR scheduling keeps the response ratios of all jobs approximately equal. At start, no job has received any CPU attention, so the response ratios are undefined. After devoting one time slice to each job, all jobs have equal elapsed and execution times. Hence their response ratios are equal. This situation would be maintained at all times during execution of jobs. The response ratio at the end of a job becomes its weighted turn around (refer to Eq. (11.1) and Tab. 11.1). Thus, all jobs would have approximately equal weighted turn arounds. Deviations from this 'fair' service arise when jobs perform IO. A job initiating IO fails to use the CPU for remainder of the time slice. However, in the next turn of scheduling it is treated on par with other jobs. Thus, an IO-bound job will have a higher weighted turn around than a CPU-bound job. The HRN policy does not suffer from this problem as it tries to keep the response ratios of all jobs equal at all times.

Not withstanding the above, the RR policy is widely used in practice due to its simplicity and efficiency. Both these properties result from the fact that it needs to perform scheduling only when a job initiates IO, or when the time slice elapses. In the HRN policy, response ratios of jobs change with time. Hence the HRN policy incurs larger overheads in recomputing the response ratios periodically. It also needs to perform scheduling far more often (see Problem 4 in Exercise 11.1).

EXERCISE 11.1.2

1. Comment on the validity of the following statement:

"The weighted turn arounds in FCFS scheduling are arbitrarily distributed while those in SJN scheduling increase monotonically."

2. Comment on the practicability of deadline scheduling. What are the practical problems governing its performance? Suggest a technique to reduce mean deadline overrun for jobs processed by such a system.
   Comment on the use of deadline scheduling in a real time OS.
3. Compare and contrast the Highest Response–ratio Next (HRN) scheduling policy with the following policies
   (a) Shortest-Time-to-Go (STG) policy.
   (b) Least-completed-Next (LCN) policy.
   (c) Round-Robin (RR) policy.
   (Hint: Think of the service provided to short and long jobs.)
4. An OS implements the HRN policy as follows: Every t seconds, response ratios of all jobs are computed. This is followed by scheduling, which selects the job with the highest response ratio. Comment on the performance and overheads of the scheduling policy for very large and very small values of t.
5. Two processes with total execution requirements of 10 and 20 seconds respectively exist in an OS using preemptive scheduling. Comment on their execution if the system uses
   (a) LCN scheduling
   (b) STG scheduling
   (c) HRN scheduling wherein the response ratios are recomputed at one second intervals.

11.2 JOB SCHEDULING

Jobs in the sense used during the 1960's and 1970's no longer exist in modern operating systems. However, equivalent features exist in the form of shell files of Unix and batch files of DOS operating systems.

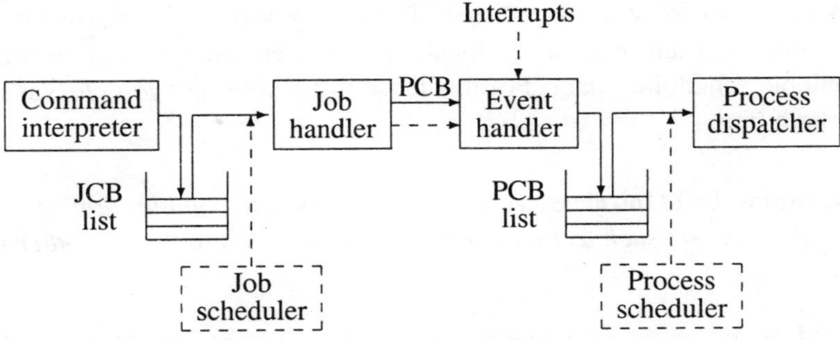

Fig. 11.2 Scheduler modules

OS modules constituting the Scheduling component are shown in Fig. 11.2. Modules in the left half of the figure, viz. *command interpreter, job scheduler* and *job handler*, constitute the job scheduling component, while modules in the right half of the figure constitute the process scheduling component. The command interpreter reads a command initiating a job, interprets it to obtain all information concerning the job, and records this information into a *job control block* (JCB). It next enters the JCB into the job scheduling list. This amounts to the arrival of a new job for processing. Figure 11.3 shows the structure of JCB. The *job location* field contains name(s) of file(s) containing the text of the job.

JCB pointer
Job identifier
Job class
Accounting information
Job location

Fig. 11.3 Job Control Block (JCB)

The job scheduler analyses the information in the JCBs existing in the scheduling list and selects a job for initiation. It passes the JCB of the selected job to the job handler. The job handler locates the text of the job and performs allocation of resources like memory, IO devices, etc. After resource allocation, a PCB is built for the primary process of the job. The PCB is handed over to the event handler, which enters it into the process scheduling list.

Job class

A job scheduler may use the following information for job scheduling: user's estimate of job execution time, memory requirements, IO device requirements, etc. In practice it is found that users lack the expertise, or the inclination, to provide good estimates of job execution times. Users may grossly overestimate the requirements or prefer certain nice values for their estimates. Hence these estimates do not form reliable scheduling data. For this reason, the notion of *job class* is often used in job scheduling.

Definition 11.2 (Job class) *A job class is a unique combination of ranges of scheduling parameters such as execution time, memory requirements, other resource requirements, etc.*

Depending on its usage environment, a system defines a limited number of job classes. While submitting a job, a user is required to assign a suitable job class to the job. This frees the user from having to specify resource requirements very precisely. It also simplifies the scheduler since it does not have to handle a large variety of resource estimates. For example, consider the following job classes for use in a university environment:

1. Long running jobs with up to two magnetic tapes
2. Long running jobs with no magnetic tapes
3. Jobs with medium execution requirements and up to 500 K bytes memory requirement
4. Jobs with very short execution requirements and up to 200 K bytes memory requirement.

The scheduler can use a priority structure in which the priorities increase from class 1 to class 4. To discourage users from specifying misleading information to obtain better turn around times (e.g. specifying a job to be of class 4, when it is in fact of class 1 or 2), the system can enforce job class discipline by cancelling a job which exceeds the resource limits specified in the job class.

Job scheduling in OS/360

The reader-interpreter module of the OS reads in a job and interprets its control statements to build a JCB. The JCB is entered into the appropriate scheduling queue according to job class. The system supports 15 job classes identified by the letters A through O. For each job, the user can specify the job class and a priority within the class. Scheduling is performed on the basis of priority amongst job classes, and then according to priority within a job class, ties being broken by arrival times of jobs. Priorities of the job classes are assigned by the system operator at the time of system initiation. Scheduling is performed by the master scheduler. The scheduled job is handed over to the initiator-terminator task of the system, which performs allocation of memory and other resources before initiating the job step. At the end of a job step, the initiator-terminator interprets the program completion code set by the job step to determine whether it is meaningful to continue execution of the job. If so, it schedules the next job step.

Job scheduling in Unix

Unix is a pure time sharing system. Hence, there is no job scheduling per se. A job is scheduled for processing immediately on arrival. Being an interactive system, a user may fire each job step of a job individually, or fire the entire job as a shell file through the command `sh` <*job_file_name*>.

The OS simply redirects standard input file of the user to <*job_file_name*>. Job step initiation commands are thus taken from the shell file. At the end of the job, the standard input file is reset to the user's terminal.

11.3 PROCESS SCHEDULING

Process scheduling involves following tasks:

1. Creating new processes

2. Monitoring processes states
3. Selecting a process for execution (*process scheduling*)
4. Allocating the CPU to the selected process (*process dispatching*)
5. Deallocating the CPU from a process and determining the new state of the process (*process preemption*)
6. Termination of processes
7. Supporting communication and synchronization requirements of processes
8. Interfacing with other OS modules which affect process states.

Function 3 is the primary function in scheduling. Functions 1, 2 and 5 (as also function 7 to some extent) involve housekeeping actions in support of process scheduling, e.g. saving process state and contents of CPU registers in PCBs.

The process scheduling component consists of three smaller components—*event handler*, *process scheduler* and *process dispatcher* (see Fig. 11.2). Process scheduler examines the information in PCB's to select a process for execution and hands over its PCB to the dispatcher. The dispatcher loads the PSR and register contents from the PCB into the CPU to initiate execution of the process. Event handler processes each interrupt occurring in the system, determines the event causing the interrupt and logs an appropriate change of state in the PCB of the affected process. This ensures that scheduling decisions are based on up-to-date information. Note that contrary to the schematic of Fig. 11.1, preemption is not shown as a separate function to be performed by the scheduler, it is merely a consequence of the event handling actions described here. This aspect is discussed in the next section.

Implementation of process preemption differs from the fundamental scheduling schematic of Fig. 11.1. Preemption is caused by an interrupt of some kind. The event handler handles the interrupt and marks a change in the state of the interrupted process (i.e. the *running* process). The process scheduler now selects the next process to be scheduled.

11.3.1 Event Monitoring

Events affecting the state of a process p_i may be internal or external to it. An internal event occurs due to some action of process p_i itself, while an external event could occur due to some action by another process in the system, or due to the action of some OS module. Examples of internal events are an IO request, a resource request, an exception occurring during execution of an instruction in p_i (for example, an addressing exception, a memory protection violation, etc.). Examples of external events are: occurrence of an interrupt, a process p_j sending a message to p_i, process p_i being swapped out, and a higher priority process p_k becoming *ready*, thereby preempting process p_i.

To understand the basics of event monitoring in an OS, consider the following observations from Chapter 9:

1. Operation of the OS is interrupt driven.

2. The OS interrupt handler gets control when an interrupt occurs.
3. The cause of an interrupt can be determined by analysing the interrupt code field in the saved PSR.

Thus, the key to event monitoring is to organize OS operations in such a way that occurrence of an event causes an interrupt to be raised. This is achieved as follows:

1. *Internal events:* Internal events can be classified into request events of some kind or exceptions occurring during the execution of an instruction. As seen in Chapter 10, a request is made through a system call, which involves execution of a *software interrupt* instruction. Exceptions occurring during execution of an instruction also lead to interrupts.
2. *External events:* External events like conditions in the hardware also cause interrupts. For example, a timer raises an interrupt when a specified interval elapses. Internal events occurring in processes other than p_i also constitute external events for p_i. For example, process p_j sending a message to p_i causes an interrupt because a *send* event involves a system call.
3. *OS actions:* OS modules other than the scheduler may also cause a change in the state of p_i. Such actions are in response to some internal events in other processes. For example, the memory manager may decide to swap out process p_i when it runs out of memory while servicing a 'request memory' event which occurred in process p_j.

When an interrupt arises, the event handler must analyse the interrupt to determine the event causing it. It must then find the process affected by the event. For example, when an IO completion interrupt arises, the OS must identify the process awaiting its completion. The notion of an *event control block* (ECB) is introduced to help perform this operation efficiently.

Event Control Block (ECB)

An ECB is used to facilitate quick identification of a process awaiting an event. It contains all information concerning an event whose occurrence is anticipated by some process in the system. Figure 11.4 shows the fields in the ECB. The *event description* field describes the event. Its contents can vary depending on the nature of the event, hence it is best to look upon this field as consisting of two parts

1. Event class
2. Event details.

OS kernel uses the *ECB pointer* field to maintain a list of ECB's. When an event occurs, it scans the list of ECB's to find an ECB with a matching event description. The *process id* field of the ECB points to the affected process. The state of the process is now changed to reflect the occurrence of the event. To speed up this action, scheduler can maintain many ECB lists, e.g. a list of ECB's for awaited

ECB pointer
Event description
process id of awaiting process

Fig. 11.4 Event Control Block (ECB)

interprocess messages, a list of ECB's for IO operations on a specific IO device, etc. Example 11.4 illustrates use of ECBs to locate the PCB of a process affected by an event.

Example 11.4 Kernel actions when process p_i requests an IO operation on some device d, and when the IO operation completes, can be described as follows:

1. Kernel creates an ECB, and initializes it as follows:
   (a) Event description = End IO on device d
   (b) Process awaiting the event = p_i.
2. The newly created ECB (let us call it ECB$_i$) is added to a list of ECB's.
3. The state of p_i is changed to *blocked* and address of ECB$_i$ is put into the 'Event information' field of p_i's PCB (see Fig. 11.5).

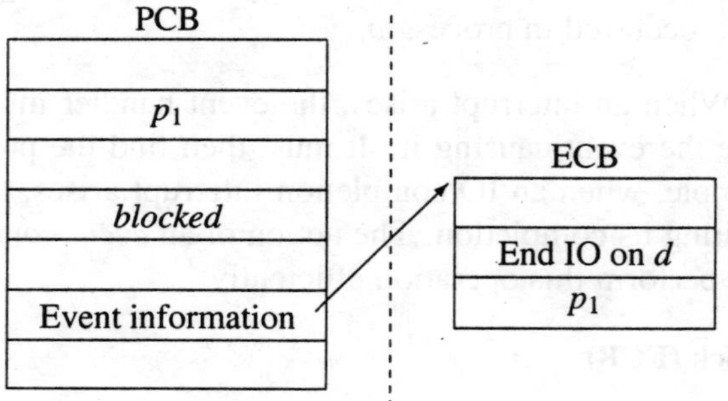

Fig. 11.5 PCB-ECB interrelationship

4. p_i's PCB may now be shifted to the appropriate scheduling list (more about this later).
5. When the interrupt 'End of IO on device d' is raised, ECB$_i$ is located by searching for an ECB with a matching event description field.
6. PCB of p_i is located from ECB$_i$. State of p_i is now changed to *ready.*

Event Handler

Figure 11.6 shows organization of the modules constituting the event handler component of Fig. 11.2. The interrupt handler gains control when an interrupt signals the occurrence of an event. It saves the PSR and contents of CPU registers in the

PCB of the interrupted process and changes the state of the process from *running* to *ready.* It then obtains the event class and event details from the *interrupt code* field in the saved PSR and invokes the event handler for the appropriate event class. The invoked handler analyses the event and performs appropriate actions. These actions typically result in the creation of a new ECB (when a process makes some request to the OS), or in a change of state for some process. At the end of its processing, the event handler module passes control to the process scheduler, which selects a process and passes its PCB to the CPU dispatcher. Example 11.5 illustrates functioning of the event handler modules.

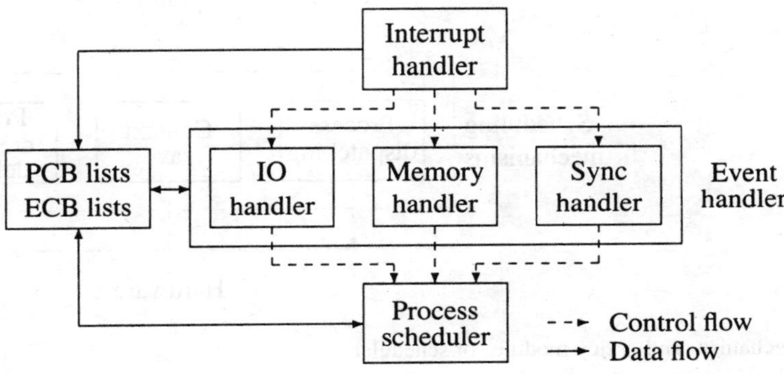

Fig. 11.6 Event handler modules

Example 11.5 Example 11.4 has described event handling actions when process p_i makes an IO request. The micro-level details of these actions are as follows:

1. The interrupt handler saves the PSR and contents of CPU registers in the PCB of p_i.
2. The interrupt handler changes the state of p_i to *ready.*
3. Control is pssed to the IO handler.
4. IO handler changes the state of p_i to *blocked* (since it knows that an IO operation is to be initiated). It also creates an ECB as described in step 1 of Ex. 11.4.
5. IO handler initiates IO for process p_i.
6. Control reaches process scheduler which selects some process p_j for execution.
7. Process p_j is dispatched.

The arrangement of interrupt handler modules shown in Fig. 11.6 implicitly handles process preemption. Ex. 11.6 illustrates this.

Example 11.6 Consider a process p_i which is in execution when an IO operation initiated by a higher priority process p_j completes and an IO interrupt is raised. The first three actions of the kernel are as shown in Ex. 11.4. The subsequent actions are as follows:

4. IO handler changes the state of p_j to ready.
5. Control reaches process scheduler which selects process p_j.

11.3.2 Process Scheduling Mechanisms

Figure 11.7 shows process scheduling mechanisms and their interaction with the process scheduling policy. The scheduling mechanisms are:

1. Process dispatching
2. Context save
3. Process creation and deletion.

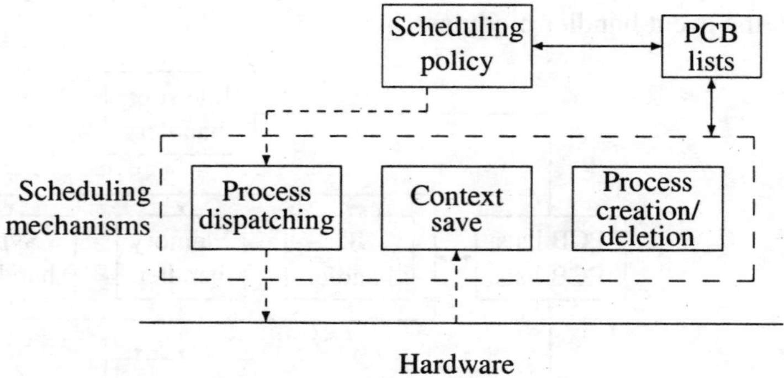

Fig. 11.7 Mechanism and policy modules of scheduler

The dispatching mechanism is activated by the scheduling policy. The context save mechanism is a part of the interrupt handler (see Fig. 11.6). It is invoked at every interrupt to save the PSR and contents of CPU registers of the interrupted process. The process creation and deletion mechanism is invoked by the application code through a kernel call, or by the command interpreter. This mechanism is not directly concerned with process scheduling. The context save and proccess creation and deletion mechanisms update the information in PCB lists. This information is used by the scheduler to select a process for execution.

11.3.3 Process Scheduling in Multiprogramming

From the discussion in Section 9.4, we can summarize the relevant features of multiprogramming as follows:

1. A mix of CPU-bound and IO-bound processes exists in the system.
2. An IO-bound process has a higher priority than a CPU-bound process.
3. Process priorities are static, i.e. they do not change with time.
4. Process scheduling is preemptive; a low priority *running* process is preempted if a higher priority process becomes *ready*. In effect, a low priority process cannot be *running* if a higher priority process exists in *ready* state.

Figure 11.8 shows the causes of process state transitions in multiprogramming. Compared to the state transitions in Fig. 10.1, the diagram contains a new transition *running* → *ready*. The need for this transition arises as follows: According to Feature 4 in the above summary, a low priority process cannot remain in the *running* state when a higher priority process makes the transition *blocked* → *ready*. The kernel implements this by forcing the transition *running* → *ready* for the low priority process. (This is performed automatically by the interrupt handler—see Ex. 11.5). The higher priority process now makes the transition *ready* → *running*.

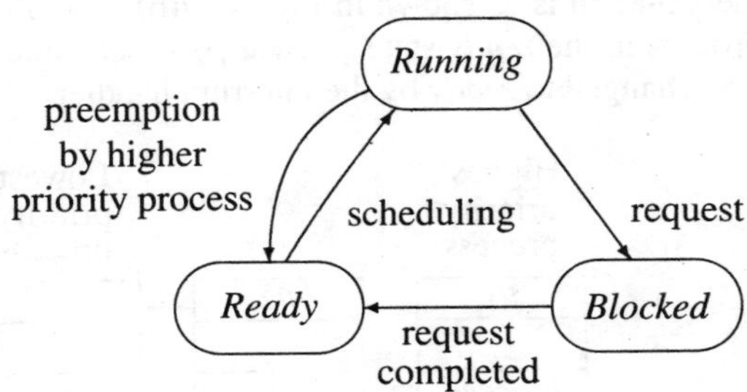

Fig. 11.8 Process state transitions in multiprogramming

The scheduler can maintain separate lists of *ready* and *blocked* processes and always select the highest priority process from the *ready* list. However, a more efficient arrangement can be designed by analysing multiprogramming Features 3 and 4 as follows: Since the scheduling decision is based on process priorities, and priorities do not change with time, the scheduler can have a single list of PCB's arranged in the order of reducing priorities. It can scan this list and simply select the first *ready* process it finds. This is the highest priority *ready* process in the system.

Thus, features of the multiprogramming scheduler can be summarized as follows:

1. A single list of PCB's is maintained in the system.
2. PCBs in the list are organized in the order of reducing priorities.
3. The PCB of a newly created process is entered in the list in accordance with its priority.
4. When a process terminates, its PCB is removed from the list.
5. The scheduler scans the PCB list and schedules the first *ready* process.

In addition to the PCB list, the scheduler maintains a pointer called *currently running process pointer* (CRP pointer). This pointer points to the PCB of the currently running process. When an interrupt occurs, the interrupt handler processes this PCB to perform the context save function.

What should the scheduler do if no *ready* processes exist in the system? It should simply 'freeze' the CPU such that it does not execute any instructions, but remains in an interruptible state so that occurrence of an event can be processed by the kernel. If the architectures lacks a 'freeze' state for the CPU, the scheduler can achieve an equivalent effect quite simply by defining a dummy process which contains an infinite loop. This process is always in the *ready* state. It is assigned the lowest priority so that it is scheduled only when no *ready* processes exist in the system. Once scheduled, this process executes till one of the user processes becomes *ready*.

Example 11.7 Figure 11.9(a) illustrates the situation when all user processes are *blocked*. The only PCB showing a process in the *ready* state is the one for the dummy process. The scheduler selects this process and dispatches it. When process p_2 becomes *ready*, the situation is as shown in Fig. 11.9(b). The PCB of p_2 is the first PCB showing a process in the *ready* state. Hence p_2 is scheduled. (The state of the dummy process was changed to *ready* by the interrupt handler.)

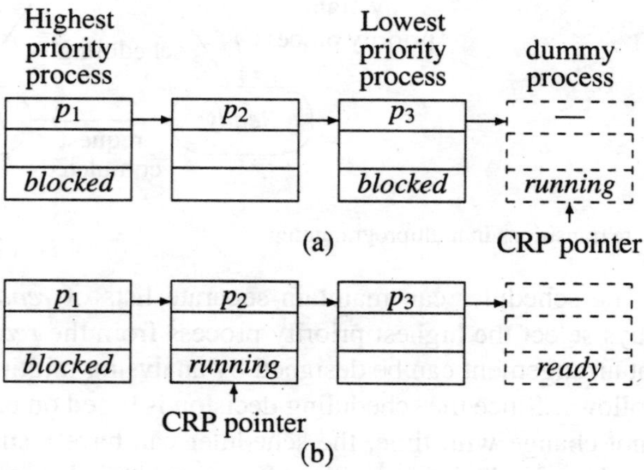

Fig. 11.9 Example of multiprogramming scheduling

11.3.4 Process Scheduling in Time Sharing

The relevant features of time sharing are:

1. Process priorities do not depend on the nature of the processes (i.e. whether the processes are CPU-bound or IO-bound).
2. Processes are scheduled in a round-robin manner.
3. A *running* process is preempted when its time slice elapses.
4. Processes may be swapped out of the memory.

Figure 11.10 shows the process state transitions in time sharing. Here the *running* → *ready* transition is caused by a timer interrupt which indicates that the time slice has elapsed. Two transitions can put a process into the *swapped out* state, viz. *ready* → *swapped out* and *blocked* → *swapped out*, however only a *swapped out* → *ready* transition can take a process out of a *swapped out* state (see problems 4 - 6 of Exercise 11.3 for some interesting points concerning these transitions).

An implication of round-robin scheduling is that the priority of a process changes dynamically during its lifetime. It is the highest priority process when it is scheduled.

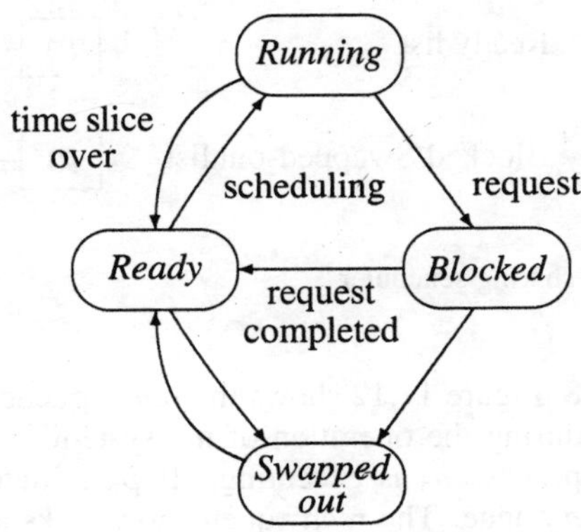

Fig. 11.10 Process state transitions in time sharing

It becomes the lowest priority process when it finishes its time slice or gets blocked due to an IO request. Its effective priority increases with time as it waits for the CPU. Processes swapped out of the memory should not be considered for scheduling.

These considerations are best handled by maintaining two lists of PCBs. One list would contain the PCBs of *ready* processes, while the other list would contain PCBs of *blocked* and *swapped out* processes. The list of *ready* processes would be organized as a queue. The relative priority of a *ready* process p_i with respect to other *ready* processes would be reflected in the position of its PCB in the *ready* queue. Advancement of p_i's PCB in the queue reflects the growing priority of p_i. It becomes the highest priority process when it reaches the head of the *ready* queue. When the state of a process changes, the scheduler has to shift the PCB of the process from one PCB list to another. Since the *blocked* and *swapped out* processes are ignored for the purpose of scheduling, their PCB list need not be maintained in any specific order.

Actions of the time sharing scheduler can be summarized as follows:

1. The scheduler maintains two separate PCB lists—one for *ready* processes and another for *blocked* and *swapped-out* processes.
2. The PCB list for *ready* processes is organized as a queue.
3. The PCB of a newly created process can be added to the end of the *ready* queue.
4. The PCB of a terminating process can be simply removed from the system.
5. The scheduler always selects the PCB at the head of the *ready* queue.
6. When a running process finishes its time slice, or makes an IO request, its PCB is moved from the *ready* queue to the *blocked/swapped-out* list.
7. When the IO operation awaited by a process finishes, its PCB is moved from the *blocked/swapped out* list to the end ot the *ready* queue.

Figure 11.11 illustrates the data structures of a time sharing scheduler.

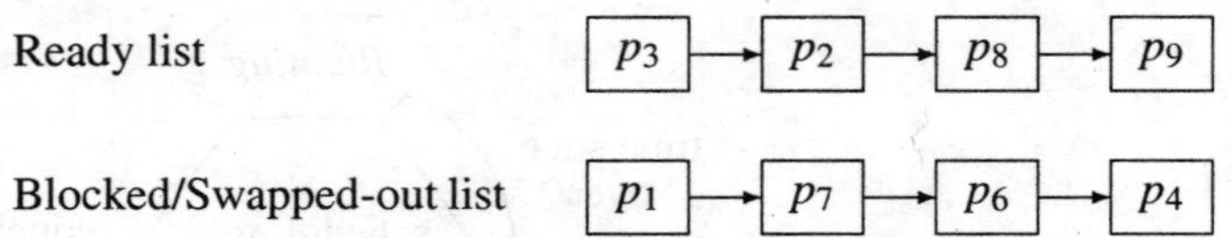

Fig. 11.11 PCB lists in a time sharing scheduler

Example 11.8 Figure 11.12 shows the *ready* queue of a time sharing scheduler at different times during the operation of the system. Figure 11.12 (a) shows the *ready* queue when process p_3 is executing. If p_3 initiates an IO operation, it is shifted to the *blocked* queue. The *ready* queue now looks as shown in Fig. 11.12(b). When the IO operation completes, p_3 is added to the end of the *ready* queue (see Fig. 11.12(c)). In the *ready* queue it is preceded by process p_7 which was added to the queue while the IO operation of p_3 was in progress.

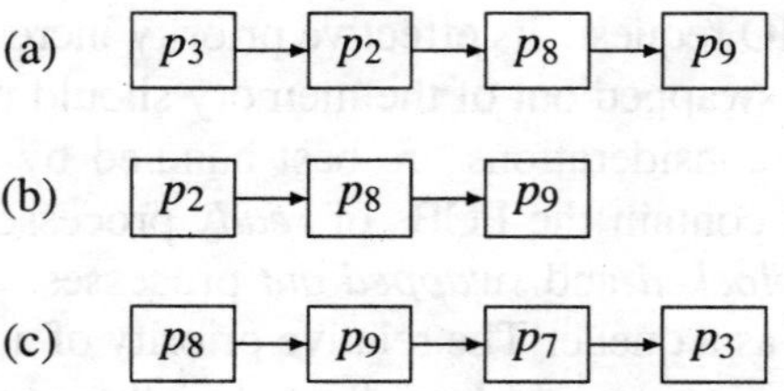

Fig. 11.12 Ready lists in a time sharing example

11.3.5 Multi-level Scheduling

Good utilization efficiency and good user service project conflicting requirements on the scheduler. Hence the scheduler must trade these features against each other. Multiprogramming and time sharing represent extreme positions in this tradeoff. Multiprogramming provides high levels of system utilization but cannot provide good user service, while time sharing provides good response times, but cannot provide high utilization efficiency.

Multi-level scheduling provides a hybrid solution to the problem of providing good system utilization and good user service simultaneously. The multi-level scheduler uses many *ready* lists. The organization and use of these lists are governed by the following rules:

1. Each *ready* list has a pair of attributes (*time slice*, *processing priority*) associated with it. Thus, processes in different lists receive different time slices and different processing priorities. The time slice provided to the processes in a list is inversely proportional to the priority of the list.
2. The processes of a list are considered for scheduling only when all higher priority lists are empty.

3. Round-robin scheduling is performed within each list.

The scheduler puts highly interactive processes into the highest priority list, where small time slice provides very good response times to these processes. Non-interactive processes are put into the lowest priority list. These processes receive large time slices. This fact reduces the scheduling and dispatching overheads in the system. Other processes occupy intermediate scheduling levels depending on how interactive they are.

Example 11.9 Figure 11.13 illustrates the *ready* lists in a multi-level scheduler. Processes p_7 and p_5 have a larger time slice than processes p_1, p_4 and p_8. However, they get a chance to execute only when p_1, p_4 and p_8 are blocked. Processes p_{10} and p_3 can execute only when all other processes in the system are blocked.

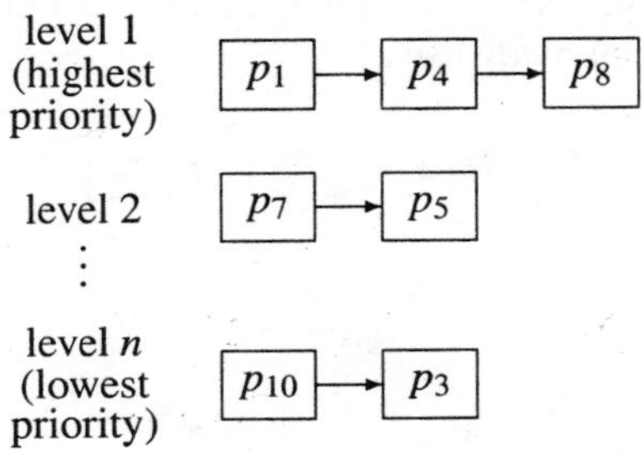

Fig. 11.13 Ready lists in a multi-level scheduler

The multi-level scheduling model inherits some drawbacks of the multiprogramming model. It requires processes to be classified according to their CPU and IO requirements. Thus, a wrong classification would degrade both user service and system performance. Further, the classification is static, i.e. a process is classified only once in its lifetime. This approach cannot handle a change in the computational or IO behaviour of a process during its lifetime. As seen in Ex. 11.9, processes also suffer from starvation.

Multi-level adaptive scheduling

A multi-level adaptive scheduler determines the correct scheduling level for a process on the basis of its CPU and IO requirements in the immediate past. This permits a process to freely enter IO-bound and CPU-bound phases during its execution, and still receive an appropriate processing priority and time slice. A change of priority is achieved by promoting or demoting a process to different scheduling levels based on its behaviour.

A well-known example of multi-level adaptive scheduling is the CTSS time sharing OS for the IBM 7094 system developed in the 1960's. The system used an eight-level priority structure, with the levels numbered 0 through 7. Level numbered n had the time slice 0.5×2^n CPU seconds associated with it. At initiation, each user process was placed at level 2 or 3 depending on its memory requirement. The promotion/demotion policy was as follows: If a process completely used up the time slice at its current scheduling level (i.e. it did not initiate an IO operation), it was demoted to the next higher numbered level, else it remained at the same level. A process was promoted to the next lower numbered level if it spent more than a minute in *ready* state without obtaining any CPU service. Further, any process performing IO on the user terminal was promoted to level 2. Subsequently, it would find the correct place for it in the priority structure through possible demotions.

Example 11.10 Figure 11.14 shows promotions and demotions in the CTSS-type multi-level adaptive scheduling. Figure 11.14(a) shows process p_3 in execution, being at the top of the highest priority *ready* list. Processes p_5, p_8 and p_7 exist in lower priority lists. At the end of the time slice, p_3 is demoted to level 2. A little later process p_7 is promoted to level 2 after spending a minute in level 3. Figure 11.14(b) shows the resulting *ready* lists.

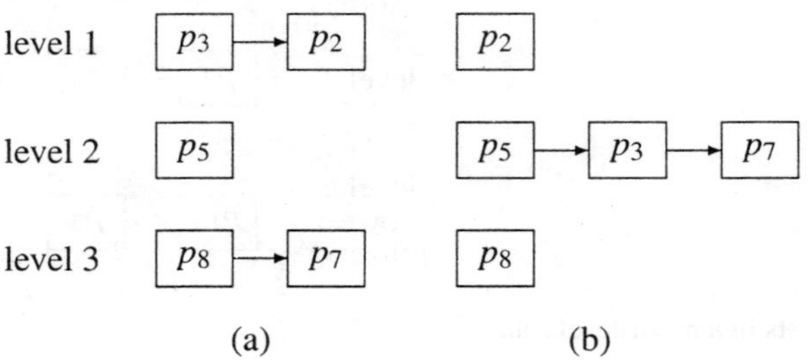

Fig. 11.14 Example of multi-level adaptive scheduling

EXERCISE 11.3

1. List the actions of the process scheduling mechanisms described in Section 11.3.2.
2. Describe the actions of the event handler modules when a time slice elapses.
3. A time sharing system uses 5 PCB lists—*ready* list, *blocked* list, *swapped out* list, *being swapped out* list and *being swapped in* list. Explain the conditions under which a PCB would be transferred from one of these lists to another.
4. List all conditions under which a process enters the *blocked* state (see Chapter 10). For which of these conditions can a blocked process make the transition *blocked* → *swapped out*? Explain why this transition cannot occur under other conditions.
5. It is proposed to add a transition *swapped out* → *blocked* to the state transition diagram of Fig. 11.10. Explain the conditions under which this transition occurs.
6. Unix splits the *swapped out* state of Fig. 11.10 into the states *blocked swapped out* and *ready swapped out*. Explain the state transitions into and out of these states.
7. Comment on the correctness of the following statements concerning multi-level adaptive scheduling:

   (a) The smallest response time for any process in the system is $(n \times \delta_{min})$, where n

is the total number of processes in the system, and δ_{min} is the smallest time slice associated with any scheduling level in the system.

(b) The largest response time any process in the system may suffer is $(n \times \delta_{max})$, where δ_{max} is the largest time slice associated with any scheduling level in the system.

11.4 PROCESS MANAGEMENT IN UNIX

Unix version 5 uses round robin adaptive scheduling. A Unix process is in one of three modes at any moment:

1. Kernel non-interruptible mode
2. Kernel interruptible mode
3. User mode.

Kernel non-interruptible mode processes enjoy the highest priorities, while user mode processes have the lowest priorities. The logic behind this priority structure is as follows: A process in the kernel mode has many OS resources allocated to it. If it is allowed to run at a priority, it is likely to release these resources sooner. Processes in the kernel mode which do not hold many OS resources are put in the kernel mode interruptible class.

The priority of a user process is varied dynamically in two ways. When a process gets blocked, the cause of blocking is used to determine the priority it should have when it wakes up. The reasoning is similar to that for the priority structure—a process that holds important OS resources should be scheduled earlier so that it can release the resources sooner.

Process priorities are also varied periodically to prevent a process from monopolizing the CPU. This requires the effective priority to vary inversely with the CPU time a process has received recently. The priority of a user process is determined from two components as follows:

$$\begin{aligned}\text{process priority} &= \text{base priority of user processes}\\ &\quad + f(\text{CPU time used});\end{aligned}$$

with larger numerical values of priority signifying lower effective priorities. Thus, of two user processes the one which has received more CPU time has lower effective priority. Since Unix is a pure time sharing system, the function '*f*' is designed to only consider the recent CPU usage rather than the total CPU usage since the start of a process. It has the form

$$f(\text{CPU time used}) = \text{recent CPU usage}/2;$$

The priority of user processes is recalculated periodically (typically once every second) resulting in migration of processes to different scheduling levels. Thus, the effect of CPU time used by a process wears off the longer it waits in the system without CPU service. For this reason, '*f*' is called a *decay* function.

An interesting feature in Unix is that a user can control the priority of a process. This is achieved through the system call

`nice (<priority value>);`

which sets the *nice value* of a user process. The effective priority of the process is now computed as follows:

$$\text{process priority} = \text{base priority of user processes} + f(\text{CPU time used}) + \text{nice value};$$

A user is required to use a zero or positive value in the `nice` call. Thus, a user cannot increase the effective priority of his process, but can lower it. This is done when the process is known to have entered a CPU-bound phase.

EXERCISE 11.4

1. Comment on the similarities and differences between the LCN scheduling policy and the Unix scheduling policy.
2. Comment on the validity of the following statement:

   "The Unix scheduling policy favours interactive processes over non-interactive processes".

11.5 SCHEDULING IN MULTIPROCESSOR OS

There are two approaches to process management in a multiprocessor OS. One approach favours centralized process management, wherein a single processor in the system is entrusted with all decisions and actions concerning process management. The other approach favours sharing of the process management responsibility amongst all CPU's in the system. These approaches differ in their performance and reliability implications.

11.5.1 Master-slave Configurations

One of the processor units is identified as the *master processor.* Only the master processor executes the OS routines and performs all control functions in the system. Thus the master processor decides which process to execute on which processor. All other processors are slaves to the master processor, they simply perform the tasks detailed to them by the master.

The advantages and disadvantages of the master–slave configuration can be summarized as follows:

1. Simplicity
2. Poor reliability
3. Poor scalability.

Simplicity results from the fact that all control functions are performed by the master processor. This implies that all interrupts generated within the OS, should be directed to it. This reduces the OS to a conventional one with a simple extension to schedule a process on each CPU in the system. However, centralization of the control function in the master processor leads to poor reliability since failure of the master processor can paralyze the entire system. Poor scalability (see Section 19.8 for a definition) results from the fact that the load on the master processor increases as more processors are added to the system. Hence the master processor may become a bottleneck in efficient utilization of other processors.

Despite the limitations of a master-slave configuration, the hardware design of a computer system often necessitates its use in practice. First, all processors in the system may not be identical in terms of their capabilities. This happens when some special purpose processors are added to a system, e.g. special purpose array processors, attach processors, etc. These processors do not have the same capabilities as the main CPU, so a master-slave configuration results quite naturally. Second, even if a computer system was designed with identical multiprocessors, cost considerations may make the processors unequal in terms of their control capability. For example, expensive processor selection logic in the form of a processor $\times$channel cross-switche is necessary (see Fig. 11.15(a)) if all processors in the system are to have identical interrupt processing capabilities. If IO channels are connected to only one processor to reduce the cost (see Fig. 11.15(b)) only that processor would be capable of IO control. Use of a master-slave configuration is quite natural in such systems.

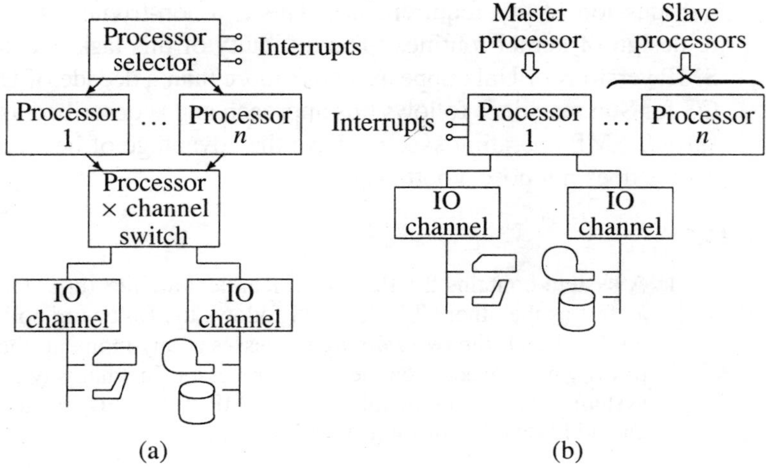

Fig. 11.15 (a) A symmetrical multiprocessor, (b) Master–slave

11.5.2 Symmetrical Multiprocessors (SMP's)

In a symmetrical multiprocessor system, processors are identical in their ability to perform control functions. Thus, any processor in the system can perform a control function. As illustrated in Fig. 11.15(a), a hardware processor-selection logic is activated whenever an interrupt is raised in the system. This logic determines which processor should handle the interrupt. This arrangement permits a malfunctioning processor to be isolated easily. The rest of the system can continue its operation, though at a lower level of performance. This provides better reliability than the master–slave arrangement.

Early OSs for symmetrical multiprocessors used a version of the master–slave arrangement wherein the master was determined dynamically. A special hardware mechanism existed to ensure that only one processor could be in the privileged mode at any given time. Thus, any processor could handle an interrupt so long as no other processor was in the privileged mode, i.e. no other processor was executing kernel code. A drawback of this approach is that it does not fully exploit the potential of multiple processors in the system. For example, IO initiation for one process and memory allocation/deallocation for another process are completely independent activities. However, they would not be performed concurrently since only one processor can execute a kernel routine at any time.

Full benefits of a symmetrical multiprocessor configuration can be obtained by permitting more than one CPU to execute kernel code simultaneously. To safeguard consistency of the kernel data, processors simultaneously executing the kernel routines should access kernel data in a mutually exclusive manner (see Section 13.2 for a discussion of this requirement). This is a non-trivial task, and requires a detailed re-design of kernel routines. The difficulty of this task is evident from the fact that SMP versions of Unix appeared after more than a decade of Unix usage. The Solaris OS for Sun machines follows this approach and is described as a *multi-threaded Unix kernel*. SMP operating systems have the advantage of better scalability since kernel access does not pose a bottleneck.

EXERCISE 11.5

1. A system contains 2 CPU's with identical architecture. One of the CPU's is twice as fast as the other CPU. The OS follows the following policy concerning the use of the CPUs: Of the two *running* processes at any moment, the process with the higher priority must execute on the faster processor. In what way does the scheduling in this system differ from scheduling in an SMP system? Does the use of this policy require any additional hardware features?

BIBLIOGRAPHY

(a) Queuing theory

Queuing theory is used in scheduling and performance evaluation. The earliest application of queuing theory was by Erlang in 1909, who applied it in the performance evaluation of a telephone exchange. Trivedi (1982) is an excellent source on all aspects of queuing theory. Earlier works include those by Kleinrock (1975, 1976) and Coffman (1976). Hansen (1973) introduces the necessary queuing background for the discussion of scheduling. Hellerman and Conroy (1975) describe its use in performance evaluation.

1. Bucholz, W. (1969): "A selected bibliography on computer system performance evaluation," *IEEE Computer Group News*, **2** (8).
2. Coffman, E.G. (ed.)(1976): *Computer and Job Shop Scheduling*, Wiley, New York.
3. Conway, R.W., W.L. Maxwell and L.W. Miller (1967): *Theory of Scheduling*, Addison-Wesley, Reading.
4. Fife, D.W. (1966): "An optimization model for time sharing," *Proceedings of AFIPS SJCC*, **28**, 97-104.
5. Hansen, P.B. (1973): *Operating System Principles*, Prentice-Hall, Englewood Cliffs.
6. Hellerman, H. and T.F. Conroy (1975): *Computer System Performance*, McGraw-Hill Kogakusha, Tokyo.
7. Kleinrock, L. (1975-1976): *Queuing Systems*, Vols. I and II, Wiley, New York.
8. Trivedi, K.S. (1982): *Probability and Statistics with Reliability - Queuing and Computer Science Applications*, Prentice-Hall, Englewood Cliffs.

(b) Job, process and processor scheduling

Literature in the public domain concentrates mostly on performance evaluation of different scheduling policies. The more practical aspects, namely, dispatching and job and process control blocks, are described only in proprietary literature. For a discussion of these aspects, the reader is referred to OS literature of a particular computer system of interest.

1. Bruno, J., E.G. Coffman and R. Sethi (1974): "Scheduling independent tasks to reduce mean finishing time," *Commn. of ACM*, **17** (7), 382-387.
2. Chamberlein, D.D. *et al* (1973): "Experimental study of deadline scheduling for interactive systems," *IBM Journal of R and D*, **17** (3), 263-269.
3. Coffman, E.G. and P.J. Denning (1973): *Operating Systems Theory*, Prentice-Hall, Englewood Cliffs.
4. Forbes, K. and A.W. Goldsworthy (1977): "The prescheduling algorithm," *Computer Journal*, **20** (1), 27-29.
5. Gonzalez, M.J. (1977): "Deterministic Processor Scheduling," *Computing Surveys*, **9** (3), 173-204.
6. Hellerman, H. (1969): "Some principles of time sharing scheduler strategies," *IBM Systems Journal*, **8** (2), 94.
7. Hume, J.N.P. and C.B. Rolphson (1968): "Scheduling for fast turn around in a job-at-a-time processing," *Proc. IFIP Congress*.
8. Mullery, A.P. and G.C. Driscoll (1970): "A processor allocation method for time sharing," *Commn. of ACM*, **13** (1), 10-14.
9. Ruschitzka, M. and R.S. Fabry (1977): "A unifying approach to scheduling," *Commn. of ACM*, **20** (7), 469-476.
10. Ryder, K.D.(1970): "A heuristic approach to task dispatching," *IBM Systems Journal*, **9** (3), 189-198.

11. Saltzer, J.H.(1974): "Protection and control of information sharing in MULTICS," *Commn. of ACM*, **17** (7), 388.
12. Schwetman, H.D. (1978): "Job scheduling in multiprogrammed computer systems," *Software – Practice and Experience*, **8** (3), 241-255.
13. Tolopka, S. and H. Schwetman (1979): "Mix dependent job scheduling," *Proc. of AFIPS NCC*, 45-49.
14. Wood, D.C. and E.H. Forman (1971): "Thruput measurement using a synthetic job stream," *AFIPS proceedings*, **39**, 51-56.
15. Wulf, W.A.(1969): "Performance monitors for multiprogrammed Systems," *Proc. of ACM Symposium on Operating System Principles*, 175-181.

(g) Multiprocessors – Architecture and Scheduling

1. Enslow, P.H.(ed.)(1974): *Multiprocessors and Parallel Processing*, Wiley, New York.
2. Enslow, P.H.(1977): "Multiprocessor organization – A survey," *Computing Surveys*, **9** (1), 103-129.
3. Gountanis, R.J. *et al* (1966): "A method of processor selection for interrupt handling in a multiprocessor system," *Proc. IEEE*, **54** (12), 1812.
4. Holley, L.H. *et al* (1979): "VM/370 asymmetric multiprocessing," *IBM Systems Journal*, **18** (4), 47-70.
5. Jones, A.K. and P. Schwarz (1980): "Experience using multiprocessor systems – a status report," *Computing Surveys*, **12** (2), 121-165.
6. Lampson, B.W.(1968): "A scheduling philosophy for multiprocessing systems," *Commn. of ACM*, **11** (5), 347-360.
7. Pariser, J.J. (1965): "Multiprocessing with floating executive control," *IEEE International Conference Record*, **3**, 266-275.
8. Peinl, P. and A. Reuter (1983): "Synchronizing multiple database processes in a tightly coupled multiprocessor environment," *Operating Systems Review*, **17** (1), 30-37.
9. Sauer, C.H. and K.M. Chandy (1979): "The impact of distributions and disciplines on multiple processor systems," *Commn. of ACM*, **22** (1), 25-33.
10. Sherman, S., F. Baskett and J.C. Browne (1972): "Trace driven modelling and analysis of CPU scheduling in a multiprocessing system," *Commn. of ACM*, **15** (12), 1063-1069.
11. Sreenivasan, K., G.A. Nelson and J.A. Maksin (1980): "An experimental study of relative throughput in a multiprocessor computer system," *Software – Practice and Experience*, **10** (12), 973-986.

CHAPTER 12

Deadlocks

Processes compete for physical and logical resources in the system (e.g. disks or files). Deadlocks affect the progress of processes by causing indefinite delays in resource allocation. Such delays have serious consequences for the response times of processes, idling and wastage of resources allocated to processes, and the performance of the system. Hence an OS must use resource allocation policies which ensure an absence of deadlocks. This chapter characterizes the deadlock problem and describes the policies an OS can employ to ensure an absence of deadlocks.

12.1 DEFINITIONS

We define three events concerning resource allocation:

1. *Resource request:* A user process requests a resource prior to its use. This is done through an OS call. The OS analyses the request and determines whether the requested resource can be allocated to the process immediately. If not, The process remains blocked on the request till the resource is allocated.
2. *Resource allocation:* The OS allocates a resource to a requesting process. The resource status information is updated and the state of the process is changed to *ready*. The process now becomes the *holder* of the resource.
3. *Resource release:* After completing resource usage, a user process releases the resource through an OS call. If another process is blocked on the resource, OS allocates the resource to it. If several processes are blocked on the resource, the OS uses some tie-breaking rule, e.g. FCFS allocation or allocation according to process priority, to perform the allocation.

Definition 12.1 (Deadlock) *A* deadlock *involving a set of processes D is a situation in which*

1. Every process p_i in D is blocked on some event e_i.

2. *Event e_i can only be caused by some process(es) in D.*

An interesting point concerning deadlocks follows from this definition. A long delay in the occurrence of an awaited event, i.e. starvation of some kind, cannot contribute to a deadlock. The important requirement is that processes capable of causing an event must themselves belong to *D*. This makes it impossible for the event to occur.

If the event awaited by each process in *D* is the granting of some resource, it results in a resource deadlock. A communication deadlock occurs when the awaited events pertain to the receipt of interprocess messages, and a synchronization deadlock when the awaited events concern the exchange of signals between processes. An OS is primarily concerned with resource deadlocks because allocation of resources is an OS responsibility. The other two forms of deadlock are seldom tackled by an OS.

Example 12.1 A system contains one tape and one printer device and two processes p_i and p_j. Both p_i and p_j require the tape and printer devices for their functioning. The processes make their resource requests in the following order:

1. Process p_i requests the tape,
2. Process p_j requests the printer,
3. Process p_i requests the printer,
4. Process p_j requests the tape.

The set of processes $\{p_1, p_2\}$ is now deadlocked.

In Ex. 12.1, the first two resource requests can be granted straightaway because a tape cartridge and a printer exist in the system. Now, p_i holds the tape and p_j holds the printer. When p_i asks for the printer, it is blocked by the OS since the printer is currently not available for allocation. p_j is similarly blocked when it asks for the tape. Since p_i holds the tape, only a release by p_i can enable p_j to come out of the *blocked* state. Similarly p_j must release the printer for p_i to come out of the *blocked* state. Hence the set of processes $\{p_1, p_2\}$ is deadlocked.

A deadlock has several consequences. Response times and elapsed times of processes in *D* suffer. A resource r_l already allocated to a process p_i in *D* remains idle. This may deny resource r_l to a process $p_k \in D$.

12.2 RESOURCE STATUS MODELLING

From Ex. 12.1, it is clear that the OS must analyse the resource request and resource allocation status of the system (hereafter simply called the 'resource status') to determine whether a set of processes is deadlocked. It is customary to model the resource status by a graph. We introduce the key concepts of graph theory before describing two graph models of resource status.

Graph concepts and notation

A graph G is an ordered pair

$$G \equiv (N, E)$$

where N is a set of *nodes* and E is a set of *edges*. A node, depicted by a circle in the graph, represents an entity of interest, while an edge, depicted by a line connecting two nodes, represents a relationship between two entities. An edge is denoted by a pair of nodes, e.g. (n_i, n_j). A *directed edge* represents an asymmetric relationship between entities, e.g. a parent-child relationship. Such an edge is depicted by an arrow in the graph and is denoted by an ordered pair of nodes (parent entity, child entity). A graph containing directed edges is called a *directed graph*. Directed edges connecting a node with other nodes of the directed graph can be classified into *in-edges* and *out-edges* depending on their direction.

A *path* $n_i - n_k - n_l - \ldots - n_j$ in a directed graph is a sequence of edges (n_i, n_k), (n_k, n_l), $\ldots(\ldots, n_j)$ such that the destination of one edge is the source of the next edge. The length of a path is the number of edges in it. A *path* $n_i - n_k - n_l - \ldots - n_j$ is a *cycle* if $n_i \equiv n_j$. A graph without cycles is called an *acyclic graph*.

Example 12.2 Figure 12.1 shows a directed graph where the nodes represent processes and edges represent relationships between processes. Edges (p_1, p_2) and (p_2, p_3) form a path between p_1 and p_3. The length of this path is 2. Node p_1 has no in-edges and two out-edges, p_2 has one in-edge and two out-edges, while p_4 has two in-edges and one out-edge. The graph is acyclic.

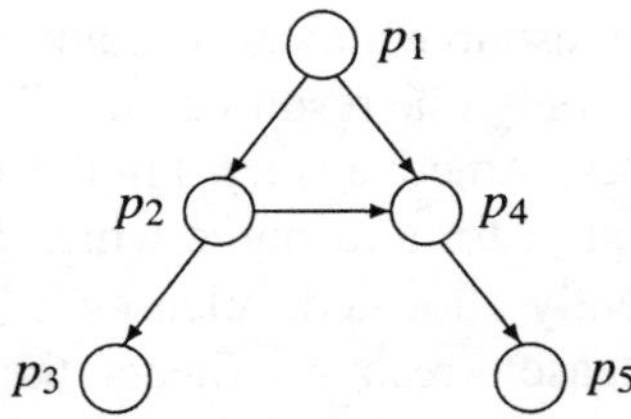

Fig. 12.1 A directed graph

Resource Request and Allocation Graph (RRAG)

An RRAG is a directed graph containing two kinds of nodes—process nodes and resource nodes. A process node, which is depicted by a circle in an RRAG, represents a user process or a system process. A resource node is depicted by a rectangle and represents one class of resources. The number of dots in a resource node indicates the number of units of that resource class. An edge can exist only between a process node and a resource node and can represent a resource allocation or a resource request. An *allocation edge* is directed from a resource node to a process node. It represents the allocation of one unit of the concerned resource class to the process. A *request edge* is directed from a process node to a resource node. It represents a pending request for one unit of the resource. A request edge is replaced by an allocation edge when one unit of the resource class is allocated to the process. An allocation edge is deleted when a process releases a resource unit allocated to it.

Example 12.3 Figure 12.2 contains an RRAG. Only one unit of resource R_1 exists in the system. It is currently allocated to process p_1. Processes p_2 and p_3 have made requests for this resource unit, and these requests are currently pending. Two units of resource class R_2 exist in the system. These are currently allocated to processes p_2 and p_3, respectively. A request by process p_4 for one unit of resource class R_2 is pending. Two paths of length 4 exist in the graph between nodes p_4 and p_1.

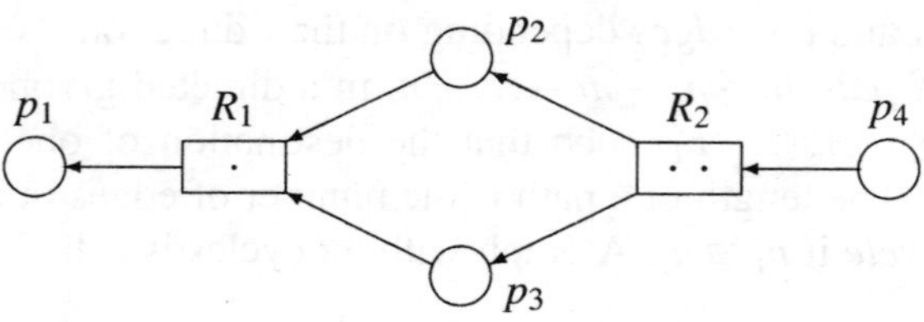

Fig. 12.2 A Resource Request and Allocation Graph (RRAG)

Wait For Graph (WFG)

An RRAG is useful when multiple units of a resource class exist in the OS. A WFG can represent the resource allocation status more concisely when every resource class in the system has only one resource unit. The WFG contains nodes of only one kind, viz. process nodes. An edge (p_i, p_j) in the WFG represents the fact that process p_i is blocked on a request for a resource which can be allocated only when process p_j, to which it is currently allocated, releases it. In other words, process p_i is waiting for process p_j to release a resource (hence the name *wait-for* edges). Representing the same information as a wait-for edge would have required two edges in an RRAG.

Example 12.4 A WFG for a system containing resource class R_1 and processes p_1, p_2 and p_3 of Fig. 12.2 is shown in Fig. 12.3. The wait for edges (p_2, p_1) and (p_3, p_1) indicate that processes p_2 and p_3 are waiting for the resource currently allocated to process p_1. Note that the WFG cannot depict the status concerning resource class R_2 for the following reason: Since two units of R_2 exist in the system, p_4's wait is satisfied when any one of p_2 or p_3 release a unit of resource R_2. Such a relationship cannot be depicted in a WFG.

Unless otherwise mentioned, in this chapter we assume that only one unit of any resource class exists in the system. This permits us to use a WFG instead of an RRAG.

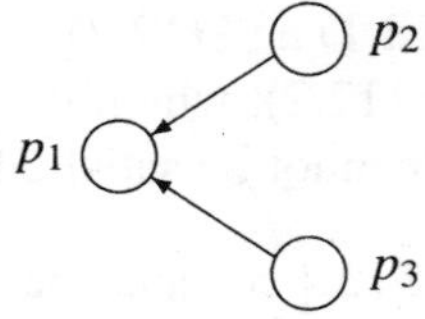

Fig. 12.3 A Wait For Graph (WFG)

12.2.1 Paths in RRAG and WFG

The nature of paths in RRAG and WFG are used to reason about the existence of deadlocks in the system. The following notation is defined for this purpose:

Blocked	:	Set of blocked processes
WF_i	:	The set of processes with which p_i has a wait-for relation.

Using this notation, Conditions 1 and 2 of Definition 12.1 can be restated as follows:

$$D \subseteq Blocked \tag{12.1}$$

$$\forall p_i \in D, WF_i \subseteq D. \tag{12.2}$$

We first consider paths in WFG. A path may grow or shrink over a period of time as resources are requested, allocated and released. Thus a path $p_1 - p_2 - \ldots - p_i \ldots p_n$ may vanish over a period of time (i.e. shrink to a length of zero) as follows: When p_n completes its execution, it would release the resource which is requested by process p_{n-1}. When p_{n-1} finishes, it would release the resource wanted by process p_{n-2}, and so on. Eventually, process p_1 may obtain the resource it needs. Alternatively the path may be replaced by another path $p_1 - p_2 - \ldots - p_i - p_k \ldots$. This would happen if process p_i, on obtaining the resource from p_{i+1}, requests another resource and waits for some other process p_k.

Consider a path $p_1 - p_2 - \ldots - p_n$ in a WFG such that p_n has no wait-for out-edges (i.e. p_n is not blocked on a resource) and p_1 has no wait-for in-edges (i.e. no process is blocked on a resource allocated to p_1). The existence of this path represents the fact that p_1 is blocked on a resource allocated to p_2, which is blocked on a resource allocated to p_3 ... and p_{n-1} is blocked on a resource allocated to p_n. Processes $\{p_1, \ldots p_n\}$ are not deadlocked because p_n is not blocked.

We can argue the absence of a deadlock when a single path $p_1 - p_2 - \ldots - p_n$ exists in a WFG, as follows: Let $D = \{p_1, p_2, \ldots p_n\}$. Deadlock does not exist because $p_n \notin Blocked$, which violates condition (12.1). Now, let $D = \{p_1, p_2, \ldots p_{n-1}\}$. Here, $WF_{n-1} = \{p_n\}$, violates condition (12.2). Hence a deadlock does not exist.

Now consider a path $p_1 - p_2 - \ldots - p_n$ in the WFG such that $p_n \equiv p_1$. This path represents a cycle in the WFG. We find that the set of processes $\{p_1, p_2, \ldots p_n\}$ now satisfy conditions (12.1) and (12.2). Hence a deadlock exists. From this we can conclude that condition (12.2), which implies existence of mutual wait-for relationships between processes, cannot be satisfied by acyclic paths.

Example 12.5 Figure 12.4 contains the WFG for Ex. 12.1. Here $WF_1 = \{p_2\}$ and $WF_2 = \{p_1\}$. $D = \{p_1, p_2\}$ satisfies conditions (12.1) and (12.2). Hence the set of processes $\{p_1, p_2\}$ is deadlocked.

Fig. 12.4 WFG for example 12.1

All observations concerning paths in WFG also hold for paths in RRAG with one small difference. A path $p_1 - R_1 \ldots p_i - R_i - p_{i+1} - \ldots p_n$ may be broken even if process p_{i+1} does not release the unit of resource class R_i. This may happen because another process p_0 may hold a unit of resource class R_i. If p_0 releases the unit allocated to it, that unit can be granted to p_i. The edge (p_i, p_{i+1}) would thus vanish.

Example 12.6 In the RRAG of Ex. 12.3, the path $p_4 - R_2 - p_3 - R_1 - p_1$ is broken when process p_2 releases a unit of resource R_2.

12.2.2 Conditions for Deadlock

Existence of a path $p_1 - p_2 - \ldots - p_n$ in a WFG represents wait-for relationships between processes. Consider process p_2. It is blocked on a resource allocated to p_3. While in the *blocked* state, it continues to hold the resources allocated to it. That is why p_1 is blocked on a resource allocated to p_2. It is clear that a wait-for relationship would not arise if processes could share their resources, or release their resources while requesting other resources. Deadlocks would also not arise if the OS could preempt allocated resources from *blocked* processes. From Section 12.2.1, it is also clear that a mutual wait-for relationship between a set of processes cannot arise unless cycles exist in the WFG, i.e. unless circular waits exist in the system.

Hence we can conclude that the following conditions are necessary for deadlocks to arise:

1. Resources cannot be shared.
2. Processes continue to hold the resources allocated to them while waiting for other resources.
3. Resources cannot be preempted from processes.
4. Circular waits exist in the system.

The first three conditions pertain to resource utilization policies. Only the fourth condition pertains to relationships between processes and the resource status at any time during system operation. Another condition implied in the discussion of deadlocks is that a process blocked on a resource request cannot unilaterally withdraw the request. This condition is not explicitly stated because most processes automatically satisfy this condition in practice.

12.3 HANDLING DEADLOCKS

Two fundamental approaches used for handling deadlocks are:

1. Detection and resolution of deadlocks
2. Avoidance of deadlocks.

In the former approach, the OS detects deadlock situations as and when they arise. It then performs some actions aimed at ensuring progress for some of the deadlocked processes. These actions constitute deadlock resolution. The latter approach focuses on avoiding the occurrence of deadlocks. This approach involves checking each resource request to ensure that it does not lead to a deadlock. The detection and resolution approach does not perform any such checks. The choice of the deadlock handling approach would depend on the relative costs of the approach, and its consequences for user processes.

12.3.1 Characterizing Deadlocks

From Section 12.2.2, a circular wait-for relationship between processes is a necessary condition for a deadlock. This manifests into a cycle in an RRAG or WFG. However, to evolve a deadlock detection strategy, we must ask the following question: Is the presence of a cycle sufficient to conclude existence of a deadlock? To answer this question, one has to consider various possibilities concerning resource status which might be encountered in practice. We introduce the following models to help us do this effectively:

1. *Resource instance models:* A resource class may be restricted to a single instance of the resource, or may be permitted to contain multiple instances of the resource. We will refer to these as *single instance* (SI) and *multiple instance* (MI) models, respectively.
2. *Resource request models:* A resource request may be restricted to a single resource class, or may extend to more than one resource class. We will refer to these as *single request* (SR) and *multiple request* (MR) models, respectively. Note that each request to a class is restricted to a single unit of that class. (This restriction is relaxed in Section 12.4.)

Use of these models leads to the following resource systems:

1. Single-instance-single-request (SISR) systems
2. Multiple-instance-single-request (MISR) systems
3. Single-instance-multiple-request (SIMR) systems

4. Multiple-instance-multiple-request (MIMR) systems.

Deadlock situations in these systems are discussed individually. Later a general characterization of deadlocks applicable to all resource systems is presented. For the sake of generality, RRAG's are used to depict the resource status of the system at any time.

SISR systems

In such a system, a circular path in the RRAG implies a mutual wait-for relationship for a set of processes. Since only single resource instances exist in the system, each *blocked* process waits for exactly one process to release the required resource. The presence of a cycle thus satisfies condition (12.2). A cycle is thus a necessary as well as a sufficient condition to conclude the existence of a deadlock.

MISR systems

In this system a cycle is a necessary but not a sufficient condition for the existence of a deadlock. This is a consequence of our observation in Section 12.2.1 that a path $p_1 - R_1 - \ldots p_i - R_i - p_{i+1} - \ldots p_n$ may be broken even if process p_{i+1} does not release a unit of resource class R_i.

Example 12.7 An OS contains one printer and two tapes, and three processes p_i, p_j and p_k. The nature of processes p_i and p_j is as depicted in Ex. 12.1. Process p_k only requires a tape unit for its execution. Let the sequence of requests in the system be:

1. Process p_k requests a tape.
2. Process p_i requests a tape.
3. Process p_j requests a printer.
4. Process p_i requests a printer.
5. Process p_j requests a tape.

Requests 1-3 are allocated while requests 4 and 5 remain pending. Figure 12.5 shows the RRAG after the fifth request. A cycle involving p_i and p_j exists in the graph, however the cycle would vanish if the following sequence of events occurs in the system: Process p_k finishes and releases the tape allocated to it. This tape is allocated to p_j which runs to completion and releases the printer allocated to it. The printer is allocated to p_i which now runs to completion. Thus there is no deadlock even though a cycle p_i- printer $-p_j-$ tape $-p_i$ exists in RRAG.

One can conclude the absence of deadlock by considering the resource status information after the fifth request, viz.

$$\begin{aligned} Blocked &= \{p_i, p_j\}, \\ WF_i &= \{p_j\}, \text{ and} \\ WF_j &= \{p_i, p_k\}. \end{aligned}$$

$WF_j \nsubseteq Blocked$ violates condition (12.2). Hence no deadlock exists in the system.

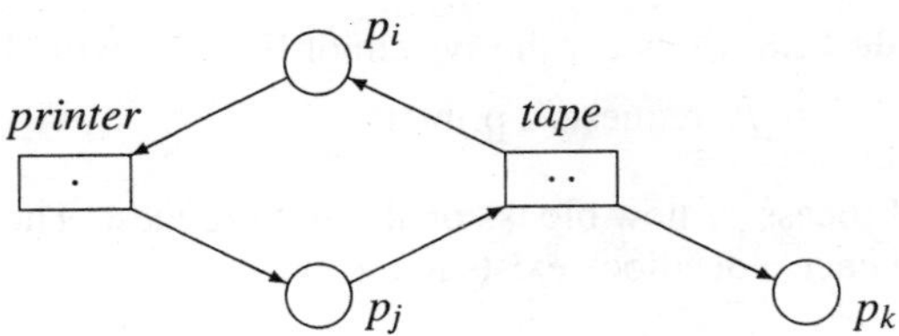

Fig. 12.5 RRAG after fifth request of example 12.7

We can explain why a cycle is not a sufficient condition for a deadlock in MISR systems as follows: Existence of a cycle $p_1 - \ldots - p_n$ such that $p_1 \equiv p_n$ implies that some processes are involved in a mutual wait-for relationship. However, since multiple units of a resource class can exist in a system it is possible that a resource unit required by some process in the cycle could be granted by a process outside the cycle. In Ex. 12.7, p_j's wait for p_i is part of the cycle involving p_i and p_j. However, p_j also waits for p_k and either of $\{p_i, p_k\}$ can release the tape needed by it. Thus, the mutual wait-for relation between p_i and p_j ceases to exist when p_k releases a tape unit. For a deadlock to exist, it is essential that no process outside of a cycle should be able to supply a resource unit required by some process in the cycle. This is the implication of condition (12.2).

Two new definitions are introduced to help characterize a deadlock in MISR systems.

Definition 12.2 (Subgraph) *A graph $G' \equiv (N', E')$ is a* subgraph *of a graph $G \equiv (N, E)$ if $N' \subseteq N$ and $E' \subseteq E$.*

A subgraph is non-trivial if $E' \neq \phi$.

Definition 12.3 (Knot) *A non-trivial subgraph $G' \equiv (N', E')$ of an RRAG is a* knot *if*

1. *$\forall n_i \in N'$ such that $(n_i, n_j) \in E$, $(n_i, n_j) \in E'$ and $n_j \in N'$.*
2. *$\forall n_i \in N'$, existence of a path $n_i - \ldots - n_j$ in G' implies existence of a path $n_j - \ldots - n_i$ in G'.*

Consider a knot $G' \equiv (N', E')$ in an RRAG. Since G' is a non-trivial subgraph, condition 2 of Definition 12.3 ensures that every process in the knot is necessarily in the *blocked* state. Note that condition 1 of Definition 12.3 applied to a resource node depicting a resource class with multiple resource units ensures that none of its resource units are allocated to any process outside the knot. Condition 2 further ensures that every process of the knot is involved in a cycle. This satisfies condition (12.2). Thus one can conclude that the presence of a knot in an RRAG is a necessary and sufficient condition for the existence of a deadlock.

Example 12.8 Consider the system of Ex. 12.7 with the following additional request:

6. p_k requests a printer.

Process p_k now blocks on the sixth request. The entire graph is a knot (see Fig. 12.6), hence a deadlock exists in the system.

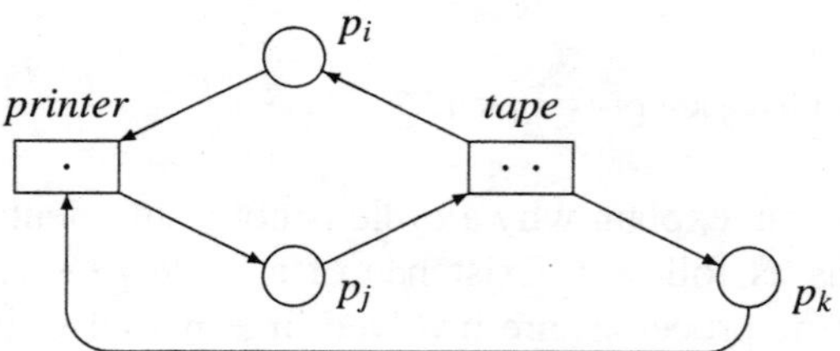

Fig. 12.6 A knot in RRAG

SIMR systems

In such a system, a cycle is a necessary and sufficient condition for the existence of a deadlock. A knot is a sufficient condition, but not a necessary one! This can be seen from Ex. 12.9.

Example 12.9 Figure 12.7 contains the RRAG for a system containing three resource classes, and three processes p_i, p_j and p_k. Process p_i holds the resource unit of class R_2 and has made a multiple request for resource units of classes R_1 and R_3. Process p_j holds a resource unit of class R_1 and has requested a resource unit of class R_2. Process p_k holds a resource unit of class R_3. No knot exists in the RRAG (since no path exists from process p_k to process p_i—see condition 2 of Definition 12.3), however a cycle involving p_i and p_j exists. Since process p_i needs a resource unit each of classes R_1 and R_3, it is clear that processes p_i and p_j are deadlocked.

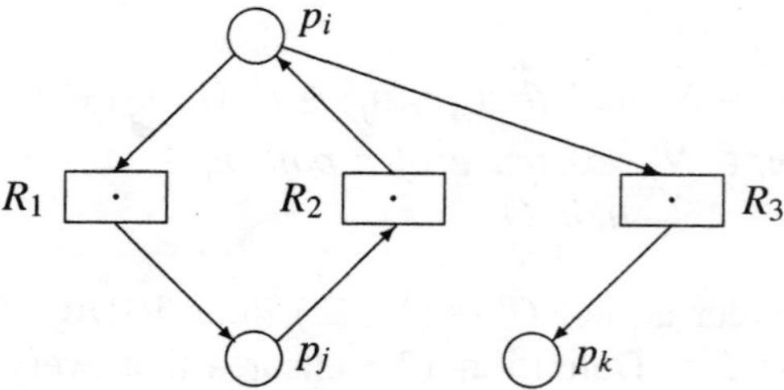

Fig. 12.7 RRAG for example 12.9

A cycle is adequate to deduce a deadlock since any node p_i in the RRAG which has an out-edge (p_i, R_k) which is not a part of the cycle is necessarily a process node involved in a multiple request—that is, p_i also has another out-edge (p_i, R_j) which is a part of the cycle. Since process p_i must have a resource unit of both resource classes, it is clear that p_i faces an indefinite wait.

We can differentiate between the MISR and SIMR systems as follows: In an MISR system, a process p_i faces an indefinite wait only if all processes in WF_i face indefinite waits. However, in an SIMR system a process p_i faces an indefinite wait if any process in WF_i faces an indefinite wait.

MIMR systems

In the MIMR model, both process and resource nodes of an RRAG can have multiple out-edges. If none of the resource nodes involved in a cycle in the RRAG has multiple out-edges, the cycle is similar to a cycle in the RRAG of an SIMR system. Hence such a cycle is a sufficient condition for the existence of a deadlock. However, if a resource node in a cycle has multiple out-edges, then a cycle is a necessary but not a sufficient condition for a deadlock. Example 12.10 illustrates this aspect.

Example 12.10 In the RRAG of Fig. 12.8, resource node R_1 contains an out-edge (R_1, p_k) which does not belong to the cycle $R_1 - p_i - R_2 - p_j - R_1$. The absence of a knot in the RRAG implies that process p_k may release an instance of resource class R_1, which could be allocated to process p_j. This will resolve the cycle in the RRAG. If R_3 had an allocation edge (R_3, p_i), we would have a knot involving p_i, p_j, p_k, R_1, R_2 and R_3, and we have a deadlock situation.

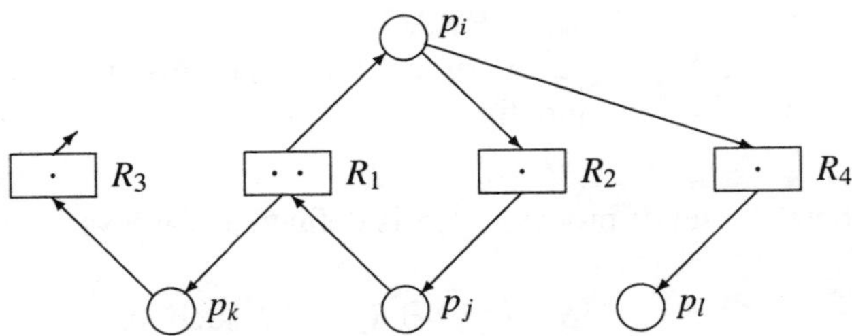

Fig. 12.8 RRAG for an MIMR system

If none of the resource nodes in a cycle has multiple out-edges, then the situation resembles either an SIMR or an MISR system. Hence a cycle is a sufficient condition for deadlock. For example, if the edge (R_1, p_k) in the RRAG of Fig. 12.8 is removed and an edge (p_j, R_3) is added, we have a deadlock situation even though a knot does not exist. From the above discussion it is clear that we must differentiate between the process and resource nodes of an RRAG. We achieve this by introducing the notion of a *resource knot*.

Definition 12.4 (Resource knot) *A non-trivial subgraph* $G' \equiv (N', E')$ *of an RRAG is a* resource knot *if*

1. *$\forall n_i \in N'$ such that n_i is a resource node and $(n_i, n_j) \in E$, $(n_i, n_j) \in E'$ and $n_j \in N'$.*
2. *$\forall n_i \in N'$, existence of a path $n_i - \ldots - n_j$ in G' implies existence of a path $n_j - \ldots - n_i$ in G'.*

The resource knot differs from a knot in that process nodes in the resource knot may possess out-edges which do not belong to the resource knot, whereas resource nodes cannot possess such out-edges. Clearly, a resource knot is a necessary and sufficient condition for the existence of a deadlock in an MIMR system. It is also a necessary and sufficient condition for deadlock in all resource systems discussed in this section.

Processes in deadlock

The set of processes D which are deadlocked when resource knot(s) exists in an RRAG can be defined using the following notation:

RR_i	:	The set of resources requested by process p_i
HP_k	:	The *holder set* of resource R_k, i.e. set of processes to which units of resource class R_k are allocated
KS	:	The set of process nodes in resource knot(s) (i.e. the *knot-set* of RRAG)
AS	:	An *auxiliary set* of process nodes in RRAG which face indefinite waits

where the set of processes AS is defined as follows:

$$AS = \{\ p_i \mid \exists\ R_k \in RR_i \text{ such that } \forall\ p_j \in HP_k,\ p_j \in (KS \cup AS)\ \}$$

We now have $D = KS \cup AS$.

Example 12.11 The cycle $p_1 - R_1 - p_2 - R_2 - p_3 - R_3 - p_1$ in the RRAG of Fig. 12.9 forms a resource knot despite the presence of edge (p_3, R_{10}) because $WF_3 = \{p_1, p_{11}\}$, and p_1 is a part of the cycle. We now have

$$\begin{aligned} KS &= \{p_1, p_2, p_3\} \\ AS &= \{p_4\} \text{ since } RR_4 = \{R_4\} \text{ and } HP_4 = \{p_1\} \\ D &= \{p_1, p_2, p_3, p_4\}. \end{aligned}$$

Process p_6 is not included in AS since all processes in $HP_6 = \{p_4, p_5\}$ are not included in $KS \cup AS$.

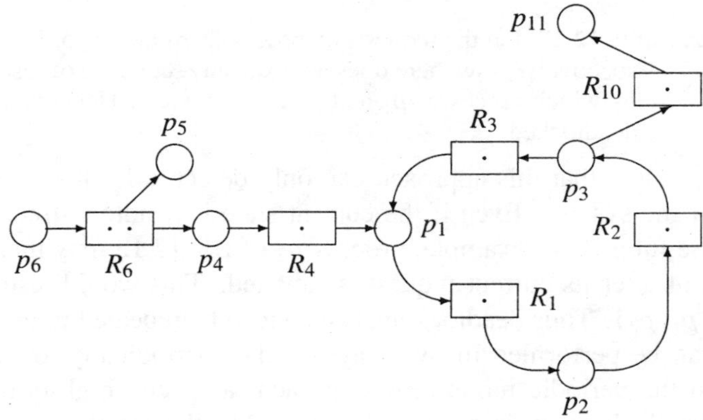

Fig. 12.9 An example of resource knot

12.4 DEADLOCK DETECTION AND RESOLUTION

The deadlock characterization developed in the previous section is not very useful in practice for two reasons. First, it involves the overheads of building and maintaining an RRAG. Second, it restricts each resource request to a single resource unit of one or more resource classes. Due to these limitations, deadlock detection cannot be implemented merely as the determination of a graph property. For a practical implementation, Definition 12.1 can be interpreted as follows: A set of *blocked* processes *D* is deadlocked if there does not exist any sequence of resource allocations and resource releases in the system whereby each process in *D* can complete. The OS must determine this fact through exhaustive analysis.

Deadlock analysis is performed by simulating the completion of a *running* process. In the simulation it is assumed that a *running* process completes without making additional resource requests. On completion, the process releases all resources allocated to it. These resources are allocated to a blocked process only if the process can enter the *running* state. The simulation terminates in one of two situations—either all *blocked* processes become *running* and complete, or some set *B* of *blocked* processes cannot be allocated their requested resources. In the former case no deadlock exists in the system at the time when deadlock analysis is performed, while in the latter case processes in *B* are deadlocked.

Example 12.12 An OS contains 10 units of some resource *R*. It has allocated 4, 4 and 2 units to 3 processes p_1, p_2 and p_3, respectively. Processes p_1 and p_2 are currently blocked on requests for 6 and 2 units of the resource respectively. Process p_3 is in the *running* state. All processes in the system can complete as follows: Process p_3 completes and releases 2 units of the resource allocated to it. These can now be allocated to p_2 which becomes *running* and completes. This releases 6 units of the resource which can now be allocated to p_1 to enable it to complete. No deadlock exists in the system since all processes can complete in this manner.

Example 12.13 Let the requests by processes p_1 and p_2 of Ex. 12.12 be for 6 and 3 units respectively. Now there does not exist any sequence of resource allocations and releases by which processes p_1 and p_2 can complete. Hence, the set of processes $\{p_1, p_2\}$ is deadlocked.

Note that this approach can only detect a deadlock existing in the current state of the system. Even if the current state is deadlock-free, a deadlock could arise in the future. For example, process p_2 of Ex. 12.12 may make a request for 1 resource unit after its current request is satisfied. This would result in a deadlock with $D = \{p_1, p_2\}$. Thus deadlock analysis has to be repeated to detect future deadlocks. This can be performed in two ways—either periodically, or in an event based manner. In the periodic monitoring approach, a special high-priority OS process performs deadlock analysis at fixed intervals. In the event based approach, the analysis is performed every time a process gets blocked on a resource request. The overheads of deadlock detection would depend on several factors like the number of processes and resource classes in the system, the frequency with which deadlock analysis is performed, etc.

12.4.1 Deadlock Detection Algorithm

Algorithm 12.1 performs deadlock detection along the lines described earlier. Consider a system containing n processes and r resources. Pending requests are represented by an $n \times r$ array. Each element of this matrix indicates the number of units of a resource class requested by a process. The current resource allocation in the system is similarly represented by an $n \times r$ array. The sets *Blocked*, *Running* and *Finished* are used to represent the set of *blocked*, *running* and *finished* processes, respectively, at any simulated instant of time. The algorithm simulates the completion of a *running* process p_j by transferring it from *Running* to *Finished*. The resources allocated to p_j are added to the pool of free resources (Step 1(c)). The algorithm now selects a *blocked* process (Step 1(d)) whose resource request can be satisfied from the currently free resources. This process is transferred from *Blocked* to *Finished*. The algorithm terminates after simulating the completion of all *running* processes. If any processes are still blocked, they must be deadlocked. The size of the *Running* and *Blocked* sets is $O(n)$, where n is the number of processes in the system. The loop of Step 1 iterates $O(n)$ times and Step 1(d) performs $O(n.r)$ work in each iteration. Hence the complexity of the algorithm is $O(n^2.r)$.

Algorithm 12.1 (Deadlock Detection)

Inputs

n	:	Number of processes;
r	:	Number of resource classes;
Blocked	:	**Set of** processes;
Running	:	**Set of** processes;

Data structures

$$
\begin{aligned}
\textit{Allocated\_resources} &: \ \textbf{array } [1..n, 1..r] \textbf{ of } \textit{integer};\\
\textit{Requested\_resources} &: \ \textbf{array } [1..n, 1..r] \textbf{ of } \textit{integer};\\
\textit{Free\_resources} &: \ \textbf{array } [1..r] \textbf{ of } \textit{integer};\\
\textit{Finished} &: \ \textbf{Set of } \textit{processes};
\end{aligned}
$$

1. **Repeat until** *Running is empty*
   (a) *Select a process* p_j *from Running*;
   (b) *Delete* p_j *from Running and add it to Finished*;
   (c) **for** $k = 1..r$
   $Free\_resources[k] := Free\_resources[k]$
   $+ Allocated\_resources[j,k]$;
   (d) (i) *Find some process* $p_l \in$ *Blocked such that*
   $Requested\_resources[l,k] \leq Free\_resources[k]$
   for $k = 1..r$
   (ii) **for** $k = 1, r$
   $Free\_resources[k] := Free\_resources[k]$
   $- Requested\_resources[l,k]$;
   (iii) *Delete* p_l *from Blocked and add it to Running*;
2. *If Blocked is non-empty* **then**
   declare processes in Blocked to be deadlocked.

12.4.2 Deadlock Resolution

Given a set of deadlocked processes D, *deadlock resolution* implies breaking the deadlock to ensure progress for some processes $\{p_i\} \in D$. This can be achieved by satisfying the resource request of a process p_i in one of two ways:

1. Terminate some processes $\{p_j\} \in D$ to free the resources required by p_i. (We call each p_j a *victim* of deadlock resolution.)
2. Add a new unit of the resource requested by p_i.

Note that deadlock resolution only ensures some progress for p_i. It does not guarantee that a p_i would run to completion. That would depend on the behaviour of processes after resolution.

Example 12.14 Figure 12.10 depicts deadlock resolution using the second approach. The WFG of Part (a) shows a deadlock involving processes p_2, p_3 and p_4. It is assumed that both processes p_3 and p_1 have requested a resource R_i held by process p_2. Part (b) of the figure shows the WFG after terminating process p_2, assuming that the resource previously allocated to p_2 is now allocated to process p_3. The resource request made by p_3 is now satisfied, and process p_1, which waited for the victim before deadlock resolution, is now shown to wait for p_3, the new holder of the resource. This fact is important for deadlock detection in future.

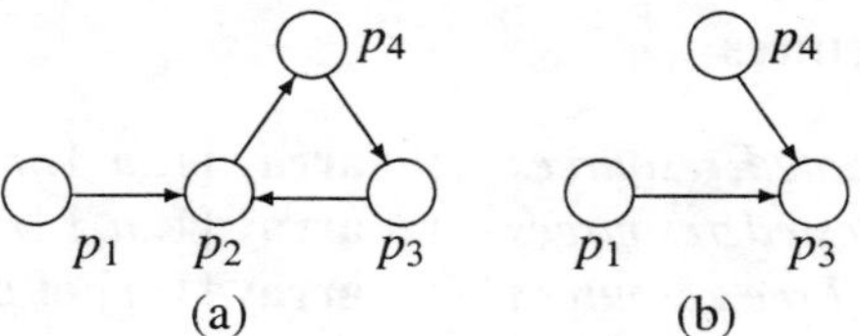

Fig. 12.10 Deadlock resolution

Adding a new resource unit is meaningless in most systems, with the exception of a system facing an interprocess communication deadlock. In this case, the system could create a dummy message for process p_i. A control flag in the message would identify it as a dummy message. On receiving such a message, process p_i is expected to retry a *receive* after a lapse of time, preferably after performing some *send*'s. This does not guarantee that the deadlock would not recur. However, it may enable a partial recovery in some applications. Forced termination of some $\{p_j\} \in D$ is a more practical approach to deadlock resolution.

Deadlock resolution can be very expensive in practice. Apart from the obvious costs, namely the overhead associated with termination of a victim process, and the cost of re-executing a victim sometime in future, the OS must also make an optimal choice of victims. This is very complex and expensive. Practical OSs either use a simple deadlock resolution policy like always terminating the least priority process, or use deadlock avoidance as described in the next section.

12.5 DEADLOCK AVOIDANCE

Deadlock avoidance approaches ensure that deadlocks cannot arise in a system. These approaches can be broadly classified into

1. *Deadlock prevention*
2. *Deadlock avoidance.*

The term *deadlock avoidance* is used as a generic term for both these approaches.

In the deadlock prevention approach the OS imposes certain constraint (called the *validity constraint*) on the resource requests which a process can make at any time. This constraint is of the form

$$f\,(<\!resource\_status\!>)$$

where $<$*resource_status*$>$ is the resource request and allocation status of the entire system. (In simple deadlock prevention algorithms, f may be a function of only the resource status of a requesting process.) This validity constraint ensures that deadlocks cannot arise in the system. Any request violating the validity constraint is rejected straightaway. The deadlock avoidance approach does not specify any validity constraints. A resource request is considered only if the OS can establish that its presence in the system as a pending or granted request cannot lead to a deadlock.

For this purpose, the resource allocation policy specifies a *safety* test. All unsafe requests are kept pending until they can be honoured. Note that a request may have to be kept pending even if the requested resources are available. We shall discuss this aspect in the context of specific algorithms.

The validity constraint or the safety criterion are implemented as a part of the resource allocation policy. The cost of deadlock avoidance consists of two components—the overheads of applying the validity constraint or the safety test, and the cost of resource idling due to the policy. Three resource allocation policies are discussed in this section—the first two policies are for deadlock prevention while the third policy is for deadlock avoidance.

12.5.1 All Requests Together

This is the simplest of all deadlock prevention policies. The validity constraint on resource requests is that a process must make all its requests together—typically, at the start of its execution. All requested resources are also allocated together, i.e. a unit of resource class R_k is allocated to a process p_i only if all resource units requested by p_i can be allocated. This constraint implies that a blocked process does not hold any resources, hence paths of length larger than 1 cannot form in the RRAG or WFG. Thus, mutual wait-for relationships cannot develop in the system and deadlocks cannot arise.

Example 12.15 For the processes of Ex. 12.1, each of the processes p_i and p_j will either receive both resources or none of them. Hence the processes are never deadlocked.

Here the validity constraint is that a process requesting a resource does not hold any other resource. The resource allocation policy can be implemented as follows: A boolean flag can be associated with each process to indicate whether any resources are allocated to it. Each resource in the system can be represented by an entry in a resource table, a field in the entry indicating whether the resource is presently free or allocated. The request of a process can be checked against the resource table to determine whether all requested resources can be granted. The simplicity of its implementation makes this policy very attractive for small operating systems.

This policy has one practical drawback. It adversely influences the efficiency of resource utilization even in cases where deadlock possibilities do not exist. Consider two processes p_i and p_j such that p_i needs a tape device and a printer, while p_j only needs a printer. It is possible that p_i requires a tape in the beginning and a printer only towards the end of its execution. However, it will be forced to request both tape and printer at the start. This will imply idling of the printer in early parts of p_i. Such resource idling may affect the effective degree of multiprogramming in the system. For example if p_i is initiated first, p_j can be initiated only after p_i completes. In turn, this would affect the efficiency of CPU utilization.

12.5.2 Resource Ranking

The resource ranking policy (also called *resource ordering*) eliminates the possibility of circular waits by using the notion of *resource ranks*. All resource classes in the system are ranked using some criterion and each resource class i is assigned a numerical rank ($rank_i$). The validity constraint on a resource request by a process is a function of the ranks of resources currently allocated to it. Let a process p_1 currently hold one or more units of resource classes i and j such that $rank_i > rank_j$. Process p_1 can only request units of resource class $rank_l$ such that $rank_l > rank_i$, i.e. it can only request a resource whose rank is larger than that of the highest ranked resource currently allocated to it. Any request violating this constraint is rejected, and a process making such a request is terminated.

It is easy to show that circular waits cannot arise in the system. Let process p_1 make a valid request for a unit of resource class l. This implies $rank_i < rank_l$ for each resource class i allocated to it. Now consider a process p_2 which holds some units of resource class l. Process p_2 cannot ask for a unit of resource class i since $rank_i \not> rank_l$. Thus, p_1 can wait for p_2 implies that p_2 cannot wait for p_1. Hence, circular waits cannot arise.

Example 12.16 For the processes of Ex. 12.1, let $rank_{printer} > rank_{tape}$. Requests 1 and 2 lead to allocation of the tape and printer to p_i and p_j. Request 3 satisfies the validity constraint, but remains pending since the printer is not available. Request 4 would be rejected since it violates the validity constraint. This implies that process p_j would be terminated if it makes this request.

The resource ranking policy works best when all processes require their resources in the order of increasing ranks. However, difficulties arise when a process requires resources in some other order. For example, if a process p_3 requires a unit of resource class m after it has been allocated units of resource classes i, j and k such that $rank_i > rank_j > rank_m > rank_k$, it would violate the validity constraint. The only way p_3 can obtain a unit of resource class m is by releasing the resources of classes i and j before making the request. It would now have to re-acquire the units of resource classes j and i (in that order). This is difficult in practice since resources are typically non-preemptible.

Processes may tend to circumvent such difficulties by acquiring lower ranking resources much before they are actually needed. In the worst case, this policy may degenerate into the 'all requests together' policy of resource allocation. For instance, processes p_i and p_j of Ex. 12.1 could request for a printer and a tape together. However, as we will see later, the OS can use the resource ranking policy for its own resource requirements since it needs the resources in a fixed order. This policy is attractive due to its simplicity once resource ranks have been assigned.

12.5.3 Banker's Algorithm

The Banker's algorithm uses an avoidance policy. Hence no validity constraint is specified, and processes are free to make any resource requests. The system uses two tests—called *feasibility test* and *safety test*—to govern its resource allocation actions when process p_j makes a request $Req_{j,k}$ for units of resource class k.

Definition 12.5 (Feasible request) *A request* $\mathrm{Req}_{j,k}$ *is a* feasible request *if, after granting the request, the total allocated resources of class k do not exceed the total number of resource units of class k in the system.*

Definition 12.6 (Safe request) *A feasible request* $\mathrm{Req}_{j,k}$ *is a* safe request *at time t if, after granting the request at time t, there exists at least one sequence of allocations and releases by which all processes in the system can complete.*

The system only grants safe requests at any time. An unsafe request is kept pending even if it is feasible. It is granted sometime in the future when it becomes both feasible and safe. The fact that all feasible requests are not automatically granted points to the possibility of resource idling in the system.

The OS uses a common-sense admission criterion while initiating a process p_j, namely that the maximum number of units of resource class k required by p_j at any time during its execution must not exceed the total number of units of resource class k in the system. The OS may initiate any number of processes satisfying the admission criterion. Thus the total resource requirements of all admitted processes may exceed the number of resource units of resource class k. The algorithm is called the Banker's algorithm presumably because bankers follow an analogous procedure while granting loans.

To motivate the Banker's algorithm, consider an OS containing a single resource class k. Let

$max_{j,k}$	:	maximum number of units of resource class k required by process p_j
$allocated\_resources_{j,k}$	:	number of units of resource class k allocated to process p_j
$requested\_resources_{j,k}$	:	number of units of resource class k requested by process p_j
$total\_alloc_k$	:	total number of allocated units of resource class k
$total\_exist_k$	:	total number of units of resource class k existing in the system

Now, we have

1. $max_{j,k} \leq total\_exist_k$ (this is the admission criterion)
2. $requested\_resources_{j,k} \leq (max_{j,k} - allocated\_resources_{j,k})$

3. $total\_alloc_k = \Sigma_j(allocated\_resources_{j,k})$
4. $total\_alloc_k \le total\_exist_k$.

The resource allocation state of the system with respect to resource class k is represented as an n-tuple

$$(allocated\_resources_{1,k}, \ldots allocated\_resources_{n,k})$$

where n is the number of processes in the system.

The notion of safety is extended to a resource allocation state as follows: A resource allocation state is a *safe allocation state* if there exists at least one sequence of allocations and releases by which all processes in the system can complete their execution.

A request by process p_j for $requested\_resources_{j,k}$ units of resource class k is processed as follows:

1. Determine the new allocation state of the system if the request is granted (we will call it the *projected state*).
2. If the projected state is both feasible and safe, the request is granted immediately. The system updates $allocated\_resources_{j,k}$ and $total\_alloc_k$ accordingly.
3. If the projected state is either infeasible or unsafe, the request is kept pending.

Note that the projected allocation state differs from the current allocation state only in that $requested\_resources_{j,k}$ have been allocated to process p_j. Hence, the projected state is feasible if $total\_exist_k - total\_alloc_k \ge 0$ in the projected state, i.e. if in the current state

$$total\_exist_k - total\_alloc_k \ge requested\_resources_{j,k}$$

The safety of the projected allocation state is determined by trying to simulate the completion of all processes in the system. Unlike the deadlock analysis of Section 12.4, a *running* process p_l can be assumed to complete only if its remaining requirements, viz. $max_{l,k} - allocated\_resources_{l,k}$ can be allocated to it, i.e. if

$$\forall k,\ total\_exist_k - total\_alloc_k \ \ge\ max_{l,k} - allocated\_resources_{l,k} \quad (12.3)$$

When it completes, it would release all the resources allocated to it. We simulate this by updating $total\_alloc_k$. Similarly, we simulate the completion of a *blocked* process p_g, i.e. a process p_g which is blocked on a request for $requested\_resources_{g,k}$ units of resource class k, if

$$total\_exist_k - total\_alloc_k \ \ge\ max_{g,k} - allocated\_resources_{g,k}$$

Thus, no distinction needs to be made between *running* and *blocked* processes while determining the safety of the projected allocation state.

Example 12.17 A system contains 10 units of resource class R_k. The resource requirements of three user processes p_1, p_2 and p_3 are as follows:

	p_1	p_2	p_3
Maximum requirements	8	7	5
Current allocation	3	1	3
Balance requirements	5	6	2
New request made	1	0	0

Using our notation, the current allocation state can be depicted as follows:

$$max = \begin{bmatrix} \dots & 8 & \dots \\ \dots & 7 & \dots \\ \dots & 5 & \dots \end{bmatrix} \qquad allocated\_resources = \begin{bmatrix} \dots & 3 & \dots \\ \dots & 1 & \dots \\ \dots & 3 & \dots \end{bmatrix}$$

$$requested\_resources = \begin{bmatrix} \dots & 1 & \dots \\ \dots & 0 & \dots \\ \dots & 0 & \dots \end{bmatrix}$$

$$total\_alloc = [\ \dots \quad 7 \quad \dots\ ]$$

$$total\_exist = [\ \dots \quad 10 \quad \dots\ ]$$

The projected allocation state is feasible since the total allocation in it does not exceed the number of resource units of R_k. The safety of the projected state is determined as follows: Equation (12.3) is not satisfied by processes p_1 and p_2. However, p_3 satisfies it since it is two units short of its maximum requirements and two unallocated units exist in the system. Hence, p_3 can complete. This will release the resources allocated to it. Now p_1 can complete since the number of unallocated units exceeds the units needed to satisfy its maximum requirement. This enables p_2 to complete. Thus, the processes can finish in the sequence p_3, p_1, p_2. This makes the projected allocation state safe. Hence the algorithm will grant the request by p_1.

This will change the allocation state to (4,1,3). Now consider the following requests:

1. p_1 makes a request for 2 tape units.
2. p_2 makes a request for 2 tape units.
3. p_3 makes a request for 2 tape units.

The requests by p_1 and p_2 are unsafe since Equation (12.3) is not satisfied by any process. However, the request by p_3 is safe. In other words, requests by p_1 and p_2 cannot be granted till p_3 completes.

We are now ready to present the Banker's algorithm for multiple resources.

Algorithm 12.2 (Banker's algorithm)

Inputs

n	:	Number of processes;
r	:	Number of resource classes;

```
Blocked     :  Set of processes;
Running     :  Set of processes;
p_req       :  Process making the new resource request;
New_req     :  array [1..r] of integer;
```

Data structures

```
Max                   :  array [1..n, 1..r] of integer;
Allocated_resources   :  array [1..n, 1..r] of integer;
Requested_resources   :  array [1..n, 1..r] of integer;
Total_alloc           :  array [1..r] of integer;
Total_exist           :  array [1..r] of integer;
Active                :  Set of processes;
Simulated_alloc       :  array [1..r] of integer;

 1. Active := Running ∪ Blocked;
 2. for k = 1..r
          Requested_resources[req,k] := New_request[k];
 3. for k = 1..r          /* Compute projected state */
          Allocated_resources[req,k] :=
                Allocated_resources[req,k] + New_request[k];
          Total_alloc[k] :=
                Total_alloc[k] + New_request[k];
 4. for k = 1..r          /* Check if allocation is feasible */
          if Requested_resources[req,k] >
                Total_exist[req,k] − Total_alloc[req,k]
                then go to step 6;
 5. Simulated_alloc := Total_alloc;
    while ∃ p_l ∈ Active such that ∀k
          Total_exist[k] − Simulated_alloc[k]
                ≥ max[l,k] − Allocated_resources[l,k]
     (a) Delete p_l from Active;
     (b) for k = 1..r
               Simulated_alloc[k] :=
                     Simulated_alloc[k] − Allocated_resources[l,k];
 6. if Active is empty then          /* Projected state is safe */
          for k = 1..r
                Requested_resources[req,k] := 0;
    else        /* Disallow projected grant and revert to current state */
          for k = 1..r
                Allocated_resources[req,k] :=
                      Allocated_resources[req,k] − New_request[k];
                Total_alloc[k] :=
```

$$Total\_alloc[k] - New\_request[k];$$

The algorithm keeps a request pending if the projected state is infeasible (Step 4). Else it simulates the grant of the new request (Step 3) and determines its safety (Step 5). If the request is safe, its grant is confirmed, else it is nullified (Step 6). Note the similarity of this algorithm to the deadlock detection algorithm. Analogously, it has the complexity of $O(n^2.r)$.

Note that the effect of applying the multi-resource Banker's algorithm is different from the effect of applying the single-resource algorithm for each resource individually. Example 12.18 illustrates this fact.

Example 12.18 A system contains 4 resources each of two resource classes R_1 and R_2, and three processes p_1, p_2 and p_3. The allocation status and maximum requirements of the processes are as follows:

	Allocated resources		*Maximum requirements*	
	R_1	R_2	R_1	R_2
Process p_1	1	0	1	1
Process p_2	1	1	2	3
Process p_3	1	2	2	2

The unallocated resources with the system are (1,1). If process p_2 were to make a request which is either (1,0) or (0,1), the system would grant it because in the former case the processes can complete in the sequence p_1, p_3, p_2 and in the latter case the processes can complete in the sequence p_3, p_1, p_2. However, if process p_2 were to make a request (1,1), the request would be rejected because no process can satisfy Equation (12.3), hence no process can complete.

12.6 MIXED APPROACH TO DEADLOCK HANDLING

The deadlock handling approaches differ in terms of their usage implications. Hence it is not possible to use a single deadlock handling approach to govern the allocation of all resources. The following mixed approach is found useful:

1. *System control blocks:* Control blocks like JCB, PCB, etc. can be acquired in a specific order. Hence resource ranking can be used here. If a simpler strategy is desired, all control blocks for a job or process can be allocated together at its initiation.
2. *IO devices, files:* Avoidance is the only practical strategy for these resources. However, in order to eliminate the overheads of avoidance, new 'devices' are added as and when needed. This is done using the concept of *spooling*. If a system has only one printer, many printers are 'created' by using some disk area to store a file to be printed. Actual printing takes place when a printer becomes available.

3. *Main memory:* No deadlock handling is explicitly necessary. The memory allocated to a program is simply preempted by swapping out the program whenever the memory is needed for another program.

EXERCISE 12.6

1. Compare and contrast the following policies of resource allocation:
   (a) All resource requests together
   (b) Allocation using resource ranking
   (c) Allocation using Banker's algorithm.

   on the basis of (a) resource idling, and (b) overheads of the resource allocation algorithm.
2. Is the allocation state (6,1,2) for the system of Ex. 12.17 safe? Would the allocation state (5,1,1) be safe?
3. An OS contains 2 resource classes. The number of resource units in these classes is 4 and 5, respectively. The current resource allocation state is as shown below:

	Allocated resources		*Maximum requirements*	
	R_1	R_2	R_1	R_2
Process p_1	1	3	2	5
Process p_2	2	1	3	2

   Would the following requests be granted in the current state?
   (a) Process p_2 requests (1,0)
   (b) Process p_2 requests (0,1)
   (c) Process p_2 requests (1,1)
   (d) Process p_1 requests (1,0)
   (e) Process p_1 requests (0,1).
4. An OS contains 3 resource classes. The number of resource units in these classes is 7, 7 and 10, respectively. The current resource allocation state is as shown below:

	Allocated resources			*Maximum requirements*		
	R_1	R_2	R_3	R_1	R_2	R_3
Process p_1	2	2	3	3	6	8
Process p_2	2	0	3	4	3	3
Process p_3	1	2	4	3	4	4

   (a) Is the current allocation state safe?
   (b) Would the following requests be granted in the current state?
      (i) Process p_1 requests (1,1,0)
      (ii) Process p_3 requests (0,1,0)
      (iii) Process p_2 requests (0,1,0).

5. A system contains 6 units of a resource, and 3 processes that need to use this resource. If the maximum resource requirement of each process is 3 units, will the system be free of deadlocks for all time? Explain clearly.

   If the system had 7 units of the resource, would the system be deadlock-free?
6. An OS uses a simple strategy to deal with deadlock situations. When it finds that a set of processes is deadlocked, it cancels all of them and restarts them immediately. Under what conditions will this approach lead to repeated deadlocks? Under what conditions the deadlocks will not occur repeatedly?
7. An OS has a single disk, which it uses (a) to create user files, and (b) to spool printer output for various user processes. Space is allocated for both on a demand basis, and a program is blocked if its disk space requirement cannot be granted. Spooled printer output is handed over to the printer when a program finishes. Is there a possibility of deadlocks in this system? If so, under what conditions? Suggest a solution to the deadlock problem.
8. A *phantom deadlock* is a situation wherein a deadlock handling algorithm declares a deadlock but no deadlock exists. Prove that phantom deadlocks are not detected by Algorithm 12.1 if processes are not permitted to withdraw their resource requests.

BIBLIOGRAPHY

Havender (1968) and Habermann(1969) are early works on deadlock handling. Since then a lot of literature has appeared on the problem of deadlock handling. Isloor and Marsland (1980) is a good survey paper on this topic. Zobel (1983) is an extensive bibliography. The deadlock problem has also been studied from the viewpoint of multi-access data bases. Refer to Ullman (1982) as a starting point for the same.

1. Coffman, E.G., M.S. Elphick, and A. Shoshani (1972): "System deadlocks, *Computing Surveys*, **3** (2).
2. Habermann, A.N. (1969): "Prevention of System deadlocks," *Commn. of ACM*, **12** (7), 373-377.
3. Habermann, A.N. (1973): "A new approach to avoidance of system deadlocks," in *Lecture notes in Computer Science*, Vol.16, Springer-Verlag.
4. Havender, J.W. (1968): "Avoiding deadlock in multitasking systems," *IBM Systems Journal*, **7** (2), 74-84.
5. Holt, R.C. (1972): "Some deadlock properties of computer systems," *Computing Surveys*, **4** (3).
6. Howard, J.H. (1973): "Mixed solutions to the deadlock problem," *Commn. of ACM*, **6** (3), 427-430.
7. Isloor, S.S. and T.A. Marsland (1980): "The deadlock problem – an overview," *Computer*, **13** (9), 58-70.
8. Rypka, D.J. and A.P. Lucido (1979): "Deadlock detection and avoidance for shared logical resources," *IEEE transactions on Software Engg*, **5** (5), 465-471.
9. Ullman, J.D. (1982): *Principles of Data Base Systems*, Pitman, London.
10. Zobel, D. (1983): "The deadlock problem – a classifying bibliography," *Operating Systems Review*, **17** (4), 6-15.

CHAPTER 13

Process Synchronization

Two kinds of synchronization were identified in Sect 10.3:

1. *Control synchronization:* Processes may wish to coordinate their activities with respect to one another such that a process performs an action only when some other processes reach specific points in their execution.
2. *Data access synchronization:* Race conditions should not arise when concurrent processes access shared data. Data access synchronization is used to ensure this by implementing mutual exclusion over accesses to shared data.

The basic technique used to implement synchronization is to block a process until an appropriate condition is fulfilled. Thus to implement control synchronization a process p_i can be blocked till some process p_k reaches a specific point in its execution. Data access synchronization is implemented by blocking a process till another process finishes accessing some shared data.

In this chapter we discuss implementation of control and data access synchronization of processes. We begin by introducing the semantics of control and data access synchronization of processes and discussing the desired properties which their implementations should satisfy. We then introduce some well-known problems in process synchronization and discuss their solutions using a variety of programming language features.

13.1 IMPLEMENTING CONTROL SYNCHRONIZATION

We first discuss control synchronization at the start or end of a process. Later we consider more general forms of synchronization.

Definition 13.1 (Process precedence) *Process* p_i precedes *process* p_j *if execution of* p_i *must be completed before* p_j *can begin its execution.*

The notation $p_i \rightarrow p_j$ is used to represent the fact that process p_i precedes process p_j. Note that the '$\rightarrow$' relation on the set of processes is transitive, i.e. $p_i \rightarrow p_j$ and $p_j \rightarrow p_k$ implies $p_i \rightarrow p_k$. The notation $p_i \xrightarrow{*} p_k$ is used to represent transitive precedences. Processes p_i and p_j are said to be *independent processes* if no direct or transitive precedence exists between them. Process precedences can be represented using process precedence graphs and process precedence sequences.

Process precedence graphs

A *process precedence graph* (PPG) is a directed graph $G \equiv (N, E)$ such that $p_i \in N$ represents a process, and an edge $(p_i, p_j) \in E$ implies $p_i \rightarrow p_j$. Thus, a path $p_1 - p_2 - \ldots - p_i$ in a PPG implies $p_1 \xrightarrow{*} p_i$. DS_i, the *dependence set* of a process p_i, contains processes which depend on p_i for their completion. Thus a process $p_j \in DS_i$ if $p_i \rightarrow p_j$. DS_i^* is the transitive closure of DS_i. It contains a process p_k if $p_i \xrightarrow{*} p_k$. In terms of the PPG, DS_i and DS_i^* are defined as follows:

$$DS_i = \{ p_k \mid \exists\, (p_k, p_i) \text{ in PPG} \}$$
$$DS_i^* = \{ p_k \mid \exists \text{ path } p_k - \ldots - p_i \text{ in PPG} \}$$

Example 13.1 Figure 13.1 shows a precedence graph. $DS_4 = \{p_2, p_3\}$ because of edges (p_2, p_4) and (p_3, p_4). $DS_4^* = \{p_1, p_2, p_3\}$ because of the paths $p_1 - p_2 - p_4$ and $p_1 - p_3 - p_4$ in PPG.

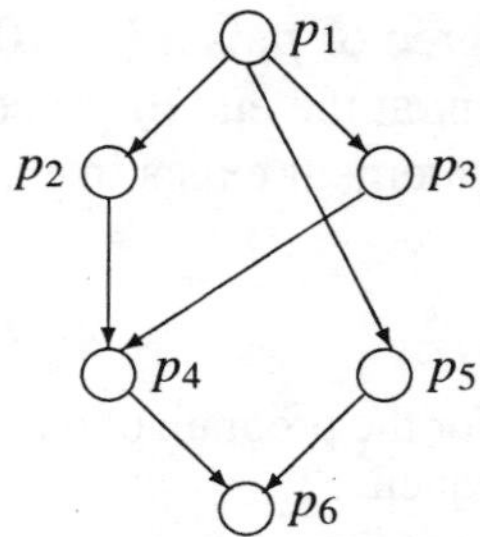

Fig. 13.1 A Process Precedence Graph (PPG)

Process precedence sequences

Process precedence relations can also be represented in the form of a *process precedence sequence*. A process precedence sequence is composed of the following elements:

1. Process names
2. Sequence operator ';'
3. Concurrency operator ','
4. Braces '{ }' which enclose precedence subsequences.

A subsequence $\{p_1; p_2\}$ represents the precedence relation $p_1 \rightarrow p_2$. The subsequence $\{p_3, p_4\}$ represents the fact that processes p_3 and p_4 can execute concurrently without any synchronization, i.e. p_3 and p_4 are independent processes.

Example 13.2 We can represent the process precedences of Fig. 13.1 as follows:

$$\{p_1\}; \{\{\{p_2, p_3\}; p_4\}, p_5\}; \{p_6\} \qquad (13.1)$$

Example 13.2 uses the nesting of precedence subsequences to represent deeper precedence relations. Note that a process precedence sequence can represent only structured process precedences. It cannot represent arbitrary precedence relations, e.g. it cannot represent the process precedence graph of Fig. 13.1 if a process p_7 and an edge (p_7, p_4) also exists in the system.

Implementing process precedences

Process precedences can be implemented through programming language constructs, or through OS calls. In Section 10.4 we have discussed the **Fork–Join** and **Parbegin–Parend** control constructs and the process initiation and termination features in Unix and OSF/1. A PPG can be implemented using **Fork–Join** by performing the following steps for each process p_i:

1. Associate a variable v_i with p_i.
2. Set the initial value of v_i to the in-degree of p_i.
3. Add the statement lab_i : **Join** v_i; at the start of p_i.
4. If the out-degree of p_i is n $(n > 0)$, put $(n-1)$ **Fork** statements followed by a **goto** statement at the end of process p_i such that $\forall\ p_j,\ p_i \in DS_j$, a **Fork** lab_j or a **goto** lab_j statement exists in p_i.

EXERCISE 13.1

1. Draw a PPG for the program of example 10.4. Can this PPG be implemented using a precedence sequence?
2. For the system of Fig. 13.2,
   (a) Identify all independent processes,
   (b) Identify all precedence relations.
3. Implement the PPG of Fig. 13.2 using
   (a) **Fork–Join**.
   (b) **Parbegin–Parend**
4. Comment on the validity of the following statement: "A PPG can be implemented using **Parbegin–Parend** only if

$$\forall p_i \in N,\ \{DS_i^* - p_j\} \equiv DS^*{}_j \text{ where } p_j = \text{parent}(p_i)\text{"}$$

5. Develop algorithms for the following:
   (a) Converting a PPG into a process precedence sequence.

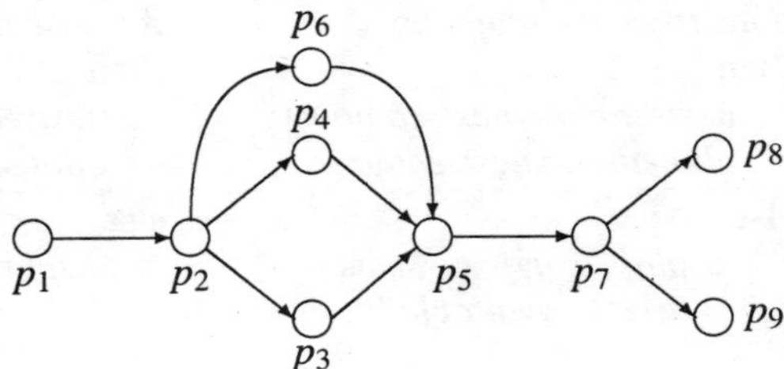

Fig. 13.2 PPG

(b) Converting a process precedence sequence into a PPG.
(c) Identifying independent processes in a PPG.

13.2 CRITICAL SECTIONS

A *race condition* on a data item arises when many processes concurrently update its value (see Section 10.3.2). Data consistency requires that only one process should update the value of a data item at any time. This is ensured through the notion of a *critical section* (CS).

Definition 13.2 (Critical Section) A critical section *for a data item d is a section of code which cannot be executed concurrently with itself or with other critical section(s) for d.*

Thus, at any moment at most one process can execute a CS for a data item. Hence a CS for a data item d is a mutual exclusion region with respect to d. Race conditions on d are avoided by performing all updates of d inside a CS for d. Further, to ensure that processes see consistent values of d, references to d should also occur inside a CS for d. If a process p_i is executing a CS on d, any other process wishing to enter a CS for d will have to wait till p_i exits from the CS.

A CS is represented by a dashed rectangular box in a program. Note that processes may share a single copy of code, in which case a single CS for d exists in the system. Alternatively, the code for each process may contain a CS for d. Definition 13.2 covers both situations.

Example 13.3 Figure 13.3 shows the use of critical sections in the airline reservations system of Fig. 10.6. Consistency of the shared variable *nextseatno* is maintained since each process queries and updates its value inside a CS.

13.2.1 Properties of a CS Implementation

An implementation of a CS for a data item d must possess the following properties:

1. *Correctness:* At most one process may execute a CS at any given moment.
2. *Progress:* When a CS is not in use, one of the processes wishing to enter it will be granted entry to the CS.

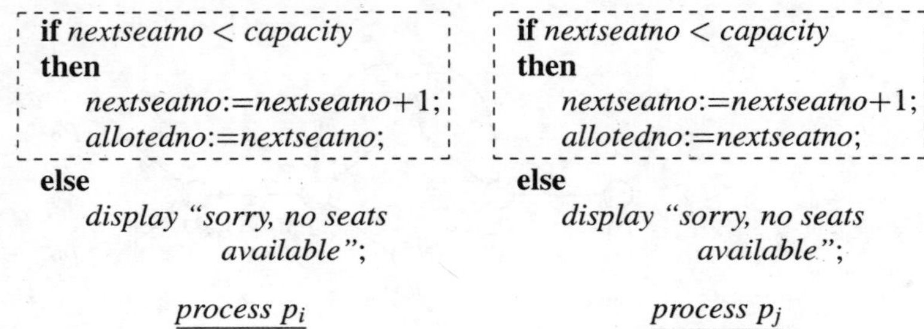

Fig. 13.3 Use of CS in airline reservations

3. *Bounded wait:* After a process p_i has indicated its desire to enter a CS, the number of times other processes gain entry to the CS ahead of p_i is bounded by a finite integer.
4. *Deadlock freedom:* The implementation is free of deadlocks.

Correctness and deadlock freedom are obvious conditions. The progress condition implies that a CS can not be kept reserved for a process that does not presently wish to enter it. This safeguards resource utilization and response times in the system. The bounded wait condition introduces an element of fairness by ensuring that no process is denied entry to a CS indefinitely.

13.2.2 History of CS Implementations

A chronological ordering of CS implementations is as follows:

1. Algorithmic approaches
2. Implementations using programming language features:
   (a) Language primitives for mutual exclusion,
   (b) Concurrent programming features of programming languages.

Algorithmic implementations depended on a complex arrangement of checks to ensure mutual exclusion. The correctness of the CS implementation thus depended on the correctness of these checks, and was hard to prove due to the complexity of the checks. This was a serious deficiency in the development of large concurrent systems. However, a major advantage of this approach was that no special hardware or software was required to implement a CS. A von Neumann computer with a single memory unit and one or more CPUs was adequate to implement a concurrent system.

A set of software primitives for mutual exclusion (e.g. the P and V primitives of Dijkstra) were developed to overcome the complexity of the algorithmic implementations. These primitives were implemented using some special hardware features of a computer. The properties of the primitives could be used to construct proofs of correctness of a software. However, experience with such primitives showed that ease of use and ease of establishing the correctness still remained major obstacles in the development of large concurrent systems.

Use of data abstraction and encapsulation features specifically suited to the construction of concurrent programs was the next important step in the history of CS implementations. These features, which were in the form of language constructs for process synchronization, had well defined semantics which were enforced by the language compiler. This made the construction of large concurrent systems more practical. The abstraction and encapsulation features were initially introduced in special purpose languages for concurrent programming. Later they found their way into general purpose languages like Ada.

Algorithmic solutions to the concurrency control problem are discussed in Section 13.2.4. Section 13.8 discusses the abstraction and encapsulation facilities necessary for concurrent programming. Section 13.9 discusses relevant features of Ada.

13.2.3 Process Synchronization With CS

Figure 13.4 shows the typical form of a process using a CS. The process is cyclic in nature. In each cycle, the process uses the CS and also performs other computations represented by the step "remainder of the cycle". When the process only wishes to access shared data, the CS is used to safeguard consistency of the data. When the process requires synchronization with other processes, the CS is used to guard the consistency of some control data introduced for the purpose of synchronization.

```
repeat forever
        ┌ - - - - - - - ┐
        |   Critical    |
        |   Section     |
        └ - - - - - - - ┘
      { Remainder of the cycle }
end
```

Fig. 13.4 A typical form of a process

Example 13.4 Consider the tasks in the real time application of Ex. 9.12 which stores data samples sent by a satellite to an earth station. The satellite link causes an IO interrupt after putting a sample in the special register. The interrupt activates a process (we will call it the *interrupt process*) which copies the sample into *buffer_area*. Another process in the application copies it from the *buffer_area* into a data base. If *buffer_area* can only hold one sample, both processes must access *buffer_area* in a mutually exclusive manner. Further, the interrupt process can access *buffer_area* only if it is empty, i.e. if the last data sample put into it has been copied out into the data base by the application process. Similarly, the application process can access *buffer_area* only if it contains a new data sample.

Figure 13.5 shows an outline of the interrupt process and the application process. The solution introduces a control variable called *buffer_status*. Processes enter the CS to test the value of *buffer_status* and decide whether to access *buffer_area*. The value *occupied* implies that *buffer_area* contains a sample which is yet to be copied into the data base. The value *free* indicates that the last data sample has been copied into the data base. Both processes use the value of *buffer_status* to determine their future course of actions. The CS is used to safeguard consistency of *buffer_status*.

```
                                   repeat
if buffer_status =                 if buffer_status =
"free" then                        "occupied" then
{ put data                         { copy data
  into the buffer }                  from the buffer }
  buffer_status :=                   buffer_status :=
    "occupied";                        "free";
                                   forever
   Interrupt process                 Application process
```

Fig. 13.5 Process synchronization with CS

A condition called *busy wait* often arises when critical sections are used to guard the consistency of control information. The application process of Fig. 13.5 suffers from this problem. Consider the case where a large time interval separates two data samples. After copying a data sample, the application process would repeatedly enter the CS to check if a new sample has arrived. This keeps the CPU busy even as the application process does nothing! A busy wait condition denies the CPU to lower priority processes in the system, hence a good solution to a process synchronization problem must not permit busy waits to arise. A process waiting for a resource should be blocked until it can be allocated the resource.

13.2.4 Algorithmic Implementation of CS

In this section we discuss various proposals for algorithmic implementation of a CS. The weaknesses of each proposal and ways to overcome them are discussed. All algorithms are shown as programs in a pseudo-language with the following features:

1. **Parbegin–Parend** control structure for creation and termination of concurrent processes
2. Declaration of shared variables
3. Declaration of local variables in a process
4. Comments enclosed within the braces '{ }'.

Algorithm 13.1

```
var   turn : integer;
begin
      turn := 1;
Parbegin
   repeat                              repeat
```

```
        while turn = 2                      while turn = 1
           do { nothing };                     do { nothing };
        { Critical Section }                { Critical Section }
        turn := 2;                          turn := 1;
        { Remainder of                      { Remainder of
          the cycle }                         the cycle }
     forever;                            forever;
Parend
end.
          Process p1                          Process p2
```

The shared variable *turn* is used to indicate which process can enter the CS next. Let process p_1 wish to enter the CS. If *turn* = 1, p_1 can enter straightaway. After completing the CS, it sets *turn* to '2' so as to enable process p_2 to enter the CS. If p_1 finds *turn* = 2 when it wishes to enter CS, it waits in the **while** loop until p_2 exits from the CS and executes the assignment *turn* := 1. Thus processes may encounter a busy wait before gaining entry to the CS.

Use of shared variable *turn* leads to some interesting behaviour of the processes. Let process p_1 be in CS and process p_2 be in the remainder of the cycle. If p_1 exits from the CS, finishes the remainder of its cycle and wishes to enter the CS once again, it would encounter a busy wait until after p_2 uses the CS. This does not violate the bounded wait condition, since p_1 has to wait for p_2 to go through the CS exactly once. However, the progress condition is violated since p_1, which is currently the only process interested in using the CS, is not able to enter it. This violation of the progress condition has the potential of delaying the processes periodically.

Algorithm 13.2

```
var    c1, c2 : integer;
begin
     c1 := 1;
     c2 := 1;
Parbegin
   repeat                                 repeat
      while c2 = 0                           while c1 = 0
         do { nothing };                        do { nothing };
      c1 := 0;                               c2 := 0;
      { Critical Section }                   { Critical Section }
      c1 := 1;                               c2 := 1;
      { Remainder of                         { Remainder of
        the cycle }                            the cycle }
   forever;                               forever;
```

Parend
end.

Process p_1 *Process p_2*

Variable *turn* of Algorithm 13.1 has been replaced by two shared variables c_1 and c_2. c_1 can be looked upon as a status flag for process p_1. p_1 sets this flag to 0 while entering the CS, and changes it back to 1 while exiting from the CS. Process p_2 checks the status of c_1 to determine whether it can enter the CS. This check eliminates the progress violation of Algorithm 10.1 by enabling a process to enter the CS again any number of times if the other process is not interested in entering the CS. However, the busy wait condition still exists (see the **while** loops). Further, this algorithm violates the correctness condition when both processes simultaneously try to enter the CS. Both c_1 and c_2 will be 1 at this point (since none of them is in the CS), hence both processes will enter the CS. To avoid this, one may consider interchanging the statements **while** $c_2 = 0$ **do** { *nothing* }; and $c_1 := 0$; in process p_1 (and similarly in process p_2), such that c_1 will be set to zero before p_1 checks the value of c_2. However, this solution suffers from deadlocks (see Problem 3 of Exercise 13.2).

The deadlock possibility can be eliminated by forcing a process to defer to another process while trying to enter the CS. Process p_1 can defer to p_2 by resetting c_1 to '1' if it finds that p_2 is also trying to enter the CS. However, this may lead to a *livelock* situation wherein both processes defer to each other indefinitely. This situation can be avoided as shown in Dekker's algorithm.

Algorithm 13.3 *Dekker's Algorithm*

```
var    c1, c2, turn : integer;
begin
        c1 := 1;
        c2 := 1;
      turn := 1;
Parbegin
   repeat                                 repeat
     c1 := 0;                               c2 := 0;
     while c2 = 0 do                        while c1 = 0 do
        if turn = 2 then                       if turn = 1 then
        begin                                  begin
           c1 := 1;                               c2 := 1;
           while turn = 2                         while turn = 1
              do { nothing };                        do { nothing };
           c1 := 0;                               c2 := 0;
        end;                                   end;
     { Critical Section }                   { Critical Section }
```

```
      turn := 2;                      turn := 1;
      c1 := 1;                        c2 := 1;
      { Remainder of                  { Remainder of
        the cycle }                     the cycle }
    forever;                        forever;
Parend
end.
        Process p1                      Process p2
```

The correctness problem of Algorithm 13.2 when both processes wish to enter the CS is avoided as follows: If $c_2 = 1$ when p_1 wishes to enter the CS, p_1 skips the entire **while** loop and enters the CS straightaway. If both processes try to enter the CS simultaneously, value of *turn* is used to force one of them to defer to the other. For example, if p_1 finds $c_2 = 0$, it defers to p_2 if *turn* = 2, else it simply waits for $c_2 =$ 1 before entering the CS. Process p_2, which is also trying to enter the CS at the same time, is forced to defer to p_1 if *turn* = 1. In this manner neither deadlock nor livelock conditions would arise.

The two process solution of Dekker's algorithm can be extended to the *n* process solution as in the algorithm by Eisenberg & McGuire [1972].

Algorithm 13.4 *An n Process Algorithm*

```
const   n = ...;
var   flag : array [0..n − 1] of (idle, want-in, in-CS);
      turn : 0 .. n − 1;
begin
Parbegin
  process pi :
    repeat
      repeat
        flag[i] := want-in;
        j := turn;
        while j ≠ i
          do if flag[j] ≠ idle
            then j := turn { Loop here! }
            else j := j + 1 mod n;
        flag[i] := in-CS;
        j := 0;
        while (j < n) and (j = i or flag[j] ≠ in-CS)
          do j := j + 1;
      until (j ≥ n) and (turn = i or flag[turn] = idle);
      turn := i;
```

```
            { Critical Section }
            j := turn +1 mod n;
            while (flag[j] = idle) do j := j + 1 mod n;
            turn := j;
            flag[i] := idle;
            { Remainder of the cycle }
        forever
    process p_k : ...
Parend
end.
```

The variable *turn* is still used to indicate which process may enter the CS next. Each process has a 3-way status flag. A process turns its flag to *want-in* whenever it wishes to enter the CS. It then checks to see whether any process from p_{turn} in modulo order, i.e. in the order p_{turn}, p_{turn+1}, $\dots p_{n-1}$, p_0, p_1, $\dots p_{turn-1}$, wishes to use the CS. If not, it turns its flag to *in-CS*. Note that many processes may reach the same conclusion simultaneously, hence another check is made to ensure correctness. The **while** loop checks whether any other process has turned its flag to *in-CS*, in which case the process changes its flag back to *want-in* and repeats the checks. All other processes, which had changed their flags to *in-CS* simultaneously change the flags back to *want-in* and repeat the checks. These processes will not tie for CS the next time because they have all turned their flags to *want-in*. The process earlier in the modulo order from p_{turn} will get in and enter CS ahead of other processes.

This implementation of CS satisfies the bounded wait condition, however there is a certain form of unfairness since processes do not enter the CS in the order in which they request entry to CS. This unfairness is eliminated in the bakery algorithm by Lamport [1974].

Algorithm 13.5 *Bakery Algorithm*

```
const   n = ... ;
var   choosing : array [0 .. n - 1] of boolean;
        number : array [0 .. n - 1] of integer;
begin
Parbegin
    process p_i :
        Repeat
            choosing[i] := true;
            number[i] := max (number[0], .., number[n - 1])+1;
            choosing[i] := false;
            for j := 0 to n - 1 do
            begin
                while choosing[j] do { nothing };
```

```
            while number[j] ≠ 0 and (number[j],j) < (number[i],i)
                do { nothing };
        end;
        { Critical Section }
        number[i] := 0;
        { Remainder of the cycle }
    forever;
  process p_j : ...
Parend
end.
```

A process requesting entry to CS is given a numbered token such that the number on the token is larger than the maximum number issued earlier. The algorithm permits the processes to enter the CS in the order of their token numbers. A problem can arise if two or more processes choose their tokens concurrently. This is resolved as follows: After choosing a token, process p_i forms a pair (*number*[i], i) and compares it with similar pairs for other processes using the *precedes* relation (represented by '<') defined as follows:

(*number*[j], j) < (*number*[i], i) if
number[j] < *number*[i], or
number[j] = *number*[i] and $j < i$.

Thus, if more than one process has obtained the same token number, the request of the process with the smaller process id is considered to be earlier. A process may enter the CS if its pair is the 'smallest' in the system, else it gets into a busy wait repeatedly checking for this condition. Thus, processes enter the CS in the order in which they raise their requests.

EXERCISE 13.2

1. Analyse Algorithms 13.1, 13.2 and comment on the CS properties violated by them. Give examples illustrating the violations.
2. Prove that the progress condition is satisfied in the case of Dekker's algorithm. (*Hint:* Consider *turn* = 2 and process p_1 trying to enter CS.)
3. It is proposed to modify Algorithm 13.2 by interchanging the statements **while** $c_2 = 0$ **do** { nothing }; and $c_1 := 0$; in process p_1 (and similarly in process p_2). Show that a deadlock possibility exists in the modified algorithm.
4. For Dekker's algorithm, prove that
   (a) Deadlock condition cannot arise
   (b) Livelock condition cannot arise.
5. In Lamport's bakery algorithm a process choosing a token later receives a larger token. Explain the need for the first **while** loop in this context.
6. In the n-process algorithm for mutual exclusion, explain the need for the last check before entering the CS, viz. **while** ($j < n$) **and** ... .

7. Explain the behaviour of a process p_i in the n-process algorithm when process p_i finishes the CS and no other process is interested in entering the CS.

13.3 CLASSICAL PROCESS SYNCHRONIZATION PROBLEMS

A solution to a process synchronization problem must possess two important properties:

1. Correctness
2. Maximum concurrency.

Correctness criteria depend on the nature of a problem. Within the constraints imposed by these criteria, a solution must provide maximum concurrency. In this section some classical problems in process synchronization are analysed to determine their correctness criteria and outline their solutions. In later sections these solutions are implemented using different implementation approaches.

13.3.1 Producers–Consumers With Bounded Buffers

A producers–consumers system with bounded buffers consists of an unspecified number of producer and consumer processes, and a finite pool of buffers. Each buffer is capable of holding one record of information. A producer produces one record of information at a time. After producing a record, it waits to obtain exclusive access to an empty buffer and writes the record into the buffer. A consumer process consumes information one record at a time. When it desires to consume, it waits to obtain exclusive access to a full buffer and copies the record from the buffer.

A solution to this problem must satisfy following conditions:

1. A producer must not overwrite a full buffer.
2. A consumer must not consume an empty buffer.
3. Producers and consumers must access buffers in a mutually exclusive manner.

Two optional conditions are sometimes imposed. These are

4. Information must be consumed in the same order in which it is put into the buffers, i.e. in FIFO order.
5. Busy waits must not occur. A producer or consumer process awaiting the availability of an empty or full buffer, respectively, must be blocked and must wake up only when a buffer is allocated to it. Thus, a process must not repeatedly check for the availability of an empty or a full buffer.

The progress and bounded wait conditions apply in an obvious way. No deadlocks can arise since each process requires only one resource—a buffer to produce in or consume from. However, indefinite blocking could result from incorrect implementation, e.g. all requesting producer(s) may be blocked while empty buffer(s) exist in the system, or all requesting consumer(s) may be blocked while full buffer(s) exist. This should be avoided.

Figure 13.6 shows the solution outline for the problem wherein the producer and consumer processes access the buffers inside the CS. An interesting situation concerning correctness Condition 5 arises as follows: The producer enters the CS and checks to see if an empty buffer exists. If so, it produces into that buffer before leaving the CS, else it merely exits from the CS. This sequence is repeated until it finds an empty buffer. The consumer similarly makes repeated checks until it finds a full buffer. This amounts to busy waits in the system. Thus, a CS by itself cannot achieve the desired synchronization between producer and consumer processes.

```
var   p_found, c_found : boolean;
begin
Parbegin
repeat                                   repeat
   p_found := false;                        c_found := false ;
   while p_found = false                    while c_found = false
   ┌─────────────────────────────┐        ┌──────────────────────────────┐
   │ if empty buffer exists      │        │ if full buffer exists        │
   │ then                        │        │ then                         │
   │    { Produce in a buffer }  │        │    { Consume a buffer }      │
   │    p_found := true;         │        │    c_found := true;          │
   └─────────────────────────────┘        └──────────────────────────────┘
   { Remainder of                           { Remainder of
     the cycle }                              the cycle }
forever;                                 forever;
Parend
end.
             Producer                                 Consumer
```

Fig. 13.6 Solution outline for producers–consumers with bounded buffers

In the desired form of solution, a producer process should check for the existence of an empty buffer only once. If none exists, the process should be blocked until an empty buffer becomes available. When a consumer consumes from a buffer, it should wake a producer which is waiting for an empty buffer. Similarly, a producer must wake a consumer waiting for a full buffer.

13.3.2 Readers and Writers

The readers–writers system consists of many processes accessing some shared data. Some processes only read the data (*reader processes*), while others write, i.e. update, the data (*writer processes*). Instances of the readers and writers problem can be found in on-line transaction processing systems, e.g. reservations and banking systems. The correctness conditions are as follows:

1. Only one writer can write at any time.
2. Reading is prohibited while a writer is writing.

3. Many readers can read simultaneously.

An optional condition is

4. Writers should have priority over readers.

Conditions 1 and 2 can be satisfied straightaway by performing all reading or writing inside a CS. However, this violates condition 3 since only one reader can read at any time. Condition 4 is also not satisfied since writers cannot be guaranteed entry to CS ahead of readers.

Figure 13.7 contains a solution outline without writer priority. If simultaneous reading by multiple readers is somehow implemented, the bounded wait condition may be violated since a stream of readers may starve a writer of an opportunity to begin writing.

```
Parbegin
    repeat                               repeat
       If a writer is writing               If reader(s) reading, or a
       then                                    writer writing then
          { wait }                             { wait }
       { read }                             { write }
       If writer(s) waiting                 If reader(s) or writer(s) waiting
       then                                 then
          wake a writer if no                  wake all readers
          readers are reading                  or one writer
    forever;                             forever;
Parend
          Reader(s)                            Writer(s)
```

Fig. 13.7 Solution outline for readers-writers without writer priority

13.3.3 Dining Philosophers

A group of philosophers sit around a table pondering over philosophical issues. To ensure that none of them dies of hunger, a plate of food is kept in front of each philosopher and a fork is placed between each pair of philosophers. To eat, each philosopher is assumed to require a fork in each hand. The problem is to design a set of processes for philosophers such that each philosopher can eat periodically and none dies of hunger.

Note that a simple solution in which each process is of the form

```
repeat
      lift the left fork;
      lift the right fork;
      { eat }
      { think }
forever
```

is not acceptable since it is prone to deadlocks (think of all philosophers lifting their left forks!). The solution outline of Fig. 13.8 avoids deadlocks because a philosopher picks up a fork only if both forks are available simultaneously. This ensures that at least some philosopher(s) can eat at any time. Since the availability of forks is checked within a CS, no races can arise. However, this solution suffers from a busy wait problem.

```
repeat
    if both forks are available then
        pick up both forks;
            { eat }
            put down both forks;
    { think }
forever
```

Fig. 13.8 Solution outline for dining philosophers

13.4 EVOLUTION OF LANGUAGE FEATURES FOR PROCESS SYNCHRONIZATION

Algorithmic implementations of critical sections suffer from the problems of cost and logical complexity. A complexity-related issue concerns the difficulty of adding a new process to the set of processes using a CS (or deleting an existing process). Most algorithmic implementations require each process to know the number and identities of processes using the CS. Hence the codes for all processes change when processes are added or deleted. This can be seen readily from Algorithms 13.1–13.5 of Section 13.2.4.

These problems can be eliminated by entrusting the correctness (and other properties) of the CS implementation to the language compiler or the OS kernel. This approach motivated the development of language features for process synchronization. The significant landmarks in this development are as follows:

1. Software primitives, e.g. Semaphores.
2. Control Structures, e.g. Critical regions and Conditional critical regions.
3. Monitors.
4. Languages for concurrent programming, e.g. Modula, Ada.

These are discussed in the following sections.

13.4.1 Structure of Concurrent Systems

A concurrent system consists of three essential components:

1. Shared data
2. Operations on shared data
3. Processes.

An *operation* is a convenient unit of code, typically a procedure in a programming language, which manipulates shared data. Thus an operation is a passive entity which is executed by an active agent. Processes represent concurrent activities in a system. They invoke operations to access and manipulate shared data.

An implementation of the producers–consumers problem with bounded buffers contains the following components:

Shared data : Set of buffers
Operations : Get and put on a buffer
Processes : Producers and Consumers

The pictorial conventions shown in Fig. 13.9 are used to depict relationships between shared data, operations on shared data and processes.

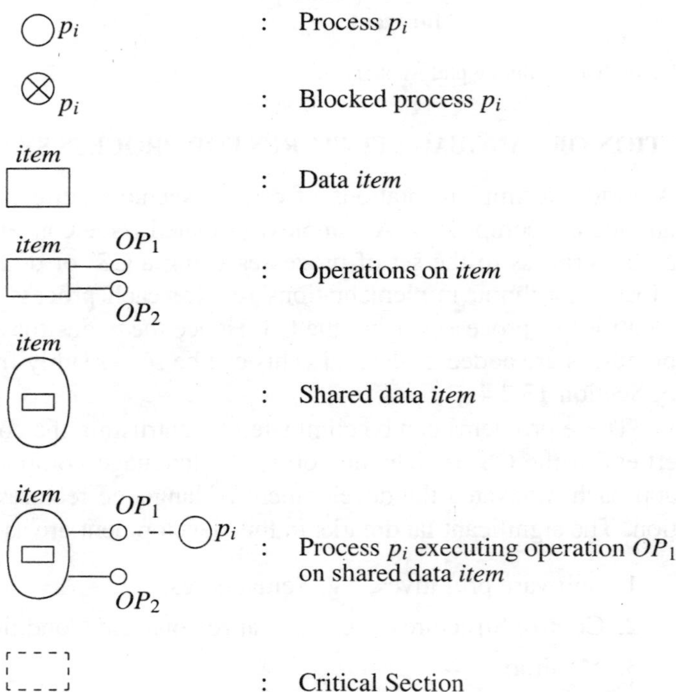

Fig. 13.9 Pictorial conventions

Example 13.5 Figure 13.10 shows a shared data named *item* with two operations OP_1 and OP_2 defined on it, and two processes p_i and p_j. Process p_i is currently engaged in performing the operation OP_2, while process p_j is currently in the *blocked* state.

In the following sections we see how the semantics of operations on shared data determine the ease, logical complexity and reliability of a concurrent system implementation.

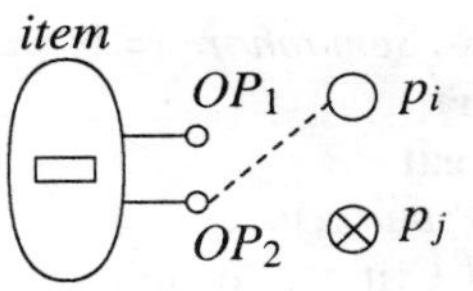

Fig. 13.10 Processes, shared data and operations

13.5 SEMAPHORES

Definition 13.3 (Indivisible operation) *An* indivisible operation *on data d is an operation whose execution cannot overlap in time with the execution of any operation on d.*

Thus, no process can access *d* while an indivisible operation on *d* is in progress. This avoids race conditions on *d*.

Definition 13.4 (Semaphore) *A* semaphore *is a shared integer variable with non-negative values which can only be subjected to the following operations:*

1. *Initialization (specified as part of its declaration)*
2. *Indivisible operations P and V.*

Indivisibility of P and V operations implies that these operations cannot be executed concurrently. This avoids race conditions on the semaphore. Semantics of P and V operations are as follows:

```
P(S)  :  if S > 0
            then S := S - 1;
            else block the process executing
                   the P operation;

V(S)  :  if there exist process(es) blocked on S
            then wake one blocked process;
            else S := S + 1;
```

Thus the P and V operations on a semaphore S either change the value of S, or suspend or wake a process performing a P operation on S. A suspended process is *blocked*, thus avoiding the *busy wait* problem of the algorithmic implementations of CS. A *binary semaphore* is one which only takes the values 0 and 1. Binary semaphores are used to implement mutual exclusion.

Example 13.6 Figure 13.11 illustrates a CS implementation using a binary semaphore. The main program declares a semaphore named *mutex* (and initializes it to 1) and initiates two concurrent processes. Each process performs a P(*mutex*) to gain entry to the CS, and a V(*mutex*) while exiting from the CS. Since *mutex* is initialized to 1, only one process can be in the CS at any time.

var *mutex* : *semaphore* := 1;	
Parbegin	
Repeat	**Repeat**
P(*mutex*);	P(*mutex*);
{ Critical Section }	{ Critical Section }
V(*mutex*);	V(*mutex*);
{ Remainder of the cycle }	{ Remainder of the cycle }
forever;	**forever**;
Parend	
end.	
Process p_i	Process p_j

Fig. 13.11 CS implementation with semaphores

Figure 13.12 illustrates the operation of this program. Note that the P and V operations on *mutex* are enclosed in a dashed rectangular box to indicate that they are mutually exclusive (see pictorial conventions of Fig. 13.9). Let both processes simultaneously attempt the operation P(*mutex*). Being an indivisible operation, only one process can perform it at any time. Let process p_i succeed in performing the operation. Figure 13.12(a) illustrates the situation at the start of p_i's P operation. Figure 13.12(b) shows the situation after p_i completes the P operation and p_j executes its P operation. p_j will be blocked since *mutex* has the value '0'. Figure 13.12(c) shows the situation after process p_i performs a V operation on *mutex*. Process p_j is awakened as a result of the V operation, however the value of *mutex* remains '0'. This is the situation when process p_j performs its V operation on *mutex*. This simply results in increasing the value of *mutex* by '1' (see Fig. 13.12(d)).

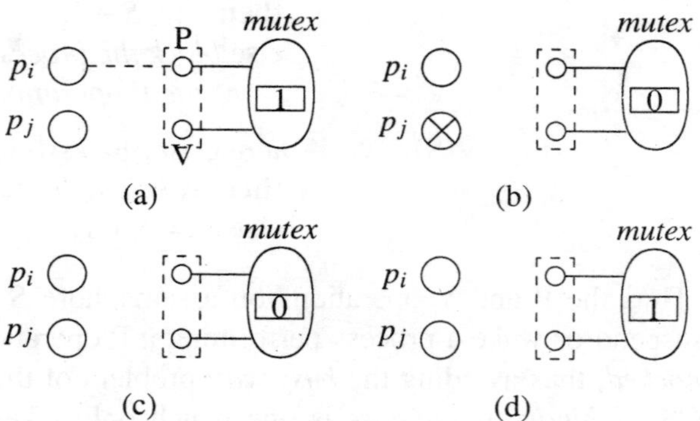

Fig. 13.12 Operation of the program of Figure 13.11

CS implementation using semaphores satisfies the progress condition since choice of the next process to enter the CS is restricted to the set of processes that have performed a P operation. However, the bounded wait condition cannot be guaranteed since the order in which a V operation wakes blocked processes is not defined. Other drawbacks of using semaphores are as follows: P and V operations are *primitives* whose semantics are limited to blocking or waking processes. While these semantics are useful in implementing critical sections, they offer no assistance in ensuring correctness of a solution. For example, the P(*mutex*) and V(*mutex*) operations in the processes of Fig. 13.11 should enclose all accesses to shared data. However, semaphores cannot offer any protection against accesses to shared data *outside* the CS. Further, there is no way to ensure that matching P's and V's exist in a program. For example, a process p_i may be erroneously written as

```
repeat
      V(mutex);
      { Critical Section }
      V(mutex);
      { Remainder of the cycle }
forever
```

using V(*mutex*) instead of P(*mutex*) prior to entering the CS. This violates the correctness condition since it enables many processes to enter the CS simultaneously. If P(*mutex*) is used in place of V(*mutex*) after the CS, a deadlock could result. In either case, a language compiler cannot offer any protection because it is unaware of the program logic.

13.5.1 Implementation of Semaphores

Blocking and awakening of processes in P and V operations requires involvement of the process management component of the OS. Hence semaphores should be implemented by the OS rather than by an application program. Typically, an OS implements semaphores using some special features provided in the machine architecture. This avoids the drawbacks of cost and complexity associated with the algorithmic implementations of CS.

Architectural features for semaphore implementation

Since mid 1960's, a variety of features have been provided in machine architectures to support the implementation of semaphores. The simplest such feature ensures that race conditions cannot arise over accesses to a memory location, i.e. all accesses to a memory location from within an instruction are implemented without permitting another CPU to access that location. This is variously achieved by locking the memory bus (Intel 80x86 processors), by providing an indivisible instruction (IBM/370 and M68000 processors), or by using an atomic swap instruction. We will use the term *indivisible instruction* as a generic term for such features.

Use of a lock variable

An indivisible instruction avoids race conditions on a variable. However the semantics of P and V operations cannot be mapped into single machine instructions. To avoid this problem the arrangement shown in Fig. 13.13 is used. The lock variable is used to ensure mutual exclusion over accesses to the value of the semaphore. Every P or V operation on the semaphore checks the value of the lock variable before accessing the value of the semaphore. This ensures indivisibility of the P and V operations. Race conditions on *lock* are avoided using indivisible instructions as discussed in Ex. 13.7

```
test:   if lock = on
            then goto test;
        lock := on;
        { Access and update the value of semaphore
          to implement a P or V operation }
        lock := off;
```

Fig. 13.13 Semaphore implementation with a lock variable

Example 13.7 IBM/370 supports an indivisible instruction called test-and-set (TS) which tests the value of a memory byte, sets the condition code to indicate whether the value was zero or nonzero, and sets all bits in the byte to 1's. This instruction can be used to implement the statements

```
test:   if lock = on
            then goto test;
```

in Fig. 13.13 as shown in Fig. 13.14. A non-zero value in `LOCK` implies that the lock is 'on'. The `TS` instruction sets the condition code according to the value of `LOCK` and also sets the lock to 'on'. The `BC 7, TEST` instruction checks the condition code and loops back to the `TS` instruction if the lock was already 'on'. The `MVI` instruction puts 0's in all bits of `LOCK`, i.e. sets the lock to 'off'.

```
TEST    TS    LOCK          Test-and-set lock
        BC    7, TEST       Loop if lock was 'on'
      { Access and update the value of semaphore to
        implement a P or V operation }
        MVI   LOCK, X'00'   Reset lock
```

Fig. 13.14 P/V operations using the test-and-set instruction

13.5.2 Producer–Consumer Using Semaphores

Figure 13.15 shows a solution of the bounded buffers problem using semaphores. This solution is a simple extension of the single buffer producer–consumer solution shown in Fig. 13.6. The values of semaphores *empty* and *full* indicate the number of empty and full buffers, respectively. The buffer pointers *i* and *j* are used to ensure that buffers are produced and consumed in FIFO order. A producer and a consumer can operate concurrently so long as some full and some empty buffer(s) exist in the system. It is easy to verify that this solution implements the correctness conditions of the bounded buffer problem described in Section 13.3.1.

```
const                          n = ... ;
type                        item = ...;
var
                            full : Semaphore := 0; { Initializations }
                           empty : Semaphore := n;
             prod_ptr, cons_ptr : integer;
                          buffer : array [0..n − 1] of item;
begin
                 prod_ptr := 0;
                 cons_ptr := 0;
Parbegin
   repeat                                    repeat
      P(empty);                                 P(full);
      buffer[prod_ptr] := ...;                  x := buffer[cons_ptr];
           { i.e. produce }                          { i.e. consume }
      prod_ptr := prod_ptr+1 mod n;             cons_ptr := cons_ptr+1 mod n;
      V(full);                                  V(empty);
   forever;                                  forever;
Parend
end.
            Producer                                  Consumer
```

Fig. 13.15 Bounded buffers using semaphores

Note that a simpler solution would result if a CS is used to control access to the entire set of buffers. However, the solution would suffer from busy waits (e.g. when a producer cannot find an empty buffer) and lack of concurrency between a producer and a consumer. The solution of Fig. 13.15 is superior in these respects. However, if multiple producer and consumer processes exist in the system, we need to add some mutual exclusion amongst producers and amongst consumers. The coding of a solution with multiple producers and consumers is left to the reader (see Problem 2 of Exercise 13.5).

13.5.3 Readers and Writers Using Semaphores

The following counters are introduced to implement readers–writers without writer priority:

1. Count of readers currently reading (a variable named *runread*)
2. Count of readers reading or waiting to read (*totread*)
3. Count of writers currently writing (*runwrite*)
4. Count of writers writing or waiting to write (*totwrite*).

Values of these counters are incremented and decremented at appropriate places in the processes. For example, a reader process increments *totread* when it decides to read and *runread* when it actually starts reading. It decrements both *totread* and *runread* when it finishes reading. The values of these counters are used as follows: A reader is allowed to begin reading when *runwrite* = 0 and a writer is allowed to begin writing when *runread* = 0 and *runwrite* = 0. The value of (*totread*−*runread*) is used to wake all waiting readers when a writer finishes writing. The solution outline of Fig. 13.7 can now be refined as follows:

```
Parbegin
    repeat                              repeat
      if runwrite ≠ 0                     if runread ≠ 0 or
      then                                runwrite ≠ 0 then
         { wait }                            { wait }
      { read }                            { write }
      if totwrite ≠ 0                     if totread ≠ 0 or
      then                                totwrite ≠ 0 then
         if runread = 0                      wake all readers
         then                                or one writer
            wake one writer
    forever;                            forever;
Parend
         Reader(s)                            Writer(s)
```

Readers and writers must be blocked until they can be allowed to start reading or writing. This is best achieved through a P operation. Two semaphores *reading* and *writing* can be used for this purpose. A reader process performs P(*reading*) before starting to read. This should block the reader process if conditions permitting it to read are not currently satisfied. Similarly, a writer process performs a P(*writing*) before writing. Who should perform V operations to wake the reader and writer processes blocked on their P operations? Obviously conditions governing the start of reading or writing were not satisfied when the reader or writer processes were blocked. These conditions change when any of the counts change, i.e. when a reader finishes reading or a writer finishes writing. Hence the processes must perform appropriate V operations after reading or writing.

Note one important issue while implementing this solution. The solution must avoid race conditions on the various counters. Hence checking of a condition to permit a read or write operation must be performed in a critical section. Now consider a reader wishing to start a read operation. It can enter a CS (say, on a semaphore named *mutex*) to check if *runwrite* = 0. If the condition is satisfied, it can increment *runread*, exit the CS and start reading straightaway. If the condition is not satisfied, it must perform P(*reading*). However, it must not perform P(*reading*) inside the

CS on *mutex*, as this would prohibit any other process from accessing the counters. (This could lead to a deadlock!) An approach called the *self-scheduling approach* is employed to overcome this problem. Let the reader always perform a P(*reading*) after exiting the CS on *mutex*. If conditions permitting the start of a read operation were satisfied when it examined the counter values inside the CS, it should have performed a V(*reading*) itself. Such a reader will get past the P(*reading*) operation on exiting the CS. A writer will similarly perform a V(*writing*) inside the CS on *mutex* under the correct set of conditions and P(*writing*) after exiting the CS. Readers and writers which get blocked on their respective P operation would wake up sometime in the future when a process performs a V operation after reading or writing. We are now ready to present the solution. This is given in Fig. 13.16. Note that the solution does not give writers priority over readers.

EXERCISE 13.5

1. Extend the Producer–consumer solution of Fig. 13.6 to permit many producer and consumer processes.
2. Rewrite Fig. 13.15 using a semaphore for mutual exclusion and full and empty as counters. Would your solution need any changes if more producer or consumer processes are to be added to the system? Explain clearly.
3. Extend the readers–writers solution of Fig. 13.16 to provide writer priority.
4. The reader process of Fig. 13.16 is modified to perform a P(*reading*) inside the CS on *mutex* (rather than performing it after the CS) when $runwrite \neq 0$. Show that a deadlock can arise due to this modification.
5. Processes in an OS often need to acquire many resources simultaneously. Two new operations *multiple_P* and *multiple_V* are proposed for this purpose as follows:

   Multiple_P(i, j): block the process if a P(i) or P(j) would have led to blocking, else perform P(i) and P(j).

   Multiple_V(i, j): perform V(i) and V(j).

   (a) Can *Multiple_P* and *Multiple_V* be implemented using P and V operations? Give reasons for your answer.
   (b) Develop a scheme to implement these new operations.
   (c) Is the scheme developed in problem 5(a) free of deadlock possibilities? Justify your answer.

13.6 CRITICAL REGIONS

The critical region (CR) is a control structure for implementing mutual exclusion over a shared variable. A concurrent program using a critical region looks as follows:

```
begin
    Var x : shared <type> := < initial_value>;
    Parbegin
        repeat                { process p_i }
            Region x do
```

```
var
    totread, runread, totwrite, runwrite : integer;
                    reading, writing : semaphore := 0;
                              mutex : semaphore := 1;
begin
    totread := 0;
    runread := 0;
    totwrite := 0;
    runwrite := 0;
Parbegin
  repeat                                  repeat
    P(mutex);                               P(mutex);
    totread := totread+1;                   totwrite := totwrite+1;
    if runwrite = 0 then                    if runread = 0 then
        runread := runread+1;                   runwrite := 1;
        V(reading);                             V(writing);
    V(mutex);                               V(mutex);
    P(reading);                             P(writing);
    { Read }                                { Write }
    P(mutex);                               P(mutex);
    runread := runread−1;                   runwrite := runwrite−1;
    totread := totread−1;                   totwrite := totwrite−1;
    if runread = 0 and                      while(runread<totread) do
        totwrite > runwrite                 begin
      then                                      runread := runread+1;
        runwrite := 1;                          V(reading);
        V(writing);                         end;
    V(mutex);                               if runread = 0 and
  forever;                                  totwrite > runwrite then
                                                runwrite := 1;
                                                V(writing);
                                            V(mutex);
                                          forever;

Parend
end.
                    Reader(s)                 Writer(s)
```

Fig. 13.16 Readers and Writers using semaphores

```
                begin
                ┌ - - - - - - - - ┐
                ¦ Access shared   ¦
                ¦   variable x    ¦
                └ - - - - - - - - ┘
                end;
              { Remainder of the cycle }
              forever
          Parend
      end
```

where the construct **Region** *x* **do** .. forms a critical region on variable *x*. Variable *x* is called the CR control variable. The keyword **shared** in the declaration of *x* indicates that it is a shared variable. Due to this, *x* can be accessed only within a **Region** *x* **do** .. construct; its use anywhere else is flagged as an error by the compiler. The compiler implements the **Region** *x* **do** .. construct as a CS on the CR control variable *x*. This implementation, possibly using P and V operations on semaphores, is invisible to the programmer.

Figure 13.17 illustrates the use of CRs in mutual exclusion. Here *info* is declared to be a shared variable, and mutual exclusion is implemented by merely using the **Region** *info* **do** ... construct. Use of *info* outside a **Region** *info* **do** ... construct would be flagged by the compiler. Thus, any program violating the correctness conditions of CS would be rejected by the compiler. A CR is very convenient for mutual exclusion. However, it is less versatile than a semaphore. It cannot be used for process synchronization since it lacks the ability to block a process for any reason other than mutual exclusion. Example 13.8 illustrates this aspect.

```
Var  info : Shared ... ;
begin
Parbegin
  repeat                                repeat
     ...                                   ...
     Region info do                        Region info do
     begin                                 begin
        { Access info }                       { Access info }
     end;                                  end;
     { Remainder of the cycle }            { Remainder of the cycle }
     ...                                   ...
  forever;                              forever;
Parend
end.
```

Fig. 13.17 Mutual exclusion with critical regions

Example 13.8 The single buffer producers–consumers problem can be implemented using critical regions as shown in Fig. 13.18. Here, the CR control variable *buffer* is a record consisting of a boolean status flag for the buffer, and a field to store the message text. As in the solution outline of Fig. 13.6, a producer enters mutual exclusion to check the status of the buffer. If the buffer is full it releases the CS without producing. This check is repeated till it finds an empty buffer to produce in. A consumer analogously suffers a busy wait when all buffers are empty. These busy wait problems cannot be avoided because the CR construct lacks a feature for blocking a process under a condition.

```
var
    buffer :  Shared record
                  full : boolean := false; { Initialization }
              message : character;
              end
begin
Parbegin
    var p_found : boolean;                  var c_found : boolean;
    repeat                                  repeat
        p_found := false;                       c_found := false;
        while (not p_found) do                  while (not c_found) do
            Region buffer do                        Region buffer do
            begin                                   begin
                if full = false then                    if full = true then
                begin                                   begin
                  { produce in                            { consume from
                    buffer.message }                        buffer.message }
                  full := true;                           full := false;
                  p_found := true;                        c_found := true;
                end;                                    end;
            end;                                    end;
        { Remainder of the cycle }              { Remainder of the cycle }
    forever;                                forever;
Parend
end.
                    Producer                                Consumer
```

Fig. 13.18 Producer-Consumer using critical regions

13.7 CONDITIONAL CRITICAL REGIONS

The conditional critical region (CCR) is a control structure with the following features:

1. It provides mutual exclusion analogous to the CR construct.
2. It permits a process executing the CCR to block itself until an arbitrary boolean condition becomes 'true'.

A concurrent program using the CCR construct looks as follows:

```
Begin
    Var x : shared <type> := < initial_value>;
    Parbegin
        repeat
            Region x do
            begin
             ┌ - - - - - - - - ┐
             |    ...          |
             |  await (B);     |
             |    ...          |
             └ - - - - - - - - ┘
            end;
        { Remainder of the cycle }
        forever
    Parend
end
```

where B is a boolean condition. Variable x is called the CCR control variable.

Semantics of a CCR on control variable x are as follows: The compiler implements the CCR as a CS on variable x. A process executing the CCR enters the CS on variable x and executes till it reaches the **await**(B) statement. If condition B evaluates to true, the process continues execution of the CS, else it releases mutual exclusion and blocks itself waiting for B to become true. Some other process can now enter the CCR. Some time in future, when condition B is true, the process blocked on B wakes up and resumes execution of the CS at the statement following **await**(B). Needless to say, the resumed execution is also performed as a CS on x.

The ability to wait on an arbitrary condition inside the CS overcomes the deficiency of the CR construct discussed in the previous section. This can be seen in Fig. 13.19 which contains a solution of the bounded buffer problem using CCRs. *full* is a shared integer in this solution. The producer produces under the condition $full < size$, while the consumer consumes under the condition $full > 0$. For maximum concurrency in the system the producer first produces in a local variable *produced_info* and enters the CCR to simply put the produced information into the buffer. Similarly the consumer copies out the information to be consumed into local variable *for_consumption*, and performs its processing outside the region. Note that the compiler guarantees mutual exclusion over the CCR control variable *buffer_pool*. This ensures consistency of its fields *full, prod_ptr* and *cons_ptr*. More producer and consumer processes can be added without any changes to the code of the producer and consumer processes.

Figure 13.20 contains a solution to the readers–writers problem using CCRs. A writer performs writing inside the CS, whereas a reader reads outside the CS. This is because writers must be mutually exclusive, while readers can be concurrent. Correctness is ensured as follows: When readers are active, $runread > 0$ blocks a writer from reaching the write statement. Similarly $runwrite > 0$ blocks a reader

```
const    n = ... ;
type  item =  ... ;
var
    buffer_pool : Shared record
                      buffer : array [0..n − 1] of item;
                        size : integer := n;
                        full : integer := 0;
                    prod_ptr : integer := 0;
                    cons_ptr : integer := 0;
                  end
begin
Parbegin
    var produced_info : char;               var for_consumption : char;
    repeat                                  repeat
       Region buffer_pool do                   Region buffer_pool do
       begin                                   begin
          await (full < size);                    await (full > 0);
          buffer[prod_ptr]                        for_consumption :=
              := produced_info;                        buffer[cons_ptr];
              { i.e. produce }                         { i.e. consume }
          prod_ptr :=                             cons_ptr :=
              prod_ptr+1 mod size;                     cons_ptr+1 mod size;
          full := full+1;                         full := full−1;
       end;                                    end;
       { Remainder of the cycle }              { Remainder of the cycle }
    forever;                                forever;
Parend
end.
                 Producer                              Consumer
```

Fig. 13.19 Bounded buffer using conditional critical regions

from reading. When a writer completes, a reader blocked on *runwrite* $= 0$ wakes up and exits the CS. This enables another reader blocked on the same condition to wake up, and so on until all readers wake up.

Note that the count *runwrite* of this solution is redundant. Its purpose is to block a reader from entering the CS if a writer is writing. However, since writing is performed inside the CS, no reader can enter CS while a writer is writing! A compact and elegant solution is obtained by eliminating the count and the **await** (*runwrite* = 0) statement in the reader process.

13.7.1 Implementation of CCR

Implementation of the **await** statement is straightforward. The compiler can generate code to evaluate the condition and make an OS call to block the process if the condition is false. How should the blocked process be awakened? As discussed in

```
type item =  ... ;
var
      read_write :  shared record
                        runread : integer := 0;
                       runwrite : integer := 0;
                    end
begin
Parbegin
    repeat                                      repeat
      Region read_write do                        Region read_write do
      begin                                       begin
        await (runwrite = 0);                       await (runread = 0);
        runread := runread+1;                       runwrite := runwrite+1;
      end;                                          { Write }
      { Read }                                      runwrite := runwrite−1;
      Region readwrt do;                          end;
        runread := runread−1;                     { Remainder of the cycle }
      end;                                      forever;
      { Remainder of the cycle }
    forever;
Parend
end.
                  Reader(s)                               Writer(s)
```

Fig. 13.20 Readers and Writers without writer priority

chapter 11, this is best achieved by linking the condition in the **await** statement with an event known to the scheduling component of the OS. In Fig. 13.19, conditions in the **await** statements (viz. *full* < *size* and *full* > 0) involve fields of *buffer_pool*. Since each CCR is implemented as a CS on *buffer_pool*, these conditions can change only due to the execution of a CCR by some process. Hence the **await** conditions of all blocked processes can be checked every time a process exits a CCR. A blocked process whose **await** condition is satisfied can now be scheduled.

However, unblocking of a process is not always so simple. The semantics of CCR permit the use of any boolean condition in an **await** statement. If the condition does not involve a field of the CCR control variable, execution of a statement outside a CCR may also change the truth value of an **await** condition. For example, conditions involving the local variables of a process, or involving values returned by OS calls like time-of-day, can become true even if no process executes a CCR. Such conditions will have to be checked periodically to wake up blocked processes. This increases the overheads of implementing CCRs, which makes them less attractive.

EXERCISE 13.7

1. Discuss whether the following primitives and constructs satisfy the bounded wait con-

dition
   (a) Semaphores
   (b) Critical regions
   (c) Conditional critical regions.
2. Modify Fig. 13.20 to implement writer priority.
3. Processes requesting a resource are required to gain access to it in a FIFO manner. Each concurrent process is coded as

```
repeat
      ...
      request-resource(resource_id);
      { Use resource }
      release-resource(resource_id);
      { Remainder of the cycle }
forever
```

Develop the procedures *request-resource* and *release-resource* using
   (a) semaphores
   (b) conditional critical regions.

13.8 MONITORS

Monitors provide abstraction and encapsulation support for structuring large concurrent systems. The features of monitors are described after introducing the fundamentals of abstraction and encapsulation.

13.8.1 Abstraction

An abstraction is a simplified description of an object that emphasizes the essential details of the object and ignores its inessential details. In program development, abstraction is used to specify the usage aspects of a program entity and to hide its implementation details. This enables the implementation of an entity to be changed without affecting its usage. Programming languages typically support *procedural abstraction* by separating the interface of a procedure (i.e. its name and parameter specification) from its implementation. A program using the procedure only needs to know its interface. This permits the procedure body to be modified without affecting its callers.

Data abstraction similarly separates the usage aspects of data from their implementation. The interface of abstract data with their users consists of the specification of legal values of data and legal operations over data (which are coded as procedures). This permits representation of data or implementation of their operations to be changed without affecting their users.

The *class* concept of Simula is the first widely-known data abstraction construct. Figure 13.21 shows a Simula class named `stack`. It consists of an array named `locations` to store the values existing in the stack, and variable `pointer` to point to the top element of the stack. Stack operations `push` and `pop` are coded as procedures.

Note that a class is a type. Many variables of this type, called *instances* of the class, can be created. Each instance contains a copy of the data structures declared in the class. In Fig. 13.21, each instance of `stack` contains an array named `locations` and a variable named `pointer`. Code of the class procedures is shared by all instances of the class. The initialization code of the class is executed for each instance of the class. It effectively initializes `pointer` to *null*.

```
type stack = class
   var
      locations :  array [1..100] of integer;
        pointer :  1..100;

   procedure entry push (element : integer);
   begin
      if pointer < 100 then
      begin
         pointer := pointer+1;
         locations[pointer] := element;
      end;
   end;

   procedure entry pop (element : integer);
   begin
      if pointer > 0 then
      begin
         element := locations[pointer];
         pointer := pointer-1;
      end;
   end;

   begin { Initialization code }
      pointer := 0;
end.
```

Fig. 13.21 A class of Simula 67

Example 13.9 Using the class `stack`, the following Simula program segment creates and uses a stack:

```
type stack = class
   ...
end;

var  nodestack : stack;
          info : integer;
begin
   nodestack.push(25);
   ...
   nodestack.pop(info);
end.
```

Declaration of `nodestack` leads to an *instantiation* of class `stack`. This involves creation of a copy of the data structures declared in the class and execution of the initialization code of the class, which will set `pointer` of `nodestack` to 0. The statement `nodestack.push(25);` invokes procedure `push` of class `stack` which pushes the value 25 on `nodestack`, while `nodestack.pop(info);` pops an element off `nodestack` and puts it into variable `info`.

In Ex. 13.9, changing the representation of the stack from an array to a linked list would not affect its usage through the stack operations `push` and `pop`.

13.8.2 Encapsulation

Abstraction separates the observable behaviour of an entity from the details of its implementation. It is useful in understanding the functioning of a complex system. However, one more feature is needed to make the implementation of a complex system reliable—the implementation details of an entity should be hidden from its users. This would ensure that one part of a system does not depend on the implementation details of another part for its correct functioning.

Encapsulation is the 'packaging' of data and procedural abstractions to provide 'localization' of an entity's implementation details. This ensures separation of the entity's interface from its implementation. Localization is achieved by 'hiding' the implementation details of a data or operation from the rest of the system; only the interface of the entity is visible in the rest of the system. Thus, a program using an encapsulated entity can access it only through its interface. This improves the reliability of a program. Hiding of the implementation details is enforced by the language compiler. It flags as an error any attempt in one entity to refer to the implementation details of another entity.

Example 13.10 Simula does not provide encapsulation. Hence it is possible for a program to 'see' the implementation details of an abstract entity. For example, consider `nodestack`, an instance of class `stack` in Ex. 13.9. A user of `nodestack` can access the array which stores the values of `nodestack`, and remove or modify an element of it. This conflicts with the semantics of class `stack`, which only permits `push` and `pop` operations to be performed. An encapsulated implementation of class `stack` would not suffer from these drawbacks as the compiler would only permit `push` and `pop` operations on it.

Encapsulation is depicted by extending the pictorial convention described in Section 13.4. A double box is used to represent encapsulated data. Figure 13.22 shows the Simula variable `nodestack` and an encapsulated stack `en_stack`. Using this convention, a semaphore should be depicted using a double oval. However, for simplicity we continue to use single boxes and ovals when encapsulation is obvious from the context.

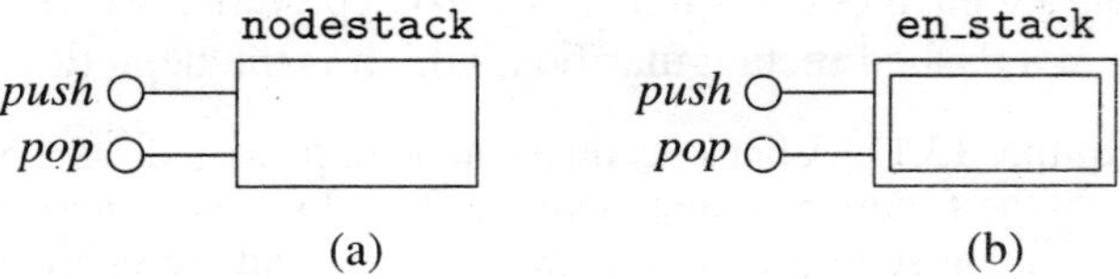

Fig. 13.22 (a) A Simula stack, (b) An encapsulated stack

13.8.3 Features of Monitors

Early language features for concurrency provided control constructs for mutual exclusion and synchronization (we will use the term *control abstraction* for these features) but did not provide data abstraction features. For example, a semaphore could be used to implement critical sections, but it had no notion of shared data. The CR and CCR constructs provided structured ways to implement a CS on shared data but permitted arbitrary manipulation of shared data within the CS. In contrast, monitors provide encapsulation support for data abstraction, control abstraction and procedural abstraction. This permits monitors to be used as building blocks in reliable construction of large concurrent systems. Early proposals for monitors were made by Brinch Hansen (1973) and Hoare (1974).

A monitor type consists of the following four components:

1. Declaration of shared data
2. Initialization of shared data
3. Operations on shared data
4. Synchronization statements.

Syntactically, the first 3 components closely resemble the corresponding components of a Simula class (see Fig. 13.21). However, their semantics are aimed at concurrency control. Encapsulation is also aimed at concurrency control.

A program can define a monitor type and create many instances of the type, each instance being a monitor. On creation of a monitor, the initialization code is executed to initialize its shared data. Operations over shared data are coded as procedures in the monitor type. These operations can be invoked by concurrent processes. They represent the only legal ways to manipulate the shared data. Each monitor is implemented as a CS to ensure consistency of its data. Thus at most one monitor procedure can be actively manipulating a monitor's data at any moment. Calls on monitor procedures are serviced in FIFO manner to satisfy the bounded wait property. This is realized by maintaining a queue of processes wishing to execute monitor procedures.

It may be noted that a monitor provides two kinds of encapsulation. The first kind supports data abstraction by encapsulating the data and operations of the monitor. The second kind encapsulates monitor operations for mutual exclusion by implementing each operation as a CS. To depict this, we enclose the operations of a monitor in a dashed rectangular box, which is the depiction of a CS (see Section 13.2).

Example 13.11 A bank account can be implemented as a monitor. The monitor would have the following components: a shared variable *current_balance*, an initialization statement setting *current_balance* to '0', and the operations *credit* and *debit*. Use of the monitor would eliminate race conditions on *current_balance* during credit and debit transactions.

Condition variables

A *condition* is similar to an event in the sense described in Section 10.2.3. A condition variable is associated with each condition. It is used to synchronize the execution of processes sharing a monitor according to the occurrence of the condition. A condition variable is declared using the syntax

var x : **condition**;

Two operations are possible on a condition variable. A process can await the occurrence of condition x using the syntax x.**wait**, or signal the occurrence of condition x using the syntax x.**signal**. When a process executing a monitor procedure encounters an x.**wait** statement, it releases mutual exclusion of the monitor and blocks on condition x. Processes blocked on the same condition are put into a queue. When a process executes an x.**signal** statement inside a monitor procedure, it activates, in FIFO manner, one process blocked on condition x. Semantics of the conditions used in a monitor differ from those of semaphores and the conditions in a conditional critical region in some vital ways. A signal is lost if no process is waiting on the condition. Thus, a process executing a **wait** is necessarily blocked until the condition is signalled. Further, only one process can wake up as a result of a **signal**. A condition may have to be signalled several times if all blocked processes are to wake up.

Note that many processes might be blocked on a monitor at a given time. Some of them might be wishing to enter the monitor through a procedure call, while others might be blocked on conditions. To ensure bounded waits in the system, the implementation favours processes blocked on conditions over those wishing to enter through procedure calls.

Example 13.12 Figure 13.23 illustrates a monitor to implement a semaphore. Variable *busy* is a status flag for the critical section. *busy* = *true* implies that some process is currently using the critical section. *busy* is initialized to *false* when monitor *Semaphore* is created.

Let the semaphore be used by three processes, p_1, p_2 and p_3, two of which are shown in Fig. 13.23. Let p_1 be the first process to perform a P operation. Since *busy* is *false*, it changes *busy* to *true* and enters the CS. If p_2 performs P while p_1 is still inside the CS, it would be blocked because of the statement *non_busy*.**wait** in procedure P. It waits in the queue associated with the condition variable *non_busy*. Process p_3 now invokes operation P. p_3 will wait in the queue associated with entry to monitor *Semaphore*. Now let p_1 perform the V operation.

```
type sem_type = Monitor
    Var
            busy : boolean;
        non_busy : condition;
    Procedure entry P;
    begin
        if busy = true then non_busy.wait;
        busy := true;
    end;
    Procedure entry V;
    begin
        busy := false;
        non_busy.signal;
    end;
    begin {initialization}
        busy := false;
end;
var Semaphore : sem_type;
begin
Parbegin
  repeat                                    repeat
     Semaphore.P;                              Semaphore.P;
     { Critical Section }                      { Critical Section }
     Semaphore.V;                              Semaphore.V;
     { Remainder of the cycle }                { Remainder of the cycle }
  forever;                                  forever;
Parend
end.
              Process p1                                Process p2
```

Fig. 13.23 Monitor implementation of a Semaphore

Figure 13.24 illustrates a snapshot of the system at the current moment of time. Queues associated with the condition variable *non_busy* and entry to the monitor contain processes p_2 and p_3, respectively. When process p_1 executes a **signal** and exits from the monitor, process p_2 will wake up since queues associated with condition variables have priority over the queue associated with entry to the monitor. Process p_3 will enter the monitor only when process p_2 completes execution of the P operation and exits the monitor. p_3 will now enter and block itself on the condition *non_busy*. It will wake up when p_2 executes the V operation.

An interesting synchronization problem arises when process p_1 of Fig. 13.23 invokes the V operation which performs a *non_busy* **.signal**. This **signal** is expected to wake up process p_2, which would resume its execution of the P operation. At the same time, process p_1 would continue its execution of the V operation. Since the monitor is implemented as a CS, only one of them can execute. So which of them

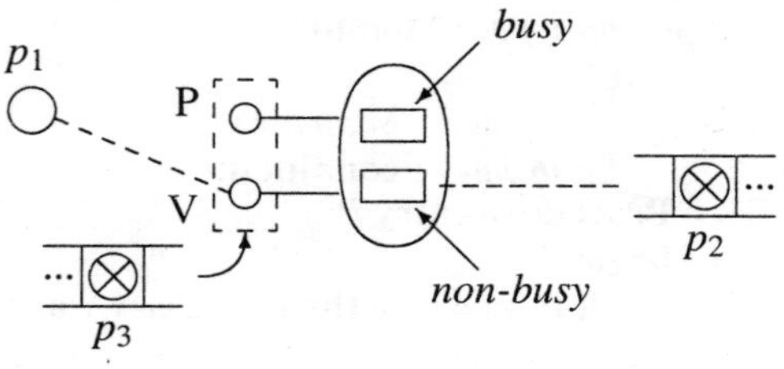

Fig. 13.24 Snapshot of the system of Example 13.12

should be scheduled? Scheduling of process p_2 would delay the signalling process p_1, which seems unfair. Scheduling of p_1 would imply that p_2 does not really wake up now. Hoare's monitors implement the first alternative. In Hansen's work, a **signal** statement is required to be the last statement of a CS. Hence the process executing **signal** exits the CS immediately. The awakened process can now enter the CS to resume its execution.

Use of condition variables has two advantages: First, a **signal** has no effect if no process is blocked on the condition variable. This simplifies the logic of the procedures as we will see in Ex. 13.13. Second, unlike the conditional critical region, processes are woken up by explicit **signal**'s. This avoids repeated checking to determine when a *blocked* process can be woken up, thus reducing the overheads of process synchronization.

Example 13.13 Figure 13.25 shows an implementation of bounded buffers using monitors. The code for procedures *Produce* and *Consume* is analogous to that using the conditional critical region except for one significant difference: A process executing a **wait** operation on a condition variable needs to be woken up explicitly. This is why corresponding to a *buff_empty*.**wait** in procedure *produce*, a *buff_empty*.**signal** has to exist in procedure *consume*. As mentioned before, a signal is lost if no process is waiting. This simplifies the solution since a process need not consider whether any process is waiting before executing a **signal**.

13.8.4 Disk Scheduler : A Case Study

A set of user processes share a moving head disk. A disk scheduler schedules IO operations on the disk to optimize its throughput (see Section 16.3.3 for a discussion of disk scheduling). To code the disk scheduler as a monitor, we identify its key elements, viz. shared data and operations on shared data.

1. *Shared data:* Data concerning pending IO operations. The data can be organized as a queue called *IO_queue*.
2. *Operations on shared data:* The following operations can be identified
   (a) Add an IO operation to *IO_queue*
   (b) Delete an IO operation from *IO_queue*
   (c) Analyse the IO operations in *IO_queue* and perform scheduling.

```
type Bounded_buffer_type = Monitor
    const   n = ... ;
    type  item = ... ;
    Var
                          buffer : array [0..n – 1] of item;
        full, prod_ptr, cons_ptr : integer;
                       buff_full : condition;
                      buff_empty : condition;
    Procedure entry produce (produced_info : item);
    begin
      if full = n then buff_empty.wait;
      buffer[prod_ptr] := produced_info; { i.e. Produce }
      prod_ptr := prod_ptr+1 mod n;
      full := full + 1;
      buff_full.signal;
    end;
    Procedure entry consume (for_consumption : item);
    begin
      if full = 0 then buff_full.wait;
      for_consumption := buffer[cons_ptr]; { i.e. consume }
      cons_ptr := cons_ptr+1 mod n;
      full := full – 1 ;
      buff_empty.signal;
    end;
    begin { initialization }
      full := 0;
      prod_ptr := 0;
      cons_ptr := 0;
end;
begin
var B_buf : Bounded_buffer_type;
Parbegin
     var msg : item;                      var area : item;
     repeat                               repeat
        B_buf.produce (msg);                 B_buf.consume (area);
        { Remainder of the cycle }           { Remainder of the cycle }
     forever;                             forever;
Parend
end
          Producer                             Consumer
```

Fig. 13.25 Bounded buffers using monitors

These operations are coded as monitor procedures *IO_request*, *IO_complete* and *IO_schedule*.

Processes are created in the program which uses the monitor. These consist of a disk scheduling process and user processes which wish to perform IO operations (see Fig. 13.26). Figure 13.27 shows the monitor type *Disk_Mon_type*. The scheduling process realizes disk scheduling by repeatedly invoking the monitor procedure *IO_schedule*. *IO_schedule* blocks the scheduling process till scheduling needs to be performed, i.e. till the first IO request arrives, or till the IO request in progress completes. A user process issues an IO request by invoking the monitor procedure *IO_request*. *IO_request* queues the request and blocks the requesting process. When the scheduling policy decides which IO request to initiate, the user process making the request is woken up and exits the monitor procedure *IO_request*. It now executes the code corresponding to the IO operation (see the step 'Perform IO operation' in Fig. 13.26), and calls the monitor procedure *IO_complete*. This call is simply intended to inform the scheduler that the IO request is completed. It awakens the scheduling process which performs a scheduling decision, completes its execution of *IO_schedule*, and calls *IO_schedule* once again to schedule the next IO request. Needless to say that the blocking and awakening of processes is performed within the monitor procedures called by them.

```
var Disk_scheduler : Disk_Mon_type;
Parbegin
    begin { User process i }
        repeat
            Disk_scheduler.IO_request (i, track);
            { Perform IO Operation }
            Disk_scheduler.IO_complete (i);
            { Remainder of the cycle }
        forever
    end;
    begin { Scheduling process }
        repeat
            Disk_scheduler.IO_Schedule;
        forever;
    end;
Parend.
```

Fig. 13.26 User processes and the scheduling process

The monitor defines an array of condition variables called *proceed*, each element of which is used to synchronize a specific user process, and a condition variable *schedule_next* which is used to synchronize the scheduling process with user processes. The scheduling process repeatedly calls procedure *IO_schedule*, which executes *schedule_next*.**wait** to await the time when the next IO request can be scheduled. When a user process p_i calls the monitor procedure *IO_request* with its own

```
type Disk_Mon_type : Monitor
    const
            n = ... ; { Size of IO queue }
            m = ... ; { Number of user processes }
    type    Q_element = record ... end;
    var
                    IO_Queue : array [1..n] of Q_element;
                    proceed : array [1..m] of condition;
                schedule_next : condition;
        IO_in_progress, count : integer;
    Procedure entry IO_request (proc_id, track_no : integer);
    begin
        { Enter proc_id and track_no in IO_Queue }
        count := count + 1;
        if count > 1 then proceed[proc_id].wait;
        IO_in_progress := proc_id;
    end;
    Procedure entry IO_complete (proc_id : integer);
    begin
        if IO_in_progress = proc_id then
        begin
            count := count − 1;
            { Remove request of this process from IO_Queue }
            IO_in_progress := 0;
            schedule_next.signal;
        end;
    end;
    Procedure entry IO_schedule;
    var k : integer;
    begin
        schedule_next.wait;
        if count > 0 then
        begin
            { Select the IO operation to be initiated. Get its proc_id
              from IO_Queue }
            proceed[proc_id].signal;
        end;
    end;
    begin { Initializations }
        count := 0;
        IO_in_progress := 0;
end;
```

Fig. 13.27 A disk monitor and a program using it

id and details of the required IO, procedure *IO_request* executes the statement *proceed*[*i*].**wait** if the IO request cannot be scheduled straightaway (i.e. if a previous IO operation is in progress). This blocks process p_i until its IO request can be scheduled. A process whose IO request has been scheduled, executes the step 'Perform IO operation' and calls the monitor procedure *IO_complete*. *IO_complete* executes a **signal** on *schedule_next* to indicate that scheduling needs to be performed. This wakes the scheduling process which resumes its execution of *IO_schedule*. *IO_schedule* now analyses all pending IO requests, determines which IO request should be initiated next, and finds the id of the process issuing the IO request. Let this be process p_j. *IO_schedule* now executes *proceed*[*j*].**signal**. This awakens process p_j, which proceeds with its IO operation. Details of IO request queuing and the scheduling policy in force are not shown explicitly.

EXERCISE 13.8

1. An airline reservation system is to be implemented using monitors. The system must process booking and cancellation requests and perform appropriate actions.
   (a) Identify the data structures, procedures and processes that must exist,
   (b) Implement the reservation system using monitors.
2. A customer wishes to give the following instructions to his bank manager: Do not credit any funds to my account if the balance in my account exceeds n, and hold any debits until the balance in the account is large enough to permit the debit.
   Implement a bank account using a monitor to implement these instructions (*Hint:* Use the monitor of Ex. 13.11).
3. An interprocess message communication system is to be implemented using monitors. The system handles messages exchanged by 4 user processes, using a global pool of 20 buffers. The system is to operate as follows:
   (a) Asymmetric communication is used, i.e. a sender names the receiver, but the receiver does not name the sender.
   (b) The system allocates a message buffer and copies the sender's message in it. If no free buffer exists, the sender is blocked until a message buffer becomes available.
   (c) When a receiver performs a *receive*, it is given messages meant for it in a FIFO manner. A message is copied into the area provided by the receiver, and the message buffer is freed. A receiver is blocked if no messages exist for it.
   (d) The system detects a deadlock if one arises.

   Write a monitor called *Communication_Manager* to perform the above functions. What are the condition variables used in it? Clearly explain how blocked senders and receivers wake up.
4. A monitor is to be written to simulate a clock manager used for real-time control of concurrent processes. The clock manager is to have an internal clock to keep track of the time of the day. A typical request made to the manager is 'wake me up at 9.00 a.m.'. The manager blocks the processes making such requests and arranges to wake them up at the designated times.

   (a) Are condition variables adequate for this purpose?
   (b) Implement the monitor.

5. In Fig. 13.25 producers and consumers always execute the statements *buf_full*.**signal** and *buf_empty*.**signal**. This is expensive in practice. Suggest and implement a method of reducing the number of **signal** statements executed during the operation of the system.
6. Nesting of monitor calls implies that a procedure in monitor A calls a procedure of another monitor, say monitor B. During execution of the nested call, the procedure of monitor A continues to hold its mutual exclusion. Prove that nested monitor calls can lead to deadlocks.
7. Write a short note on the implementation of monitors. Your note must discuss
   (a) how to achieve mutual exclusion between the monitor procedures.
   (b) whether monitor procedures need to be coded in a re- entrant manner.

13.9 CONCURRENT PROGRAMMING IN ADA

Ada is a programming language designed for embedded system applications. The 'package' construct of Ada provides encapsulation of abstract data and operations. Ada facilitates top down programming by separating the specification of a program unit, e.g. a package or a procedure, from its implementation. A program utilizing a package only needs to know the details in its 'specification' part. The implementation is contained in its 'body' part which can be compiled separately. This arrangement simplifies the updating or substitution of a package or procedure body without affecting other components of a software system, so long as its specification remains unchanged.

Figure 13.28 illustrates an implementation of a stack in the form of an Ada package. The package has 2 parts—a specification part and a body part. Note the close similarity of this package with the Simula class `stack` of Fig. 13.21, the only significant difference being the presence of a specification part for the package. The statement **with stack** enables the use of entities declared in package `stack`. These entities can now be referenced using a qualified name, e.g. `stack.push(..)`. Entities declared in the package body are visible only to the procedures of the package body. Additionally, procedures can define local entities for their own use. The **begin** part of the package body is executed when the package body is elaborated, i.e. instantiated. It is used to initialize data declared within the package body. An entity (data or procedure) can be encapsulated by prefixing its declaration with the keyword **private**. Figure 13.29 shows encapsulation of a stack; the entities declared in it cannot be accessed from outside.

13.9.1 Tasks in Ada

A *task* is the unit of concurrency in an Ada program. Tasks are encapsulated within a package or within a procedure. Execution of a task is initiated when the package containing the task is instantiated or when the procedure containing the task is called.

```
Package stack is -- Package specification
   Procedure Push(x : in Integer);
   Function Pop return Integer;
end stack;

Package body stack is -- Package body
   S : array (1..100) of Integer;
   Top_of_stack :  Integer range 1..100;

   Procedure push(x : in Integer) is
      if top_of_stack < 100 then
      begin
         Top_of_stack := Top_of_stack + 1;
         S(Top_of_stack) := x;
      end;
   end push;

   Function pop return Integer is
      val :  Integer;
      if Top_of_stack > 0 then
      begin
         val := S(Top_of_stack);
         Top_of_stack := Top_of_stack - 1;
      return val;
      end;
   end pop;

      begin -- initialization
      Top_of_stack := 0;
end stack;

                                          -- package use
with stack
   stack.push(..);
```

Fig. 13.28 Definition and use of an Ada package

Tasks encapsulated within a procedure or a package can share some nonlocal data.

The *rendezvous* mechanism implements synchronization between a pair of tasks. A task declares an 'entry' and associates some code, called the rendezvous code, with it. For example, consider a task B which declares an entry `comp`. Rendezvous between tasks A and B takes place only when task A invokes entry `comp` and task B executes the statement `accept comp`. The rendezvous code is now executed by task `B`. The rendezvous mechanism is asymmetric in that the calling task (task `A`) is suspended while the rendezvous code is executed by the called task (task `B`).

Figure 13.30 contains an Ada package for buffered processing of an input file.

```
Package stack is -- Package specification
   type stack_type is private;
   Procedure Push(x : in Integer);
   Function Pop return Integer;
   private
      type stack_type is
         record
            S : array (1..100) of Integer;
            Top_of_stack : Integer range 1..100;
         end record;
end stack;
```

Fig. 13.29 Private data in Ada

Two tasks `buf_inp` and `calculate` are encapsulated within the body of procedure `xyz`. Both tasks start executing when the procedure is called. Task `buf_inp` reads and buffers the next record of the standard input file. `calculate` invokes entry `Get` of `buf_inp` to obtain the next input record. `buf_inp` hands over the buffered record to `calculate` in the rendezvous code associated with `Get`.

When `calculate` and `buf_inp` start executing, they both run freely until they encounter the need for rendezvous. Let task `buf_inp` read one record of the input file and encounter the **accept** statement before task calculate reaches the call on `Get`. Task `buf_inp` would now be suspended until the rendezvous materializes. When task `calculate` executes the statement `buf_inp.Get(x);` a rendezvous is realized and task `calculate` is suspended. `buf_inp` now wakes up and executes the rendezvous code which transfers one input record to variable `x` of `calculate`. After the rendezvous code is executed, both tasks run freely again. `buf_inp` now reads the next input record and holds it in a buffer until the next rendezvous. If task `calculate` is faster, it might reach the call on `Get` before `buf_inp` has reached the **accept** statement. In that event it will be suspended until `buf_inp` reaches the **accept** statement and completes execution of the rendezvous code.

Note that control would exit from procedure `xyz` only after both the tasks terminate. Many other tasks (defined in procedure `xyz`) could also call entry `Get`. These calls would be entered in a queue and serviced in a FIFO manner.

13.9.2 Real Time Programming in Ada

Ada emphasizes embedded system applications. A major characteristic of such systems is their need for real time response. Apart from synchronization of tasks, this requires an ability to select one of many alternative actions possible at a moment (we will call this *selective rendezvous*). Further, a real-time system should be able to prioritize its activities such that it performs low priority activities only when no high priority activities are possible. The **select** control structure permits *conditional rendezvous* and timed calls to meet these requirements.

The **select** structure in Fig. 13.31 encloses many **accept** statements. Each **accept**

```
Procedure xyz is
   type item is ...

   task buf_inp is
      entry Get(V : out item);
   end buf_inp;

   task calculate;

   task body buf_inp is
      temp : item;
      begin
         while not End_of_file (Standard_input)
         loop
            Read (temp);
            accept Get(V : Out item);
            do -- rendezvous code
               V := temp;
            end Get;
         end loop;
   end buf_inp;

   task body calculate is
      x : item;
      begin
         while ... loop
            buf_inp.Get(x);
            ...
         end loop;
      end calculate;

   begin
         -- body of procedure xyz
end xyz;
```

Fig. 13.30 Ada tasks for buffered file processing

is under a *guard*, which is a boolean condition mentioned in the **when** clause. A rendezvous can materialize on an **accept** only if the governing guard evaluates to 'true'. When control reaches the **select** statement, all guards in it are evaluated. Only **accept** statements governed by guards that evaluate to *true* are considered for execution. If more than one **accept** can be executed then the system makes a non-deterministic choice. If none of the alternatives can be executed, execution of the **select** statement is blocked until at least one guard can evaluate to *true*. At this point, a rendezvous materializes. The statement **delay** 100; avoids such blocking. It implies that task `mult_action` will wait for a rendezvous till 100 time units have elapsed.

At the end of the interval, the rendezvous attempt will be abandoned and the task will exit from the **select** statement.

```
task body mult_action is
    ...
    select
       when a < 10 =>
          accept ent1 ( ... ) do
       or when x < y =>
          accept ent2 ( ... ) do
       or delay 100;
       end select;
    ...
    end mult_action;
```

Fig. 13.31 Choice of action in a **Select** structure

Note that alternatives in the **select** statement are mutually exclusive in that at most one of them can execute at a time. In fact this is one way to achieve mutual exclusion in Ada. Figure 13.32 illustrates a solution to the bounded buffer problem using the **select** statement. The *produce* and *consume* actions are coded here as two accept statements within a **select** structure. This ensures basic mutual exclusion of the produce and consume actions. The guards on these actions ensure that the actions will be performed only under appropriate conditions. Non-determinism built into the **select** control structure by the language implies that if both producer and consumer wish to access the buffer when 0 < `full` < n, the system will arbitrarily choose one of them. In this case the choice is immaterial since correctness is preserved either way.

Ada provides a variety of other useful facilities, e.g. conditional rendezvous and timed entry calls. A conditional rendezvous is implemented as follows:

select `controller.produce(msg)` **else** *<statement>*

Here a rendezvous will take place with `produce` if entry `produce` is waiting for such a rendezvous. If the rendezvous cannot materialize immediately, the calling task does not wait. Instead it goes ahead with the execution of the statement in the **else** clause. In a real time system, this is important for prioritizing the various concurrent activities. For example, a database system might want to perform some backup actions when no transactions are taking place.

Timed calls are implemented by using a delay statement as in the following:

select `controller.produce(msg)` **else delay** `50;`

Here rendezvous with `produce` would be attempted for the next 50 time units. If it does not materialize during this time, the calling task would continue with the execution of the next statement.

```
n : constant := ..  ;
type item is array (1..100) of character;

task Consumer;
task Producer;

task controller is
   entry produce(msg : in item);
   entry consume(msg_area : out item);
end controller;

task body controller is
   buffer : array (0..n-1) of item;
   i, j, full : integer;
   select
      when full < n =>              -- -- produce
         accept produce (msg : in item)
            buffer(i) := msg;
            i := i+1 mod n;
            full := full+1;
      or when full > 0 =>                -- -- consume
         accept consume (msg_area :  out item)
            msg_area := buffer(j);
            j := j+1 mod n;
            full := full-1;
   end select;
end controller;

task body consumer is
   loop
      controller.consume(area);
         -- Remainder of the cycle
   end loop;
end Consumer;

task body producer is
   loop
      controller.produce(msg);
         -- Remainder of the cycle
   end loop;
end Producer;
```

Fig. 13.32 Bounded buffers in Ada

Ada also maintains a count of tasks waiting for rendezvous on a particular **accept** statement. This count can be used in a boolean condition, e.g. to govern an **accept** statement. Figure 13.33 is an Ada implementation of the readers–writers problem. Here `write'count` gives the number of tasks waiting for rendezvous with the entry `write`. Note the simplicity of this solution of the readers-writers problem with writer priority vis-a-vis the earlier solutions.

Note that use of the count attribute would be hazardous when conditional or timed rendezvous is attempted. Value of `count` may be inexact at a given moment if some of the calls on `write` are conditional. In such cases, use of `count` in guards could lead to deadlocks.

EXERCISE 13.9

1. Implement the P and V operations of semaphores in Ada.
2. Implement the airline reservation system of Problem 1 in Exercise 13.8 in Ada. Is it possible to process the cancellations at a higher priority than bookings? If so, explain how this can be done.
3. Implement the Interprocess Communication system of Problem 3 in Exercise 13.8. In what way does your solution differ from the solution using monitors?
4. Implement the Clock Manager of Problem 4 in Exercise 13.8 (*Hint* : Use the `count` attribute).

BIBLIOGRAPHY

(a) Critical regions, conditional critical regions and monitors

Hoare (1972) and Hansen (1972) discuss the critical and conditional critical regions. Hansen (1973) and Hoare (1974) describe the monitor concept. Buhr *et al* (1995) describe different monitor implementations.

1. Buhr, M., M. Fortier and M.H. Coffin (1995): "Monitor classification," *ACM Computing Surveys*, **27** (1), 63-108.
2. Hansen, P.B. (1972): Structured multiprogramming, *Commn. of ACM*, **15** (7), 574-578.
3. Hansen, P.B. (1973): *Operating System Principles*, Prentice-Hall, Englewood Cliffs, New Jersey.
4. Hoare, C.A.R. (1972): "Towards a theory of parallel programming," in *Operating Systems Techniques*, Hoare, C.A.R. and R.H. Perrot (ed), Academic Press, London, 1972.
5. Hoare, C.A.R (1974): "Monitors : an operating system structuring concept," *Commn. of ACM*, **17** (10), 549-557.
6. Schmid, H.A. (1976): "On the efficient implementation of conditional critical regions and the construction of monitors," *Acta Informatica*, **6** (3), 227-279.

```
type item is array(1..100) of character;
V : item; -- Used by readers/writers.

task controller is
   entry start_read;
   entry stop_read;
   entry write ( x :  in item);
end controller;
task reader;
task writer;

task body controller is
   select
      when write'count = 0 =>
         -- # of tasks waiting on entry 'write'
         accept start_read;
            readers := readers + 1;
      or
         accept stop_read;
            readers := readers - 1;
      or when readers = 0 =>
         accept write(x :  in item) do
            V := x;
         end write;
   end select;
end controller;

task body reader is
   loop
      controller.start_read;
      { Read }
      controller.stop_read;
   end loop;
end reader;

task body writer is
   msg :  item;
   loop
      controller.write(msg); -- { i.e.  write }
   end loop;
end writer;
```

Fig. 13.33 Readers and writers in Ada

(b) Methodology of concurrent programming

Ben Ari (1982) describes the evolution of mutual exclusion algorithms, and provides a proof of Dekker's algorithm. Lamport (1974, 1977, 1979) describes and proves the bakery algorithm. Owicki and Gries (1976) and Francez and Pneuli (1978) deal with the methodology of proving the correctness of concurrent programs. Hansen (1973, 1977) discusses the methodology for building concurrent programs.

1. Ben Ari, M. (1982): *Principles of Concurrent Programming*, Prentice-Hall International, Englewood Cliffs, New Jersey.
2. Chandy, K.M. and J. Misra (1988): *Parallel Program Design : A Foundation*, Addison-Wesley, Reading.
3. Francez, N. and A. Pneuli (1978): "A proof method for cyclic programs," *Acta Informatica*, **9**, 133-157.
4. Hansen, P.B. (1973): *Operating System Principles*, Prentice-Hall, Englewood Cliffs, New Jersey.
5. Hansen, P.B. (1977): *The Architecture of Concurrent Programs*, Prentice-Hall, Englewood Cliffs, New Jersey.
6. Lamport, L. (1974): "A new solution of Dijkstra's concurrent programming problem," *Commn. of ACM*, **17**, 453-455.
7. Lamport, L. (1977): "Proving the correctness of multiprocess programs," *IEEE transactions on Software Engineering*, **3**, 125-143.
8. Lamport, L. (1979): "A new approach to proving the correctness of multiprocess programs," *ACM Transactions on Programming Languages and Systems*, **1**, 84-97.
9. Owicki, S. and D. Gries (1976): "Verifying properties of parallel programs : An axiomatic approach," *Commn. of ACM*, **19**, 279-285.

(c) Concurrent programming languages

The class concept of SIMULA (Dahl *et al*, 1968) is a good starting point for readings on data abstraction. Wirth (1977) describes the concurrent programming language MODULA. Hansen (1975, 1977) develops the language Concurrent Pascal, and reports its use in developing operating systems. Other important languages for concurrent programming are Mesa (Lampson and Redell, 1980), Communicating Sequential Processes (Hoare, 1979) and distributed processes (Hansen, 1978). CSP is widely used for theoretical work in this field. Ada (Ichbiah *et al*, 1981) holds considerable interest as a general purpose language supporting synchronization primitives.

1. Dahl, O.J., B. Myhrhaug and K. Nygaard (1968): "The SIMULA 67 common base language," *Technical report*, Norwegian computing center, Oslo, Norway.
2. Ichbiah, J. *et al* (1981): *The Programming Language Ada : Reference Manual*, Lecture Notes in Computer Science, Vol. 106, Springer-Verlag, Berlin.
3. Gehani, N. (1984): *Ada – an Advanced Introduction*, Prentice-Hall, New Jersey.
4. Hansen, P.B. (1975): The Programming language concurrent Pascal, *IEEE Transactions on Software Engineering*, **1** (2), 199-207.
5. Hansen, P.B. (1977): *The Architecture of Concurrent Programs*, Prentice-Hall, Englewood Cliffs, New Jersey.

6. Hansen, P.B. (1978): "Distributed processes : a concurrent programming concept," *Commn. of ACM*, **21** (11), 934-941.
7. Hoare, C.A.R. (1978): "Communicating sequential processes," *Commn. of ACM*, **21** (8), 666-677.
8. Lampson, B.W. and D.D. Redell (1980): Experience with processes and monitors in MESA, *Commn. of ACM*, **23** (2), 105-117.
9. Pyle, I.C. (1981): *The Ada Programming Language*, Prentice-Hall International, London.
10. Wegner, P. (1980): *Programming with Ada*, Prentice-Hall, Englewood Cliffs, New Jersey.
11. Welsh, J. and A. Lister (1981): "A comparative study of task communication in Ada," *Software – Practice and Experience*, **11**, 257-290.
12. Wirth, N. (1977): "Modula : a programming language for modular multiprogramming," *Software – Practice and Experience*, **7** (1), 3-35.

CHAPTER 14

Interprocess Communication

Data access synchronization and control synchronization provide a structured form of communication to implement pre-defined interaction between processes. This form of communication lacks generality, e.g. it cannot handle situations in which a process can alter the course of execution of another process. Interprocess communication in the form of textual messages provides generality. A textual message does not have standard semantics; it must be interpreted by its receiver to deduce its meaning.

14.1 INTERPROCESS MESSAGES

Figure 14.1 shows a model of communication using interprocess messages. Process p_i sends a message to process p_j by executing the OS call *send*. The OS copies the message into a buffer and awaits execution of a *receive* call by process p_j. When p_j executes a *receive*, the OS delivers the message to p_j. Process p_j interprets the message and takes appropriate action determined by its contents. This may result in a reply being sent to p_i. If no message has been sent to p_j by the time p_j executes a *receive* call, the OS blocks p_j till a message arrives for it. If many messages have been sent to p_j, the OS queues them and delivers them in FIFO order when p_j executes *receive*'s.

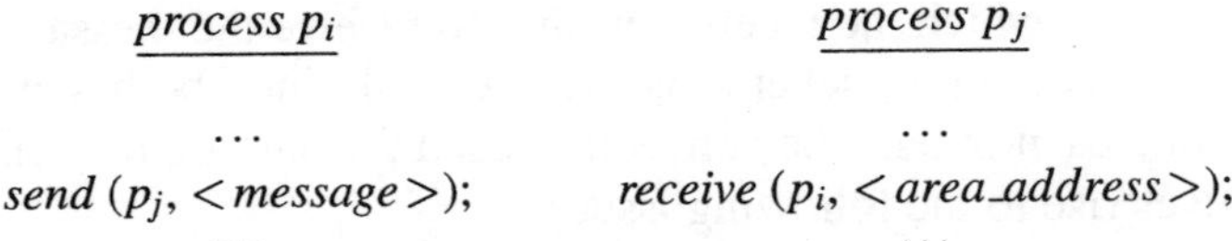

Fig. 14.1 Interprocess communication through messages

In principle, such communication can be performed using shared variables. Processes p_i and p_j can leave messages for each other in some shared variables. However, this would require a process to use different sets of variables to communicate with different processes in the system. The sender as well as the receiver process would have to share the knowledge concerning the name and address of the variables. Interprocess messages do not suffer from these problems. Further, messages become indispensable in a distributed system environment where the shared variables approach is not feasible. Other advantages of interprocess messages have been described in Section 10.3.3.

14.2 IMPLEMENTATION ISSUES

The following implementation issues arise in interprocess communication:

1. *Naming of the sender and receiver processes:* Naming conventions used in the send and receive calls provide answers to some key questions—How does the sender process know the name of the receiver? (One may even ask whether it needs to know the name.) How does the receiver know the name of the sender?
2. *Message delivery protocols:* Protocols determine the message data formats and actions of processes while sending and receiving messages.
3. *OS responsibilities:* Buffering of messages, blocking and waking of processes, etc.

These issues are discussed in the following sections.

14.2.1 Naming

Typical formats for the send and receive calls are:

`send` (*process_id*$_1$, *message*);
`receive` (*process_id*$_2$, *ad*(*message_area*));

where

–*process_id*$_1$ *process_id*$_2$ are names of the receiver and sender processes, respectively (these are typically process id's assigned by the OS)
–*message* is the textual form of the message to be sent
–*ad*(*message_area*) is the address of a memory area in which the receiver wishes to receive the message.

This naming scheme is symmetrical since both sender and receiver processes name each other. The convention used for naming the sender and receiver processes gives rise to the following issues:

1. How do the sender and receiver processes know each other's id?
2. Is it essential to name the sender and receiver process?

The first issue concerns the scope of process names in the system. It is easy for concurrent processes within a program to know each other's names. However, processes belonging to different programs do not possess this ability. The OS must provide some arrangement by which a process can find the name of any other process in the system.

The second issue concerns the need for communicating processes to know each other's names. When two user processes communicate, it is natural to expect knowledge of each other's names. However, this is inconvenient for server processes. For example, if a print server is only required to print the files deposited in its queue, knowledge of a senders' name is unnecessary. For this reason, an *asymmetric naming* convention is often used in practice. The `send` and `receive` calls in this form of communication have the following formats:

`send` (*process_id*$_1$, *message*);
`receive` (*ad*(*message_area*));

Here the receiver does not name the process from which it wishes to receive a message, however the sender process must still know the name of the receiver process.

14.2.2 Message Delivery Protocols

Definition 14.1 (Protocol) *A* protocol *is a set of rules and conventions shared by communicating entities.*

Essential aspects of a message delivery protocol are:

1. Conventions concerning data formats
2. Rules concerning actions to be performed by a sender and receiver process until a message is delivered
3. Rules for handling exceptional conditions.

Aspects 2 and 3 are discussed in the following.

Blocking and Nonblocking Protocols

In a *blocking protocol*, a sender process is blocked till the message is delivered to the receiver. A *non-blocking protocol* permits a sender to continue execution after performing a `send` irrespective of whether the message is delivered. In both protocols a process performing a `receive` must wait till a message can be delivered to it. These protocols are also known as *synchronous* and *asynchronous* protocols, respectively.

A blocking protocol has certain nice properties for both user processes and the OS. A sender process has a guarantee that the message sent by it is delivered before it continues its execution. The OS responsibilities are also simpler since it can allow a message to remain in the sender's memory area until it is delivered. However blocking of the sender may pose unnecessary waits in certain situations—for example, while communicating with a print server—resulting in poor response times.

A non-blocking protocol has the advantage that a sender is free to continue its execution immediately after sending a message. However, a sender has no means of knowing when (and whether) its message is delivered to the receiver; a sender does not know when it is safe to reuse the memory area containing the text of a message. To overcome this problem, the OS does not hold undelivered messages in a sender's memory area. It allocates a *buffer* in the system area and copies the message into the buffer. This involves substantial memory commitment when many undelivered messages exist. It also consumes CPU time as a message has to be copied twice—once into a system buffer at a *send*, and later into the message area of the receiver at the time of message delivery.

Example 14.1 Consider a process `process-i` with the following text:

```
Send (process-j, " ... ");
...
Send (process-k, " ... ");
...
```

If `send`'s are blocking, the process would be blocked on the first `send` until process `process-j` performs a matching `receive`. Thus, its progress would depend on when processes `process-j` and `process-k` perform their `receive`'s. If `send`'s are non-blocking, `process-i` can make progress independent of `process-j` and `process-k`. At any moment, the system must buffer all undeclared messages sent by `process-i`.

Exceptional Conditions

Message delivery protocols should provide for handling of exceptional conditions during *send* and *receive* calls. We begin by listing a few such conditions in the order of reducing severity.

1. In symmetric communication the process from which a message is to be received does not exist.
2. The process to which a message is to be sent does not exist.
3. The OS cannot accept a *send* call because it has run out of buffer memory.
4. No message exists for a process when it executes a *receive* call.

In cases 1 and 2, the process executing the *send* or *receive* call which leads to the exception may be cancelled and its termination code may be set to describe the exceptional condition. In case 3, the sender process may be blocked till some buffer space becomes available due to *receive*'s executed by other processes. Case 4 is really not an exception if *receive*'s are blocking (they generally are!), but it may be treated as an exception to provide some flexibility to the receiving process. For example, the OS may return from a *receive* call with an appropriate status code. If the status code is 'no messages available', the receiver process has the choice to wait for the arrival of a message, or attempt a *receive* after performing some other actions. In the former case, it may repeat the *receive* call with a flag to indicate that occurrence of this condition should be suppressed. The format for a *receive* call would thus be one of the following:

1. for symmetric communication:
   `receive` (*sender*, *flags*, *ad*(*status_area*), *ad*(*message_area*));
2. for asymmetric communication:
   `receive` (*flags*, *ad*(*status_area*), *ad*(*message_area*));

where *ad*(*status_area*) is the address of the area where the status information should be returned by the OS.

More severe exceptions belong to the OS domain. These include communication deadlocks, wherein processes enter into a mutual wait condition due to *receive*'s, or certain-more-difficult-to-handle situations like a process waiting a very long time on a *receive* call.

14.2.3 Buffering of Interprocess Messages

When a process p_i sends a message to some process p_j using a non-blocking protocol, the system builds an *interprocess message packet* (IMP) to store all relevant information (see Fig. 14.2). The packet contains some control information, viz. names of the sender or receiver and the length of the message, and the text of the message. The packet is allocated a buffer in the system area, which is entered into a list using the *IMP pointer* field. When process p_j executes a *receive* call, the kernel copies the message from the appropriate IMP into the message area provided by p_j. The kernel can use the *IMP pointer* field of the packet to form different lists of packets, e.g. a list of packets for each recipient process (see Fig. 14.3). This helps in efficiently locating the relevant IMP when a process performs a *receive*.

IMP pointer
Sender id
Receiver id
Message length
Message text or address

Fig. 14.2 Interprocess message packet (IMP)

In a blocking protocol, the OS can hold the message in the memory area of the sender. However, it may be preferable to use an IMP even in this case because a sender process may be swapped out as it waits for the message to be delivered. The memory requirements are not very large because only one buffer is needed per sending process. This scheme becomes further simplified if fixed message lengths are used in the system. If message lengths are variable, or a non-blocking protocol is in use, the system may have to reserve a considerable amount of memory for interprocess messages. In such cases, the OS may consider saving message texts on

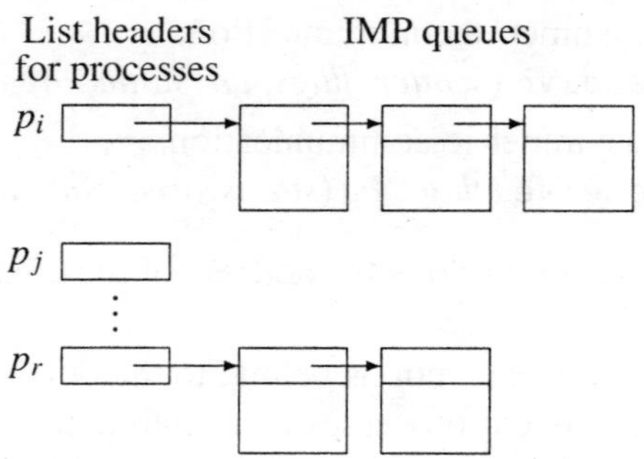

Fig. 14.3 List of undelivered messages

the disk. An IMP would then contain the disk address of a message, instead of the message text.

14.2.4 Delivery of Interprocess Messages

Two possibilities arise when a process p_i sends a message to process p_j:

1. Process p_j has already performed a *receive* and is in the *blocked* state.
2. Process p_j may perform a *receive* sometime after the *send*.

In the former case, the OS must arrange to deliver the message to p_j, and change its state to *ready*. In the latter case, the message would remain undelivered until process p_j performs a matching *receive*.

Clearly, OS actions concerning message delivery are analogous to its actions on the occurrence of an event. In the first case discussed above, occurrence of a *send* event in one process is awaited by another process. In the second case, the *receive* event causes the delivery of an already sent message. Thus, the first situation anticipates a send event while the second anticipates the *receive* event. The OS can organize the delivery of messages using event control blocks (ECB's) for the *send* and *receive* events. The event information field can contain the IMP (or a pointer to it).

Figure 14.4 shows the arrangement of ECB's when process p_i sends a message to process p_j using a blocking protocol. Figure 14.4(a) illustrates the case when process p_i executes a *send* call before p_j executes a *receive* call. An ECB is created for the *send* event. It contains the id of p_j. Figure 14.4(b) illustrates the case when process p_j executes a *receive* call after p_i executes a *send* call. An ECB for a receive event is created. It contains the id of p_i to indicate that the state of p_i would be affected when the receive event occurs. As described in Section 11.3.1, standard event handling procedure now triggers the actions concerning message delivery and activation of the sender and receiver processes.

Figure 14.5 shows the actions to be executed by the OS kernel for *send* and *receive* calls in a blocking protocol. For reasons concerning process swapping men-

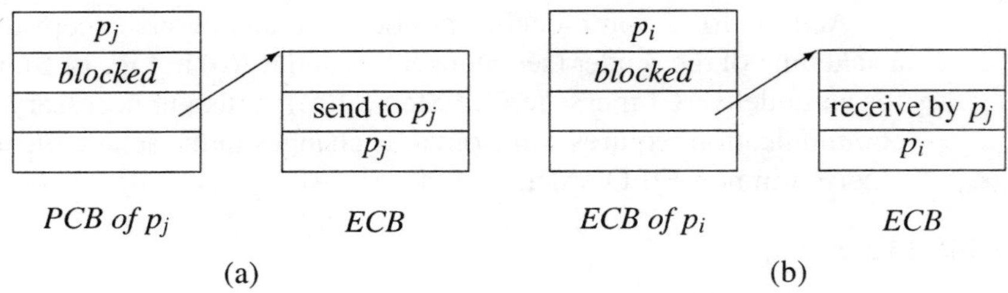

Fig. 14.4 ECBs in message communication

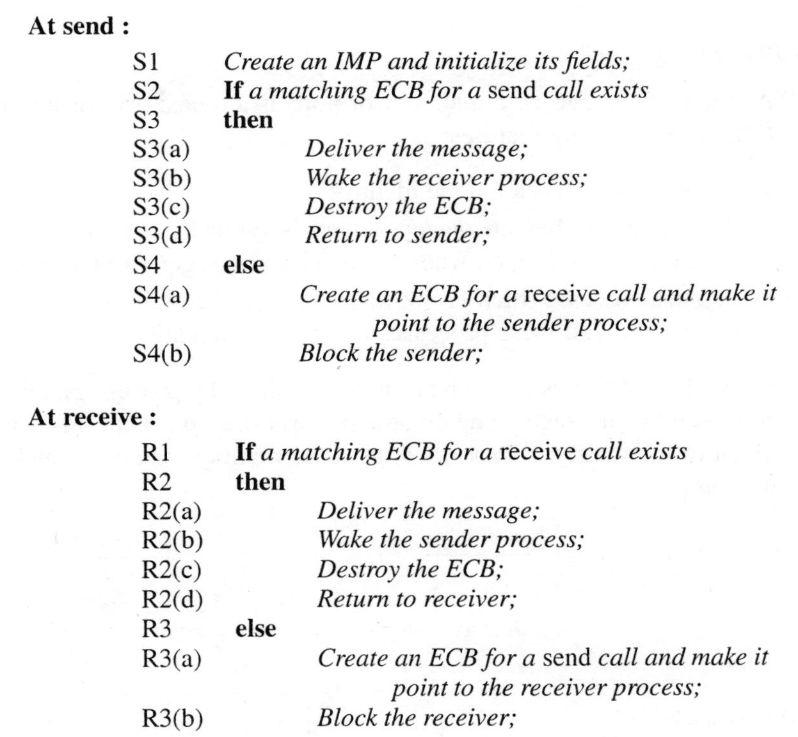

At send :

S1 *Create an IMP and initialize its fields;*
S2 **If** *a matching ECB for a* send *call exists*
S3 **then**
S3(a) *Deliver the message;*
S3(b) *Wake the receiver process;*
S3(c) *Destroy the ECB;*
S3(d) *Return to sender;*
S4 **else**
S4(a) *Create an ECB for a* receive *call and make it point to the sender process;*
S4(b) *Block the sender;*

At receive :

R1 **If** *a matching ECB for a* receive *call exists*
R2 **then**
R2(a) *Deliver the message;*
R2(b) *Wake the sender process;*
R2(c) *Destroy the ECB;*
R2(d) *Return to receiver;*
R3 **else**
R3(a) *Create an ECB for a* send *call and make it point to the receiver process;*
R3(b) *Block the receiver;*

Fig. 14.5 OS actions in a blocking protocol

tioned before, the OS creates an IMP even though the protocol blocks the sender or receiver process till message delivery. Action S3 immediately delivers the message being sent if the receiver already awaits a message. The receiver's state is changed from *blocked* to *ready*. Action S4 blocks the sender till the message can be received by the receiver. Action R2 implements immediate delivery if a message has been sent before a *receive* is executed. Action R3 blocks the receiver pending a matching *send*.

Actions for a non-blocking protocol are analogous except for the blocking and awakening of the sender (see Steps S4(b) and R2(b) in Fig. 14.5). Creation of an ECB for an undelivered message (see Step S4(a)) is also unnecessary. Use of symmetric communication requires some obvious changes in the schematic as messages may be received in non-FIFO order.

EXERCISE 14.2

1. In Fig. 14.5 a process may be blocked due to lack of memory to create an IMP or ECB. Modify the scheme to block and unblock the processes on this condition.
2. Modify the scheme of Fig. 14.5 to implement symmetric communication.

14.3 MAILBOXES

As the name suggests, a mailbox (or port) is a repository for interprocess messages. It has the following features:

1. A mailbox has a unique identity.
2. A mailbox has an *owner*, which is typically the process which created the mailbox. Only the owner can receive messages from a mailbox.
3. Any process which knows the identity of a mailbox can send messages to it. We will call these processes the *users* of a mailbox.

Figure 14.6 illustrates creation of a mailbox by process p_i, and its use by process p_j to send a message. The creator process, i.e. p_i, mentions a unique name to be given to the mailbox. Process p_j uses the mailbox name, instead of a process id, in its *send*.

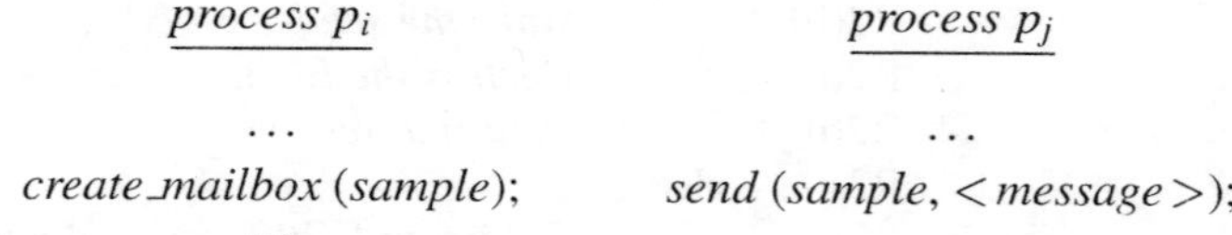

Fig. 14.6 Mailbox example

14.3.1 Implementation of a Mailbox

Answers to two key questions motivate alternative implementations of mailboxes:

1. How does a process know the name of a mailbox?
2. Where does the system buffer the messages sent to a mailbox?

An OS may provide a set of pre-fixed mailbox names, or may permit user processes to create names of their choice. A process creates a mailbox through a *create_mailbox* call. A user of a mailbox can simply *send* a message to a mailbox. Both calls would return with status codes to indicate the success or failure of a call. The OS may associate a fixed set of buffers with each mailbox, or may allocate buffers from a common pool of buffers when a message is sent. For better control over creation and destruction of mailboxes, an OS may require a user to explicitly 'connect' to a mailbox before starting to use it, and to 'disconnect' at the end of its communication.

Apart from creation and use of mailboxes, the OS may permit the ownership of a mailbox to be transferred to another process. OS may also permit an owner to destroy a mailbox. In that case, it has the responsibility to inform all users of the mailbox accordingly.

14.3.2 Advantages of Mailboxes

Interprocess communication using mailboxes differs from communication where the sender and receiver processes directly name each other in the following respects:

1. Mailboxes permit anonymity of the receiver process; a sender need not know the name of the receiver.
2. A process may own many mailboxes. This permits it to segregate different kinds of messages sent to it.

Anonymity of the receiver process can be used to hand over a function from one process to another. Consider an OS which wishes to use different process scheduling criteria during different periods of the day. Interrupts relevant to the process scheduling function can be modelled as messages sent to a mailbox named `scheduler`. At any time one system process would own the `scheduler` mailbox. When the process scheduling policy is to be changed, this process can release the mailbox. A new process can now claim ownership of the mailbox. Since all messages relevant to scheduling are directed to the `scheduler` mailbox rather than to a scheduling process by name, the new owner of `scheduler` can now receive all scheduling related messages. Functionalities of OS servers can be similarly transferred. For example, all print requests can be directed to the laser printer instead of the dot matrix printer by simply changing the ownership of the `print` mailbox.

Although communication to a mailbox is anonymous, it is often necessary to know the identity of the sender of a message. For example, a server would like to return some kind of status code for each request made to it. This can be achieved by passing the sender's id along with the text of the message. Alternatively, each user process may be required to put its own id as part of the message. In both these alternatives the sender of a message must receive the server's reply using an asymmetric `receive`. If this is not desired, *send_to_mailbox* can be provided as a blocking call with an implicit return message. Now, return of a status code would become a part of the protocol for a server call.

The possibility of many mailboxes being owned by a single process can be used to optimize the functioning of a multi-function server as illustrated in Ex. 14.2.

Example 14.2 An airline reservations system consists of a centralized data base and a set of passenger booking processes, each process representing one booking agent. A booking process interrogates the data base to determine availability of seats to satisfy a passenger's requirements before issuing a booking request. A typical message sequence for a booking is as follows:

```
if a booking request then
    send(enquire, '....');
    if seats available then
        send(book, '....');
        if successful then
            inform the passenger;
else
    if a cancellation request then
        send(cancel, '....');
```

where the three mailboxes *enquire*, *book* and *cancel* are owned by the reservations server, and communication is implemented using a blocking protocol. Figure 14.7 shows the reservations server. The flags $flags_1$, $flags_2$ and $flags_3$ in the reservations server indicate that the *receive* calls should return with an error-code if no message exists. Thus, the server processes all pending cancellations before it processes a booking or an enquiry. Further, bookings are processed at a higher priority over enquiries. All this is made possible by segregating the three kinds of messages into the mailboxes *book*, *enquiry* and *cancel*.

```
repeat
    while receive (book, flags1, ad(msg_area1)) returns a message
        while receive (cancel, flags2, ad(msg_area2)) returns a message
            process the cancellation;
        process the booking;
    if receive (enquire, flags3, ad(msg_area3)) returns a message then
        while receive (cancel, flags2, ad(msg_area2)) returns a message
            process the cancellation;
        process the enquiry;
forever
```

Fig. 14.7 Airline reservations server using three mailboxes

EXERCISE 14.3

1. A mailbox facility may not support flags (as in Ex. 14.2) to test the presence of undelivered messages. In such a case, a process must design its own means to obtain an equivalent effect. This can be achieved by sending a message to itself. If this message is delivered to the process on a *receive*, it can conclude that no undelivered messages exist. Rewrite the reservations application using this approach.

14.4 INTERPROCESS MESSAGES IN UNIX

Unix 5.4 supports the concept of a *message queue* which is analogous to the concept of a mailbox. A message queue is created and owned by one process. Other processes can send or receive messages to or from a queue in accordance with the access permissions specified by the creator of the message queue. The format used for specifying these permissions is the same as file permissions in Unix. A message queue has a finite capacity in terms of the number of bytes it can buffer.

A message queue is created by a `msgget` call with the following syntax:

`msgget`(*key*, *flag*);

where *key* specifies the name of the message queue and *flag* indicates some options. The OS maintains an array of message queues and their keys. The first `msgget` call with a given key results in creation of a new message queue. The process executing the call becomes the owner of the message queue. The position of the message queue in the system array (called the *message queue id*) is returned by the `msgget` call. Every subsequent call with the same key simply returns the message queue id. This id is used in a `send` or `receive` call.

Each message consists of a message type (which is an integer) and a message text. The OS maintains a list of message headers to represent the messages sent to a message queue (but not yet received). A message header contains the size of a message, its type and a pointer to the memory area where the message text is copied from the sender's memory area.

The `send` and `receive` calls have the following syntax:

`msgsnd`(*msgqid, msg, count, flag*);
`msgrcv`(*msgqid, msg_struct_ptr, maxcount, type, flag*);

The *count* and *flag* parameters of a `msgsnd` call specify the number of bytes in a message, and the actions OS should take if sufficient space is not available in the message queue (e.g. block the sender, or return with an error code). In the `msgrcv` call, *msg_struct_ptr* is the address of a structure to be used to receive the message, *maxcount* is the maximum length of the message, and *type* indicates the type of the message to be received. When a message is sent to a message queue on which many processes are waiting, the OS wakes all processes. The type parameter in a `msgrcv` call, which is an integer, is used to perform selective receive's of messages. When the type specified is positive, the OS returns the first message with a matching type. If the type is negative, the OS returns the lowest numbered message with the type value less than the absolute value specified in the call.

Example 14.3 Figure 14.8 illustrates the coding of the reservations server using the message passing primitives of Unix 5.4. The cancellation, booking and enquiry messages are assigned the types 1, 2 and 3 respectively. The `msgrcv` call with *type* = −3 and *flag* = "*no wait*" returns a cancellation message (if present), or a bookings message (if present) or an enquiry message (if present). This results in priority processing of cancellations as desired, while obviating the need for three separate mailboxes as suggested in Fig. 14.7.

```
server()
{
   msgqid=msgget(reservations_data, flags);
    ...
   repeat
      msgrcv(msgqid,&msg_struct,200,−3,"no wait");
      if ...           /* a message exists */
      then ...          /* process it;*/
   while(true);
}
```

Fig. 14.8 A reservations server in Unix 5.4

EXERCISE 14.4

1. Modify the scheme of Fig. 14.5 to implement Unix interprocess communication.

14.5 INTERPROCESS MESSAGES IN MACH

Mach is a multiprocessor OS kernel which forms the basis of operating systems of the Open Systems Foundation (OSF). The interprocess communication facilities of Mach are centered around *ports*. A port is basically a mailbox. Ports are connected to processes rather than to threads. The messages sent to a port are stored in a message queue. The port owner can set the maximum number of messages a port can contain. At creation, a port is assigned a unique numerical id which is used in all subsequent operations. Mach supports the notion of *port sets*, which is a set of ports. A server can issue a read on a port set. This is more convenient than reading from each of the ports individually. When a process dies, all ports owned by it are destroyed irrespective of whether they contain buffered messages.

Mach supports a single OS call to send and receive messages. The format of the call is as follows:

`mach_msg` (*hdr_addr, options, send_size, rcv_size, rec_port, timeout, notify_port*);

hdr_addr points to the message to be sent, or the memory area where a message is to be received. The message contains a header, and the text of the message. The header identifies the port to which the message is to be sent. *options* specify whether a message is to be sent or received, and whether a timeout interval is specified. *timeout* indicates the maximum amount of time a process may be blocked on the `send` or `receive` call. After the timeout interval elapses, the call fails and returns an error code.

One interesting feature of Mach ports concerns a mismatch between the expected and actual size of a message. Two options are provided concerning the situation when the message size is larger than the size specified in the receive call. One option is to discard the message altogether. The second option is for the call to fail but return the actual size of the message. The receiver process can now re-attempt the call with the correct size. Some peculiar situations arise because Mach ports are connected to processes rather than threads. More than one thread can now wait on the same port. When a message arrives, Mach awakens one of these threads. It is not possible for the program to specify any options in this regard.

EXERCISE 14.5

1. Design a scheme to implement the 'time out' feature of Mach interprocess communication by extending the event handling mechanism of the OS.

BIBLIOGRAPHY

This topic is mostly found in proprietary literature. Some literature in the public domain is listed below.

1. Bach, M.J. (1986): *The Design of the Unix Operating System*, Prentice-Hall, Englewood Cliffs.
2. Barnett, J.K.R. (1980): "The design of an inter-task communication scheme," *Software-Practice and Experience*, **10**(10), 801-816.
3. Bernstein, P.A. and N. Goodman (1979): "Approaches to concurrency control in distributed data base systems," *Proc. AFIPS NCC*, **48**, 813-820.
4. Morenoff, E. and J.B. Mclean (1967): "Inter-program communications, program string structures and buffer files," *Proc. AFIPS SJCC*, **30**, 175-183.
5. Silberschatz A. and P. Galvin (1994): *Operating System Concepts* (4th edition), Addison-Wesley, Reading.
6. Tsichritzis, D.C. and P.A. Bernstein (1974): *Operating Systems*, Academic Press, New York.
7. Walden D.C.(1972): "A system for interprocess communication in a resource sharing computer network," *Commn. of ACM*, **15** (4), 221-230.

CHAPTER 15

Memory Management

The memory hierarchy of a computer system consists of secondary memories like disks and tapes, the primary memory (i.e. RAM), and buffer or cache memories. Of these, management of a secondary memory is under the control of the file system. Cache memories are captive to the hardware subsystems and are not accessible to a user program. Hence the term *memory management* in the context of OS functions typically implies management of the primary memory.

OS responsibilities in memory management include memory allocation and deallocation, efficient utilization of memory and protection of the memory allocated to a program or process from interference by other programs or processes. Two kinds of memory management are performed during the operation of an OS. These involve allocation and deallocation of memory

1. to programs or processes
2. *within* a program or process

Different allocation and deallocation issues arise in these two kinds of memory management. Allocation to user programs and processes is performed by the kernel. This activity is characterized by the fact that program and process sizes vary over a wide range of values. This makes efficient utilization of memory rather difficult. In fact, in later parts of this chapter we will see how the need for efficient utilization of memory by user programs and processes led to the development of a new concept in computer architecture called *virtual memory*. Protection is a very important issue in this kind of memory management as programs and processes are independent entities and have to be protected against mutual interference.

Memory management within a program or a process faces wide variations in the size of a memory request. However, some obvious differences exist when compared with the allocation for programs and processes. Allocation and deallocation is done using run-time support of the programming language in which a program or process is coded. The run-time support is implemented by the run-time library of the language. Allocation and deallocation requests are made by calling appropriate routines of the run-time library. The library routines allocate memory out of a large block of memory set aside for this purpose. This block exists in the memory area already allocated to the program by the kernel. Thus, the kernel is not involved in this kind of memory management. In fact it is oblivious to it. Examples of such of allocation are the `new` call of Pascal, and `malloc` and `calloc` calls of C. Issues of memory protection do not arise in this form of memory management since all allocations made by the library in response to requests by a user program are within the large memory block already allocated to the program or process by the kernel. Protection of the block of memory used for this purpose against interference by other programs or processes is performed by the kernel as an aspect of the first function mentioned above.

This chapter discusses only the first kind of memory management explicitly since it is implemented by the OS. Memory management of the second kind, i.e. within a program, is performed by the run-time support of the programming language in which a program is coded using the techniques described in Section 15.1. We discuss memory management in two parts

1. *Contiguous memory management:* A program's data and instructions are assumed to occupy a single contiguous memory area.
2. *Noncontiguous memory management:* A program's data and instructions may occupy noncontiguous areas of memory.

In each part fundamental functions which devolve on the memory management component of the OS, and hardware and software provisions necessary to implement the OS functions are discussed. Various alternative techniques used to implement the OS functions and their practical implications are also discussed.

The term *memory handler* is used for the memory management component of the OS. As with other OS components, only certain functions of the memory handler need to be implemented in the OS kernel. Other functions of the memory handler can execute in the non-kernel mode.

15.1 MEMORY ALLOCATION PRELIMINARIES

The discussion in this section assumes the background of the stack and heap data structures discussed in Chapter 2.

15.1.1 Reuse of Memory

Two fundamental concerns in the design of a memory allocator are speed of allocation and efficient utilization of memory. The latter concern has two facets

1. Minimizing the memory overheads of allocation
2. Reusing the memory released by programs.

Memory overheads concern the amount of memory which is used by the memory allocator for its own operation, i.e. to help itself in allocation and deallocation of memory. Reuse of memory attempts to ensure that at any moment the total memory used up by a memory allocator is very close to the total memory allocated to requesting programs. In the case of a stack the memory overheads are caused by the reserved pointers used in each entity. Reuse of memory is automatically achieved since the memory which is released when an entity is popped off the stack is used the next time an entity is pushed on the stack.

Example 2.12 illustrates how free areas (or 'holes') develop in memory as a result of allocations and deallocations in the heap. Memory management for a heap thus consists of identifying the free memory areas and reusing them while making fresh allocations. These aspects of heap memory management are discussed in the following.

Identifying free memory areas

Two popular approaches used to identify and reuse free memory areas in a heap are:

1. Use of reference counts
2. Garbage collection.

In the reference count technique, a *reference count* is associated with each memory area to indicate the number of its active users. The number is incremented when a new user gains access to that area and is decremented when a user finishes using it. The area is known to be free when its reference count drops to zero. The reference count method can be implemented by providing two library routines `allocate` and `free` to implement memory allocation and deallocation, respectively, and a *free list* to keep track of free areas in memory. The `allocate` routine performs the following actions: If a request for new memory is received it searches the free list and finds a free memory area of appropriate size to satisfy the request. It then deletes this area from the free list, allocates it to the calling program, sets its reference count to 1 and returns its address to the calling program. If the requested area has already been allocated it simply increments its reference count by 1 and returns its address to the calling program. (The conditions to determine whether an area has already been allocated are application-specific hence these will not be discussed here.) The `free` routine decrements the reference count by 1. If the count becomes 0, it enters the area in the free list. The reference count technique is simple to implement and incurs incremental overheads—that is, overheads at every allocation and deallocation.

The garbage collection approach performs reuse of memory differently. It reclaims memory returned by programs only when it runs out of free memory to allocate. The garbage collection algorithm makes two passes over the memory to identify unused areas. In the first pass it traverses all pointers pointing to allocated areas and *marks* the memory areas which are in use. In the second pass it finds all unmarked areas and declares them to be *free*. It can now enter these areas in a *free list*. In this approach the `allocate` and `free` routines do not perform any actions aimed at reuse of memory. Hence the garbage collection overheads are not incremental. Thus allocation and release of memory are very fast. Garbage collection overheads are incurred every time the system runs out of free memory to allocate to fresh requests. The overheads become very heavy when most of the available memory is allocated to programs because the garbage collector has to do more work in its mark and free passes and needs to run more often.

It is best to use part of each free area to maintain the pointers in the free list. This way extra memory does not need to be commited to maintain the free list. This reduces the memory overheads of the allocator. The free list may be maintained as a singly linked list, with each area in the list pointing to the next free area in the list. This facilitates the search for an area of appropriate size when a fresh allocation is needed. Now free areas are added to the head of the list. It is useful to organize entries in the free list in the increasing order by size. This helps in finding the 'best' area to allocate to a memory request. Example 15.1 illustrates use of a singly linked free list. (The free list can also be maintained as a doubly linked list to facilitate addition of new areas in the correct place.)

Example 15.1 Figure 15.1 shows free area management using a singly linked free list. Part (a) shows five areas named `a`-`e` in active use, and three free areas named `x`, `y` and `z`. The system has a *free area descriptor* permanently allocated. The descriptor is used as a list header for the free list. The first word in each area is used to hold the count of words in the area and a pointer to the next free area in the list. Part (b) shows the free list in which the area `c` is added at the start of the free list consisting of `x`, `y` and `z`.

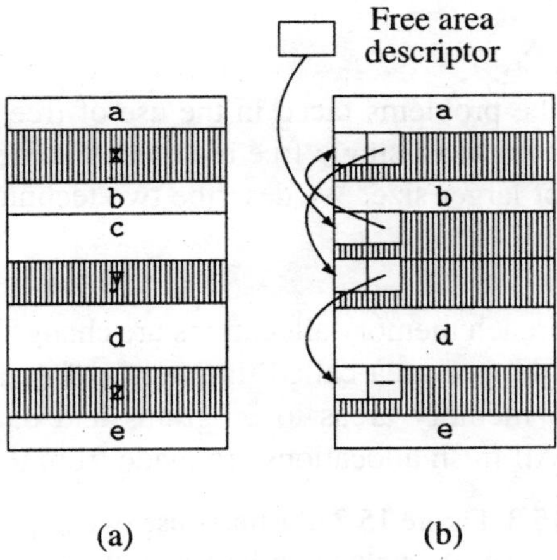

Fig. 15.1 (a) allocation status of heap, (b) free list.

Performing fresh allocation using free list

Two techniques can be used to perform a fresh allocation from a free list:

- First fit technique
- Best fit technique.

The first fit technique selects the first free area whose size is $\geq n$ words, where n is the number of words to be allocated. The remaining part of the area is put back into the free list. This technique suffers from the problem that memory areas become successively smaller, hence requests for large memory areas may have to be rejected. The best fit technique finds the smallest free area whose size $\geq n$. This enables more allocation requests to be satisfied. However, in the long run it, too, may suffer from the problem of numerous small free areas.

Example 15.2 Let the free list consist of two areas called $area_1$ and $area_2$ of 500 words and 200 words, respectively. Let allocation requests for 100 words, 50 words and 400 words arise in the system. The first fit technique will allocate 100 words from $area_1$ and 50 words from the remainder of $area_1$. The free list now contains areas of 350 words and 200 words. The request for 400 words cannot be granted. The best fit technique will allocate 100 words and 50 words from $area_2$, and 400 words from $area_1$. This leaves two areas of 100 words and 50 words, respectively, in the free list.

Example 15.2 illustrates a situation in which the best fit technique performs better than the first fit technique. However, this does not mean that best fit is superior to first fit. It is possible to design situations where the first fit technique performs better than the best fit technique. In fact Knuth (1973), who discusses methods of overcoming the problems faced by first fit and best fit techniques, concludes that the first fit technique is superior in practice.

Merging free areas

To avoid the problems faced in the use of free lists an OS may attempt to combine all free areas into a single free area, or to combine some adjoining free areas into a free area of larger size. We describe two techniques of merging free areas.

Memory compaction

In this approach memory allocations are changed such that all free areas can be united into a single free area called the merged free area. This is achieved by allocating alternative memory areas to programs and data existing in the allocated areas of memory. All fresh allocations are made from the merged free area.

Example 15.3 Figure 15.2 illustrates use of compaction to merge free areas. Part (a) shows a free list containing four free areas named c, x, y and z. Part (b) shows the situation after compaction. The *free area descriptor* describes the single free area resulting from compaction. The first word in this area contains a count of words in the area and a *null* pointer.

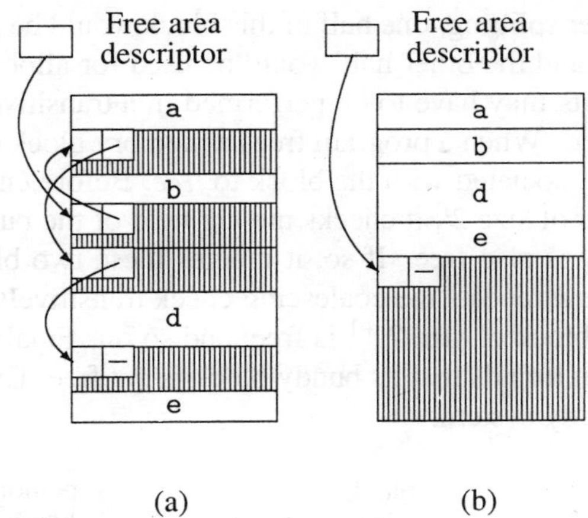

Fig. 15.2 Memory compaction

Buddy system

The buddy system aims at facilitating the merging of a pair of adjacent free blocks to make larger free blocks. A set of standard block sizes are defined in the system. Each memory request is satisfied by allocating a standard sized block. The standard sizes are 2^n for different value of $n \geq t$, where t is some machine-specific threshold value which ensures that blocks are meaningfully large in size. Each block b has a *buddy block*. This block has the same size as b and appears in a physically adjoining position, i.e. it either immediately precedes b in memory or succeeds it. A single tag field is associated with each memory block. This field indicates the allocation status of a memory block, i.e. whether the block is *allocated* or *free*. The tag fields are stored separately in a bit map. The system always tries to coalesce a free block with its buddy provided the buddy block is also free. This yields a larger free block. Coalescing actions thus ensure that blocks do not get progressively smaller in size.

To facilitate speedy allocation, the system maintains many lists of free blocks. Each free list is maintained as a doubly linked list and consists of free blocks of identical size. Thus, a list contains blocks of size 2^k for some $k \geq t$. A list header block points to the start of a list. Thus list headers exist for lists of blocks with sizes $\geq 2^t$ and $\leq 2^u$ for some u. Figure 15.3 illustrates this arrangement for $t = 2$. The following actions are performed when a program requests for a memory block of size 2^i. The system looks into the list of blocks with size 2^i. If the list is non-empty it allocates the first block from the list to the program and changes the tag field of the block from *free* to *allocated*. If the list is empty it looks into the list for blocks of size 2^{i+1}. It takes one block off the list, and splits it into two halves of size 2^i. It puts one block into the free list for blocks of size 2^i and uses the other block to satisfy the request. If a block of size 2^{i+1} is not available, it looks into the list for blocks of size

2^{i+2}. After splitting, one half of this block would be put into the free list for blocks of size 2^{i+1} and the other half would be used for allocation as described before. Thus, many splits may have to be performed in a transitive manner before the request can be satisfied. When a program frees a memory block of size 2^i the system changes the tag field associated with the block to *free*. Before entering the block into the free list for blocks of size 2^i, it checks the tag field of the buddy of this block to see whether the buddy is also free. If so, it merges these two blocks into a single block of size 2^{i+1}. It now repeats the coalescing check transitively, it checks to see if the buddy of this new block of size 2^{i+1} is free, and so on. Finally, it enters a block on a free list only when it finds that its buddy block is not free. Example 15.4 illustrates operation of the buddy system.

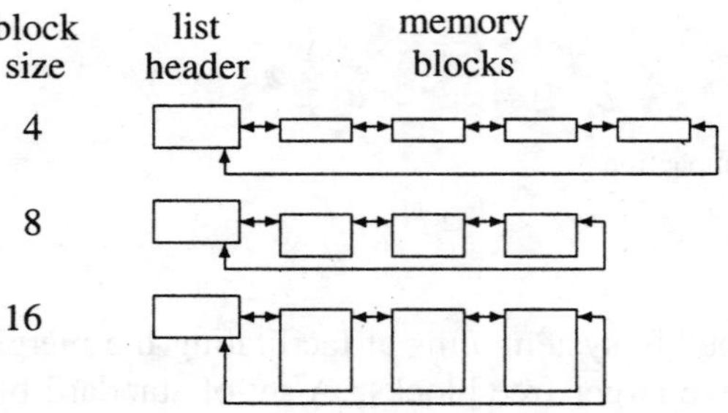

Fig. 15.3 Buddy system

Example 15.4 Figure 15.4 illustrates the operation of a buddy system. Parts (a) and (b) of the figure show status of the system before and after the block marked with the '⇓' symbol is released by a program. The left half of each part of the figure shows the free lists while the right half shows the allocation status of the memory. Blocks allocated to programs have been marked with hash lines in the right half of the figure and free blocks have been numbered in both halves of the figure to show their correspondence. The block being released has a size of 4 bytes. Its buddy is the free block numbered 1 in Fig. 15.4(a). When the block is released by a program the buddy system checks the status of block 1 and finds that it is free. It now deletes block 1 from the free list of blocks of size 4 bytes and merges it with the block being released to form a free block of 8 bytes. This block has block 2 as its buddy. Since it, too, is free, the system deletes block 2 from the free list of blocks of size 8 bytes and merges it with the new block to form a free block of size 16 bytes. The buddy of this new block is not free. Hence the system enters this new block of 16 bytes, which is numbered 5 in Fig. 15.4(b), in the appropriate free list.

A buddy system's operation starts with a single free memory block of size 2^s, for some $s > t$. It exists in the free list for blocks of size 2^s. Efficiency of allocation is obvious since no lists need to be searched during allocation. Efficiency of deallocation depends on the speed with which the system can check the allocation status of the buddy of the block being freed. This is aided by two factors. Existence of a buddy

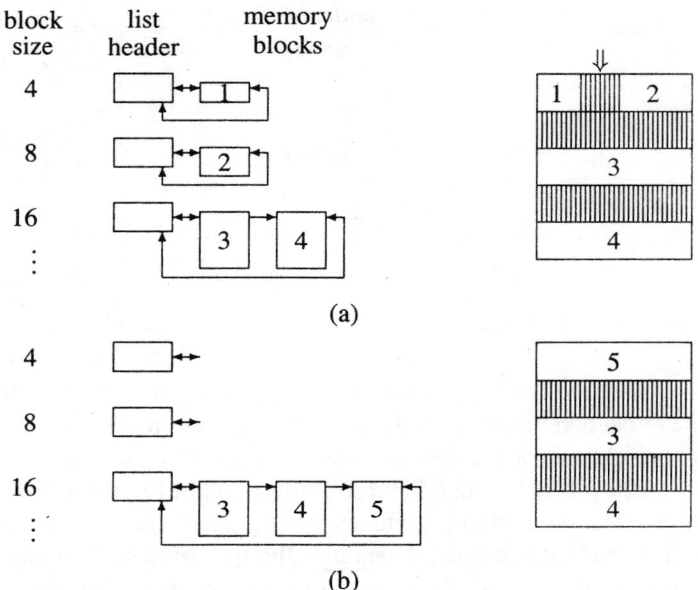

Fig. 15.4 Buddy system operation

is guaranteed for all blocks except for the block with size 2^s with which the system operation started. The tag field of the buddy can be accessed from the bit map once the address of buddy block is known. But how does the system know the address of the buddy block? Address determination is aided by the fact that all block sizes are powers of 2. Hence a block of size 2^k must have an address whose binary form has zeroes in the last k bit positions. For example, the address of a block of size 64, i.e. 2^6, would be of the form ...000000. The addresses of the buddy blocks of size 64 are therefore of the form ...0000000 and ...1000000 where ... is a string of 0s and 1s, i.e. the addresses differ only in the 7th least significant bit (see Figure 15.5). So if the address of a block of size 64 is $\ldots x000000$, where x is 0 or 1 then the address of its buddy block is $\ldots y000000$ where $y = 1 - x$. This address can be obtained by performing an exclusive or operation with a number 000... 1000000, which makes it easy to compute.

Powers-of-two free lists method

In this approach memory allocation is done in blocks whose sizes are powers of 2. Like in the buddy system, separate free lists are maintained for blocks of different sizes. However the similarity with the buddy system ends there. Each block contains a header element which is used for two purposes. It contains a status flag to indicate whether the block is currently allocated or free. If a block is free, another field in the header contains size of the block. If allocated, the header contains the address

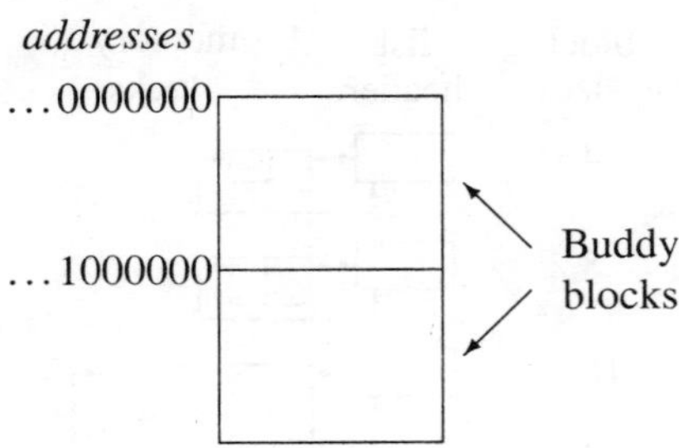

Fig. 15.5 Addresses of buddy blocks

of the free list to which it should be added when it becomes free. These provisions are needed because unlike the buddy system there is no relation between the size and the address of the block. When a request is made for n bytes, the system finds the smallest block which is large enough to hold n bytes. This is done by first searching the free list containing blocks whose size is the smallest power of 2 larger than n. If this free list is empty, it searches the list containing blocks which are the next higher power of 2 in size. An entire block is allocated to a request, i.e. no splitting of blocks takes place as in the buddy system. Also, no effort is made to coalesce adjoining blocks to form larger blocks.

System operation starts by forming list headers for all block sizes of interest. Formation of blocks can be done statically by forming blocks of desired size and entering them into the appropriate free lists. It can also be done dynamically whenever the system runs out of blocks of a given size, or when no block can be allocated to a request.

Comparison of memory reuse methods

Memory reuse methods can be compared on the basis of speed of allocation and efficiency of memory utilization. The buddy and power-of-two methods are superior to the first-fit or best-fit methods in terms of the speed of allocation because they avoid searches in the free lists to find a block which can satisfy a request.

Memory utilization can be compared by computing a memory utilization factor as follows

$$\text{Memory utilization factor} = \frac{\text{memory in use}}{\text{total memory committed}}$$

where *memory in use* is the amount of memory in use by requesting programs, and the total memory committed includes allocated memory, free memory existing with the memory management system and the memory occupied by its own data structures. The largest value of the utilization factor depicts the best case performance of a system and the smallest value depicts the worst case performance. It can be seen that the buddy and power-of-two allocators do not fare very well in terms of the utilization factor because they insist on allocating blocks whose sizes are a power of 2. Some memory in an allocated block would be unused unless a program requests a memory area whose size is a power of 2. These allocators also use up additional memory to store the list headers. Allocators using the first-fit or best-fit techniques would perform better since no wasted memory exists internal to an allocated block. However, the first-fit and best-fit allocators suffer from the problem that free blocks existing with them may be too small to satisfy any requests. Powers-of-two allocators suffer from another drawback. While the size of a block is a power of two, the header element cannot be used by a program to which the block is allocated. Thus the useful portion of a block is somewhat smaller than a power of 2. If a memory request is for an area which is a power of 2 in size, this method uses up exactly twice the amount of memory because the request can be satisfied only by allocating a block whose size is the next power of 2.

15.1.2 The Memory Allocation Model

During the execution of a program or process, the memory allocated to it contains the following components:

- Code of the program
- Static data of the program
- Program controlled dynamic data (PCD data)
- Stack.

The *code* component consists of the code of the main procedure and the functions and procedures which together constitute the program. Data declared in a program consists of the variables declared in the main procedure and the functions or procedures. The arrangement of these data items, as also their existence and visibility at a specific time in the execution of a program or process, would depend on the scope rules of the language in which the program is coded. The data can be divided into static data and dynamic data. The *static data* is created as a separate component of the program by the compiler. *Dynamic data* is allocated by the run-time support of a language like Pascal, C, Ada or C++. Allocation of this data is automatically done whenever a function or procedure is invoked. Apart from static and dynamic data the program may request additional data space during its execution through language features similar to the `new` statement of Pascal, C++ or Ada, or the `malloc`, `calloc` statements of C. Such data is also dynamically allocated however its allocation and deallocation is explicitly controlled by the program. Hence we call it *program controlled dynamic data* (PCD data) and its allocation as *program controlled dynamic allocation* (PCD allocation). Contents of the *stack* component are machine- and compiler-specific in nature. In most architectures the stack contains parameters of procedures or functions which have been called but have not been exited from, and return addresses to be used while exiting from procedures or functions. The language compiler puts the dynamic data on the stack as well. The sizes of the PCD data and the stack vary during the execution of a program. This happens because new entities may be created in these components and existing entities may be destroyed or may cease to exist during the execution of a program.

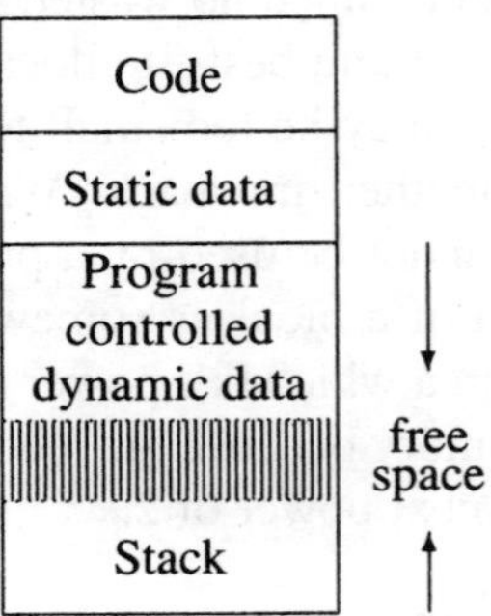

Fig. 15.6 A program during execution

Sizes of the code and static data components in a program are known at the time of compilation. The compiler puts this information in the compiled form of a program (see the discussion of object modules in Section 7.1.3). Hence there is no difficulty in making this information available to the OS. However, sizes of the PCD data and stack components cannot be predicted at compilation time. So how does the OS know how much memory to allocate to a program or process? In general, it does not know. It can either guess the sizes of these dynamic components or allocate a certain fixed amount of memory and hope that the program can manage within the allocated area of memory. In the former case, it has to guess the sizes of the PCD data and stack components separately. An obvious problem is that the execution of the program would be in danger if the OS underestimates the sizes of these components, and the memory would be used inefficiently if it overestimates the sizes. To avoid facing these problems individually for each of the components, operating systems follow the second alternative and use the memory allocation model depicted in Fig. 15.6. The code and static data components in the program are allocated memory areas which exactly match their sizes. The PCD data and the stack share a single large area of memory but grow in the opposite directions when memory is allocated to new entities. The PCD data is allocated starting at the low address end of this area while the stack is allocated starting at the high address end of the area. Thus the stack grows *downwards* in memory while the dynamically created data grows *upwards* in memory. The memory between these two components is free. It is used to create new entities in these components. In this model it is not necessary to guess the sizes of the components individually. The execution of a program is in danger only if these two components tend to overlap and destroy each other. This happens only when their individual sizes add up to a number which is larger than the size of the memory area allocated to them.

15.2 CONTIGUOUS MEMORY ALLOCATION

This approach uses the classical program model wherein each program is allocated a single contiguous area in memory. The memory allocation decision is made *statically*, i.e. before the execution of a program begins. Variations in this approach concern the scope of the decision—whether the allocation is made for a job as a unit or separately for each job step, i.e. each program, in the job.

Practical issues in contiguous memory allocation are as identified in sections 9.4.1 and 9.4.3.2, viz.

1. *Protection* of programs from one another
2. *Static relocation* of a program to execute from the allocated memory area
3. *Memory fragmentation* and measures to overcome it.

15.2.1 Memory Protection

Memory protection is used to avoid interference between programs existing in memory. Implementation of memory protection requires support from a machine's architecture in the form of memory bound registers or memory protection keys associated with different areas of memory.

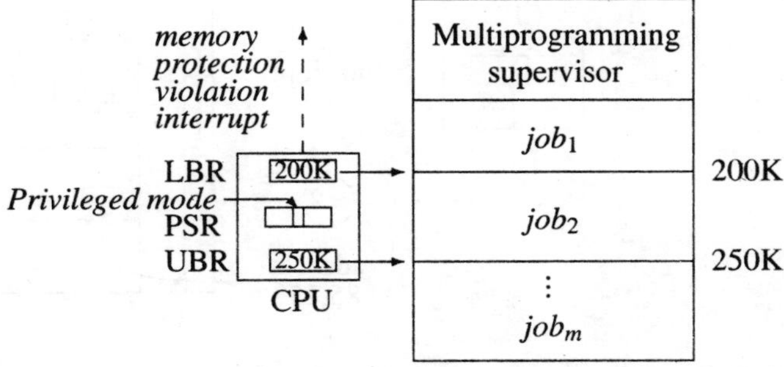

Fig. 15.7 Memory protection through memory bounds registers

Memory bound registers

As discussed in Section 9.4.1 and illustrated in Fig. 15.7, memory protection using memory bound registers is implemented as follows: When a program is in execution, two special CPU registers, viz. the *lower bound register* (LBR) and the *upper bound register* (UBR), contain the start and end addresses of the memory area allocated to it. The memory protection hardware compares every memory address used by the program with the contents of these registers to ensure that it lies within the allocated memory area. A *memory protection violation* interrupt is generated if an address lies outside the allocated area. On sensing this interrupt, the OS kernel can terminate the erring program.

Memory protection keys

Figure 15.8 illustrates memory protection based on the protection keys. Each memory protection key is a small integer. The memory of the system is conceptually divided into sections of equal size called *memory blocks*. While allocating a memory block to a program, the OS kernel assigns a *memory protection key* to the memory block. Protection keys for all blocks are stored in a separate memory called the protection key memory. Each program is also assigned a unique protection key (we will call it the *authorized protection key* (APK) of the program). This authorizes the program to access any memory block whose protection key matches its APK. Memory protection is implemented as follows: During the execution of a program, its APK is put in the *memory protection info* (MPI) field of the PSW (see Fig. 9.9). We will refer to this value as the program's APK (PAPK, for short). For every address *aaa* used by the program during its execution, the memory protection hardware compares PAPK with the protection key assigned to the memory block containing *aaa*. The access to *aaa* is legal if the two match. Else a memory protection violation has occurred. An interrupt is raised to indicate this fact to the OS kernel.

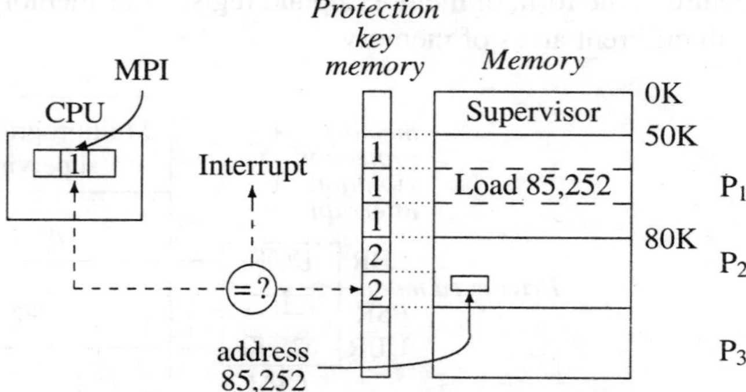

Fig. 15.8 Memory protection through memory protection keys

Example 15.5 In Fig. 15.8, P_1's APK is '1'. Hence memory blocks allocated to P_1 have the memory protection key '1', and the MPI field of PSW contains '1' when P_1 is in execution. Consider an access to a memory location with address 85252. The memory protection hardware obtains the protection key assigned to the memory block containing this address, and compares it with the value in MPI. Since the values are different, a memory protection violation is raised.

Kernel actions

Kernel actions concerning memory protection are aimed at initializing the memory protection hardware when a program is scheduled. When using bound registers based memory protection, the start and end addresses of the memory area allocated to a program should be loaded into the MPI field of the PSW while scheduling the program. No other actions are needed to support memory allocation. If protection keys are being used, the PAPK value should be loaded in the MPI field of the PSW. Use of protection keys also requires use of a privileged instruction to set the protection key of a memory block, e.g. the Set Storage Key (SSK) instruction in the IBM mainframe architecture. Figure 15.9 summarizes the kernel actions to implement memory protection.

a) Bound registers scheme:

1. *While allocating memory:* Put the start and end addresses of the memory area allocated to a program in the program's PCB.
2. *While dispatching:* Load PSR with contents of relevant fields of the program's PCB.

b) Protection key scheme:

1. *While allocating memory:*
   (a) Set a program's APK as the memory protection key for each memory block allocated to the program.
   (b) Put the program's APK value into the program's PCB.
2. *While dispatching:* Load PSR with contents of relevant fields of the program's PCB.

Fig. 15.9 Kernel actions for memory protection

As seen in Section 10.2.4 contents of certain fields in a programs's PCB are loaded into the PSW when the program is scheduled. This fact is used to load the memory protection information into the PSW. Thus, the memory bounds information or the PAPK value for a program are put into its PCB. Relevant fields of the PCB get loaded into the PSW when the program is scheduled. Certain kernel functions require access to the entire memory of the computer system. This is achieved by temporarily changing the information in the protection hardware using privileged instructions. In the bound registers approach, it is sufficient to change the contents of the LBR and UBR to the start and end addresses of the memory. Architectures using memory protection keys make a special provision to disable protection checks. In the IBM mainframe architectures, a '0' in the MPI field of the PSW disables all protection checks.

15.2.2 Program Relocation

A linker 'binds' a program to a set of memory addresses starting on the load origin of the program. This makes the program *address sensitive*, i.e. the program can execute correctly only if it occupies a memory area whose start address equals its load origin. To make a program execute correctly from any other memory area, it has to be 'relocated' by changing all memory addresses used in it (see Section 7.1.1). Since an OS cannot guarantee that programs would be allocated memory areas matching their load origins, every program would require relocation. This could be very expensive.

Some systems provide a special register in the CPU called a *relocation register* to aid in program relocation. Every address used in a program is relocated as follows:

Effective address = Address used by the program + contents of relocation register.

Example 15.6 Consider a program P with a linked origin of 50000. Let the memory area allocated to it have the start address of 70000. The value to be loaded in the relocation register is determined as follows:

The value to be loaded in relocation register
= start address – load origin
= 70000 – 50000 = 20000.

Figure 15.10 illustrates execution of an instruction with the address 61000. The instruction accesses a memory location with the link-time address of 65784. Since the relocation register contains 20000, the effective address is 65784 + 20000 = 85784. Hence the actual memory reference is performed at the address 85784. Note that memory protection considerations should be applied to the address 85784. Thus, it should lie in the range of addresses defined by LBR and UBR, or the memory protection key of the memory block containing it should match the program's APK.

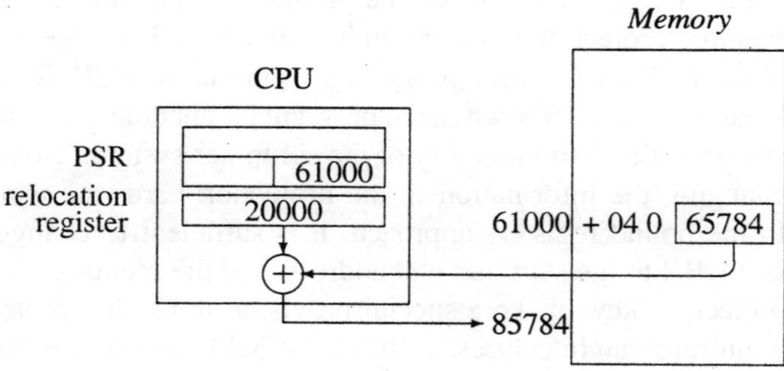

Fig. 15.10 Dynamic relocation using relocation register

Note that memory protection using memory bound registers becomes simpler if every program has the linked origin of '0000'. Now LBR can itself be used as the relocation register. This obviates the need to compare the effective address with the address in LBR. This scheme also aids in dynamic relocation of a program as we shall see in Section 15.2.3.

15.2.3 Memory Fragmentation

In Section 9.4.3.2, memory fragmentation is defined as the presence of unusable memory areas in a computer system. *External fragmentation* arises when free memory areas existing in a system are too small to be allocated to programs. *Internal fragmentation* arises when memory allocated to a program is not fully utilized by it. In this section we discuss techniques used to overcome the problem of memory fragmentation.

Memory compaction

To eliminate external fragmentation, OS can periodically perform memory compaction. This produces a single unused area in memory. This area may be large enough to accommodate one or more new programs.

Example 15.7 Figure 15.11 illustrates memory compaction. Initially, programs A, B, C and D are in execution (Fig. 15.11(a)). Compaction is performed when program B terminates. This produces a single unused memory area of 48 K bytes at the high end of memory (Fig. 15.11(b)). Program E with a size of 46 K bytes can now be initiated in this memory area. This leaves a single unused area of 2 K bytes (Fig. 15.11(c)).

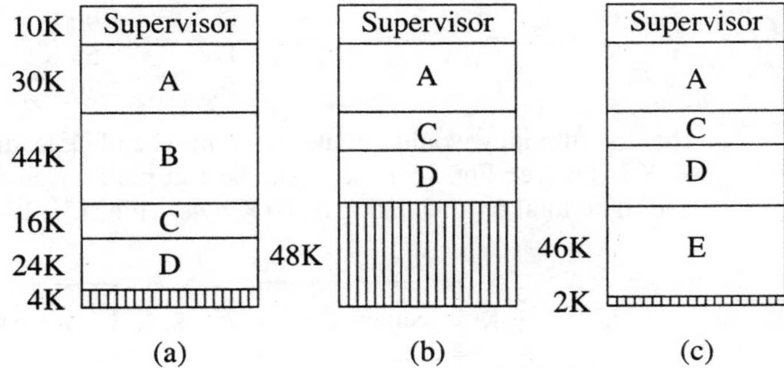

Fig. 15.11 Memory compaction

Compaction involves movement of programs in the memory during their execution. This is *dynamic relocation* of a program. This can be achieved quite simply in computer systems using a relocation register. Consider program C of Fig. 15.11(a). Assuming its linked origin to be '0000', relocation register should contain the address 84 K. During memory compaction (see Fig. 15.11(b)) it is moved to the memory area with start address 40 K. To implement this dynamic relocation, relocation register would be loaded with the address 40 K whenever program C is scheduled. This is achieved by storing the value 40 K in a relevant field of program C's PCB.

Garbage collection

Garbage collection is aimed at selective reuse of memory fragments. When a program terminates and releases its allocation of, say, z memory units, the OS searches through the list of programs awaiting memory allocation and selects a program that can be executed in this memory area. The following two criteria can be used to select a program:

1. First fit criterion
2. Best fit criterion.

The first fit criterion selects the first program it can find which can execute in the free area, i.e. the first program with size $\leq z$. The remaining portion of the free area may be too small to accommodate any other program. In due course, the number of such unusable areas (i.e. 'holes' in the allocation) may increase. The best fit strategy finds the largest program with size $\leq z$. This leads to a smaller hole in the allocation, thus reducing the amount of unusable memory. This strategy has the drawback that holes become smaller and smaller as system operation progresses. Knuth (1974) discusses methods of overcoming this problem.

Example 15.8 Consider a system which has 170 K bytes available for user programs. Let the following programs await memory allocation:

Program name	*Size*
C	40 K
D	90 K
E	55 K
F	70 K

The first fit policy would initiate programs C and D, leading to total fragmentation of 40 K bytes (see Fig. 15.12(a)). The best fit policy would initiate programs D and F, leading to total fragmentation of 10 K bytes (Fig. 15.12(b)).

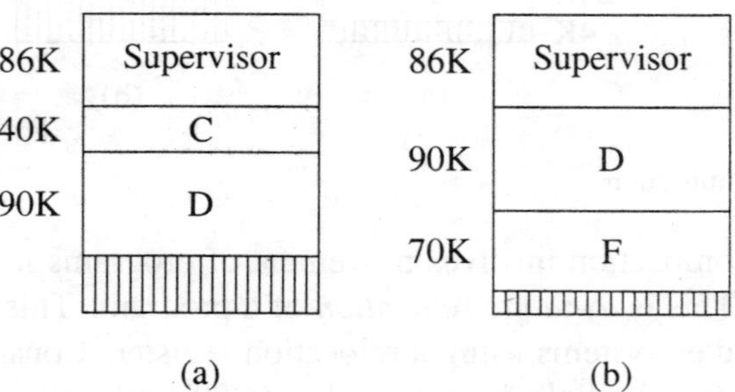

Fig. 15.12 Program selection by (a) first fit criterion, (b) best fit criterion

Garbage collection avoids overheads of program relocation. It also does not require special hardware provisions like a relocation register. However, use of garbage collection may cause delays in the initiation of programs. In Ex. 15.8, use of the best fit policy would delay initiation of job C until the memory contains a free area which is large enough to accommodate it, but not large enough to accommodate a larger program.

15.2.4 Program Initiation

In a contiguous memory allocation system, an OS must decide how to allocate memory to different programs. The basic approach followed is to partition the memory and allocate a memory partition to each program. A choice exists between keeping the partition sizes and boundaries fixed for all time or varying them during the operation of the system. The former restricts OS overheads by performing the allocation decision only once at system boot time, while the latter enables better memory utilization by performing the allocation function repeatedly during system operation.

Fixed partitioned allocation

The sizes and boundaries of memory partitions are fixed for all time. This also fixes the degree of multiprogramming. During job scheduling, a job is assigned to a memory partition. All steps of a job execute in the same partition. Hence the partition should be large enough to accommodate the largest job step. This implies that some memory in the partition may remain unused during other job steps, i.e. internal fragmentation is present most of the time.

Example 15.9 Figure 15.13 shows the usage of a memory partition of 200 K bytes by different job steps of a job. Internal fragmentation of 50 K bytes, 80 K bytes and 100 K bytes exists during the compilation, linking and execution of a program.

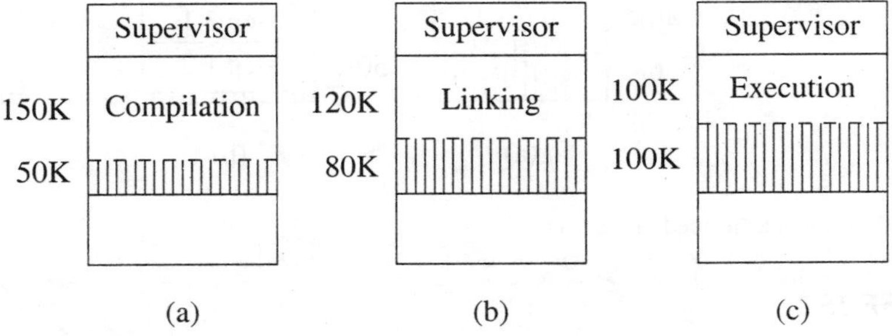

Fig. 15.13 Internal fragmentation in fixed partitioned allocation

Despite the drawback of internal fragmentation, many small multiprogramming OSs used the fixed partitioned allocation strategy in 1960's,, e.g. the IBM/360 DOS and OS/MFT operating systems. Partition sizes were standardized based on the prevailing job classes. From the OS point of view, the main advantage of this approach is its simplicity. The overheads are also low, since no memory allocation or deallocation actions are needed during system operation.

Variable partitioned allocation

In this approach, partition sizes and boundaries are varied during system operation. Each job (and each job-step of a job) is allocated a partition whose size matches its memory requirements. Hence no internal fragmentation exists. However, external fragmentation may arise due to the existence of holes which are too small to accommodate a job step. This leads to a curious effect—the initiation of a job step may be delayed even while the total unused memory in the system exceeds its memory requirements.

Example 15.10 The IBM OS/MVT operating system used variable partitioned allocation. Figure 15.14(a) shows three jobs in execution. Step 1 of job 1 (denoted as step 1.1 in the figure) has been initiated in a partition of size 30 K bytes. This is based on the specification REGION = 30 K indicated in a control command of the job step. Similarly, job steps 2.1 and 3.1 have been initiated in partitions of size 44 K and 40 K bytes, respectively. 56 K bytes are currently unused because the system operator had fixed the degree of multiprogramming at 3.

Let job step 1.1 terminate and let step 1.2 require a partition of size 50 K bytes. The old partition is too small to accommodate this job step, hence it is released. The OS looks for a partition large enough to accommodate a 50 K byte program, which it finds at the higher end of memory (see Fig. 15.14(b)). After job step 2.1 terminates, job step 2.2 is initiated as shown in Fig. 15.14(c)).

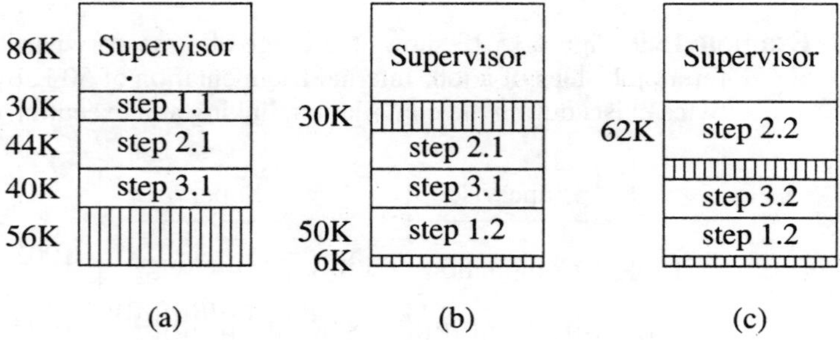

Fig. 15.14 Variable partitioned allocation

EXERCISE 15.2

1. Write short notes on
   (a) influence of memory allocation policy on job scheduling,
   (b) memory protection overheads in swapping.
2. During the execution of a program, memory allocation is required for the following components: code, stack and heap. The stack grows as activation records are created during procedure calls. The heap grows as the program creates new data objects (e.g. using `malloc` of C or `new` of Pascal) during its execution. Suggest ways to accommodate these components in a single partition in the partitioned memory allocation model.
3. An OS intends to use memory compaction. List the conditions which must be satisfied to enable dynamic relocation. Compare these with the conditions for swapping a program out of the computer's memory (see problem 6 of Exercise 9.5.2). What are the significant differences between them?

15.3 NONCONTIGUOUS MEMORY ALLOCATION

The classical contiguous memory allocation model requires a program to be allocated a single contiguous area of memory. This causes memory fragmentation as we saw in the previous section. An effective solution of the fragmentation problem therefore lies in permitting a program to occupy noncontiguous areas of memory. Example 15.11 illustrates how noncontiguous allocation helps to avoid fragmentation.

Example 15.11 Four unallocated memory areas of 50, 30, 80 and 60 K bytes exist in the memory as shown in Fig. 15.15(a). A program P requiring a total of 140 K bytes is loaded into three of these areas as shown in part (b). We refer to the parts of P existing in these different areas as P-1, P-2 and P-3, respectively. Free memory areas now exist following part P-3 and program D in memory. These areas could be utilized to initiate another program of size $\leq$ 80 K bytes. This avoids external fragmentation.

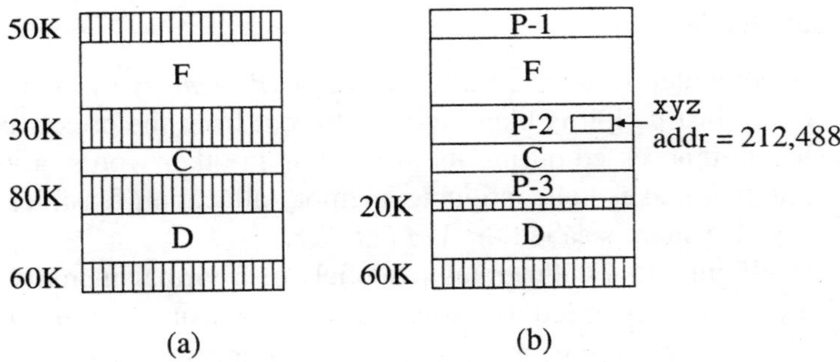

Fig. 15.15 Noncontiguous memory allocation

Note that program P of Ex. 15.11 would have been compiled and linked assuming the classical contiguous memory allocation model. So how can it execute from noncontiguous areas of memory? It is clear that an address generated by an instruction of P would have to be 'corrected' to point at the appropriate memory location. For example, let program P have the linked origin of '0', and let a data area `xyz` in P have the address 62488. Since the program parts P-1, P-2 and P-3 in Fig. 15.15 have the sizes of 50, 30 and 60 K bytes, `xyz` lies in P-2 and has the memory address of, say, 212488. An instruction in P-1 uses the address 62488 to access `xyz`. This address should be corrected to 212488. Note that this correction needs to be applied *during* the execution of P. This is best done by a hardware unit that is located on the path to memory. For reasons which will become clear shortly, the process of 'correcting' an address is called *address translation*. The address of the memory location where an operand is actually located is called the *effective memory address* of the operand.

Figure 15.16 illustrates program execution when the noncontiguous memory allocation model is used. The firm arrow shows an access of `xyz` by an instruction of program P. The dotted arrows show how the access is actually implemented during an execution of P. A hardware unit called the *address translation unit* (ATU) 'corrects' the address of xyz to point at the actual memory location where xyz exists. The ATU corrects each memory address generated by the program in this manner.

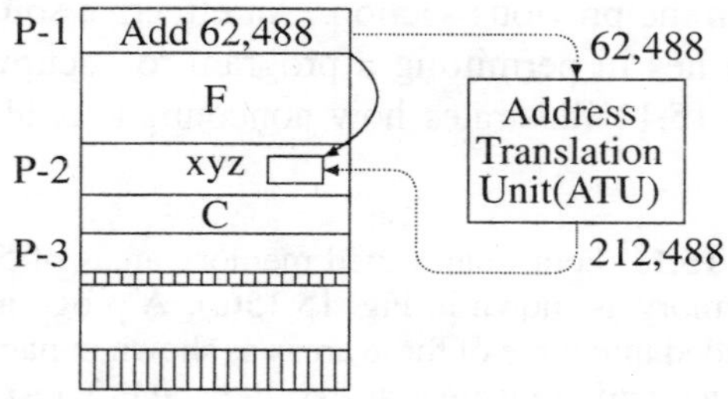

Fig. 15.16 Address translation in noncontiguous allocation

15.3.1 Virtual Memory

A computer system is said to use *virtual memory* (VM) if a memory address used by an instruction is likely to be different from the effective address of the memory location accessed during its execution. In other words, a virtual memory system is one that makes noncontiguous memory allocation feasible. The memory handler in a VM system is called the *VM handler*.

Figure 15.17 illustrates essentials of a virtual memory system. While loading a program for execution, it is viewed as a sequential arrangement of abstract parts called *program components*. Each component is allocated a single contiguous area of memory. However, areas allocated to different components can be noncontiguous with one another. An address used in an instruction of a program, say, an operand address, is considered to consist of two parts—the id of the program component containing the address, and the id of the word within the component. Each address is represented by the pair $(comp_i, word_i)$. In an address (10, 349), $comp_i = 10$ and $word_i = 349$. It is thus the address of the 349th word in the 10th program component.

Address translation

Let us see the basics of address translation with the help of an address (10, 349). Consider program component 10 to be allocated the memory area starting at address 27000. Then,

Effective memory address corresponding to the address (10, 349)

$$\begin{aligned} &= \text{(start address of component 10)} + 349 \\ &= 27000 + 349 = 27349 \qquad (15.1) \end{aligned}$$

Address translation can be performed in a table based manner where the table contains start addresses of various components of a program. In an address $(comp_i, word_i)$, $comp_i$ is used to index this table to obtain its start address in memory.

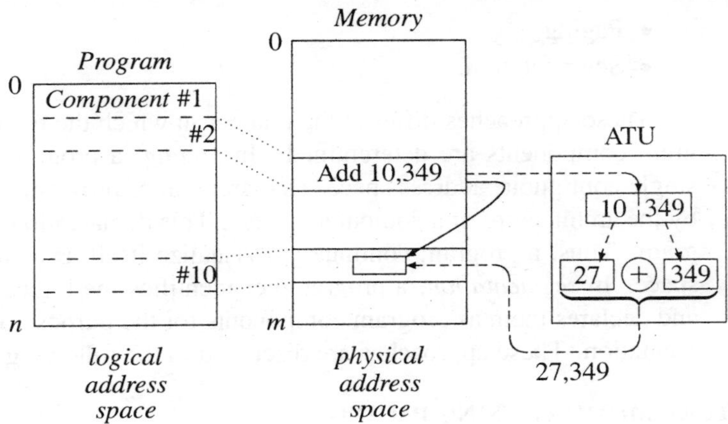

Fig. 15.17 Virtual memory essentials

This is used to perform address translation as shown in Eq. (15.1). Note that $comp_i$ and $word_i$ can be numeric or symbolic in nature. When the id's are numeric, as in the address (10, 349), address translation simply involves a table lookup. However, numeric id's may require certain binding actions to precede the start of program execution. This imposes some restrictions as we see in Section 15.4.7. Use of symbolic id's permits use of addresses of the form `(alpha, beta)` in a program. This is less restrictive as we see in Section 15.5.5.

Logical and physical addresses

A *logical address* is the address of an instruction or data word as used by a program. (This address may be obtained using index, base or segment registers.) A *physical address* is the effective memory address of an instruction or data word, viz. the address obtained by the address translation equation, Eq. (15.1). The set of logical addresses used by a program constitute the *logical address space* of the program. The set of physical addresses generated during the operation of a system constitute the *physical address space* of the system. These terms are used to formulate a definition of a virtual memory system.

Virtual memory system

Definition 15.1 (Virtual memory system) *A* virtual memory system *is a system wherein the logical address of an instruction or data word is likely to be different from its physical address.*

This definition presumes the presence of an ATU to translate a logical address situated in the logical address space of a program into a physical address. Two fundamental approaches used in implementing virtual memory systems are

- Paging
- Segmentation.

These approaches differ in the manner in which the boundaries and sizes of program components are deteremined. In *paging*, a program is visualized to have a single contiguous address space. Demarcation of program components is performed by the architecture of a computer system. This demarcation is transparent to the program. Thus, a program continues to visualize itself as a single contiguous address space. In *segmentation*, a programmer identifies the logical entities in his program and declares them as program components for the purpose of virtual memory implementation. These approaches are discussed in the following sections.

15.4 VIRTUAL MEMORY USING PAGING

15.4.1 Pages, Page Blocks and Address Translation

In a paged virtual memory system, an OS views the logical address space of a program to be a linear arrangement of fixed sized components called *pages*. Each logical address used in a program is thus considered to be a pair

$$(p_i, w_i)$$

where p_i, w_i are numeric in nature, i.e. p_i is a page number and w_i is the word number within p_i. Pages in a program, as also words in a page, are numbered from 0 onwards.

Consider a program P of size z words and a load origin of 0. If the size of a page is s words, the logical address space of P consists of pages $0 \ldots n-1$, such that

$$n = \lceil \frac{z}{s} \rceil \tag{15.2}$$

where '$\lceil \ \rceil$' indicates a rounded integer quotient. Pages 0 to $n-2$ contain s words each, while the last page may contain less than s words. Thus the logical address space of P consists of a linear arrangement of logical addresses from (0, 0) to $(n-1, z-(n-1).s-1)$. Note that the architecture demarcates pages of P by fixing the page boundaries at $k \times z$ for $k = 0, \ldots, n-2$. The architecture also specifies a method of obtaining the address pair (p_i, w_i) from every logical address generated during the execution of a program. We describe this method in the following.

The physical memory of the computer system is viewed to consist of *page blocks* (also called *page frames*), each capable of holding exactly one page of a program. Thus each page block also has a size of s words. At any moment, a page block may be free, or it may contain a page of some program. The size of a page (and hence that of a page block) is chosen to be a power of 2. This permits a logical address to be viewed as a juxtaposition of p_i and w_i. For example, if logical addresses are l_1 bits in length and $s = 2^m$, $(l_1 - m)$ higher order bits form p_i, and lower order m bits form w_i as follows

$\leftarrow l_1 - m \rightarrow$	$\leftarrow m \rightarrow$
p_i	w_i

This choice of page size also simplifies construction of the effective physical address, which we assume to be l_2 bits in length. This comes about as follows: Let a page p_i of a program be allocated page block q_i. Since the sizes of pages and page blocks are identical, m bits are needed to address the words in a page block. Physical address of word '0' of page block q_i is thus

$\leftarrow l_2 - m \rightarrow$	$\leftarrow m \rightarrow$
q_i	0······0

Physical address of word w_i in page block q_i is thus given by

$\leftarrow l_2 - m \rightarrow$	$\leftarrow m \rightarrow$
q_i	w_i

ATU can obtain this address simply by juxtaposing q_i and w_i to obtain an l_2 bit address.

Example 15.12 IBM/370 used 24 bit logical addresses. The page size could be 2 K or 4 K bytes. When 2 K byte pages were used, 11 bits were adequate to address the bytes in a page. Thus, higher order 13 bits in a logical address represented p_i and 11 lower order bits represented w_i. For a physical memory size of 1 M bytes, $l_2 = 20$. Thus, higher order 9 bits in a physical address represented q_i. If $p_i = 130$, $w_i = 600$ and $q_i = 48$, the logical and physical addresses look as follows:

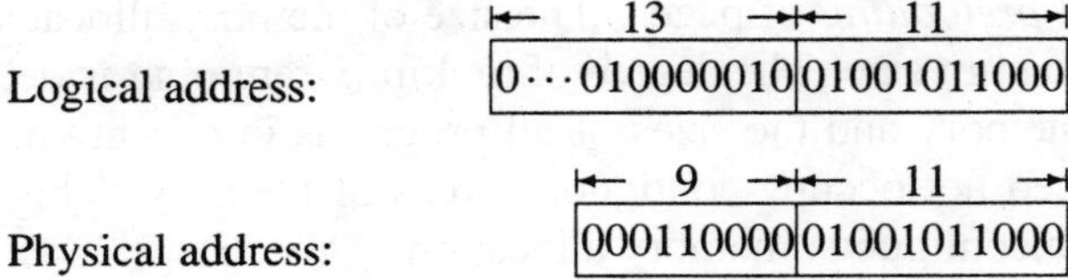

Note that l_1 and l_2 do not have any specific relation with one another. If $l_1 > l_2$, the logical address space is larger than the physical address space, and we have a very useful way to execute large programs on a computer system with limited memory. However, this is not a necessary condition for virtual memory systems. Systems with $l_1 < l_2$ also exist, e.g. the PDP/11 system.

To implement address translation, the ATU employs a simple mapping technique using a *page map table* (PMT) for a program. The PMT of a program has one entry for each page of the program, showing the page block number in memory where the page presently resides. This information is put here by the VM handler while performing memory allocation. Address translation now consists of the following four steps illustrated in Fig. 15.18. (For simplicity, addresses are shown in decimal and page size is assumed to be 1000 words.)

1. The logical address is viewed as a pair (p_i, w_i).
2. p_i is used to index the PMT.
3. Id of the memory block where page p_i resides is obtained from the *block number* field of the PMT entry. (15.3)
4. The physical address is obtained by juxtaposing q_i and w_i.

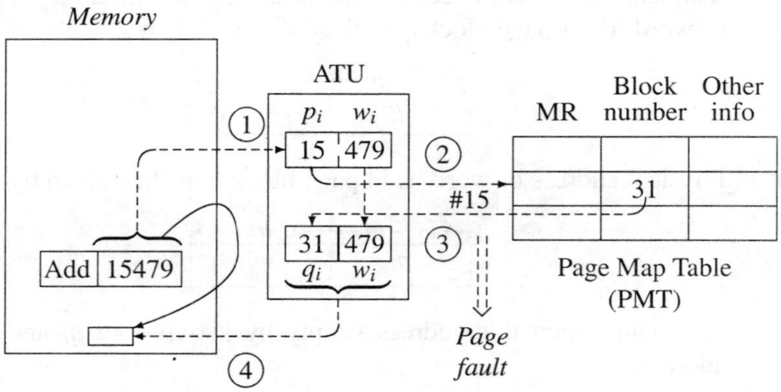

Fig. 15.18 Address translation in paged virtual memory

15.4.2 Demand Paging

All pages of a program can be loaded in memory before the program is initiated. This is called *preloading* of pages. The size of memory allocated to a program thus equals the program size. The degree of multiprogramming is determined by the size of physical memory and the sizes of all programs in execution. Note that pages of a program need not occupy contiguous areas of memory. This model captures the essence of noncontiguous memory allocation.

It is possible to improve on the memory utilization provided by this model using the technique of *demand paging*. This can be explained as follows: For correct execution of an instruction which uses a logical address *aaa*, it is necessary that the page containing address *aaa* should exist in memory. Other pages of the program need not exist in memory. This fact can be used to reduce the amount of memory allocated to a program. Thus, even though a program consists of *n* pages, a smaller number of pages may exist in the memory at any given time. When a program refers to a page which does not exist in memory, the OS must arrange to load this page in memory. Thus, a page is loaded on demand. Hence the term *demand paging.* The degree of multiprogramming in a demand paged system is determined by the number of pages of executing programs loaded in memory rather than by the sizes of the executing programs.

The following provisions are needed to implement demand paging:

- Page faults,
- Page-in and page-out operations.

Page faults

A field in the PMT entry of page p_i indicates whether the page currently exists in memory. If p_i does not exist in memory when referenced, ATU raises a *missing page interrupt*, also called a *page fault*. This transfers control to the VM handler for necessary actions.

Page-in and page-out operations

When a page fault occurs during a reference to page p_i, the VM handler finds a free page block in memory and loads p_i in it. This is called a *page-in* operation for p_i. If no free block exists in memory, some page p_k existing in the memory is written out onto a secondary memory to free its page block. This is a *page-out* operation for p_k. The page-in and page-out operations required to implement demand paging constitute *page IO*. Note that page IO is distinct from IO operations performed by programs, which we will call *program IO*. The term *page traffic* is used to describe the movement of pages in and out of memory.

The PMT entry of a page contains additional fields to support demand paging. Figure 15.19 illustrates these fields. The *memory resident* (MR) field indicates whether the page exists in memory. The *other information* field contains useful information for page-out operations. The use of these fields is discussed in Section 15.4.4.

Memory resident ?	*Block number*	*Other information*

Fig. 15.19 PMT entry

The operation of a demand paged virtual memory system is described with the help of an instruction which refers to logical address *aaa* situated in program page p_i. Steps in implementing this reference are as follows:

1. If the MR field of the PMT entry of page p_i indicates that p_i exists in memory, ATU translates the logical address *aaa* into a physical address using the *block number* field of the PMT entry (see Steps 1-4 of (15.3)).
2. If p_i does not exist in memory
   (a) A page fault is raised during Step 3 of Section 15.4.1.
   (b) If necessary, VM handler performs a page-out operation for some page p_k to free a memory block.
   (c) VM handler allocates a page block to p_i and performs a page-in operation for it.

(d) Execution of the interrupted instruction is now resumed at Step 3 of Section 15.4.1.

While step 2 is being performed for one program, the CPU is switched to the execution of another program.

Page replacement

Definition 15.2 (Page replacement) Page replacement *of a page p_i by page p_j is removal of page p_i from some page block q_i followed by a page-in operation for p_j into page block q_i.*

Page replacement becomes necessary when a page fault occurs and no free page blocks exist in memory. An important issue in page replacement is deciding which page to replace. If a replaced page is referenced in immediate future, it would cause another page fault. This would affect performance of the program. System efficiency would also be affected if many programs encounter such situations. Thus the issue amounts to knowing or predicting which page is likely to be referenced in immediate future. However, we rejected this possibility when we rejected preloading of pages. So how can we safeguard program performance and system efficiency during page replacement? Fortunately, favourable empirical evidence exists concerning behaviour of programs in a paged virtual memory system. This evidence which is used to formulate the principle of locality of reference, helps to ensure good program performance.

Locality of reference

The principle of locality of reference states that the logical address generated during the execution of an instruction in a program is likely to be in close proximity of logical addresses used in the previous few instructions of the program.

Locality can be explained as follows: Program execution is predominantly sequential in nature (excepting branch instructions). Thus, the next instruction to be executed typically follows the previous instruction in memory. References to non-scalar data, e.g. arrays, also tend to be in close proximity of previous references. Consider two pages p_1 and p_2 of a program P. Let t_1 and t_2 be the periods of time for which p_1 and p_2 have not been referenced during the execution of P. Let $t_1 > t_2$. From the principle of locality, it follows that page p_1 is less likely to be referenced in the next instruction than page p_2.

The principle of locality implies that the page containing the next logical address used by a program is likely to be one of the pages containing the previous few logical addresses. Thus too many page faults may not occur during the execution of a program, hence one can expect VM systems to operate with reasonable levels of efficiency. Note, however, that locality does not imply an absence of page faults. These occur from time to time when instructions or data referenced by a program are not in close proximity of the previous few instructions or data. We attribute this effect to a shift in the locality of a program.

A page replacement policy must possess two important properties: First, it must not disregard locality of reference, i.e. it must not remove a page that is likely to be accessed again in immediate future. Second, it must possess the page fault characteristic depicted by the graph of Fig. 15.20. This graph shows that the page fault rate of a program, i.e. the number of page faults per unit time, should decrease when we increase the number of page blocks allocated to the program. This characteristic implies that the performance of a program will not degrade with an increase in its memory allocation. The OS uses this property to plan a corrective action when high page fault rates arise in the system. We discuss this in the next section.

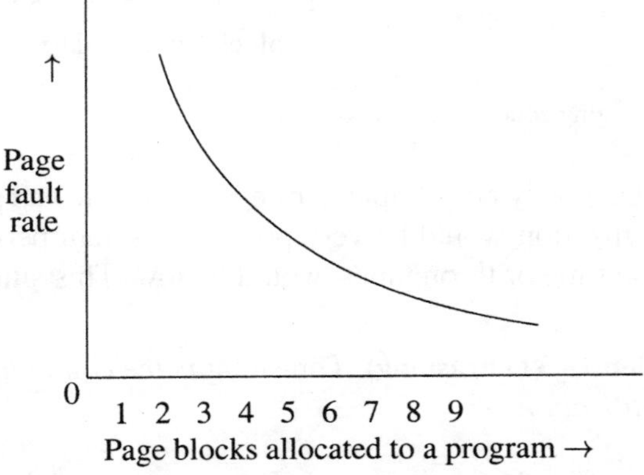

Fig. 15.20 Desirable variation of page fault rates with memory allocation

Memory allocation to a program

How much memory should the OS allocate to a program? Two opposite factors influence this decision. From Fig. 15.20, we see that an over-commitment of memory would imply a low page fault rate, hence good program performance. However it would mean that a smaller number of programs would exist in memory at any time. This could cause CPU idling. An under-commitment of memory would cause a high page fault rate, which would lead to poor program performance. Hence we need to define a desirable operating zone for a program which would ensure moderate to medium page fault rates (see Fig. 15.21).

Thrashing

Consider a program which is operating to the left of the desirable operating zone, i.e. in the region of high page fault rates. Such a program is not in a position to use the CPU effectively. It also causes high page traffic, which increases OS overheads. If all programs in the system similarly operate in high page fault rate zones, the CPU

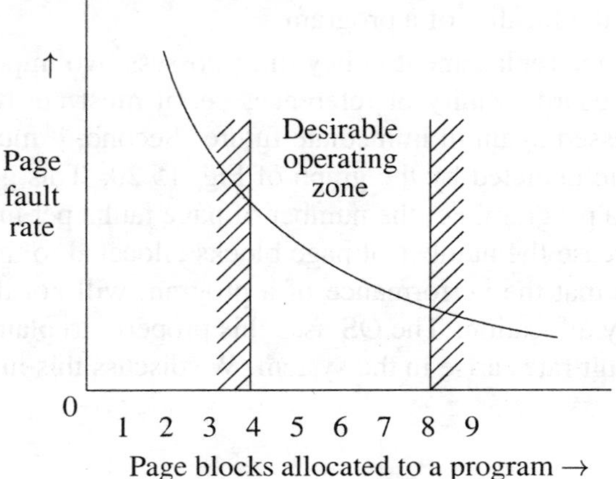

Fig. 15.21 Desirable operating zone

would be mostly busy implementing page traffic and performing program scheduling. CPU utilization would be very poor and system performance, measured in terms of response time or throughput, would be low. This situation is called *thrashing*.

Definition 15.3 (Thrashing) Thrashing *is the coincidence of high page traffic and low CPU utilization.*

From Fig. 15.21, it is seen that the cause of thrashing is an under-commitment of memory to programs. The cure is to increase the memory allocation for each program. This may have to be achieved by removing some programs from the memory—that is, by reducing the degree of multiprogramming.

Note that this reasoning is qualitative in nature. It does not help us in deciding how much memory we should allocate to a program. The main problem in deciding the memory allocation for a program is that the page fault characteristic of Fig. 15.20, i.e. the slope of the curve and the page fault rates, differ for different programs. In fact, even for the same program the characteristic is likely to be different at different times. Thus it is reasonable to assume that the optimum amount of memory for a program would have to be determined dynamically. This issue is discussed in Section 15.4.6.

15.4.3 Paging Hardware

Paging hardware performs the following functions:

1. Address translation and page fault generation
2. Support for page replacement
3. Memory protection.

Function 1 is the fundamental function performed by the paging hardware. It is implemented by the ATU. Function 2 involves collection of information that aids in page replacement. Function 3 involves protecting user programs from one another. However, certain new facets enter the picture because of noncontiguous memory allocation.

Address translation and page fault generation

The fundamentals of address translation have been discussed in Section 15.4.1 (see Fig. 15.18). A Page Map Table (PMT) is maintained for every program, showing the page blocks allocated to its pages. ATU uses the page number in a logical address to index the PMT.

Address translation buffers

Address translation would consume one memory cycle if PMTs are located in the memory. Some systems use *address translation buffers* to speed up address translation (see Fig. 15.22). Address translation buffers hold information concerning the page numbers and block numbers used in the last few page references. During address translation, the buffers are searched in an associative manner using the page number as the key. This search is performed concurrently with the normal address translation procedure through the PMT (see arrows marked 2′ and 3′ in Fig. 15.22). The PMT look-up is aborted if search in the buffers is successful. This makes address translation very fast for logical addresses involving recently referenced pages.

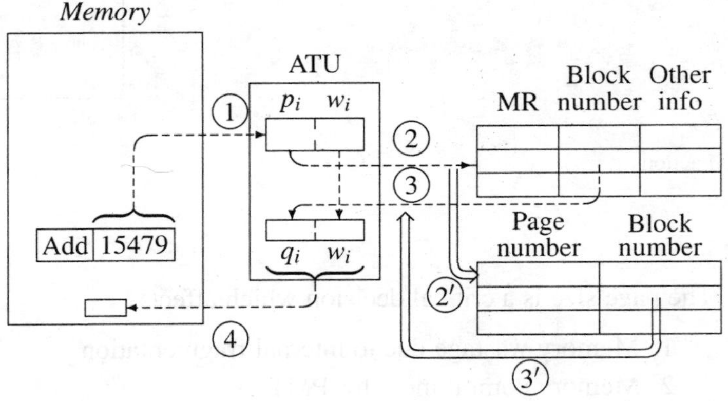

Fig. 15.22 Address translation buffers

ATU actions

Figure 15.23 shows actions of the ATU in more detail. PMTs for many programs exist in the memory. A special register of the CPU called the *PMT address register* (PMTAR) points at the PMT of the currently executing program. The PMT address for a program now becomes a part of the information in its PCB. It is loaded into PMTAR whenever the program is scheduled. As shown in Fig. 15.19, each PMT entry now contains two fields in addition to the page block number field. These are the *memory resident* (MR) field and the *other information* field. The MR field is a single bit indicating whether a program page is currently in the memory. It is used as follows:

1. When a page-in operation is performed, the field is set to 'resident' (i.e. 'R').
2. When a page-out operation is performed, the field is set to 'not resident' (i.e. 'NR').
3. During address translation, the field is used to check whether the page exists in memory. A page fault is raised if the MR field reads 'not resident'.

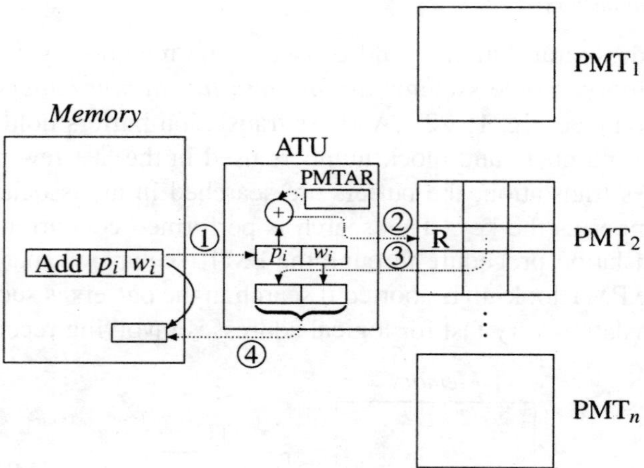

Fig. 15.23 ATU actions

Optimal page size

The page size is a critical decision which affects

1. Memory wastage due to internal fragmentation
2. Memory commitment for PMT
3. Influence on page fault rates.

To see this, consider a program of size z words. A page size of s words will imply that the program has pages $0 \ldots n-1$, such that $n = \lceil z/s \rceil$. Internal fragmentation will be $s/2$ memory words because the last page would be half empty on the average. The number of entries in the PMT would be n. Thus internal fragmentation varies directly with the page size, while PMT size varies inversely with it. To see how the page fault rate varies with the page size, consider memory allocation for P to be fixed. The number of pages of P in memory varies inversely with the page size. Now, one can find the page fault frequency from the characteristic of Fig. 15.20. For small page sizes, page fault rates would be small because more pages of the program would be in the memory at any time. Large page sizes would imply larger page fault rates.

We can compute the page size which minimizes the memory penalty due to the first two factors. If $s \ll z$, and each PMT entry occupies one word of memory, the optimal page size works out to be $s = \sqrt{2z}$. Thus, the optimal page size is 400 bytes for a program size of 80 K bytes, and only 200 bytes for a program of 20 K bytes. Practical systems tend to use larger page sizes (of the order of 1 K bytes) due to the following reasons:

1. PMT entries tend to occupy more than one memory word.
2. Hardware costs are high for smaller page sizes. For example, the cost of address translation increases due to the large number of bits used to represent a page number, and the cost of protection key memory increases due to increased size.
3. The secondary memory devices used to support paging also tend to operate less efficiently for smaller block sizes.

The decision to use larger page sizes than the optimal value implies somewhat larger page fault rates during the execution of a program. This fact represents a tradeoff between the hardware cost and program efficiency.

Paging device

At program initiation time, a copy of its logical address space is loaded onto a paging device. Page-in and page-out operations transfer program pages between the paging device and the memory. For efficient operation of the system, a paging device must possess the following properties:

1. High data transfer rates
2. Small access times
3. Large capacity and low cost.

High data transfer rates necessitate high recording densities. The *access time* is the time taken by the device to initiate data transfer after an IO command is given to it. In a continuously rotating medium such as a disk or a drum, this includes rotational latency (which can be as high as the time taken for one complete rotation of the surface (see Chapter 16)). Early paging systems used special purpose paging drums which could read or write one page during one rotation of the drum. These could provide a page transfer time of about 2 milliseconds. Contemporary systems tend to use sectored disk devices with multiple read/write heads to achieve better page transfer times.

Support for page replacement

A good page replacement policy must exploit locality of reference. The following information is needed for this purpose:

1. Time at which the last use of a page occurred.
2. Whether the page is clean or dirty, i.e. whether a write operation was performed on any word in the page.

The former helps to decide whether a page has been used in the recent past (i.e. whether it is a part of the *current locality* of a program). The latter is used to decide whether a page-out operation is necessary during page replacement. For a dirty page, a page-out operation must be performed because the copy existing in the paging device is outdated. If a page is clean, an up-to-date copy already exists on the paging device. Hence its copy in the memory can be simply overwritten by a new page.

The paging hardware typically collects page replacement information in the 'other information' field of the PMT. A single bit is sufficient to indicate whether a page is clean or dirty, whereas a number of bits are necessary to record the time when a page was last used.

Memory protection

Presence of the ATU greatly simplifies memory protection. Since every logical address is translated using the PMT, it is not easy for a program to access the memory allocated to another program. Hence protection exceptions can only arise in the following ways:

1. A program may generate an address that lies outside its logical address space.
2. A program might attempt to access a page in an invalid manner.

The former could manifest itself in the form of a very large page number. Unless this is detected, the ATU might access the contents of some other PMT. In the latter situation, a program may exceed its access privileges while accessing a page. For example, the program may have a read privilege to a page, but may attempt to modify it. This can happen in a system which permits controlled sharing of pages. We discuss two alternative approaches to memory protection which differ in whether protection is implemented *before* (or *during*) the translation of a logical address or *after* its translation. The former approach is termed as protection in the logical address space and the latter as protection in the physical address space.

Protection in the logical address space

Use of an address lying outside the logical address space of a program can be trapped during address translation. Figure 15.24 shows the use of a special CPU register, called the *PMT size* register, for this purpose. The ATU checks each page number against this register during Step 1 of address translation, i.e. before accessing the

PMT and raises a protection fault if page number exceeds PMT size. The PMT size information is maintained in the PCB of a program and loaded in the CPU when the program is scheduled.

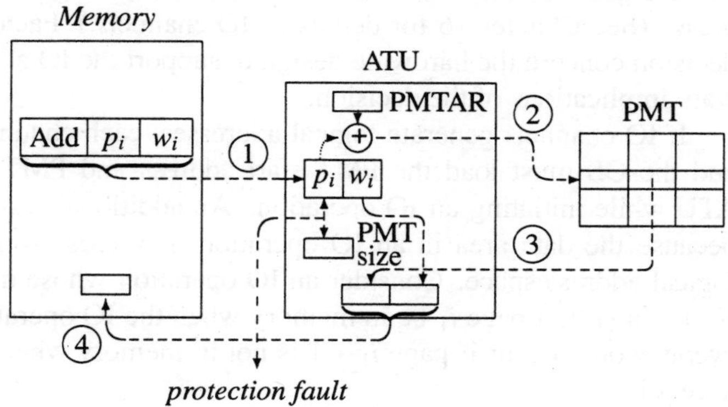

Fig. 15.24 Protection in logical address space

Protection against invalid accesses to a page can be implemented by using the PMT entry of a page to store the access privilege of a program for the page. Bits in the *other info* field can be used for this purpose. Each bit in the field corresponds to one kind of access to the page (e.g. read, write, etc.). The bit is set 'on' if the program possesses the corresponding access privilege to the page. During program execution, the ATU can perform this check during step 3 of address translation.

Protection in the physical address space

In this approach, standard memory protection hardware is used to implement protection after a logical address has been translated into a physical address. The bounds register schematic is not useful here since the program does not occupy a single contiguous area of memory. The protection key method can be easily adapted for this purpose as follows: The protection key memory stores the pair

(protection key, access privileges)

for each page block. A program whose PAPK matches the protection key of a block can access the contents of the page block in a manner consistent with the access privileges.

This approach has the advantage of not requiring any special hardware for protection in a virtual memory system. However, it has the limitation that all programs sharing a page must have identical access privileges for the page. For example, it is not possible to provide some program P_1 with a *read* access for a page if another program P_2 has a *read-write* access privilege for it.

IO operations in a paged environment

The major issue concerning IO operations in virtual memory systems is whether an address generated by the IO channel should be a logical address, or a physical address. (See Chapter 16 for details of IO channels.) Factors influencing this design decision concern the hardware design to support the IO addressing scheme, and software implications of the decision.

If IO channels generate logical addresses, each channel must have its own ATU and the OS must load the PMT start address and PMT size information into the ATU while initiating an IO operation. An additional responsibility rests on the OS because the data area in an IO operation may cross some page boundaries in the logical address space. Consider an IO operation whose data area extends (i_1, w_1) to $(i_1 + 1, w_2)$. Let page i_1 be in memory when the IO operation begins. The following events would occur if page $i_1 + 1$ is not in memory when the IO operation needs to access it:

1. The IO channel would raise a page fault.
2. The page fault would be serviced by the OS by loading the page in memory. (This may involve a page-out operation.)
3. The IO operation would be resumed.

However it may not be possible to suspend an IO operation while the required page is being loaded. For example, a read or write operation cannot be suspended. To avoid this problem, the OS would have to ensure that no page faults can occur during an IO operation. This can be achieved by preloading all pages of the data area of an IO operation into the memory. This involves page IO, which would delay the initiation of an IO operation. Furthermore, none of these pages can be removed from memory until the IO operation is completed.

If the hardware cost of using multiple ATUs is very high, the only feasible alternative is to let IO channels generate physical addresses while accessing the data area involved in an IO operation. Since a channel generates contiguous addresses during an IO operation, the data area must be contiguous in the memory. The OS can ensure this contiguity as follows:

1. The OS prefetches all pages of the data area involved in the IO operation into contiguous page blocks of the main memory.
2. All logical addresses used in the IO instruction(s) and IO command(s) (see Section 16.1) are converted to physical addresses.
3. The IO operation is now initiated. The IO channel uses physical addresses, i.e. it accesses the memory without any address translation.

When this alternative is chosen, physical memory protection is imperative, irrespective of whether logical address space protection is implemented. In both alternatives, the VM handler should be made aware that these pages should not be removed until the IO operation is complete. (This is called *IO fixing* of pages.)

Case studies of paging hardware

IBM/370

Address translation is performed by a hardware unit called the *Dynamic Address Translation* (DAT) unit. DAT can support two page sizes, viz. 2 K and 4 K bytes. The page size to be used must be indicated at system boot time. PMT(s) reside in main memory. A hardware register points to the PMT of the executing program. Address translation is performed using the PMT as illustrated in Fig. 15.22. A *translation look-aside buffer* (TLB) is used to speed up address translation. The buffer has a minimum of eight page entries.

Page replacement information is stored against a page block. Memory protection using the protection key schematic is also enforced at the page block level. The protection key memory contains one byte for each page block (see Fig. 15.8), which contains the following information:

1. A four bit memory protection key (in the range 0-15)
2. A fetch (i.e. *read*) protection bit
3. A reference bit
4. A write (i.e. *modify*) bit.

Memory protection keys are used to implement write protection. Thus, to write into a page block a program must have a matching protection code in its Program Status Word (PSW). Protection code '0' is a privileged protection code. A program possessing this code in its PSW can write into any page block. This facility is used to provide special memory access privileges to kernel programs. Read protection is implemented through the fetch protection bit. When this protection is enabled for a page block, only a program with a matching protection code (or the privileged code '0') can read from the page block. The reference bit is set 'on' every time the page block is referenced for a read or write purpose. This bit is the only hardware provision to support a page replacement policy. When a new page needs to be loaded, a page whose reference bit is 'off' is the obvious candidate for replacement. When all pages have their reference bits 'on', all the bits have to be turned 'off'. Thus no differentiation is possible between pages having their reference bits identically 'on' or 'off'. The write bit indicates whether a page is clean or dirty. This is used to decide whether a page-out operation is necessary while replacing the page.

VAX/11

VAX/11 uses a page size of 512 bytes. Both memory protection and information collection to support page replacement are implemented in the Page Table (PT). Protection is based on a protection code stored in each PT entry. All programs in the system are divided into four categories. All programs of a category have identical access privileges to a page based on the protection code stored in a page table entry. In the reducing order by privileges, these categories are: OS Kernel, OS executive,

OS supervisor and User. If a category possesses a certain access right to a page (e.g. read only, write only or read/write), all more privileged categories also possess that access right to the page. A page table length register is provided for implementing protection in the logical address space.

EXERCISE 15.4

1. Compare the use of following schemes to implement protection at the level of a page block
   (a) Protection through bounds registers
   (b) Protection through memory protection keys.
2. An OS designer wishes to determine the optimum page size on the basis of expected page fault rates for various page sizes. Assuming a fixed amount of memory to be available for the pages of a program, draw a graph of page size *vs.* expected page fault rate. Justify the nature of the graph qualitatively.
3. Comment on possible loss of protection if, after program switching, the new program uses old contents of the address translation buffers. Propose a solution to this problem. Explain which aspects of this solution can be handled by hardware.
4. A computer's memory has an access time of 1.0 microsecond. The PMT is stored in main memory. An associative memory is used to speed up address translation. It can hold 8 PMT entries at any time and has an access time of 0.1 microsecond. During the execution of a program, it is found that 85% of the time a required PMT entry exists in the associative memory and only 2% of the references lead to page faults. What is the average memory access time?
5. An OS designer considers the following design approaches
   (a) Make the OS supervisor permanently memory resident.
   (b) Page the supervisor in a manner analogous to the paging of user programs.
   (c) Make the supervisor a compulsory part of the logical address space of every program in the system.

   Which alternative would you recommend? Give reasons.

15.4.4 Paging Software

Paging software performs the following functions:

1. Implementation of the logical address space for a program
2. Management of the physical memory
3. Protection of programs
4. Collection of information to aid in page replacement
5. Page replacement
6. Control of memory allocation for a program
7. Implementation of page sharing.

Figure 15.25 illustrates the typical arrangement used for this purpose. It consists of the following three tables:

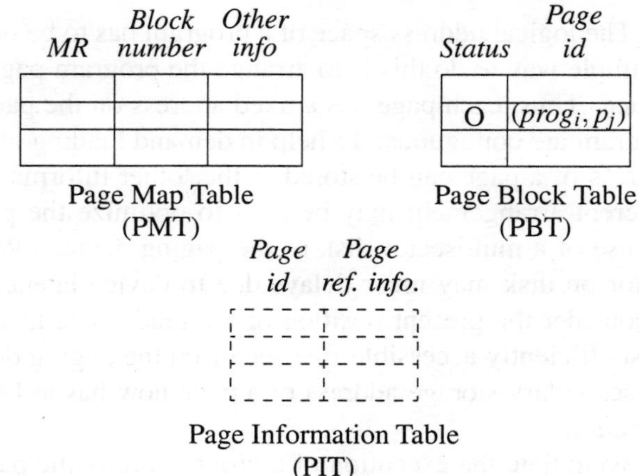

Fig. 15.25 Paging tables

1. The page map table (PMT),
2. The page block table (PBT),
3. The page information table (PIT).

PMT is used to implement address translation. This has been discussed before. A PBT entry shows the status of each page block in memory, that is (i) whether a page block is presently occupied, and (ii) if so, the identity of the page occupying it. We will represent the former by 'O' (i.e., occupied) or 'NO' (i.e., not occupied). The latter is represented by the pair

(program id, page number)

PIT contains the information regarding page usage collected by the paging hardware. Note that this table is shown by broken lines in Fig. 15.25. This is because the information and entry formats in this table differ from system to system. For example, IBM/370 collects the information against page blocks in memory, while VAX/11 collects it against a program page. Thus, depending on the details of the hardware, PIT may be a part of PBT or PMT, or may exist independently as shown.

The first four functions performed by the paging software are discussed in this section. The remaining functions are described in separate sections.

Implementation of the logical address space of a program

Implementation of the logical address space of a program involves the following sub-functions:

1. Organize a copy of the program's instructions and data on the paging device
2. Perform program initiation
3. Maintain the page map table, and perform page-in and page-out operations.

The logical address space of a program has to be organized on the paging device. A simple way to do this is to arrange the program pages contiguously on the paging device. Thus, each page has a fixed address on the paging device, and all pages of a program are contiguous. To help in demand loading of a page, the secondary storage address of a page can be stored in the 'other information' field of its PMT entry. A different arrangement may be used to optimize the paging performance. Consider the use of a multisector disk as the paging device. Writing out a page to a specific sector on disk may incur delays due to device latency. A better strategy would be to consider the present position of the read–write heads and write out a page at the most efficiently accessible free sector on the paging device. Information concerning the secondary storage address of a page now has to be updated after every page-out operation.

To initiate the execution of a program, only the page containing its start instruction needs to be loaded in the memory. Other pages would be brought in on demand. Details of PMT and the page-in and page-out operations have been discussed in sections 15.4.1 and 15.4.2.

Management of the physical memory

Management of the physical memory involves maintaining up-to-date information in the Page Block Table (PBT). Whenever a page p_i of $program_j$ is loaded into page block q_k, the OS writes the pair

$$(program_j,\ p_i)$$

into the q_k^{th} entry of the PBT. The hardware mechanism for gathering page reference information, e.g. the reference and modification bits, is initialized. At a page-out operation, the page block can be simply marked 'free'. Other fields of the PBT are now irrelevant until a new page is loaded into the block.

Protection

The program protection function involves the following:

1. Determining the protection information to be stored in various OS tables
2. Initializing the protection hardware.

When protection is implemented in the logical address space, the protection information exists mostly in a PMT and consists of access privileges of the pages. Initialization of the protection hardware simply amounts to loading the PMT start address and PMT size information into appropriate registers while scheduling a program. As seen before, this is achieved by putting these items of information in a program's PCB. When protection is implemented in the physical address space, little protection information exists in OS tables. The protection key of every page block allocated to a program is initialized to the APK of the program. This must be performed while initiating a program, and also after every page-in operation. While scheduling a program, the PMT start address and PMT size must be loaded into appropriate registers.

Collection of information to aid in page replacement

This function simply involves initializing the page reference and modify bits when a page-in operation is performed. The information is actually collected by the hardware. Peculiarities of the paging hardware may necessitate certain additional housekeeping functions. For example, the IBM/370 provides a single bit to indicate when a page was last referenced. This cannot differentiate between two pages whose reference bits are 'on'. When the reference bits for all pages of a program become 'on', the software must turn them all 'off'.

15.4.5 Page Replacement

Page replacement involves the following functions:

1. Determine which page is to be removed from the memory.
2. Perform a page-out operation.
3. Perform a page-in operation.

Functions 2 and 3 involve housekeeping operations on the paging tables PMT and PBT as described in the previous section. In fact, these functions are mechanisms of page replacement. Function 1 involves a policy decision, which is taken by a page replacement algorithm. Figure 15.26 depicts the arrangement of policy and mechanism modules of the VM handler. The page-in and page-out mechanisms interact with the paging hardware to implement their functionalities. They also update the paging tables to reflect their actions. The paging policy in force uses the information in paging tables to invoke the page-in and page-out mechanisms.

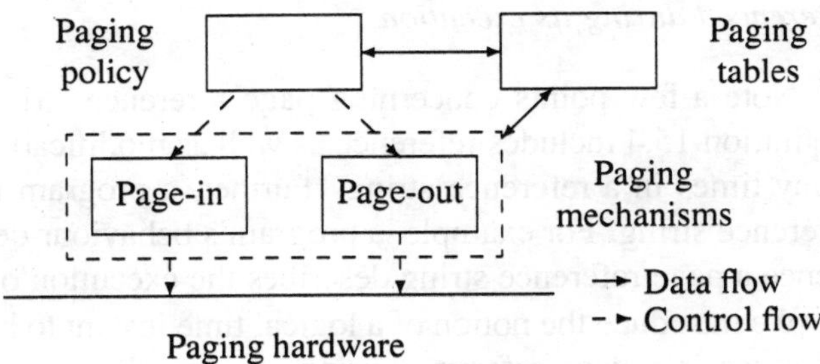

Fig. 15.26 VM handler modules in a paged VM system

15.4.5.1 Page Replacement Policies

In Section 15.4.2 we discussed two requirements which should be satisfied by a page replacement policy. These are:

1. Non-interference with the program's locality of reference—that is, the page replacement policy must not remove a page which may be referenced in the immediate future.
2. The page fault rate must not increase with an increase in the memory allocation for a program.

The following notation is used while discussing page replacement policies:

$alloc_i$	:	Amount of memory (i.e. number of page blocks) allocated to $prog_i$. The subscript is omitted when only one program is under consideration.

We evaluate different page replacement policies on the basis of the first requirement, by making the tacit assumption that the amount of memory allocated to a program (i.e. the value of $alloc_i$) is fixed during its execution. This implies that a page of the same program is removed from memory to load a new page. (Change in the value of $alloc_i$ is considered separately in Section 15.4.6.) We also define a property that must be possessed by a page replacement policy if it is to satisfy the second requirement. The discussion in this section shows that the LRU page replacement policy satisfies both the requirements.

Page reference strings

We introduce the notion of a page reference string to help us examine the performance of different page replacement policies.

Definition 15.4 (Page reference string) *A* page reference string *of a program is a sequence of page numbers, arranged in the chronological order in which the pages are referenced during its execution.*

Note a few points concerning page reference strings. The word 'reference' in Definition 15.4 includes reference as well as modification. A page number can occur many times in a reference string. Further, a program may not have a unique page reference string. For example, a program's behaviour depends on the data input to it. Hence a page reference string describes the execution of a program on a given data.

We introduce the notion of a logical time instant to help us refer to a specific page reference in a page reference string, A *logical time instant* is the time in a logical clock of the program, i.e. in a clock which is advanced only when the program is in the *running* state. Thus, the logical time instants at which different instructions of a program are executed form a sequence of consecutive integers. These are referred to as $t_0, t_1, \ldots$. A logical time instant is used as an index into a page reference string. For ease of use, the logical time instants are shown as a string associated with the page reference string. This string is called the *reference-time string*.

Example 15.13 A page reference string and its reference-time string for a program P are as follows:

$$page\ reference\ string \ : \ 1, 1, 2, 1, 1, 1, 3, 1, 3 \ldots \tag{15.4}$$

$$reference\ time\ string \ : \ t_0, t_1, t_2, t_3, t_4, t_5, t_6, t_7, t_8 \ldots \tag{15.5}$$

Here, page 1 was referenced at the logical time instants t_0, t_1, t_3, t_4, t_5 and t_7.

In the following, we describe the three page replacement policies and discuss their practical performance:

1. Optimal page replacement policy
2. First-in-First-out (FIFO) page replacement policy
3. Least Recently Used (LRU) page replacement policy.

Optimal page replacement

The optimal page replacement policy makes the optimum page replacement decision at every page fault. It achieves this by analysing all the page references in a string—the past as well as the future references. In other words, this policy requires future knowledge concerning the behaviour of a program. This makes optimal page replacement infeasible in practice. However, this policy provides a very useful basis for studying the performance of other page replacement policies.

(a)

PMT

	MR	*Block number*	*Other info*
1	R	*i*	
2	R	*i*+1	
3	NR		

PBT

	Status	*Page id*
i	O	(P,1)
i+1	O	(P,2)

PIT

Page id	*Page ref info*
(P,1)	–
(P,2)	–
(P,3)	–

(b)

PMT

	MR	*Block number*	*Other info*
1	R	*i*	
2	NR		
3	R	*i*+1	

PBT

	Status	*Page id*
i	O	(P,1)
i+1	O	(P,3)

PIT

Page id	*Page ref info*
(P,1)	–
(P,2)	–
(P,3)	–

Fig. 15.27 Optimal page replacement

Example 15.14 Figure 15.27(a) shows the paging tables after time instant t_5 in the page reference string (15.4) when program P is executed with *alloc* = 2. At t_6, the reference to Page 3 leads to a page fault. The replacement policy analyses future references of the pages in memory, viz. Pages 1 and 2, and decides to remove Page 2 from memory since it is not referenced in the immediate future while Page 1 is (see Fig. 15.27(b)). Note that PIT is not used by the optimal page replacement policy.

FIFO page replacement

In FIFO page replacement, the PIT entry of a page is used to record the time when the page was last loaded into memory. When a page fault occurs, this information in PIT is used to determine p_{early}, the earliest loaded page of a program. This page is replaced by the required page.

Example 15.15 Figure 15.28 illustrates the performance of the FIFO replacement policy assuming *alloc* = 2. Part (a) of the figure shows the paging tables after time instant t_5. When a reference to Page 3 leads to a page fault at t_6, Page 1 is removed from memory since it was loaded earlier than Page 2. It is now replaced by Page 3 (see Fig. 15.28(b)). However, page 1 is referenced again at the very next instant, i.e. at t_7. This leads to another page fault. Page 2 is now removed, and page 1 is loaded in its place (see Fig. 15.28(c)). This leads to more page faults than in Ex. 15.14.

PMT:

	MR	*Block number*	*Other info*
1	R	i	
2	R	i+1	
3	NR		

PBT:

	Status	*Page id*
i	O	(P,1)
i+1	O	(P,2)

PIT:

Page id	*Page ref info*
(P,1)	t_0
(P,2)	t_2
(P,3)	–

(a)

1	NR		
2	R	i+1	
3	R	i	

i	O	(P,3)
i+1	O	(P,2)

(P,1)	–
(P,2)	t_2
(P,3)	t_6

(b)

1	R	i+1	
2	NR		
3	R	i	

i	O	(P,3)
i+1	O	(P,1)

(P,1)	t_7
(P,2)	–
(P,3)	t_6

(c)

Fig. 15.28 FIFO page replacement

LRU page replacement

The LRU policy uses the principle of locality of reference as the basis for its replacement decisions. Its operation can be described as follows: At every page fault the *least recently used* (LRU) page is replaced by a new page. This results in a high probability that the next page reference will not cause a page fault. The PIT entry of a page records the time when the page was last referenced. When a page fault occurs, PIT is searched to locate the page p_{lru} whose last reference is earlier than that of all other pages. This page is replaced with the new page.

Example 15.16 Figure 15.29 illustrates the performance of the LRU replacement policy when *alloc* = 2. Part (a) of the figure shows the PIT information after time instant t_5. At t_6, page 2 is replaced by page 3 since its last reference precedes the last reference of page 1 (see Fig. 15.29(b)). Thus no page fault occurs when page 1 is referenced again at the very next instant, i.e. at t_7.

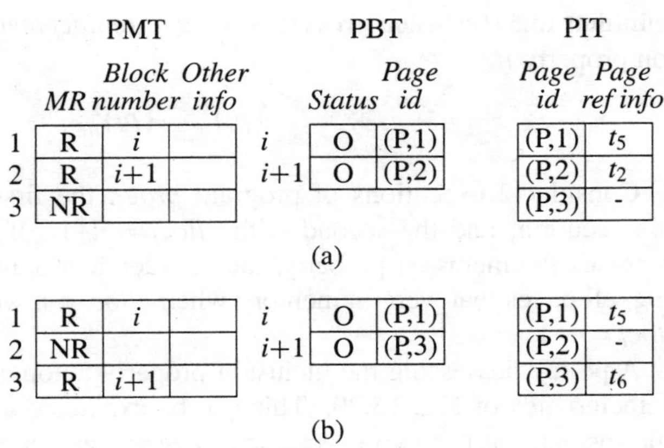

PMT
PBT
PIT
MR
Block number
Other info
Status
Page id
Page id
Page ref info
1 R i
2 R i+1
3 NR
i O (P,1)
i+1 O (P,2)
(P,1) t5
(P,2) t2
(P,3) -
(a)
1 R i
2 NR
3 R i+1
i O (P,1)
i+1 O (P,3)
(P,1) t5
(P,2) -
(P,3) t6
(b)

Fig. 15.29 LRU page replacement

From Ex. 15.14 and 15.16 it can be seen that the memory configuration at time instant t_7^- is identical in optimal replacement and LRU replacement. From this, can one conclude that the LRU policy can perform as well as the optimal policy? This is obviously not true. LRU does not possess future knowledge, hence at t_6 it does not know that Page 1 will be referenced earlier than Page 2 in page reference string (15.4). It replaced 2 instead of 1 simply because 2 had not been referenced for a longer period of time than 1.

Optimal page replacement is infeasible in practice. Hence the choice of the page replacement policy is limited to the FIFO and LRU policies. Let us analyse why LRU performed better than FIFO in examples 15.15 and 15.16. At time instant t_6, the FIFO policy removed Page 1 because it had been loaded earlier, whereas LRU removed Page 2 because it had not been referenced for a longer period of time than 1. This is in keeping with the principle of locality which stipulates that the probability of being referenced after t_6 is higher for Page 1 than for Page 2. Thus, LRU does not interfere with the locality of a program whereas FIFO does.

Now consider the question of whether FIFO and LRU possess the desirable page fault characteristic of Fig. 15.20, i.e. whether the page fault rate can increase with an increase in the memory allocation to a program. To answer this question, we define a property called the inclusion property.

Inclusion property in page replacement

We introduce the following notation to help in discussing the performance of a page replacement policy for different values of $alloc_i$:

$\{p_i\}_n^k$: Set of program pages existing in memory at time instant t_k^+ if $alloc_i = n$ all through the execution of program $prog_i$ (t_k^+ implies after time instant t_k but before t_{k+1}).

Definition 15.5 (Inclusion property) *A page replacement policy possesses the* inclusion property *if*

$$\{p_i\}_n^k \subseteq \{p_i\}_{n+1}^k.$$

Consider 2 executions of program $prog_i$, the first with $alloc_i = n$ all through the execution, and the second with $alloc_i = n+1$. If the page replacement policy possesses the inclusion property, then at identical points during these executions of $prog_i$ all pages that were in memory when $alloc_i = n$ would also be in memory when $alloc_i = n+1$.

A policy possessing the inclusion property automatically satisfies the page fault characteristics of Fig. 15.20. This can be explained as follows: Consider identical time instants during two executions of $prog_i$ with n and $n+1$ pages, respectively. If the policy possesses the inclusion property, all n pages which were in memory when $alloc_i = n$ are also in memory when $alloc_i = n+1$. Thus, when $alloc_i = n+1$, the memory contains one page in addition to the n pages when $alloc_i$ had the value n. This additional page may (or may not) avoid some page faults from arising. In any case, the number of page faults cannot be larger than when $alloc_i = n$. Thus, the page fault rate does not increase when the allocation for a program is increased. However, if a policy does not possess the inclusion property, then $\{p_i\}_{n+1}^k$ does not contain some page(s) contained in $\{p_i\}_n^k$. References to this page would result in page faults. This may lead to a larger number of page faults when $alloc_i = n+1$ than when $alloc_i = n$.

It is easy to prove that the LRU policy possesses the inclusion property. Example 15.17 shows that the FIFO policy does not possess the inclusion property.

Example 15.17 Consider the following page reference and reference time strings for a program:

$$page\ reference\ string \ : \ 5, 4, 3, 2, 1, 4, 3, 5, 4, 3, 2, 1, 5, \ldots \qquad (15.6)$$

$$reference\ time\ string \ : \ t_0, t_1, t_2, t_3, t_4, t_5, t_6, t_7, t_8, t_9, t_{10}, t_{11}, t_{12}, \ldots \qquad (15.7)$$

Figure 15.30 shows the behaviour of the FIFO page replacement policy. Each column of boxes shows page blocks allocated to the program. Numbers in the boxes indicate pages in memory *after* executing the memory reference marked under the column. Page references marked with '*' cause page faults and result in page replacement, which is performed by replacing the earliest loaded page existing in memory.

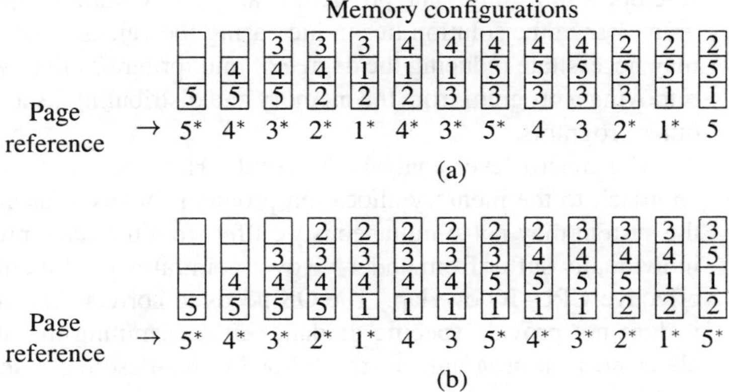

Fig. 15.30 FIFO allocation: (a) *alloc* = 3, (b) *alloc* = 4

From Fig. 15.30, we have $\{p_i\}_4^{11} = \{2, 1, 4, 3\}$, while $\{p_i\}_3^{11} = \{1, 5, 2\}$. Thus, FIFO page replacement does not possess the inclusion property. This leads to a page fault at t_{12} when $alloc_i = 4$. Thus, a total of 11 page faults arise in 13 time instants when $alloc_i = 4$, while 10 page faults arise when $alloc_i = 3$.

15.4.6 Controlling the Memory Allocation to a Program

Section 15.4.2 described how an over-commitment or under-commitment of memory to a program can adversely affect system performance. An over-commitment leads to good program performance but lower degree of multiprogramming, hence poor CPU–IO overlap. An under-commitment leads to poor program performance, hence high page fault rates and heavy page traffic. In this situation we notice an increase in the paging and scheduling overheads, high page IO and a reduction in the overlap of CPU activities with program IO (we will call this the *effective* CPU-IO overlap).

How should the OS avoid under-commitment or over-commitment of memory to a program and keep a program within the desirable operating zone of Fig. 15.21? We will discuss this issue at two levels: At the *micro* level we discuss this issue from the viewpoint of a program, while at the *macro* level we discuss it from the viewpoint of the OS. At the micro level, the page fault rate of a program $prog_i$ is determined by the value of $alloc_i$ and the page fault characteristic of Fig. 15.20. Thus a high page fault rate implies an under-commitment of memory.

At the macro level the OS must carefully differentiate between the following situations

1. Low page fault rates and low effective CPU–IO overlap.
2. High page fault rates and low effective CPU–IO overlap.

The former situation arises due to a lower degree of multiprogramming resulting from over-commitment of memory to programs. The OS can try smaller values of *alloc* in the hope of increasing the degree of multiprogramming. The latter situation resembles thrashing. The problem is an under-commitment of memory to each program, hence the solution lies in increasing the values of *alloc* for all programs. This may necessitate reducing the degree of multiprogramming, which can be achieved by removing a program from the memory and distributing its allocated memory amongst other programs.

The macro level analysis is useful. However, it does not provide a practical approach to the memory allocation problem for two reasons. First, all programs in the system may not simultaneously suffer from the same problem. A program could individually suffer from under- or over-commitment of memory without causing low effective CPU–IO overlap. The OS needs to correct this situation as well. Second, it does not provide specific guidance in determining the amount of memory to be allocated to a program. In the following we describe a scientific approach to this problem.

Working set

Definition 15.6 (Working set) *The* working set *of a program is the set of program pages which will be referenced in the next w instructions of the program, where w is a system defined constant.*

The next w instructions are said to constitute the *working set window*. We introduce the following notation for our discussion:

WS_i	:	Working set for program $prog_i$.
WSS_i	:	Size of the working set for program $prog_i$, i.e. the number of pages in WS_i (note that $WSS_i \leq w$ because a page may be referenced more than once in a window).

WS_i obviously varies with time. We will optionally use a superscript to denote the time at which the working set information is determined. Thus, WS_i^j is the working set at time instant t_j^-. Program $prog_i$ would execute without page faults if all pages in WS_i^j are in memory at every time instant t_j. The value of WSS_i could be used to determine the amount of memory to be allocated to $prog_i$. For example, one can set $alloc_i$ = WSS_i^j at every time instant t_j^-. This will eliminate the problem of overcommitment or undercommitment of memory described earlier. However, this approach suffers from two practical difficulties. First, it is very expensive to determine WSS_i^j at every time instant t_j. Second, the approach requires knowledge about the future behaviour of a program, which is not available in practice. These difficulties are addressed in the following.

A memory allocator based on the notion of working set can periodically determine WSS_i and adjust the value of $alloc_i$ accordingly. Following the determination of working sets at a time instant t_j, the degree of multiprogramming should be decreased if

$$\Sigma_{prog_k} WSS_k^j > s_m$$

where s_m is the size of memory and $prog_k$ is a program in memory. The number of programs in memory can be decreased by removing some programs until $\Sigma_{prog_k} WSS_k^j \leq s_m$. The degree of multiprogramming can be increased at time instant t_j if $\Sigma_{prog_k} WSS_k^j < s_m$ and there exists a program $prog_g$ such that

$$WSS_g^j \leq (s_m - \Sigma_{prog_k} WSS_k^j).$$

Note that in this model the working set of a program is determined periodically rather than continuously. This reduces the overheads of memory management. However, it is now possible for $WSS_i^{j'}$ to exceed $alloc_i$ at some time instant $t_{j'} > t_j$. The second difficulty is lack of knowledge about the future behaviour of a program. However, future behaviour of a program related to page references can be predicted reasonably well using the principle of locality of reference. Hence a practical approximation of WS_i (and WSS_i) is obtained from the pages referenced in the previous w machine instructions of the program.

Fig 15.31 illustrates the implementation of working sets. Part (a) of the figure illustrates the concept. The working set is the set of pages referenced in the next w instructions, where w is the size of the working set window. Part (b) shows the implementation of working sets. The working set window now includes the *previous* w instructions executed by the program.

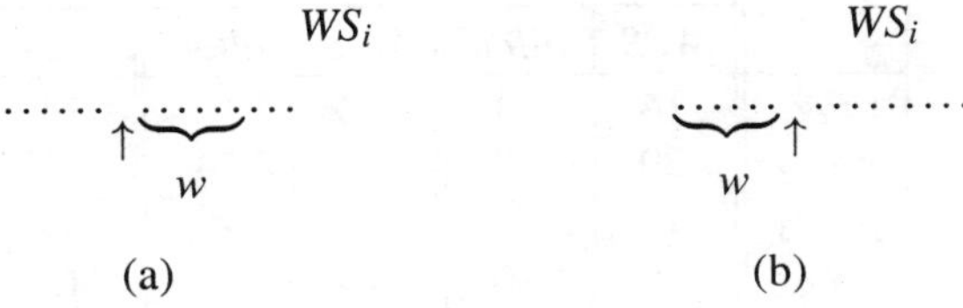

Fig. 15.31 Working set : (a) concept, and (b) implementation

The working set is computed periodically for each executing program. The memory allocator uses the working set information to determine the allocation for a program. For a program $prog_i$, $alloc_i$ is set to WSS_i. If the program has to be suspended due to shortage of memory, $alloc_i$ is set to '0' and its pages are moved to the paging device. Note that page faults will occur due to two reasons. First, $WSS_i^{j'}$ may exceed $alloc_i$ since working sets are determined periodically rather than continuously. Second, working sets are determined approximately rather than exactly (see Fig. 15.31). The page faults will be serviced without increasing $alloc_i$. Thus, page replacement algorithms like LRU would be applied locally to each program.

Performance of a VM handler using the notion of working sets is sensitive to the value of w. If w is too large, the memory would contain some pages which are not likely to be referenced. This would result in overcommitment of memory to programs. This would force the VM handler to reduce the degree of multiprogramming, thereby affecting system performance. If w is too small, there is a danger of undercommitment of memory to programs, leading to a rise in page fault frequency and the possibility of thrashing.

Example 15.18 An OS has 60 page blocks available for allocation to user programs. For simplicity we assume that the working sets of all programs which are in memory are recomputed at time instants $t_j^+, j = 1,2\ldots$. Following the computation of working sets, the VM handler processes each program $prog_i$ as follows: It sets $alloc_i = WSS_i$ if it can allocate WSS_i memory blocks to it, else it sets $alloc_i = 0$ and swaps out $prog_i$. For each program, the value of $alloc$ assigned at t_j^+ is held constant till t_{j+1}. The process of computing working sets and determining $alloc_i$ for all programs is repeated at t_{j+1}^+.

Figure 15.32 illustrates operation of the system. The Figure shows values of $alloc_i$ and WSS_i for all programs $prog_i$ at time instants $t_{11}^+,\ldots,t_{14}^+$. At t_{11}^+, $WSS_4 = 10$ and $alloc_4 = 0$. This implies that $prog_4$ is swapped out. At t_{12}^+, values of $WSSi$, $i = 1,\ldots,3$ are recomputed. The value of WSS_4 is carried over from t_{11}^+ since $prog_4$ has not been executed in the interval t_{11}–t_{12}. $alloc_i$, $i = 1,\ldots,3$ are now assigned new values. $prog_4$ still cannot be swapped in for lack of memory. At t_{13}, $prog_i$ is swapped in, however it is swapped out again at t_{14}. Note that the smallest allocation for $prog_2$ is 11 page blocks and the largest allocation is 25 page blocks during the interval t_{11}–t_{14}. This variation is performed to adjust its allocation to its recent behaviour.

	t_{11}		t_{12}		t_{13}		t_{14}	
	WSS	*alloc*	*WSS*	*alloc*	*WSS*	*alloc*	*WSS*	*alloc*
$prog_1$	14	14	12	12	14	14	13	13
$prog_2$	20	20	24	24	11	11	25	25
$prog_3$	18	18	19	19	20	20	18	18
$prog_4$	10	0	10	0	10	10	12	0

Fig. 15.32 Operation of a working set memory allocator

15.4.7 Sharing of Pages

An OS must provide support for sharing of programs and data. Such sharing can be static or dynamic in nature. In *static sharing*, which is performed by a linker or loader before the execution of a program begins, one program includes other programs as its parts. Thus, if two Programs A and B statically share another Program C, C is included to become a part of both A and B. If A and B are executing concurrently, two copies of Program C exist in the memory. For example, one copy of the 0'th page of Program C may exist in page block k as page i of Program A. Another copy may exist in page block l as page j of Program B.

Dynamic sharing is implemented during the execution of programs. The sharing of Program C by Programs A and B is implemented as follows (see Fig. 15.33): Consider Program A to begin its execution earlier. When it needs to use Program C in a shared mode, the OS includes C into the logical address space of Program A by assigning the page numbers i, i+1 ... to the pages of C. These pages are loaded into the memory on an on-demand basis. When Program B needs to use Program C, the OS similarly includes C into the logical address space of B, and assigns the page numbers j, j+1 ... to it. While paging C into the memory, OS attempts to share a single copy of C's pages between Programs A and B. Thus, if B page faults for page j (which is page 0 of Program C), the OS checks to see if a copy of this page, viz. page i of Program A, exists in memory. If so, it shares the same copy of the page between Programs A and B.

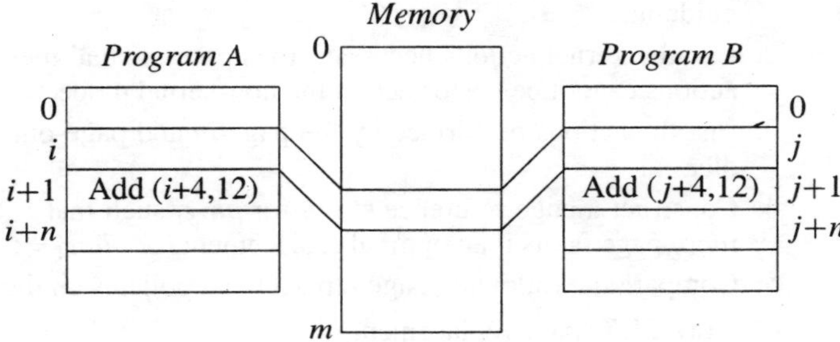

Fig. 15.33 Dynamic sharing of pages

What are the constraints on the dynamic sharing of programs and data? A data page can be freely shared, so long as the sharing programs synchronize their updates to avoid race conditions. However, certain special conditions have to be satisfied when the shared pages contain a program. The program should be re-entrant. This condition, which ensures that a program can be executed by concurrent processes without mutual interference, is carried over from program sharing in nonpaged environments. The second condition pertains to the position of the shared program in the logical address spaces of the sharing programs. Consider an instruction 'Add (4,12)' located in Page '1' of program C. This instruction stands for addition of word 12 of Page 4 of the program. When Page '1' of Program C is included as page i+1 of Program A, this instruction is modified to 'Add (i+4,12) (see Fig. 15.33). When page '1' of program C is included as logical page j+1 of program C, the same instruction has to be changed to 'Add (j+4,12)'. Hence programs A and C cannot share the same copy of the page in memory unless $i = j$. This gives rise to the requirement that the pages of a dynamically shared program should occupy identical positions in the logical address spaces of sharing programs. In the present case, program C must start on the same page, say page k, in both A and B.

Sharing of pages can be implemented by making the PMT entries of sharing programs point at the same page block. However, this approach has two drawbacks: PBT organization has to be changed since the PBT entry of a shared page will need to contain many (*program id*, *page no*) pairs (see Fig. 15.25). Page replacement algorithm also becomes more complex if LRU information is collected against a PBT entry of a page block since many programs access this page. A better method would be to maintain the information concerning shared pages in a separate *shared pages table* (SPT). This will also permit the use of a different page replacement criterion for managing shared pages.

EXERCISE 15.4

1. Develop a set of guidelines for a programmer to improve the page fault behaviour of a program in a paged virtual memory system. Describe the rationale behind each guideline.
2. List the kernel actions necessary to support virtual memory operation. Explain why actions cannot be performed in the non-kernel mode.
3. List the actions performed by the page-in and page-out mechanisms of the VM handler.
4. Construct a page reference string for $prog_i$ such that LRU replacement will produce more page faults than optimal replacement for $alloc_i = 5$.
5. Compare the following page replacement policies on the basis of OS overheads:
   (a) FIFO page replacement
   (b) LRU page replacement.
6. Show that the LRU page replacement policy possesses the inclusion property.
7. An OS uses LRU page replacement. It is proposed to modify the policy as follows:
   (a) The page size is made half of the original page size.
   (b) The total memory allocated to a program is maintained at the same value as in the original policy.
   (c) All other aspects remain unchanged.

   Compare the performance of the modified policy with the original page replacement policy.
8. An OS implementing dynamic sharing permits different access privileges, e.g. read, read–write, etc., to the programs sharing a page
   (a) Describe the housekeeping actions performed by the OS in the following situations
      (i) When a page fault arises in the system. (*Hint:* Page faults can arise for both shared and nonshared pages.)
      (ii) When a shared page drops out of the working set of one of the programs sharing it.
   (b) How should memory protection be implemented? In this context, discuss the advantages and disadvantages of
      (i) Protection in the logical address space

(ii) Protection in the physical address space.

15.4.8 Memory Management in Unix

Early versions of Unix did not use noncontiguous memory allocation. Memory allocation was on a first-fit basis and an entire process was swapped out when sufficient memory was not available to accommodate all processes. Shared code segments were not swapped out.

Berkeley Unix 4.2 uses demand paged virtual memory allocation on the VAX/11, using a page size of 1 K bytes (although the hardware permits a page size of 512 bytes). The page replacement policy is hampered by the fact that the system does not possess any features assisting in LRU replacement. For speedy servicing of a page fault, the OS always keeps a certain number of page blocks free. A global page replacement policy is used by scanning all memory resident pages in a fixed order. When the scan reaches a page, it is marked for removal and its page table entry is marked invalid. It may be some time before the page is actually overwritten. If a program faults for that page in the meanwhile, it can be re-connected to the program without involving any page IO. The scan stops if the number of free blocks in the memory reaches the desirable number of free page blocks. Care is taken to see that the number of page blocks for a program does not become too small. The notion of working set is not used, instead the memory allocation for a process is held at a certain fraction of its size.

15.5 VIRTUAL MEMORY USING SEGMENTATION

In a segmented virtual memory system, a programmer views a program to be a collection of program components called *segments*. Each segment is a *logical* unit of a program as defined by the program's designer. In programming terms, a segment usually consists of a set of procedures or data and forms a module of some software system. The motivation for segmentation is to group together procedures and data which possess common attributes for sharing by other procedures. This is advantageous for implementing protection in a large software system.

Each logical address in a segmented program is viewed to be a pair

$$(s_i, w_i)$$

where s_i and w_i are the segment id and word id, respectively. During execution, an ATU converts this reference into a physical address using the schematic of Fig. 15.34. Several similarities with the paged virtual memory system (see Fig. 15.23) can be noted. A special hardware register called the *segment table address register* (STAR) points to the *segment table* (ST) of a program. This is accessed with s_i as an index. If the segment is present in the memory, address translation is completed using the memory start address found in its segment table entry. Else, a 'missing segment' fault is raised. Segmentation differs from paging in one significant respect. Being logical units, segments have different lengths. Hence memory cannot be allocated in

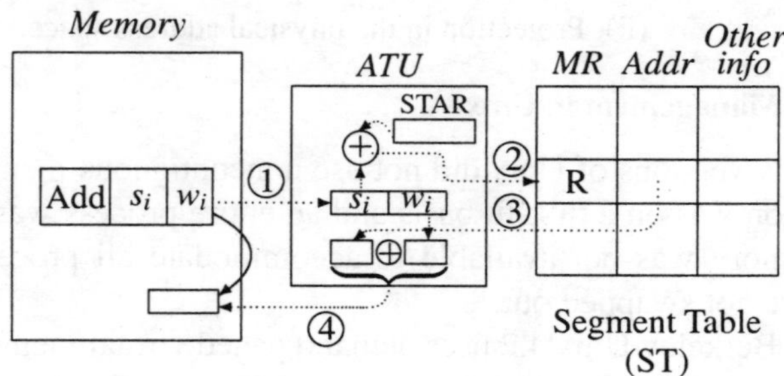

Fig. 15.34 Virtual memory implementation using segmentation

terms of fixed sized blocks. Each segment table entry therefore contains a complete physical memory address rather than simply a block number. Address translation now involves an addition cycle rather than mere bit juxtaposition as in paging.

Important variations exist concerning the manner in which s_i and w_i are indicated in a program instruction. One alternative is to use numeric identifiers for each of them. The logical address thus consists of a segment number and a word number, and address translation is performed as described earlier. Alternatively, s_i and w_i could be specified in a symbolic form, i.e. as names. A typical logical address in this case would be

`(alpha, beta)`

where `alpha` is the name of a segment and `beta` is the name of a word in it. In this case, an associative mapping has to be used to obtain the start address of the segment in memory. Another associative mapping is required to obtain the offset of the word within the segment. Both numerical and symbolic id's have been used in practical segmented VM systems. For simplicity, the discussion in this section (as also the illustrations) will presume the use of numerical identifiers. Use of symbolic identifiers, and their influence on various OS functions is discussed as part of the MULTICS case study in Section 15.5.5.

15.5.1 Constituting Multi-segment Programs

Readying a program for use in a segmented virtual memory system involves a certain amount of preprocessing during linking. The central issue in preprocessing concerns the resolution of a symbolic reference, e.g. a reference to a symbol `xyz`, into the logical address (s_i, w_i). Consider a reference to `xyz` from within a procedure P. Let us assume that the segment in which P is located has been assigned the segment id seg_i. We now have to decide whether `xyz` is to be represented by a pair like (seg_i, $word_i$) or (seg_j, $word_j$), i.e. whether `xyz` lies within the same segment as the reference to it, or lies in some other segment. In the latter case, we have to determine seg_j.

A multi-segment program could be constituted through static or dynamic linking. In a statically linked multi-segment program, the linker assigns segment id's to the segments during linking. As in the linking of non-segmented programs, symbolic references to procedures or data located in other segments are resolved at this time. Simultaneously, each symbolic reference is converted into the two-part logical address (s_i, w_i). (This can be achieved simply by storing the logical address of a symbol in NTAB—see Section 7.2.) In such systems it is convenient to use numeric identifiers in a logical address. As already described, this speeds up address translation. The processing involved closely resembles the processing in a conventional linker.

In dynamically linked multi-segment programs, inter-segment references are resolved during program execution. Such systems typically use symbolic identifiers for segments and words. Linking can be performed through an explicit kernel call. For example, `Link alpha` is a call for linking Segment `alpha` with the program. Alternatively, linking could be performed individually for every inter-segment reference. This would be done the first time such a reference is encountered during program execution. For example, when a reference to `xyz` is encountered for the first time, the system must resolve it into the pair (s_i, w_i). This would require OS intervention. Subsequent executions of the reference do not require OS intervention since linking need not be repeatd. Note that linking actions do not have any connection with segment faults, which could occur for the first or subsequent executions of a reference.

15.5.2 Management of Physical Memory

Many similarities exist with memory management in paged virtual memory systems. The memory allocation for a program could be determined using the notion of working sets. A segment which drops out of the working set of a program can be removed from memory. Additionally, a segment may be removed from the memory on an LRU basis while servicing segment faults.

Some differences with paged virtual memory are as follows: Segment sizes can differ subject to the maximum size determined by the number of address bits for w_i in a logical address. This implies that it may not be possible to replace one segment existing in the memory by another segment. This can lead to memory fragmentation. Fragmentation can be tackled either through compaction, which is aided by the presence of an ATU, or through the first fit or best fit strategies. Some segmented VM systems permit a segment to grow or shrink in size dynamically. This is possible because segmented logical address space is inherently two-dimentional, rather than linear in nature—that is, the last word of one segment does not 'precede' the 0th word of the next segment in a program. Because of this, a change in the size of a segment does not cause any difficulties in addressing. From the viewpoint of memory management, dynamic growth in the size of a segment can be handled by allocating a larger memory area to a segment when its size increases. A segment can be permitted to grow in its present location in memory if adjoining free areas exist in memory.

15.5.3 Protection and Sharing

Two important issues in the protection and sharing of segments are:

1. Protection against exceeding the size of a segment
2. Static and dynamic sharing of segments.

Unlike the pages of a paged virtual memory system, segments can have different sizes. Hence, it is necessary to ensure that an addressed word lies within a segment. For example, if the size of s_i is $size_i$, use of a $w_i > size_i$ should be detected. This check is performed by the ATU during address translation.

Being a logical entity in terms of program design, a segment is a very convenient unit for sharing. Use of numerical segment id's imply an ordering of segments in the logical address space. When segments are shared, this ordering gives rise to the same requirement concerning the positions of segments in a program as in the case of a paged virtual memory system (see Fig. 15.33). No such restrictions arise when symbolic identifiers are used. Protection in the logical and physical address spaces is analogous to that in paged virtual memory systems.

15.5.4 Segmentation with Paging

Paging can be superimposed on a segment oriented addressing mechanism to obtain efficient utilization of the memory. A generalized logical address in such a system has the following form:

$$(s_i, p_i, w_i)$$

Each segment consists of a number of pages. Hence each segment table entry points to the start of the PMT for that segment (see Fig. 15.35). Address translation now involves two levels of indirection. This requires two memory references if the STs and PMTs are held in memory. To speed up address translation, address translation buffers would have to be employed for both the ST and PMT references. Alternatively, a single set of address translation buffers may be employed, each buffer containing a pair

$$(s_i, p_i)$$

and the corresponding page block number. Protection can be implemented using the ST entries alone, because page level access validation is not necessary. Address translation buffers could therefore contain access validation information as copied from the ST entries.

15.5.5 Case Studies

IBM 360/67

IBM 360/67 uses segmentation with paging. Segment id's are numeric, hence ordering is important in a program's ST. A peculiar feature is that addressing in the

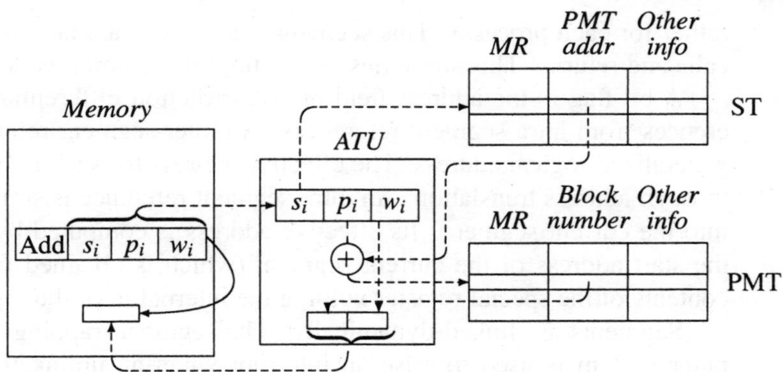

Fig. 15.35 Address translation in segmentation with paging

logical address space is considered to be contiguous, i.e. one dimensional rather than two dimensional. Hence the last word of segment s_i is followed by the 0th word of segment s_i+1 in the logical space. This implies that indexing can affect the segment number used in a logical address. The number of segments in a program is restricted to 16. While this reduces the size of ST and the number of PMTs, it often leads to packing of unrelated procedures and data into a segment. This dilutes the advantages of segmentation from the viewpoint of sharing.

An associative map is used to speed up address translation of operands, whereas an instruction fetch always implies access through the segment and page table entries residing in memory. Protection is not implemented in the segment space; protection key hardware is used at the page level.

MULTICS

MULTICS (Multiplexed Information and Computing Service) is a general purpose time-sharing system implemented on the GE-645 computer system during the 1960's. Its design has profoundly influenced many systems, including the file system of Unix. MULTICS uses symbolic id's for segments and pages, and implements virtual memory using segmentation with paging. Whenever a segment is linked to a program, it is allotted an entry in its ST, and its entry number in ST is remembered as the *internal id* of the segment. This id is put into a special hardware register for use in implementing references to words within the current segment, i.e. intra-segment references, as described later.

Since symbolic id's are used, no segment ordering restrictions exist on the logical address spaces of programs sharing a segment. A symbol table and a linkage segment is associated with each segment seg_i to facilitate dynamic linking. It contains the logical address of each external reference made by the segment. The linkage segment also contains code which would help other segments to transfer control to entry points located within seg_i. A separate stack segment is allocated for each program (or rather for each process). This segment is used for parameter passing and procedure calls and returns. This simplifies the writing of re-entrant code for shared segments.

A bit flag in the address field of an instruction differentiates inter-segment references from intra-segment references. An inter-segment reference is specified as a generalized logical address. The effective address for such a reference is determined through address translation. An intra-segment reference is simply a numerical offset into the current segment. Its effective address is computed by adding this offset to the start address of the current segment (which is obtained from the ST using the contents of the special register holding the internal id of the segment).

Segments are linked dynamically. The segment trapping hardware of the computer system is used to raise an interrupt when an unlinked external reference is encountered. To link the inter-segment reference

`(alpha, beta)`

the OS first searches for segment `alpha`. It then locates `alpha`'s symbol table and searches for `beta` to obtain `beta`'s offset within `alpha`. Actual linking of segments is described in the following.

Figure 15.36 shows a program P executing segment `S`. The symbol table of `S` and a linkage segment for `S` exist in the memory. If `S` itself is shared, a copy of the linkage segment is created for every program sharing `S`. Let L_S^P be the copy of the linkage segment of `S` for program P. Let segment `S` refer to symbol `A` in segment `T` using the following instruction

`LOAD (T,A)`

The following provisions are made while assembling this instruction

1. The logical address `(T,A)` is stored in some word of L_S^P (say, word w_k).
2. A special 'trap' flag is turned 'on' in word w_k of L_S^P.
3. The `LOAD` instruction is assembled to contain an indirect reference to word w_k of L_S^P.

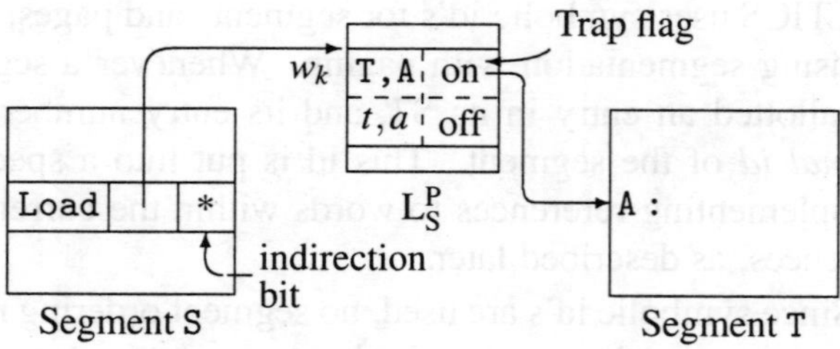

Fig. 15.36 Segment linking in Multics

When the external reference is executed by `S` (on behalf of program P or any other program) for the first time, the following sequence of events occur:

1. The 'trap' field causes an addressing trap to occur. Control now passes to the memory handler.
2. The OS locates the symbol table of segment `T` and finds the offset of `A` from it. Let this be a, and let the internal id of `T` be t. (If `T` is not already in memory, it is loaded now and an internal id is assigned to it.)
3. The logical address `(T,A)` in w_k is replaced by the internal address specification (t,a), and the trap bit is turned 'off'.
4. Address translation of the instruction making the indirect reference through w_k is now resumed to realize the inter-segment reference.

Subsequent executions of the instruction do not cause an addressing trap. The internal address specification (t,a) in word w_k of L_S^P is simply used to perform the effective address calculation.

Implementation of an inter-segment transfer of control requires some additional actions. Let the instruction making the control transfer be

```
Branch (T,B)
```

The logical address `(T,B)` is resolved analogous to the resolution of `(T,A)` above. This involves use of L_S^P. However, before actually transferring control to the address (t,b), it is necessary to set the machine register containing the internal id of the currently executing segment to point to segment `T`. This is achieved using a copy of the linkage segment of segment `T`. Let us call this L_T^P. As mentioned before, this segment contains code for transferring control to each entry point in `T`. As shown in Fig. 15.37, this code sets the hardware register to the internal id of `T` before transferring to word `B` of segment `T`.

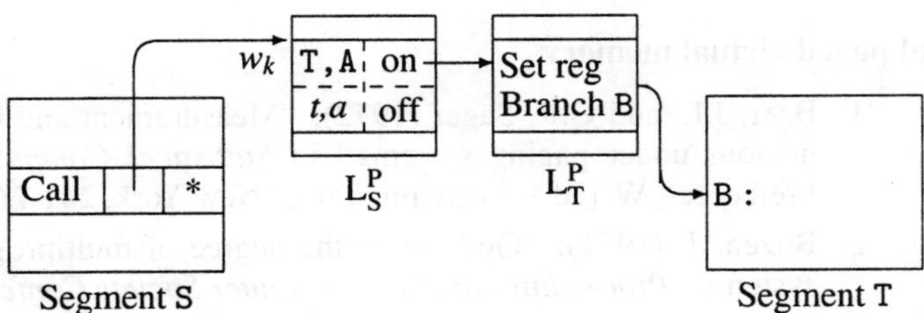

Fig. 15.37 Multics control transfer

EXERCISE 15.5

1. Compare and contrast the sharing of segments with the sharing of pages.
2. Write a short note on the advantages and disadvantages of using symbolic segment id's and word id's in a segmented virtual memory system.
3. Compare the following memory management proposals in a VM system using segmentation with paging.

(a) Use LRU policy within a program.
(b) Use LRU policy within a segment.

BIBLIOGRAPHY

Hoare and Mckeag (1971) survey various memory management techniques. Randell (1969) is an early paper on the motivation for virtual memory systems. Denning (1968) introduces the fundamental working set model. Buzen (1971) and Ghanem (1975) consider memory partitioning in a multiprogrammed virtual memory system. Hatfield (1971), Baer and Sager (1972) and Comeau (1976) consider aspects of program performance in a virtual memory system. Smith (1978) is a bibliography on paging and related topics. Bensoussen *et al* (1972) describes MULTICS virtual memory.

(a) Storage structures and memory management

1. Hoare, C.A.R. and R.M. Mckeag (1971): "A survey of store management techniques," in *Operating Systems Techniques*, by C.A.R. Hoare and R.H. Perrott (eds.) Academic Press, London.
2. Knuth, D.E. (1973): *The Art of Computer Programming*, Vol. III : Sorting and Searching, Addison-Wesley, Reading.
3. Kuck, D.J. and D.H. Lowrie (1970): "The use and performance of memory hierarchies," in *Software Engineering*, **1**, J.T. Tou (ed.), Academic Press, New York.
4. Mattson, R.L., J. Gecsei, D.R. Slutz and I.L. Traiger (1970): "Evaluation techniques for storage hierarchies," *IBM Systems Journal*, **9** (2), 78-117.
5. Randell, B.(1969): "A note on storage fragmentation and program segmentation," *Commn. of ACM*, **12** (7), 365-369.
6. Sayre, D. (1969): "Is automatic folding of programs efficient enough to displace manual?," *Commn. of ACM*, **12** (12), 656-660.

(b) Paging and paged virtual memory

1. Baer, J.L. and G.R. Sager (1972): "Measurement and improvement of program behaviour under paging systems," in *Statistical Computer Performance Evaluation*, Freiberger, W. (ed.), Academic Press, New York, 241-264.
2. Buzen, J. (1971): "Optimizing the degree of multiprogramming in demand paging systems," *Proceedings of IEEE Computer Society Conference*, 141-142.
3. Case, R.P. and A. Padegs (1978): "Architecture of the IBM/370," *Commn. of ACM*, **21** (1), 73-96.
4. Chu, W. W and H. Opderbeck (1972): "The page fault frequency replacement algorithms," *Proc. AFIPS FJCC*, **41**, 547-609.
5. Comeau, L.W. (1976): "A study of the effects of user program optimization in a paging system," *Proc. ACM Symposium on Operating System Principles*.
6. Guertin, R.L.(1972): "Programming in a paging environment," *Datamation*, **18** (2), 48-55.
7. Smith, A.J. (1978): "Bibliography on paging and related topics," *Operating Systems Review*, **12** (4), 39-56.

(c) Locality, working set and replacement algorithms

1. Aho, A.V., P.J. Denning and J.D. Ullman (1971): "Principles of optimal page replacement," *Journal of ACM*, **18** (1), 80-93.
2. Batson, A.P. and A.W. Madison(1976): "Characterization of program localities," *Commn. of ACM*, **9** (5), 285-294.
3. Belady, L.A.(1966): "A study of replacement algorithms for virtual storage computers," *IBM Systems Journal*, **5** (2), 78-101.
4. Bryant, P. (1975): "Predicting working set sizes," *IBM Journal of R and D*, **19** (5), 221-229.
5. Denning, P.J. (1968a): "The working set model for program behaviour," *Commn. of ACM*, **11** (5), 323-333.
6. Denning, P.J. (1968b): "Thrashing : Its causes and prevention," *Proc. AFIPS FJCC*, **33**, 915-922.
7. Denning, P.J. and S.C. Schwartz (1972): "Properties of the working set model," *Commn. of ACM*, **15** (3), 191-198.
8. Ghanem, M.Z.(1975): "Dynamic partitioning of the main memory using the working set concept," *IBM Journal of R and D*, **19**, 445-450.
9. Rosell, J.R. and J.P. Dupuy (1973): "The design, implementation and evaluation of a working set dispatcher," *Commn. of ACM*, **16**, 247-253.
10. Schneider, P.(1976): "Working set restoration – a method to increase the performance of multilevel storage hierarchies," *Proc. AFIPS NCC*, **45**, 373-380.
11. Smith, A.J. (1976): "A modified working set paging algorithm," *IEEE Transactions on Computers*, **25** (9), 907-914.
12. Spirn, J.R. and P.J. Denning (1972): "Experiments with program locality," *Proc. AFIPS*, **41**, 611-621.

(d) Virtual memory in general

1. Abu-Sufah, W., D. Kuck and D. Lawrie (1979): "Automatic program transformations for virtual memory computers," *Proc. AFIPS NCC*, **48**, 969-974.
2. Bensoussen, A., C.T. Clingen and R.C. Daley (1972): "The MULTICS virtual memory-concepts and design," *Commn. of ACM*, **15** (5), 308-318.
3. Daley, R.C. and J.B. Dennis (1968): "Virtual memory, processes and sharing in MULTICS," *Commn. of ACM*, **11** (5), 305-322.
4. Denning, P.J.(1970): "Virtual Memory," *Computing Surveys*, **2** (3), 153-189.
5. Ferrari, D.(1976): "The improvement of program behaviour," *Computer*, **9** (11), 39-47.
6. Ghanem, M.Z. (1975): "Study of memory partitioning for multiprogramming systems with virtual memory," *IBM Journal of R and D*, **19**, 451-457.
7. Hatfield, D.J. and J. Gerald (1971): "Program restructuring for virtual memory," *IBM Systems Journal*, **10** (3), 169-192.
8. Hellerman, H., and T.F. Conroy (1975): *Computer System Performance*, McGraw-Hill Kogakusha, Tokyo.
9. IBM: "Introduction to virtual storage in system/370," No. GR20-4260-1, IBM Corpn.
10. Orgnick, E.I. (1972): *The MULTICS System*, MIT Press, Mass.

11. Parmelee, R.P. et.al. (1972): "Virtual storage and virtual machine concepts," *IBM Systems Journal*, **11** (2), 99-130.
12. Traiger, I.L. (1982): "Virtual memory management for database systems," *Operating Systems Review*, **16** (4), 26-48.

CHAPTER 16

IO Organization and IO Programming

Like other OS components the IO management component also consists of mechanisms and policies. IO mechanisms are concerned with the implementation of IO operations in the system. IO policies are concerned with performance issues, or user-oriented issues like sharing and protection of files.

The IO management module of the OS can be structured into the following layers:

1. Physical Input Output Control System (PIOCS)
2. Logical Input Output Control System (LIOCS)
3. File System (FS).

The IO management layers form the hierarchy shown in Fig. 16.1.

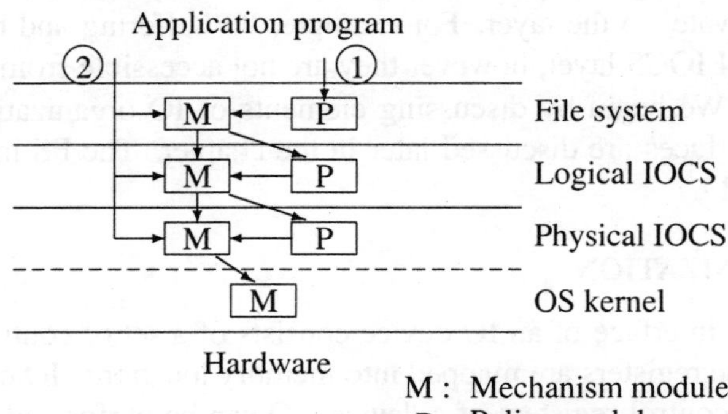

Fig. 16.1 IO management layers

The PIOCS layer is closest to the hardware of the computer system, while the FS layer is closest to an application program. Each layer provides an interface to the higher level through which its facilities can be accessed. The mechanisms and policies of the layer are implemented using the facilities of the lower layer.

Notice one peculiarity of the IO management layers in Fig. 16.1. Unlike in other OS modules, e.g. the memory handler (see Fig. 15.26), the policies and mechanisms of a layer do not form a strict hierarchy. Thus, a higher layer can access both mechanisms and policies of a lower layer. Thus, a program written in a conventional higher level language uses the FS interface (see arrow marked ① in Fig. 16.1), while a program wishing to use special IO devices or special file organization techniques can access facilities of the PIOCS or LIOCS layers directly (see arrow marked ② in Fig. 16.1).

This facility enables IO modules, e.g. device drivers or even file systems, to be added or changed to suit specific operating environments. The default facilities provided by the OS are accessible through the policy module of each layer. In this chapter and the next, we are concerned with the design of the default facilities provided by IO layers.

Most operating systems distinguish between the FS layer and the IOCS layers. The number of IOCS layers and their internal boundaries typically differ from system to system. The demarcation between the PIOCS layer and the OS kernel also varies across different OS's. Table 16.1 summarizes the mechanisms and policies implemented by the different IOCS layers. The PIOCS layer implements device-level IO through its mechanisms. It also ensures good device throughput. The LIOCS layer provides mechanisms which support file level IO. These mechanisms are implemented using the PIOCS mechanisms for device level IO. Optionally, these mechanisms use the PIOCS policies for optimizing the performance of a file. The FS layer implements sharing and protection of files using the LIOCS mechanisms for file IO. Note that Tab. 16.1 mentions only those mechanisms which are accessible from a higher layer. Other mechanisms may exist in a layer, however they might be 'private' to the layer. For example, IO buffering and blocking mechanisms exist in the LIOCS layer, however they are not accessible from the file system layer.

We begin by discussing elements of IO organization. The PIOCS and LIOCS interfaces are discussed later in the chapter. The FS interface is discussed in Chapter 17.

16.1 IO ORGANIZATION

The interface of an IO device consists of a set of control registers. In some systems these registers are mapped into memory locations. IO can be initiated by writing into the control registers of a device. IO can be performed in a *programmed manner*, or in a manner which utilizes the *direct memory access* (DMA) feature. In programmed IO, transfer of every byte of data has to be initiated by the CPU, whereas a DMA device can transfer a block of data without CPU intervention.

Table 16.1 Mechanisms and Policies implemented by IO modules

1. Physical IOCS (PIOCS) layer
   (a) Mechanisms
      - IO initiation
      - IO operation status
      - IO completion processing
      - IO error recovery

   (b) Policies
      - Optimization of IO device performance
2. Logical IOCS (LIOCS) layer
   (a) Mechanisms
      - Label processing
      - File open and close
      - File read and write

   (b) Policies
      - Optimization of file access performance
3. File System (FS) layer
   (a) Mechanisms
      - Directory maintenance mechanisms

   (b) Policies
      - Sharing and protection of files

Figure 16.2 illustrates the IO organization used in contemporary computer systems. IO devices are connected to *IO channels.* (In some systems, IO channels are called *IO processors.*) Channels are capable of DMA-mode operation for servicing block devices. Each channel is given a unique numeric channel id in the system. Similarly, each device in a channel has a unique numeric device id. A device address is thus a pair (*channel_id, device_id*) which is unique in the system.

An IO operation consists of a sequence of elementary IO tasks. It is initiated by an *IO instruction*. The CPU, the IO channel and the IO device participate to realize an IO instruction. An IO task is implemented by an *IO command*, which requires participation of the IO channel and the IO device, but not the CPU. IO commands which do not involve data transfer do not require participation of the IO channel. Such IO commands are called *IO orders*. Thus execution of IO commands and IO orders is independent of the CPU.

Example 16.1 Reading of a disk record involves the following:

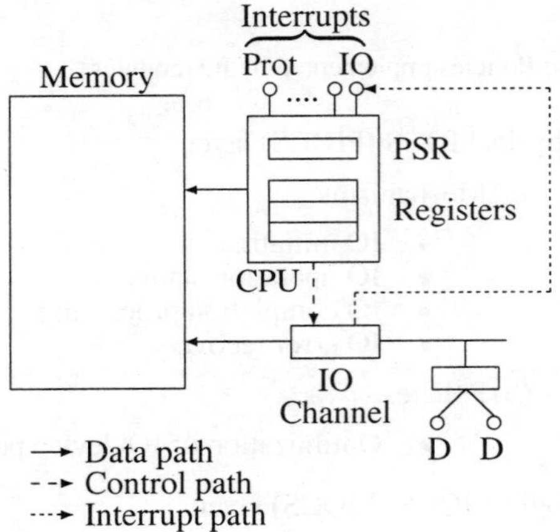

Fig. 16.2 IO organization

Start IO on (*channel_id, device_id*)
Position disk heads on track *track_id*
Read record *record_id*

'Start IO' is an IO instruction which requires participation of the CPU, the IO channel and the IO device for its execution. 'Position disk heads' is an IO command which does not involve data transfer (i.e., it is an IO order), while 'read record' is an IO command involving data transfer. The CPU is not involved during the execution of the commands 'position disk heads' and 'read record'.

When an IO operation is initiated, the channel decodes each IO command of the IO operation, extracts some information for its own use and passes the command to the appropriate IO device for execution. For example, if the command was *read*, the channel would prepare itself for organizing a data transfer from the device to the memory. If a command involves data transfer, the IO channel remains involved with the command throughout its implementation. Depending on the speed at which the data transfer takes place, a channel may be able to concurrently implement command(s) of other IO operation(s); this is called the *multiplexed mode* of IO operation. A command which does not involve data transfer frees the channel immediately after it is initiated.

In our discussion it is assumed that a computer system supports the following IO instructions and commands

1. *IO-init* (*ch, d*), *command_address* : Initiation of IO
2. *IO-term* (*ch, d*) : Forced termination of IO
3. *IO-status* (*ch, d*) : Obtaining device status
4. Appropriate IO commands for device specific operations.

where (*ch, d*) is the device address and *command_address* is the address of the memory location where the first command of the IO operation is stored. We assume that the IO commands describing an IO operation exist in consecutive memory locations.

Example 16.2 The IO operation of Ex. 16.1 is implemented by issuing the command

IO-init (channel_id, device_id), addr

where *addr* is the address of the memory area containing the 'position disk heads' and 'read record' commands.

IO programming

The details of IO initiation are quite complex. An *IO-init* instruction has to be executed by the CPU with the physical device address and the address of the first IO command as its operands. (Some systems fetch the IO command address from a standard memory location when the *IO-init* instruction is executed.) The CPU identifies the required channel and sends the device address to it. The channel interrogates the device to check its availability. This process is called *device selection.* The channel informs the result of device selection actions to the CPU, which sets an appropriate condition code in its condition code register. The *IO-init* instruction completes as soon as the condition code is set. The CPU is now free to execute other instructions. If device selection is successful, the channel immediately starts the IO operation by accessing and decoding the first IO command.

Consider an application program using a 'bare machine'. In such a machine, no software layers separate the application program from the machine's hardware. Hence all actions required to initiate an IO operation must be performed by the program itself. After executing an *IO-init* instruction, the program must determine whether IO has started as intended. If not, it has to take some corrective action based on the nature of the failure. Device selection can fail if the channel or device is busy with some other operation, or if a hardware malfunction occurs. These conditions are indicated by different condition code settings. If the channel or device was busy, the program can retry IO initiation sometime in future. If a malfunction has occurred, the program can report the condition on the operator's console. The term *IO programming* is used to describe all actions concerning initiation and completion of an IO operation. Example 16.3 shows the details of IO programming.

Example 16.3 Figure 16.3 illustrates the basic actions involved in IO programming. Consider the *IO-init* instruction followed by three `BC` instructions. The *IO-init* instruction sets condition code cc_1 if the IO initiation is successful. In that event, the program goes on to execute the instructions at `PROCEED`. Condition code cc_2 indicates that the channel or device is busy. In that event the program retries the IO instruction till initiation succeeds. Condition code cc_3 indicates an IO error situation.

IO programming also involves checking for completion of the IO operation. This is performed as follows: Before initiating the IO operation, the program sets `IO_FLAG` to '1' to indicate that the IO operation is in progress. At `PROCEED`, it loops while `IO_FLAG` is still '1'. The IO interrupt routine starting at the instruction `IO_INT` changes `IO_FLAG` to '0' when the IO operation completes. This brings the program out of the busy wait at `PROCEED`.

```
                SET        IO_FLAG, '1'
RETRY :         IO_init    (ch, d), COMMANDS
                BC         cc1, PROCEED
                BC         cc2, RETRY
                BC         cc3, ERROR

PROCEED :       COMP       IO_FLAG, '1'
                BC         EQ, PROCEED
                ...

COMMANDS :      ...        {IO commands}
                ...
IO_INT :        SET        IO_FLAG, '0'
                ...
```

Fig. 16.3 IO programming

16.2 IO DEVICES

From a programmer's viewpoint, IO devices can be classified into

- Input, print and storage devices
- Sequential and random access devices.

Input and print devices are typically sequential in nature because the IO medium moves through the IO device in a fixed direction. Storage devices can be both sequential and random access.

A unit of IO medium is called a *volume*. Thus a tape cartridge and a disk can be called a tape volume and disk volume respectively. The information written (or read) in one IO operation is said to form a *record*. The following notation is used while discussing IO operations:

t_{io} : *io time*, i.e. time interval between the execution of an *io-init* instruction and the completion of IO.

t_a : *access time*, i.e. time interval between the issue of a read or write command and the start of reading or writing.

t_x : *transfer time*, i.e. time taken to transfer the data during a read or write operation

The io time for a record is the sum of its access time and transfer time, i.e.

$$t_{io} = t_a + t_x. \tag{16.1}$$

Magnetic tapes and cartridges

The IO medium is a strip of magnetic material. In a tape or cartridge drive, an array of magnetic heads is positioned transversely across the strip, each head recording a specific data bit of a byte or a parity bit used for error detection (see Fig. 16.4). Thus nine tracks of information are written on the IO medium. As an additional error detection measure, a cyclic check sum is formed for all the bytes of a record. This sum is itself recorded at the end of the record. Adjoining records on a tape are separated by an *inter-record gap*. This provides for the start–stop motion of the medium between the reading or writing of successive records. The access time during a read or write operation (t_a) consists of the time to achieve uniform velocity motion of the IO medium before the data transfer can be initiated.

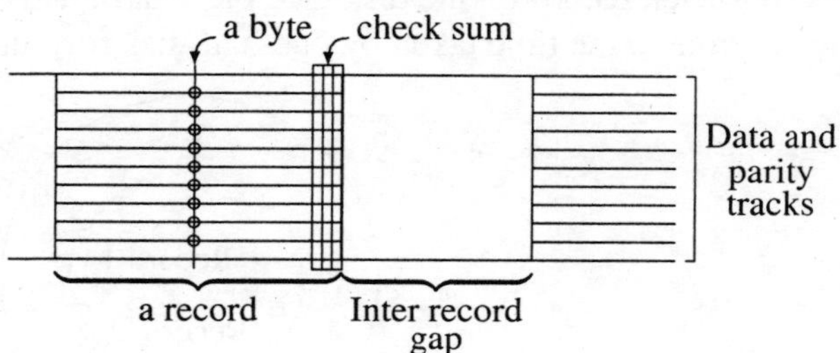

Fig. 16.4 Recording on tapes and cartridges

Total IO time for a record of size s bytes is given by

$$\begin{aligned} t_{io} &= t_a + t_x \\ &= t_a + s/(d.v) \end{aligned} \quad (16.2)$$

where d is the recording density and v is the velocity of the IO medium.

Tapes and cartridges are sequential access devices, i.e. they can perform operations only with respect to the current position of the heads. These operations are:

read (*addr* (*IO_area*))
write (*addr* (*IO_area*))
skip (i.e. ignore a record)
rewind

where *addr* (*IO_area*) is the address of a memory area to which data transfer is to take place from the IO medium (or vice versa).

Disks

The disk is a circular magnetic surface in continuous motion around its own axis. The position of the read–write head is varied radially over the magnetic surface to form circular tracks of information. The disk is a random access storage device, which uses the record address (*track_no, record_no*) to access a record.

The access time for a disk record is given by

$$t_a = t_s + t_r \quad (16.3)$$

where

t_s : *seek time*, i.e. time to position the head on the required track

t_r : time to access desired record on the track (*rotational latency*)

The seek time is due to the mechanical motion of the head, while the rotational latency is due to the time taken by the required record to pass under the head. To minimize the latter, the record address can be stored in a record descriptor which precedes each record on the disk (see Fig. 16.5). This reduces the average rotational latency time to the time taken by one-half disk revolution.

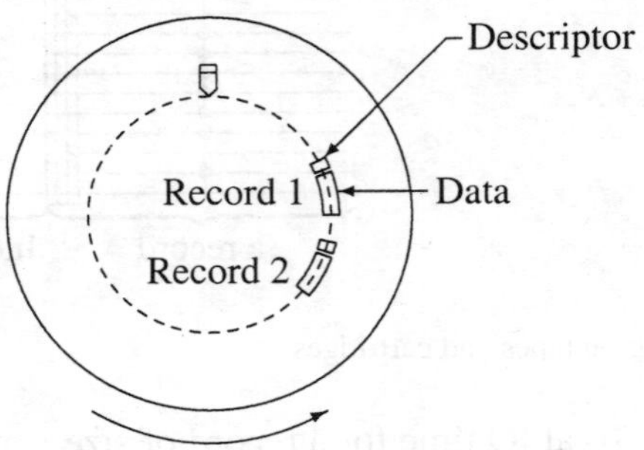

Fig. 16.5 Disk record

Variations in disk organization have been motivated by the desire to improve the access speed and capacity of a disk and to make optimum use of disk surface. To provide fast access, a head can be provided for every track on the disk surface. Such disks, known as Head Per Track (HPT) disks, were used as paging devices in early virtual memory systems. Higher capacities can be obtained by using multiple disk surfaces to form a disk pack (see Fig. 16.6). One read/write head services each disk surface. All heads of the disk pack are mounted on a single mechanical arm which moves radially to access different tracks. Thus, at any given moment the heads are positioned on identically numbered tracks of different surfaces. These tracks can be accessed without changing the arm position. We can thus look upon the disk pack as consisting of a set of concentric *cylinders*. A record address is now specified as

(*cylinder number, surface number, record number*).

This speeds up accesses to sequentially stored data.

Sectored disk organization is used to optimize use of the disk surface. A sector is a disk record with a standard size. The sector size is chosen to ensure minimum wastage of recording capacity due to inter-record gaps on the surface. Sectoring can be made a part of the disk hardware (hard sectoring), or could be implemented by the software (soft sectoring).

The commands supported by a disk device are:

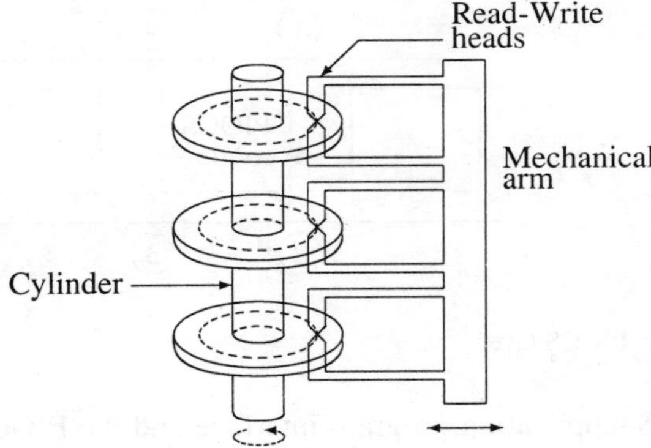

Fig. 16.6 Multiple surface disk pack

`read` (*record address, addr (IO_area)*)
`write` (*record address, addr (IO_area)*)
`seek` (*cylinder number, surface number*)

EXERCISE 16.2

1. The record descriptor for disk records shown in Fig. 16.5 contains the following information
   (a) Track number
   (b) Record number on track.

   Comment on how this would reduce rotational latency of the device. If the above information is not recorded in the descriptor then how would IO be performed? (*Hint:* Study the literature of a few disk devices to answer this question.)

16.3 PHYSICAL IOCS (PIOCS)

The physical IOCS layer provides facilities to manage device level IO in an OS. This has the following three aspects:

1. *Make the IO sequence easier:* This is achieved by providing simple means to perform IO initiation and IO interrupt handling. It has the effect of requiring less specialized knowledge to perform device level IO.
2. *Ensure good system performance:* PIOCS interfaces with the process management component to block a program which is waiting for the completion of an IO operation. This avoids the busy wait following IO initiation in Ex. 16.3.
3. *Ensure good device performance:* This is performed by scheduling the IO operations aimed at a device in an appropriate order.

Figure 16.7 illustrates how an application program uses the PIOCS layer to perform its IO. Requests and responses flow across two interfaces in the program—the

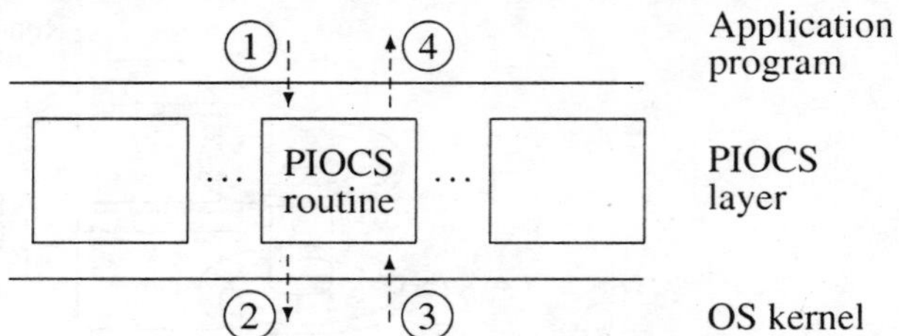

Fig. 16.7 Actions of the PIOCS layer

PIOCS–application program interface and the PIOCS–kernel interface. The typical flow of control, depicted by numbered arcs in Fig. 16.7, is as follows:

1. The application program makes a request by invoking a functionality provided by the PIOCS interface. Control is now transferred to a relevant PIOCS routine.
2. The PIOCS routine makes a request to the OS kernel to implement the program's request.
3. OS kernel sends a reply to the PIOCS routine.
4. The PIOCS routine sends a reply to the application program.

Table 16.2 shows some typical requests and responses concerning the PIOCS layer. Note that responses may be in the form of information or actions. We elaborate on the PIOCS functions in the following section.

16.3.1 PIOCS Functions

The Physical IOCS layer provides the following functionalities:

1. IO initiation, completion and error recovery
2. Use of logical devices
3. Awaiting the completion of an IO operation
4. Optimization of IO device performance.

The first two PIOCS functionalities provide basic support for IO programming and additional convenience to the application programmer, respectively. The third functionality ensures good system performance by blocking a program while it awaits the completion of an IO operation. The fourth functionality ensures good device performance. These functionalities are described with reference to Fig. 16.7 and Tab. 16.2.

IO initiation, completion and error recovery

PIOCS support for IO programming makes the channel and device intricacies 'transparent' to the problem program. The application program only needs to specify the following:

Table 16.2 Requests and responses across the PIOCS interfaces
(*note* : AP stands for application program)

Request made by	*Request made to*	*Request details*	*Response*
PIOCS	kernel	IO init	Initiate IO on the device
PIOCS	kernel	Get Device status	Status information
PIOCS	kernel	Block the program	Program is put in the *blocked* state
Appln. program	PIOCS	Start IO	Return to the program after noting IO request in PIOCS data structures (If possible, IO is initiated immediately)
Appln. program	PIOCS	Await IO completion	Return to the program after IO is complete

1. Device address
2. IO operation details.

PIOCS notes the details of the IO operation and returns control to the application program. The IO operation is performed asynchronously with the application program. When an interrupt pertaining to the device arises, PIOCS performs appropriate IO completion and error recovery actions.

Logical devices

A program using the instruction *IO-init* (*ch, d*), *command address* depends on the availability of the specific IO device (*ch, d*). Such a program would have to be modified if some other IO device is to be used instead of (*ch, d*). The concept of a *logical device* is introduced to avoid this problem. A logical device is an abstract IO device with a symbolic name. A program avoids the mention of a physical device address in a program by using a logical device name. For example, a program may make a PIOCS request with the following parameters:

1. The logical device name `mydisk`
2. IO operation details.

A physical device (*ch, d*) of an appropriate device class should have been assigned to `mydisk` before issuing this call. IO commands aimed at logical device `mydisk` are now implemented on the device (*ch, d*) by the PIOCS. Many OSs have a fixed set of standard names for logical devices, while some OSs permit an application program to choose its own logical device names.

PIOCS provides a functionality to perform the assignment of physical devices to the logical devices. This functionality may be invoked through the OS command processor before starting the execution of a program, or may be invoked dynamically by an application program through an OS call.

Awaiting completion of an IO operation

Since PIOCS returns control to a program after noting its IO request, the program can execute concurrently with the IO operation until it reaches a point where it must synchronize with the completion of the IO operation. For example, a higher level language program

```
read a, b, c;
...
result := a + 5.2;
```

must ensure the completion of the `read` operation before accessing the value of variable `a` in the assignment statement. To achieve this, the program invokes PIOCS with the device address and IO operation details. PIOCS tests the completion of the IO operation, and returns to the application program if the IO operation is complete. Otherwise, it requests the kernel to block the program. This avoids the busy wait seen in Ex. 16.3.

Optimization of IO device performance

Since all IO requests are made to the PIOCS, it knows all IO operations pending on an IO device. It can use this knowledge to maximize the device throughput by scheduling the IO operation appropriately. For example, the rotational latency and mechanical motion of disk heads can be minimized by performing the IO operations in a suitable order. This function is performed automatically by the PIOCS; it is not explicitly invoked by an application program.

16.3.2 PIOCS Data Structures

Following the discussion of PIOCS functions in the previous section, we design the following data structures for use by PIOCS:

1. Physical device table (PDT)
2. Logical device table (LDT)
3. IO control block (IOCB)
4. IO queue (IOQ).

Figure 16.8 illustrates the relationship between the PIOCS data structures. PDT contains information concerning all physical devices in the system. The important fields of this table are *device address*, *device type* and *IOQ pointer*. One LDT is created for each active program in the system (it should be accessible from its PCB).

The LDT contains one entry for each logical device, which contains the fields *logical device name*, and *physical device address*. Note that for certain classes of devices (e.g. disks), the mapping from logical devices to physical devices can be many-to-one. Thus, many logical devices, possibly belonging to different user programs, can share the same physical device.

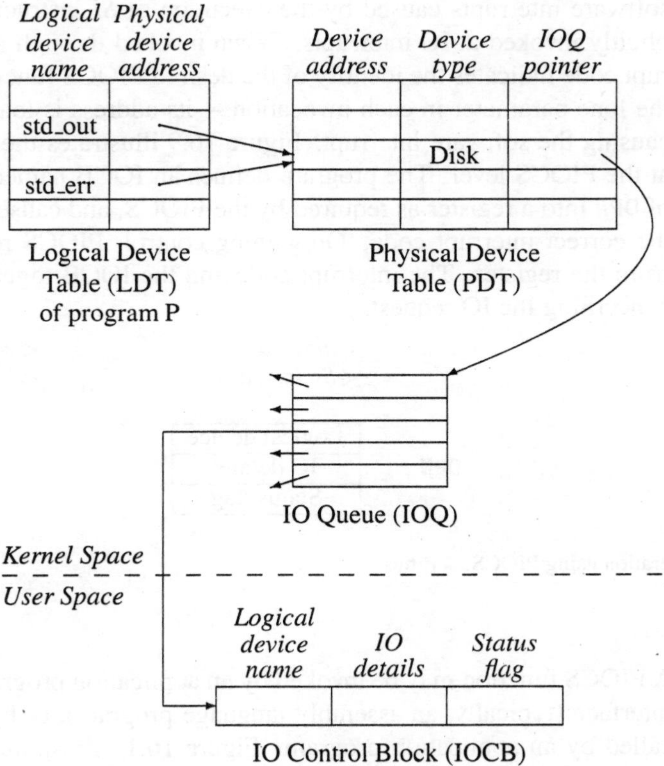

Fig. 16.8 PIOCS data structures

An IOCB contains all information pertaining to an IO operation. The important fields in IOCB are *logical device name*, *IO details* and *status flag*. The IO details field contains the addresses of all IO commands involved in the IO operation. The status flag indicates whether the IO operation is 'in progress' or 'completed'. The IOQ of a device contains IOCB addresses of all IO operations pending on the device. This information is used for optimizing the IO device performance. Note that the PDT entry of a physical device, rather than the LDT entry of a logical device, points to the IOQ. This is because a physical device may be assigned to many logical devices.

The PDT, LDT and IOQ data structures exist within the OS kernel. An IOCB exists in the address space of an application program. The program creates an IOCB, initializes its fields, and uses it as a parameter in a PIOCS call. Its presence in the application program's address space permits the status of the IO operation to be checked without having to invoke the kernel.

16.3.3 Implementation of PIOCS Functions

Some PIOCS functions are explicitly invoked by an application program through software interrupts caused by the execution of *SI* instructions, while others are implicitly invoked at IO interrupts. When invoked through an SI instruction, the interrupt code indicates the identity of the desired PIOCS function. Typically, an IOCB is the lone parameter in each invocation —its address is loaded into a register prior to causing the software interrupt. Figure 16.9 illustrates the details of an IO operation at the PIOCS level. The program defines an IOCB named `OPN`. It loads the address of `OPN` into a register as required by the PIOCS, and causes a software interrupt with the correct interrupt code. On gaining control, PIOCS retrieves the IOCB address from the register. The interrupt code and the IOCB together define all information concerning the IO request.

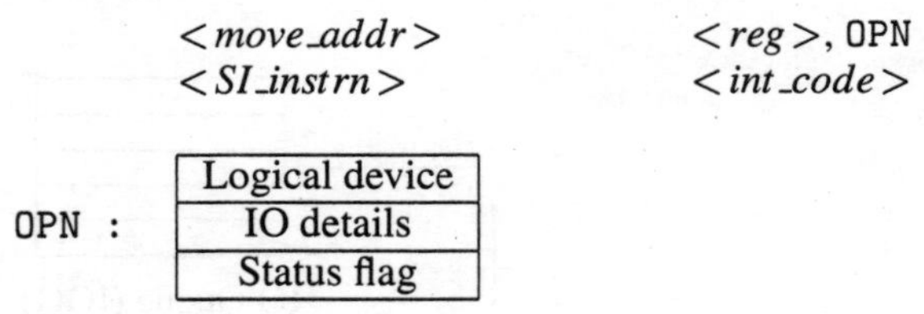

Fig. 16.9 IO operation using PIOCS facilities

PIOCS library

A PIOCS function may be invoked by an application program operating at the PIOCS interface (typically, an assembly language program), or by a PIOCS library module called by an application program. Figure 16.10 illustrates these variations. In part (a), an application program invokes the PIOCS function through an SI instruction, while in part (b) the program calls a PIOCS library module with the IOCB address as a parameter and the library module executes the SI instruction. (The PIOCS library module would have been linked with the application program by the linker.) In the latter case, the program may directly call the PIOCS library module, or it may call a module of a higher layer (viz. LIOCS or FS module) which calls the PIOCS library module. For simplicity, in the following discussion we assume that all invocations of PIOCS functions are performed through PIOCS library modules. We define the following PIOCS library modules for this purpose:

1. **`start-io`** (*IOCB_address*);
2. **`await-io`** (*IOCB_address*);

Some PIOCS functions are implicitly invoked by IO interrupts. These include the following:

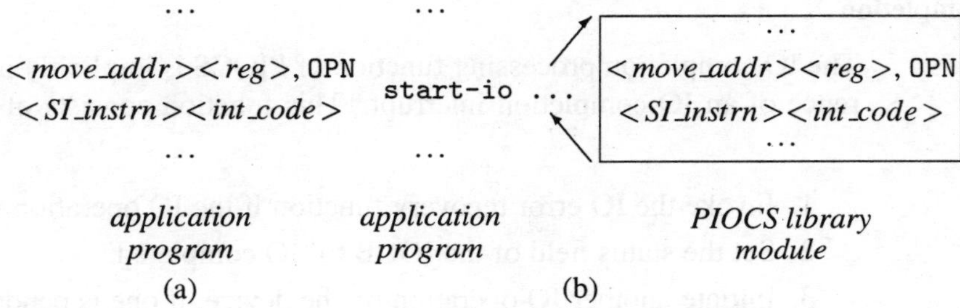

Fig. 16.10 PIOCS invocation schematics

1. IO completion processing is invoked by an interrupt indicating successful completion of an IO operation.
2. IO error recovery is invoked when an interrupt indicates IO malfunctioning.
3. IO Initiation (for a pending IO operation) is invoked on completion of the current operation on a device.

IO Initiation

To initiate an IO operation, a program (or a library module working on its behalf) puts all information concerning the IO operation into an IOCB and calls the PIOCS library module

`start-io` (*IOCB_address*);

The `start-io` module causes a software interrupt which directs execution control to the IO initiation function as shown in Fig. 16.7. PIOCS now executes the following steps:

1. Set the status flag of the IOCB to 'in progress'.
2. Enter the IOCB address into the IOQ of the physical device.
3. Initiate the IO operation, if possible.
4. Return to the invoker.

To enter the IOCB address in an IOQ, PIOCS extracts the logical device name from an IOCB, obtains the address of the physical device assigned to it from the LDT of the program, obtains the address of the IOQ for the physical device from the PDT entry of the device and adds the IOCB address at the end of the IOQ. The IO operation can be initiated straightaway if no other entries exist in the IOQ. If other entries exist, the operation would be initiated sometime in future (see description of IO completion for details).

IO initiation is performed using the details of IO programming described in Section 16.1. The *status flag* of an IOCB is used in a manner analogous to the use of IO_FLAG in Ex. 16.3.

IO Completion

The IO completion processing function of PIOCS is implicitly invoked by the occurrence of an IO completion interrupt. This function consists of the following steps:

1. Invoke the IO error recovery function if the IO operation was unsuccessful.
2. Set the status field of the IOCB to 'IO completed'.
3. Initiate another IO operation on the device, if one is pending.
4. If the program issuing the IO operation is blocked on its completion, interact with the process scheduler to change its state to *ready*.

IO completion processing is implemented as follows: The interrupt hardware provides two items of information—address of the physical device raising an IO interrupt, and IO status code describing the reason for an interrupt. The device address is used to locate the PDT entry of the device. The IOCB address of the IO operation is extracted from the IOQ of the device (typically, this is the first entry in the IOQ). If the IO status code indicates a malfunction, PIOCS consults the *device type* field of the PDT entry and activates an appropriate IO error recovery routine. The IOCB address is passed to the IO error recovery routine. If the IO completion was normal, PIOCS changes the *status flag* in the IOCB to 'IO completed'. The IOCB address is removed from the IOQ. If IOQ is not empty, another IO operation is now initiated.

Interaction with the process scheduler is required if the program issuing the IO operation is blocked on its completion. An interesting point here concerns the identity of the program issuing the IO operation. The IO management module is not concerned with the program's identity, hence none of its data structures can provide this information. This problem can be solved in one of two ways: An additional field called *requester's id* can be added to an IOCB. PIOCS can deposit the *process id* of the requester here when a `start-io` call is made. Alternatively, interaction with the process scheduler can be implemented through the event handling mechanism as follows: When the program makes an `await-io` call, the process management module creates an ECB for the IO completion event. This ECB contains the id of the program waiting for the end of IO, and describes the awaited event as 'successful IO completion' event. Occurrence of this event is signalled by the IO completion handler when it finds that a normal end of IO has occurred. The event handling mechanism locates the ECB for this event, extracts the id of the program awaiting the end of IO, and marks an appropriate change in its state. The latter alternative is 'cleaner' as we see in the following.

Awaiting the completion of an IO operation

An application program invokes this function through the PIOCS library call

`await-io` (*IOCB_address*);

which contains the IOCB address of the awaited IO operation as a parameter. PIOCS merely tests the status flag in the IOCB, and returns to the program if the flag has the value 'IO completed'. If not, the PIOCS library routine requests the kernel to block it on the event 'successful IO completion'. The library routine is woken up at the completion of the IO operation and returns to the user program.

PIOCS can make some minor error checks while implementing this function. For example, it can check whether the IOCB exists in the IOQ of the concerned device. This will avoid indefinite wait due to a programming error if a program waits for the completion of an IO operation which it never initiated!

Optimization of IO device performance

The throughput of an IO device is the number of data bytes transferred between the device and the memory per unit time. Low throughput could arise either due to idling of the device or due to large access times in IO operations. In the case of disks, PIOCS can try to reduce the effect of the latter by scheduling IO operations in an order which reduces the mechanical motion of the disk heads. PIOCS has an opportunity to do this whenever more than one IO operation exists in the IOQ of a disk device.

Some interesting scheduling algorithms which can be considered for this purpose are:

1. FCFS scheduling
2. Shortest seek time (SST) scheduling
3. SCAN scheduling.

The first two algorithms are similar to the FCFS and SJN job scheduling algorithms, respectively. Their performance characteristics are also analogous to the FCFS and SJN job schedulers, viz. FCFS is easy to implement but does not guarantee good throughput, while SST scheduling achieves good throughput but may starve some requests. One difference between the SST and SJN algorithms is that, unlike the SJN job scheduling algorithm, the SST algorithm is feasible in practice since the seek times involved in moving the disk heads from one position to another can be calculated precisely. However, note one difference between job scheduling and disk scheduling. The schedule lengths, i.e. the elapsed times to complete the processing of all requests, are identical for all job scheduling policies, whereas the schedule lengths differ for different disk scheduling policies. This is because the seek time of a disk record does not have an absolute value; it depends on the current position of the heads (see Ex. 16.4).

The SCAN algorithms try to keep the disk heads moving in one direction as far as possible. This avoids reversal of the disk head motion, which involves large seek times. In a simple SCAN algorithm, the disk heads make a sweep from one end of the disk to the other end, say the lowest numbered track to the highest numbered track. It services whatever IO operations it can in this sweep. At the end of the sweep, the direction of head motion is reversed and a reverse sweep is initiated. Another variant of the SCAN algorithm never reverses the direction of head movement. Instead, it simply initiates another sweep by positioning the heads at the starting point of the sweep. This is repeated over and over again. This algorithm is called the circular scan algorithm (CSCAN for short).

Tradeoffs between the different disk scheduling algorithms are obvious. SST algorithms are not very popular because of larger overheads and the starvation property. SCAN algorithms can be efficiently implemented if the IOQs are maintained in sorted order by track number. Example 16.4 illustrates a situation in which SCAN performs better than other algorithms. However, note that none of the algorithms is a clear winner in practice.

Example 16.4 Figure 16.11 summarizes the performance of the disk scheduling algorithms for five IO requests arriving at different instants of time. It is assumed that the previous IO operation completes when the system clock reads 150 ms. The summary further assumes that the transfer time in each IO operation is 5 ms. and that the time required for the disk heads to move from $track_1$ to $track_2$ is a linear function of the difference between their positions, viz.

$$t_{hm} = t_c + \mid track_1 - track_2 \mid \times t_{pt}$$

where t_c is a constant, t_{pt} is the per-track head movement time and t_{hm} is the total head movement time. Note that the total seek times of different scheduling algorithms vary greatly. SST is better than FCFS, however it suffers from oscillations in head movement. SCAN has the smallest total seek time in this example. It is better than CSCAN because it can reverse the direction of traversal after completing the IO operation on track 100.

Use of logical devices

The mapping of a logical device name into a physical device address using the LDT has been described already. LDT entries represent the logical device assignments in force at any moment. Entries are added to the LDT when assignments are made to logical devices, and existing entries are removed when assignments are nullified. PIOCS checks for assignment conflicts while making new assignments. For example, only one assignment can be in force for a non-sharable device like a printer. The device type field of the PDT is used to determine whether sharing is feasible for a device. A device assignment may be nullified by a program through a PIOCS call. In addition, PIOCS nullifies all device assignments of a program at the end of its execution.

Putting it together

Figure 16.12 summarizes the PIOCS functionalities. Each box represents a PIOCS module. Modules above the broken line execute in the user mode, while those below the line execute in the kernel mode. The kernel mode modules are invoked through interrupts. The module called 'IO scheduler' contains the disk scheduling algorithm

t_c	=	0 ms.
t_{pt}	=	1 ms.
Present position of head	=	Track 55
Direction of last head movement	=	Towards higher numbered tracks
Current clock time	=	150 ms.

IO requests:

Serial number	*Track number*	*Time of arrival*
1	12	0
2	85	50
3	40	100
4	100	120
5	75	180

Scheduling details:

FCFS		*SST*		*SCAN*		*CSCAN*	
Track no.	*Seek time*	*Track no.*	*Seek time*	*Track no.*	*Seek time*	*Track no.*	*Seek time*
12	43	85	30	85	30	85	30
85	73	75	10	100	15	100	15
40	45	100	25	75	25	12	88
100	60	40	60	40	35	40	28
75	25	12	28	12	28	75	35
Total	246		153		133		196

Fig. 16.11 Disk scheduling summary

in force. PIOCS functionalities are activated in one of three ways: Calls on the PIOCS library modules `start-io` or `await-io` by an application program, or occurrence of an IO completion interrupt. When a user program invokes `start-io`, `start-io` invokes the IO initiation functionality of PIOCS. After device address translation, IO scheduler enters the request in the IOQ of the physical device. IO initiator is invoked to start the IO operation immediately if no other IO operations exist in the device IOQ. Control is passed to the process scheduler which returns it to the program making the request. When the `await-io` module of PIOCS is invoked, it checks the status flag of the IOCB. If IO is complete, control returns to the application program, else the library module makes a kernel call to block itself. At an IO completion interrupt, an error recovery routine is invoked in the event of an IO error, else the status flag of the IOCB is set to 'IO completed' and the IO scheduler is called to initiate the next IO operation. The ECB-PCB arrangement is used to wake a program (if any) awaiting the IO completion. Control is now handed over to the process scheduler.

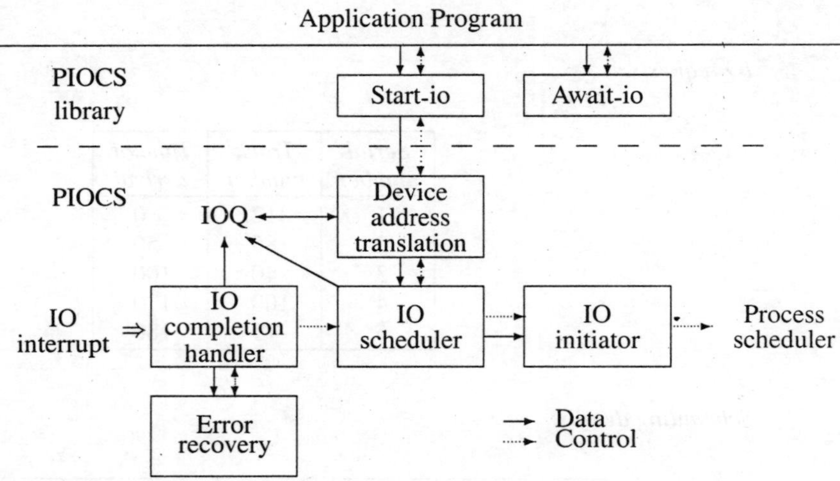

Fig. 16.12 Summary of PIOCS functionalities

16.3.4 Device Drivers

The PIOCS design described so far has one drawback—it assumes that PIOCS has sufficient knowledge to handle IO initiation, completion and error recovery for each device class. This assumption restricts the classes of IO devices which can be connected to the system, thus limiting the evolution of its IO hardware.

In an alternative design, PIOCS only provides generic support for IO operations. It invokes a specialized *device driver* (DD) for implementing IO operations on a specific class of devices. Now, device drivers need not be a part of the PIOCS. DD's for some crucial devices, e.g. the system disk, can be loaded at system boot time. Other DD's can be loaded on a demand basis during system operation. This arrangement supports addition of new IO devices by developing device drivers for them. Figure 16.13 illustrates this arrangement. The PDT entry of a device shows the name of its device driver instead of the name of its device class. Disk_DD, the device driver for the system disk, has been loaded at system boot time. Other DD's, viz. Tape_DD, would be loaded on demand. Each DD contains entry-points to support the fundamental PIOCS functions on the devices controlled by it, e.g. entry points for IO initiation, interrupt processing, etc. When PIOCS is invoked, it updates its data structures where necessary and passes control to the appropriate entry point of the relevant DD. (If DD does not already exist in memory, it is loaded at this point.) The DD performs device-specific operations and returns control to the PIOCS. For example, details of an IO initiation request are entered in IOQ before the IO-init entry point of DD is called. DD uses the information in PIOCS data structures to perform its functions.

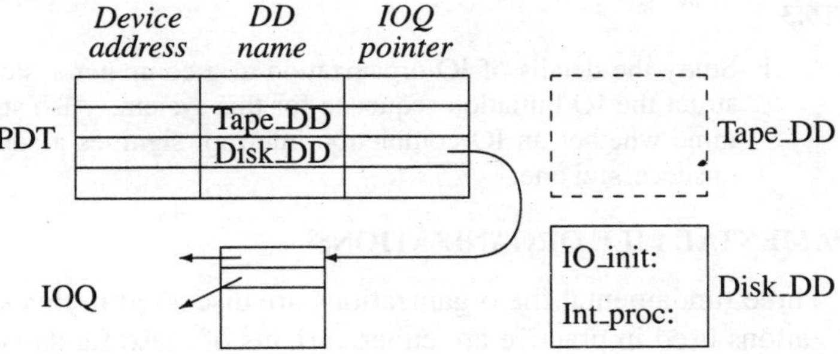

Fig. 16.13 Device drivers

A device driver combines the functionalities of four modules in Fig. 16.12 for one class of IO devices. These modules are IO scheduler, IO initiator, IO completion handler and Error recovery. To implement interrupt processing, the OS kernel needs to know the interrupt processing routine of a DD. Loading of a DD is therefore performed by the kernel rather than by the PIOCS.

16.3.4.1 Device Drivers in Unix

A Unix device driver (DD) is structured into two halves called *top half* and *bottom half*. The top half consists of routines that initiate IO operations on the devices in response to the *read*, *write*, *open* or *close* operations issued by an application program, while the bottom half consists of the interrupt handler for the device class serviced by the driver. Thus the top half corresponds to the IO scheduler and IO initiator modules in Fig. 16.12, while the bottom half corresponds to the IO completion handler and Error recovery modules.

The OS defines a standard DD interface consisting of a set of pre-defined entry points into the DD routines. Some of these are:

1. *<ddname>_init* : DD initialization routine
2. *<ddname>_read/write* : Routines to Read or Write a character
3. *<ddname>_int* : Interrupt handler routine.

The *<ddname>_init* routine is called at system boot time. It initializes various flags used by the DD. It also checks for the presence of various devices, sets flags to indicate their presence and may allocate buffers to them. Character IO is performed by invoking the *<ddname>_read* and *<ddname>_write* routines. The device driver has to provide a strategy routine for block data transfers. The strategy routine is roughly equivalent to the IO scheduler shown in Fig. 16.12. A call on the strategy routine takes the IOCB address as a parameter. The strategy routine adds this IOCB to an IOQ, and initiates the IO operation if possible. If immediate initiation is not possible, the IO operation is initiated subsequently by the interrupt handler.

EXERCISE 16.3

1. Study the details of IO organization of a computer system accessible to you. Construct the IO initiation sequence for this system. Also study how the OS can determine whether an IO completion interrupt signifies a successful IO operation or an unsuccessful one.

16.4 FUNDAMENTAL FILE ORGANIZATIONS

Three fundamental file organizations are discussed in this section. Other file organizations used in practice are either variants of these fundamental organizations or are special purpose organizations which suit specific IO devices.

16.4.1 Sequential File Organization

In this organization, records are always stored and accessed in a sequential manner. When an application program issues a `read` or `write` command, the *next* record in a file is read or written. Use of a sequential file requires data to be sorted in a desired order before storing or processing it. For example, if a master file uses sequential organization, the transaction data should be sorted in the same order before processing. In practice, sequential files are used if applications are sequential by nature or data can be presorted conveniently. Since most IO devices are capable of sequential operation, sequential files can be made device independent (see problem 1 of Exercise 16.4 for a definition of device independence). This facilitates portability of application programs.

16.4.2 Direct File Organization

Direct files are recorded on disk devices. An application program using a direct file uses explicit record addressing to access a record. This is performed by applying some transformation to the key field of a required record to generate a (*track_no*, *record_no*) address. To perform a read or write operation, disk heads have to be positioned on track *track_no* before issuing a read or write command on record *record_no*. Consider a master file of employee information organized as a direct file using an employee number as the key. Let p records be written on one track of the disk. Assuming the employee numbers and the cylinder, track and record numbers of the master file to start from 1, the address of the record for employee number n is

$$(track\ number\,(t_n),\ record\ number\,(r_n))$$

where

$$t_n = \lceil n/p \rceil \tag{16.4}$$

$$r_n = n - (t_n - 1) \times p \tag{16.5}$$

and $\lceil \ldots \rceil$ indicates a rounded-up integer value. A record address with the format

$$(cylinder\ number(c_n),\ surface\ number(s_n),\ record\ number(r_n))$$

can be similarly calculated.

Direct file organization provides access efficiency when records are not processed in sequential order. However, it has the following drawbacks compared to a sequential file:

1. Record address calculation consumes CPU time.
2. More movement of disk heads occurs than in sequential file organization.
3. Poor utilization of the IO media results from the need for dummy records (see Ex. 16.5).

Example 16.5 Figure 16.14 shows the arrangement of employee records in the sequential and direct file organizations. The direct file needs to contain a record for employee number 3 even after the employee has left the organization. This is necessary to satisfy the address calculation formulae (16.4)–(16.5).

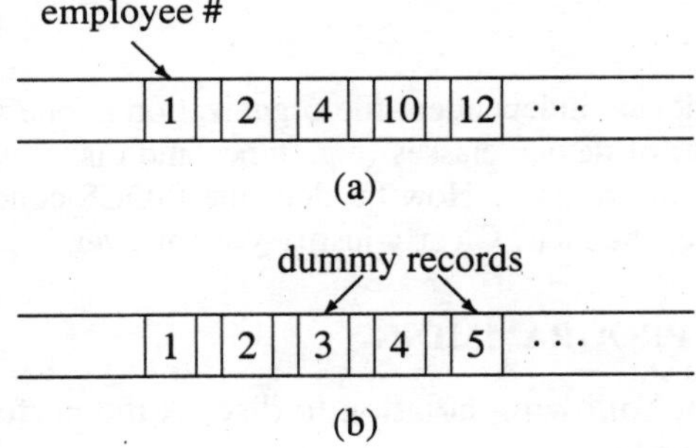

Fig. 16.14 Records in (a) sequential file, (b) direct file

One practical problem in the use of direct files is excessive device dependence. Characteristics of an IO device are explicitly assumed and used by the address calculation formulae (16.4)–(16.5). Rewriting the file on another device with different characteristics will imply modifying the address calculation formulae.

16.4.3 Index Sequential File Organization

The index sequential file organization is a hybrid organization which uses elements of the sequential and direct file organizations. It uses a hierarchical index to locate a group of records which may contain a desired record. The records in this group are searched sequentially to locate the desired record. This arrangement provides access efficiency comparable to the direct file organization while ensuring IO media economy comparable to a sequential file organization.

Figure 16.15 illustrates an index-sequential file. Records are stored in ascending order by employee number. The track index indicates the lowest and highest employee number located on a specific track. This index is used to locate the track which may contain a desired record. This track is searched to find and access the record. Note that analogous to the sequential file, a record may simply not exist. For large files, a higher level index may be used to speed up the search. For example, the higher level index could locate a group of tracks which may contain a desired record. The track index for that group of tracks would now be used to locate a track. This track would be searched to locate a record.

Track	*Low*	*High*
1	1	13
2	16	31
⋮		

Track #	employee #					
1	1	2	4	10	11	13
2	16	17	18	21	24	31
⋮						

Fig. 16.15 Track index in an index sequential file

EXERCISE 16.4

1. A device independent file organization is one which can use a device of any one of a set of device classes (e.g. tapes and disks) without requiring changes to an application program. How far does the PIOCS concept of logical devices support device independence? Clearly justify your answer.

16.5 ADVANCED IO PROGRAMMING

We use the following notation to discuss the performance of a program processing a sequential file.

t_{io} : *IO-time per record* (see Eqs. (16.1) and (16.2))

t_p : *processing time per record* (i.e. the CPU time spent by the application program in processing a record)

t_w : *IO-wait time per record* (i.e. the time during which the application program is blocked on a *read* operation for a record)

t_e : *effective elapsed time per record* (i.e. the clock time since the application program issues a *read* operation for a record to the end of processing of the record)

A typical sequence of IO operations to perform file processing is shown in Fig. 16.16. Here it can be seen that $t_w = t_{io}$ and $t_e = t_{io} + t_p$. t_{io} depends on the file organization and characteristics of the IO device while t_p depends on characteristics of the application program. Techniques of buffering and blocking are used to match

```
while (not end_of_file(f)) do
begin
    read (f, area);
    wait on read;
    process the record;
end
```

Fig. 16.16 File processing using PIOCS facilities

t_{io} and t_p to minimize (and sometimes even eliminate) t_w in a program, i.e. to reduce $(t_e - t_p)$.

16.5.1 Buffering of records

Definition 16.1 (IO buffer) *An* IO buffer *is a memory area temporarily used to implement an IO operation.*

Buffering is used to increase the overlap of the IO and CPU activities in a program, that is, to overlap t_{io} and t_p, so as to reduce t_w. This is achieved by

- *Pre-fetching* an input record into an IO buffer, or
- *Post-writing* an output record from an IO buffer.

Pre-fetching implies reading a record before a program needs it, so that the program does not have to wait on a *read* operation. In post-writing, the record to be written is simply copied into a buffer when the application program issues a *write* operation. Actual output is performed from the buffer sometime later. Thus the program does not have to wait on a *write* operation.

To consider the influence of buffering on the elapsed time of a program, let us analyse the performance of P, a program which reads and processes 100 records from a sequential file F. Let $t_{io} = t_p = 50$ ms. We will consider two versions of program P. The unbuffered version of P (we will call it *Unbuf_P*) uses a single area of memory called *Rec_area* to read and process a record of F. The buffered version of P (called *Buf_P*) uses two buffers called Buf_1 and Buf_2 for reading and processing the records of file F.

Program *Unbuf_P* uses the sequence of IO operations shown in Fig. 16.16. A time chart for the operation of this program is illustrated in Fig. 16.17(a). The chart consists of two parts showing the CPU and IO activities, respectively. Showing *Rec_area* in the IO activity part implies that an IO operation is in progress for *Rec_area*, while showing it in the CPU activity part implies that the program is currently processing the record situated in *Rec_area*. As seen before, $t_w = t_{io} = 50$ ms, hence $t_e = (t_w + t_p) = 100$ ms. The total elapsed time of *Unbuf_P* is thus 100 × 100 ms = 10 seconds.

Figure 16.17(b) illustrates the operation of *Buf_P*. To start with, *Buf_P* initiates IO on Buf_1 and Buf_2 by issuing two *read* operations. PIOCS queues these operations

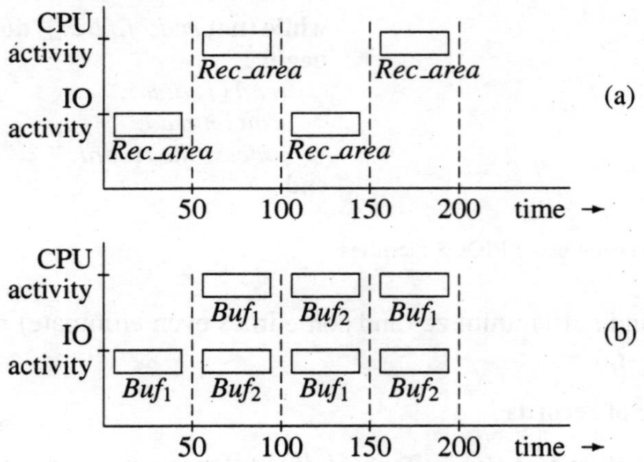

Fig. 16.17 Performance of (a) program *Unbuf_P*, and (b) program *Buf_P*

and initiates the first IO operation. *Buf_P* alternately uses Buf_1 and Buf_2 using the following 3-step procedure to perform file processing

1. Await IO on a buffer.
2. Process the record read into the buffer. (16.6)
3. Initiate IO on the buffer.

Thus during the period $t = 0$ to $t = 50$ ms, IO is in progress on Buf_1 while *Buf_P* is blocked at step 1 above. At $t = 50$ ms, the IO operation completes and Buf_1 is handed over to CPU processing. PIOCS initiates the queued IO operation on Buf_2. Since $t_{io} = t_p$, IO on Buf_2 completes at $t = 100$ ms. *Buf_P* also finishes processing the record in Buf_1 and initiates IO on it at $t = 100$ ms (see Step 3 of (16.6)). This pattern repeats every 50 ms. Thus, *Buf_P* does not face an IO wait in step 1 any time after the first record. The IO channel and CPU keep switching between the use of Buf_1 and Buf_2 without encountering any IO waits. We now have $t_e = t_p = 50$ ms. The total elapsed time of *Buf_P* is thus 50 + 100 × 50 ms = 5.05 seconds.

Buffering cannot always be so effective. In general, when a program using two buffers makes IO requests at a uniform rate, its performance is governed by the larger of t_{io} and t_p. This is because the CPU is expected to process a record in one buffer, while IO is in progress to read a new record in the other buffer. In effect, execution of step 2 on one buffer is expected to overlap with IO to read a new record in the other buffer. Both the activities must complete before CPU can start processing the new record and IO can begin on the next buffer. When $t_{io} > t_p$, IO will still be in progress on a buffer when the CPU performs step 2 of (16.6) on it. This will result in an IO wait time given by $t_w = t_{io} - t_p$.

Example 16.6 Let $t_{io} = 75$ ms and $t_p = 50$ ms. To start with, the CPU has to wait till the IO on Buf_1 completes. Thus, it faces an initial wait of 75 ms. When it begins processing the record in Buf_1, IO on Buf_2 is in progress. Both activities must complete before CPU can start processing the next record in Buf_2 and IO can begin on Buf_1. Hence the CPU incurs a wait of 25 ms before processing the second and every subsequent record.

The performance of a buffered program processing q records can be summarized as follows:

$$t_w = t_{io} - t_p, \; if \; t_{io} > t_p \quad (16.7)$$

$$t_w = 0, \; if \; t_{io} \le t_p \quad (16.8)$$

$$t_e = t_w + t_p$$

$$Total\ elapsed\ time = t_{io} + (q-1) \times t_e + t_p \quad (16.9)$$

where the terms t_{io} and t_p in Eq. (16.9) represent the time to perform IO for the first record and the time to perform processing of the last record, respectively.

Using multiple buffers

The above outline can be extended to obtain a version of *Buf_P* which uses n buffers, $n > 2$ (see Fig. 16.18). At the start of file processing, *Buf_P* initiates IO on all n buffers. Inside the file processing loop, it uses all n buffers in turn, always following the steps of (16.6) to process a record in a buffer. Excepting the value of n, this part of the program is analogous to the two buffers case.

```
        for k := 1 to n do
            Init-io on k^th buffer;
        k := n;
loop:   k := (k mod n) +1;
        Await-io on k^th buffer;
        if end_of_file goto over;
        { Process the record in k^th buffer }
        Init-io on k^th buffer;
        goto loop;
over:   --
```

Fig. 16.18 File processing using n buffers

Figure 16.19 illustrates a typical situation during the execution of *Buf_P*. The CPU is busy processing the record contained in Buf_i. IO has been initiated on all other buffers. Some of the IO operations, viz. those on $Buf_{i+1} \ldots Buf_{j-1}$, are already complete. IO is currently in progress for Buf_j, while $Buf_{j+1} \ldots Buf_n$, $Buf_1 \ldots Buf_{i-1}$ are currently in the queue for IO initiation. Thus $(j-i)$ buffers are full at the moment, IO is in progress for one buffer and $(n-j+i-1)$ buffers are in the queue for IO.

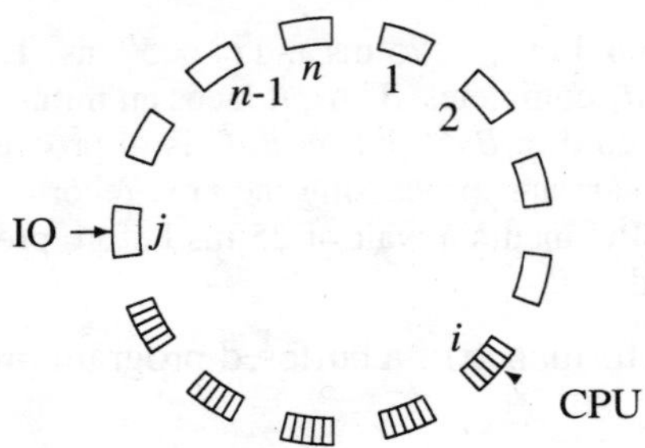

Fig. 16.19 Use of buffers in *Buf_P*

The value of $(j-i)$ would depend on the values of t_{io} and t_p. If $t_{io} < t_p$, we can use the reasoning that led to Eq. (16.8) and conclude that buffers $Buf_{i+1} \dots Buf_n$, $Buf_1 \dots Buf_{i-2}$ would be full, and Buf_{i-1} would be either full or under IO when Buf_i is being processed by the CPU. If $t_{io} > t_p$, the steady state situation would be that buffer Buf_{i+1} would be under IO and buffers $Buf_{i+2} \dots Buf_n$, $Buf_1 \dots Buf_{i-1}$ would be empty when Buf_i is being processed by the CPU.

Thus, presence of more than two buffers makes no difference to the performance of *Buf_P* because the relation $t_e = t_w + t_p$ continues to hold as in the two buffers case. So why should we use >2 buffers? The n buffer arrangement, $n > 2$, is useful to satisfy the peak requirement of records of a file in a program.

Definition 16.2 (Peak requirement of records) *The* peak requirement *of records of a file in a program is the largest number of records of that file which are likely to be processed together by the program.*

Example 16.7 illustrates how buffering can be used to satisfy the peak requirement of records.

Example 16.7 A compiler is designed to read an entire statement before starting its processing. If a statement may contain up to l lines, and each line is a record of a file F, the compiler may process upto l records together. Thus, its peak requirement is l records. In this case IO wait for the compiler can be eliminated only if

1. $t_{io} \leq t_{pl}$, and
2. $l \leq n-1$

where t_{pl} is the average processing time for each line of a statement. These conditions ensure that at least l buffers are full at any time.

16.5.2 Blocking of Records

From Eqs. (16.7)–(16.8) it is clear that $t_w > 0$ if $t_{io} > t_p$. In other words, buffering cannot eliminate IO waits if $t_{io} > t_p$. Hence we must consider ways to reduce t_{io}. Now, from Eq. (16.1), $t_{io} = t_a + t_x$ and both t_a, t_x depend on the file organization and characteristics of an IO device. So, how can we reduce t_{io}? Consider what would happen if two records are read or written in one IO operation. The IO time for the operation which reads two records (t^*_{io}) is given by

$$t^*_{io} = t_a + 2 \times t_x \tag{16.10}$$

In effect, the IO time per record is given by

$$\begin{aligned} t_{io} &= \frac{t^*_{io}}{2} \\ &= \frac{t^*_a}{2} + t_x \end{aligned}$$

which shows that t_{io} can be reduced by writing more than one record in an IO operation.

A *logical record* is a record as seen from an application program's viewpoint, and a *physical record* (also called a *block*) is a record as written on an IO medium. A file is said to employ *blocking* of records if a physical record consists of more than one logical record. We define the term *blocking factor* to describe the characteristics of a file employing blocking.

Definition 16.3 (Blocking factor) *The* blocking factor (m) *of a file is the number of logical records in one physical record.*

Example 16.8 A program SALARY produces the salary records of an organization for every pay period. Information concerning the employees of the organization is available in a master file. Each logical record of the file contains information concerning one employee, whereas a physical record in the master file contains information concerning 3 employees. The blocking factor is thus 3.

Deblocking actions

Figure 16.20 shows a program which processes a file with blocked records in an unbuffered manner. Each physical record read from the IO device contains m logical records. Thus, m records can be processed following an IO operation on *Rec_area*. A running index l points at the next logical record within a physical record. When l exceeds m, the blocking factor, the next physical record is read and l is reset to 1. Actions of extracting a logical record from a physical record are collectively called *deblocking actions*.

Choice of blocking factor

Generalizing on the previous discussion, if s_{lr}, s_{pr} represent the size of a logical and physical record, respectively, then $s_{pr} = m.s_{lr}$. The total IO time per physical record is

$$(t_{io})_{pr} = t_a + m \times t_x.$$

```
        l := m;
loop:   l := (l mod m) +1;
        if l = 1 then
            Init-io on Rec_area;
            Await-io on Rec_area;
        if end_of_file then goto over;
        { Extract l^th record in Rec_area and process it }
        goto loop;
over:   ...
```

Fig. 16.20 Processing of a file with blocked records

and the IO time per logical record is

$$(t_{io})_{lr} = \frac{t_a}{m} + t_x \tag{16.11}$$

Thus blocking reduces the effective IO time per logical record. If $t_x < t_p$, with an appropriate choice of m it may be possible to reduce $(t_{io})_{lr}$ such that $(t_{io})_{lr} \leq t_p$. An appropriate number of buffers can then be used to eliminate IO waits for the program.

Example 16.9 Table 16.3 shows how $(t_{io})_{lr}$ reduces for various values of m for a disk device with t_a = 10 ms, transfer rates of 800 Kbytes/sec and s_{lr} = 200 bytes. If t_p = 3 ms, $m \geq 4$ makes $(t_{io})_{lr} < t_p$.

Table 16.3 Variation of $(t_{io})_{lr}$ with m (transfer rate = 800 K bytes)

blocking factor (*m*)	*block* *size*	t_a *ms*	$m \times t_x$ *ms*	$(t_{io})_{pr}$ *ms*	$(t_{io})_{lr}$ *ms*
1	200	10	0.25	10.25	10.25
2	400	10	0.50	10.50	5.25
3	600	10	0.75	10.75	3.58
4	800	10	1.00	11.00	2.75

The value of m is bounded on the lower side by the desire to make $(t_{io})_{lr} \leq t_p$. On the higher side, it is bounded by the following considerations:

- Main memory commitment for file buffers.
- Size of a disk track or sector.

A practical value of the blocking factor is the smallest value of m which makes $(t_{io})_{lr} \leq t_p$. Two buffers are now sufficient to eliminate IO waits. As explained before, a larger number of buffers may be considered to meet the peak requirements of records in an application program.

EXERCISE 16.5

1. Explain how (and whether) buffering and blocking of records would be beneficial for files with following organizations:
   (a) Sequential organization
   (b) Index Sequential organization
   (c) Direct organization.
2. An *update* file is one which is read and modified during processing. Typically, a record would be read by a program, modified in memory and then written back into the file.
   (a) What are the IO devices which can be used for recording an update file?
   (b) Is blocking of records useful for an update file?
   (c) Is buffering useful for an update file?

   Justify your answers.
3. A program processes a sequential file using two buffers. The IO and processing times for each record in the file are as follows:

processing time per record	=	10 ms
access time of device	=	10 ms
transfer time per record	=	6 ms

   (a) If two buffers are used, find the value of the smallest blocking factor which can eliminate all IO waits.
   (b) If two buffers and a blocking factor of '5' is used, calculate the peak requirement of records in a program which this blocking and buffering arrangement can satisfy.
4. A sequential file is to be designed to use optimal blocking and buffering of records. Characteristics of the IO device and the application program are as follows:

Access time (average)	=	25 ms
Transfer time per record	=	5 ms
Peak requirement of records by the program	=	5 records
Processing time per record	=	10 ms

   Determine optimal values of the blocking factor and the number of buffers.
   What changes, if any, would you make in your design if the peak requirement of records were (i) 3 records, (ii) 8 records?
5. Comment on the validity of the following statement: "By judicious selection of the blocking factor and the number of buffers, it is always possible to eliminate IO waits completely."
6. Discuss the influence of disk scheduling algorithms on the effectiveness of IO buffering.
7. An input file is being processed using n buffers. When the end-of-file condition is detected, some more IO requests would have been already made by the program. Comment on how this situation can be handled.
8. In case of a system failure during the execution of a job, it is desirable to resume execution from the point at which the failure occurred. Comment on the ease with which this can be done if the program was processing a file with blocked records and a large number of buffers.

16.6 LOGICAL IOCS

The LIOCS layer supports creation and efficient access of files using the facilities provided by the PIOCS layer. Operating at the LIOCS interface, a programmer need not perform IO programming (i.e. IO initiation and IO interrupt processing), or advanced IO programming (i.e. buffering and blocking). In effect, all details shown in Sections 16.1–16.5 become the responsibility of LIOCS.

16.6.1 LIOCS Functions

LIOCS provides the following functions to perform file processing:

1. `liocs-open` (<*file_name*>, <*processing_mode*>);
2. `liocs-close` (<*file_name*>);
3. `read/write` (<*file_name*>, <*record_info*>, <*IO_area addr*>);

where we use the names `liocs-open` and `liocs-close` to differentiate the LIOCS calls from the `open` and `close` calls of the file system.

Figure 16.21 shows a typical program for processing an existing file. File processing is initiated by the `liocs-open` call in the program, which has the effect of 'connecting' the file to the program. Since the file processing mode is 'read', LIOCS performs the following actions when an `liocs-open` call is executed:

1. Obtain information concerning the size and location of the file (e.g. device id and track numbers).
2. Allocate buffers for the file.
3. Issue *IO-init* for *read* operations on all buffers.

```
liocs-open (f, 'read');
while ( not end_of_file (f) ) do
    read (f, <record_info>, area);
liocs-close (f);
```

Fig. 16.21 File processing using LIOCS facilities

A `read` call makes the next logical record of the file available to a program. For a sequential file, the `read` call involves deblocking actions and IO initiation actions at appropriate times. The `liocs-close` call releases the file buffers.

When a new file is being created by a program, the `liocs-open` call involves obtaining space on a disk for writing the file, followed by allocation of buffers. A `write` call involves blocking actions and issuing of *IO-init* for *write* operations at appropriate times. The `liocs-close` call involves more work than in the case of a read file, viz.

1. Ensure that information in all buffers is written into the file.
2. Release output buffers.
3. Save information concerning size and location of the file.

Space allocation for a new file is typically not performed by LIOCS itself; it expects its invoker to perform this function. FS performs allocation prior to invoking the LIOCS. If LIOCS is directly invoked by an application program, the program is expected to perform space allocation in some manner.

16.6.2 LIOCS Modules

Programs using the LIOCS interface must contain a file declaration specifying various attributes of the file, e.g. record size, blocking factor, etc. Figure 16.22 shows file declarations in different programming languages for files containing fixed length records. The PL/I file declaration is shown to indicate the logical device name (SYS003) and device type (*dddd*). In other languages, the device name is implied by the file id (e.g. in Fortran), or can be specified through the OS command processor in some manner (e.g. an 'assign' command). The number of buffers may be explicitly indicated, or may be a default in the language.

Cobol
```
FD INFO
BLOCK CONTAINS 500 CHARACTERS
RECORD CONTAINS 50 CHARACTERS
RECORDING MODE IS F
```
PL/I
```
DECLARE INFO FILE RECORD
SEQUENTIAL OUTPUT BUFFERED
ENVIRONMENT (MEDIUM(SYS003,dddd)
F(500,50) BUFFERS(2));
```
Fortran
```
DEFINE FILE 8 (1000,    50,      L,        ID1)
         File # no.of    record  format    pointer to
                records  size    indicator next record
```

Fig. 16.22 File declarations in different languages

The attributes of a file determine the nature of LIOCS actions required to handle its IO operations. For example, consider the processing of a sequential file. The actions at a `read` call are determined by whether the file uses blocking of records and whether it is being processed in a buffered manner. LIOCS provides a library of IO modules to handle files with different combinations of attributes. To handle the fundamental file organizations described in Section 16.4, it is adequate to provide modules for the following:

1. Unbuffered sequential IO
2. Buffered sequential IO
3. Direct IO
4. Unbuffered index sequential IO

5. Buffered index sequential IO.

While processing a file declaration in a program, the language translator analyses the file attributes to determine which LIOCS module should be used to process the file. Attributes like the number of buffers, blocking factor, etc., become parameters of the module. Each LIOCS module contains entry points for liocs-open, liocs-read, liocs-write and liocs-close operations. These entry points have the standard names `file-open`, `file-read`, `file-write` and `file-close`.

16.6.3 LIOCS Data Structures

LIOCS uses two data structures—file labels, and file control blocks. A file label describes a file existing in the system while a file control block describes the state of processing of a file in an application program.

File Label

A file label for file `alpha` ($label_{\texttt{alpha}}$) is a descriptor for `alpha`. Its lifetime in the system is never less than the lifetime of `alpha`. It contains the following information:

1. File name
2. File location
3. File size
4. Information concerning file owner, protection status, etc.

LIOCS must locate the label of file `alpha` while processing the call `liocs-open (alpha)`. To enable this, the labels of all files existing in an IO volume are stored in a standard place. The labels of disk files are stored in a special area called the Volume Table of Contents (VTOC) (see Fig. 16.23). Since a file may occupy many non-contiguous areas on the disk, the location information in a disk file label consists of many (address, size) pairs, each pair describing one disk area.

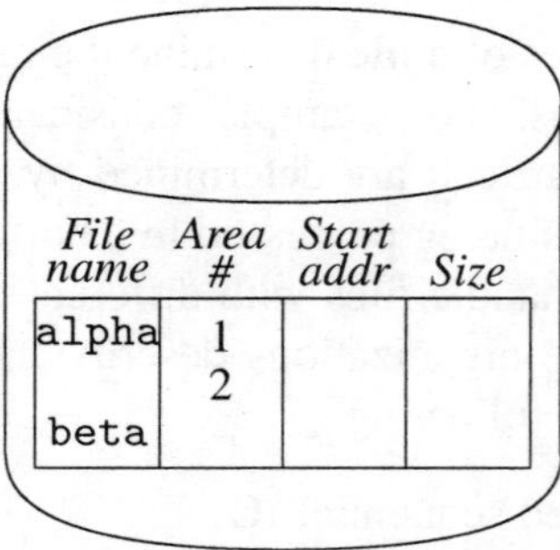

Fig. 16.23 Volume table of contents (VTOC)

The information in a file label is used for two purposes—to locate the data in a file and to protect it against accidental overwriting while creating a new file. The second function is needed because LIOCS expects its invoker to indicate where (e.g. in which disk area) to create a new file. It is very important when the LIOCS interface is directly used by an application program. (It is redundant when the LIOCS layer is invoked by the FS layer—see Section 17.3 for details of how FS manages free space on disks.) Both the functions are performed by `liocs-open`.

File control block (FCB)

A file control block $fcb_{\texttt{alpha}}$ is created when an application program opens file `alpha` for processing. Thus, an FCB contains all information necessary to perform IO on file `alpha`. Figure 16.24 shows the fields in the FCB. The information in the FCB is derived from the following three sources:

1. A language translator puts in the following information while creating the FCB—file name, record size, blocking factor, and name of the LIOCS module (the linker uses the name to obtain its address).
2. The LIOCS module copies certain information from the file label when the file is opened, e.g. address of the first and last record of an input file.
3. Certain information is filled in by the LIOCS module, e.g. addresses of the buffers.

1. File name,
2. Address of first byte/record of the file,
3. Address of last byte/record of the file,
4. Address of the next byte/record,
5. Size of a record,
6. Blocking factor,
7. Addresses of the buffers,
8. Device type and address, and
9. Address of the LIOCS module.

Fig. 16.24 File control block (FCB)

The FCB of file `alpha` can be destroyed after processing the call `liocs-close(alpha)`.

16.6.4 Implementation of LIOCS Functions

Implementation of LIOCS functions is centered around FCBs. An FCB is created at an `liocs-open`. Information from various sources is used to initialize its fields. The FCB undergoes modification as the file is processed. At `liocs-close`, information in the FCB is used to update the file label. Figure 16.25 shows LIOCS actions during the execution of a HLL program. As described earlier, the file declaration for `alpha` is used to determine the name of the LIOCS module needed to process **alpha**. Actions of the LIOCS module during the execution of the program are described in the following.

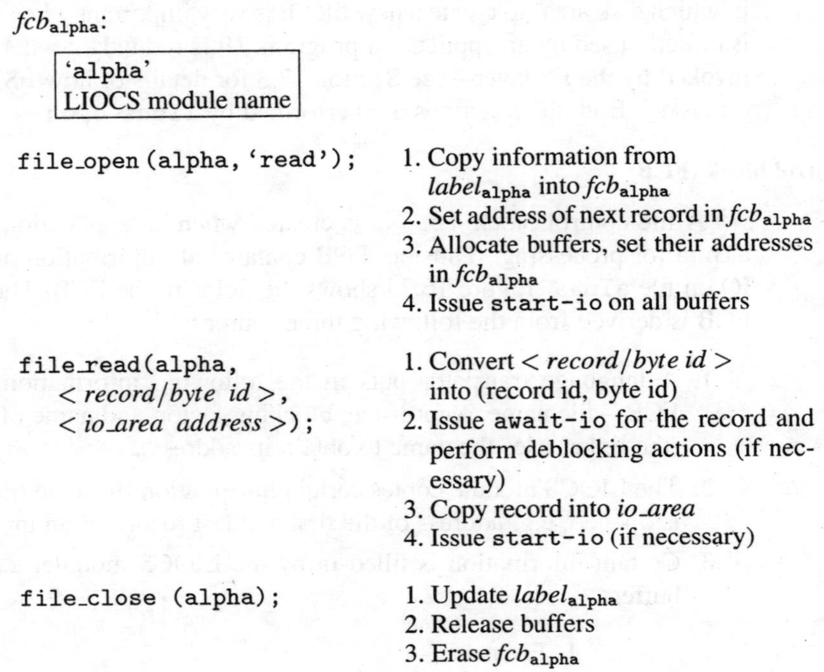

fcb_{alpha}:
'alpha'
LIOCS module name
file_open (alpha, 'read');
1. Copy information from $label_{alpha}$ into fcb_{alpha}
2. Set address of next record in fcb_{alpha}
3. Allocate buffers, set their addresses in fcb_{alpha}
4. Issue start-io on all buffers
file_read(alpha, < record/byte id >, < io_area address >);
1. Convert < record/byte id > into (record id, byte id)
2. Issue await-io for the record and perform deblocking actions (if necessary)
3. Copy record into io_area
4. Issue start-io (if necessary)
file_close (alpha);
1. Update $label_{alpha}$
2. Release buffers
3. Erase fcb_{alpha}

Fig. 16.25 Actions of the LIOCS modules during file processing

File open

An open call

```
liocs-open(alpha ...   );
```

in a program is translated into a call on the entry point 'file_open' of the LIOCS module named in fcb_{alpha}. fcb_{alpha} is itself passed as a parameter to file_open. LIOCS checks whether the file exists by locating $label_{alpha}$ on the logical device named in fcb_{alpha}. It then performs the following functions:

1. Copy the location and size of `alpha` into fcb_{alpha}.
2. Initialize certain fields of fcb_{alpha}, e.g. set the address of the next record to the address of the first record of the file.
3. For a buffered file, allocate file buffers and put their addresses in fcb_{alpha}.
4. Issue `start_io(...)` calls of PIOCS on all buffers for an input file.

If `alpha` is an output file, in step 2 LIOCS enters the address of the secondary storage area allocated to `alpha` into $fcb_{\texttt{alpha}}$ after checking for conflicts with existing files. Other actions are analogous to the opening of an input file.

File IO

While processing file `alpha`, a program makes calls with the following format

`read/write (alpha,` <*record/byte id*>, <*io_area address*>`);`

Each such call is converted into a call on the 'file_read' entry point of the LIOCS module named in $fcb_{\texttt{alpha}}$, with $fcb_{\texttt{alpha}}$ and <*record/byte id*> as parameters. The module uses the information in $fcb_{\texttt{alpha}}$ to convert the <*record/byte id*> into a pair (*record id*, *byte id*). This pair is actually used to perform the IO operation. The address of the next record in $fcb_{\texttt{alpha}}$ is updated at the end of the operation.

Converting <*record/byte id*> into the pair (*record id*, *byte id*) requires knowledge of the space allocation strategy which is under the control of the invoker, i.e. the application program itself or an IOCS layer located higher than the LIOCS. LIOCS can call a routine provided by the invoker to achieve this conversion. Alternatively, the LIOCS interface could require the invoker to provide the pair (*record id, byte id*) instead of the <*record/byte id*>.

File close

A close call

`liocs-close(alpha ...);`

is translated into a call on the entry point 'file_close' of the LIOCS module with $fcb_{\texttt{alpha}}$ as the parameter. While executing the file close operation, LIOCS writes the information concerning file size, address of the last record, etc. into the file label. For a disk file, this amounts to updating the information in $label_{\texttt{alpha}}$, which exists in the VTOC of the IO device. Any disk area allocated to `alpha` but not used by it can be returned to the OS at this stage. After updating the file label, $fcb_{\texttt{alpha}}$ is destroyed to protect against its accidental misuse.

EXERCISE 16.6

1. An operating system wishes to support true device independence at the LIOCS level. The designer is considering the following alternatives to implement this feature.
   (a) Code a general purpose LIOCS routine which can handle any device type existing in the system. When a file declaration contains the specification `devtype=any`, the compiler puts the address of this routine in the FCB (see Fig. 16.24).
   (b) The compiler will generate code to make a system call at `liocs-open`. The kernel will specify the address of a specific routine depending on the assigned device.

   Which alternative would you recommend? Comment on efficiency and link/load complexity of the alternative suggested by you.

16.7 FILE PROCESSING IN UNIX

Unix only supports plain files, i.e. sequential files without any structure. The files are considered to be streams of characters. Unix SVR4 uses the following LIOCS data structures to implement file processing:

1. inode
2. File descriptors
3. Buffer cache.

Figure 16.26 illustrates the relationship between an inode and a file descriptor. The inode is a file label. It holds addresses of disk blocks which contain file data. (The format of inode is described later in Chapter 17.) When a file is opened in a program, its inode is copied into memory and a file descriptor is allocated to the program. The memory copy of the inode acts like an FCB. The file descriptor contains two fields—displacement of the next record (i.e. byte) in the file, and the inode pointer. Thus the inode and the file descriptor together contain all information necessary to access a file. This arrangement also simplifies concurrent sharing of a file by programs. Figure 16.26 shows two programs sharing file `alpha`. Since each sharing program has its own file descriptor containing the displacement of the next record, the programs do not interfere with each other's file processing. To avoid race conditions while accessing an inode, a lock field is provided in the memory copy of an inode. A program trying to access an inode must sleep if the lock is set by some other program. The programs must use their own arrangements to avoid race conditions on file data.

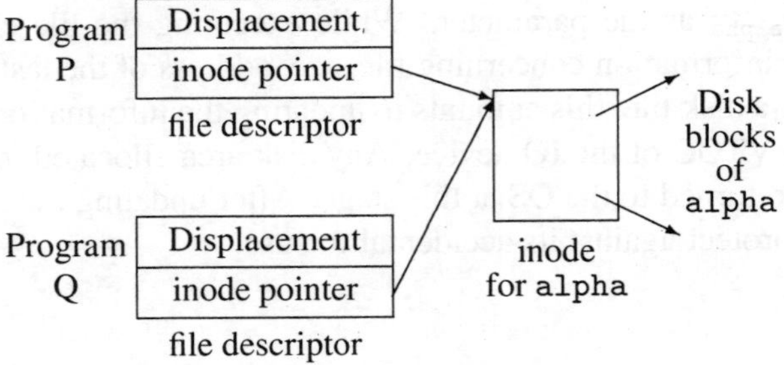

Fig. 16.26 Unix data structures

The buffer cache consists of a pool of buffers to be shared by all open files in the system. Thus, a buffer may be empty or may contain a disk block belonging to some file in the system. Each buffer has a header describing the contents of the buffer. For a buffer in use, this contains the pair (*device address, disk block address*), a status flag indicating whether IO is in progress for the buffer, and a *busy* flag to indicate whether a program is currently accessing the contents of the buffer. To implement an IO operation for some program P, Unix performs the following actions:

1. Form the pair (device address, disk block address) for the record required by P.
2. Search the buffer pool to check whether a buffer in use has a matching pair in its header.
3. If not, allocate a free buffer, put the (*device address, disk block address*) information in its header, set the status flag to 'IO in progress', queue the buffer for IO and put P to sleep on completion of IO.
4. If a buffer with matching header exists, return to P if the flags indicate that IO is complete and the buffer is 'not busy'. Else, put P to sleep on completion of IO on the buffer or buffer 'not busy' condition.

This schematic reduces IO traffic when files are shared as it is likely that the block required by P may have been read in for some other program Q. It also enables pre-fetching of data on a per-program basis for shared files. This can be performed in step 2 by initiating an IO for the next disk block of the file, unless it happens to exist in the memory. The buffers in the buffer pool are re-allocated on an LRU basis. This is implemented in an interesting way. All buffers in use are entered in a free list. A buffer is moved to the end of the list whenever its contents are referenced. Thus least recently used buffers move to the head of the free list. In step 3, Unix always allocates the buffer at the start of the free list unless the buffer contains some modified data which is yet to be written into the file. In that case, it queues a write operation for the buffer and uses the next buffer in the list. To speed up the search of step 2 above, Unix maintains a variant of a 'hash with overflow chaining' table according to the (*device address, disk block address*) information.

Figure 16.27 illustrates the above arrangement. To search for a disk block with address *bbb*, *bbb* is hashed to obtain the entry number $e = h(bbb)$. Buffers in the chain starting on this entry are searched to find the buffer with *bbb* in its header. If the buffer is present in the chain, it is moved to the end of the free list and its contents are used. Else the buffer at the head of the free list is allocated and disk block *bbb* is loaded in it. The buffer is moved to the end of the free list.

Example 16.10 In Fig. 16.27, if program P needs to access data residing in disk block 18, the buffer containing block 18 would be moved to the end of the free list. If P now needs data in disk block 21, the buffer containing block 13 would be allocated to it. This buffer would be moved to the end of the free list after loading block 21 in it.

EXERCISE 16.7

1. The `lseek` command of Unix indicates the offset of a byte in a sequential file which is to be read/written next.
   (a) What is the advantage of using the `lseek` command in a program (i.e. in what way is it better than issuing a `read` with the byte offset)?
   (b) Indicate the sequence of actions which should be executed when a program issues an `lseek` command.

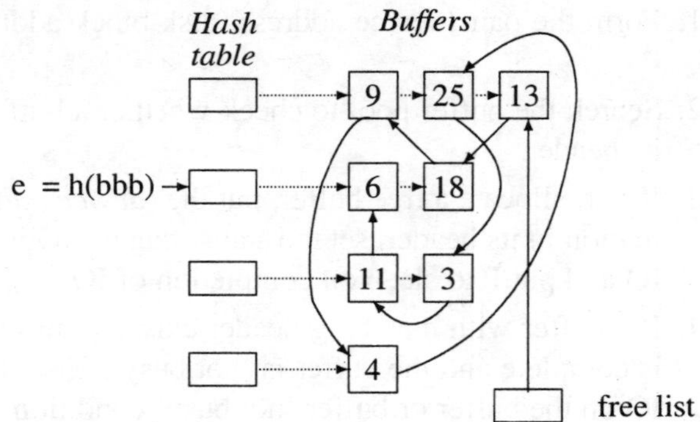

Fig. 16.27 Unix buffer cache

BIBLIOGRAPHY

(a) IO devices and device level scheduling

1. Flores, I. (1973): *Peripheral Devices*, Prentice-Hall, Englewood Cliffs.
2. Freeman, D.E. and O.R. Perry (1977): *IO design*, Hayden, New Jersey.
3. Fuller, S.H.(1972): "An optimal drum scheduling algorithm," *IEEE Transactions on Computers*, **21** (11), 1153-1165.
4. Gear, C.W. (1980): *Computer Organization and Programming*, McGraw-Hill Kogakusha, Tokyo.
5. Gold, D.E. and D.J. Kuck (1974): "A model for masking rotational latency by dynamic disk allocation," *Commn. of ACM*, **17** (5), 278-288.
6. Hofri, M. (1980): "Disk scheduling: FCFS *vs.* SSTF revisited," *Commn. of ACM*, **23** (11), 645-53.

(b) File organization

1. Bach, M.J. (1986): *The design of the Unix operating system*, Prentice-Hall, Englewood Cliffs.
2. Bradley, J. (1982): *File and Data-base Techniques*, Holt, Rinehart & Winston, New York.
3. Gear, C.W. (1980): *Computer Organization and Programming*, McGraw-Hill Kogakusha, Tokyo.
4. Hanson, O. (1982): *Design of Computer Data Files*, Pitman, London.
5. Johnson, L.F. and R.H. Cooper (1981): *File Techniques for Data Organization in Cobol*, Prentice-Hall, Englewood Cliffs.
6. Mullin, J.K. (1972): "An improved index sequential access method using hashed overflow," *Commn. of ACM*, **15** (5), 301-307.
7. Orgass, R.J. (1981): "Files in an interactive environment," *Software—Practice and Experience*, **11**, 1265-1271.
8. Roberts, D.C. (1972): "File organization techniques" in *Advances in Computers*, Vol.12, Academic Press, 115-174.

CHAPTER 17

File Systems

IO management layers of the OS form the hierarchy shown in Fig. 17.1. PIOCS is the lowest layer of the hierarchy, hence also the most machine dependent. As seen in Chapter 16, the PIOCS layer provides the means to perform device level IO without having to know the intricacies of IO programming. the knowledge of IO hardware and device specific details. The LIOCS layer provides two features to support file processing in application programs. First, label processing ensures that files would not be accidentally destroyed through overwriting. Second, a library of LIOCS modules is provided to perform efficient file processing. This obviates the need for advanced IO programming in an application program. The LIOCS layer uses the facilities provided by the PIOCS layer to implement its functions.

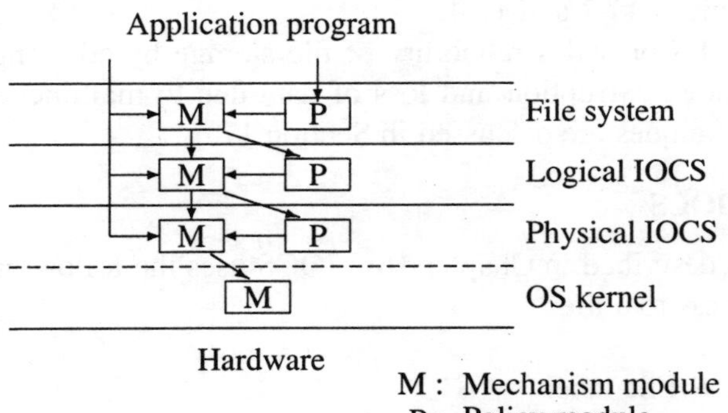

Fig. 17.1 IO management layers

The file system (FS) layer provides the following facilities to application programs:

1. File naming freedom

2. File sharing
3. Protection against illegal file accesses
4. Reliable storage of files.

The FS layer uses facilities provided by the LIOCS layer to implement its functions. This hides all details of IO organization and LIOCS module interfaces from the application program. It is thus independent of the hardware and software of a computer system.

The fundamental difference between LIOCS and FS can be summarized as follows: LIOCS views a file as an entity which is created or manipulated by application programs, whereas FS views a file as an entity which is *owned* by a user, can be *shared* by a set of authorized users, and has to be *reliably stored* over an extended period of time. The difference between the LIOCS and FS views can be seen in the context of the four FS functions mentioned above. Let two users A and B create files named `alpha`. If A wishes to open his file `alpha` using the LIOCS interface, LIOCS will simply open the first file `alpha` it can find in the VTOC of a disk. This could well be B's file! The only way to avoid this problem is for A and B to somehow ensure unique names for their files. FS, on the other hand, provides complete file naming freedom to users. It achieves this by using directories to differentiate between the files created by different users. Directory structures are discussed in Section 17.1.

The presence of directories enables FS to support file sharing and protection. Sharing is simply a matter of permitting a user to access the files existing in some other user's directory, e.g. user C may access A's files in this manner. Protection is implemented by permitting the owner of a file, say user B in the above example, to specify which other users may access his files. File protection is discussed in sections 17.2 and 17.4.

FS provides reliability of file storage by adopting specific techniques to guard against corruption and loss of data due to malfunctions in the system. Reliability techniques are discussed in Section 17.6.

Interface with LIOCS

As described in Chapter 16, LIOCS uses the following data structures to implement access to a file:

- File label
- File control block (FCB).

File labels for all files existing in a disk volume are contained in its volume table of contents (VTOC). Each file label contains information concerning the size and location of a file. LIOCS visualizes the VTOC to be *flat*, i.e. without any structure. The label of a file to be `open`'ed is located in the VTOC and relevant information is copied from it into the file's FCB. File processing can now begin.

By contrast, the file system is aware of the existence of different users in the system. Hence it organizes its information in a structured form. This structure provides the necessary support for the fundamental functions mentioned at the start of this chapter, viz. file naming freedom. However, FS must use LIOCS facilities for file processing. This involves use of LIOCS data structures. To achieve this, FS simply performs an intelligent mapping function between file names used by different users and the entries of the VTOC. Once this is achieved, it can hand over the actual file processing to LIOCS.

Figure 17.2 illustrates the mapping function performed by FS when an application program executed by user A opens a file named `alpha` for reading. Note that the VTOC may contain two or more entries for file `alpha`. FS maps the name `alpha` used by user A into the correct VTOC entry. This entry contains $label_{\texttt{alpha}}$. FS now invokes `liocs-open` with $label_{\texttt{alpha}}$ as a parameter. LIOCS copies the location information from $label_{\texttt{alpha}}$ into $fcb_{\texttt{alpha}}$. File processing now proceeds as shown in Fig. 16.25. If a file is opened for writing, FS comes into the picture once again for disk space allocation.

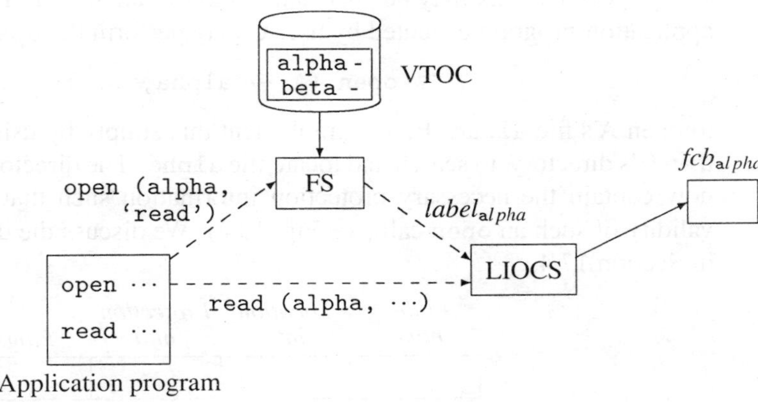

Fig. 17.2 File name mapping

17.1 DIRECTORY STRUCTURES

A directory contains information about files. Thus, it is central to the functioning of FS. To implement the mapping function of Fig. 17.2, FS may use a separate directory, called a *user directory* (UD), for files owned by each user. Figure 17.3 shows the UD's for users A and B. When a program executed by user A performs the open call

```
open(alpha, ...);
```

FS searches for `alpha` in A's UD. If the statement `open(alpha, ...)` was executed by some program executed by B, FS would have searched B's UD for `alpha`. This arrangement ensures that the correct file would be accessed even if many files with

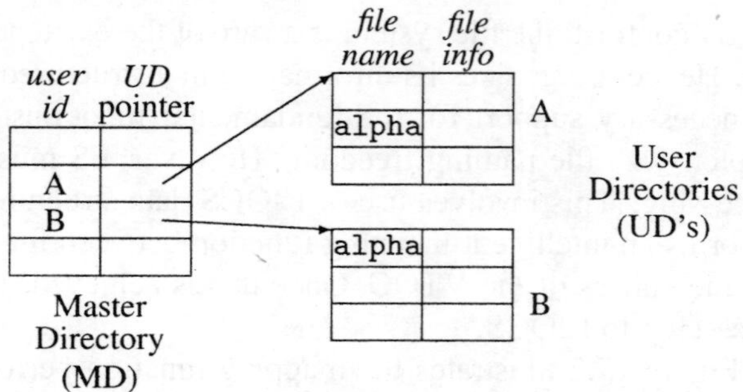

Fig. 17.3 Master and user directories

identical names exist in the system. FS uses a *master directory* (MD) to store the information concerning different UDs (see Fig. 17.3). Given this use of directories by FS, it is not necessary to have a separate VTOC for the FS disk. Thus, the information typically contained in a file label can now be stored in a relevant directory entry.

A special syntax may be provided to refer to another user's file. For example, an application program executed by user C may perform the `open` call

```
open (A → alpha, ...);
```

to open A's file `alpha`. FS can implement this simply by using A's directory, rather than C's directory, to search and locate file `alpha`. The directory entry of a file should now contain the necessary protection information such that FS can determine the validity of such an `open` call (see Fig. 17.4). We discuss the details of file protection in Section 17.4.

File name	*Location info*	*Protection info*	*Flags*

Fig. 17.4 Directory entry

The arrangement of Fig. 17.3 can be generalized in many interesting ways, each providing more flexibility to the organization of user data in the file system. We will consider the following generalizations:

1. Provide a hierarchy of directories
2. Consider the directory itself as a file
3. Provide a generalized syntax for accessing files.

Directory hierarchies

In Fig. 17.3, the directory is depicted as a means of grouping the files owned by a user. This notion of grouping can be extended to permit grouping of files according to some user defined criteria. For example, a user engaged in many distinct activities may desire to group the files related to each activity separately. The FS can provide a tree structure of directories for this purpose. The number of levels in a directory hierarchy of a user is best left to the user himself. This can be achieved by generalizing on the notion of a directory. Since a directory contains data (about files), it can itself be viewed as a file. With this generalization, it is no longer necessary to differentiate between the MD and UDs. To start with, FS provides a directory for each user. The user can develop his own directory hierarchy by creating data and directory files to suit his convenience. Figure 17.5 shows the directory tree for user A. Flag ='D' indicates that the file is a directory file. The directory trees of all users together constitute the directory tree of FS. The root of this tree is called the FS root directory.

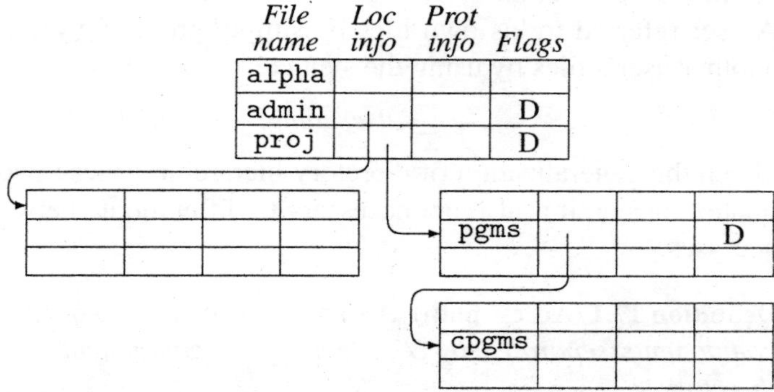

Fig. 17.5 Directory tree for user A

Current and home directories

At any moment of time, a user is said to be 'in' a specific directory. This is called the *current directory* of the user. Any filename specified by the user is searched for in this directory. While registering a user with the OS, a directory in the FS directory hierarchy is specified as his *home directory*. The OS puts a user into his home directory at log-in time, i.e. the user starts with his home directory as the current directory.

A user may change his current directory to any other directory through a *change directory* command.

Example 17.1 Examples of Unix change directory commands:

`cd ..`	Change to parent of the current directory.
`cd proj`	Directory `proj`, defined in the current directory, becomes the current directory

To facilitate traversal of the FS directory hierarchy, each directory points to its parent in the hierarchy. Figure 17.6 shows the directory format.

Self	*Parent*	*File name*	*Loc info*	*Prot info*	*Flags*

Fig. 17.6 Directory

Access paths

At the start of Section 17.1, two ways to access the files in the system were described. A user referred to his own files by simply providing the file name, and referred to another user's files by using the syntax

<username> → *<filename>*

Given the generalization of directory hierarchies, these two ways are no longer adequate. Further, it is also not necessary to differentiate between these two kinds of file accesses.

Definition 17.1 (Access path) *An* access path *is a sequence of one or more access components separated by '/', each access component being a reference through a directory.*

An access path is an unambiguous way of referring to a file. Thus identically named files created by different users differ in their access paths.

Example 17.2 Some examples of access paths:

`alpha`	file `alpha` in the current directory.
`proj/beta`	file `beta` in the directory `proj` contained in the current directory.

Absolute access paths

Access paths starting on the current directory (see Ex. 17.2) are called *relative access paths*. FS may also permit its users to specify access paths starting on the root of the FS directory hierarchy. Such access paths are called *absolute access paths*. Some systems also permit short forms in the access paths.

Example 17.3 Consider the following absolute access paths in Unix:

```
/xyz/new
~A/alpha/..
```

In the first access path, absence of an access component preceding the first '/' indicates that the access path starts on the FS root directory. `~A` in the second specification is a short form for the words 'home directory of user A'.

Links

The access path information described so far has been based on the parent-child relationships in the FS directory hierarchy. This can make some access paths long and cumbersome to write. A *link* is a directed connection in the FS hierarchy between two existing files. A link is an ordered triple

(<*from_filename*>, <*to_filename*>, <*link_name*>)

where <*from_filename*> is a directory file, <*to_filename*> could be a directory or data file and <*link_name*> is a symbolic name for the link. Once the link is established, the <*to_filename*> can be accessed as if it were a child of <*from_filename*>, i.e. as if it were a file named <*link_name*> in the directory <*from_filename*>. The entry of <*link_name*> in the directory <*from_filename*> is marked with flag = 'L' to indicate that it is the name of a link.

Example 17.4 Figure 17.7 contains the link

```
(~A,~A/proj/pgms/cpgms, s_ware)
```

This link permits `~A/proj/pgms/cpgms` to be accessed by the name `~A/s_ware`.

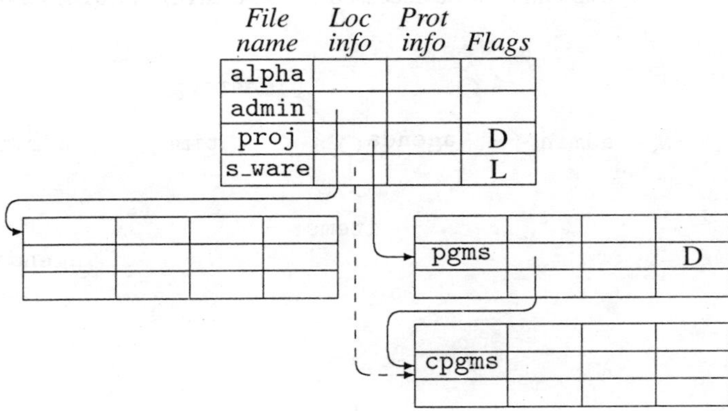

Fig. 17.7 Link

Note that the existence of links makes the directory structure a generalized graph rather than a tree. A file may have multiple access paths in the FS. In fact, access paths may even contain loops. This makes the FS actions for `open` more complex.

Directory mount points

A link is a directed association between a directory and a file. A technique called *FS mounting* provides an equivalent effect under control of the system administrator.

The technique is implemented as follows: Certain files in the FS hierarchy are designated as *mount points*. Any part of FS hierarchy can be mounted at a mount point by a command

mount (<*FS_name*>, <*mount_point_name*>);

where <*FS name*> and <*mount point name*>, both of which are access paths, designate the root of the hierarchy to be mounted and the mount-point respectively. After a mount operation mount (<*FS_name*>, ap_m) has been performed, any file with the access path ap_i in <*FS name*> can be accessed by the access path ap_m/ap_i. The effect of the mount operation is nullified by a command

unmount (<*FS name*>, ap_m);

Thus access paths of the form ap_m/ap_i are invalid following the unmount command shown above.

Example 17.5 Figure 17.8(b) shows the effect of a mount command

mount (meeting,~A/admin);

where the FS hierarchies at meeting and admin are as shown in Fig. 17.8(a). File items can now be accessed as ~A/admin/meeting/agenda/items.

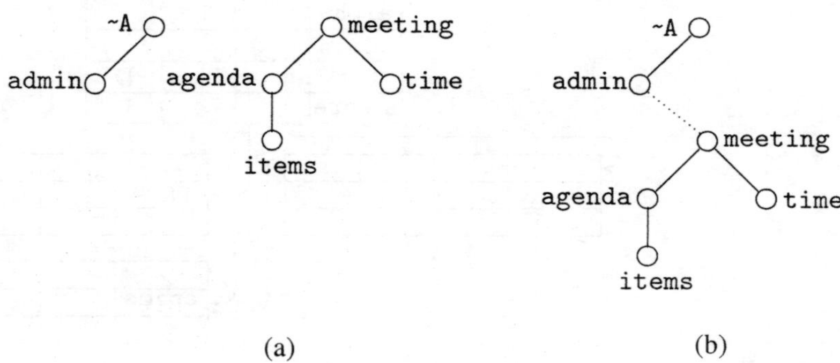

Fig. 17.8 FS mounting

FS mounting is useful when more than one FS exists in the system (see Section 17.7), or when a user of a distributed system wishes to access files located in a remote machine (see Section 19.8).

EXERCISE 17.1

1. Write a short note on the actions to be performed during a file deletion operation if links exist in the FS directory hierarchy.

17.2 FILE PROTECTION

File sharing is facilitated by permitting a user to traverse the FS directory hierarchy. Protection is implemented by using the *protection info* field in directory entries (see Fig. 17.4). The protection information can be stored in the form of an *access control list*, each element of the list being an access control pair

(*<user_name>*, *<list_of_access_privileges>*)

When a program executed by some user X tries to perform an operation *<opn>* on file `alpha`, FS checks to see if *<opn>* is contained in *<list_of_access_privileges>* of X. The program is aborted if this is not the case. For example, a write attempt by X would be rejected if the entry for user X in the access control list is (`X`, read).

However, it is infeasible to use an access control pair for every user if a system contains a large number of users. To reduce the size of protection information, the users can be classified in some convenient manner and an access control pair can be used for each user class rather than for each individual user. Now an access control list has only as many pairs as the number of user classes. Chapter 18 discusses file protection in detail.

Example 17.6 The Unix operating system limits the size of the access control list of a file `alpha` by dividing all users in the system into the following three classes:

Class 1	:	Owner of a file `alpha`
Class 2	:	Users in the same group as the owner of `alpha`
Class 3	:	All other users in the system

The directory entry of `alpha` contains the user id's of its owner, and access privileges assigned to each user class.

17.3 ALLOCATION OF DISK SPACE

In Section 16.6.3, we mentioned that disk space allocation is performed by the file system. While creating or updating a file an LIOCS module expects FS to supply the address of a disk block in which a record should be written. For simplicity, early file systems adapted the contiguous memory allocation model (see Section 15.2) to disk space allocation. Thus a new file was allocated a single contiguous area on a disk when it was opened for creation. This approach required an application program to provide an estimate of file size while creating a new file, which created an obvious difficulty for users. It also led to fragmentation of disk space. Later systems avoided the first problem by allocating fixed sized disk blocks during creation or update of a file. Fragmentation was avoided by adapting the noncontiguous memory allocation model (see Section 15.3) to disk space allocation.

In the following two approaches to noncontiguous disk space allocation are discussed. Following Section 17.1, the discussion assumes that the directory entry of a file contains the space allocation information.

Linked allocation

A file is represented by a linked list of disk blocks. Each disk block has two fields in it, *data* and *control info* (see Fig. 17.9). The *data* field contains the file data, while *control info* contains the id of the next disk block allocated to the file. The *location info* field of the directory entry of a file points to the first disk block of the file. Other blocks are accessed by following the list of disk blocks. Free space on the disk is represented by a *free list*. When a disk block is needed to write a new record of a file, a block is taken off the free list and added to the file's list of disk blocks. To delete a file, the file's list of disk blocks is simply added to the free list.

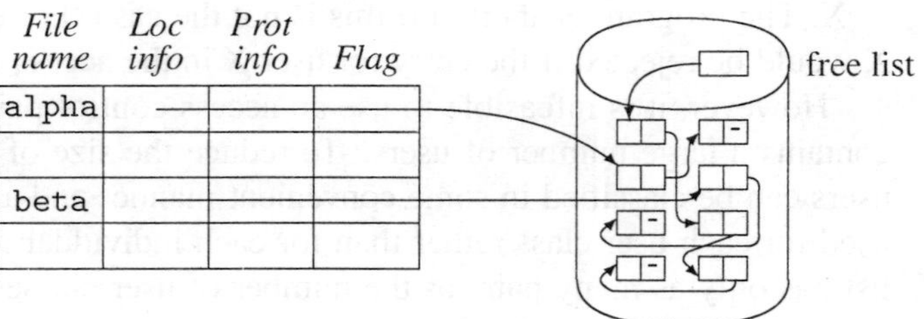

Fig. 17.9 Linked allocation

This arrangement is simple to implement, and involves low overheads for allocation and deallocation of disk blocks. It also supports sequential files. However, direct access files cannot be accessed efficiently. Reliability is also poor since corruption of a single pointer field in a disk block may lead to loss of data in the entire file. Similarly FS operation may be disrupted if a pointer in the free list is corrupted. We discuss FS reliability issues in Section 17.6.

Indexed allocation

Noncontiguous disk space allocation shares many features with a paged virtual memory system (see Section 15.4). Hence the indexed allocation model uses data structures and algorithms which closely resemble those used in paged VM systems. A file is allocated an integral number of disk blocks of fixed size. A *file map table* (FMT) is maintained for each file. Each entry in an FMT points to a disk block allocated to the file. Each disk block contains a single field—the data field. The *loc info* field of a directory entry points to the FMT for a file (see Fig. 17.10). For small FMT sizes, the directory entry may itself contain the FMT. In the following discussion, we use the notation $fmt_{\texttt{alpha}}$ to refer to the FMT of file `alpha`.

Management of disk space requires an arrangement analogous to the page block table of a paged virtual memory system. We will call this the *disk status map* (DSM). DSM has one entry for each disk block, indicating its status (whether free or allocated). Unlike the page block table of a paged VM system, each DSM entry can be a single bit. This is possible because the identity of the file using a disk block need

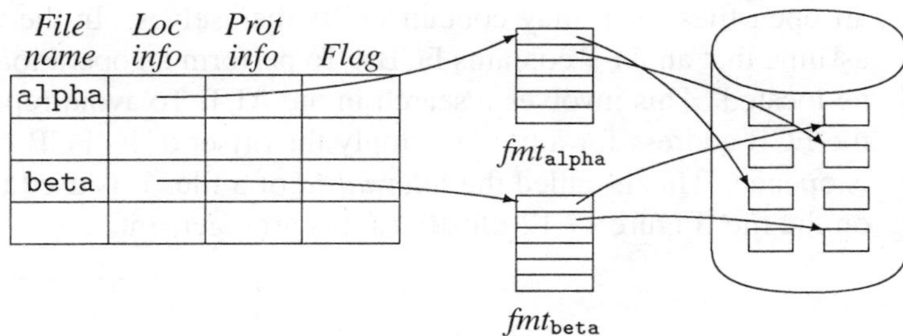

Fig. 17.10 Indexed allocation

not be maintained in the DSM entry. Figure 17.11 illustrates DSM. A '1' in an entry indicates that the corresponding disk block is free. An alternative to the use of a DSM is to use a free list of disk blocks as in linked allocation.

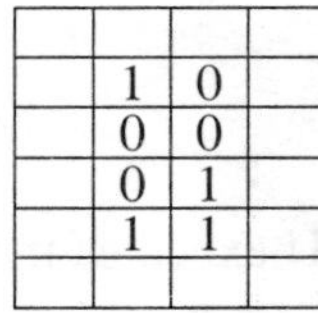

Fig. 17.11 Disk status map (DSM)

Allocation of disk space to file `alpha` is performed on demand during creation or updating of `alpha`. DSM is searched to locate a free block, and the address of the block is added to $fmt_{\texttt{alpha}}$. Deallocation is performed when `alpha` is deleted. All disk blocks pointed to by $fmt_{\texttt{alpha}}$ are marked free before $fmt_{\texttt{alpha}}$ and the directory entry of `alpha` are erased.

This approach reduces the severity of the reliability problem faced in linked allocation since corruption of an entry in an FMT or DSM leads to limited damage. Compared to linked allocation, access to sequential files is less efficient since the FMT of a file has to be accessed to obtain the address of the next disk block. However, direct file access is more efficient since the address of the disk block containing a file record can be obtained directly from an FMT.

17.4 IMPLEMENTING FILE ACCESS

Data structures

The use of directory and FCB data structures in implementing a file access has already been discussed. Another key data structure is the *active files table* (AFT). This table contains the description of all files which are open at any moment of time.

AFT can be structured in two ways—it may contain pointers to the FCBs of all open files, or it may contain FCBs themselves. In the following discussion we assume that an AFT contains FCBs. To perform an operation on a file, its FCB has to be located. This involves a search in the AFT. To avoid repeated searches, FS notes the FCB address for a file, or simply the offset of its FCB in the AFT, when the file is opened. This is called the *internal id* of a file. It is used to perform all operations on the file. Figure 17.12 illustrates this arrangement.

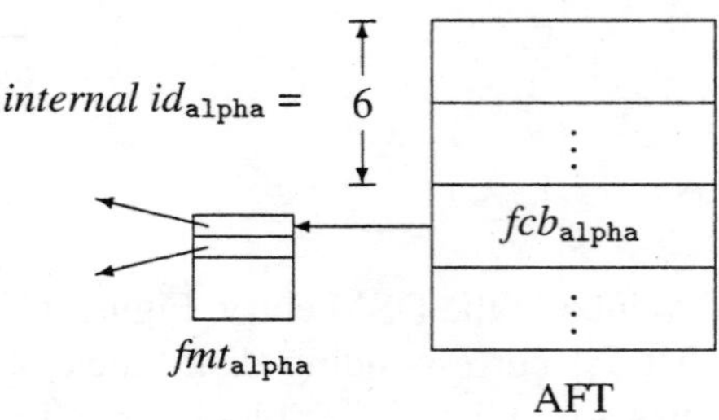

Fig. 17.12 Active files table (AFT)

17.4.1 FS Actions at Open

When a user program U executes the call

`open` (<*filename*> ..) ;

where <*filename*> is an access path for a file, FS determines two items of information:

1. Pointer to FCB of the directory containing the file (*directory FCB pointer*)
2. *Internal id* of the file.

The internal id is passed back to the application program for use during file processing. The directory FCB pointer is used to update the directory while closing a newly created file. FS uses the following procedure to determine these items of information:

1. If the access path is absolute, locate the FCB of the FS root directory. Else, locate the FCB of the current directory. Set a pointer called *directory FCB pointer* to point at this FCB.
2. (a) Search for the next component of the access path in the directory represented by *directory FCB pointer.* Give an error if the access path is not valid,
   (b) Create an FCB in a new entry of the AFT for the file described by the access path component.
   (c) Set a pointer called *file FCB pointer* to point at this FCB,
   (d) If more components exist in the access path, set *directory FCB pointer* = *file FCB pointer* and repeat Step 2.

(e) Set *internal id* of the file to the offset of *file FCB pointer* in AFT.

3. (a) For an existing file, initialize its FCB using the information in the directory entry of the file. This includes copying the pointer to the FMT of the file.

   (b) For a new file, allocate a disk block to contain its FMT. Set the address of this disk block in the FCB.

4. Return the *internal id* of the file <*filename*> to the application program.

Step 2 is called *access path resolution*. In the interests of access efficiency, FS may copy some part of the FMT into memory while opening the file (i.e. in Step 3).

Example 17.7 Figure 17.13 shows the result of FS actions after executing the call

```
open ("/info/alpha", ..);
```

FS creates FCBs for `info` and `alpha` in the AFT. The directory FCB pointer points to $fcb_{\texttt{info}}$ and the file FCB pointer points to $fcb_{\texttt{alpha}}$. The call returns with the internal id of `alpha`. Since `alpha` is an existing file, FMT is copied into $fcb_{\texttt{alpha}}$ from the directory entry of `alpha`.

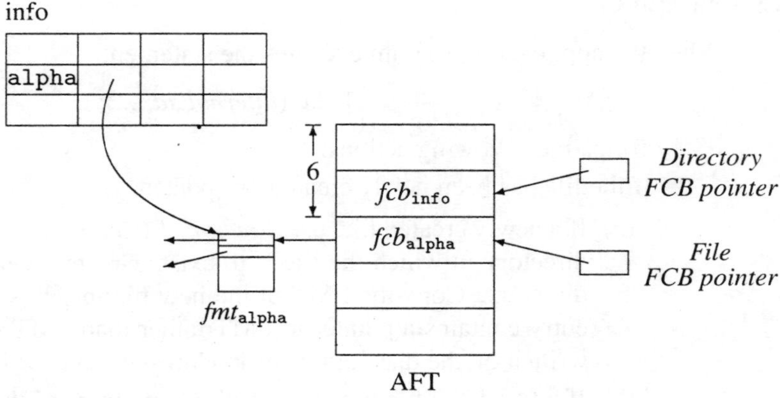

Fig. 17.13 FS actions at `open`

17.4.2 FS Actions at a File Operation

After opening a file, a program performs some read or write operation on <*filename*>. This is translated into a call

<*opn*> (*internal_id*, *byte_id*, ...);

where *internal_id* is the internal id of <*filename*> returned by the `open` call. (Note that *byte_id* may be absent in the case of a sequential file as this information is contained in the FCB.) FS takes the following actions to process this call:

1. Locate the FCB of <*filename*> in the AFT using *internal_id*.

2. Search the access control list of <*filename*> for the pair (U, ...). Give an error if <*opn*> does not exist in the list of access privileges for U.
3. Determine the correct LIOCS module for performing the operation <*opn*>. Let this be `liocs-`<*opn*>. Make the call

`liocs-`<*opn*> (*internal_id*, *byte_id*);

For a `read` operation, the call `liocs-read` obtains the FMT from FCB and converts *byte_id* into a pair (*disk block id, byte offset*) by using the FMT. If execution of operation `liocs-`<*opn*> requires a new record to be written into the file, the LIOCS module may have to call an appropriate module of FS to allocate a new disk block. The address of this disk block is added to the FMT.

Example 17.8 Following the `open` call of Ex. 17.7, a statement `read` (alpha, `...`) in the HLL program would be translated into `read (6, 2675)`. If disk blocks have a size of 1000 bytes each, LIOCS converts *byte_id* into disk block number = 3 and byte offset = 675. Disk block id of the third disk block is obtained by referring to FMT.

17.4.3 FS Actions at Close

When the application program executes the statement

`close` (*internal_id*, ...);

FS performs the following actions:

1. If the file has been newly created or updated,
   (a) If a newly created file, use *directory FCB pointer* to locate the FCB of the directory in which the file is to exist. Create an entry for the file in this directory. Copy the FMT of the new file into this entry. If the directory entry contains a pointer to FMT rather than FMT itself, the FMT is first written on the disk and its disk address is entered in the directory entry.
   (b) If an updated file, update the directory entry of the file (in the directory pointed to by *directory FCB pointer*) to reflect the change in size, etc.
   (c) *file FCB pointer* := *directory FCB pointer*;
   directory FCB pointer :=
   Address (FCB of the parent of the Directory);
   If necessary, repeat Step 1(b).
2. The FCB of the file and the FCB's of the directories containing it are erased from the AFT. Internal id's assigned to them can now be reused for other files.

Example 17.9 Figure 17.14 illustrates the FS actions while executing the command `close info/alpha` assuming `alpha` to be a new file. An entry is created for `alpha` in directory `info` and a pointer to $fmt_{\texttt{alpha}}$ is put in the *Loc info* field of this entry. This may involve updating the FMT of `info` (see steps 1(b) and 1(c) of actions at `close`).

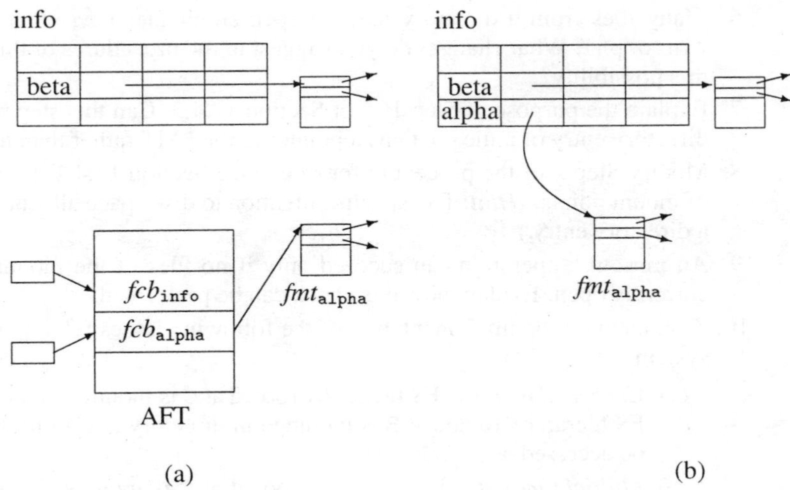

Fig. 17.14 FS actions at `close`

EXERCISE 17.4

1. In order to reduce the overheads of file access validation (see Step 2 of Section 17.4.2), an OS designer proposes to perform validation only at file 'open' time. In the `open` statement, a user is required to specify the kind of accesses he proposes to make to the file, e.g. `open (abc) read;` where the keyword `read` indicates that only *read* access is proposed.

   Is a single access validation check at file open time adequate? If not, explain why. In either case, suggest an implementation outline.
2. The Amoeba distributed operating system avoids file updates *in situ*, i.e. it writes an updated file as a new file, and deletes its old copy.

   Comment on the advantages of this approach for disk space allocation and its implementation difficulties, if any.
3. Discuss the influence of noncontiguous allocation of disk space on the feasibility and efficiency of the fundamental file organizations discussed in Section 16.4.
4. Step 2 of Section 17.4.1 creates an FCB for every directory appearing in an access path.
   (a) Are these entries sufficient in the case of a relative access path?
   (b) Are these entries necessary if a file is being opened for reading (see problem 1)?
5. A file named `data` is frequently accessed by users in a system. The following alternatives are proposed to simplify access to `data`:
   (a) Set up links from every user's home directory to `data`.
   (b) Copy `data` into every user's home directory.

   Which alternative would you recommend? Why?

6. Many files from a directory may be open simultaneously, viz. `/info/alpha` and `/info/phi`. What changes do you suggest in the procedures of this section to handle this possibility?
7. Explain the purpose of Step 1(c) of Section 17.4.3. Can this step be eliminated if the directory entry of a file contains a pointer to the FMT rather than the FMT itself.
8. Modify Step 2 of the procedure for `open` (see Section 17.4.1) to handle the crossing of mount points. (*Hint:* Pay specific attention to disk space allocation and updating of a directory entry.)
9. An `unmount` operation can succeed only if no files of the mounted file system are currently open. Explain how this check can be performed.
10. Comment on the implementation of the following issues relating to mounting of file systems:
    (a) *Cascaded mounts:* FS hierarchy rooted at `C` is mounted at mount point `B`. Later, FS hierarchy rooted at `B` is mounted in directory `A`. Can files in the hierarchy `C` be accessed as `..A/B/C/..`?
    (b) *Multiple mounts:* FS hierarchy rooted at `C` is mounted at many mount points simultaneously.

17.5 FILE SHARING

In Section 17.2 we discussed file protection, which controls the kinds of accesses users are permitted to make to a file. By contrast, file sharing determines the manner in which authorized users of a file may share a file and the manner in which the results of their file manipulations are visible to one another. Different file sharing modes have different implications for users and for the FS.

Some popular file sharing modes are

1. Sequential sharing
2. Concurrent sharing
    (a) Immutable files
    (b) Single image mutable files
    (c) Multiple image mutable files

In the following discussion, we assume that a file `alpha` is to be shared by application programs P1 and P2. In sequential sharing, file accesses by P1 and P2 are spaced out over time, i.e. only one program can access `alpha` at any point in time. The arrangement of Fig. 17.13 can be extended for this purpose as follows: A lock field is added to each directory entry. Setting and resetting of the lock at file open and close ensures that only one program can use the file at any time. Creation and destruction of FCB is performed as discussed in Section 17.4.

When programs share a file concurrently, it is essential to avoid mutual interference between them. Since an FCB contains the address of the next record to be processed, it is essential to create an FCB for each program. This can be achieved simply by following the procedure of Section 17.4.1 at every `open` of file `alpha`. When `alpha` is shared in the immutable mode, none of the sharing programs can modify it. This mode has the advantage that sharing programs are independent of one another—the order in which records of `alpha` are processed by P1 is immaterial to the execution of P2.

Two important issues arise in the case of mutable files. These are:

1. Visibility of file updates to other programs.
2. Interference between sharing programs.

In single image mutable files, changes made by one program are immediately visible to other programs. To implement this mode, it is essential that a single copy of FMT should be used by all sharing programs. This is best achieved by keeping a pointer to the FMT, rather than the FMT itself, in an FCB. Figure 17.15 shows concurrent sharing of file `alpha` using such an arrangement. Two FCB's denoted as $fcb^{P1}_{\mathtt{alpha}}$ and $fcb^{P2}_{\mathtt{alpha}}$ exist for `alpha`, both pointing to the same copy of FMT. Hence, no mix-up in the processing of `alpha` by P1 and P2 arises. Each FCB contains the address of the next record to be processed by a program. Interference between P1 and P2 may arise if the set of records processed by them overlap, e.g. if both programs update the same record. The sharing programs would have to evolve their own conventions to avoid such problems. The Unix file system uses this file sharing mode (see Section 17.7).

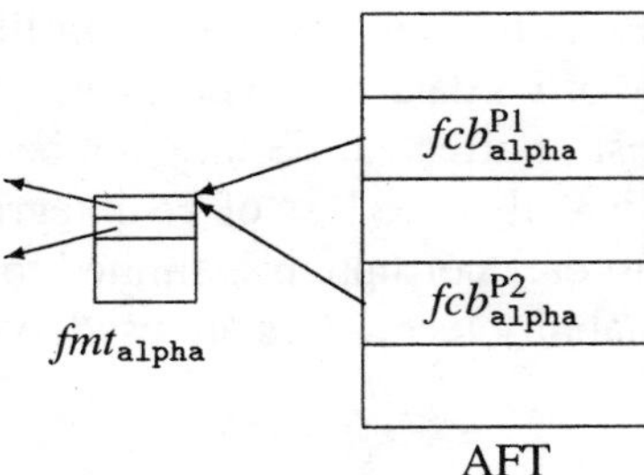

Fig. 17.15 Shared mutable files

In multiple image mutable files, many programs can concurrently update `alpha`. Each updating program creates a new version of `alpha` which is distinct from other versions created by concurrent programs. In this scheme, a distinct $fmt_{\mathtt{alpha}}$ must exist for each FCB. Further, each $fmt_{\mathtt{alpha}}$ should point to an exclusive copy of the file. This is best implemented by making a copy of `alpha` (and its FMT) for each program concurrently updating it. Figure 17.16 shows how this is achieved when programs P1 and P2 open `alpha` for updating. Processing by P1 uses $fcb^{P1}_{\mathtt{alpha}}$ and $fmt^{P1}_{\mathtt{alpha}}$ to access $\mathtt{alpha}^{P1}$. To arrive at a unique implementation scheme, the file sharing semantics must specify how `alpha` would be accessed by programs which only wish to read it, i.e., which version they would access. Note that this sharing mode can only be used in applications where concurrent updates and the existence of multiple versions are meaningful.

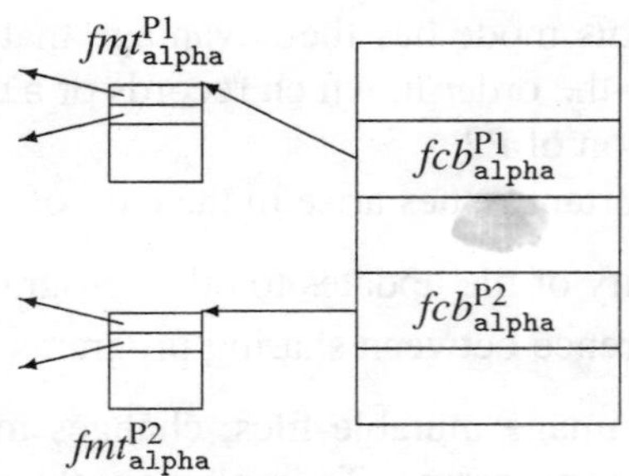

Fig. 17.16 Multiple versions of a file

17.6 FILE SYSTEM RELIABILITY

FS reliability concerns ability of FS to function correctly despite failures in the system. There are two aspects to ensuring FS reliability:

1. Ensuring the correctness of file creation, deletion and updates.
2. Preventing the loss of data in user files.

System crashes due to power failures and data corruption in disk blocks are the common causes of reliability problems in file systems. System crashes may affect the consistency of FS data, while data corruption may cause loss of FS or user data. If FS data is lost or affected, FS may not be able to continue meaningful operation. This situation is called the loss of FS integrity. The damage caused by the loss of user data due to data corruption is limited to a single user file, and is therefore less serious. FS reliability techniques are used to prevent the loss of FS integrity.

17.6.1 Loss of FS Integrity

The term *FS integrity* represents the correctness and consistency of FS control data, viz. directories, FMTs, DSM and AFT. Loss of integrity arises if FS control data is lost or damaged. The data in a file may become inaccessible if the control field of a disk block in a linked allocation is damaged or an FMT block in an indexed allocation is lost or corrupted. More serious situations arise when such loss or damage leads to a mix-up of user files.

As an example of the loss of FS integrity, consider the loss of control data due to a system crash. For efficient operation, FS maintains certain control data in the memory of the system rather than on a disk. This includes the AFT, containing FCB's of open files, and the DSM or free lists of disk blocks. The following data structures would exist in the memory while an application program run by user `U` is updating file `alpha`:

1. $fcb_{\texttt{alpha}}$ exists in AFT
2. Part of $fmt_{\texttt{alpha}}$

3. Part of DSM.

This data would be lost if the system crashes. When the system recovers, copies of $fcb_{\texttt{alpha}}$, $fmt_{\texttt{alpha}}$ and DSM existing on the disk would be accessible, however they would not contain up-do-date information. The loss of control data may cause one or more of the following:

1. Some data from file `alpha` may be lost.
2. Part of file `alpha` may become inaccessible.
3. Contents of two files may get mixed up.

It is easy to visualize a situation of the first kind. For example, let a system crash occur after a new disk block has been added to file `alpha`. The disk copy of $fmt_{\texttt{alpha}}$ would not contain this block's id, hence data in the newly added block is lost when a crash occurs. To see situations of the second and third kind, let us consider the operation of Algorithm 17.1 which adds a new disk block to a file in an FS using the linked allocation scheme.

Algorithm 17.1 (Add block d_j between blocks d_1 and d_2)

Input:

d_1, d_2, d_j : **record**
  next : ...; { id of next block }
  data : ...;
end

1. $d_j.next := d_1.next$;
2. $d_1.next :=$ address(d_j);
3. *Write d_1 to disk.*
4. *Write d_j to disk.*

Algorithm 17.1 adds a new block d_j between blocks d_1 and d_2. Figure 17.17(a) shows the file before execution of the algorithm. Parts of the file may become inaccessible if a system crash occurs between steps 3 and 4 of Algorithm 17.1. This happens because new contents have been written into block d_1, but not into block d_j. $d_1.next$ now points to d_j which does not contain the correct control information (see Fig. 17.17(b)). Blocks $d_2, d_3 \ldots$ are not accessible as parts of the file any more.

Contents of two files may get mixed up if FS writes control data to disk while closing a file, and *not* after every file operation. Now, let a program delete a disk block d_k from some file `beta`. d_k would be returned to the free list (or would be marked free in DSM). Let a new record be added to another file `alpha`. FS allocates a new disk block d_j for this purpose, and adds it before disk block d_m in file `alpha` (see Fig. 17.18(a)). Now consider the situation when $d_j = d_k$ and the following events occur in the system:

1. Processing of `alpha` is completed.

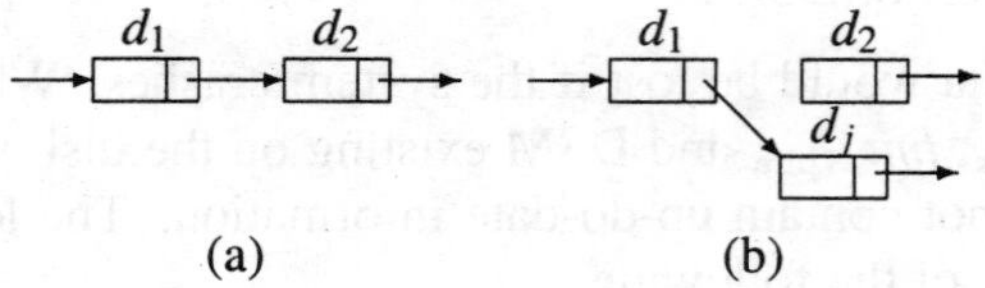

Fig. 17.17 Failure while adding a disk block to a file

2. FS updates the disk copy of file `alpha` and $fcb_{\texttt{alpha}}$. This involves adding disk block d_j to file `alpha`.
3. A crash occurs.

The disk contains an old copy of `beta` which contains block d_k. It also contains the new copy of `alpha` which contains block d_j. Since $d_j = d_k$, `alpha` and `beta` now share disk block d_j and all other blocks accessible through it (see Fig. 17.18(b)). All disk blocks of file `beta` previously accessible through d_k are now inaccessible. In effect, some data is common to files `alpha` and `beta`, while some data of `beta` has been lost.

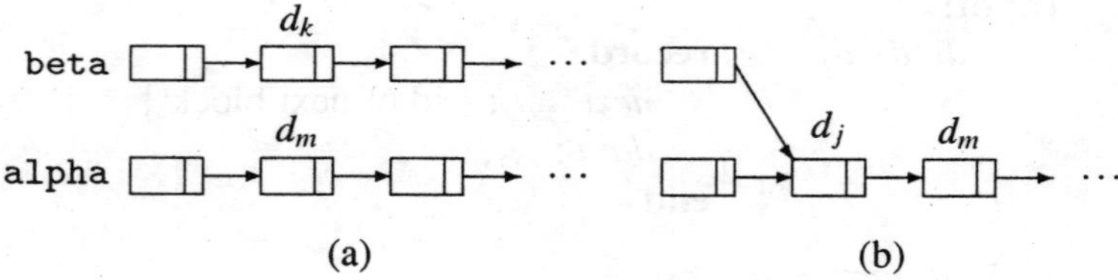

Fig. 17.18 (a) Files `alpha` and `beta`, (b) when $d_j = d_k$ and `alpha` is closed

17.6.2 FS Reliability Techniques

The reliability techniques used in file systems can be divided into fault tolerance techniques and recovery techniques. Fault tolerance techniques aim at tolerating failures as and when they arise during FS operation—that is, they aim at ensuring uninterrupted and correct operation of FS despite failures. Recovery techniques aim at restoring a consistent version of FS after a failure. These techniques have different implications concerning overheads.

Fault tolerance techniques

From the discussion at the start of this section, we can conclude that FS reliability can be improved by taking two precautions—prevent loss of data due to device malfunction, and prevent inconsistency of control data.

These precautions are implemented using the fault tolerance techniques of disk mirroring and atomic actions.

Disk mirroring

The *stable storage* technique proposed by Lampson provides reliability of a data record in the presence of a single failure. This is achieved using redundancy. Two copies of a record, called its *primary* and *secondary* copy, are maintained on a disk. A *write* operation updates both copies—the primary copy is first updated, followed by the secondary copy. For a *read*, the disk block containing the primary copy is accessed if it is readable, else the block containing the secondary copy is accessed. Since only single failures are assumed to occur, one of the blocks is sure to contain readable data. Note that the secondary copy may contain old data if a failure occurred while updating the data.

The technique of disk mirroring applies the stable storage technique to entire files. However, high overheads make the technique very expensive for general use in an FS. Application programs may selectively use it to protect their own data.

Atomic actions

Definition 17.2 (Atomic action) *An action A_i consisting of a set of sub-actions $\{sb_i\}$ is an* atomic action *if for every execution of A_i either*

1. *Each sb_i is successfully performed, or*
2. *None of the sb_i's is performed.*

Thus an atomic action A_i has an *all-or-nothing* property which rules out any partial executions. Figure 17.19 shows Algorithm 17.1 coded as an atomic action named *add_a_block*. An atomic action is said to *commit* when it executes the **end atomic action** statement. This implies that the effect(s) of its execution (e.g. file updates) must be reflected into the files used by it. An atomic action may fail to commit for one of two reasons—the application program performing the atomic action may terminate its execution by executing an `abort` statement, or the system may crash before executing `end atomic action`. No effect(s) of the atomic action must be reflected into the files in any of these cases. Thus, when the atomic action *add_a_block* is executed, we have the guarantee that its execution would lead to one of two possibilities:

begin atomic action *add_a_block;*
  $d_j.next := d_1.next;$
  $d_1.next := address(d_j);$
  write d_1;
  write d_j;
end atomic action *add_a_block;*

Fig. 17.19 Atomic action *add_a_block*

1. Disk block d_j is added to file `alpha`, i.e. `alpha` consists of disk blocks $d_1, d_j, d_2, \ldots$.

2. Disk block d_j is not added to file `alpha`, i.e. `alpha` continues to consist of disk blocks $d_1, d_2, \ldots$.

Consistency of FS control data can be preserved by updating all FS data structures using atomic actions. Data base systems use atomic actions to ensure certain other properties as well; this discussion is restricted to FS reliability only.

The following approach can be used to implement atomic actions: To simplify the processing of aborts, file updates are *not* made on the disk as the sub-actions are executed. Instead details of the updates to be made are noted in a list which we will call the *intentions' list*. The information in the intentions' list is used to perform updates when the action commits. This is called *commit processing*. This arrangement automatically tolerates failures occurring before an atomic action commits since no updates are made until commit. While making updates, it is necessary to ensure that all updates would be completed even if failures occur during commit processing. To achieve this a *commit flag*, which is a boolean variable, is associated with each atomic action. The value in the flag indicates whether the action has committed at any point of time. The flag is destroyed after all updates have been carried out. In the event of a crash, the system examines each commit flag when it recovers. If a commit flag exists and has the value 'committed', it implies that the crash occurred before commit processing was completed. Entire commit processing is now repeated. Note that in this arrangement an update may be carried out more than once. To ensure that this does not affect consistency of the files being updated, each entry in the intentions' list is simply a pair

(disk block id, new contents)

While updating, the new contents are simply written into the disk block. Repetition of this action now does not alter the values in the disk block. Both the intentions' list and the commit flag are maintained in stable storage to protect them against data corruption and loss due to a system crash. Algorithm 17.2 implements an atomic action.

Algorithm 17.2 (Implementation of an atomic action)

1. *Execution of an atomic action:*
   (a) *commit flag* := 'not committed';
   intentions' list := 'empty';
   (b) For every file update made by a sub-action, add a pair (d, v), where d is a disk block id and v are its new contents, to the intentions' list.
   (c) *commit flag* := 'committed';
2. *Commit processing:*
   (a) For every pair (d, v) in the intentions' list, write v in the disk block with the id d.

   (b) Erase the intentions' list and the commit flag.

3. *After a system crash:*
   If the commit flag for an atomic action exists,
   (a) Erase the commit flag and the intentions' list if commit flag = 'not committed'.
   (b) If commit flag = 'committed', then
   perform Step 2.

Example 17.10 Figure 17.20 shows the intentions' list when Algorithm 17.2 is applied to the atomic action of Fig. 17.19. New contents of disk blocks d_j and d_1 are kept in the intentions' list until commit processing. Atomicity of the action is ensured as follows: If a disk crash occurs during Step 1, none of the file updates are reflected on the disk. Hence the file contains the sequence of disk blocks $d_1, d_2, \ldots$. A disk crash in Step 2 can corrupt some data, however the intentions' list and the commit flag are not affected since they exist in stable storage. System failures in Step 2 lead to repeated commit processing. This does not interfere with data consistency since new contents are simply written into disk blocks during commit processing. Thus, the file contains the sequence of disk blocks $d_1, d_j, d_2 \ldots$ at the end of commit processing.

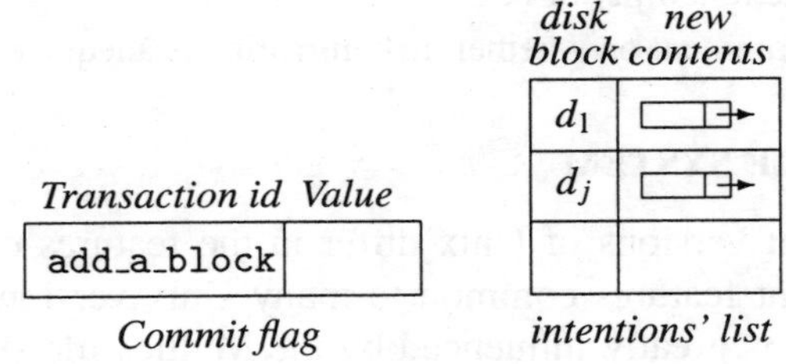

Fig. 17.20 Implementation of the atomic action add_a_block

FS Recovery techniques

FS recovery techniques are based on the periodic recording of back-ups of an FS. An *FS state* is the collection of all user and control data in FS at an instant of time t_i. A *back-up* of FS contains a recording of an FS state. FS recovery is implemented as follows: FS periodically produces back-ups during its operation. Let t_{lb} represent the time at which the latest back-up was produced. In the event of a failure, say, at time t_f, FS restores itself to the state recorded in its latest back-up. This recovers all file updates performed prior to t_{lb}. However, file updates performed between t_{lb} and t_f are lost. Programs performing these updates must be re-executed following FS recovery.

FS Recovery actions involve two kinds of overheads—overheads of creating back-ups, and overheads of re-processing. The latter is the cost of program re-execution to reproduce lost updates. An interesting way to reduce the overheads is to use a combination of incremental and full back-ups of FS. An *incremental back-up* only contains the copies of files and data structures which have been modified since the last full or incremental back-up was created. FS creates full back-ups at large intervals of time, e.g. a few days or a week. Incremental back-ups are created at shorter intervals, e.g. at every file close operation, and are discarded when the next full back-up is created. This strategy reduces the overheads of creating back-ups. After a crash the system is restored from the latest full back-up. Incremental back-ups are then processed in the same order in which they were created. Thus files whose modification was completed before the failure would be recovered in full. Files that were being modified at the point of failure would not be completely restored. Some reprocessing cost would be incurred to re-execute the programs engaged in file processing at the time of system failure. The disk space overhead would however increase as many incremental back-ups need to coexist with a full back-up.

EXERCISE 17.6

1. An *audit trail* is a technique used to reduce the cost of file recovery following a system failure. Every time a file is updated, a record is written into the audit file containing (i) record id of the updated record, and (ii) new contents of the record. Indicate how the audit file can be used in conjunction with full and incremental back-ups to increase the reliability of FS.
2. Comment on whether disk mirroring is adequate to prevent the loss of FS integrity.

17.7 THE UNIX FILE SYSTEM

Different versions of Unix differ in the features of the file system. In this section important features common to many Unix versions are described. The file system of Unix is greatly influenced by the Multics file system. The directory structure of Unix is analogous to the directory structure discussed in Section 17.1. Directory hierarchies are formed by treating directories themselves as files. Access paths are used to name files in FS. For protection purposes, three user groups are defined as discussed in Ex. 17.6.

Unix uses indexed disk space allocation, with a disk block size of 4 K bytes. Each file has a *file allocation table* analogous to FMT, which is maintained in its inode. The allocation table contains 15 entries (see Fig. 17.21). Twelve of these entries directly point to data blocks of the file. The next entry in the allocation table points to an indirect block, i.e. a block which itself contains pointers to data blocks. The next two entries point to double and triple indirect blocks. In this manner, the total file size can be as large as 2^{42} bytes. However, the file size information is stored in a 32-bit word of the inode. Hence file size is limited to $2^{32}-1$ bytes, for which the direct, single and double indirect blocks of the allocation table are adequate. For file sizes smaller than 48 K bytes, this arrangement is as efficient as the flat FMT arrangement discussed in Section 17.3. Such files also have a small allocation table which can fit into the inode itself. The indirect blocks permit files to grow to very large sizes, although their access involves traversing the indirection in the file allocation table.

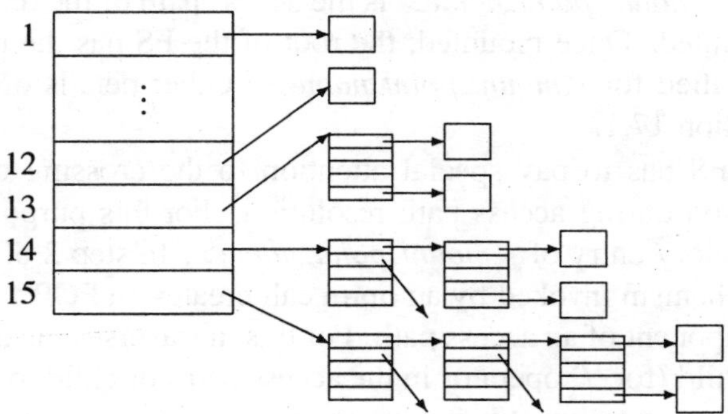

Fig. 17.21 Unix file allocation table

The file system maintains a free list of disk blocks. The free list consists of a list of blocks, with each block containing the id's of free disk blocks (analogous to an indirect block in FMT), and the id of the next block in the list. Blocks are removed from the free list as records are written into files, and are added as records are removed from files. A lock field is associated with the free list to avoid race conditions. A file system program named `mkfs` is used to form the free list when a new file system is created. `mkfs` lists the free blocks in ascending order by block number while forming the free list. This ordering is lost as disk blocks are added to and deleted from the free list during FS operation. FS makes no effort to restore this order. Thus the blocks allocated to a file may be haphazardly distributed on the disk.

Unix maintains the root of every file system, called the *super block*, in main memory in the interest of efficiency. The inodes of all open files are also copied into the memory. The super block contains the size of the file system, the free list and the size of the inode list. The super block is copied onto the disk periodically. However, this arrangement implies that some part of FS state is lost in the event of a system crash. FS can reconstruct some of this information, e.g. the free list, by analysing the disk status. This is done as part of the system booting procedure.

A Unix file system exists on a logical disk device. A physical disk can be divided into many logical devices and a file system can be constructed on each of them. Each logical device has to be mounted before being accessed. Only a super user, typically the system administrator, can mount a logical device. This arrangement provides some protection, and also prevents a user from occupying too much disk space. Each file system consists of a super block, an inode list and the data blocks.

The mounting and unmounting of file systems works as follows: A logical disk containing a file system is given a device special file name. A file system can be mounted in any directory by specifying its access path in a `mount` command, e.g.

```
mount (<FS_name>, <mount_point_name>, ...);
```

where <*FS_name*> is the device special filename of the file system to be mounted, and <*mount_point_name*> is the access path of the directory in which the FS is to be mounted. Once mounted, the root of the FS has the name given by the access path specified for <*mount_point_name*>. Other details of mounting are as described in Section 17.1.

FS has to pay special attention to the crossing of a mount point in either direction during access path resolution. For this purpose, it sets a special flag in the directory entry of <*mount_point_name*>. In step 2 of Section 17.4.1, the file access mechanism invoked by an `open` call creates an FCB for the file represented by every component of an access path. For this, it traverses the directory hierarchy from parent to child (for '/' operator in the access path) or child to parent (for the '..' operator) as the case may be. When a mount point is encountered during such traversal, FS must know where (i.e. in which file system) the parent or child of the current file is located. For this purpose, FS maintains a *mount table* to store all relevant information. An entry is made in this table when a `mount` call is processed. While processing an unmount call, a relevant entry from this table is destroyed.

File sharing

The dynamic file sharing semantics of Unix are as follows:

1. When a shared file is updated by one program, the updates are immediately visible to all other programs sharing the file,
2. Two or more programs can share the same file pointer.

The first feature is handled analogous to the handling of single image mutable files described in Section 17.5. The second feature relates only to parent and child processes, whereby a child process is permitted to use the file pointer defined in the parent process. No explicit provision is needed in the FS to support this feature.

EXERCISE 17.7

1. Explain how the byte offset into a Unix file can be converted into the pair (disk block id, offset in block).
2. Unix defines standard assignments for the files *infile* and *outfile* for each process. The redirection operators '<' and '>' can be used to override the standard assignments. The 'redirect and append' operator '>>' appends the output of a process to the end of an existing file. These features can be implemented by permanently associating two FCB's with each process.
   (a) indicate FS actions involved in implementing the standard assignments for *infile* and *outfile* and the redirection operators '<' and '>'.
   (b) indicate the FS actions involved in implementing the '>>' operator.
3. Can processing of the `link` and `unlink` commands of Unix lead to deadlocks? Discuss how such deadlocks can be avoided.
4. Discuss how file sharing semantics of Unix can be implemented.

BIBLIOGRAPHY

(a) File systems

1. Bach, M.J. (1986): *The design of the Unix operating system*, Prentice-Hall, Englewood Cliffs.
2. Fraser, A.G. (1971): "The integrity of a disc based file system," in *Operating Systems Techniques*, by Hoare, C.A.R., Perrot, R.H.(eds.), Academic Press, London.
3. Hanson, D.R.(1980): "A portable file directory system," *Software— Practice and Experience*, **10** (8), 623-634.
4. Organick, E.I.(1972): *The MULTICS System*, MIT Press, Mass.

(b) Sharing, authorization and access control

1. Brereton, P. (1983): "Detection and resolution of inconsistencies among distributed replicates of files," *Operating Systems Review*, **17** (1), 10-15.
2. Ehrsam, W.F.(1978): "A cryptographic key management scheme for implementing the data encryption standard," *IBM Systems Journal*, **17** (2), 106-125.
3. Friedman, T.D.(1970): "The authorization problem in shared files," *IBM Systems Journal*, **9** (4), 258-280.
4. Gladney, H.M., E.L. Worley and J.J. Myers (1975): "An access control mechanism for computing systems," *IBM Systems Journal*, **14** (3), 212-228.
5. Graham, R.M.(1968): "Protection in an information processing utility," *Commn. of ACM*, **11** (5), 365-369.
6. Saltzer, J.H. (1974): "Protection and control of information sharing in MULTICS," *Commn. of ACM*, **17** (7), 388-402.
7. Simmons, G.J. (1979): "Symmetric and Asymmetric encryption," *Computing Surveys*, **11** (4), 305-330.
8. Stiegler, H.G.(1979): "A structure for access control lists," *Software – Practice and Experience*, **9** (10), 813-819.

CHAPTER 18

Protection and Security

Sharing of programs and data among users of a computer system necessitates strong emphasis on protection and security measures in an OS. We have already discussed protection of OS resources allocated to a program against interference by other programs in the system, e.g. memory protection, IO protection, etc. In this chapter we discuss protection and security of user created data or program entities against illegal forms of access or use.

Both *protection* and *security* imply guarding against some kind of interference in an OS. However, in keeping with the convention followed in OS literature, the following distinction is maintained in the use of these terms:

1. *Protection:* guarding a user's data and programs against interference by *internal* entities of a system, viz. other authorized users of the system.
2. *Security:* guarding a user's data and programs against interference by entities *external* to a system, e.g. unauthorized persons.

Policy issues in protection and security are limited to specifying who should have access to other users' data and programs. These issues are mostly handled outside the domain of an OS—either by the system administrator while deciding the composition of user groups in the system, or by individual users while creating new files. Hence most discussion in this chapter is confined to mechanisms for protection and security.

Note that data accesses are performed by a process (or a set of processes) comprising a computation initiated by a user. However, in the interest of simplicity we will not differentiate between a user and his/her computation. Thus we will use the phrase 'a user accesses data' instead of the more appropriate term 'a user process accesses data'.

18.1 ENCRYPTION OF DATA

Encryption is a fundamental technique for protecting confidentiality of data. Hence it forms the basis of many protection and security mechanisms to be discussed in this chapter. The branch of science dealing with encryption techniques is called *cryptology*.

Definition 18.1 (Encryption) Encryption *is the application of an algorithmic transformation to data.*

The original form of data is called the *plaintext* form and the transformed form of data is called the *encrypted* or *ciphertext* form. Encryption is performed by applying an encryption algorithm E with a specific encryption key k chosen by a user or an application program. A ciphertext has to be decrypted using a decryption algorithm D with the same key k to obtain its plaintext form. Figure 18.1 illustrates encryption and decryption of data.

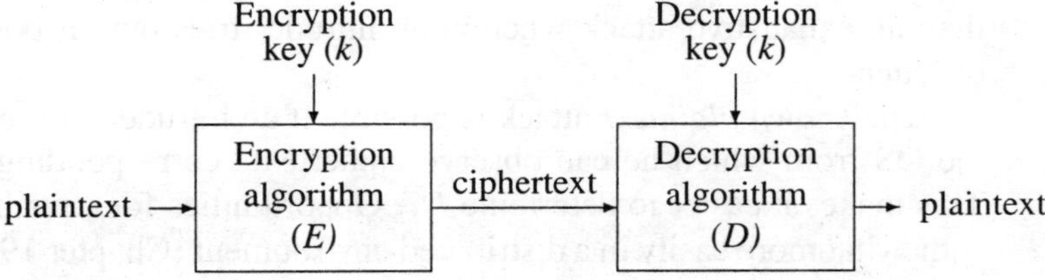

Fig. 18.1 Encryption and decryption of data

We represent encryption and decryption of data using algorithms E and D with key k as the application of functions E_k and D_k, respectively.

$$\begin{aligned} E_k(d) &: \ d \text{ encrypted by algorithm } E \text{ using key } k \\ D_k(e) &: \ e \text{ decrypted by algorithm } D \text{ using key } k \end{aligned}$$

Functions E_k and D_k now satisfy the relation

$$D_k(E_k(d)) = d, \text{ for all } d.$$

It is clear that no person can access or manipulate encrypted data without knowing D_k.

18.1.1 Attacks on Cryptological Systems

Encryption is used to protect confidentiality of data in the face of adversarial attacks. An adversary here is an *intruder*, i.e. a person who does not possess legal access to data. The aim of an encryption technique is to perform high quality encryption at low cost, where quality refers to the ability of the encryption technique to withstand attacks aimed at determining the decryption function D_k.

Definition 18.2 (One-way function) *A* one-way function *is a function whose inverse is far more difficult to compute than the function.*

In principle, it is possible to find D_k by exhaustive trial and error. However this is considered infeasible due to the large computational costs involved. Hence an intruder may use one of the following approaches to determine D_k:

1. Ciphertext only
2. Known plaintext
3. Chosen plaintext.

In the *ciphertext only* approach, an intruder has to bank on extraneous knowledge of ciphertexts in order to guess D_k. For example, an intruder may perform frequency analysis of ciphertexts to find the byte-values which occur frequently. Knowledge of relative frequencies of letters in a language may now be used to guess the encryption algorithm. D_k is then devised as the inverse of this algorithm. This is more efficient than an exhaustive attack wherein an intruder tries out all possible transformations of letters.

The *known plaintext* attack is possible if an intruder can secure a position within the OS from which he can observe ciphertexts corresponding to known plaintexts. This makes it easier to determine D_k. Opportunities for launching such attacks arise somewhat more easily in a distributed environment (Chapter 19), than in a centralized one. In the *chosen plaintext* attack, an intruder is able to observe the encrypted form of any data of his choice. In effect he can choose any d and observe $E_k(d)$. This permits on-line guessing and refinement of guesses during the attack.

Security through encryption is believed to improve with an increase in the number of bits in key k. The Data Encryption Standard (DES) of the National Bureau of Standards uses a 56 bit key, which was believed to make it computationally secure from attacks when it was developed in the 1970's. However, powerful mathematical techniques, e.g. differential analysis, can be employed to guess D_k much more easily than in an exhaustive attack. It is therefore estimated that by the turn of the century keys will need to be over 1000 bits in length to ensure that encryption functions are one-way functions.

18.1.2 Encryption Techniques

Encryption techniques can be classified into:

1. Block cipher techniques
2. Stream cipher techniques.

Block cipher techniques are an extension of the classical *substitution cipher* techniques. In a substitution cipher, each letter in a plaintext is replaced by some other letter of the alphabet to obtain a ciphertext. A block cipher technique visualizes a plaintext to consist of a number of fixed sized components of, say, n bits each. Each component (called a *block*) is encrypted with key k to obtain an n bit component of ciphertext (see Fig. 18.2). These components are assembled to obtain the ciphertext. Block cipher techniques are simple to implement, however they suffer from a serious drawback. Encryption performed by block ciphers is context-independent, i.e. identical components in a plaintext yield identical components in the ciphertext. This permits attacks based on execution frequencies.

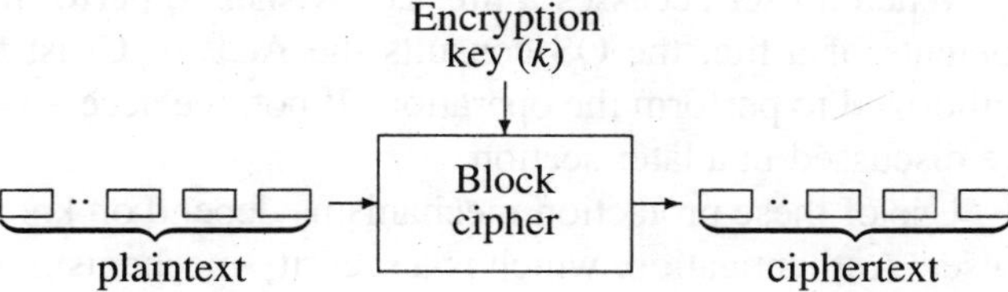

Fig. 18.2 Block cipher

Stream cipher techniques consider a plaintext as well as the encryption key to be streams of bits. The key stream can be a fixed stream, or could itself be derived from a ciphertext. Figure 18.3 illustrates a stream encryption technique. The key stream here consists of an initial stream of bits which is externally specified. The ciphertext is used as the subsequent bits in the key stream. Stream ciphers have the characteristic that encryption is context-dependent. This defeats attacks based on frequency analysis of ciphertexts. DES can function in both block and stream cipher modes.

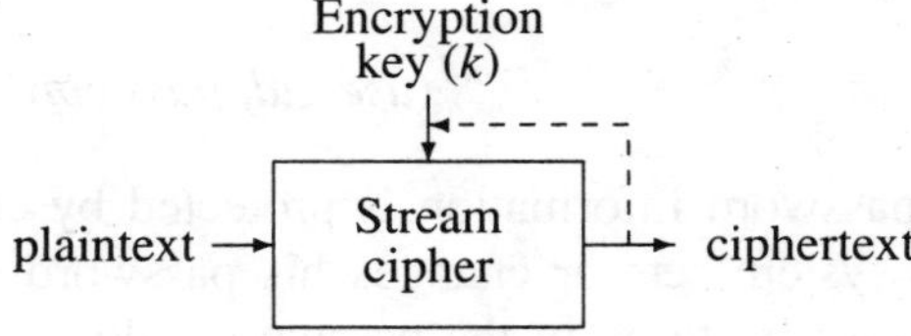

Fig. 18.3 Stream cipher

18.2 PROTECTION AND SECURITY MECHANISMS

18.2.1 Protection Mechanisms

The following mechanisms are commonly used for protecting files containing programs and data:

1. Access control lists (ACL's)
2. Capability lists (C-lists).

These lists are used to ensure that users only access files which they are explicitly authorized to access. These files include

(a) Files created by a user himself/herself. (Such files are said to be *owned* by the user.)

(b) Files owned by others, for which a user possesses explicit access privileges granted by their owners.

When a user accesses a file, i.e. wishes to perform an operation <*opn*> on the contents of a file, the OS consults the ACL or C-list to check whether the user is authorized to perform the operation. If not, the access is denied. Details of these lists are discussed in a later section.

Use of these protection mechanisms depend on knowledge of the true identity of a user. Authentication, which is a security mechanism, provides this knowledge.

18.2.2 Security Mechanisms

Authentication is the primary security mechanism.

Definition 18.3 (Authentication) Authentication *is the act of verifying the identity of a user.*

Authentication is used to eliminate the possibility of impersonation of an authorized user by another person. Authentication is typically performed through passwords at login time. A person is considered to be an authentic user if he or she can provide the correct password. The system stores the password information in a system file as a set of pairs of the form

$$(user\_id,\ password\_info)$$

The password information is protected by encryption. When a registered user X of the system sets or changes his password to, say, pw_x, the encoded form of the password is stored in the passwords file, i.e. $password\_info = E_k(pw_x)$. When a user performs a login, he is required to submit his password. Let this be called *presented_password*. The system performs the check

$$E_k(presented\_password) = password\_info\ ? \qquad (18.1)$$

The user is considered to be authentic if the check is successful.

18.3 PROTECTION OF USER FILES

Three techniques for protection of user files are:

1. Encryption of data in user files
2. Access control of user files
3. Capability lists for users.

Techniques 2 and 3 are equivalent in terms of the kind of protection provided. However, they have different implications in terms of ease of use and OS overheads.

18.3.1 Encryption of Data in User Files

In this technique a ciphertext form of data is stored in a file to ensure its confidentiality. This approach has the following characteristics:

1. A user must remember the encryption key used for each file.
2. A user file must be decrypted before every use and encrypted after every update. This imposes large computational overheads.
3. A malicious user can perform a *write* operation on another user's file. This could lead to corruption and loss of data. Thus, encryption does not make data tamper-proof.

Hence encryption of data is not a practical protection technique for an OS to use. However, encryption preserves confidentiality of data even if a person manages to access a file in an illegal manner. Hence users can use encryption as an additional means of protecting sensitive data over and above the protection provided by an OS.

18.3.2 Access Control of User Files

Access control information is maintained against each user file, typically in its directory entry. This information indicates who can access the file in what manner. Whenever a user opens a file, the OS checks the user's access privileges for the file and aborts the user process if he or she lacks the necessary access privileges. (Actually, the file system of the OS makes this check. However, in the interest of uniformity throughout this chapter, we will consider the OS to be making all protection checks.)

Access control of user files through passwords

A user X, who owns a file `alpha`, associates a password $pw_{\texttt{alpha}}$ with the file. The password information is registered with the OS, which stores it in the *protection info* field of the file's directory entry (see Fig. 18.4). To authorize some user Y to access file `alpha`, X gives the password $pw_{\texttt{alpha}}$ to Y. When Y wishes to access `alpha`, he or she submits the password $pw_{\texttt{alpha}}$. The system checks this against the password of `alpha` registered with it and permits Y to proceed only if the two match.

File name	*Location info*	*Protection info*	*Flags*
`alpha`		$pw_{\texttt{alpha}}$	

Fig. 18.4 File protection through passwords

The main drawback of this scheme is that the owner uses *external* means to authorize others to use his files. The OS does not know which users are authorized to access file `alpha`. Hence any user who can supply the correct password information for a file is automatically permitted to access the file. This feature can severely undermine protection in the system if a person shares the knowledge of a password with others, e.g. if Y passes $pw_{\texttt{alpha}}$ to Z. The only way the owner can minimize the damage in such situations is by frequently changing the passwords. However, this is hard to implement since X will have be give the new password of `alpha` to all users who are to be permitted to access it. Due to this reason, password protection of files has fallen into disuse since the mid-1970s.

Access Control Lists (ACL's) for user files

When user X creates a file `alpha`, he registers the access control information for `alpha` with the system. This information, which is in the form of a set of pairs

$$\{(user\_id,\ access\ privileges), ..\},$$

constitutes the *access control list* (ACL) for `alpha`. For example, Fig. 18.5 shows the access control list for `beta` to be {(`Y`, read), (`Z`, read/ write)}. This indicates that user Y can only read file `beta`, while user Z can read as well as write into the file. User X is not permitted any kind of access to `beta`, since no entry for X exists in the ACL for `beta`.

File name	*Location info*	*Protection info*	*Flags*
`alpha`			
`beta`		{(Y,r), (Z,r,w)}	

Fig. 18.5 Access control list

When a user wishes to access file `beta`, the system permits the access to go through only if the access control information in the ACL contains the necessary access privilege for the user. The steps involved for user Y to access file `beta` are as follows:

1. User Y performs a login.
2. The system authenticates user Y by asking for his password.
3. The process initiated by user Y issues the call `open(beta, ..)`.
4. OS performs the protection check by ensuring that the ACL of file `beta` contains the necessary access privilege for Y.

Note that impersonation cannot take place during file access since user Y has been authenticated by the system in step 2. The procedure by which the owner of a file can grant or withdraw some access privileges to other users is easier compared to the scheme using passwords for files, and fully involves the OS. Thus protection is fool-proof.

Use of access control lists faces some practical problems. Presence of a large number of users in a system leads to large ACL sizes, and thereby to large space overheads in the file system. The time overheads are also high due to ACL searches for validating a file access. Most file systems devise some ways to limit the size of ACLs. The Unix operating system achieves this by assigning access privileges to user groups rather than to individual users. All users in the system are divided into the following three classes:

1. The file owner
2. Users belonging to the same user group as the file owner
3. All other users in the system.

Thus, an ACL contains only three pairs. The identity of the file owner is stored in a field of its directory entry. The identities of users belonging to the same user group are implicit in the assignment of user id's in the system, hence there is no need to store any user id's in the ACL. Further, Unix defines only three access privileges—*r*, *w* and *x* (representing read, write and execute, respectively). Thus, ACL only needs to record the presence of a total of 9 privileges. This can be bit-encoded into a 9 bit field in the directory entry of a file. Figure 18.6 shows the Unix ACLs as reported in a directory listing. File `alpha` can be read by any user in the system, but can be written only by its owner and by users in the same user group. `beta` is a read-only file for all categories of users, while `gamma` has the read, write and execute privileges only for its owner. Validation of a file access proceeds as described before, and is very efficient due to bit-encoding of the ACL.

```
rw-rw-r--    alpha
r--r--r--    beta
rwx------    gamma
```

Fig. 18.6 Unix ACL

18.3.3 Capability Lists (C-lists) for Users

A capability is a file access privilege. Information concerning capabilities possessed by a user is stored in a *capability list* (C-list). A C-list is thus a set of pairs

$$\{(file\_id,\ access\ privileges), ..\}.$$

Figure 18.7 shows the C-list {(`alpha`, read), (`beta`, read/write)} for user X stored in a tabular form. It indicates that X can only read file `alpha`, and can read as well as write into file `beta`. User X has no access to file `info`, since no entry for `info` exists in the C-list. When X wishes to access some file, the OS implements the access only if X's capability list contains the necessary access privilege for the file.

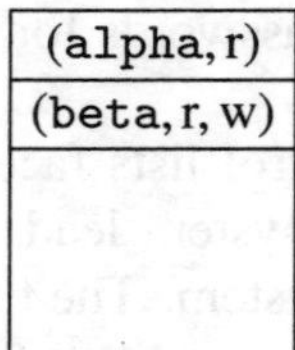

Fig. 18.7 A capability list

As in the case of ACLs no impersonation problems arise since a user is authenticated by the system at login time. C-lists are usually small in size. This limits the space and time overheads in using them to control file access. Due to this, most industry-standard general purpose operating systems do not use C-lists. ACLs are a more popular choice.

18.4 CAPABILITIES

The concept of a capability [Dennis, Van Horn, 1966] was proposed as a general mechanism for sharing and protection. Capabilities in a C-list used for file protection (see Section 18.3.3) are an adaptation of this general mechanism.

Definition 18.4 (Capability) *A* capability *is a token representing certain access privileges for an object.*

An object is any hardware or software entity in the system, e.g. a laser printer, a CPU, a file, a program, or a data structure generated during the execution of a program. A capability is possessed by a process. A process possessing a capability for an object can access the object in a manner consistent with the access privileges described in the capability. Note that many capabilities for an object may exist in the system. These may be held by different processes, and may be identical or different.

We use the notation obj_i to refer to an object, and $Cap^k(obj_i)$ to refer to k'th capability for obj_i. Note that k is used to simply differentiate between the capabilities for an object. It does not have any temporal significance. For simplicity, we omit k in situations involving a single capability of an object.

Example 18.1 The following capabilities exist for obj_i:

1. Process p_3 holds $Cap^1(obj_i)$,
2. Process p_1 holds $Cap^2(obj_i)$, and
3. Process p_2 holds $Cap^4(obj_i)$.

Of these, $Cap^1(obj_i)$ and $Cap^4(obj_i)$ confer identical access privileges (e.g. a read privilege) on processes p_3 and p_2, while $Cap^2(obj_i)$ may confer different access privileges (e.g. read and write privileges) on process p_1.

Format of a capability

The Format of a capability is illustrated in Fig. 18.8. The capability consists of two fields—*access privileges* and *object id*. The access privileges information is typically stored in a bit-encoded form, i.e. each bit in the access privileges field represents a specific access privilege. The bit value of '1' implies presence of the access privilege represented by a bit, while the value '0' implies absence of the access privilege. Each object has a unique object id in the system.

access privileges	*object id*

Fig. 18.8 Format of a capability

18.4.1 Capability Based Computer Systems

A capability based computer system is a system whose architecture implements capability based addressing and protection for all objects in the system. This includes long-life objects like files and short-life objects like data structures and copies of programs in memory. Many experimental and commercial capability based systems have been built. The Intel iapx-432 is an example of a well known commercial processor with a capability based architecture.

Figure 18.9 shows a schematic of a capability-based system. Each process has a C-list describing its access privileges for various objects in the system. A process can only access an object for which it holds a capability. A capability based system differs from conventional computer systems in following respects:

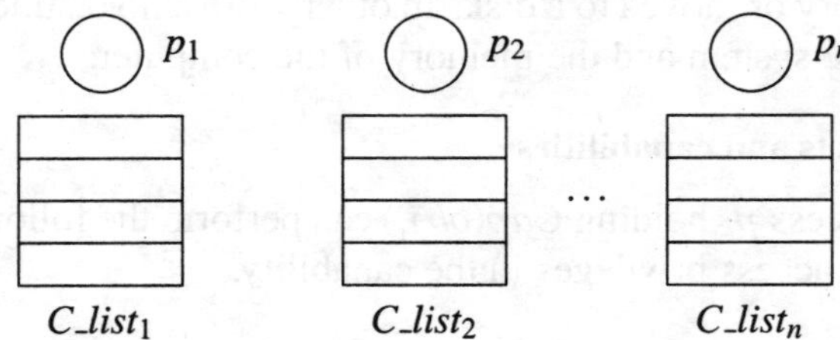

Fig. 18.9 Schematic of a capability based system

1. It provides a uniform addressing mechanism for long and short-life objects.
2. It does not explicitly associate 'memory' with processes; it associates C-lists with processes.
3. A process may access objects existing anywhere in the system (i.e. in memory or on disk); the location of an object is immaterial to a process.

Capability based addressing

Figure 18.10 shows a schematic of capability based addressing of objects. A process p_1 performs an operation *<opn>* on an object `alpha` by using an instruction of the form

$$<opn>\ d_{Cap(\texttt{alpha})}$$

where $d_{Cap(\texttt{alpha})}$ is the displacement of *Cap*(`alpha`) in p_1's C-list. The system uses the displacement to locate *Cap*(`alpha`). The object id in the capability is used as an index into a system wide *object table* (OT). The *object address* field of the OT entry indicates the address of the object in the computer's primary or secondary memory. This address is used to implement the operation *<opn>* on `alpha`. Special techniques analogous to address translation buffers (see Section 15.4.3), viz. capability registers and caches, are used to make object access more efficient.

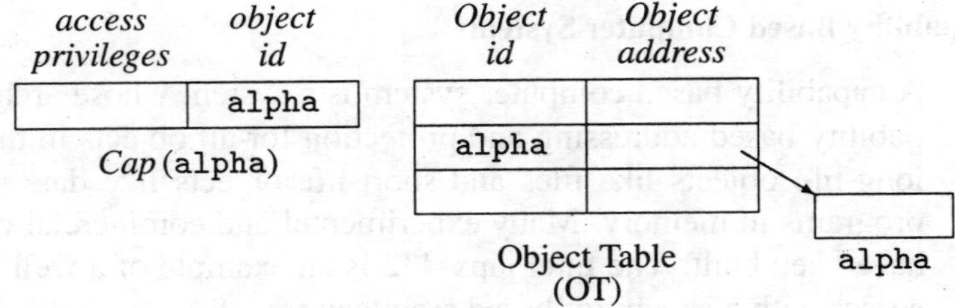

Fig. 18.10 Capability based addressing

Uniform addressing of all objects in this manner provides more flexibility to the OS. For example, the OS can freely decide whether an object should be held in the memory or moved to a disk. In other words, no distinction needs to be made between the file system and the memory of the computer.

Operations on objects and capabilities

A process p_k holding $Cap(obj_i)$ can perform the following operations on obj_i subject to the access privileges in the capability.

- Read the object
- Modify the object
- Destroy the object
- Copy the object
- Execute the object.

Further, p_k can perform the following operations with $Cap(obj_i)$:

- Make a copy of the capability

- Create a 'subset' capability
- Use the capability as a parameter in a procedure or function call
- Pass the capability for use by another process
- Delete the capability.

In many capability based systems, these operations are themselves protected through access privileges in a capability. Thus, a process may be able to create a subset capability of $Cap(obj_i)$ only if $Cap(obj_i)$ contains the access privilege 'create subset capability'.

Note that process p_k cannot modify $Cap(obj_i)$, even if it owns object obj_i. This makes capabilities tamper-proof and unforgeable. This is essential to support protection.

18.4.2 Sharing and Protection of Objects

The steps involved in the manipulation and protection of objects in a capability based system are as follows:

1. When process p_i wishes to perform operation op_1 on an object Obj_i, it executes an instruction of the form

$$<op_1> \; d_{Cap(obj_i)} \tag{18.2}$$

   where $<op_1>$ is the operation code for op_1.
2. The CPU checks if execution of op_1 is consistent with the access privileges contained in $Cap(obj_i)$. If so, it performs the operation, else it raises a protection violation interrupt.
3. If execution of op_1 leads to creation of a new object, the CPU makes an entry for it in the OT and puts a capability for it in the C-list of p_i.

Example 18.2 Figure 18.11(a) depicts the C-list of process p_1 and the object table. Note that $d_{Cap(obj_i)} = 6$ When process p_1 wishes to make a copy of obj_i, it executes the instruction

```
copy 6
```

The CPU creates a copy of obj_i (let us call it obj_j), enters it in the OT, enters $Cap(obj_j)$ in the C-list of p_1, and returns with the offset of $Cap(obj_j)$ in the C-list of p_1, i.e. with 9. Since process p_1 owns obj_j, all access privileges are enabled in $Cap(obj_j)$.

Sharing of objects can be performed as follows:

1. Process p_1 creates an object obj_i. The OS returns a capability $Cap^1(obj_i)$ to p_1. This capability typically confers all access privileges to its holder.
2. p_1 creates a subset capability of $Cap^1(obj_i)$ containing the read privilege. Let us call this $Cap^2(obj_i)$.

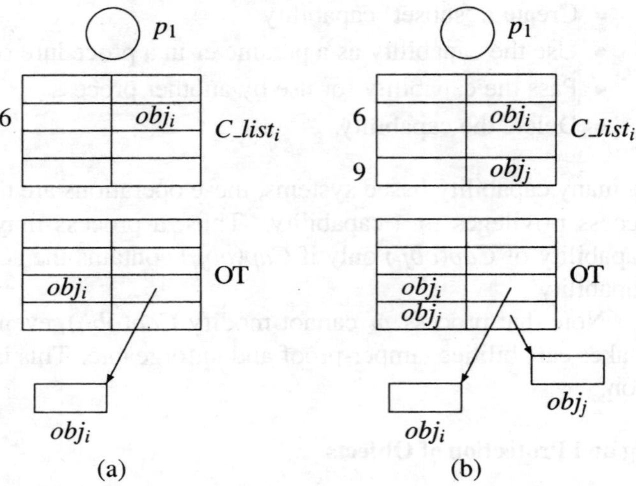

Fig. 18.11 Object manipulation in a capability based system

3. p_1 passes $Cap^2(obj_i)$ to process p_2. It is entered in the C-list of p_2.
4. p_2 uses capability $Cap^2(obj_i)$ to perform a read access to obj_i.

Process p_1 can ensure that the right to read obj_i is confined to process p_2 alone by turning off the 'pass the capability' privilege in $Cap^2(obj_i)$. Figure 18.12 illustrates the resulting C-lists of p_1 and p_2. Sharing is implicit in the fact that both C-lists contain a capability for obj_i. Protection is implicit in the fact that these capabilities confer different access privileges on processes p_1 and p_2.

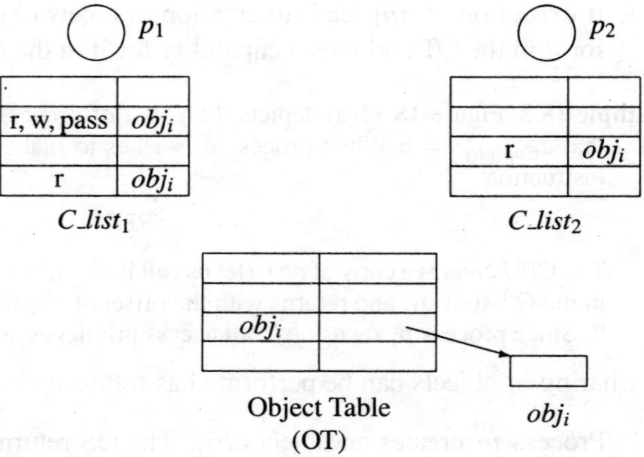

Fig. 18.12 Capability based object sharing and protection

Protection of capabilities

Capability based systems can be broadly divided into two groups based on the manner in which capabilities are protected. These are:

1. Tagged architectures
2. Capability segments.

In a tagged architecture, protection is based on *tags* associated with an object. Viewed simply, each tag is the equivalent of a 'type' in a programming language. The run-time representation of a data item consists of a tag and a value. The machine architecture checks the validity of an operation op_i on a data object d by checking the compatibility of op_i with d's tag. For example, a fixed point operation will fail if applied to a float value. A capability is itself viewed as an object, hence a tag 'cap' is associated with a memory word containing it. Thus capabilities and objects coexist in the memory (see Fig. 18.13). Only the capability related operations mentioned in Section 18.4.1 are valid on memory words with the tag 'capability'. Since none of these operations permit modification of a capability, there is no way in which a program may tamper with a capability.

tag	*object*
int	−246
float	···
cap	$Cap\,(obj_i)$

Fig. 18.13 Tag based capability protection

When protection is based on the notion of capability segments, capabilities are distinguished from instruction and data objects in a system. Distinct address spaces exist in the system to house capabilities, instruction objects and data objects. Due to this arrangement, the *object address* field of the object table (see Fig. 18.10) can never contain the address of a capability. This prevents tampering with capabilities.

In both approaches privileged instructions exist for the OS to set the various fields in a capability.

18.4.3 Software Capabilities

The OS for a non-capability based architecture can implement capabilities in the software. The arrangement of objects and capabilities can be analogous to the arrangement shown in Fig. 18.11, however the manipulation and protection of objects is now performed by a component of OS—an *object manager*—rather than by the CPU of the system.

A program indicates its object manipulation requirements to the OS in a manner similar to instruction (18.2), viz. by a call of the form

<opn> $(Cap(obj_i))$

Before performing *<opn>*, the object manager verifies that $Cap(obj_i)$ contains the necessary access privileges. As important issue in the use of software capabilities is that of protecting the capabilities against tampering. This is typically addressed using encryption. We describe a simplified version of the capability protection scheme used in the distributed operating system Amoeba. An encryption key key_i is assigned to obj_i at object creation time. The object table entry of an object contains an additional field to hold this key. A capability has a third field *number* in addition to the *object id* and *access privileges* fields (see Fig. 18.14). This field contains a number which is used to protect the capability.

A capability for obj_i is created using the following procedure:

access privileges	*object id*	*number*

Fig. 18.14 An Amoeba-like capability

1. The *object id* and *access privileges* fields of the capability are set appropriately.
2. key_i is obtained from the object table entry of obj_i. The strings *access privileges* and key_i are concatenated. Let *cat* denote the resulting string.
3. Contents of the *cat* string are encrypted by key_i. The result is put in the *number* field of the capability. Thus, $number = E_{key_i}(access\ privileges\ .\ key_i)$, where '.' denotes concatenation.

To manipulate obj_i, a process must submit a capability for obj_i to the object manager. The object manager verifies the validity of the capability as follows:

1. key_i is obtained from the object table entry of obj_i,
2. The *access privileges* string from the capability and the key_i string are concatenated and the result is encrypted using key_i as the key.
3. The capability is valid only if the result of encryption in step 2 is identical with the *number* field in the capability.

Any tampering with the *object id* or *access privileges* fields of a capability would lead to failure of the check in step 3.

Comparison with capability based systems

The major strength of software capabilities, viz. independence from the underlying hardware, is also its major weakness. Many actions performed by the hardware of a capability based system, e.g. creation of subset capabilities, need to be performed in the software. In addition, it is necessary to validate every capability before use. All these requirements add to the overhead of using software capabilities.

BIBLIOGRAPHY

Lempel (1979) and Pfleeger (1989) discuss techniques and algorithms in cryptology. Dennis and Van Horn (1966) is the fundamental paper on the concept of capabilities. Levy (1984) describes a number of capability based systems. Mullender and Tanenbaum (1986) and Tanenbaum(1992) describe the software capabilities of Amoeba.

1. Dennis, J.B. and E.C. Van Horn (1966): "Programming semantics for multiprogrammed computations," *Commn. of ACM*, **9** (3).
2. Lempel, A.(1979): "Cryptology in transition," *Computing Surveys*, **11** (4), 285-303.
3. Levy, H.M. (1984): *Capability Based Computer Systems*, Digital Press, Mass.
4. Mullender, S.P. and A. Tanenbaum (1986): "The design of a capability based distributed operating system," *Computer Journal*, **29** (4).
5. Pfleeger, C.P. (1989): *Security in Computing*, Prentice Hall, 1989.
6. Tanenbaum, A.S. (1992): *Modern Operating Systems*, Prentice-Hall, N.J.
7. Wofsey, M.M. (1983): *Advances in Computer Security Management*, John Wiley, New York.

CHAPTER 19

Distributed Operating Systems

Distributed systems provide the following advantages:

- Resource sharing
- Reliability
- Computation speed-up
- Communication
- Incremental growth.

Resource sharing has been the traditional motivation for distributed systems. The earliest form of a distributed system was a computer network which enabled the use of specialized hardware and software resources by geographically distant users. Resource sharing continues to be an important aspect of distributed systems today, however the nature of distribution and sharing of resources has changed due to advances in the networking technology. Sharing of resources is now equally meaningful in a local area network (LAN). Thus, low-cost computers and workstations in an office or a laboratory can share some expensive resources like laser printers.

A distributed environment can be used to enhance the *reliability* of a system. There are two aspects to this—*availability* of a resource and *reliability* of data. Resource availability implies continued availability and usability of data despite failures in the system. This is ensured through redundancy. For example, availability of a disk resource can be increased by having two or more disks located at different sites in the system. Now if one disk is unavailable due to a disk or site failure, a program can use some other disk. Availability of a data resource, e.g. a file, can be similarly enhanced by keeping copies of the file at various sites in the system. The second aspect is *data reliability* which implies guarding against corruption and loss of data. Basic data reliability can be implemented through fault tolerance techniques like disk mirroring and atomic operations (see Section 17.6.2). However, these techniques need to be augmented to handle consistency of file copies residing at different sites in a distributed system.

Computation speed-up implies obtaining better response times or turn around times by distributing a computation between different computers in a distributed system. For example, the computation of Fig. 10.5 can be speeded up by executing processes p_2 and p_5 in different computers.

Communication between users at different locations is greatly facilitated using a distributed system. There are two important aspects to communication. First, users have unique id's in a distributed system. Their use in communication automatically invokes the security mechanisms of the OS. Thus, no separate authentication is needed to safeguard confidentiality of communication. Second, use of a distributed system also implies continued availability of communication when users travel between different sites of a system.

Distributed systems are capable of *incremental growth*, i.e. the capabilities of a system (e.g. its processing power) can be enhanced at a price proportional to the nature and size of the enhancement. A major advantage of this feature is that enhancements need not be planned in advance. This is in contrast to the classical mainframe architectures where enhancements often took the form of upgradation—that is, replacement of subsystems by more powerful ones—hence enhancement costs tended to be disproportionate to the nature and size of an enhancement.

Distributed systems today cover a wide spectrum of computer hardware, software and topological configurations; resource sharing services range from off-line access to real-time access and topologies vary from locally distributed to geographically distributed. In this chapter, we shall discuss major issues in the design of distributed operating systems without reference to these hardware, software and topological differences. Hence we will adopt a definition of a distributed system which emphasizes the essential features of a distributed system and ignores the non-essential ones. This will enable us to focus on the generic design issues in distributed systems.

19.1 DEFINITION AND EXAMPLES

Definition 19.1 (Distributed System) *A* distributed system *is a system consisting of two or more nodes, each node being a computer system with its own memory, some communication hardware, and a capability to perform some control functions of an OS.*

The definition does not specify the nature of control functions a node may perform. Thus a node may have its own OS, or may perform certain control functions of a system-wide OS. Similarly, a node may perform all file system operations in a local file system, may perform only some operations on behalf of a central file system, or may not perform any file system operations at all. Note that a tightly coupled multiprocessor system—that is, a multiprocessor system containing a shared memory and no local memories for processors—may be a part of a distributed system, but cannot constitute a distributed system by itself.

Figure 19.1 illustrates a schematic of a distributed system. The system consists of a set of individual computer systems and workstations connected via communication systems. Individual computer systems connected to communication system are called *hosts*. A *local area network* (LAN) consists of a number of servers, workstations and low-cost processors located at the same geographical site, e.g. an office or a laboratory, such that the inter-node distances are of the order of a few meters or tens of meters. A *wide area network* (WAN) connects systems and LANs located at geographically distant sites. A gateway provides connectivity between LANs and WANs. Intermediate nodes called *communication processors* (CPs) are used to facilitate communication.

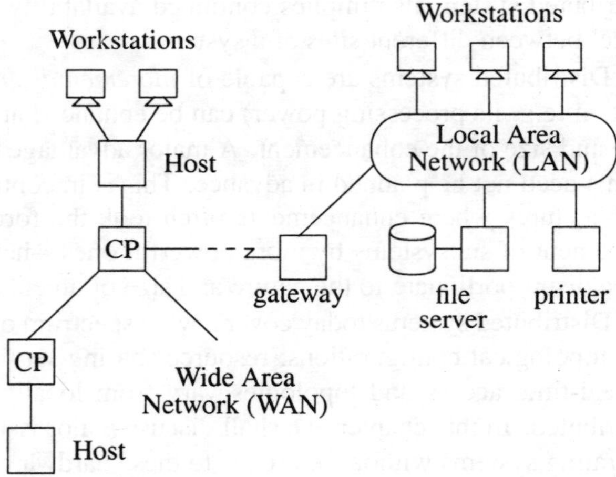

Fig. 19.1 A distributed system

19.1.1 A Distributed System Model

It is convenient to model a distributed system as an undirected graph

$$S = (N, E)$$

where N is the set of nodes, each node representing a computer system and E is the set of edges, each edge representing a communication path. Note that the words 'node' and 'site' often have the same connotation in our discussion; in such cases we will use these terms interchangeably.

Each node is assumed to have an *import list* describing non-local resources and services which the node can utilize, and an *export list* describing local resources of the node which are accessible to other nodes. In practice, a distributed OS contains a component called a *name server* which provides a service to locate a non-local entity required by a process. Processes in a node use the name server to locate the entities in their import lists. For simplicity the name server is not included in the system model.

It is convenient to adapt the graph model to suit specific analysis or design tasks. For example, since each computer or workstation contains many concurrent activities, it is sometimes convenient to treat a process as a node in the graph. Graph edges then represent interprocess communication paths in the system. We shall use such a model while discussing distributed control algorithms for use in a distributed OS.

19.1.2 Examples of Distributed Operating Systems

In this section we outline the features of some distributed operating systems. The systems mentioned here have been chosen with the specific intent of illustrating the evolution of distributed OSs.

ARPA-net [McQuillan, Walden, 1977] was the first well-known computer network. It was set up by the Defense Advanced Research Projects Agency of USA. This network was an interconnection of heterogeneous computer systems, analogous to the network of Fig. 19.1, except that the communication processors were called Intermediate Message Processors—IMPs. When some process A wished to send a message to process B, the host OS where process A was executing handed over the message to an IMP. IMP used the destination information to send the message over the network.

A major emphasis of the Arpanet design was on file sharing and transmission of messages over the network. Every IMP maintained routing tables, which contained information concerning alternative routes to a given destination. These tables were consulted while dispatching a message. The system maintained statistics regarding the current traffic density and transmission delays along every communication link. A message was sent along the route that promised quickest delivery. Use of this routing strategy permitted the network to withstand IMP and link failures. The filing systems of different computers were entirely local. Though sharing of files and programs over the network was intended, Arpanet only supported a "remote login" and file transfer facility between network nodes.

LOCUS [Walker *et al*, 1983] was an OS with a single network-wide filing system. It was thus possible to access local and distant files in a uniform manner. This feature enabled a user to log in at any node of the network and utilize the resources in the network without reference to his/her location in the system. MICROS [Wittie, Van Tilborg, 1980] provided for sharing of resources in an automatic manner. Jobs and parts of jobs were dispatched in different nodes of the system in an effort to balance the load on different nodes. This led to higher throughput and improved response times in the system. The manner in which a job executed in the system was transparent to the user. The system provided enhanced availability and reliability since many identical functional units were available. If one node crashed, a computation could be moved to another node at the cost of a short delay. Multiplicity of units also led to the possibility of graceful degradation—that is, the system could continue to operate despite failures, though with lesser efficiency.

Amoeba and Mach are modern distributed operating systems [Tanenbaum, 1992]. Resource transparency and optimum utilization of system resources are the key elements of Amoeba design. Resources are uniformly accessible independent of a user's location in the system. The system determines how best to implement a user computation, hence parts of a computation may be dispatched to different CPU's in order to obtain good response times.

Two important design aims of Mach are supporting parallelism in the hardware and software, and providing a base for implementing other OSs. The former extends support to multiprocessors, which few other OSs support. The latter takes the form of a small micro-kernel. Emulators for different OSs can be implemented on top of the micro-kernel to give the look and feel of different OSs.

The trend manifested in the above examples is towards increasing integration of OS functions over different nodes of a network. Arpanet is an example of a Network Operating System (NOS). Here every node of the network has its own local OS. In addition, it also contains some component of the network OS which performs operations over the network, e.g. transfer of files or migration of jobs. Here, the emphasis is on interconnecting a set of autonomous computers to provide convenient and cost-effective execution of jobs at the user's initiative. The system is heterogeneous, and the user is responsible for ensuring that requests for data and job migration are meaningful. Local operations, including management of local files, remain a responsibility of the local OS. The NOS simply provides another layer of services which is accessible through explicit calls. This enables exploitation of resources existing at different nodes of a network.

The other operating systems mentioned above are examples of distributed OS. They are designed to support meaningful distribution of resources. All OS services and hardware or software resources are uniformly accessible from different sites in the system. The key issue here is one of transparency of the network mechanisms. The user need not know the identities and locational details of resources in order to use them. This leads to a user-friendly computing environment which facilitates user mobility in the system. It also raises the possibility of optimizing the utilization of resources in the OS.

19.2 DESIGN ISSUES IN DISTRIBUTED OPERATING SYSTEMS

Two significant differences between a distributed and a conventional OS are the distribution of OS functions between different nodes of the system and the handling of distributed resources. These differences give rise to the following user and system oriented issues:

1. Transparency of resources and services
2. Distribution of control functions of the OS

3. System performance
4. Reliability.

Transparency of resources and services

Transparency implies the ability to access a resource or a service without having to know its location in the system. Lack of transparency leads to non-uniformity of resource access from different sites—for example, a user may have to use different access paths for a file when operating from different sites. This affects user mobility within the system. It also implies that the location of a resource cannot be changed without affecting the manner in which it is accessed by users. This constrains the performance optimization function of the OS, which may have wanted to change the location of a resource to improve its utilization or performance. The transparency issue in distributed file systems is described in Section 19.8.1.

Distribution of control functions

Implementation of control functions for a shared memory multiprocessor system does not differ significantly from that in a conventional OS. State information can be maintained in the shared memory and any CPU can perform a control function by accessing this information. It is only necessary to ensure that mutual exclusion is implemented over the state information.

In a distributed OS, presence of local memories in different nodes and communication delays between nodes make it impossible to obtain consistent state information concerning all entities in the system (see Section 19.5). This situation, called the *lack of global state*, necessitates use of special algorithms to perform the control functions in a distributed manner. Examples of such algorithms are—distributed mutual exclusion algorithms, distributed deadlock handling algorithms, etc. Some important distributed control algorithms are described in Section 19.7.

System performance

The computational loads in different nodes of a distributed system may be different. Hence there is more to the performance of a distributed system than mere CPU scheduling. For example, some node N_1 may have a large number of running processes, while another node N_2 may have none. Thus, the CPU of N_1 is heavily loaded while that of N_2 is idle.

For good system performance, a distributed OS must perform *load balancing* to ensure that all nodes in the system are equally loaded at any moment of time. This involves migrating some user processes from one node to another, e.g. from node N_1 to node N_2 in the above example. If resource transparency exists in the system, an OS may similarly migrate data resources to improve system performance.

The design of a distributed system must be *scalable*, i.e. the performance of a system must not deteriorate with increasing size. In other words, delays and overheads incurred due to the distribution of control functions must not be allowed to degrade system performance.

Reliability

Apart from resource availability and data reliability mentioned at the start of this chapter, a distributed system must address two other aspects of reliability. These concern progress of computations in the presence of failures, and security of data.

Progress of computations in the presence of failures

A distributed OS may move different parts of a computation to different nodes of a system. This may be done either because the computation uses specialized resources located in different nodes, or because the system performs load balancing to ensure good performance. When a node or link failure occurs during the execution of such a computation, the system must determine the impact of the failure on the computation and decide on the least expensive way to recover from it. This requires new techniques to ensure that parts of the computation not affected by a failure should be able to continue their execution.

Consider the following failures during the execution of an application:

1. A remote node fails
2. A communication link connecting a node to the rest of the system fails.

These failures are often indistinguishable to the rest of the application, however they require different recovery actions. In the former case, the subcomputation performed by the failed node would have to be repeated, possibly at some other node in the system. In the latter case, unknown to the rest of the application, the computation may have been completed at the remote node. Hence re-initiating it elsewhere in the system presents data consistency problems (e.g. an update may be performed twice!) or wastes CPU time. Conventional fault tolerance techniques do not offer a solution to this problem, hence special techniques have to be designed for reliability in a distributed OS.

Security of data in a distributed system

Authentication of a user or a service acquires a new dimension in a distributed system. The conventional model of authenticating a user at log in time is not adequate because a user may log in at one node and access data or resources located in another node. Since inter-node messages pass through many CP's, possibly under the control of different operating systems, user authentication becomes a very complex issue. Special techniques and algorithms have to be evolved for this purpose. Reliability and security issues are described in Sections 19.9 and 19.10, respectively.

EXERCISE 19.2

1. Load balancing can be performed in one of two ways:

(a) Initiate the processes of a computation in different nodes of the system.
(b) Move the processes of a computation to different nodes of the system. This is called *process migration*.

Discuss how each of these approaches can be implemented. What are the practical difficulties in their implementation? (*Hint:* Think of the environment of a process.)

19.3 NETWORKING ISSUES

Networking hardware and software form a vital component of a distributed system. Reliability and throughput of a distributed system is influenced by the following aspects of networking:

1. Network topology
2. Communication over the network
3. Switching techniques in the network
4. Routing of network traffic.

19.3.1 Network Topology

Figure 19.2 illustrates different network topologies. In the star topology, each node is connected to the central node of the system. This topology is useful when the distributed system has one major computational site. Reliability of a star network depends on reliability of the central node. Communication delays between a node and the central node, or between two nodes, depend on contention at the central node. In the ring network, messages are passed along the ring till they reach their destination. The ring network is immune to single node and link failures, however the communication load on each node is high. In the fully connected network, each node is connected to all other nodes. Communication between a pair of nodes in the fully connected network is immune to failure of other nodes, or failure of up to $(n-2)$ link failures, where n is the number of nodes in the network. A partially connected network reduces the cost of communiation links. However, such a network suffers from partitioning with fewer node or link failures than a fully connected network.

19.3.2 Communication

Communication is achieved through mutual cooperation between nodes of a network. Conventions used to implement communication in a network are collectively called *network protocols*. The ISO reference model for network communication (see Tab. 19.1) specifies a hierarchy of layers for use by communicating nodes. Each layer in the hierarchy implements one protocol. The purpose of this model is to make all details of data semantics, switching, routing and error detection transparent to the application program. This is achieved as follows: The application layer accepts data from an application program or presents it in the form expected by an application program. The session layer establishes communication between two processes. The presentation layer maintains consistency of data between sites, performing change of

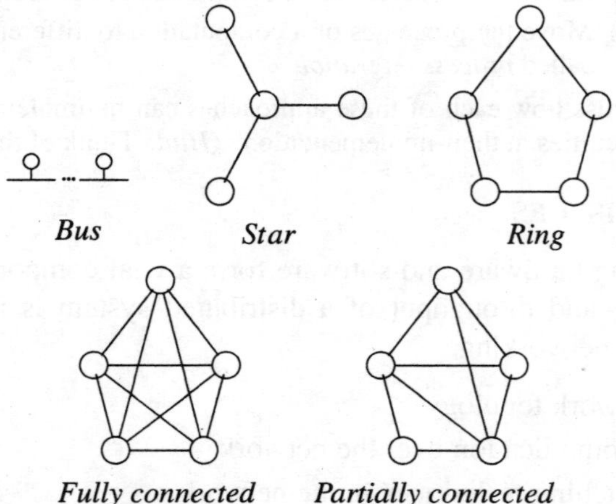

Fig. 19.2 Network topologies

representation, compression and coding or decoding where necessary. The first four layers handle networking related issues.

The layers of the ISO reference model carry out the following functions for an outgoing message (see Fig. 19.3): A message originates in the application layer and passes through the presentation and session layers. The transport layer splits the message into packets and hands over the packets to the network layer. The network layer determines the link on which each packet is to be sent and hands over the link id and the packet to the data link layer. The data link layer views the packet as a string of bits and adds error detection and correction information to it. This is handed over to the physical layer for actual transmission. Converse actions are performed when a message is received.

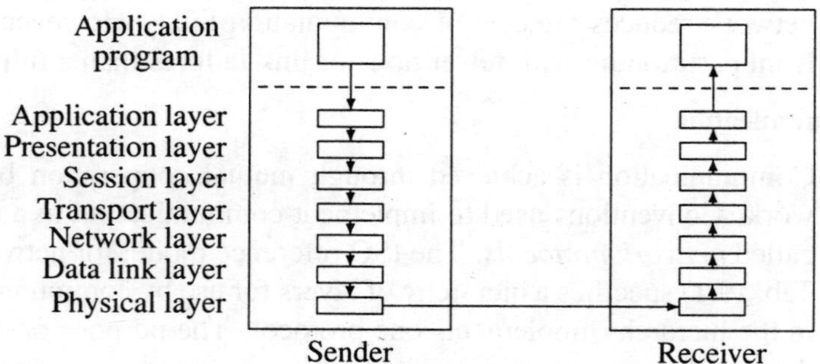

Fig. 19.3 Operation of the ISO protocol

Table 19.1 The ISO Protocol

Layer No.	*Name*	*Function*
1.	Physical Layer	Provides electrical and physical mechanisms for bit transmission.
2.	Data Link Layer	Organizes received bits into packets. Performs error detection on packets.
3.	Network Layer	Establishes a route for the travel of packets.
4.	Transport Layer	Forms outgoing packets. Assembles incoming packets. Performs error detection, retransmission.
5.	Session Layer	Establishes logical connection between processes.
6.	Presentation Layer	Implements data semantics by performing change of representation and compression, coding or decoding where necessary.
7.	Application Layer	Provides network interface for applications.

19.3.3 Switching Strategies

A distributed system provides a connection to implement communication between a pair of processes. A switching technique determines *when* a connection should be set up between a pair of processes, and for how long the connection should remain in existence. Choice of a switching technique determines efficiency of communication between a pair of processes and the throughtput of communication links.

Circuit switching

In circuit switching, a connection carries all messages between a pair of communicating processes. Each connection is a point-to-point circuit (much like a telephone connection), which is exclusive to a pair of communicating processes. Message transmission is efficient once a circuit is established. However, a circuit ties up a set of communication resources. Hence use of circuit switching is meaningful only if traffic exists between a pair of processes but the overall message density in the system is low.

Message switching

Message switching establishes a connection for every message exchanged between a pair of processes. Thus its use incurs repetitive overheads but does not tie up communication resources between two messages. Use of message switching is justified if heavy message traffic does not exist between a pair of processes. Since a connection is destroyed between two messages, some other processes may use the same connection, or some links in the connection, for their communication. Traffic in the network should be heavy enough to exploit this possibility.

Packet switching

In packet switching, a message is split into units of fixed length, called *packets*. A connection is established for each packet. A packet carries the following identification information with it:

1. Id of the message to which it belongs
2. Sequence number within the message
3. Process id of the sender process
4. Process id of the destination process.

Packets belonging to different messages and different pairs of processes may coexist in any communication node. Message transmission and reassembly is the responsibility of the network software. Packet switching increases the throughput of communication links since links are not monopolized by specific pairs of processes. Consequently, response times improve. This makes packet switching attractive for interactive communication. All process pairs receive fair and unbiased service. However, the amount of control information to be carried increases.

19.3.4 Routing

A routing strategy determines which communication links should belong to a connection. Thus routing involves making a choice between alternative paths in a network. Choice of a routing technique influences the ability of a distributed system to adapt to changing traffic patterns in the system.

Fixed routing

A path is permanently specified for every pair of nodes in the system. Each node contains a table showing paths to all other nodes in the system. This table is consulted whenever a connection is to be set up between processes located in different nodes of a system. Fixed routing reduces the overheads of setting up a connection. However, it can lead to delays or low throughputs. in the presence of node or link failures and fluctuations in traffic densities.

Virtual circuit

A path is selected at the start of every session. Different sessions between the same pair of processes may thus use different paths. Information concerning traffic densities along different links in the system is used to determine the best path for a session. This leads to improvements in network throughput and response times. This strategy can adapt to changing traffic patterns in the network.

Dynamic routing

A path is determined only when a message or a part of a message is to be sent. Different messages of a session and different packets of a message may thus use different paths. Dynamic routing provides adaptability and improves throughput and response times. In Arpanet, information concerning the traffic density and communication delay along every link is constantly exchanged between the nodes. At every node this information is used to determine the current best path to a given destination node.

19.4 COMMUNICATION PROTOCOLS

Node and link failures tend to disrupt communication in a distributed system. Communicating processes therefore use special conventions to ensure reliable message communication. Such conventions are called *communication protocols*. The basic reliability means adopted in communication protocols are:

1. *Acknowledgements:* An acknowledgement is used to indicate that a message or a reply has reached its destination.
2. *Retransmission of messages and replies:* A message is retransmitted if it is feared that it may not have reached its destination. This is typically done after waiting a certain amount of time for a reply or acknowledgement of the message. A reply is similarly retransmitted if an acknowledgement is not received.

Communication protocols aim at implementing an *exactly-once* semantics, whereby a request is processed exactly once by a receiver and its reply is received exactly once by the sender. This makes communication failures transparent to both senders and receivers.

19.4.1 A Blocking Protocol

Consider a blocking, i.e. *synchronous*, protocol consisting of the following steps:

1. A sender stores a request in a buffer before sending it to the intended receiver. It then blocks waiting for a reply.
2. The receiver processes the message, stores its reply in a buffer and sends it to the sender. It then waits for an acknowledgement from the sender.
3. The sender retransmits the request if it does not receive a reply within a stipulated interval of time called the *time-out interval*.

4. The sender sends an acknowledgement on receiving a reply.
5. The receiver retransmits the reply if it does not receive an acknowledgement within the stipulated interval.
6. The sender and receiver release their buffers on receiving the reply and the acknowledgement, respectively.

Figure 19.4 depicts the blocking protocol where numbers in circles indicate steps in the protocol. This protocol may be called a 'reliable protocol' since it guarantees delivery of a request and receipt of a reply before a sender can proceed with its computations. A sender needs a single buffer. A receiver may require many buffers if it receives messages from many senders. It also needs explicit acknowledgement of every reply. Some simplification is possible due to the fact that a sender awaits a reply before proceeding with its computations. When a receiver receives a new message from a sender, it knows that the sender has received the reply to its previous message. Hence, explicit acknowledgements can be dispensed with for all but the last reply; a receiver now buffers a reply till it receives an acknowledgement or a new request from the same sender.

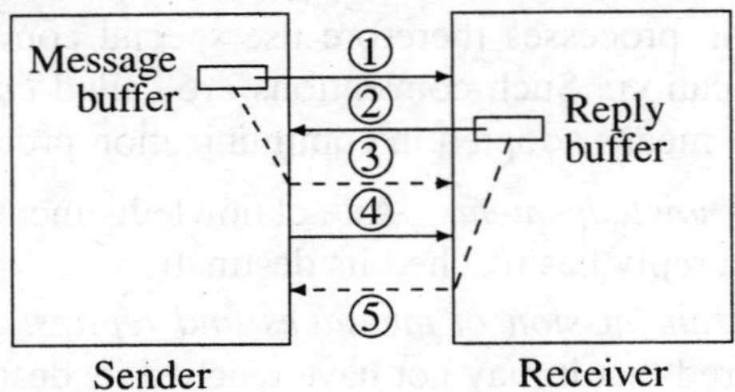

Fig. 19.4 A blocking protocol

19.4.2 A Non-blocking Protocol

The steps in a non-blocking (i.e. *asynchronous*) protocol are as follows:

1. A sender stores a request in a buffer, sends it to a receiver and proceeds with its computation.
2. The receiver stores its reply in a buffer and sends it to the sender.
3. A sender retransmits a request if it does not receive a reply within the *time-out interval*.
4. The sender is interrupted when a reply arrives. It now releases the buffer in which the corresponding request was stored.

Figure 19.5 depicts the protocol. A weakness of this protocol concerns the release of buffers in the receiver. The communication is asynchronous, i.e. the sender does not wait for the reply to a message. Arrival of some message m_j from a sender therefore does not imply that the sender has received replies for previous messages, i.e. $\forall m_i, i < j$. Hence a receiver does not know when it can release a buffer. The protocol also requires a special arrangement to avoid duplicate processing when a request is retransmitted. Each request is given a unique request id, which could be a pair like (*sender id, serial number*) or (*sender id, time of sending*). Each entry in the receiver's buffer consists of two fields—a *header* field containing the id of the request, and a *reply* field containing the reply. On receiving a request, the receiver checks if it is a retransmitted request by comparing its id with the headers of all entries in the buffer. If it is a retransmitted request, the receiver simply retransmits the contents of the reply field without processing the request. This is called *suppression of duplicate requests*. Apart from saving processing time, it also avoids problems like duplicate updates of data.

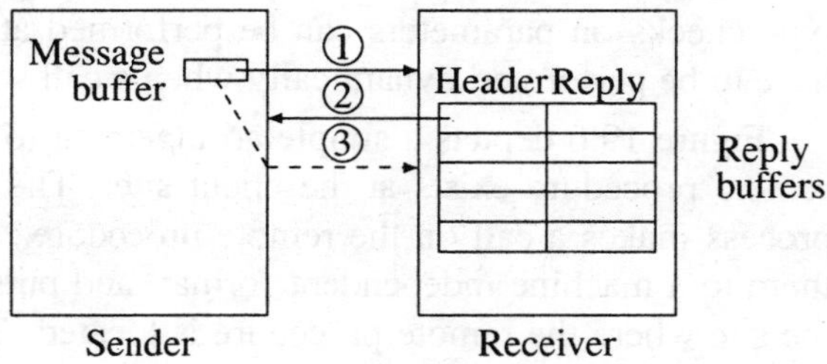

Fig. 19.5 A non-blocking protocol

The problem concerning release of buffers can be solved by introducing acknowledgements for replies received by a sender. Alternatively, a receiver can be permitted to process a retransmitted request as if it were a fresh request. Now, the receiver does not need to buffer its replies. Whenever it receives a request (including a retransmitted one), it computes a reply and sends it to the sender of the request. However, the computations performed by the receiver must satisfy two conditions. First, the computation must be inexpensive so that recomputation of a reply does not impose large overheads. Second, the computation must be *idempotent*, i.e. repeating the computation must yield exactly identical results. For example, the computation $i := 5$ is idempotent whereas $i := i + 1$ is not.

19.4.3 Remote Procedure Calls

A remote procedure call (RPC) is a language feature designed for distributed computing. It has the syntax

`call` *<proc_id>* (*<message>*);

where *<proc_id>* is the id of a process which may exist in any node of the system and *<message>* may be a list of parameters. The call results in sending *<message>* to the desired procedure. The reply returned by process *<proc_id>* is modelled as the result of the call. RPC is analogous to the conventional procedure call since it is implemented using a blocking protocol. We term the caller process as a *clinet* and the called process as a *server*.

Implementation of RPCs gives rise to two important issues. First, it is necessary to find the location of the remote procedure to be called. This is the issue of naming, which is implemented using a name server. The second issue concerns passing of parameters. In a heterogeneous distributed system, the hardware and software architecture of the node at which the procedure is located may be different from that of the calling node. Hence the RPC mechanism must perform appropriate conversion of value parameters. For reference parameters, the caller would have to construct system-wide capabilities for the parameters. These capabilities would be transmitted to the remote procedure in the message. Integration between the caller and the callee is another issue in implementing RPC. If integration is static and language based, type checks on parameters can be performed at compilation time. Otherwise they have to be performed dynamically when a call statement is executed.

Figure 19.6 depicts a simple arrangement to implement RPC's. A 'stub' for the remote procedure exists at the client site. The stub gains control when the client process makes a call on the remote procedure. It collects the parameters, converts them to a machine independent format, and puts them into a message to be sent to the site where the remote procedure is located. The identity of the site at which the server process exists is determined with the help of a name server and the message is sent to the server site using a blocking protocol. At the server site, another stub receives the message, converts the parameters to the machine specific format suitable for the site and transfers them to the called procedure. The results of the procedure call are sent back to the caller in a like manner.

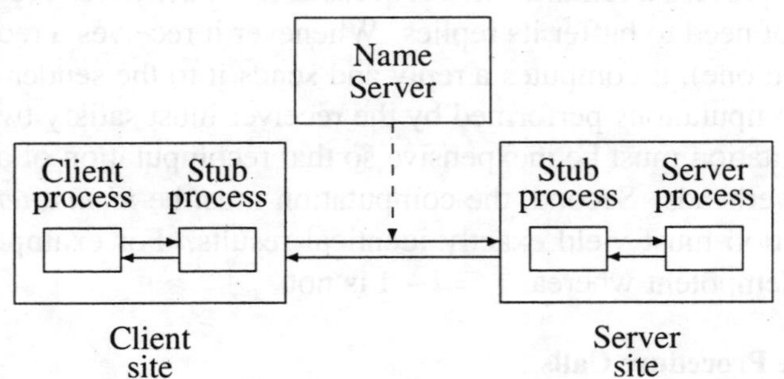

Fig. 19.6 Implementation of a remote procedure call (RPC)

Ideally, RPCs must possess exactly-once semantics. This would make them equivalent to the conventional procedure calls. However, exactly-once semantics are very expensive to implement. At-most-once is an alternative semantics for RPCs in which a remote call may or may not be completed, but it is guaranteed that its execution would not to be repeated. The caller would have to repeat the call if it finds that its execution was not completed.

EXERCISE 19.4

1. Write a short note on reliability and overheads in protocol design.
2. Explore the possibility of implementing the blocking and non-blocking protocols using monitors. What are the difficulties in the implementation?
3. An important aspect of the blocking protocol of Section 19.4.1 is the re-transmission of messages and replies when a time-out occurs. Write a short note on the factors that influence the size of the time-out interval.
4. Compare the following asynchronous protocol with the blocking and non-blocking protocols of sections 19.4.1 and 19.4.2:
   (a) A sender sends a message and continues processing.
   (b) Receiver sends a reply.
   (c) Sender sends an acknowledgement when it receives a reply.

19.5 SYSTEM STATE AND EVENT PRECEDENCE

To implement a control function, an OS needs to know the current state of the system, and the sequence in which events have occurred in the system. For example, CPU scheduling in a node requires knowledge of all *ready* processes in the node, while load balancing requires knowledge of *ready* processes in all nodes. Resource allocation needs to know the sequence in which resource requests are made, as also the resource allocation status in the system.

19.5.1 System State

Each component and entity in a system has its own state. Such a state is called the *local state* of a component or entity. For example, the local state of a memory cell is the value contained in it. The states of all components and entities in the system at a time instant t constitute the state of the system at t. This is called the *global state* of the system. The global state thus contains states of all processes, memories, IO devices and other resources, and all communication channels in the system.

Presence of the communication subsystem poses difficulties in collecting the local states of the nodes of the system precisely at time instant t. As a result, the global state cannot be obtained by simply putting together the local states of the nodes. To see this, consider what happens when the OS component situated in node N_1 wishes to record the system state at time instant t using the following procedure:

1. Node N_1 records its own state. This includes the state of all processes and resources located in N_1.
2. N_1 sends a message to each neighbouring node to record its state. We will call this a 'recording message'.
3. On receiving a recording message, a node
   (a) Records its own local state, if it is not already recorded. (Note that a node

may receive recording messages from many neighbours.)

(b) Records the state of the channel over which it received the recording message.

(c) Sends a recording message to each neighbour.

Note that a node $N_i, i \neq 1$ would receive the message to record its state at some time instant $t_i > t$. Hence what is recorded is not the system state at time instant t!

It is incorrect to consider such collections of local states to form the global state of a system because the local state information may not be mutually consistent. For example the state of node N_2 may mention that a message m_1 has been received from N_1, while the state of N_1 may not mention sending such a message! Problems in collecting consistent global states can be solved using special algorithms for global state collection. Alternatively, OS functions can be designed so as not to require knowledge of the global state. In Section 19.7.3, we will see examples of this approach in connection with deadlock detection.

19.5.2 Event Precedence

Let S_i represent the state of the system at time instant t_i. We say state S_i *precedes* state S_j, represented as $S_i < S_j$, if $t_i < t_j$. State S_i is said to be a recording state for event e_k (represented as *Recording_state* $(e_k) = S_i$) if S_i records e_k as having occurred and none of its preceding states do so. Event e_k is said to precede event e_l (represented as $e_k < e_l$) if *Recording_state* $(e_k) <$ *Recording_state* (e_l). Note that the precedence relation over events is transitive, i.e. if $e_1 < e_2$ and $e_2 < e_3$ then $e_1 < e_3$.

Event ordering implies arranging a set of events in a sequence such that each event in the sequence precedes the next one. In essence, it implies determining the order in which events have occurred in a system. We say a *total order* exists with respect to the precedence relation '<' when all events in the system can be ordered using '<'. A *partial order* implies that only some events can be ordered.

Difficulties in recording the global state of a system lead to difficulties in defining a total order on events. For example, consider a process p_1 executing in node N_1 which asks for a remote resource R. Let another process p_2 executing in node N_2 also ask for the same resource. It may be difficult to determine which request has occurred earlier. Such difficulties lead to fairness problems in resource allocation.

An ordering can be determined for events which possess a cause-and-effect relationship amongst them, for example:

1. Start and end of an IO operation in some process p_1.
2. Process p_4 sends a message to process p_3, and process p_3 receives the message from p_4.

Here, due to the nature of IO and message transmission, start IO is known to precede end IO, and the event 'send to p_3' in process p_4 is known to precede the event 'receive from p_4' in process p_3. Such precedences and the transitive nature of the precedence relation can be used to determine precedences between events not directly connected by cause-and-effect relationships. For example, $e_i < e_j$ if an event e_i precedes the 'send message to p_3' event in process p_4, and an event e_j is preceded by the 'receive message' event in process p_3. Events e_i, e_j are said to be *concurrent events* if neither $e_i < e_j$ nor $e_j < e_i$.

A *timing diagram* is useful in determining event precedences using the transitiveness of the 'precedes' relation. The diagram shows activities of different processes against time. Example 19.1 illustrates the use of timing diagrams.

Example 19.1 Figure 19.7 shows activities in processes p_1 and p_2. Event e_{23} is a 'message send' event while e_{12} is a 'message receive' event. The transitive nature of '<' leads to the precedence relations $e_{22} < e_{13}$ and $e_{21} < e_{13}$. Event e_{11} is concurrent with event e_{21}. It is also concurrent with e_{22} and e_{24}.

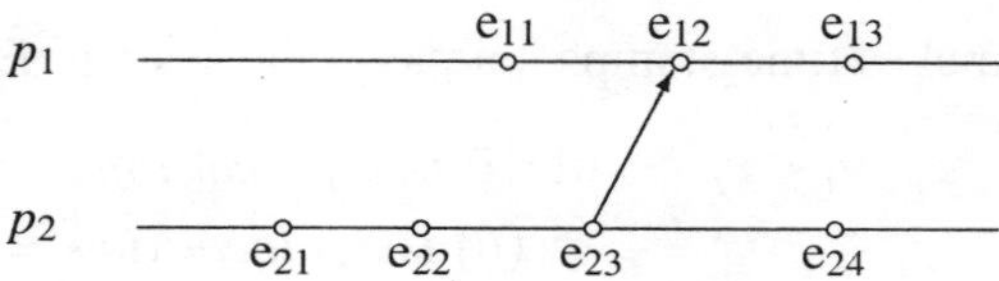

Fig. 19.7 Event precedence via timing diagram

19.5.3 Generating Useful Time Stamps

Event ordering based on event precedences is unsatisfactory for two reasons—it is expensive to determine the order, and a total order on events is not guaranteed. An alternative is to use *time-stamp ordering*. In this method an 'occurrence time' is associated with each event, which is called its time-stamp. Let $ts(e_i)$ represent the time-stamp of event e_i. An ordering is defined on events according to their time-stamps, i.e. $\forall e_i, e_j \,:\, e_i < e_j$ if $ts(e_i) < ts(e_j)$ and $e_i > e_j$ if $ts(e_i) > ts(e_j)$. This yields a total order if time-stamps are unique.

Due to communication delays it is infeasible to use a central clock to obtain the occurrence times of events. Hence a local clock is used in each node and the time-stamp of an event is defined as follows:

$$ts(e_i) \quad = \quad \text{local time of the node when event } e_i \text{ occurred in that node}$$

Clocks in different nodes may show different times due to drift. This would affect the reliability of time-stamp based event ordering. Hence, clocks of all nodes are synchronized using the cause-and-effect relationship of interprocess messages as follows:

1. Each message m includes the time-stamp of the 'send m' event in the sender process.
2. Process p_i receiving message m performs the action

   if *local clock*(p_i) < *time-stamp*(m) then
   local clock(p_i) := *time-stamp*(m) + δ;

where *local clock*(p_i) is the local clock in the node where process p_i executes, *time_stamp*(*m*) is the time-stamp in message *m* and δ is the average communication delay in the network.

This procedure can keep the local clocks of the nodes loosely synchronized. (Note that such clocks may not show 'real' time. Hence they are called *logical clocks*.) The time-stamps obtained using such clocks have the property that $ts(e_i) < ts(e_j)$ if $e_i < e_j$. However, two or more events occurring in different nodes may obtain identical time-stamps from local clocks, hence a total order cannot be obtained over events occurring in the system. To overcome this problem, a time-stamp is defined to be the following pair:

$$ts(e_i) \equiv (process\ id,\ local\ time)$$

which makes time-stamps unique in the system. Event precedence is now defined as

$$\begin{aligned} e_i < e_j \quad \text{iff } & (i)\ ts(e_i).local\ time < ts(e_j).local\ time,\ or \\ & (ii)\ ts(e_i).local\ time = ts(e_j).local\ time\ and \\ & \quad ts(e_i).process\ id < ts(e_j).process\ id \end{aligned} \qquad (19.1)$$

where $ts(e_i)$.*process id* and $ts(e_i)$.*local time* are the process id and local time in $ts(e_i)$, respectively.

EXERCISE 19.5

1. Given the following events occurring in a system consisting of three processes:

process p_1	*process* p_2	*process* p_3
event e_1;	*event* e_3;	*event* e_5;
– –	– –	– –
Send message to p_2;	Receive message from p_3;	Send message to p_2;
event e_2;	Receive message from p_1;	*event* e_6;
	– –	Receive message from p_2;
	event e_4;	– –
	Send message to p_3;	*event* e_7;

   (a) Draw a timing diagram for the system.
   (b) Show the event precedences in this system.
   (c) List the concurrent events.

19.6 RESOURCE ALLOCATION

The problem of resource allocation in a distributed system is to make a resource r_k situated at some site N_k available to a process p_i at site N_i. There are two aspects to this problem:

1. Locating the required resource in the system.
2. Determining availability of the resource.

The first aspect is handled using a name server. The second aspect is complicated by the absence of global state, since the state of a resource may change by the time its state information reaches a remote node. In this section we discuss how a resource may be allocated using a centralized resource manager. In Section 19.7.2 we shall discuss a distributed algorithm for mutual exclusion which may be used to query the state of a resource and perform resource allocation in a distributed manner.

The issue of locating a required resource is related to the naming issue in a distributed system. An OS may encompass many administrative domains, each domain containing a set of sites and communication links. If a resource required by a process p_i is available in node N_i where p_i executes, or within the same domain as N_i, it can be located and accessed easily. However, p_i would need help to locate resources situated in other nodes or in other domains of the system. This service is provided by a name server. The name server accepts the name of a resource or service and maps it to a name in another domain. It may also be able to provide the name of the process that handles the resource or service. Each site in the system may have a name server which contains information concerning all services in the system. Alternatively each domain may have its own name server, or the OS may have a single name server.

Figure 19.8 illustrates centralized resource allocation in a distributed system. The system contains a single resource manager which consists of a name server and a resource allocator. The steps in the allocation and use of a resource res_j by process p_i are as follows:

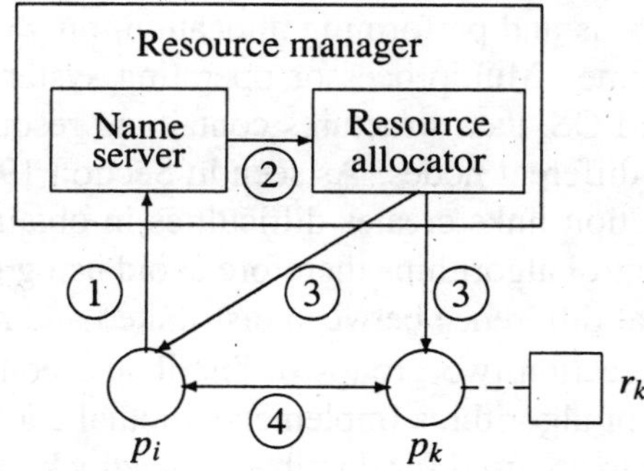

Fig. 19.8 Resource allocation in a distributed system

1. When p_i wishes to use res_j, it constructs a tuple (res_j, <*attributes*>, p_i) and forwards it to the resource manager. The resource manager receives the request and hands it over to the name server.
2. The name server locates the resource using its name and attributes, and constructs the tuple (r_k, N_k, p_i) where res_j is resource r_k at node N_k. The tuple is handed over to the resource allocator.

3. The resource allocator finds whether resource r_k of node N_k is available. If so, it passes the id of process p_k, which handles resource r_k of node N_k, to p_i and sends an allocation message containing the id of p_i to p_k. If the resource is not available, it stores the request in a queue of pending requests. The allocation is performed sometime in future when the resource becomes available.
4. Process p_k interacts with process p_i to fulfill p_i's service requests.
5. After completing its use of the resource, process p_i informs the resource manager accordingly.

This resource allocation approach has the advantage of simplicity. Existence of a single name server simplifies addition and deletion of resources. The resource manager is the only entity performing resource allocation and de-allocation. It may use a resource table to keep track of the status of resources in the system. Drawbacks of this approach are poor reliability due to centralization, and delays in resource allocation.

19.7 ALGORITHMS FOR DISTRIBUTED CONTROL

In a distributed operating system using a symmetric design for its kernel, each node in the system has identical capabilities with respect to each OS control function. This provides availability of the function in the presence of failures, and reduces delays involved in performing a control function. However, a symmetric design requires synchronization of activities in various nodes to ensure absence of race conditions over OS data structures. For example, even if each node is capable of querying the resource status and performing allocation, only one node should be permitted to do so at any time. Multiprocessor operating systems use this approach. However, in a distributed OS, data structures containing resource status information may be distributed in different nodes. As seen in Section 19.5, presence of local memories and communication links creates difficulties in obtaining global state information. Distributed control algorithms therefore avoid using global state information. This is the fundamental difference between distributed and non-distributed control algorithms.

In this section two groups of distributed control algorithms are discussed. The first group of algorithms implements mutual exclusion in the OS. Algorithms of the second group are used for distributed deadlock handling.

19.7.1 Understanding Distributed Control Algorithms

A *distributed control algorithm* (DCA) implements control activities in different nodes of a system. Each DCA provides a service of some kind, e.g. providing mutual exclusion, and has clients which can be user or OS processes. A DCA performs some actions when a client needs its service, or when an event related to its service occurs in the system. The following terminology is introduced to differentiate between the actions of a DCA and its clients:

1. Execution of a DCA constitutes a *control computation.* A control computation involves processes in different nodes of the system. These processes communicate with each other through *control messages.*
2. Execution of a client constitutes a *basic computation.* A basic computation could involve processes in same or different nodes of the system. These processes communicate with each other through *basic messages.*

It is convenient to visualize a control computation as being superimposed on the basic computation. Accordingly, a client process p_i is viewed to consist of two parts—a *basic part* (bp_i) and a *control part* (cp_i). The control part of a process is never blocked. The basic part of a process interacts with the system through its control part. Thus cp_i is aware of the sends and receives of basic messages by bp_i and, thereby, of bp_i's current state. Depending on the nature of the control computation, bp_i may also make explicit requests to cp_i. cp_i makes use of control messages to determine when a request made by bp_i can be satisfied. Figure 19.9 shows the system model used while discussing distributed control algorithms. Each node represents a process. Firm edges represent basic communication between processes while dotted edges depict control communication. Note that the firm and dotted edges need not be identical.

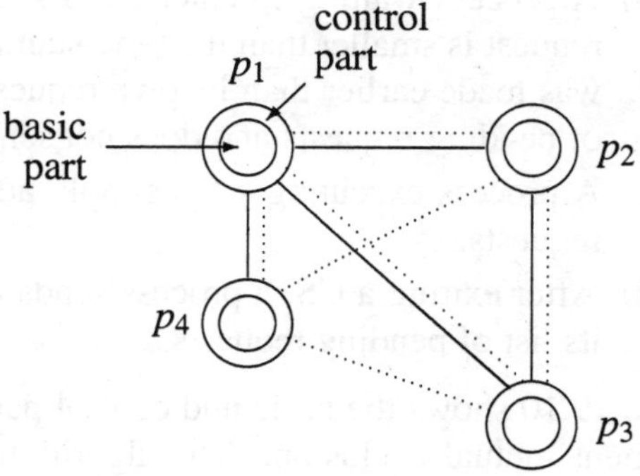

Fig. 19.9 A view of the system for distributed control

Example 19.2 Processes $\{p_i\}$, $i = 1, \ldots, 4$ in a banking application depicted by Fig. 19.9 need to access shared data D in a mutually exclusive manner. When process p_1 wishes to access D, bp_1 makes a request to cp_1 and gets blocked. cp_1 communicates with $cp_2, \ldots, cp_4$ to determine when p_1 may access D and wakes bp_1 appropriately.

19.7.2 Algorithms for Distributed Mutual Exclusion

The distributed mutual exclusion algorithms can be divided into two classes —fully distributed algorithms, and token based algorithms. In the former class of algorithms a process wishing to enter the mutual exclusion region, i.e. a critical section, needs permission from all other processes. In the latter class of algorithms an abstract entity called a *privilege token* exists in the system. Only a process possessing this token (called the *token holder*) can enter a critical section. When a new process wishes to enter, it sends a request to the token holder and waits till it receives the token.

19.7.2.1 A Fully Distributed Algorithm

In a fully distributed algorithm, all processes existing in the system participate to determine the order in which requesting processes should enter the critical section.

Algorithm 19.1 (Ricart Agrawala algorithm)

1. A process desirous of entering a CS sends a request to all other processes in the system. Each request carries a time-stamp. The requester enters CS only after receiving a 'go ahead' reply from every other process in the system, i.e. after receiving $(n-1)$ replies, where n is the number of processes.
2. On receiving a request,
   (a) A process not desirous of entering a CS immediately sends a 'go ahead' reply.
   (b) A process waiting to enter a CS sends a reply if the time-stamp of the request is smaller than the time-stamp of its own request (i.e., the request was made earlier than its own request), else it adds the request to its list of pending requests and does not send a reply to the requesting process.
   (c) A process executing a CS simply adds the request to its list of pending requests.
   (d) After exiting a CS, a process sends a 'go ahead' reply to all requests in its list of pending requests.

Figure 19.10 shows the basic and control parts of a process using this algorithm to implement mutual exclusion. The algorithm ensures FIFO entry to the critical section (see Step 2(b)) and has a message complexity of $O(n)$.

19.7.2.2 Raymond's Token Based Algorithm for Mutual Exclusion

Raymond's algorithm visualizes processes in the system to form an *abstract inverted tree*. The word 'abstract' here implies that the tree structure does not really exist in the system, it is simply defined and used by the DCA for its own purposes. The system continues to be a graph $G = (N,E)$ as defined in Section 19.1.1 with each node representing a process. The process in possession of the privilege token is called p_{hold}. The algorithm has three invariants concerning the abstract inverted tree:

1. Process p_{hold} is the root of the tree.
2. Each process belongs to the tree.

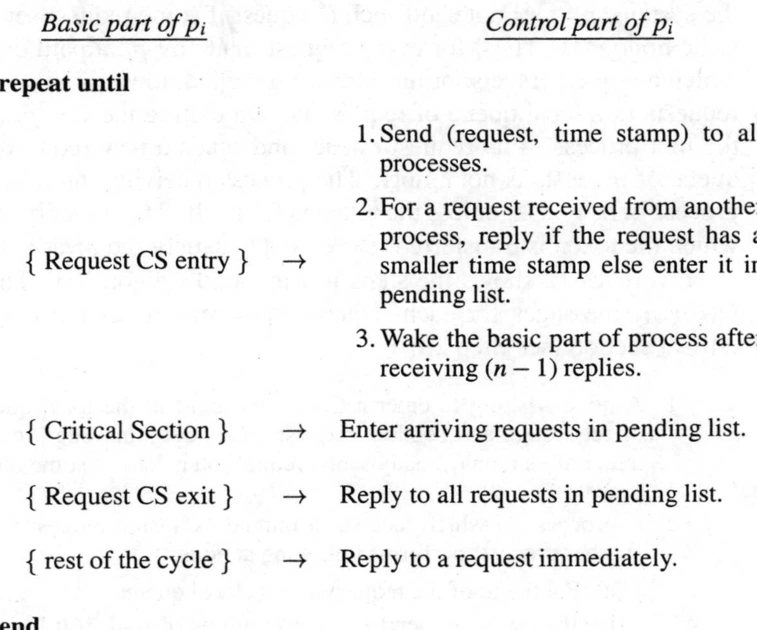

Basic part of p_i		*Control part of p_i*
repeat until		
{ Request CS entry }	$\rightarrow$	1. Send (request, time stamp) to all processes. 2. For a request received from another process, reply if the request has a smaller time stamp else enter it in pending list. 3. Wake the basic part of process after receiving $(n-1)$ replies.
{ Critical Section }	$\rightarrow$	Enter arriving requests in pending list.
{ Request CS exit }	$\rightarrow$	Reply to all requests in pending list.
{ rest of the cycle }	$\rightarrow$	Reply to a request immediately.
end		

Fig. 19.10 Basic and control actions in distributed mutual exclusion

3. Each process $p_i \in N - \{p_{hold}\}$ has exactly one out-edge which has the form $(p_i, parent(p_i))$ where $parent(p_i)$ is the parent of p_i in the tree.

Thus, for every process $p_i \in N - \{p_{hold}\}$, a path from p_i to p_{hold} exists in the system. Figure 19.11 depicts an abstract inverted tree in a system involving six processes. Process p_5 holds the token, hence it is at the root of the tree.

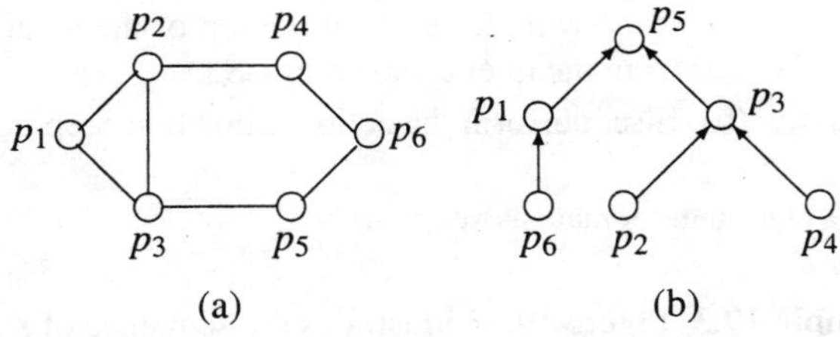

Fig. 19.11 (a) System graph, and (b) Abstract tree

The working of Raymond's algorithm can be summarized as follows: To enter a CS, a process p_i sends a request along its out-edge. The request contains a single field *requester_id* (which, in this case, is p_i). A process p_r receiving the request from p_i enters the *requester_id* in a local queue of requesters. It then sends a request along its out-edge with *requester_id* $= p_r$. To minimize the number of request messages in the system, p_r does not send such a request if some request sent earlier by it has yet to be honoured. Thus, for every request made by p_i, a path exists in the tree along which a request travels, or has already travelled, towards p_{hold}. p_{hold} enters all such requests in a local queue of requesters. On exiting the CS, p_{hold} sends the token to the first process in its request queue, and sends a new request to that process if its queue of requests is not empty. The process receiving the token sends it to the first process in *its* queue, unless the token is for itself. The direction of the tree edge along which the token is transferred is reversed to satisfy the invariants of the algorithm.

Figure 19.12 shows the steps in Raymond's algorithm. The algorithm requires $O(log\ n)$ messages for each request, however it does not ensure FIFO entry to a critical section (see Step 2(b)).

1. A node wishing to enter a CS enters its id in the local queue of requesters and sends a request on its outgoing edge in the tree, unless it has already sent a request on behalf of some other process.
2. A process p_r, which receives a mutual exclusion request from another process, performs following actions:
   (a) Put the id of the requester in its local queue.
   (b) If $p_r \neq p_{hold}$, send a request with its own id (if it has not already made or sent one) on its outgoing edge.
3. On completing the execution of a CS, p_{hold} performs following actions:
   (a) Send the token to p_i, the first process in its local queue.
   (b) Reverse the tree edge (p_i, p_{hold}).
   (c) Erase p_i from the local queue of requesters.
   (d) If its local queue is not empty, send a request with its own id to p_i.
4. A process receiving the token performs following actions:
   (a) If its own request is at the top of the local queue, erase it from the queue and enter CS.
   (b) Else, perform the actions shown in Step 3(a)-(d).

Fig. 19.12 Raymond's algorithm for mutual exclusion

Example 19.3 Figure 19.13 illustrates the sequence of steps in the execution of Raymond's algorithm when processes p_1 and p_4 of Fig. 19.11 make requests to enter a CS. Figure 19.13(a) shows the situation after the requests made by p_1 and p_4 have reached p_5, the holder of the privilege token (see Steps 1 and 2 of Fig. 19.12). When process p_5 releases the CS, it passes the token to p_3 and reverses the tree edge (p_3, p_5). p_5 now erases p_3 from its queue and makes a request to p_3 since its own queue is not empty (see Step 3). p_3 performs similar actions (see Step 4), which result in transferring the token to process p_4, reversal of the edge (p_4, p_3) and sending of a request by p_3 to p_4. (see Fig. 19.13(b)). p_4 now enters CS. After p_4 completes the CS, the privilege token

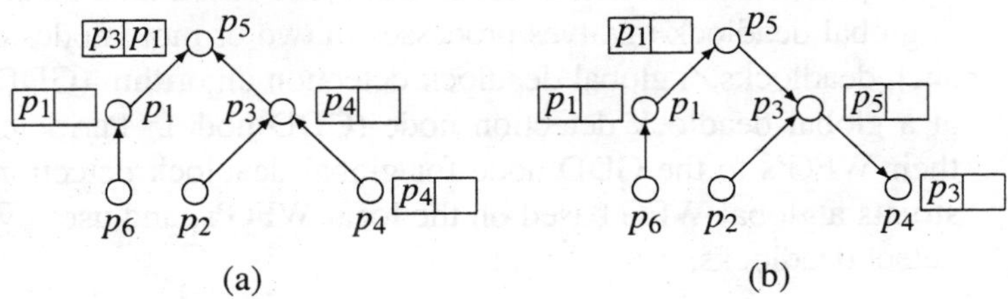

Fig. 19.13 An example of Raymond's algorithm

is transferred to process p_1 in an analogous manner, which enables p_1 to enter CS.

EXERCISE 19.7

1. Construct an example where Raymond's algorithm does not exhibit FIFO behaviour for entry to a CS.
2. Show actions of the basic and control parts of a process to implement Raymond's algorithm.

19.7.3 Distributed Deadlock Handling

In Section 12.3, we have classified the deadlock handling approaches into the following:

1. Deadlock detection
2. Deadlock prevention
3. Deadlock avoidance.

Of these approaches, deadlock prevention does not require knowledge of system state, while the deadlock detection and avoidance algorithms explicitly use system state information. In deadlock detection, state information is represented in the form of RRAG or WFG, which is used to determine the presence of resource knots. In deadlock avoidance, resource status information is used to determine the feasibility and safety of granting a resource request. These approaches can be trivially extended to the distributed environment by adopting the centralized resource manager schematic of Section 19.6, but will need modification if a distributed resource allocation policy is adopted.

We discuss distributed deadlock detection and deadlock prevention approaches in this section. No distributed deadlock avoidance approaches have been discussed in OS literature. For simplicity this discussion is restricted to the SISR model of resource allocation (see Section 12.3).

Hierarchical Deadlock Detection

A simple way to extend the deadlock detection techniques of Section 12.4 is to use a hierarchical arrangement. A local deadlock detection algorithm existing in each node performs detection of local deadlocks based on a local wait-for-graph (WFG). A global deadlock involves processes in two or more nodes of the system. To detect such deadlocks, a global deadlock detection algorithm (GDD algorithm) is executed at a global deadlock detection node (GDD node). Periodically, all nodes transmit their WFG's to the GDD node for global deadlock detection. The GDD node constructs a global WFG based on the local WFG's, and uses cycle or knot detection to detect deadlocks.

Example 19.4 The sequence of events in a system consisting of two nodes and containing three processes p_1, p_2 and p_3 is as follows:

1. Process p_1 requests and obtains resource r_3 in node C.
2. Process p_2 requests and obtains resource r_2 in node B.
3. Process p_3 requests and obtains resource r_1 in node B.
4. Process p_2 requests resource r_1 in node B.
5. Process p_1 requests resource r_2 in node B.
6. Process p_3 requests resource r_3 in node C.

Figure 19.14(a) shows the WFG's in nodes B and C of the system. Local deadlocks do not exist in either node. When nodes B, C send their WFG's to the GDD node, the GDD node merges the WFG's of individual nodes to obtain a system-wide WFG (see Fig. 19.14(b)). Since the system-wide WFG contains a cycle, the GDD node will declare a deadlock involving processes $\{p_1, p_2, p_3\}$.

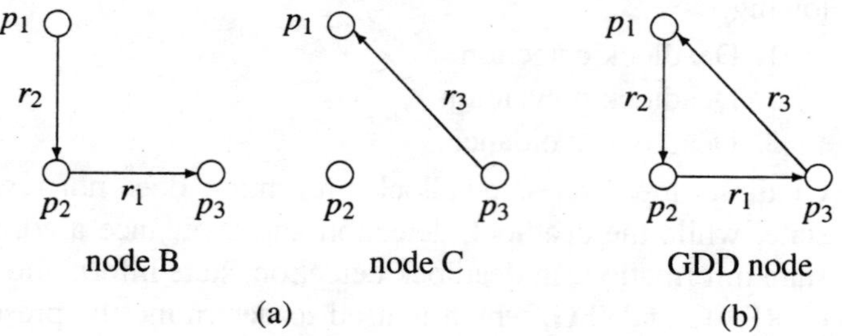

Fig. 19.14 (a) Local WFG's, (b) Global WFG

This scheme suffers from the weakness that the global WFG may not correctly represent wait-for relationships in the system due to problems analogous to those encountered in obtaining the global state. This could lead to failure in detecting deadlocks, and detection of *phantom* (i.e. non-existent) deadlocks. The former problem arises if information sent to the GDD node is outdated by the time the GDD node constructs the global WFG, e.g. if some resource requests are not represented in the WFG. This failure is not very serious since the deadlock may be detected the next time the GDD node constructs the WFG. The latter problem arises because the nodes may construct the local WFG's at different instants of time. Thus, inconsistent information may be represented in the global WFG, resulting in the detection of a deadlock which does not really exist in the system. Due to these problems, a different approach has to be used for deadlock detection in a distributed environment.

Example 19.5 The sequence of events in a system consisting of three processes p_4, p_5 and p_6 is as follows:

1. Process p_5 requests and obtains resource r_5 in node B.
2. Process p_6 requests and obtains resource r_4 in node B.
3. Process p_5 requests and obtains resource r_6 in node C.
4. Process p_4 requests resource r_5 in node B.
5. Process p_5 requests resource r_4 in node B.
6. Node B sends its local WFG to the GDD node.
7. Process p_6 releases resource r_4 in node B.
8. Process p_6 requests resource r_6 in node C.
9. Node C sends its local WFG to the GDD node.

Figures 19.15(a) and (b) show the local WFG's at steps 6 and 9, respectively. It can be seen that no global deadlock exists in the system at any of these times. However, the global WFG constructed by the GDD node (see Fig. 19.15(c)) contains the cycle $\{p_5, p_6\}$. This leads to detection of a phantom deadlock.

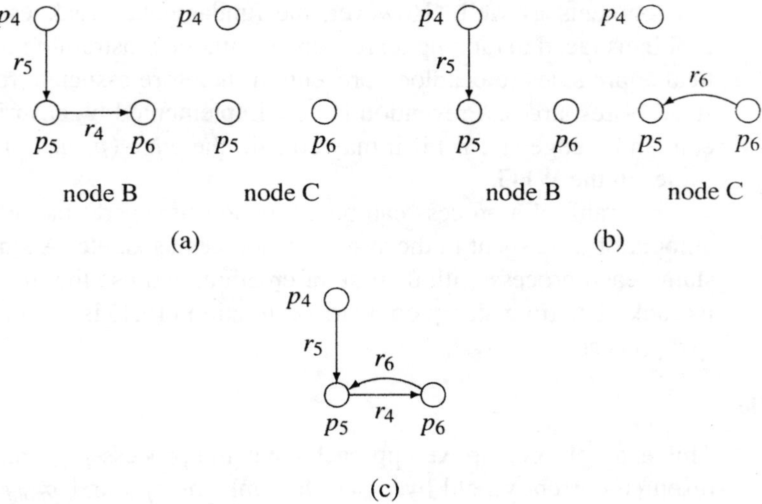

Fig. 19.15 Phantom deadlock : (a),(b) Local WFG's at steps 6 and 9, (c) Global WFG

Distributed Deadlock Detection

In this approach, the existence of a closed path of pending resource requests is detected through interprocess messages called *probes*. The deadlock detection algorithm is initiated every time a process p_{req} blocks on some resource r. p_{req} sends a probe to the process holding that resource (process p_{hold}). Thus the probe travels over one edge of the WFG. p_{hold} ignores the message if it is not blocked on a resource, else it forwards p_{req}'s probe to the process for which it is waiting. Thus the probe travels along edges in the WFG. If a closed path exists in the WFG, the probe would be received back at p_{req}, which declares a deadlock. This approach is called *edge chasing* approach since the probe traverses edges in the WFG. The processes involved in a deadlock could be identified by requiring each process to append its process id to the probe before forwarding it. One of these processes can be terminated to eliminate the deadlock.

The practical issues involved in this approach are:

1. Communication cost in terms of the number of probes
2. Delay in detecting a deadlock
3. Storage cost of probes
4. Correctness of the algorithm, i.e. absence of undetected deadlocks and phantom deadlocks.

Distributed Deadlock Prevention

The resource ordering approach to deadlock prevention is applicable in distributed environments as well. However, the fundamental weakness of the approach, viz. problems faced in ranking all resources without constraining the users, persists. Practical approaches to deadlock prevention therefore associate ranks with processes instead of resources. Prevention is now implemented by ensuring that a WFG cannot contain an edge (p_i, p_j) if it may contain the edge (p_j, p_i). This ensures absence of cycles in the WFG.

The rank of a process can be a function of several factors, e.g. process priority, amount of time spent in the system, resources used, etc. A simple scheme is to time-stamp each process with its time of creation, and use the time-stamp of a process as its rank. The time-stamp comparison relation (19.1) is used to compare the ranks of two processes.

Wait-or-die

This is a non preemptive approach. When a process p_{req} makes a request for some resource currently held by p_{hold}, the ranks of p_{req} and p_{hold} are compared. If p_{req} has a greater rank than p_{hold}, it is permitted to wait for the resource, else it is killed. A killed process is re-initiated sometime in the future.

Wound-or-wait

This is a preemptive approach. If p_{req} has a smaller rank than p_{hold}, it is allowed to wait for the resource held by p_{hold}. Else p_{hold} is preempted. The requested resource now becomes free and can be allocated to p_{req}. p_{hold} will have to be reinitiated sometime in the future.

When time-stamps are used as ranks, preempted processes may be permitted to retain their old time-stamps when they are re-initiated. This avoids starvation of processes.

EXERCISE 19.7

1. It is proposed that processes may themselves perform the resource allocation function. Discuss how this can be implemented using the distributed mutual exclusion algorithms described in this section.
2. Discuss practical difficulties in implementing distributed resource allocation as described in problem 1.
3. Discuss the influence of the wait-or-die and wound-or-wait schemes on response times and deadlines for different processes.
4. It is proposed to modify the distributed deadlock detection algorithm as follows: An unblocked process stores all probes received by it and forwards them when it blocks on a resource request. Discuss the effect of this modification on (i) memory requirements, and (ii) delays in detecting a deadlock.
5. It is proposed to use a probe based deadlock detection algorithm for deadlocks arising in message based process communication. When a process gets blocked on a 'receive message' request, a probe is sent to the process from which it expects the message. If that process is blocked, it forwards the probe to the process for which it is waiting, and so on.
   Comment on the suitability of the above algorithm for
   (a) Symmetric communication.
   (b) Asymmetric communication.

19.8 FILE SYSTEMS

The issue of transparency (see Section 19.2) is of paramount importance while accessing files in a system. Lack of transparency would hamper user mobility in the system as it would require users to be aware of their positions relative to the files being accessed. Centralized naming conventions can be used to provide transparency. However, this has to be done in a manner which does not cause inconvenience to users performing local computing, i.e. users operating completely within the confines of a node.

19.8.1 File System Transparency

Three approaches for implementing file sharing in a distributed system are discussed. These approaches have different implications for transparency of files.

Independent file systems in nodes

Each node N_i in the system has its own independent file system FS_i. Each file system performs file protection and recovery individually. A user X in node N_1 can access file `alpha` located in node N_2 by performing a *remote login* to node N_2 and making a copy of file `alpha`. `alpha` is now processed locally.

File sharing in this manner faces many practical difficulties. A user is required to possess a login id and a password for every node. Authentication is performed during remote login and file transfer. A user is responsible for the consistency of file copies in different nodes. Dynamic sharing of files is similarly a user issue. Since each node has an independent file system, the OS has no control over the location of a file in the system.

Combining file systems of nodes

Each node N_i in the system has its own file system FS_i. A distributed file system is built by creating an abstract 'super' node which has the file systems of all real nodes as its children. A user at some node N_1 can access files at another node N_2 by traversing the file system hierarchy. File access is thus location dependent, however it is more convenient than in the case of independent file systems in nodes. If we assume `B` to be the name of the root directory at node B, a user X of node A can access file `alpha` at node B by using the access path `../B/alpha`. In this approach, file sharing does not entail copying of files. Hence no consistency problems concerning file copies arise. Further, the concurrency issue can be handled by the OS, and need not concern the users.

Use of file `alpha` of node B by user X at node A can be implemented as follows: Stub processes called *server agent* and *client agent* exist in every system node (see Fig. 19.16). When user X in node A accesses a non-local file `../B/alpha`, the request is handed over to the server agent in node A. The server agent communicates the request to the client agent in node B. The client agent makes the request to FS_B, which opens `alpha` and builds $fcb_{\texttt{alpha}}$. Whenever user X performs a read or write operation on file `alpha`, the operation is implemented through a message between the server agent and client agent processes of nodes A and B. IO buffers for the file exist at node B, and only one record at a time gets passed to node A. This arrangement is particularly convenient since issues of dynamic sharing of a file would be resolved by FS_B. It also simplifies FS design since a file system need not differentiate between local and non-local file accesses.

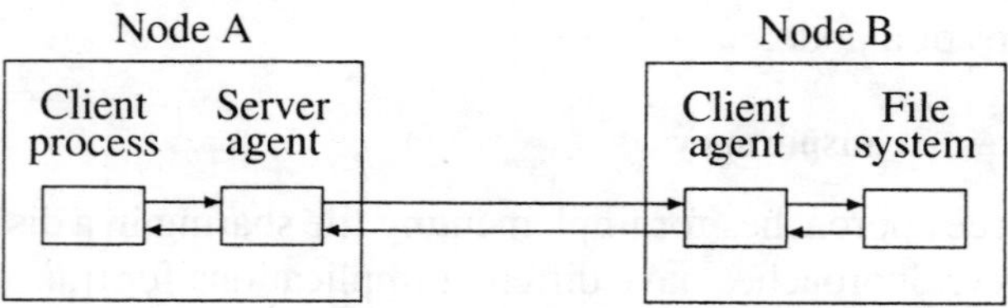

Fig. 19.16 Combining the file systems of nodes

A certain amount of flexibility can be offered to users by permitting *remote mount* commands (see Section 17.1). This would enable user A to mount FS_B at any node in his own FS hierarchy.

Distributed file systems

When an OS has a single file system, each user has a single system wide id and password. This reduces the issue of protection to the kind of checks that have to be performed in a conventional OS. The file system is fully transparent. Hence a user enjoys complete mobility in the system, and FS enjoys complete control over the location of files. Depending on the frequency and kind of usage, the file system may decide to move a file to another site in the system, or to maintain multiple copies of a file. Issues of consistency of file copies and concurrent access to files have to be resolved by FS rather than by a user.

File servers

A *file server* is a node which contains a complete file system (see Fig. 19.17). This arrangement simplifies the issues of file location, file consistency and concurrency control. However reliability of the system is affected by the fact that failure of the file server would cripple the entire system.

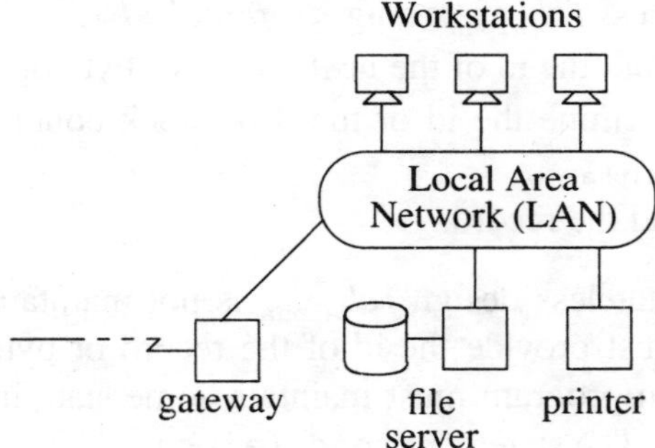

Fig. 19.17 A file server

19.8.2 Design Issues in Distributed File Systems

Performance requirements give rise to two important design issues in distributed file systems. These are:

- Stateful *vs.* stateless design
- Scalability.

Stateful vs. stateless design

The state of a file system consists of the states of all ongoing file processing activities. FCBs of all open files (i.e. entries of AFT) contain the state information. An FS is said to be *stateful* if it maintains and utilizes the state information to implement file accesses, and *stateless* if it does not use state information to implement file accesses.

In a stateful design, the state information provides an implicit context between FS and an application program. This reduces the amount of control information which must accompany each FS call made by an application program. It also reduces the amount of processing performed by FS. Consider the following file processing program:

```
open (alpha);
while not end_of_file (alpha)
   read (alpha, ...);
close (alpha);
```

When the statement `open (alpha, ..);` is executed, the OS creates $fcb_{\texttt{alpha}}$ in an entry of AFT, initializes it and returns its offset in AFT as the internal id of `alpha`. The statement `read (alpha, ...);` is translated into an FS call

`read (`<*internal_id*>, ...);

FS implements the `read` operation as follows:

1. Access $fcb_{\texttt{alpha}}$ using <*internal_id*>.
2. Obtain the id of the next record or byte of `alpha` from $fcb_{\texttt{alpha}}$.
3. Determine the id of the disk block containing the next byte or record using $fmt_{\texttt{alpha}}$.
4. Read the record.

In a stateless design $fcb_{\texttt{alpha}}$ is not maintained by the file server. Hence each FS call must provide the id of the record or byte to be read. This implies that the application program must maintain some state information, for example the record or byte id. The statement `read (alpha, ..);` in the program now must lead to the FS call

```
read ("alpha", <record/byte id>, <io_area address>);
```

At this call, FS opens file `alpha`, locates its FMT and uses it to convert <*record/byte id*> into the pair (*record id, byte id*). It then reads the record. Thus, many actions are repeated at every file access, leading to more overheads. Also, the application program is now required to keep some state information for the file processing activity.

Properties of the stateless design can be summarized as follows:

1. FS memory requirements are lower than for a stateful design.
2. FS has to perform more work to implement an IO operation.
3. FS is more reliable. If the node containing the FS crashes, the application program can simply resume its operation when FS is restored. As against this, the crash of a stateful server completely disrupts the execution of an application program due to loss of state.

Clearly, this design issue provides a tradeoff. Reliability and performance are both important issues. Which one should an FS favour? Some FS designs use a compromise. The FS maintains an AFT, but uses it as a help rather than a necessity. The application program maintains some state information for a file processing activity, and provides a record id for each IO operation. If the FCB and FMT of the file are accessible, FS uses them to obtain the position of the record, else it proceeds as in a stateless design. This arrangement has reliability properties analogous to a stateless design and processing efficiency analogous to a stateful design.

Scalability

Scalability requires that the performance of FS should not degrade with increase in its size. This is a very important requirement given the rapid growth in the size of distributed systems. An important principle in scalable FS design is to ensure that the network traffic only grows linearly with size of the system. This is ensured through the design principle of *caching of files*. Caching implies making a copy of the complete file at a remote node when the file is opened by a process in that node. This reduces the network traffic when the file is accessed. However, it gives rise to the issue of cache consistency when a file is simultaneously updated by many programs. This is solved by using a cache validation protocol which ensures that the cache contains up-to-date copy of the file when it is accessed.

EXERCISE 19.8

1. Write a short note on the influence of stateful and stateless file server design on fault tolerance in the presence of client and server failures in the system.
2. *Session semantics*, a semantics for use in a distributed environment, is defined as follows:
   (a) Write's performed to a file are visible immediately to local clients who have the same file open concurrently, but are invisible to non-local clients.
   (b) When a file is closed, changes made to it are visible only to non-local sessions starting after the `close` operation.

   Design a scheme to implement session semantics.
3. Discuss whether file buffers should be maintained at the server site or at a client site. What is the influence of this decision on the Unix file sharing semantics (see Section 17.7) and session semantics?
4. Discuss the influence of file caching on the implementation of the Unix and session semantics for dynamic file sharing.
5. Compare the effect of concurrent mounting of the same file system by different processes in a system when the Unix and session semantics are used.

19.9 RELIABILITY

Reliability in a distributed system has two facets—availability, and reliability of computations and data. Availability implies that a system and its resources should be accessible and usable when required. Redundancy is the basic technique used to ensure availability of system resources in the presence of failures. For example, the presence of multiple disk units provides better availability of disks. Availability of data is similarly ensured through redundancy—that is, by maintaining multiple copies of data.

Reliability of a computation is concerned with correctness of system operation in the presence of failures. In a distributed system, reliability of a computation acquires a new dimension because a computation may be distributed in different nodes. Consistent updating of different data files thus becomes a key issue. Reliability of data implies that the system should be able to store and manipulate data over long periods of time without data corruption or loss of data. When redundancy is used to enhance data availability, consistency between the copies of data becomes a new reliability issue.

19.9.1 Hierarchy of Reliability Techniques

The reliability techniques used in practice form a hierarchy consisting of the following:

1. Data recovery techniques
2. Fault tolerance techniques
3. Resiliency techniques.

Recovery techniques are at the lowest level of the hierarchy and resiliency techniques are at the highest level. As we see in the following discussion, each level in the hierarchy provides a certain form of reliability and involves a certain amount of reprocessing when a failure occurs. Higher levels of the hierarchy incur lower reprocessing costs.

Recovery techniques guard against loss of data in a file when a failure occurs. A recovery technique typically restores a file to the last back-up taken before a failure (see Section 17.6.2). This involves loss of some updates performed on the file. Hence it requires re-execution of all computations performed since the back-up. *Tolerance* techniques emphasize uninterrupted operation of a system in the presence of failures. Tolerance has the implication that the results of a computation that was completed prior to a failure would not be lost. However, it is possible that computations which were in progress at the time of failure need to be re-executed. *Resiliency* techniques ensure that even the effect of computations which were in progress at the time of failure would not be entirely lost. Thus, the emphasis is on retaining useful partial results produced by a computation which is in progress at the time of a failure.

19.9.2 Recovery of Data

In Section 17.6.2, we discussed the recovery techniques based on file back-ups, which restore a file to an earlier state. All file updates made since the backup was created have to be reprocessed. The stable storage technique of Lampson maintains two copies of every record in the file, one of which is guaranteed to survive a disk crash. However, a practical difficulty is that the stable storage technique cannot indicate whether the copy contains information before or after an update was performed by the computation. Hence it is difficult to decide whether a computation in progress at the time of failure should be re-executed.

19.9.3 Tolerance of Failures

Like atomic actions used in file systems, an application program can use *atomic transactions* to reliably update one or more files. An atomic transaction has the all-or-nothing property which ensures that the transaction either fails completely leaving all files accessed by it in their initial states, or it succeeds and leaves all files consistently updated. A transaction is deemed to have failed if a system failure occurs before the transaction commits. The reprocessing cost is thus the re-execution of a transaction which is in progress at the time of failure. When all files or records updated in a transaction are located in one node of the system, atomic transactions can be implemented as discussed in Section 17.6.2.

Multi-site transactions

A *multi-site transaction* (also called a *distributed transaction*) involves files or records located at different sites. This can be implemented as follows (see Fig. 19.18): One site S_j is designated to be the control site for transaction T_j. This site maintains the commit flag for the transaction. All participating sites maintain an intentions' list for the file updates made on behalf of transaction T_j. To ensure mutually exclusive access to file records, a lock is put on every record accessed by the transaction. Deadlocks can be assumed not to occur (some prevention or avoidance strategy may be used).

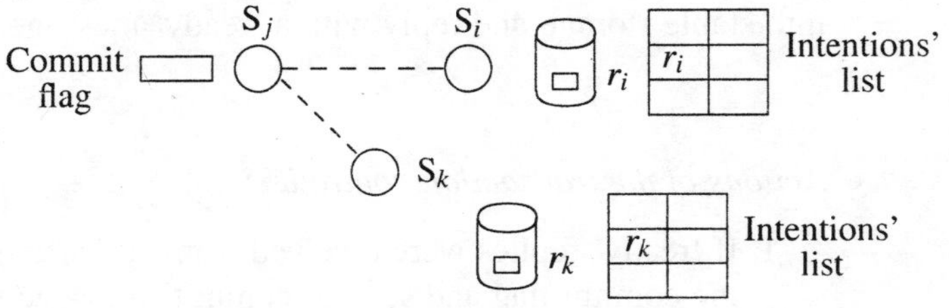

Fig. 19.18 A multi-site transaction

The following sequence of events illustrates reliability issues in multi-site transactions:

1. Transaction T_j updates some record r_i at a remote site S_i. The intentions' list at S_i now contains an entry for r_i.
2. The system is partitioned due to failure of link S_i-S_j. However, T_j makes no

further references or updates of record r_i, hence it is unaware that site S_i is inaccessible.

3. Transaction T_j commits.

Now, we might have a situation wherein record r_i is not updated because site S_i is unaware that T_j has committed, however all other records involved in T_j are updated. This situation violates the atomicity requirement. This problem is solved using the *two phase commit protocol*. In the first phase, the transaction controller checks if all records involved in a transaction are accessible for updating. It aborts the transaction if this is not the case. The second phase consists of commit processing. The details of the protocol are described in Algorithm 19.2.

Algorithm 19.2 (Two phase commit protocol)

Phase 1:

- *Actions of the transaction controller:*
  1. Set a time-out interval Δ.
  2. Send a 'are you ready to commit?' message to each participating site. Wait till either
     (a) 'ready' replies are received from all participating sites, or
     (b) time-out occurs.
  3. Enter phase 2 of the protocol.
- *Actions of the participating site:*

  On receiving an 'are you ready to commit?' message, write the intentions' list into stable storage and reply with a 'ready' message.

Phase 2:

- *Actions of the transaction controller:*
  1. If 'ready' replies were received from all participating sites in phase 1, set the commit flag and send a 'commit' message to all participating sites.
  2. If a time-out had occurred in phase 1, send an 'abort' message.
- *Actions of the participating site*
  1. On receiving a 'commit' message, perform commit processing.
  2. On receiving an 'abort' message, discard the intentions' list.

Example 19.6 If link $S_i - S_j$ fails during the multi-site transaction shown in Fig. 19.18, the transaction controller will not receive a 'ready' reply from site S_i. Hence it will abort the transaction. All participating sites will discard the intentions' list and no file updates will be performed.

Data Replication

Replication of data (i.e. maintaining multiple copies of data) enhances data availability. No reliability issues arise from replication if the replicated data is immutable, i.e. read-only. For mutable data, special care has to be taken during updates. A simple approach is to use the two-phase commit protocol to update all copies of data. However, this approach would delay updates if failures occur during an update. An alternative is to use a *quorum protocol*. This approach requires that a pre-specified number of copies should participate in a file operation. This is called the *quorum* for the operation. Let n copies of data exist in a system and let q_r and q_w be the quorums for *read* and *write* operations. Then the following values of q_r and q_w will ensure that *write*'s are exclusive and a *read* will always see a latest value:

$$q_w \geq \lceil \frac{n+1}{2} \rceil \tag{19.2}$$

$$q_r \geq (n - q_w) + 1 \tag{19.3}$$

Equation (19.2) ensures that concurrent *write*'s are not possible. Equation (19.3) ensures that a *read* cannot be concurrent with a *write*, and also that a *read* will always access at least one copy of the latest value. Concurrent reading is possible if $q_r < n/2$.

19.9.4 Resiliency

The effect of a failure in a distributed system is intrinsically different from that in a centralized system. There are two aspects to this difference:

1. Failures are partial, i.e. failures affect only some activities in the system.
2. It is difficult to determine the nature of a failure and its influence on ongoing activities in the system.

Consider the effect of a node failure on a distributed computation. Parts of the computation executing in other nodes are not affected by this failure. To minimize the reprocessing cost it is essential to use the results produced by the unaffected parts of the computation, and reprocess only the affected parts. The second issue arises due to the presence of the communication component in the system. Consider a computation which is executing in nodes N_i and N_j of the system when link (N_i, N_j) fails. It is difficult to detect the failure because a failed link appears analogous to a heavily loaded link. For example, if some process p_i in N_i has sent a message to a process in N_j, failure of (N_i, N_j) leads to a time-out in process p_i. Failure of node N_j also leads to a similar situation. Hence handling of failures in a distributed system involves dealing with such uncertainties. Resiliency techniques handle failures in a distributed system by utilizing the results produced by computations unaffected by a failure, and by dealing with uncertainties without leading to data consistency problems.

We illustrate interesting resiliency issues with reference to Fig. 19.19. The figure shows that a process at site A has made a request to a process at site B and is currently awaiting a reply. Site B implements the required computation as an atomic action. The communication protocol used provides a time-out to the sender when a response is delayed. The following possibilities can arise:

1. A time-out occurs at site A. Possible causes of the time-out are:
   (a) Site B never received the request, so never started processing it.
   (b) Site B is still processing the request, i.e. the processing is taking longer than expected.
   (c) Site B started processing the request but failed before completing it.
   (d) Site B completed the processing of the request but its reply to A was lost.
2. Site A crashed before receiving a reply from site B.

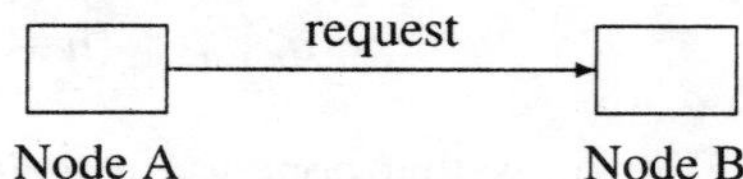

Fig. 19.19 Resiliency issues in a remote request

In case 1 site A may decide to either abandon the request, or to repeat it. In either case, the previous request to site B becomes an *orphan*. In situations 1(b) and 1(d) the computation in site B should not be permitted to commit, else we will have a data consistency problem if the request is repeated. In case 2 also the computation at B is an orphan and a way has to be found to prevent it from committing.

Data consistency can be maintained by killing the orphan at site B and reinitiating the computation when the request is received again from A, or by retaining the results of the orphan at B, and simply forwarding them when an identical request (i.e. a 'duplicate' request) is received from A. The latter alternative implements resiliency as we have defined it. Some resiliency techniques reported in the literature are cited at the end of this chapter.

EXERCISE 19.9

1. Should the commit flag of an atomic transaction be stored in stable storage? Justify your answer.
2. Write short notes on the following aspects of the two-phase commit protocol for multi-site transactions:

   (a) Influence of time-outs on the throughput of the system,
   (b) Deadlock handling in multi-site transactions.
3. Explain the working of the two-phase commit protocol when
   (a) The transaction controller fails before commit.
   (b) The transaction controller fails after each participating node sends a 'ready' reply.
   (c) A remote node fails after sending a 'ready' reply.
4. A system keeps five copies of a data item in five nodes to enhance availability. Two transactions T1 and T2 access the values of this data item.
   (a) Show how availability is enhanced by having five copies instead of one.
   (b) Can T1 and T2 access the different copies concurrently? Justify your answer.
   (c) Show how no consistency problems will arise if both transactions use the quorum rules (19.2-19.3) for updating the values of the data item.

19.10 SECURITY

A conventional OS authenticates a user at the time of log in. No authentication is necessary when processes running on behalf of a user make resource requests or communicate with other processes in the system. In a distributed system, however, it may become necessary to authenticate a user more often. In this section, we discuss the reasons for frequent authentication and consider techniques aimed at reducing the authentication overheads.

Figure 19.20 depicts a network communication model showing processes in secure nodes communicating over a network. A secure node here implies a node which is under the control of a distributed OS. Other nodes in the network may be communication processors (CPs) under the control of a local operating system. These nodes are susceptible to penetration by an intruder. If an intruder can locate himself in a CP (the easiest way to achieve this is for an intruder to load his own version of OS in the CP!), he could interfere with messages passing through it. This could lead to the following security threats:

1. Release of message contents to unauthorized user(s).
2. Modification of message contents.
3. Impersonation of a user by an intruder.

The first two threats, termed threats to message security, are countered using encryption techniques. Impersonation can be countered by authenticating the sender of every message. This requires repeated authentication of a user which is time consuming and expensive. In Section 19.10.4 an arrangement to avoid repeated authentication is discussed.

19.10.1 Countering Threats to Message Security

Approaches to counter threats to message security can be classified into link oriented approaches, and end-to-end approaches. In link oriented approaches, protection mea-

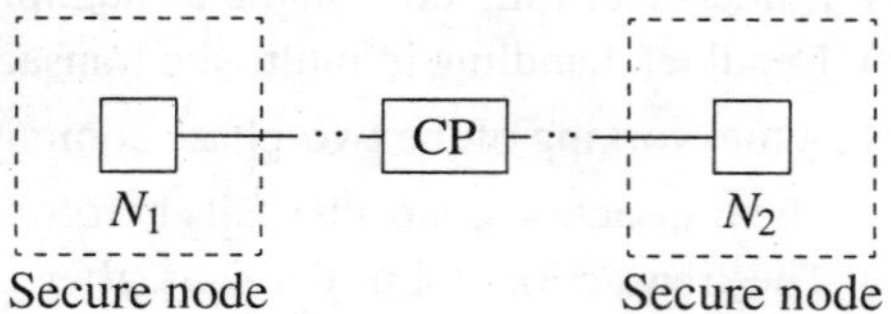

Fig. 19.20 Security in a communication network

sures are applied at every link of a communication path. This approach tends to be expensive since its cost depends on the number of links over which a message travels. For example, if a message between process p_i located at node N_1 and process p_j located at node N_3 passes along the path $N_1 - N_2 - N_3$, it has to incur security overheads for links $N_1 - N_2$ and $N_2 - N_3$. The protection measures are embedded in the networking software. This requires all nodes to be under control of the distributed OS, and requires all communication in the system to bear the security overheads. In the end-to-end approach, security measures can be employed selectively by the nodes or processes in the system. This permits users to employ security measures with varying degrees of cost and sophistication. In the following discussion, it is assumed that end-to-end measures are used.

Encryption is the standard technique used to counter the threats of release or modification of message contents. Conventional encryption is symmetric in nature, hence it requires the sender and receiver processes to agree on an encryption key. This is impractical because it would require some entities, e.g. OS servers like a print server, to agree upon an encryption key with every user in the system. We discuss two alternative techniques which associate a unique key with every entity, rather than with every pair of communicating entities. This reduces the number of distinct keys in the system.

Private key encryption

Each process p_i has a private key V_i known to itself and to a few other processes in the system. Any process sending a message to p_i encrypts it with V_i. On receiving a message, p_i decrypts it with V_i. The advantages of this scheme are that the number of keys is limited to n, where n is the number of communicating entities in the system, and a process receiving a message need not know the identity of the sender. However, a sender process needs to know the private key of the receiver process. This requirement makes it difficult to change the process keys over a period of time.

This scheme is not useful for message security in general due to the need to know the private key of a receiver. It is therefore only used by OS processes while dealing with user processes—the private key of a user process is naturally known to OS processes.

Public key encryption

Each process p_i has a pair of keys (U_i, V_i). U_i is the *public key* of p_i, which is made known to all processes in the system. V_i is the *private key* known only to process p_i. The public and private keys are so chosen that

$$D_{V_i}(E_{U_i}(m)) = m \tag{19.4}$$

The steps involved in the transmission of a message m from process p_i to process p_j are as follows:

1. Process p_i encrypts the message with the public key of the recipient process p_j (i.e. with U_j).
2. The encrypted message is transmitted over the network and is received by process p_j.
3. Process p_j decrypts the received message with its own private key (i.e. V_j).

Rivest-Shamir-Adelman encryption

The Rivest-Shamir-Adelman (RSA) encryption algorithm uses mod n arithmetic where n is the product of two large prime numbers p and q. Typically, p and q are 100 digits each which makes n a 200 digit number. Two keys d and e are used for encryption and decryption as follows:

$$\begin{aligned} E_e(m) &= m^e \bmod n \\ D_d(m) &= m^d \bmod n \end{aligned}$$

To use this method of encryption, it is necessary that m should be an integer $< n$. The algorithm is used as a block cipher with n as the block size.

Since encryption and decryption are analogous, (d, e) or (e, d) can be used as the public and private keys of a process p_i. Assuming (d, e) to be the public and private keys, to satisfy relation (19.4), e should be relatively prime to $(p-1) \times (q-1)$ and d should satisfy the relation

$$d \times e \; mod \; [(p-1) \times (q-1)] = 1.$$

To make public key encryption suitable for short-life entities, e.g. processes, it should be possible to obtain the public key information interactively rather than through a manual process. This functionality is provided by a key distribution centre.

19.10.2 Distribution of Encryption Keys

The *key distribution centre* (KDC) is a trusted OS process which provides an interactive service concerning encryption keys for processes in the system. The existence of this service makes it possible for a process to change its encryption key frequently in order to enhance the level of message security.

Distribution of private keys

When a process p_i wishes to find the private key of a process p_j, the following exchange of messages takes place between p_i and the KDC

$$\begin{array}{lcl} p_i \rightarrow \text{KDC} & : & p_i, p_j \\ \text{KDC} \rightarrow p_i & : & E_{V_i}(p_j, V_j) \end{array}$$

First p_i sends its own id, and that of p_j, to KDC. KDC replies by sending the private key of p_j encrypted with the private key of p_i. p_i decrypts the message received from the KDC to obtain V_j, and uses it while communicating with p_j. Note that the message from p_i to KDC is not encrypted because process p_i does not know the private key of KDC. This message is susceptible to modification by an intruder. However, this does not cause any serious damage since the reply from KDC contains the id of the destination process (i.e., p_j) along with its key and is encrypted with the key of p_i. Thus any modification would be noticed by p_i straightaway.

Distribution of public keys

$$\begin{array}{lcl} p_i \rightarrow \text{KDC} & : & E_{U_{kdc}}(p_i, p_j) \\ \text{KDC} \rightarrow p_i & : & E_{U_i}(p_j, U_j) \end{array}$$

where U_j is the public key sought by p_i, i.e. the public key of process p_j. p_i can obtain U_j by decoding the message with its own private key V_i. Note that p_i's message to KDC is now encoded with U_{kdc}, which protects it against modification.

19.10.3 Countering Message Playback Attacks

Encryption foils attempts at release or modification of message contents. It also defeats any attempt by an intruder at fabricating messages and making them look genuine, i.e. sending a message to p_j and making it appear as if it originated in p_i. It is however possible for the intruder to trick a receiver into believing that the intruder is an authentic user process. This can be achieved through *message playback*. Here an intruder simply copies messages passing through it, and 'plays them back' in the future. For example, it may play back an old message m from p_i to p_j. In a system using public key encryption, this has the form $E_{U_j}(m)$. When p_j receives the message, it concludes that p_i is initiating a communication with it. The intruder can play back an entire session in this manner. This could mislead p_j into taking wrong or duplicate actions which may affect data consistency.

This threat is countered by using a *challenge-response* scheme. This scheme works as follows: When process p_j receives a message from p_i it sends some bit string, called the *challenge string* to p_i. p_i is expected to transform the challenge string in some pre-determined manner and send it back to p_j. (A standard response is to add '1' to the challenge string and return it.) If p_j finds that the response matches with its expectations, it concludes that the dialogue is being performed in real time with p_i, else it concludes that it is being subject to a playback attack and ignores all subsequent communication from p_i. Note that every challenge string must be different for this scheme to work reliably. This may be achieved by using the current time of the day as the challenge string. Since the message traffic copied by the intruder will have been generated at an earlier time, p_j will be able to detect all message playback attacks.

19.10.4 Kerberos

An *open system* is a system which conforms to standard, well-specified interfaces with other systems. Any system with matching interfaces can access the resources and services of an open system. This implies that the computers in a system may not be under the same organizational control. Kerberos is a third-party authenticator developed in project Athena at MIT for use in an open system environment. It enables a user to prove his identity to the servers in an open system without being subject to repeated authentication.

Overview of Kerberos

Kerberos assigns a private key for each user and server in the system. Only Kerberos knows the private keys, hence a message received by a user (or on his behalf) or server is considered genuine if it is encrypted with its private key. A user communicates with a server using a *session key* which is generated by Kerberos for each session.

In Kerberos terminology, a program executing on behalf of a user is called a *client*. Let C be a client executing on behalf of a user with the id *User_id*. Two things are necessary for C to use a server S_j. C must possess a *ticket* for S_j. The ticket contains the session key assigned to the communication session between C and S_j, and the *lifetime* during which the ticket is valid. To use a service, client C must present a ticket for S_j along with an *authenticator* which establishes the identity of C in a manner which eliminates playback attempts. S_j provides the service only if the authenticator is valid, and the lifetime in the ticket has not expired. Thus stolen tickets cannot be used to obtain a service. Each authenticator can only be used once. A new authenticator must be prepared and presented to obtain another service from the server. Each process obtains the initial ticket from the Kerberos server and the subsequent tickets from a ticket granting server.

The formats of the ticket and the authenticator are shown in Fig. 19.21. The ticket is encrypted using the key of the server, while the authenticator is encrypted using the session key included in the ticket. This protects both of them from modification or forgery. The ticket and the authenticator are used as follows: The server decrypts the ticket using its own key and obtains the session key. It checks the timestamp and lifetime of the ticket to ensure that the ticket is valid. It then uses the session key to decrypt the authenticator, and checks its timestamp to ensure that the request has originated in real time and within the validity period of the ticket. The server

Ticket : E_{server_key} (server, client, client-address, timestamp, lifetime, session key)

Authenticator : $E_{session\_key}$ (client, client-address, timestamp)

Fig. 19.21 Formats of Kerberos ticket and authenticator

performs the service requested by the client only if all these checks succeed.

A user obtains a ticket for a desired server using the Kerberos authentication protocol described below. Client C maintains the server ticket on behalf of the user and forwards them to the server whenever a service is required.

Working of Kerberos

The Kerberos system has two main components: Kerberos Authentication Server (KAS), and Ticket Granting Server (TGS). KAS authenticates a user at log in time using an authentication database and provides him with a ticket to TGS. TGS enables the client to obtain tickets to other servers in the system. Three stages are involved in the use of servers and resources in the system.

1. *Initial authentication:* The user is authenticated at log in time as follows:

$$\begin{aligned} User \rightarrow C &: \; User\_id, password \\ C \rightarrow KAS &: \; User\_id, TGS \\ KAS \rightarrow C &: \; E_{V_{User}}(T_{TGS}, SK_{User,TGS}, timestamp, lifetime) \end{aligned}$$

where T_{TGS} is a ticket for TGS encrypted with the key of TGS, and $SK_{User,TGS}$ is a session key for the session between the user and TGS. V_{User} is the private key of the user, which KAS retrieves from the authentication database using *User_id*. The private key satisfies the relation $V_{User} = f(password)$ where f is a one-way function known to C. C obtains V_{User} by applying f to *password* and decrypts the reply received from KAS. This is the authentication step. Authentication fails if the decryption is unsuccessful. This is equivalent to the test (18.1) in chapter 18.

2. *Obtaining a ticket for a server:* To obtain a ticket for a desired server, client C uses the following protocol

$$\begin{aligned} C \rightarrow TGS &: \; <Server\_id>, T_{TGS}, AU \\ TGS \rightarrow C &: \; E_{SK_{User},TGS}(T_S, SK_{User,S}, <Server\_id>, timestamp, lifetime) \end{aligned}$$

where <*Server_id*> is the name of the server it wishes to use, AU is an authenticator, $SK_{User,S}$ is a session key for the session between the client and the desired server, and T_S is the ticket for the desired server encrypted using the key of the server. Before replying to the client, TGS verifies that the ticket presented by the client is valid, and that the request has originated in real time and within the validity period of the ticket.

3. *Obtaining the service:* Client C sends the details of the service required by the user to the server, along with the ticket for the server and an authenticator.

$$\text{C} \rightarrow \text{Server} \quad : \quad E_{SK_{User,S}}(T_S, AU, <\textit{service request}>)$$

The server performs the service if it can establish that the request has originated in real time.

Comments

Kerberos provides a low granularity authentication support, where granularity refers to the time period during which an arrangement remains valid. This is achieved by generating new keys for each session, and by specifying a lifetime for each session key and each ticket in the system. This reduces the damage caused by accidentai leakage of keys. Playback attempts are foiled using time stamps in the authenticators. This requires loosely synchronized clocks at all sites.

EXERCISE 19.10

1. Devise a public key cipher for $n = 77$ using the RSA approach.

BIBLIOGRAPHY

(a) Distributed operating systems

Tanenbaum and Renesse (1985) is a good starting point for the study of distributed operating systems. It discusses the major design issues and contains a survey of some distributed operating systems. Tanenbaum (1981) discusses the design principles of computer networks. Fortier (1988) discusses the design aspects of distributed operating systems. Tanenbaum (1992) discusses some distributed operating systems in detail, while Silberschatz and Galvin (1994) contains a useful chapter on this subject.

Lin and Gannon (1985) discuss the reliability issues in remote procedure calls. The issue of synchronizing multiple processes in a distributed system is discussed in Reed and Kanodia (1979) and Schneider (1982).

1. Coulouris, G., J. Dollimore and T Kindberg (1994): *Distributed Systems – Concepts and Design*, Addison-Wesley, New York.
2. Goscinski, A. (1991) : *Distributed Operating Systems – The Logical Design*, Addison-Wesley, New York.
3. Fortier, P.J. (1988): *Design of Distributed Operating Systems*, McGraw-Hill, New York.

4. Lin, K. and J.D. Gannon (1985): "Atomic remote procedure call," *IEEE Transactions on Software Engineering*, **11** (10), 1126-1135.
5. McQuillan, J.M. and D.C. Walden (1977): "The ARPA network design decisions," *Computer Networks*, **1**, 243-289.
6. Silberschatz, A. and P. Galvin (1994): *Operating System Concepts* , (4 th edition), Addison-Wesley, Reading.
7. Reed, D.P. and R.K. Kanodia (1979): "Synchronization with event counts and sequences," *Commn. of ACM*, **22** (2), 115-123.
8. Schneider, F.B. (1982): "Synchronization in distributed programs," *ACM Transactions on Programming Languages and Systems*, **4** (2), 125-148.
9. Singhal, M. and N.G. Shivaratri (1994): *Advanced Concepts in Operating Systems*, McGraw-Hill, New York.
10. Spector, A.Z. (1982): "Performing remote operations efficiently on a local computer network," *Commn. of ACM*, **25** (4), 246-260.
11. Tanenbaum, A.S. (1981): *Computer Networks*, Prentice-Hall, N.J.
12. Tanenbaum, A.S. (1992): *Modern Operating Systems*, Prentice-Hall, N.J.
13. Tanenbaum, A.S. and R. Van Renesse (1985): "Distributed Operating Systems," *ACM Computing Surveys*, **17** (1), 419-470.

(b) Distributed control algorithms

Raymond (1989) discusses a token based algorithm for distributed mutual exclusion. Dhamdhere and Kulkarni(1994) discuss resilient distributed mutual exclusion algorithms which can function correctly despite a pre-specified number of failures in the system.

Chandy, Misra and Haas (1983) and Knapp (1987) review distributed deadlock detection algorithms. Chandy and Lamport (1985) describe a distributed algorithm for determining the global state of a system. Sinha and Natarajan (1985), Choudhary *et al* (1989), Singhal (1989) and Bharát Shyam and Dhamdhere (1990) discuss edge chasing algorithms for distributed deadlock detection. These algorithms use a special message called a probe, and aim at eliminating the use of the global system state to detect deadlocks.

1. Bharat Shyam and D.M. Dhamdhere (1990): "A new priority based distributed deadlock detection algorithm using probes, *Technical report TR-15-90*, Computer Science & Engineering Department, Indian Institute of Technology, Bombay.
2. Chandy, K.M., J. Misra and L.M. Haas (1983): "Distributed deadlock detection, *ACM Transactions on Computer Systems*, **1** (2), 144-156.
3. Chandy, K.M. and L. Lamport (1985): "Distributed snapshots: determining global states of distributed systems," *ACM Transactions on Computer Systems*, **3** (1), 63-75.
4. Choudhary, A.N. *et al* (1989): "A modified priority based probe algorithm for distributed deadlock detection and resolution," *IEEE Transactions on Software Engineering*, **15** (1), 10-17.
5. Dhamdhere, D.M. and S.S. Kulkarni (1994): "A token based *k*-resilient mutual exclusion algorithm for distributed systems," *Information processing letters*, **50**, 151-157.
6. Knapp, E. (1987): "Deadlock detection in distributed databases," *ACM Computing Surveys*, **19** (4), 203-328.
7. Raymond, K. (1989): "A tree based algorithm for distributed mutual exclusion," *ACM Transactions on Computer Systems*, **7** (1), 61-77.

8. Ries, D.R. and G.C. Smith (1982): "Nested transactions in distributed systems," *IEEE Transactions on Software Engineering*, **8** (3), 167-172.
9. Singhal, M (1989): "Deadlock detection in distributed systems," *IEEE Computer*.
10. Sinha, M.K. and N. Natarajan (1985): "A priority based distributed deadlock detection algorithm," *IEEE Transactions on Software Engineering*, **11** (1), 67-80.

(c) Reliability

Svobodova (1984) discusses the design aspects of file servers for distributed systems, and contains a useful review of some well-known file servers. Svobodova (1986) identifies the reliability issues in distributed transaction processing and discusses the techniques to ensure resiliency of a distributed computation. Herlihy and McKendry (1989) describe an algorithm for orphan elimination in a distributed system. Liskov (1982) discusses the language issues for distributed programming.

1. Herlihy, M.P. and M.S. McKendry (1989): "Time stamp based orphan elimination," *IEEE Transactions on Software Engineering*, **15** (7), 825-831.
2. Liskov, B. (1982): "On linguistic support for distributed programs," *IEEE Transactions on Software Engineering*, **8** (3), 203-210.
3. Svobodova, L. (1984): "Resilient distributed computing," *IEEE Transactions on Software Engineering*, **12** (3), 257-268.
4. Svobodova, L. (1986): "File servers for network-based distributed systems," *ACM Computing Surveys*, **16** (4), 353-398.

(d) Security

Voydock and Kent (1983) discuss the security issues in distributed systems and the techniques used to tackle them in practice. Mullender and Tanenbaum (1986) discuss some hardware solutions to the security problem.

Pfleeger (1989) explains the theory behind RSA encryption.

1. Mullender, S.J. and A. Tanenbaum (1986): "The design of a capability based operating system," *Computer Journal*, **29** (4), 289-299.
2. Pfleeger, C.P. (1989): *Security in computing*, Prentice Hall, N.J.
3. Steiner, J.G., C. Newman and J.I. Schiller (1988): "Kerberos : an authentication service for open network system," *Proceedings of the Winter USENIX conference*.
4. Voydock, V.L., S.T. Kent (1983): "Security mechanisms in high level network protocols," *ACM Computing Surveys*, **15** (2), 135-171.
5. Walker, B. *et al* (1983): "The LOCUS distributed operating system," *Operating System Review*, **17** (5), 49-70.
6. Wittie, L.D. and A. M. Van Tilborg (1980): "MICROS – a distributed operating system for MICRONET," a reconfigurable network computer, *IEEE Transactions on Computers*, **9**, 1133-1144.
7. Woo, T.Y.C. and S.S. Lam (1992): "Authentication for distributed systems," *IEEE Computer*.

Index